Peterson's®

MASTER THE PSAT/NMSQT® EXAM

6TH EDITION

PETERSON'S

About Peterson's

Peterson's®, a Nelnet company, has been your trusted educational publisher for over 50 years. It's a milestone we're quite proud of, as we continue to offer the most accurate, dependable, high-quality educational content in the field, providing you with everything you need to succeed. No matter where you are on your academic or professional path, you can rely on Peterson's for its books, online information, expert test-prep tools, the most up-to-date education exploration data, and the highest quality career success resources—everything you need to achieve your education goals. For our complete line of products, visit www.petersons.com.

For more information, contact Peterson's, 3 Columbia Circle, Suite 205, Albany, NY 12203, 800-338-3282 Ext. 54229; or find us online at www.petersons.com.

© 2017 Peterson's, a Nelnet company

ISBN-13: 978-0-7689-4157-9

Printed in the United States of America
10 9 8 7 6 5 4 3 2 1   19 18 17

Sixth Edition

Contents

PART III   PSAT/NMSQT® EXAM READING TEST STRATEGIES

PART IV   PSAT/NMSQT® EXAM WRITING AND LANGUAGE TEST STRATEGIES

PART V   PSAT/NMSQT® MATH TEST STRATEGIES

Contents

PART VI PRACTICE TESTS FOR THE PSAT/NMSQT® EXAM

Before You Begin

Congratulations on taking the first major step in PSAT/NMSQT® exam prep by acquiring this book and dedicating yourself to doing what it takes to get a top score.

Much like training for a marathon, ideal PSAT/NMSQT® preparation takes time, practice, and commitment. Armed with the goal of success and this book in hand, you'll have all you need to improve your skills to earn a score that gives you an indication of your potential SAT® exam scores and that can open the door to scholarships and other financial aid resources to make your education goals a reality.

HOW TO USE THIS BOOK

Here's a roadmap to Peterson's *Master the PSAT/NMSQT® Exam* and how you can use it as your main study plan.

Top 10 Strategies to Raise Your Score lists the ten key test-taking tips to keep in mind as you approach practice questions, practice tests, and then the real PSAT/NMSQT® exam.

Part I gives you all the information you need to know about the exam: its structure, where to take it, and how it's scored. We'll walk you through every test section so you know exactly what question types to expect, and break down the timing so you start to get a sense of how test day will progress. Finally, we'll lay out study plans for you to follow, depending on how much time you have left to study.

Part II is a Diagnostic Test. This practice exam mirrors the PSAT/NMSQT® exam, and taking it will give you a good sense of where your strengths and weaknesses lie. Take this exam before you begin your review of the test content, and use the results of this exam to determine where you need to focus your studying.

Parts III though V give you a review of all topics tested on the Reading, Writing & Language, and Mathematics sections of the exam. In each review chapter, we go into detail on all the question types you will see on the exam, with test-like examples and detailed answer explanations. Each chapter ends with a practice set of questions to test the skills you've learned.

Part VI lets you put what you've learned to the test, with two full-length practice exams. Try to take each under the conditions of a real exam. Then, like the diagnostic, you can use the results to go back and sharpen any skills where you're still having trouble.

SPECIAL STUDY FEATURES

Throughout this guide, we've included several features to make your studying as user-friendly and helpful as possible.

Overview

Each chapter begins with a bulleted overview listing the major topics covered within the chapter. This will allow you to quickly target certain areas, or easily return to specific topics for review.

Summing It Up

Each chapter ends with a bulleted review section, which summarizes the most important concepts covered. These summaries are a great way to review once you've finished a chapter, or to go back and refresh in the days leading up to the test.

Bonus Information

As you work your way though the chapters, be on the lookout in the page margins for special advice in the following forms:

- **Notes** highlight need-to-know information about the format, structure, and language of the PSAT/NMSQT® exam.

- **Tips** provide valuable strategies and information from test experts on the best way to use and remember what you are learning and apply it to PSAT/NMSQT® exam questions.

- **Alerts** signal areas where test-takers commonly make mistakes. We've seen these errors made again and again, and want you to take extra care when faced with the trickiest concepts and test questions.

We created Peterson's *Master the PSAT/NMSQT® Exam* with one end goal in mind—to make sure you know exactly what to expect on the exam.

GIVE US YOUR FEEDBACK

Peterson's publishes a full line of books—test prep, career preparation, education exploration, and financial aid. Peterson's publications can be found in high school guidance offices, college libraries and career centers, and at your local bookstore and library. Peterson's books are also available online at *www.petersonsbooks.com*.

We welcome any comments or suggestions you may have about this publication. Your feedback will help us make education dreams possible for you—and others like you.

TOP 10 STRATEGIES TO RAISE YOUR SCORE

When it comes to taking any standardized test, friends, teachers, and family will likely bombard you with all sorts of test-taking tips. Depending on your study style, some pieces of advice will do you more good than others. We've sorted through all the information to nail down the tried-and-true tips that always lead to top results.

Here's our pick for the top 10 strategies to raise your score:

1. **Create a study plan and follow it.** The right PSAT/NMSQT® study plan will help you get the most out of this book in whatever time you have. Before you dive in, create a plan (check out our ideas in Chapter 1). Organization is key to test day success.

2. **Don't get stuck on any one question.** Since you have a specific amount of time to answer questions, you can't afford to spend too much time on any one problem. Make a mark, make sure you skip the correct line on your answer sheet, and come back to it.

3. **Learn the directions in advance.** If you already know the directions, you won't have to waste your time reading them. You'll be able to jump right in and start answering questions as soon as the testing clock begins.

4. **For the Writing and Language questions, think about the simplest, clearest way to express an idea.** If an answer choice sounds awkward or overly complicated, chances are good that it's wrong.

5. **For Vocabulary-in-Context questions, as you read, try to predict what word should go in each blank.** Before you even look at the choices, rephrase the sentence containing the tested word in your own words. Then, scan the answer choices, look for a word that's similar to the one you've predicted, and then eliminate the answer choices that don't match up.

6. **For Reading questions, skim the passage first to see what it's about.** Don't worry about the details; you can always look them up later if you need to. Look for the main ideas then tackle the questions that direct you straight to the answer by referring you to a specific line in the passage. If you have time afterward, you can try solving the harder questions.

7. **For some of the math multiple-choice questions, you're allowed to use a calculator, but it won't help you unless you know how to approach the problems.** If you're stuck, try substituting numbers for variables. You can also try plugging in numbers from the answer choices. Start with the middle number. That way, if it doesn't work, you can strategically choose one that's higher or lower.

8. **For the math grid-ins, you come up with an answer and enter it into the grid.** Like the multiple-choice questions, you won't be penalized for wrong answers, so make your best guess even if you're not sure. Any answer is better than no answer.

9. **If you aren't sure about an answer but know something about the question, eliminate what you know is wrong and make an educated guess.** Ignore the answers that are absolutely wrong, eliminate choices in which part of the answer is incorrect, check the time period of the question and of the answer choices, check the key words in the question again, and revisit remaining answers to discover which seem more correct.

10. **Finally, relax the night before the test.** Don't cram. Studying at the last minute will only stress you out. Go to a movie or hang out with a friend—anything to get your mind off the test! Just make sure to get home in time for a good night's sleep.

PART I
PSAT/NMSQT®
EXAM BASICS

Chapter 1   All About the PSAT/NMSQT® Exam

All About the PSAT/NMSQT® Exam

OVERVIEW

- What Is the PSAT/NMSQT® Exam?

- When You Can Take the PSAT/NMSQT® Exam

- How Many Times Should You Take the PSAT/NMSQT® Exam?

- How to Register for the PSAT/NMSQT® Exam

- Test Day: What to Bring, and What to Leave Home

- How Your Scores Are Reported

- Get to Know the PSAT/NMSQT® Exam Format

- The PSAT/NMSQT® Exam Evidence-Based Reading and Writing Section

- The PSAT/NMSQT® Exam Math Section

- The PSAT/NMSQT® Exam Answer Sheet

- How the PSAT/NMSQT® Exam Is Scored

- How to Use Your PSAT/NMSQT Exam Scores

- Strategies for PSAT/NMSQT® Exam Success

- Making Your PSAT/NMSQT® Exam Study Plan

- Measuring Your Progress

- Summing It Up

WHAT IS THE PSAT/NMSQT® EXAM?

While the SAT® exam is used directly in college admissions decisions, the Preliminary Scholastic Aptitude Test/National Merit Scholarship Qualifying Test (PSAT/NMSQT®) is a bit different. As a standardized test typically taken by high school sophomores and juniors, the PSAT/NMSQT® scores are used to determine whether a student is eligible and qualified for the National Merit Scholarship Program. The National Merit Scholarship Program is an academic competition that offers recognition and scholarships to a number of high-scoring students every year. You do not need to do anything specific to be eligible for National Merit Scholarship recognition—the scores of everyone who takes the test are automatically screened for consideration.

The PSAT/NMSQT® exam is a paper-based multiple-choice test with two main goals: testing the skills you've learned so far in high school and preparing you for college and the college admission tests you'll need to take (including the SAT® exam). It's similar in format to the SAT® exam and covers the following content areas:

- Reading
- Writing and Language
- Math

There's no essay component on the PSAT/NMSQT® exam, so you won't need to write any essays or take any supplemental tests.

WHEN YOU CAN TAKE THE PSAT/NMSQT® EXAM

You should expect to take the PSAT/NMSQT® exam in the fall of your junior year, although sophomores can also take the test.

The PSAT/NMSQT® exam is offered on a weekday every fall, typically in October or November. There is only one primary test date for the exam across the country. There are also two alternate test dates (one on a weekday and one on a Saturday), but it's important to note that these other dates are not for students who missed the test or want to retake it. Rather, these alternate dates are meant to accommodate schools that can't offer the PSAT/NMSQT® exam on the national test date. For the most up-to-date info on upcoming test dates, be sure to check the College Board website and then ask your school counselor to confirm when your school will be offering the test.

HOW MANY TIMES SHOULD YOU TAKE THE PSAT/NMSQT® EXAM?

Most students take the PSAT/NMSQT® exam once, but, if you take the test as a sophomore, you can retake the test in your junior year. In fact, you can take the test up to three times during high school. So, if you really want to, you can take the test your freshman, sophomore, and junior years. However, it's important to note that only juniors qualify for the National Merit Scholarship competition. So if you take the test multiple times, only your eleventh grade score will count toward National Merit Scholarships and recognition.

What If I Miss the Test?

If you miss the primary PSAT/NMSQT® test date in your junior year, don't panic! You may still be able to qualify for a National Merit Scholarship. If you miss the primary test day due to illness or emergency, notify the National Merit Scholarship Corporation (NMSC) in writing no later than March 1 following the missed exam to request information about alternate entry into the National Merit Scholarship Program. The request can be submitted by either you or a school official. Your request for alternate entry should include your name and address; the contact information of the person (either you or the school official) making the request; the name, address, and code of your high school; and a brief explanation of why you missed the PSAT/NMSQT® exam. The NMSC will then give you alternate entry materials and information about next steps.

You can fax your request to:
(847) 866-5113
Attn: Scholarship Administration

You can mail your request to:
National Merit Scholarship Corporation
Attn: Scholarship Administration
1560 Sherman Avenue, Suite 200
Evanston, IL 60201-4897

The sooner you contact NMSC after the missed test date, the greater your chances will be of meeting the requirements for alternate entry.

If you aren't expecting to qualify for a National Merit Scholarship and miss the exam, simply move on. To get a similar experience and level of prep, you can do a timed practice test on your own to simulate the PSAT/NMSQT® exam.

HOW TO REGISTER FOR THE PSAT/NMSQT® EXAM

Because the PSAT/NMSQT® exam is offered through your high school, your school will handle the necessary registration and test scheduling. You should check with your school counselor to make sure you're registered and to confirm your school's next test date.

If you're homeschooled or otherwise not affiliated with a school, you can contact your local high school about taking the PSAT/NMSQT® exam there.

Test Fees

The PSAT/NMSQT® exam costs schools $15 per student. Many schools cover these fees for their students, but others don't. Some schools may also require that students pay an additional processing fee. It's important to check with your school counselor to see what your school's policy is and whether you will need to pay to take the exam.

TEST DAY: WHAT TO BRING, AND WHAT TO LEAVE HOME

On test day, plan to bring the following items with you:

- A valid school ID or government ID with a photograph
- Two No. 2 pencils with erasers
- An approved calculator for the math section. Approved calculators include:
  - A graphing calculator
  - A scientific calculator
  - A four-function calculator (although this type is not recommended by the College Board)
- Your Social Security number (optional)

Although you will be allowed to have your pencils, test booklet, answer sheet, and calculator when the test begins, you should avoid bringing the following items, because they won't be allowed:

- Smartphones or other devices that can take photos or record video/audio
- Pens, highlighters, or colored pencils
- Books or papers of any kind (scratch paper will be provided)
- Rulers, compasses, or protractors
- Food or drink (not even bottled water), unless you've received approval from the College Board's Services for Students with Disabilities

---

Special Accommodations

If you have a documented disability and need additional accommodations, you should plan ahead and make sure you get approval from the College Board for:

- Extra testing time
- Extra/extended breaks
- Reading/seeing accommodations (example: large-print or braille test booklets)
- Special seating

If you have approval from the College Board ahead of time, you'll be good to go on test day. If you don't get approval, you may not get the accommodations on test day, and the College Board might cancel your scores if you use the accommodations anyway. So as you get your checklist in order ahead of test day, make sure you also think about any accommodations for which you'll need early approval.

If you have a cell phone or alarm with you or in your bag, it should be turned off and stowed away during the test. You should also double check with your school counselor to make sure that these items are allowed in the room with you. The safest option is to leave them at home!

HOW YOUR SCORES ARE REPORTED

Score reporting is especially important with the PSAT/NMSQT® exam because your scores are your official entry into the National Merit Scholarship Program. After you take the test, your scores are calculated and sent directly to your school—and possibly also your city and state, depending on your state's policy. Your school will then pass the report along to you, along with an explanation of what your scores mean and whether you might qualify for National Merit Scholarships and recognition. If you don't want to wait until you get the official score report from your school, you can also log in to the College Board website about two months after your test date to see how you did on the exam.

Because the PSAT/NMSQT® exam is the official entry for National Merit Scholarships, your scores are shared with certain programs to see if you qualify for certain scholarship and academic recognition programs. Your scores will be automatically released to these programs:

- National Scholarship Service
- National Hispanic Recognition Program
- Telluride Seminar Scholarships

If you don't want your scores released to these scholarship organizations for any reason, be sure to notify the PSAT/NMSQT® exam program in writing by October 31 of the fall you take the test. You can send a notification letter to the following address:

P.O. Box 6720
Princeton, NJ 08541-6720

Unlike the SAT® exam, your PSAT/NMSQT® exam scores will not be released to any colleges. They won't even be included on your high school transcript that will eventually be sent to colleges, unless you (if you're over 18) or your parent/guardian gives specific permission. PSAT/NMSQT® exam scores are used for scholarships and to help identify skills and subjects for you to work on in high school, so they are not typically a factor in the college admission process.

GET TO KNOW THE PSAT/NMSQT® EXAM FORMAT

The PSAT/NMSQT® exam is primarily a multiple-choice test, broken out into two main sections: Evidence-Based Reading and Writing (which includes the Reading Test and the Writing and Language Test) and Math. The overall test takes 2 hours and 45 minutes. That sounds like a long stretch, but don't worry—there are breaks between sections. Let's look at how the test breaks down.

Evidence-Based Reading and Writing

Section	Minutes Allotted	Number of Questions	Score Range
Reading	60	47	160-760
Writing and Language	35	44	160-760

Evidence-Based Reading and Writing questions will include single or paired (related) passages covering topics in the following areas:

- Literature
- History
- Social Science
- Science

Each section has a score ranging from 160 to 760 points.

For the Reading and Writing and Language tests, question types are pretty straightforward: they're all multiple-choice, with four answer choices each.

Math

Section	Minutes Allotted	Number of Questions	Score Range
Math	70	48	160-760

Math questions will mainly cover three basic areas:

- Algebra
- Problem Solving and Data Analysis
- Complex Equations

For the Math section, you'll receive a score ranging from 160 to 760 points.

Most of the Math Test questions you'll see are multiple-choice, but there may be a few "grid-in" questions for which you'll need to come up with an answer yourself and fill in circles in a grid that correspond with the digits in the answer, instead of selecting one from four different options.

THE PSAT/NMSQT® EXAM EVIDENCE-BASED READING AND WRITING SECTION

The first two tests you'll see on the PSAT/NMSQT® exam make up the Evidence-Based Reading and Writing section: the Reading Test and the Writing and Language Test. Together, these tests assess your verbal skills, giving you text passages, charts, and graphs to evaluate. These tests are exclusively multiple-choice, so you'll see passages throughout the Reading and Writing and Language tests that are underlined and/or numbered to correspond to specific questions.

On the Reading Test, you'll be asked to read passages and sometimes interpret related graphs or charts. These graphs will never require you to do math or scientific analysis, but rather are included to provide outside information in addition to the passage or relate to specific concepts within the passage. Reading Test questions may ask you to draw conclusions about the passage or read between the lines to determine what the writer is trying to say. In every Reading Test, you should expect to see the following:

- A passage/excerpt from literature (classic or contemporary)
- A passage or two paired passages from a U.S. historical document (like the Constitution or Declaration of Independence) and/or work that is derived from it (for example, a speech or essay that draws on the same concepts)
- A passage related to the social sciences (economics, sociology, psychology, etc.)
- A passage or two paired passages about science concepts and developments (biology, chemistry, earth science, or physics)

On the Writing and Language Test, you'll be reading passages and answering multiple-choice questions as well. (There's no actual writing on your part, despite the name of the test!) The Writing and Language passages are different from the Reading passages because they focus only on nonfiction narratives in these areas:

- Career/professional life
- History
- Social Studies
- Humanities
- Science

Each Writing passage will accompany multiple-choice questions that ask you to examine a particular word, phrase, or sentence and decide if it's correct according to standard written English conventions. If it's not, you will select the best replacement word, phrase, or sentence. Other questions in this test will have you look at the passage as a whole and/or interpret a graph (or other supplemental info) to identify themes or draw conclusions. In this test, you're basically an editor deciding if information is presented correctly or, if it's not, how it *should* be presented. You don't need to know specific facts, vocabulary words, or information for this test—you just need to be able to read and evaluate information presented to you.

Both the Reading and the Writing and Language tests are designed to assess your skills in specific areas: Command of Evidence, Analysis in History/Social Studies and in Science, and Words in Context. The Reading Test will always include a passage (or a pair of passages) from U.S. founding documents or a text from the great Global Conversation they stimulated. The Writing and Language test also assesses skills in Expression of Ideas and Standard English Conventions.

Command of Evidence

The PSAT/NMSQT® exam measures your ability to understand the information you're given and use it to draw your own conclusions and make predictions. For the Reading Test, this means you'll need to find relevant details in the passage that support your answers to questions. For the Writing and Language Test, this means you'll be asked to improve the way information is organized or presented in the passage so it makes the most logical sense and creates the most powerful passage. These questions may ask you to:

- Find and select relevant details in the passage
- Decide which information would be relevant to add to the passage
- Summarize the author's argument

TIP

Good news! The PSAT/NMSQT® exam does not require you to memorize specific information for the test. All of the information you need to answer will be right there in front of you in the passages. Any vocabulary questions will ask you to determine the meaning based on the context of the passage.

- Identify how information is used to support (or contrast with) the author's argument
- Identify relationships between the passage and any supporting information (graphs, charts, etc.)
- Draw conclusions based on information presented in the passage

Analysis in History/Social Studies and in Science

In college, you'll need to apply critical-thinking skills across all disciplines and be able to read and interpret all sorts of different content. That's why, since the 2015 test redesign, a big focus of the PSAT/NMSQT® exam is on testing students' ability to analyze real-world science, history, and social studies issues. In the Evidence-Based Reading and Writing section of the exam, this means you'll be given written/graphical information to read and make sense of the perspectives given. So, whether the topic is developments in space science or a controversial political issue, the PSAT/NMSQT® exam is designed to determine if you can read, interpret, and improve (if necessary) the way the information is presented. These questions may ask you to:

- Interpret data and information given
- Draw conclusions about the implications of that information or the author's argument
- Examine hypotheses and determine how well they're supported

Words in Context

You don't have to worry about coming to the test with your head crammed full of specific vocabulary words and definitions. Instead, you should come prepared to figure out a word's meaning based on the context of the words around it. This isn't your parents' standardized test, where students would have to memorize complicated words and Latin roots just to get through a Verbal section. These days, the PSAT/NMSQT® exam is much more focused on making sure you understand *how* to get to the meaning of a word, rather than the word itself. These questions may ask you to:

- Use clues in a passage to figure out the meaning of a word or phrase
- Think about how word choice can affect meaning, style, and tone in a passage

U.S. Founding Documents and the Great Global Conversation

As part of the redesigned test, the PSAT/NMSQT® exam includes a reading passage taken from one of the United States' founding documents (including the Constitution, the Declaration of Independence, and the Federalist Papers) or a piece inspired by those documents and ideas. By doing this, the PSAT/NMSQT® exam assesses your ability to read the text and draw meaningful conclusions from it…whether you agree with it or not. The end goal here is building the kind of close reading skills you'll need in college—reading, reflecting, and responding to issues that are significant and relevant to American life. These questions may ask you to:

- Compare and contrast the ideas presented in the documents with commentary on those ideas
- Draw conclusions of your own about the text
- Identify a writer's perspective and how it informs the passage

Expression of Ideas

The PSAT/NMSQT® exam tests your ability to discern whether a passage's organization could be improved and how it can best be done. These questions may ask you to:

- Determine which changes in a passage's words or structure are needed to improve its impact
- Evaluate how well sentences and paragraphs work together to present a well-organized passage

Standard English Conventions

Recognizing when a piece of writing is structured correctly—and knowing how to correct it when it is not—are valuable skills you will use in college writing and future business communication. The PSAT/NMSQT® exam tests your knowledge of the foundations of writing: punctuation, sentence structure, and usage.

These questions may ask you to:

- Recognize and correct errors in clause and sentence structure
- Recognize and correct errors in verb tense, parallel construction, and subject-verb agreement
- Recognize and correct errors in punctuation

The questions you'll see in the Evidence-Based Reading and Writing sections are designed to see how well you read and interpret information you may not have seen before.

THE PSAT/NMSQT® EXAM MATH SECTION

The PSAT/NMSQT® exam Math section presents you with the kinds of math you'll actually use the most—no gotchas or super-complex math concepts that you'll never use. The test focuses on the types of problem-solving and modeling skills that will help you through college math courses and in everyday life after that.

The Math section is divided into two subsections: Math Test—No Calculator and Math Test—Calculator. In the Math Test—No Calculator portion of the test, you'll be tested on how fluent you are in math and logic and your understanding of general math concepts, as well as math technique and number sense. In the Math Test—Calculator portion of the test, you'll use your graphing or scientific calculator (remember, no smartphones or tablets!) to answer questions about complex modeling and reasoning.

The PSAT/NMSQT® exam Math Test goes in-depth in three main areas of math:

- Heart of Algebra (linear equations and systems)
- Problem Solving/Data Analysis (interpreting data and patterns to apply math concepts to real world problems)
- Passport to Advanced Math (complex equations)

In addition to these major areas, there may also be questions about geometry and trigonometry (called Additional Topics in Math) that relate to real-world problems:

- Volume
- Trigonometric ratios

Even on the Calculator portion of the Math Test, you're not obligated to use your calculator for any question. And, in fact, sometimes it's better not to use one at all. If the question is about math reasoning rather than a specific number, it might be quicker to just work your way through and move on to the next question.

- Pythagorean theorem
- Complex number operations
- Degrees and radians
- Circle theorems for arc lengths, angle measures, chord lengths, and areas of sectors
- Congruence and similarity theorems for lines, angles, and triangles
- Similarity, right triangles, and trigonometric ratios for the sine and cosine of complementary angles
- Two-variable equations for a circle in the coordinate plane

With its focus on useful, real-world math, the PSAT/NMSQT® exam Math Test assesses skills in the following areas:

- **Fluency.** You understand what the problem is asking and can quickly apply math procedures to solve the problem.

- **Conceptual Understanding.** You have a grasp of general math concepts, operations, and relationships and can apply these concepts to a variety of contexts.

- **Application.** You can take abstract math concepts and recognize how they apply to a real-world problem.

THE PSAT/NMSQT® EXAM ANSWER SHEET

On test day, you'll be given an answer sheet along with your test booklet. This answer sheet is a big grid, where each question number is accompanied by either a set of four ovals (multiple-choice questions) or a set of write-in boxes and ovals where you can enter your answer (grid-ins).

For the multiple-choice questions, remember:

- **Mark your answer choices very clearly with your Number 2 pencil.** These answer sheets are graded by machines, so if your answer is unclear, there's no pair of human eyes there to give you the benefit of the doubt by saying, "hmm, it looks like she meant to pick choice C."

- **Fill in the bubbles; don't make Xs or check marks.** Again, you want your answer to be clear for the machines, so make sure you've fully filled in the oval for your answer choice.

- **Be careful when you skip a question.** If you can't answer a question, there's nothing wrong with moving on—but be sure that you list the skipped question number on your scratch paper, so you don't accidentally fill in #4 when you really meant to leave #4 blank for now and fill in #5.

- **Double-check your bubbles.** If B is your answer, make sure you're filling in the B oval. If you move too fast or fill carelessly, the scoring machine will never know you had the right answer and will mark it wrong.

For grid-in answers, the process is a little more complex. Some of the questions will require you to fill in answers, rather than picking from a set of four options. For these, your answer sheet will look a little different.

At the top of the grid, you'll write in the numerical answer. The slashes that appear in the second row are used for answers with fractions. If you need one of these fraction lines in your answer, darken one of the circles. The circles with the dots are for answers with decimal points—use these circles just as you do the fraction line circles. In the lower part of the grid, fill in the numbered circles that correspond to the numbers in your answer.

Here are some examples. Note that for grid-in responses, answers can begin on the left or the right.

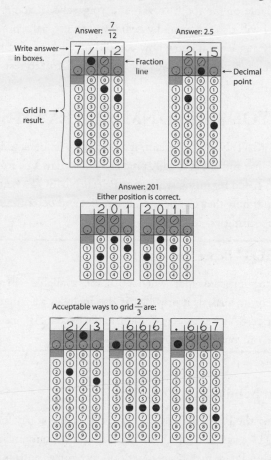

Once you understand the following six rules, you can concentrate on just solving the math problems in this section.

1. Write your answer in the boxes at the top of the grid.

2. Mark the corresponding circles, one per column.

3. Start in any column.

4. Work with decimals or fractions.

5. Express mixed numbers as decimals or improper fractions.

6. If more than one answer is possible, grid any one.

HOW THE PSAT/NMSQT® EXAM IS SCORED

Now that you know how to fill in your answer sheet, what happens to those sheets after your 2 hours and 45 minutes are up? At the end of the testing time, your answer sheets will be collected and sent by your school to the College Board.

The Evidence-Based Reading and Writing section of the test (Reading/Writing and Language) and the Math section each get their own raw score, which is then converted into a scaled score of 160–760 points. These are added together to get your total PSAT/NMSQT® score, which will range from 320–1520.

Your scores will be available online (both to you and your school) about two months after your test date, and your school will also follow up by giving you an official score report and walking you through the results. They can let you know how you did on each section and help you determine your strengths and weaknesses as you get ready for other standardized tests and college prep.

HOW TO USE YOUR PSAT/NMSQT® EXAM SCORES

As you prepare for the PSAT/NMSQT® exam, it's helpful to understand exactly what's at stake and why it's worth your time and effort to fully prepare for test day. The following information will get you completely up to speed regarding what your PSAT/NMSQT® exam scores, subscores, and cross-test scores mean, and how they can be used to predict and determine future success—as well as open doors to new opportunities.

Your PSAT/NMSQT® Score Report

Pay careful attention to your score report when it becomes available—in addition to the wealth of information and scoring analysis it provides, it also includes information on how to access free SAT® exam practice, SAT® exam registration, and a look at AP® exam courses that might be right for you based on your performance.

The National Merit Scholarship Program

Did you know that taking the PSAT/NMSQT® exam can help you pay for college? Students who take the PSAT/NMSQT® exam and meet the official entry requirements are entered into the National Merit Scholarship Program. This competition recognizes outstanding students who score exceptionally well on the PSAT/NMSQT® exam with commendations and possible scholarships, to help cover the costs of college. These include National Merit Scholarships as well as a variety of corporate-sponsored and college-sponsored scholarship awards.

For a comprehensive list of scholarships and entry requirements, visit the official College Board website.

Use Your Scores to Prepare for the SAT® Test

Your performance on the PSAT/NMSQT® exam will help you build an effective study plan for the SAT® exam. Although these two exams have different score ranges (the SAT® score range is 400–1600, while the PSAT/NMSQT® score range for is 320–1520), the good news is that the skill areas tested overlap and the tests use a common scoring scale. What does this mean? It means that your PSAT/NMSQT® scores are a good indication of how you might do on the SAT® exam. This is extremely valuable information!

Success on the SAT® exam—an important exam that will help determine what colleges you'll be eligible to attend—requires a solid study plan, and your PSAT/NMSQT® scores will help you build an effective plan for SAT® test success. Once you receive your scores, analyze them to understand your key areas of strength and weakness. Chances are, they'll also be your strong and weak areas on the SAT® exam, so use this information when you begin preparing for test day.

Are you strong in math but struggle with evidence-based reading? Are you better at comprehending and answering questions based on history passages than those based on science topics? Use this information to guide your study, giving extra time and attention to your weak areas. Be sure to make building your skills in your weak test areas and maintaining and strengthening your skills in your stronger areas a key goal of your SAT® exam study plan.

Prepare for College and Career Success

The PSAT/NMSQT® exam is designed to test and measure the foundational skills that are critical for success beyond high school—both in college and in your chosen career path. Your test scores will indicate your current abilities in each of the skill areas tested. Use this information wisely as you prepare for future success.

You're well aware of the importance of having strong reading, writing, and math skills in the classroom—these skills are at the core of nearly any course of study you choose to pursue, so if you want to be ready for college then be sure to address any areas of weakness that your PSAT/NMSQT® scores reveal.

Did you know that the skills tested on the PSAT/NMSQT® exam are also good predictors of success in your chosen career path? It's true! Therefore, understanding your scores and using them to make improvements can really have positive long-term effects on your future. Determine any weak areas you may have based on your section scores, subscores, and cross-test scores, and devote some attention to building your skills so that you're at your best when you enter college and the world of work.

Here's an example: Are your evidence-based reading and writing skills strong but your math skills without a calculator need some improvement? Then be sure to devote some time and focus on building your math skills. Drill down deeper, using your subscores and cross-test scores to focus your skill-building efforts. Are you proficient in problem solving and data analysis but struggle with algebra and advanced math? Target your skill-building in these specific areas.

Remember, learning and skill-building can happen both in the classroom and out—there are a wealth of learning resources available that can help you address and attack any weak areas you may have. Once you're aware of the areas you need to focus on, be sure to take full advantage of them.

Using Your Practice Scores—The Bottom Line

We know that you're eager to do well on the PSAT/NMSQT® exam—that's precisely why you're using this book—and we're with you on your journey towards test day success. But we're also here to help take your journey a step further, to help you take full advantage of what your performance on the PSAT/NMSQT® exam means and how you can make the most of the information your scores provide—for long-term life success in high school, college, and beyond.

STRATEGIES FOR PSAT/NMSQT® EXAM SUCCESS

The PSAT/NMSQT® exam isn't a huge mystery and neither is getting a good score. If you put in the time and effort to prepare, you're doing yourself huge favors on test day. Because there are scholarships and other academic honors on the line, don't you want to do everything you can to make you and your skills shine through? Here are some tips for your PSAT/NMSQT® exam prep.

Practice, Practice, Practice

If you're reading this, you've already taken a very important first step! Take full advantage of the practice tests in this book and online to get yourself used to the timing and types of questions you'll face on test day.

Watch the Clock

When you do your PSAT/NMSQT® exam practice, make sure you're timing yourself. The last thing you want to do on test day is get through ten questions out of forty-four, only to find you're totally out of time (and options for finishing up). Plan accordingly: if you know you have 30 minutes and forty-five questions, make sure you're spending only about 40 seconds on each question. Here's where all that practice comes in handy. Test yourself on particular question types. If you find that you're lagging on certain kinds of questions, come up with an attack plan to either a) cut down your time or b) work as fast as you can through the question types that take less time, and then go back for the harder ones.

If you don't wear a watch, now's the time to invest in one, and get used to wearing it while you take practice tests. On test day, you may find yourself in a room without a clock…and you can't bring in any cell phones or devices, so you'll need to keep track of time somehow. An old-school watch does the trick quite nicely—just make sure it's not a fancy calculator watch or one with a lot of bells or whistles, because you might have it taken away on test day before you ever fill in a bubble.

Know When to Bail

Sometimes you're just going to come up to a question that stumps you. Don't let that bog down the rest of your test. If you know early on that it's a lost cause, make a guess and move on—you've got plenty of other things to do!

Skip the Directions on Test Day

"But," you say, "how will I know what to do?" Here's another place where your prep comes in handy. Familiarize yourself with the test directions well before test day, in this book and online. The PSAT/NMSQT® test makers aren't trying to trip you up—the directions will be the same on test day. One less thing you have to read when your time is precious!

Do the Easy Math Questions First

In the Math section, the questions are usually laid out with the easiest questions first and the hardest questions last. The faster you move through the easy questions, the more time you'll have for the trickier ones at the end.

Don't Panic

One of the most important things you can practice ahead of test day is keeping calm. If you feel like you're not getting answers right away, do everything you can to eliminate choices. If you can't even do that, skip the question and go back later. Practicing breathing exercises can help, too. Don't let one small part of the test derail your whole test day.

MAKING YOUR PSAT/NMSQT® EXAM STUDY PLAN

There's no magic solution to acing the PSAT/NMSQT® exam. If you've got time and are willing to put in the prep work of learning the ins and outs of the test, identifying and improving your weaknesses, and coming up with strategies that work for you on each section of the test, you'll be in great shape. Let's look at a couple of sample study plans you can use, depending on how much time you have before test day. (And if the answer to that question is "not much," don't worry—one of the two is an accelerated plan for you to follow.)

If you have several months before the test…

- Review this chapter carefully to make sure you understand what the test is like and what's expected.
- Take the diagnostic test to figure out what you do well, what you need to work on, and how the test works.
- Read each strategy and content review chapter, and work through the examples and practice sections.
- Read all answer explanations.
- Take full-length practice tests.
- Go back to the chapters where you still need some work.

If you have only a month or less to prepare…

- Review this chapter carefully to make sure you understand what the test is like and what's expected.
- Take the diagnostic test to figure out what you do well, what you need to work on, and how the test works.
- Once you know your problem areas, read the chapters that focus on that material. Make sure you work through all examples and practice sections in these chapters.
- Read all answer explanations.
- Take as many practice exams as you can in the weeks or days leading up to the test.

MEASURING YOUR PROGRESS

So how do you know whether all this is working? There's only one test day, and it can be tough to see where all of your hard work is leading. Here are some benchmarks you can set along the way to make sure you're moving along at the right pace. The most important thing you can do is to police yourself, making sure that you're setting aside enough time for prep, and taking your time with each area of the test. Your progress plan will look something like this:

Start

Take the diagnostic test, and make some notes about where you really need to beef up your skills and knowledge. Then start working on the book chapters. If you have a lot of time before test day, you can work through all chapters. If you have only a month or so, target your study based on the areas where you need some extra work.

One-Third of the Way Through

Take a full practice test. If you're doing better than you did on your diagnostic, great! If you still have areas for improvement, go back to the specific chapters and work through them again. If your math scores are right up there but your Reading and Writing and Language scores are still below where you'd like them to be, it's time to really start focusing on those tests.

Two-Thirds of the Way Through

Take a second practice test. This is another chance to see exactly how far you've come and what review you still need to go back and do. Did the extra review boost your scores? Are you still strong in the areas where you were strong before? If the answer to both of those is "yes," then that's fantastic. Keep doing what you're doing with your practice, but you probably don't have to spend as much time reviewing content. If the answer is "no," you still have time to do some emergency review and practice.

The Final Countdown to the Test

Crunch time. At this point (about a week before the test), it's getting awfully late to be learning new geometry concepts or grammar skills. Take timed practice tests if you have not already, answer all practice questions, and make sure you're getting the *feel* of the exam down, now that you've hopefully had time to review all of the content tested on the exam.

The timing for your progress plan really depends on you and how much time you have before the test. Before you do anything, make sure you have a clear plan in your head for milestones you can achieve between now and test day. ("By August, I will have taken three practice tests," for example.)

The Night Before

Okay, so once you've done all of your prep, all of your practice, and all of your positive-thinking exercises for test day, what do you need to do the night before? Here's your checklist for test day success.

- **Prep your "go bag,"** with your photo ID, your Number 2 pencils, your calculator, and your watch. If the next morning is a rush, you don't want to risk forgetting any of those things.

- **Get a good night's sleep.** If you're groggy, you won't be performing as well as you can on test day, so get as much sleep and rest as you can the night before.

- **Plan to wear layers.** If the test room is boiling, you don't want to be roasting in a heavy sweater. Or if someone left the air conditioning on high, it's going to be difficult to do math while you're shivering. Dress in weather-appropriate layers so you can shed them or add them as necessary.

- **Pack a healthy snack.** You can't eat in the testing room, but you will get two short, 5-minute breaks out in the hallway.

- **Set your alarm.** You don't want to be that cautionary-tale student who overslept and missed the test altogether. Make sure you get up and are at school on time so that you don't miss any instructions or important info before the test.

- **Eat a normal breakfast.** You don't need to carb-load (this isn't a marathon!), but you should make sure that you eat something healthy and in line with your usual breakfast plan.

SUMMING IT UP

- The PSAT/NMSQT® exam is an essential step on your path to finishing high school strong and preparing for college. While your scores aren't used for your college applications, they can qualify you for prestigious National Merit Scholarship grants and honors that can be extremely helpful in your future college career.

- The PSAT/NMSQT® exam is taken primarily by high school sophomores and juniors, but you can take it up to three times throughout your high school career. However, only the junior year scores count for the National Merit Scholarship Program.

- Exam scores are available online about two months after the test, but you will also receive an official score report from your school. They will walk you through the results and what they mean for your college prep.

- Your school hosts the test and handles registration for students, so you should confirm dates and registration with your school counselor. Some schools pay the $15 test fee for students but not all schools do, so be sure to double-check your own school's policy.

- On test day, don't bring phones, tablets, or computers. All you'll be allowed to have in the test room with you are your test booklet, your answer sheet, a piece of scratch paper (which will be given to you), your pencils, and your College Board-approved calculator.

- The Evidence-Based Reading and Writing section of the PSAT/NMSQT® exam focuses on your ability to read, interpret, and edit information presented in passages. You won't need to write anything; you will be reading information in various types of passages (literary, history, science, and social science) and making decisions about how to present that information in the best possible way.

- The Math section of the PSAT/NMSQT® exam targets the kind of math you can apply to real-world problems, not abstract concepts that you'll never have to face after high school. It tests your fluency, problem-solving abilities, and math techniques. The Math section is the only section of the test that has some grid-in answers in addition to multiple-choice questions.

- The most important thing you can do ahead of test day is practice like crazy. Take advantage of all of the tools available to you (diagnostic test, chapters, examples, practice sets, and full-length practice tests) to get in shape for test day. Know your test-taking style and the areas where you need to pay extra close attention. And timing is crucial as well—make sure you're prepping for test timing as well as the test itself.

- Whether you have one month or three months before test day, never fear—there's a study plan for you. If you have several months of prep time, you can pace yourself through the comprehensive PSAT/NMSQT® prep materials. If you have less time, you can condense your study plan by taking a diagnostic test and laser-focusing your prep on the areas where you need the most work.

- Keep track of your progress throughout. Set milestones (practice tests, chapter reviews, score goals), so that you're making steady progress toward test day.

PART II
DIAGNOSING STRENGTHS AND WEAKNESSES

The Diagnostic Test

OVERVIEW

- Introduction to the Diagnostic Test
- The PSAT/NMSQT® Exam Answer Sheet
- Section 1: Reading Test
- Section 2: Writing and Language Test
- Section 3: Math Test—No Calculator

- Section 4: Math Test—Calculator
- Answer Keys and Explanations
- Using Your Diagnostic Test Results
- Subscores, Test Scores, and Cross-Test Scores

INTRODUCTION TO THE DIAGNOSTIC TEST

Before you start your preparation and review for the PSAT/NMSQT® exam, it's important for you to understand your strengths and weaknesses. That way, you can tailor your studying to hit the areas where you need the most work.

The key to creating a study plan that gets results is to not waste precious time—that's where this diagnostic test comes in. The test that follows mirrors the actual PSAT/NMSQT® exam you will see on test day. As you take it, make a note of which sections give you trouble and which, if any, you are able to complete with some ease. After completing the test and calculating your score, you will have a better sense of where you should focus your studying.

Preparing to Take the Diagnostic Test

Aim to take this diagnostic test as you would a real PSAT/NMSQT® exam. If possible, take the test in one sitting—find a quiet room, set aside a block of 3 hours, and minimize all distractions. The actual test is 2 hours and 45 minutes, and you'll be allowed to take three short breaks.

It may seem like overkill to plan a practice test so strictly, but you really will want to get a sense of how long you can spend on each question in each section. Then you can begin to work out a pacing schedule for yourself.

Gather all the things you will need to take the test. These include:

- No. 2 pencils, at least three
- A calculator with fresh batteries
- A timer

Have a snack, turn off your phone, and get to work! Don't forget to set your timer for the time specified for each section, which is noted at the top of the first page of each test section. Stick to that time, so you are simulating the real test.

When you're done with the test, turn to page 79 for extensive answer explanations for every test question and to calculate your final score.

Good luck!

PSAT/NMSQT® EXAM ANSWER SHEET

Section 1: Reading Test

1. Ⓐ Ⓑ Ⓒ Ⓓ	11. Ⓐ Ⓑ Ⓒ Ⓓ	21. Ⓐ Ⓑ Ⓒ Ⓓ	30. Ⓐ Ⓑ Ⓒ Ⓓ	39. Ⓐ Ⓑ Ⓒ Ⓓ
2. Ⓐ Ⓑ Ⓒ Ⓓ	12. Ⓐ Ⓑ Ⓒ Ⓓ	22. Ⓐ Ⓑ Ⓒ Ⓓ	31. Ⓐ Ⓑ Ⓒ Ⓓ	40. Ⓐ Ⓑ Ⓒ Ⓓ
3. Ⓐ Ⓑ Ⓒ Ⓓ	13. Ⓐ Ⓑ Ⓒ Ⓓ	23. Ⓐ Ⓑ Ⓒ Ⓓ	32. Ⓐ Ⓑ Ⓒ Ⓓ	41. Ⓐ Ⓑ Ⓒ Ⓓ
4. Ⓐ Ⓑ Ⓒ Ⓓ	14. Ⓐ Ⓑ Ⓒ Ⓓ	24. Ⓐ Ⓑ Ⓒ Ⓓ	33. Ⓐ Ⓑ Ⓒ Ⓓ	42. Ⓐ Ⓑ Ⓒ Ⓓ
5. Ⓐ Ⓑ Ⓒ Ⓓ	15. Ⓐ Ⓑ Ⓒ Ⓓ	25. Ⓐ Ⓑ Ⓒ Ⓓ	34. Ⓐ Ⓑ Ⓒ Ⓓ	43. Ⓐ Ⓑ Ⓒ Ⓓ
6. Ⓐ Ⓑ Ⓒ Ⓓ	16. Ⓐ Ⓑ Ⓒ Ⓓ	26. Ⓐ Ⓑ Ⓒ Ⓓ	35. Ⓐ Ⓑ Ⓒ Ⓓ	44. Ⓐ Ⓑ Ⓒ Ⓓ
7. Ⓐ Ⓑ Ⓒ Ⓓ	17. Ⓐ Ⓑ Ⓒ Ⓓ	27. Ⓐ Ⓑ Ⓒ Ⓓ	36. Ⓐ Ⓑ Ⓒ Ⓓ	45. Ⓐ Ⓑ Ⓒ Ⓓ
8. Ⓐ Ⓑ Ⓒ Ⓓ	18. Ⓐ Ⓑ Ⓒ Ⓓ	28. Ⓐ Ⓑ Ⓒ Ⓓ	37. Ⓐ Ⓑ Ⓒ Ⓓ	46. Ⓐ Ⓑ Ⓒ Ⓓ
9. Ⓐ Ⓑ Ⓒ Ⓓ	19. Ⓐ Ⓑ Ⓒ Ⓓ	29. Ⓐ Ⓑ Ⓒ Ⓓ	38. Ⓐ Ⓑ Ⓒ Ⓓ	47. Ⓐ Ⓑ Ⓒ Ⓓ
10. Ⓐ Ⓑ Ⓒ Ⓓ	20. Ⓐ Ⓑ Ⓒ Ⓓ			

Section 2: Writing and Language Test

1. Ⓐ Ⓑ Ⓒ Ⓓ	10. Ⓐ Ⓑ Ⓒ Ⓓ	19. Ⓐ Ⓑ Ⓒ Ⓓ	28. Ⓐ Ⓑ Ⓒ Ⓓ	37. Ⓐ Ⓑ Ⓒ Ⓓ
2. Ⓐ Ⓑ Ⓒ Ⓓ	11. Ⓐ Ⓑ Ⓒ Ⓓ	20. Ⓐ Ⓑ Ⓒ Ⓓ	29. Ⓐ Ⓑ Ⓒ Ⓓ	38. Ⓐ Ⓑ Ⓒ Ⓓ
3. Ⓐ Ⓑ Ⓒ Ⓓ	12. Ⓐ Ⓑ Ⓒ Ⓓ	21. Ⓐ Ⓑ Ⓒ Ⓓ	30. Ⓐ Ⓑ Ⓒ Ⓓ	39. Ⓐ Ⓑ Ⓒ Ⓓ
4. Ⓐ Ⓑ Ⓒ Ⓓ	13. Ⓐ Ⓑ Ⓒ Ⓓ	22. Ⓐ Ⓑ Ⓒ Ⓓ	31. Ⓐ Ⓑ Ⓒ Ⓓ	40. Ⓐ Ⓑ Ⓒ Ⓓ
5. Ⓐ Ⓑ Ⓒ Ⓓ	14. Ⓐ Ⓑ Ⓒ Ⓓ	23. Ⓐ Ⓑ Ⓒ Ⓓ	32. Ⓐ Ⓑ Ⓒ Ⓓ	41. Ⓐ Ⓑ Ⓒ Ⓓ
6. Ⓐ Ⓑ Ⓒ Ⓓ	15. Ⓐ Ⓑ Ⓒ Ⓓ	24. Ⓐ Ⓑ Ⓒ Ⓓ	33. Ⓐ Ⓑ Ⓒ Ⓓ	42. Ⓐ Ⓑ Ⓒ Ⓓ
7. Ⓐ Ⓑ Ⓒ Ⓓ	16. Ⓐ Ⓑ Ⓒ Ⓓ	25. Ⓐ Ⓑ Ⓒ Ⓓ	34. Ⓐ Ⓑ Ⓒ Ⓓ	43. Ⓐ Ⓑ Ⓒ Ⓓ
8. Ⓐ Ⓑ Ⓒ Ⓓ	17. Ⓐ Ⓑ Ⓒ Ⓓ	26. Ⓐ Ⓑ Ⓒ Ⓓ	35. Ⓐ Ⓑ Ⓒ Ⓓ	44. Ⓐ Ⓑ Ⓒ Ⓓ
9. Ⓐ Ⓑ Ⓒ Ⓓ	18. Ⓐ Ⓑ Ⓒ Ⓓ	27. Ⓐ Ⓑ Ⓒ Ⓓ	36. Ⓐ Ⓑ Ⓒ Ⓓ	

Section 3: Math Test—No Calculator

1. Ⓐ Ⓑ Ⓒ Ⓓ	4. Ⓐ Ⓑ Ⓒ Ⓓ	7. Ⓐ Ⓑ Ⓒ Ⓓ	10. Ⓐ Ⓑ Ⓒ Ⓓ	12. Ⓐ Ⓑ Ⓒ Ⓓ
2. Ⓐ Ⓑ Ⓒ Ⓓ	5. Ⓐ Ⓑ Ⓒ Ⓓ	8. Ⓐ Ⓑ Ⓒ Ⓓ	11. Ⓐ Ⓑ Ⓒ Ⓓ	13. Ⓐ Ⓑ Ⓒ Ⓓ
3. Ⓐ Ⓑ Ⓒ Ⓓ	6. Ⓐ Ⓑ Ⓒ Ⓓ	9. Ⓐ Ⓑ Ⓒ Ⓓ		

answer sheet

Section 3: Math Test—No Calculator

14.
15.
16.
17.

Section 4: Math Test—Calculator

1. Ⓐ Ⓑ Ⓒ Ⓓ   7. Ⓐ Ⓑ Ⓒ Ⓓ   13. Ⓐ Ⓑ Ⓒ Ⓓ   18. Ⓐ Ⓑ Ⓒ Ⓓ   23. Ⓐ Ⓑ Ⓒ Ⓓ

2. Ⓐ Ⓑ Ⓒ Ⓓ   8. Ⓐ Ⓑ Ⓒ Ⓓ   14. Ⓐ Ⓑ Ⓒ Ⓓ   19. Ⓐ Ⓑ Ⓒ Ⓓ   24. Ⓐ Ⓑ Ⓒ Ⓓ

3. Ⓐ Ⓑ Ⓒ Ⓓ   9. Ⓐ Ⓑ Ⓒ Ⓓ   15. Ⓐ Ⓑ Ⓒ Ⓓ   20. Ⓐ Ⓑ Ⓒ Ⓓ   25. Ⓐ Ⓑ Ⓒ Ⓓ

4. Ⓐ Ⓑ Ⓒ Ⓓ   10. Ⓐ Ⓑ Ⓒ Ⓓ   16. Ⓐ Ⓑ Ⓒ Ⓓ   21. Ⓐ Ⓑ Ⓒ Ⓓ   26. Ⓐ Ⓑ Ⓒ Ⓓ

5. Ⓐ Ⓑ Ⓒ Ⓓ   11. Ⓐ Ⓑ Ⓒ Ⓓ   17. Ⓐ Ⓑ Ⓒ Ⓓ   22. Ⓐ Ⓑ Ⓒ Ⓓ   27. Ⓐ Ⓑ Ⓒ Ⓓ

6. Ⓐ Ⓑ Ⓒ Ⓓ   12. Ⓐ Ⓑ Ⓒ Ⓓ

28.
29.
30.
31.

SECTION 1: READING TEST

60 Minutes • 47 Questions

Turn to Section 1 of your answer sheet to answer the questions in this section.

> **Directions:** Each passage (or pair of passages) below is followed by a number of questions. After reading each passage, select the best answer to each question based on what is stated or implied in the passage or passages and in any supplementary material, such as a table, graph, or chart.

Questions 1–9 are based on the following passage.

This passage is adapted from *The Lost World*, by Sir Arthur Conan Doyle, originally published in 1912.

The peaceful penetration of Maple White Land was the pressing subject before us. We had the evidence of our own eyes that the place was inhabited by some unknown creatures, and there was that of Maple White's sketch-book to show that more dreadful and more

Line dangerous monsters might still appear. That there might also prove to be human occupants
5 and that they were of a malevolent character was suggested by the skeleton impaled upon the bamboos, which could not have got there had it not been dropped from above. Our situation, stranded without possibility of escape in such a land, was clearly full of danger, and our reasons endorsed every measure of caution which Lord John's experience could suggest. Yet it was surely impossible that we should halt on the edge of this world of mystery when our very
10 souls were tingling with impatience to push forward and to pluck the heart from it.

We therefore blocked the entrance to our zareba by filling it up with several thorny bushes, and left our camp with the stores entirely surrounded by this protecting hedge. We then slowly and cautiously set forth into the unknown, following the course of the little stream which flowed from our spring, as it should always serve us as a guide on our return.

15 Hardly had we started when we came across signs that there were indeed wonders awaiting us. After a few hundred yards of thick forest, containing many trees which were quite unknown to me, but which Summerlee, who was the botanist of the party, recognized as forms of conifera and of cycadaceous plants which have long passed away in the world below, we entered a region where the stream widened out and formed a considerable bog. High
20 reeds of a peculiar type grew thickly before us, which were pronounced to be equisetacea, or mare's-tails, with tree-ferns scattered amongst them, all of them swaying in a brisk wind. Suddenly Lord John, who was walking first, halted with uplifted hand.

"Look at this!" said he. "By George, this must be the trail of the father of all birds!"

An enormous three-toed track was imprinted in the soft mud before us. The creature,
25 whatever it was, had crossed the swamp and had passed on into the forest. We all stopped to examine that monstrous spoor. If it were indeed a bird—and what animal could leave such a mark?—its foot was so much larger than an ostrich's that its height upon the same scale must be enormous. Lord John looked eagerly round him and slipped two cartridges into his elephant-gun.

30   "I'll stake my good name as a shikarree," said he, "that the track is a fresh one. The creature has not passed ten minutes. Look how the water is still oozing into that deeper print! By Jove! See, here is the mark of a little one!"

Sure enough, smaller tracks of the same general form were running parallel to the large ones.

35   "But what do you make of this?" cried Professor Summerlee, triumphantly, pointing to what looked like the huge print of a five-fingered human hand appearing among the three-toed marks.

"Wealden!" cried Challenger, in an ecstasy. "I've seen them in the Wealden clay. It is a creature walking erect upon three-toed feet, and occasionally putting one of its five-fingered

40 forepaws upon the ground. Not a bird, my dear Roxton—not a bird."

"A beast?"

"No; a reptile—a dinosaur. Nothing else could have left such a track. They puzzled a worthy Sussex doctor some ninety years ago; but who in the world could have hoped— hoped—to have seen a sight like that?"

45   His words died away into a whisper, and we all stood in motionless amazement. Following the tracks, we had left the morass and passed through a screen of brushwood and trees. Beyond was an open glade, and in this were five of the most extraordinary creatures that I have ever seen. Crouching down among the bushes, we observed them at our leisure.

There were, as I say, five of them, two being adults and three young ones. In size they

50 were enormous. Even the babies were as big as elephants, while the two large ones were far beyond all creatures I have ever seen. They had slate-colored skin, which was scaled like a lizard's and shimmered where the sun shone upon it. All five were sitting up, balancing themselves upon their broad, powerful tails and their huge three-toed hind-feet, while with their small five-fingered front-feet they pulled down the branches upon which they browsed.

55 I do not know that I can bring their appearance home to you better than by saying that they looked like monstrous kangaroos, twenty feet in length, and with skins like black crocodiles.

1. The passage characterizes Maple White Land as fantastical in that

   A. it is not a real place.

   B. large birds live there.

   C. people are exploring it.

   D. dinosaurs exist there.

2. Which choice provides the best evidence for the answer to the previous question?

   A. Line 1 ("The peaceful … before us.")

   B. Lines 24-25 ("The creature … forest.")

   C. Line 40 ("Not a … bird.")

   D. Line 42 ("No … track.")

3. What does Challenger's reaction to the tracks say about him?

   A. Challenger is open to incredible possibilities.

   B. Challenger is extremely close-minded.

   C. Challenger is very unrealistic.

   D. Challenger has a great sense of humor.

4. As used in line 1, "penetration" most nearly means

   A. saturation.

   B. entrance into.

   C. comprehension.

   D. insight.

5. Based on the passage, when Lord John says he found the trail of "the father of all birds" (line 23), Lord John most probably means that he thinks he has found

   A. evidence of the earth's first bird.

   B. a bird that recently had chicks.

   C. the bird responsible for every other bird.

   D. a large heap of handsome feathers.

6. As used in line 30, "fresh" most nearly means

   A. novel.

   B. refreshing.

   C. new.

   D. ancient.

7. Based on the passage, which character most likely identified the high reeds as equisetacea?

   A. Lord John

   B. Challenger

   C. Summerlee

   D. the narrator

8. Which choice provides the best evidence for the answer to the previous question?

   A. Lines 7-8 ("our reasons … suggest.")

   B. Lines 17-18 ("but which … below")

   C. Lines 19-20 ("High reeds … equisetacea")

   D. Line 38 ("Wealden! … ecstasy.")

9. In the context of the passage, the main purpose of line 45 ("His words … amazement.") is to show that the party

   A. was losing consciousness.

   B. was having a hallucination.

   C. had been immobilized by force.

   D. is stunned by what they see.

diagnostic test—Reading

Questions 10–18 are based on the following passage and supplementary material.

This passage is adapted from *A Negro Explorer at the North Pole*, by Matthew A. Henson, originally published in 1912.

The story of the winter at Cape Sheridan is a story unique in the experience of Arctic exploration. Usually it is the rule to hibernate as much as possible during the period of darkness, and the party is confined closely to headquarters. The Peary plan is different; and *Line* constant activity and travel were insisted on.

5   There were very few days when all of the members of the expedition were together, after the ship had reached her destination. Hunting parties were immediately sent out, for it was on the big game of the country that the expedition depended for fresh meat. Professor Marvin commenced his scientific work, and his several stations were all remote from headquarters; and all winter long, parties were sledging provisions, equipment, etc., to Cape 10 Columbia, ninety-three miles northwest, in anticipation of the journey to the Pole. Those who remained at headquarters did not find life an idle dream. There was something in the way of work going on all of the time. I was away from the ship on two hunting trips of about ten days each, and while at headquarters, I shaped and built over two dozen sledges, besides doing lots of other work.

15   Naturally there were frequent storms and intense cold, and in regard to the storms of the Arctic regions of North Greenland and Grant Land, the only word I can use to describe them is "terrible," in the fullest meaning it conveys. The effect of such storms of wind and snow, or rain, is abject physical terror, due to the realization of perfect helplessness. I have seen rocks a hundred and a hundred and fifty pounds in weight picked up by the storm and 20 blown for distances of ninety or a hundred feet to the edge of a precipice, and there of their own momentum go hurtling through space to fall in crashing fragments at the base. Imagine the effect of such a rainfall of death-dealing boulders on the feelings of a little group of three or four, who have sought the base of the cliff for shelter. I have been there and I have seen one of my Esquimo companions felled by a blow from a rock eighty-four pounds in weight, 25 which struck him fairly between the shoulder-blades, literally knocking the life out of him. I have been there, and believe me, I have been afraid. A hundred-pound box of supplies, taking an aërial joy ride, during the progress of a storm down at Anniversary Lodge in 1894, struck Commander Peary a glancing blow which put him out of commission for over a week. These mighty winds make it possible for the herbivorous animals of this region to exist. They sweep 30 the snow from vast stretches of land, exposing the hay and dried dwarf-willows, that the hare, musk-oxen, and reindeer feed on.

The Esquimo families who came north to Cape Sheridan with us on the *Roosevelt* found life much more ideal than down in their native land. It was a pleasure trip for them, with nothing to worry about, and everything provided. Some of the families lived aboard ship all 35 through the winter, and some in the box-house on shore...

There were thirty-nine Esquimos in the expedition, men, women and children; for the Esquimo travels heavy and takes his women and children with him as a matter of course. The women were as useful as the men, and the small boys did the ship's chores, sledging in fresh water from the lake, etc. They were mostly in families; but there were several young,

40 unmarried men, and the unattached, much-married and divorced Miss "Bill," who domiciled herself aboard the ship and did much good work with her needle. She was my seamstress and the thick fur clothes worn on the trip to the Pole were sewn by her. The Esquimos lived as happily as in their own country and carried on their domestic affairs with almost the same care-free irregularity as usual.

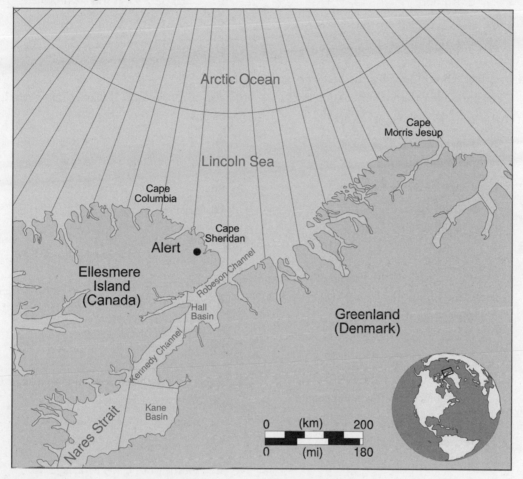

10. Which choice best supports the author's claim that the winter at Cape Sheridan was "unique in the experience of Arctic exploration" (lines 1-2)?

   A. The explorers planned to take a journey to the North Pole.

   B. The explorers continued to work through the dark season.

   C. The explorers had to face frequent storms and intense cold.

   D. The explorers saw storms carry away 150-pound rocks.

11. As used in line 7, "game" most nearly means

   A. sport.

   B. amusement.

   C. wild animals.

   D. willing.

12. Based on the passage, the storms at Cape Sheridan
    A. made the work harder to perform.
    B. occurred every day during the expedition.
    C. were essentially harmless.
    D. disturbed the narrator deeply.

13. Which choice provides the best evidence for the answer to the previous question?
    A. Line 15 ("Naturally … cold")
    B. Lines 17-18 ("The effect … helplessness.")
    C. Lines 18-20 ("I have seen … precipice")
    D. Lines 23-24 ("I have been … weight")

14. Over the course of the passage, the main focus shifts from
    A. the storms at Cape Sheridan to the plants hare, musk-oxen, and reindeer eat.
    B. the environment at Cape Sheridan to the habits of the Esquimo people.
    C. Professor Marvin's scientific work to the journey to the North Pole.
    D. hunting trips to the construction of sledges.

15. Which choice provides the best evidence for the answer to the previous question?
    A. Lines 28-30 ("These mighty … land.")
    B. Lines 33-34 ("It was … provided.")
    C. Lines 34-37 ("Some … course.")
    D. Lines 38-39 ("The women … lake, etc.")

16. As used in line 27, "progress" most nearly means
    A. journey.
    B. improvement.
    C. evolution.
    D. develop.

17. According to the passage and the map, the explorers were stationed near
    A. Greenland.
    B. Ellesmere Island.
    C. Cape Morris Jesup.
    D. Montreal.

18. According to the passage and the map, the explorers were stationed
    A. northeast of Cape Sheridan.
    B. northwest of Greenland.
    C. southeast of Cape Morris Jesup.
    D. southeast of Cape Columbia.

Questions 19–28 are based on the following passage and supplementary material.

This passage is adapted from *The Story of the Living Machine,* by H.W. Conn, originally published in 1899.

…animals and plants show relationships. This fact is one of the most patent and yet one of the most suggestive facts of biology. It has been recognized from the very beginning of the study of animals and plants. One cannot be even the most superficial observer without seeing
Line that certain forms show great likeness to each other while others are much more unlike.
5 The grouping of animals and plants into orders, genera, and species is dependent upon this relationship. If two forms are alike in everything except some slight detail, they are commonly placed in the same genus but in different species, while if they show a greater unlikeness they may be placed in separate genera. By thus grouping together forms according to their resemblance the animal and vegetable kingdoms are classified into groups subordinate to
10 groups. The principle of relationship, i.e., fundamental similarity of structure, runs through the whole animal and vegetable kingdom. Even the animals most unlike each other show certain points of similarity which indicates a relationship, although of course a distant one.

The fact of such a relationship is too patent to demand more words, but its significance needs to be pointed out. When we speak of relationship among men we always mean
15 historical connection. Two brothers are closely related because they have sprung from common parents, while two cousins are less closely related because their common point of origin was farther back in time…

This subject of comparative anatomy includes a consideration of what is called homology, and perhaps a concrete example may be instructive both in illustration and as
20 suggesting the course which nature adopts in constructing her machines. We speak of a monkey's arm and a bird's wing as homologous, although they are wonderfully different in appearance and adapted to different duties. They are called homologous because they have similar parts in similar relations. This can be seen in Figs. 47 and 48, where it will be seen that each has the same bones, although in the bird's wing some of the bones have been fused
25 together and others lost. Their similarity points to a relationship, but their dissimilarity tells us that the relationship is a distant one, and that their common point of origin must have been quite far back in history. Now if we follow back the history of these two kinds of appendages, as shown to us by fossils, we find them approaching a common point. The arm can readily be traced to a walking appendage, while the bird's wing, by means of some
30 interesting connecting links, can in a similar way be traced to an appendage with its five fingers all free and used for walking…one of these connecting links represent[s] the earliest type of bird, where the fingers and bones of the arm were still distinct, and yet the whole formed a true wing. Thus we see that the common point of origin which is suggested by the likenesses between an arm and a wing is no mere imaginary one, for the fossil record has
35 shown us the path leading to that point of origin. The whole tells us further that nature's method of producing a grasping or flying organ was here, not to build a new organ, but to take one that had hitherto been used for other purposes, and by slow changes modify its form and function until it was adapted to new duties.

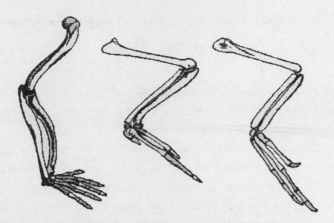

FIG. 47.—The arm of a monkey, a prehensile appendage.
FIG. 48.—The arm of a bird, a flying appendage. In life covered with feathers.
FIG. 49.—The arm of an ancient half-bird half-reptile animal. In life covered with feathers and serving as a wing.

19. The main purpose of the passage is to
   A. prove that there are similarities among the bodies of all animals.
   B. show that animals and plants are related to each other.
   C. explain the similarities between wings and arms.
   D. suggest that birds and mammals belong to the same species.

20. As used in line 6, "slight" most nearly means
   A. delicate.
   B. thin.
   C. minor.
   D. insult.

21. The statement "The fact of such a relationship is too patent to demand more words" (line 13) mainly serves to show that
   A. the passage's central claim is an obvious one.
   B. using too many words can make a description confusing.
   C. the rest of the passage can be ignored.
   D. illustrations can be more descriptive than words.

22. According to the passage, what is the direct result of two people who share the same parents?
   A. They are considered to be closely related.
   B. They are considered to be brothers.
   C. They are considered to be members of a new species.
   D. They are considered to be animals.

23. Which choice provides the best evidence for the answer to the previous question?
   A. Lines 13-14 ("The fact … out.")
   B. Lines 14-15 ("When … connection.")
   C. Lines 15-16 ("Two … parents")
   D. Lines 16-17 ("while … time")

24. According to the passage, one way a monkey's arm and a bird's wing are different is that they
   A. do not both contain bones.
   B. the monkey's bones are fused together.
   C. the bird's wing contains more bones.
   D. have different purposes.

25. Which choice provides the best evidence for the answer to the previous question?

   A. Lines 21-22 ("although … duties.")

   B. Lines 22-23 ("They … relations.")

   C. Lines 24-25 ("in the … lost.")

   D. Lines 25-26 ("Their … one.")

26. The main purpose of the final paragraph of the passage is to

   A. state the passage's main idea clearly.

   B. prove that monkeys and birds are closely related.

   C. serve as evidence to support the passage's main idea.

   D. define the term "homology."

27. Which of the following is information that can be learned only from the diagram and not from the passage?

   A. The earliest bird is the *Archaeopteryx lithographica*.

   B. The earliest birds had wings.

   C. The earliest birds' wings were similar to arms.

   D. The earliest birds were related to reptiles.

28. Which claim from the passage is most directly supported by the diagram?

   A. The monkey's arm can be traced to a walking appendage.

   B. The fingers of the earliest birds were distinct.

   C. The monkey's arm and the bird's wing are adapted to different duties.

   D. The ancient bird's wing was covered in feathers.

Questions 29–37 are based on the following passage.

This passage is adapted from *Jailed for Freedom,* by Doris Stevens, originally published in 1920.

When all suffrage controversy has died away it will be the little army of women with their purple, white and gold banners, going to prison for their political freedom, that will be remembered. They dramatized to victory the long suffrage fight in America. The challenge of
Line the picket line roused the government out of its half-century sleep of indifference. It stirred
5 the country to hot controversy. It made zealous friends and violent enemies. It produced the sharply-drawn contest which forced the surrender of the government in the second Administration of President Wilson.

The day following the memorial deputation to the President, January 10th, 1917, the first line of sentinels, a dozen in number, appeared for duty at the White House gates. In
10 retrospect it must seem to the most inflexible person a reasonably mild and gentle thing to have done. But at the same time it caused a profound stir. Columns of front page space in all the newspapers of the country gave more or less dispassionate accounts of the main facts. Women carrying banners were standing quietly at the White House gates "picketing" the President; women wanted President Wilson to put his power behind the suffrage amendment
15 in Congress. That did not seem so shocking and only a few editors broke out into hot condemnation.

When, however, the women went back on the picket line the next day and the next and the next, it began to dawn upon the excited press that such persistence was "undesirable" …

"unwomanly" … "dangerous." Gradually the people most hostile to the idea of suffrage in any
20 form marshaled forth the fears which accompany every departure from the prescribed path.
Partisan Democrats frowned. Partisan Republicans chuckled. The rest remained in cautious
silence to see how "others" would take it. Following the refrain of the press, the protest-
chorus grew louder.

"Silly women" … "pathological" … "They must be crazy" … "Don't they know anything
25 about politics?" … "What can Wilson do? He does not have to sign the constitutional
amendment." … So ran the comment from the wise elderly gentlemen sitting buried in their
cushioned chairs at the gentlemen's club across the Park, watching eagerly the "shocking,"
"shameless" women at the gates of the White House. No wonder these gentlemen found
the pickets irritating! This absorbing topic of conversation, we are told, shattered many an
30 otherwise quiet afternoon and broke up many a quiet game. Here were American women
before their very eyes daring to shock them into having to think about liberty. And what was
worse—liberty for women. Ah well, this could not go on, —this insult to the President. They
could with impunity condemn him and gossip about his affairs. But that women should stand
at his gates asking for liberty that was a sin without mitigation.

35 Disapproval was not confined merely to the gentlemen in their Club. I merely mention
them as an example, for they were our neighbors, and the strain on them day by day, as our
beautiful banners floated gaily out from our headquarters was, I am told, a heavy one.

Yet, of course, we enjoyed irritating them. Standing on the icy pavement on a damp,
wintry day in the penetrating cold of a Washington winter, knowing that within a stone's
40 throw of our agony there was a greater agony than ours there was a joy in that!

There were faint rumblings also in Congress, but like so many of its feelings they were
confined largely to the cloak rooms. Representative Emerson of Ohio did demand from the
floor of the House that the "suffrage guard be withdrawn, as it is an insult to the President,"
but his protest met with no response whatever from the other members. His oratory fell on
45 indifferent ears. And of course there were always those in Congress who got a vicarious thrill
watching women do in their fight what they themselves had not the courage to do in their
own. Another representative, an anti-suffrage Democrat, inconsiderately called us "Iron-
jawed angels," and hoped we would retire. But if by these protests these congressmen hoped
to arouse their colleagues, they failed.

29. As used in line 3, "challenge" most nearly means

   A. test
   B. confrontation
   C. brave
   D. dispute

30. Stevens makes which point about the suffrage protests?

   A. They did not surprise the press and were soon forgotten.
   B. They caused the world to be aware of the suffrage movement.
   C. They caused President Wilson to support the suffrage amendment.
   D. They were inherently harmless yet provoked strong reactions eventually.

31. Which choice provides the best evidence for the answer to the previous question?
    A. Lines 9-11 ("In retrospect … stir.")
    B. Lines 13-14 ("Women carrying … President")
    C. Lines 14-15 ("women wanted … Congress.")
    D. Lines 15-16 ("That did … condemnation.")

32. According to the majority of the press, women who fought for suffrage should have
    A. fought harder.
    B. given up.
    C. chosen a different cause.
    D. been more hostile.

33. Which choice provides the best evidence for the answer to the previous question?
    A. Lines 17-18 ("When, … next, …")
    B. Lines 18-19 ("it began … dangerous")
    C. Lines 19-20 ("Gradually … path")
    D. Line 21 ("Partisan … chuckled.")

34. As used in line 26, "ran" most nearly means
    A. streamed.
    B. jogged.
    C. operated.
    D. sequenced.

35. Which choice most closely captures the meaning of the figurative "buried in their cushioned chairs" referred to in lines 26-27?
    A. trapped within furniture
    B. spending their money
    C. wasting their time
    D. indulging in lazy luxury

36. The main purpose of the sixth paragraph (lines 38-40) is to
    A. explain what women most enjoy during protests.
    B. prove that the protest conditions were unfavorable.
    C. describe how the women who fought for suffrage felt about their efforts.
    D. show that one must endure great suffering to enact change.

37. The central claim of the final paragraph (lines 41-49) is that
    A. Congressmen only voiced their opposition to women's suffrage in cloak rooms.
    B. Representative Emerson thought that women's suffrage was an insult to President Wilson.
    C. the opponents to women's suffrage failed to generate much support.
    D. the nickname "Iron-jawed angels" is insulting to women.

38. As used in line 48, "retire" most nearly means
    A. cease working.
    B. withdraw.
    C. lose hope.
    D. go to bed.

diagnostic test—Reading

Questions 39–47 are based on the following passages.

Passage 1 is adapted from *Geology: The Science of Earth's Crust,* by William J. Miller, originally published in 1922. Passage 2 is adapted from *Principles of Geology,* by Sir Charles Lyell, originally published in 1853.

Passage 1

Earth features are not fixed. The person of ordinary intelligence, surrounded as he is by a great variety of physical features, is, unless he has devoted some study to the subject, very likely to regard those features as practically unchangeable, and to think that they are now
Line essentially as they were in the beginning of the earth's history. Some of the most fundamental
5 ideas taught in this book are that the physical features of the earth, as we behold them today, represent but a single phase of a very long-continued history; that significant changes are now going on all around us; and that we are able to interpret present-day earth features only by an understanding of earth changes in the past.

Geology, meaning literally "earth science," deals with the history of the earth and its
10 inhabitants as revealed in the rocks. The science is very broad in its scope. It treats of the processes by which the earth has been, and is now being, changed; the structure of the earth; the stages through which it has passed; and the evolution of the organisms which have lived upon it.

Geography deals with the distribution of the earth's physical features, in their relation
15 to one another, to the life of sea and land, and human life and culture. It is the present and outward expression of geological effects.

As a result of the work of many able students of geology during the past century and a quarter, it is now well established that our planet has a definitely recorded history of many millions of years, and that during the lapse of those eons, revolutionary changes in earth
20 features have occurred, and also that there has been a vast succession of living things which, from very early times, have gradually passed from simple into more and more complex forms. The physical changes and the organisms of past ages have left abundant evidence of their character, and the study of the rock formations has shown that within them we have a fairly complete record of the earth's history. Although very much yet remains to be learned about
25 this old earth, it is a remarkable fact that man, through the exercise of his highest faculty, has come to know so much concerning it.

Passage 2

Geology is the science which investigates the successive changes that have taken place in the organic and inorganic kingdoms of nature; it inquires into the causes of these changes, and the influence which they have exerted in modifying the surface and external structure of
Line our planet.

5 By these researches into the state of the earth and its inhabitants at former periods, we acquire a more perfect knowledge of its present condition, and more comprehensive views concerning the laws now governing its animate and inanimate productions. When we study history, we obtain a more profound insight into human nature, by instituting a comparison between the present and former states of society. We trace the long series of events which

10 have gradually led to the actual posture of affairs; and by connecting effects with their causes, we are enabled to classify and retain in the memory a multitude of complicated relations— the various peculiarities of national character—the different degrees of moral and intellectual refinement, and numerous other circumstances, which, without historical associations, would be uninteresting or imperfectly understood. As the present condition of nations is the result

15 of many antecedent changes, some extremely remote, and others recent, some gradual, others sudden and violent, so the state, of the natural world is the result of a long succession of events; and if we would enlarge our experience of the present economy of nature, we must investigate the effects of her operations in former epochs.

39. As used in line 1 in Passage 1, "fixed" most nearly means

  A. repaired.

  B. rigid.

  C. unchanging.

  D. flexible.

40. Which choice provides the best evidence for the answer to the previous question?

  A. Lines 1-4 ("The person … earth's history.")

  B. Lines 5-6 ("the physical … long-continued history")

  C. Lines 6-7 ("significant … around us.")

  D. Lines 7-8 ("we are … past.")

41. According to Passage 2, one similarity between studying geology and studying history is that they both

  A. teach us about human nature.

  B. involve violent changes.

  C. inquire into changes in nature.

  D. teach us about the present.

42. Which choice provides the best evidence for the answer to the previous question?

  A. Lines 1-4 ("Geology … planet.")

  B. Lines 5-7 ("By these … productions.")

  C. Lines 7-9 ("When we … society.")

  D. Lines 14-18 ("As the … epochs.")

43. As used in line 9 of Passage 2, "trace" most nearly means

  A. draw.

  B. follow.

  C. find.

  D. suggestion.

44. The primary purpose of each passage is to

  A. explain how geology depends upon changes that occurred in the past.

  B. compare geology to another similar branch of science.

  C. define "geology" for students who had never heard the term.

  D. provide an introduction to the study of geography.

45. Both authors would most likely agree with which statement about geology?

    A. It deals with the distribution of the earth's physical features.

    B. It illustrates different degrees of moral refinement throughout history.

    C. It has a lot in common with history.

    D. It has a lot in common with geography.

46. In the passages, a significant difference in how the two authors discuss geology is that the author of Passage 2

    A. contrasts it with other sciences.

    B. uses a comparison to explain it.

    C. explains that it means "earth science."

    D. makes assumptions about how other people may view it.

47. Assuming that he agrees with the assumptions in the first paragraph of Passage 1, the author of Passage 2 would most likely recommend which course of action to "a person of ordinary intelligence"?

    A. Remember that both geography and geology are studies of the earth.

    B. Understand that rocks are living organisms.

    C. Study geology as you would study history.

    D. Try to classify and remember a multitude of complicated relations.

STOP!
IF YOU FINISH BEFORE TIME IS CALLED, YOU MAY CHECK YOUR WORK ON THIS SECTION ONLY.
DO NOT TURN TO ANY OTHER SECTION.

SECTION 2: WRITING AND LANGUAGE TEST

35 Minutes • 44 Questions

Turn to Section 2 of your answer sheet to answer the questions in this section.

Directions: Each of the following passages is accompanied by a set of questions. For some questions, you will consider how the passage might be revised to improve the expression of ideas. For other questions, you will consider how the passage might be edited to correct errors in sentence structure, usage, or punctuation. A passage or a question may be accompanied by one or more graphics (such as a table, chart, graph, or photograph) that you will consider as you make revising and editing decisions.

Some questions will direct you to an underlined portion of a passage. Other questions will direct you to a location in a passage or ask you to think about the passage as a whole.

After reading each passage, choose the answer to each question that most effectively improves the quality of writing in the passage or that makes the passage conform to the conventions of standard written English. Many questions include a "NO CHANGE" option. Choose that option if you think the best choice is to leave the relevant portion of the passage as it is.

Questions 1–11 are based on the following passage.

The Human Computer

Known as "The Human Computer," mathematician Katherine Johnson is widely [1] known now for her many [2] contributions to NASA's space program that spanned the second half of the 20th century. That wasn't always the case, however. For many years, she worked as a brilliant mind behind the scenes, working to launch more high-profile names into space.

Born in 1918 in the small town of [3] White Sulphur Springs West Virginia Johnson was, as a child, fascinated by the power of numbers. "I counted everything. I counted the steps to the road, the steps up to church, the number of dishes and silverware I washed … anything that could be counted, I did," she later said. Her love of math led her to burn through her school's math curriculum and rocket past her classmates. By age 13, Johnson was taking advanced math classes at the nearby West Virginia State College—and by 18, she was a full-time student there. [4]

[5] Johnson was a civil rights pioneer as well. After graduating from the historically black college with highest honors, Johnson accepted a teaching position. Only two years into her teaching career, [6] although, Johnson was selected as one of the first African American students in the graduate program to integrate the previously segregated West Virginia University. At the school, Johnson kept studying and researching in the mathematics program until she left to get married and have a family.

After her three daughters were older, Katherine stepped back onto the path that would define her career. She joined [7] the aeronautics laboratory, analyzing data from flight tests. In 1957, with the successful launch of the USSR's satellite *Sputnik*, her work began to take on a more other-worldly focus. Her math became the basis for American space missions, including Alan Shepard's historic 1961 mission Freedom 7, which put an American in [8] Space for the first time.

Johnson's mathematical work made her a pioneer in the space science industry, particularly as an African American woman. [9] Throughout her career, she did invaluable work for NASA's space programs. [10] When NASA first used computers to calculate orbits and trajectories, astronaut John Glenn reportedly refused to fly a mission until Johnson (whom he'd requested by name) personally verified the calculations.

In the decades since then, Johnson has become famous as a math and aerospace pioneer. In 2015, at the age of 97, she was awarded the Presidential Medal of Freedom for her achievements. As of 2016, you can also visit NASA's Katherine G. Johnson Computational Research Facility in Hampton, Virginia, dedicated in her honor. [11]

1. **A.** NO CHANGE
   B. anonymous
   C. celebrated
   D. vilified

2. **A.** NO CHANGE
   B. NASA's space program contributions, which spanned
   C. contributions to NASA's space program, which spanned
   D. contributions to NASA's space program, that spanned

3. **A.** NO CHANGE
   B. White Sulphur Springs West Virginia,
   C. White Sulphur Springs, West Virginia,
   D. White Sulphur Springs, West Virginia

4. Based on the details about Johnson given in this paragraph, which of the following choices would be a relevant detail to add at the end of this sentence?
   A. studying her favorite subject under her mentor, Dr. W.W. Shieffelin Claytor.
   B. making her a proud resident of West Virginia.
   C. long before her time working on NASA's space program.
   D. taking advanced math classes that were far beyond what students her age were taking.

5. Which of the following would be an effective opening sentence for this paragraph?

   A. So yeah, Johnson was a very successful student, but that wasn't her only achievement.

   B. As a student and academic, her stellar grades were not her only major achievement.

   C. As a civil rights pioneer in addition to her academic success as a mathematician, had many talents.

   D. Johnson was not just a successful student of mathematics.

6. A. NO CHANGE

   B. though

   C. still

   D. so

7. A. NO CHANGE

   B. a

   C. some

   D. the NASA

8. A. NO CHANGE

   B. space

   C. the Space

   D. the space

9. Which choice most effectively supports the writer's statement that "she did invaluable work for NASA's space programs"?

   A. Johnson was an employee of NASA for more than 30 years.

   B. Johnson continues to live in Virginia and has 6 grandchildren and 11 great-grandchildren.

   C. Johnson is profiled in the 2016 movie *Hidden Figures*.

   D. Johnson published twenty-six papers about the math and calculations involved in space launches.

10. Which of the following detail points would be the strongest addition to the passage at this point?

    A. She was very well liked by her colleagues, who often commented on her kind demeanor.

    B. She calculated the trajectory for the 1969 *Apollo 11* mission that put American astronauts on the moon.

    C. Her many honors and accolades show how valuable she was to the space program.

    D. Stopping work to get married and raise a family did not stand in her way as a professional.

11. Which choice most effectively establishes the central point of the passage?

    A. Also in 2016, the movie *Hidden Figures* celebrated the contributions of Johnson and other female African American mathematicians and scientists who worked for NASA during the 1960s.

    B. As we look to the future of space travel, who will step up and be the next Katherine Johnson?

    C. There are books and movies that detail the many contributions of Katherine Johnson to American space travel and history.

    D. Katherine Johnson's lifetime of work as "The Human Computer" has become well known as an important and undeniable part of America's twentieth-century history.

diagnostic test— Writing and Language

Questions 12–22 are based on the following passage and supplementary material.

The following passage is an excerpt from a report on drought conditions in the United States.

[12] As of January 2014, the entire state of California was determined to be in a drought. It was made official by an announcement by Governor Jerry Brown, who continued to issue executive orders about water use and conservation to help resolve this water crisis. These executive orders included restrictions on how much water Californians could use in their households, as well as limits for water use at government facilities.

As temperatures rise around the globe, drought (a condition where drier-than-normal land and weather conditions lead to a lack of available water) has become a major problem for many countries. In the United States, being declared a drought zone means a state must have a [13] severe lack of precipitation, soil moisture, or low groundwater levels. Any of these factors can indicate a drought, but many droughts are characterized by a combination of factors. [14] Droughts are considered emergencies. They endanger drinking water supplies. They also endanger animal populations that depend on water sources, and limit farmers' ability to grow crops.

For example, the recent drought in California was seen as the result of warmer-than-normal temperatures leading to declines in soil moisture and groundwater levels.

[15] In general, water restrictions are a key short-term solution for a state or country to help conserve the water they do have, until conditions improve and moisture levels return closer to normal. The U.S. Environmental Protection Agency (EPA) recommends that communities facing water crises adopt a number of policies to help conserve water, including:

Limiting outdoor watering (lawns and plants)

Recommending short periods of water usage in the home, like for bathing

[16] Install household appliances designed to reduce water usage [17]

Adapting farm irrigation systems to maximize water usage and avoid water waste

Of these recommendations, the ones most likely to have an impact on drought conditions are [18] the domestic household changes. [19]

On a [20] largest level than state water usage, experts are seeking to understand more about the causes of drought so that they can better resolve crises as they happen and prevent and reduce the severity of droughts. Many of these experts see the rise in drought emergencies as a consequence of climate change. Higher temperatures around the world lead to increased rates of evaporation in the water cycle. As a result, [21] fewer water is available on the Earth's surface. [22]

Image 1

How Much Water Do We Use?

Shower 16.8%
Toilet 26.7%
Faucet 15.7%
Leaks 13.7%
Clothes Washer 21.7%
Other 5.3%

Source: American Water Works Association Research
Foundation, "Residential End Uses of Water." 1999

Image 2

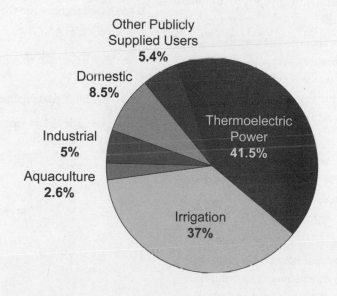

U.S. Freshwater Withdrawals (2005)

Other Publicly Supplied Users 5.4%
Domestic 8.5%
Industrial 5%
Aquaculture 2.6%
Thermoelectric Power 41.5%
Irrigation 37%

*Livestock and Mining combined use approximately
1% of total use and are not included

*Data comes from U.S. Geological Service Circular
1344: Estimated Use of Water in the United States in
2005 by Joan F. Kenny, Nancy L. Barber, Susan S.
Hutson, Kristin S. Linsey, John K. Lovelace, and Molly
A. Maupin, available at http://pubs.usgs.gov/circ/1344/

diagnostic test— Writing and Language

12. **A.** NO CHANGE

    B. As of January 2014, California governor Jerry Brown declared that his state was officially suffering from drought conditions. The announcement was followed by

    C. January 2014: California governor Jerry Brown declares state is in a drought. Brown would then

    D. The state of California has been in a drought since January 2014, when they

13. **A.** NO CHANGE

    B. severe lack of precipitation, soil moisture, or groundwater

    C. severe lack of precipitation levels, soil moisture levels, or groundwater levels

    D. severe lack of precipitation.

14. Which is the most effective way to combine these sentences?

    A. Droughts are considered emergencies: because they endanger drinking water supplies, animal populations that depend on water sources, and farmers' ability to grow crops.

    B. Drinking water supplies, animal populations that depend on water sources, and farmers' ability to grow crops all depend on water.

    C. The reason droughts are considered emergencies is because they endanger drinking water supplies and animal populations that depend on water sources and limit farmers' ability to grow crops.

    D. Droughts are considered emergencies; they endanger drinking water supplies and animal populations that depend on water sources and limit farmers' ability to grow crops.

15. **A.** NO CHANGE

    B. In California,

    C. Unquestionably,

    D. Although

16. **A.** NO CHANGE

    B. Installing

    C. Installed

    D. Please install

17. Which choice completes the sentence using accurate data based on the chart in Image 1?

    A. such as leaks, shower heads, clothes washers, and toilets

    B. such as yard sprinklers and faucets

    C. such as yard sprinklers

    D. such as faucets, shower heads, clothes washers, and toilets.

18. Which choice completes the sentence using accurate data based on the chart in Image 2?

    A. NO CHANGE

    B. the thermoelectric power plant changes.

    C. the industrial changes.

    D. the agricultural irrigation changes.

19. Based on Image 2, which sentence should be added here?

   A. Changes in domestic water usage can help make a difference in concert with other measures.

   B. Domestic water usage is a huge part of water conservation, and should be the highest-priority solution.

   C. Together, domestic and industrial water usage account for 40 percent of overall fresh water usage.

   D. While thermoelectric power is the biggest water user (as it accounts for more than 41 percent of all fresh water use), household changes can be an important part of the overall water conservation.

20. A. NO CHANGE

   B. larger

   C. large

   D. more larger

21. A. NO CHANGE

   B. more

   C. less

   D. few

22. Which of the following makes the most effective order for the passage?

   A. NO CHANGE

   B. Paragraph 2, Paragraph 3, Paragraph 4, Paragraph 1

   C. Paragraph 2, Paragraph 3, Paragraph 1, Paragraph 4

   D. Paragraph 4, Paragraph 3, Paragraph 4, Paragraph 1

Questions 23–33 are based on the following passage and supplemental material.

Coding: The Skill of the Future

As the world becomes [23] more and more and more digital or electronic, the workforce will need to keep up with that trend, or risk becoming obsolete. By 2016, 8 of the top 25 jobs were in tech fields. And while the U.S. Bureau of Labor Statistics predicts that the number of traditional computer programming jobs may decline about 8% over the next ten years, the demand for people with computer coding and programming skills will increase. [24] As companies look for ways to save on overhead costs, they will likely be turning to contract and freelance employees to fill their tech needs.

While the format of these tech jobs may be changing, the basics stay the same: computer [25] programmers, and other tech industry professionals will still need the most up-to-the-minute technical skill sets. In these fields, computer coding [26] (writing the technical instructions that make computer programs and applications run) is one of the most essential skills for a programmer or computer engineer to have. [27] One of the most portable skills, a computer programmer can be found working almost anywhere in healthcare, at a tech startup, in a large corporation, at a small nonprofit, etc. Most industries need to have qualified programmers as part of their tech teams, so people with those skills are rarely confined to one narrow career path.

As tech careers grow to meet the demands of a world that is [**28**] <u>producing</u> more digital media by the hour, the Bureau of Labor Statistics has identified some of the fastest-growing roles that require coding. [**29**]

Video game designers use coding language to create worlds within games, and manage teams of engineers, designers, and developers to make that vision come to life. [**30**] <u>Knowing the underlying code, how it can be changed</u>, allows video game designers to be more flexible and creative in their designs.

User experience designers take online products and make sure they are [**31**] <u>easy for users to use</u>. They take feedback, and work with the underlying code in a website or app to make [**32**] <u>it</u> look more user-friendly.

Environmental scientists bring coding with them into the lab. These scientists analyze data and trends in the environment, and create computer simulations of events. Coding and programming languages come in handy for processing complicated data into a format that can be used to draw conclusions.

Civil engineers use complicated calculations to find answers to real-world problems like building safety, water management, and construction planning. Being able to code their own software programs lets them go beyond what existing apps and programs can do, and help the engineers find better solutions, faster.

In fact, coding is a skill in such high demand that many schools and companies have launched "coding boot camps" that teach the basics to students or employees to make them more versatile. This is a trend that will continue to define the job market for years to come. [**33**]

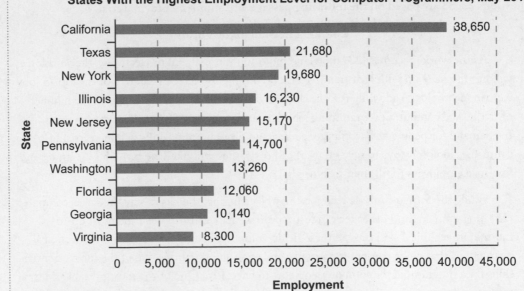

States With the Highest Employment Level for Computer Programmers, May 2015

Source: Bureau of Labor Statistics

23. **A.** NO CHANGE
    B. more…digital or electronic
    C. more and more digital
    D. more etc. digital or electronic

24. At this point, the writer is considering deleting the underlined sentence. Should the writer do this?
    A. No, because it supports the main point of the passage.
    B. Yes, because it has little to do with the main point of the passage.
    C. No, because it acts as a transition to the next paragraph.
    D. No, because it provides a necessary detail.

25. **A.** NO CHANGE
    B. programmers: and
    C. programmers and,
    D. programmers and

26. **A.** NO CHANGE
    B. writing the technical instructions that make computer programs and applications run
    C. or writing the technical instructions that make computer programs and applications run
    D. or, writing the technical instructions that make computer programs and applications run

27. **A.** NO CHANGE
    B. Computer programmers have portable skills, so
    C. The good thing is these skills are portable,
    D. With these portable skills,

28. **A.** NO CHANGE
    B. rejecting
    C. paraphrasing
    D. enjoying

29. Which of the following choices could the writer add here as a relevant sentence?
    A. Not all of them are traditional IT roles—many also bring in elements from the arts, marketing, and sales.
    B. User experience designers are tasked with making complex programs more user-friendly.
    C. Jobs that do not require coding are on the rise as well.
    D. Knowing graphic design software is essential for all of these jobs as well.

30. **A.** NO CHANGE
    B. Knowing the underlying code and how it can be changed
    C. Knowing the underlying code, because of how it can be changed,
    D. Knowing the underlying code, and so how it can be changed,

31. **A.** NO CHANGE
    B. easier for users to use
    C. easy for users
    D. used in a way that's easy for users

32. **A.** NO CHANGE
    B. the code
    C. the product
    D. coding

diagnostic test— Writing and Language

33. Which detail would be relevant to add to the passage, based on the chart?

   A. States like Georgia and New York are likely to be hotspots for computer programming jobs in the near future.

   B. If you have strong coding skills, you might want to consider living in areas like California and Texas because computer programming jobs are booming there.

   C. Only ten states have jobs for people with coding skills, so you should consider moving somewhere like Texas or New York.

   D. With nearly 40,000 computer programmer jobs, New Jersey in particular is a big magnet for people with computer coding skills.

Questions 34–44 are based on the following passage.

Will the Real William Shakespeare Please Stand Up?

William Shakespeare (1564-1616) is credited as one of the most famous playwrights of all time—and one of the most [34] prohibitive, having written at least 38 plays and 154 sonnets over the course of his life. Originally a humble stage actor in Elizabethan England, Shakespeare would go on to be known as one of the world's legendary writers, as well. Yet while [35] he is handed down from generation to generation, there have long been rumblings that this wonderfully insightful and productive writer may not have been all he seemed. [36] That in fact, he might not have been the writer at all.

As long as there has been analysis of Shakespeare's many plays, there has been speculation that the man himself did not write all of them. [37] Some theories say that there were a number of writers sharing "William Shakespeare" as a nom-de-plume. Others suggest that Shakespeare's work was really that of another writer living in London around the same time. The possible candidates over the years have included other playwrights like Francis Bacon, Christopher Marlowe, and Edward De Vere. [38]

(1) The current accusations (or at least questions) about Shakespeare's authorship [39] has been fueled mostly by historical inconsistencies uncovered by scholars over the years. (2) There are very few records or accounts of Shakespeare's personal life, leaving question marks about whether someone of his social standing would have received the level of formal education suggested by his sophisticated writing. (3) Shakespeare was the son of a farmer, and would have received a very basic education in reading and writing, according to the customs of the time. [40]

Many experts also question how a stage actor who likely spent his entire life in London would have so much insight into complex human emotions around the [41] world? Shakespeare's plays are set in a variety of places and times throughout history, suggesting a writer [42] that has completed advanced studies and traveled widely. There is also little information when Shakespeare started writing his plays, leaving open the question about whether the plays were the product of a younger writer with a strong imagination, or a wiser writer with deeper life experience.

(1) Even as the debate rages on, the issue [43] was haunted by a lack of evidence. (2) There is nothing concrete to suggest that any of the other potential writers were "William Shakespeare" after all. (3) Without that evidence, the simplest answer is that Shakespeare was merely a remarkable writer, who created an extraordinary body of work as history has suggested. [44]

34. A. NO CHANGE

    B. professional

    C. prolific

    D. proud

35. A. NO CHANGE

    B. his plays are

    C. his plays is

    D. his name is

36. A. NO CHANGE

    B. He might not, in fact, have been the writer at all.

    C. The writer might not have been him at all.

    D. In fact, he might not have been the writer at all.

37. Which of the following is a relevant detail the writer could add here?

    A. *Julius Caesar* is by far my favorite Shakespearean play.

    B. About 230 years after Shakespeare's death, speculation began to emerge among scholars.

    C. Shakespeare's plays were a mix of comedies, tragedies, and histories.

    D. Shakespeare is buried in his hometown of Stratford-on-Avon in England.

38. Which addition to the paragraph most effectively maintains the paragraph's focus on relevant information and ideas?

    A. Like Shakespeare, these writers were all living and writing in England around the same time, but held higher social ranks or had more formal education.

    B. Christopher Marlowe was also a playwright, though lesser-known than Shakespeare these days.

    C. Queen Elizabeth was England's reigning monarch during most of Shakespeare's life.

    D. Shakespeare's Globe Theater in London has been a major reconstruction project in recent decades.

39. A. NO CHANGE

    B. had

    C. will have

    D. have

40. Which of the following sentences should the writer delete from the paragraph?

    A. NO CHANGE

    B. Sentence 1

    C. Sentence 2

    D. Sentence 3

41. **A.** NO CHANGE
    B. world!
    C. world.
    D. world…

42. **A.** NO CHANGE
    B. which
    C. what
    D. who

43. **A.** NO CHANGE
    B. is
    C. will be
    D. would be

44. The writer wants to add the following sentence. Where in the paragraph should it be placed?

    Regardless, we may never truly know whether Shakespeare was the playwright we always believed him to be, or whether there were other hands holding the quills that wrote these plays and sonnets.

    A. Before Sentence 1
    B. After Sentence 1
    C. After Sentence 2
    D. After Sentence 3

STOP!
IF YOU FINISH BEFORE TIME IS CALLED, YOU MAY CHECK YOUR WORK ON THIS SECTION ONLY.
DO NOT TURN TO ANY OTHER SECTION.

SECTION 3: MATH TEST—NO CALCULATOR

25 Minutes • 17 Questions

Turn to Section 3 of your answer sheet to answer the questions in this section.

> **Directions:** For **Questions 1–13,** solve each problem, choose the best answer from the choices provided, and fill in the corresponding circle on your answer sheet. For **Questions 14–17,** solve the problem and enter your answer in the grid on the answer sheet. Please refer to the directions before **Question 14** on how to enter your answers in the grid. You may use any available space in your test booklet for scratch work.

NOTES:

1. The use of a calculator is **not permitted.**

2. All variables and expressions used represent real numbers unless otherwise indicated.

3. Figures provided in this test are drawn to scale unless otherwise indicated.

4. All figures lie in a plane unless otherwise indicated.

5. Unless otherwise indicated, the domain of a given function f is the set of all real numbers x for which $f(x)$ is a real number.

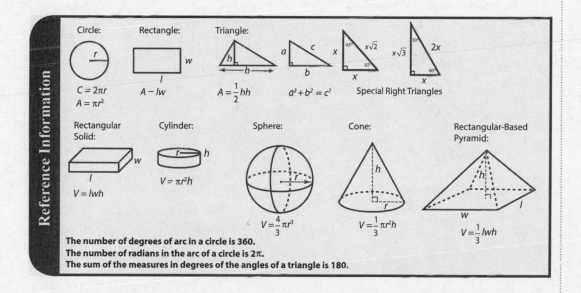

1. Consider the following boxplot.

SHOW YOUR WORK HERE

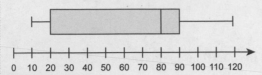

What is the average of the first and third quartiles?

A. 55

B. 70

C. 80

D. 105

2. A newly discovered species of locust has begun to decimate corn crops nationwide. Initially, there are 580 million square feet of area devoted to corn crops in the nation. If left unchecked, the locust population will triple each month and devour the corn crops at the same rate. Which of the following functions $c(t)$ describes the number of square feet untouched by the locust population? Assume t is measured in months and the output is measured in millions of square feet.

A. $c(t) = 580\left(\dfrac{2}{3}\right)^t$

B. $c(t) = 580\left(\dfrac{1}{3}\right)^t$

C. $c(t) = 580(3)^t$

D. $c(t) = 580\left(\dfrac{3}{2}\right)^t$

3. What is the *y*-intercept of the linear function pictured below?

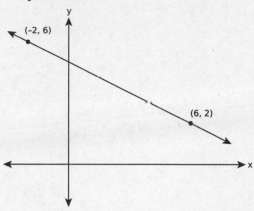

SHOW YOUR WORK HERE

A. (0, 2)

B. (0, 5)

C. (0, 7)

D. (0, 10)

4. Consider the following triangle:

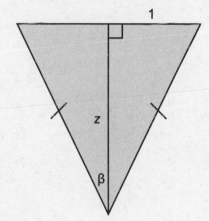

Which expression equals $\sin \beta$?

A. $\dfrac{\sqrt{1+z^2}}{1+z^2}$

B. $\sqrt{1+z^2}$

C. $\dfrac{1}{z}$

D. $\dfrac{z\sqrt{1+z^2}}{1+z^2}$

5. A farmer raises ninety hens to produce eggs. From his experience, he knows that z% of the hens will produce one egg daily. Of these, p% of the eggs produced will be multicolored. And of these, q% will have two yolks. Which expression describes the number of eggs expected daily that are multicolored but NOT double-yolked?

A. $\dfrac{9pqz}{10^5}$

B. $\dfrac{9zq(100-p)}{10^5}$

C. $\dfrac{9pz(100-q)}{10^5}$

D. $\dfrac{9z(100-p)(100-q)}{10^5}$

6. A furniture company manufactures end tables in the shape of circular cylinders. The height of each table should be 6 inches greater than the diameter. Which of the following describes the surface area of such a table as a function of its radius, R? (Note: The surface area S of a right circular cylinder with base radius R and height H is $S = 2\pi R^2 + 2\pi RH$.)

A. $S(R) = 4\pi R(R+3)$

B. $S(R) = 6\pi R(R-2)$

C. $S(R) = 2\pi R^2(R+3)$

D. $S(R) = 6\pi R(R+2)$

7. An electronics manufacturer imports the outer casing for its MP3 players from an offshore company. The weekly number of outer casings they order is 42,000. With the holiday seasoning approaching, the company increases its order to 60,000. Which expression represents the percent increase incurred?

SHOW YOUR WORK HERE

A. $\dfrac{60,000 - 42,000}{42,000}\%$

B. $100 \times \dfrac{60,000 - 42,000}{42,000}\%$

C. $\dfrac{60,000 - 42,000}{60,000}\%$

D. $100 \times \dfrac{60,000 - 42,000}{60,000}\%$

8. The change machine at an indoor amusement park provides quarters and dollar bills. The manager wants the machine to have at least $75 worth of quarters during peak hours. Also, the machine must contain less than $350 at any time. If the number of quarters placed in the machine is x and the number of dollar bills y, then which system of inequalities could be used to determine the possible number of quarters and dollar bills used to stock the change machine?

A. $\begin{cases} 0.25y \le 75 \\ 0.25x + y < 350 \end{cases}$

B. $\begin{cases} 25x + y < 350 \\ 25x \le 75 \end{cases}$

C. $\begin{cases} 25x \le 75 \\ x + 25y < 350 \end{cases}$

D. $\begin{cases} 0.25x \ge 75 \\ 0.25x + y < 350 \end{cases}$

diagnostic test — Math — No Calculator

9. Suppose c_1 and c_2 are positive real numbers. Which of the following quadratic equations has two distinct real solutions?

   SHOW YOUR WORK HERE

   A. $c_1 x^2 + c_2 = 0$

   B. $(c_1 x + c_2)^2 = 0$

   C. $(x - c_1)^2 + c_2 = 0$

   D. $c_1 x (x + c_2) = 0$

10. For what real value of k does the following system have no solution?

$$\begin{cases} 2y + kx = 1 \\ 4 - 6y = 2kx \end{cases}$$

   A. 0

   B. $\dfrac{1}{2}$

   C. 1

   D. 2

Use the following information for Questions 11 and 12.

Four hundred eighty residents of a small section of a rural southwestern state, divided into three townships, cast their votes for 1 of 2 potential representatives or a third-party candidate for state government. The data, separated by township, is summarized below.

Township	Candidate A	Candidate B	Third-Party Candidate
McCracken	100	73	1
Dunley	29	33	4
Samoa	89	101	50

11. If a vote was cast for Candidate B, what is the probability that it came from a voter in Samoa township?

    A. $\frac{101}{207}$

    B. $\frac{101}{480}$

    C. $\frac{101}{240}$

    D. $\frac{101}{106}$

12. If a ballot is chosen at random from this sample, what is the probability that either a vote was cast for a third-party candidate or that it came from a voter in McCracken township?

    A. $\frac{11}{96}$

    B. $\frac{29}{80}$

    C. $\frac{19}{40}$

    D. $\frac{229}{480}$

SHOW YOUR WORK HERE

diagnostic test— Math— No Calculator

13. The energy, I, radiated by a blackbody per unit surface area per unit time is related to the temperature T of the surface by the formula $I = \sigma T^4$, where σ is a constant. If the temperature is decreased by 50 percent, the resulting energy is $\overline{I}$. What fraction of the original energy is $\overline{I}$?

A. $\dfrac{1}{2}$

B. $\dfrac{1}{4}$

C. $\dfrac{1}{8}$

D. $\dfrac{1}{16}$

SHOW YOUR WORK HERE

Directions: For **Questions 14–17,** solve the problem and enter your answer in the grid, as described below, on the answer sheet.

1. Although not required, it is suggested that you write your answer in the boxes at the top of the columns to help you fill in the circles accurately. You will receive credit only if the circles are filled in correctly.

2. Mark no more than one circle in any column.

3. No question has a negative answer.

4. Some problems may have more than one correct answer. In such cases, grid only one answer.

5. **Mixed numbers** such as $3\frac{1}{2}$ must be gridded as 3.5 or $\frac{7}{2}$. If $3\frac{1}{2}$ is entered into the grid

   as 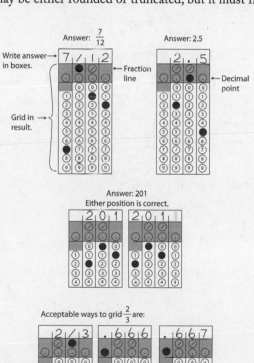 it will be interpreted as $\frac{31}{2}$, not $3\frac{1}{2}$.

6. **Decimal answers:** If you obtain a decimal answer with more digits than the grid can accommodate, it may be either rounded or truncated, but it must fill the entire grid.

Answer: $\frac{7}{12}$ Answer: 2.5

Write answer in boxes.   Fraction line   Decimal point

Grid in result.

Answer: 201
Either position is correct.

Acceptable ways to grid $\frac{2}{3}$ are:

14. The sum of three consecutive even integers is 60. What is the largest of these three integers?

15. A start-up company designs a revolutionary chair that it claims will create total gaming immersion. The company starts off in debt and needs to sell a certain number of chairs to break even (meaning the profit is $0 dollars). Thereafter, every chair it sells will yield an actual profit. The quadratic function graphed below describes the company's profit:

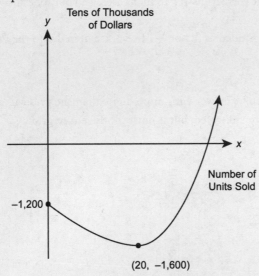

How many chairs must the company sell to break even?

16. Rick owns his own lawn care business. Each week during last summer, he spent 60 hours doing various landscaping activities. He determined that the number of hours he spent mowing grass and the number of hours he spent pruning trees were in a 7:3 ratio. This year, he gained several new customers and predicts he will now spend 70 hours a week on lawn care, with the ratio for his two main activities being the same. If his prediction is correct, what will be the approximate percent increase in time he will spend on pruning trees from last year to this year?

17. Consider the function $q(x) = 3(x + 4)^2 - 2$. What positive value of a ensures that the minimum value of the function $m(x) = q(x - a) - 2a$ is -9?

SHOW YOUR WORK HERE

STOP!
IF YOU FINISH BEFORE TIME IS CALLED, YOU MAY CHECK YOUR WORK ON THIS SECTION ONLY.
DO NOT TURN TO ANY OTHER SECTION.

diagnostic test — Math — No Calculator

SECTION 4: MATH TEST—CALCULATOR 🖩

45 Minutes • 31 Questions

Turn to Section 4 of your answer sheet to answer the questions in this section.

> **Directions:** For **Questions 1–27,** solve each problem, choose the best answer from the choices provided, and fill in the corresponding circle on your answer sheet. For **Questions 28–31,** solve the problem and enter your answer in the grid on the answer sheet. Please refer to the directions before **Question 28** on how to enter your answers in the grid.

NOTES:

1. The use of a calculator is **permitted.**

2. All variables and expressions used represent real numbers unless otherwise indicated.

3. Figures provided in this test are drawn to scale unless otherwise indicated.

4. All figures lie in a plane unless otherwise indicated.

5. Unless otherwise indicated, the domain of a given function f is the set of all real numbers x for which $f(x)$ is a real number.

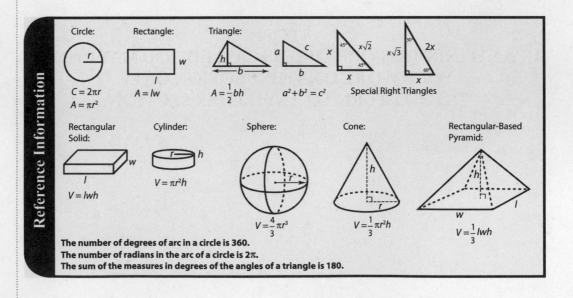

1. Suppose that a third-degree polynomial $p(x)$ has zeros -2, 0 and 3. If $p(x) = x^3 + Bx^2 + Cx$, what is the value of $\dfrac{B}{C}$?

   A. $\dfrac{1}{6}$

   B. 0

   C. $-\dfrac{1}{6}$

   D. -6

2. Natasha wants to broaden the advertisement of her PC repair shop business. She creates a page on a social media site and asks that past customers post their impressions of her work. Based on the results of others advertising in this manner, she expects each testimonial post to gain her 4 new followers. The data also suggest that each time someone shares her business page to their personal page, she will gain 2 new followers. She would like to achieve more than 750 new followers. Which inequality represents the various combinations of the number of testimonials, T, and number of shares, S, that Natasha needs to achieve her goal?

   A. $2T + 4S > 750$

   B. $2T + 4S \geq 750$

   C. $4T + 2S > 750$

   D. $4T + 2S \geq 750$

SHOW YOUR WORK HERE

diagnostic test — Math — Calculator

3. A family-owned tractor company produces a diesel model and hybrid model. The standard model requires 50 hours of labor to produce, while the deluxe model requires 80 hours to produce. The company can devote at most 1,800 hours of labor weekly to manufacture these tractors. The plant's storage capacity is no more than thirty tractors weekly, and it then sends them to various distributors. Which of the following systems can be used to determine the number of diesel tractors, x, and hybrid tractors, y, the company should manufacture each week?

SHOW YOUR WORK HERE

A. $\begin{cases} 50x + 80y \leq 1,800 \\ x + y = 30 \end{cases}$

B. $\begin{cases} 50x + 80y \leq 1,800 \\ x + y \leq 30 \end{cases}$

C. $\begin{cases} 50x + 80y < 1,800 \\ x + y \leq 30 \end{cases}$

D. $\begin{cases} 50x + 80y = 1,800 \\ x + y = 30 \end{cases}$

4. Let a be a positive real number. If a linear function $f(x)$ passes through the points $(-2a, a)$ and $(4a, 2a)$, what is its equation?

A. $f(x) = \frac{1}{6}x + \frac{4}{3}a$

B. $f(x) = \frac{1}{6}x + \frac{2}{3}a$

C. $f(x) = \frac{1}{6}x + 3a$

D. $f(x) = \frac{1}{6}x - a$

5. Consider the following scatterplot relating variables *X* and *Y*. Which of the labeled points *J*, *K*, *L*, and *M* least conforms to the trendline?

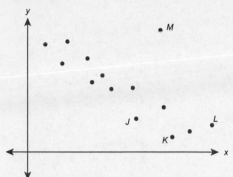

SHOW YOUR WORK HERE

   A. Point *J*

   B. Point *K*

   C. Point *L*

   D. Point *M*

6. If *z* is the solution of the equation $-z + 2\{z - 3(2 - 3z)\} = z - 30$, what is the value of $\left(\frac{z}{1-z}\right)^{-1}$?

   A. -2

   B. $-\frac{1}{2}$

   C. $\frac{1}{2}$

   D. Undefined

7. For what pair of values of *m* and *b* does the following nonlinear system have precisely one solution?

$$\begin{cases} y = mx + b \\ x^2 + y^2 = 16 \end{cases}$$

   A. $m = 1, b = 0$

   B. $m = 0, b = 4$

   C. $m = 0, b = -16$

   D. $m = -1, b = 1$

8. After a week of very high temperatures, a cold front passes through a coastal state, producing a significant rainfall. The difference in temperatures causes a thick fog to blanket that portion of the state for hours. The visibility (in miles) versus the number of hours after the rain stopped is described by the linear function $v(t)$, graphed below:

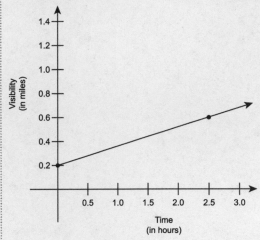

How many hours elapse after the rain stops before the visibility reaches 3.4 miles?

A. 20

B. 15

C. 10

D. 5

9. The luminosity L of a star is related to its radius R and its temperature T by the formula $L = 4\pi R2\sigma T^4$, where σ is a certain physical constant. Which of the following formulas is NOT equivalent to this given formula?

A. $\sqrt{\dfrac{L}{4\pi\sigma}} = RT^2$

B. $\dfrac{\sqrt{L}}{2\pi\sigma T^2} = R$

C. $1 = \dfrac{4\pi R^2 \sigma T^4}{L}$

D. $\dfrac{L}{\pi\sigma} = \left(2RT^2\right)^2$

SHOW YOUR WORK HERE

10. An immunologist is studying the potential healing effects of a new skin cream. One thousand participants take part in the study. Half of the participant pool has had severe psoriasis in the past year, while the other half has not. The skin cream is applied daily for one month, and then skin quality is assessed and compared to the quality prior to the application of the skin cream regimen. The summary of the data collected is shown in the following table:

	Skin quality declined	Skin quality remained the same	Skin quality improved
Have had severe psoriasis in the past year	20	355	125
Have not had severe psoriasis in the past year	65	380	55

What is the probability that a randomly selected participant's skin quality declined?

SHOW YOUR WORK HERE

A. 0.20

B. 0.17

C. 0.13

D. 0.085

11. For which linear system is the solution set given by the following graph?

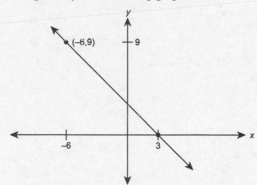

A. $\begin{cases} y = x + 3 \\ y = x - 3 \end{cases}$

B. $\begin{cases} 9 - y = x \\ 2y = -2x + 18 \end{cases}$

C. $\begin{cases} y + x = 3 \\ -3y + 9 = 3x \end{cases}$

D. $\begin{cases} 3y + x = 1 \\ y + 3x = 1 \end{cases}$

Use the following information for Questions 12 and 13.

After a patient returns home from having heart surgery, she is instructed to monitor her blood pressure every 2 hours daily for two weeks. The following graphs show her readings for the first day. Here, $t = 0$ corresponds to midnight.

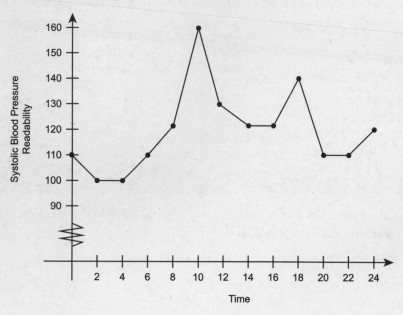

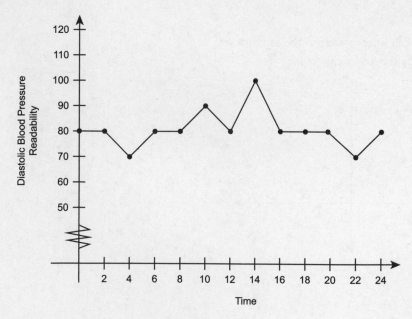

The following are the classifications of blood pressure readings provided by the American Heart Association.

Category	Systolic (top number)		Diastolic (bottom number)
Normal	Less than 120	AND	Less than 80
Pre-hypertension	120 – 139	OR	80 – 89
High Blood Pressure STAGE 1	140 – 159	OR	90 – 99
High Blood Pressure STAGE 2	160 or higher	OR	100 or higher
Hypertensive Crisis	Higher than 180	OR	Higher than 110

http://www.heart.org/HEARTORG/Conditions/HighBloodPressure/AboutHighBloodPressure/Understanding-Blood-Pressure-Readings_UCM_301764_Article.jsp/#.WITmSn3D_hA)

12. For how many of the measurement times are the blood pressure readings normal?

    A. 2

    B. 3

    C. 6

    D. 8

13. What proportion of the readings have a classification of High Blood Pressure—STAGE 1?

    A. $\frac{4}{13}$

    B. $\frac{3}{13}$

    C. $\frac{2}{13}$

    D. $\frac{1}{13}$

SHOW YOUR WORK HERE

14. Which of the following is equivalent to the

    product $\dfrac{2-x}{x^3-4x} \cdot \dfrac{x-4}{x^2-16} \cdot x^2$?

    SHOW YOUR WORK HERE

    A. $-\dfrac{1}{2x+8}$

    B. $\dfrac{x}{(x-2)(x+4)}$

    C. $\dfrac{-x}{(x+2)(x+4)}$

    D. $-\dfrac{x-2}{x^2-16}$

15. During the winter months, a horse owner offers carriage rides around the city to see the holiday lights. The driver charges a $25 flat fee plus $1.50 per half-mile. If you have $40 to spend on the carriage ride, which inequality can be used to determine the maximum number of miles, m, of your ride?

    A. $25 + 1.5m \le 40$

    B. $75m \le 40$

    C. $25 + 0.75m \le 40$

    D. $25 + 3m \le 40$

16. Purified kerosene is used for jet fuel. Pollutants are removed from the kerosene using a special filtering tank. The kerosene mixes through the filtering tank, removing 15 percent of the pollutants each minute. If P_0 is the initial amount of pollutants (measured in grams) present in the kerosene, then which equation can be used to determine the number of minutes, t, it takes for the filtering tank to reduce the amount of pollutants in the kerosene to 20 percent of the initial amount present?

    A. $0.20P_0 = P_0(0.85)^t$

    B. $0.20P_0 = P_0(0.15)^t$

    C. $0.20P_0 = P_0 e^{0.85t}$

    D. $0.85P_0 = P_0(0.20)^t$

17. Membership in a worldwide environmental group increased by 75 percent each year from 2009 to 2016. If the membership in 2013 was z, what was the membership in 2010?

   A. $(1.75)^{-2}z$

   B. $(1.75)^{-3}z$

   C. $(0.75)^{-3}z$

   D. $(1.75)^{3}z$

18. If the sum of the edges of a cube is 240 inches, what is the area of one of its faces?

   A. 20 square inches

   B. 40 square inches

   C. 400 square inches

   D. 8,000 square inches

19. What is the solution set for the equation

$$2 + \sqrt{x-1} = 6 - \frac{1}{10}x\ ?$$

   A. $\{10\}$

   B. $\{-10\}$

   C. $\{10, 170\}$

   D. $\{-10, -170\}$

SHOW YOUR WORK HERE

diagnostic test — Math — Calculator

20. A homeowner needs to purchase firewood for heating her home during the winter months. She wants a mixture of cherry wood and maple wood. The company where she intends to place an order charges $20 per maple log and $35 per cherry log. She has $1,500 to spend on firewood and has room to store forty such logs. Which system can be used to determine the number of maple logs, x, and the number of cherry logs, y, that she can purchase?

SHOW YOUR WORK HERE

A. $\begin{cases} x = 40 + y \\ 20x + 35y = 1,500 \end{cases}$

B. $\begin{cases} x + y = 40 \\ 7x \cdot y = 15 \end{cases}$

C. $\begin{cases} y = 40 - x \\ 4x + 7y = 300 \end{cases}$

D. $\begin{cases} x + y = 1,500 \\ 4x + 7y = 40 \end{cases}$

21. A *parsec* is a unit of measure often used in astronomy to measure very large distances between stars. One parsec is equal to about 3.26 light years, and 1 light year is about 6 trillion miles. The Andromeda Galaxy is approximately 4.75×10^{19} miles away from the earth. Which of the following is closest to this distance in parsecs?

A. 2.43×10^5 parsecs

B. 2.43×10^6 parsecs

C. 2.58×10^7 parsecs

D. 2.58×10^5 parsecs

22. Suppose a and b are positive real numbers. What is the slope of a line in the xy-plane that passes through the points $\left(\frac{3}{4}a, -\frac{2}{5}b\right)$ and $\left(-\frac{1}{6}a, -\frac{1}{10}b\right)$?

    A. $-\frac{11b}{40a}$

    B. $\frac{55a}{18b}$

    C. $-\frac{6b}{7a}$

    D. $-\frac{18b}{55a}$

23. Two angles are supplementary. The measure of one of them is 20 degrees less than three times the other one. What is the measure of the smaller angle?

    A. $40°$

    B. $50°$

    C. $130°$

    D. $140°$

24. Assume that b is a positive real number. What is the solution set of the quadratic equation $(bx)^2 + b = 0$?

    A. $\left\{\pm\frac{\sqrt{b}}{b}\right\}$

    B. $\{\pm i\}$

    C. $\left\{\pm i\frac{\sqrt{b}}{b}\right\}$

    D. $\left\{-b \pm i\sqrt{b}\right\}$

25. An object has mass m and volume v. If the volume is doubled and the mass is halved, how does the density change?

    A. The density would be half of the original density.

    B. The density would be a quarter of the original density.

    C. The density would double the original density.

    D. The density would quadruple the original density.

SHOW YOUR WORK HERE

diagnostic test— Math— Calculator

Use the following information for Questions 26 and 27:

The following boxplots show the average number of miles per gallon used in highway driving and city driving for various models of hybrid SUVs in 2015.

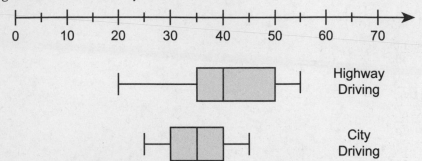

26. What is the difference in interquartile ranges for these two boxplots?

    A. 5

    B. 10

    C. 15

    D. 25

27. Which of the following comparisons of the average miles per gallon attained during highway driving and the average miles per gallon attained during city driving is correct?

    A. The median gas mileage is the same for highway driving and city driving for the sample of hybrid SUVs used in this study.

    B. The lowest gas mileage for any model hybrid SUV included in this study occurred for city driving.

    C. The ranges for both boxplots are the same.

    D. There is considerably more variation in gas mileage for highway driving for various models of hybrid SUVs than there is for city driving.

SHOW YOUR WORK HERE

Directions: For **Questions 28–31,** solve the problem and enter your answer in the grid, as described below, on the answer sheet.

1. Although not required, it is suggested that you write your answer in the boxes at the top of the columns to help you fill in the circles accurately. You will receive credit only if the circles are filled in correctly.

2. Mark no more than one circle in any column.

3. No question has a negative answer.

4. Some problems may have more than one correct answer. In such cases, grid only one answer.

5. **Mixed numbers** such as $3\frac{1}{2}$ must be gridded as 3.5 or $\frac{7}{2}$. If $3\frac{1}{2}$ is entered into the grid as 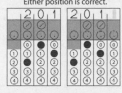 it will be interpreted as $\frac{31}{2}$, not $3\frac{1}{2}$.

6. **Decimal answers:** If you obtain a decimal answer with more digits than the grid can accommodate, it may be either rounded or truncated, but it must fill the entire grid.

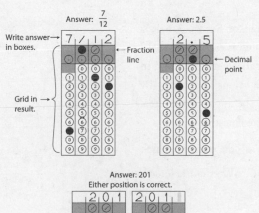

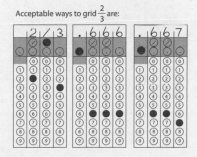

diagnostic test — Math — Calculator

28. A pharmacist has 4 liters of a 15 percent solution containing the active ingredient *dextromethorphan* to control coughs. If she wants to weaken this to a 10 percent solution, how much water would need to be added?

29. In materials science, the Brinell hardness test is a measure of a material's resistance to permanent deformation at the surface using a ball bearing. A version of the formula that gives the Brinell hardness number (BHN) is $BHN = \dfrac{2}{\pi D\left(D - \sqrt{D^2 - d^2}\right)}$, where D is the indenter ball diameter and d is the mean indent diameter. Find the approximate Brinell hardness number, accurate to the hundredths place, if the indenter ball diameter is 5mm and the mean indent diameter is 3 mm.

30. The legend of a map of South America indicates that 0.75 inch is equivalent to 12 miles. If a country can be encapsulated in a rectangle with dimensions 1.25 inches by 2.25 inches, what is the approximate area, in square miles, of the country?

31. Consider the following diagram in which $\overline{FQ}$ is parallel to $\overline{BC}$. What is the length of $\overline{AB}$?

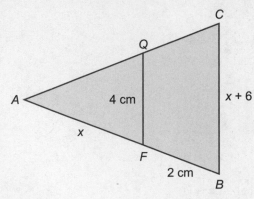

SHOW YOUR WORK HERE

ANSWER KEYS AND EXPLANATIONS

Section 1: Reading Test

1. D	9. D	17. B	25. A	33. B	41. D
2. D	10. B	18. D	26. C	34. A	42. D
3. A	11. C	19. A	27. D	35. D	43. B
4. B	12. D	20. C	28. B	36. C	44. A
5. A	13. B	21. A	29. B	37. C	45. C
6. C	14. B	22. A	30. D	38. B	46. B
7. C	15. A	23. C	31. A	39. C	47. C
8. B	16. A	24. D	32. B	40. A	

1. **The correct answer is D.** A fantastical place is a place that could not exist in reality. A place in which dinosaurs exist could not exist in reality. Choice A merely defines "fantastical"; it does not show what makes Maple White Land fantastical. Real places might have large birds or people might explore them, so choices B and C are incorrect.

2. **The correct answer is D.** These are the lines that most explicitly show that there are dinosaurs in Maple White Land. Choice A merely introduces that setting. Choices B and C describe the animals in terms that are not especially fantastical.

3. **The correct answer is A.** Challenger believes that the tracks were created by a dinosaur, which is an incredible possibility since dinosaurs have been extinct for millions of years. Choice B is the opposite of the correct answer. The fact that the party sees dinosaurs shortly afterward makes choice C incorrect. Challenger is not joking, so choice D is incorrect.

4. **The correct answer is B.** Each answer choice can be used as a synonym of *penetration*, but only choice B makes sense in this particular context, which describes how the adventurers plan to enter into Maple White Land.

5. **The correct answer is A.** Based on the passage, it is clear that extinct animals can be found in Maple White Land. The earth's first bird would likely be extinct, and possibly even the size of a dinosaur, so choice A is the best interpretation of Lord John's figurative phrase. Choices B and C are too literal. There is no evidence to support choice D.

6. **The correct answer is C.** Lord John uses *fresh* to refer to a newly made footprint. Choices A and B are both synonyms of *fresh*, but neither makes sense in this particular context. Choice D is an antonym of *fresh*.

7. **The correct answer is C.** Evidence in the passage supports the conclusion that Summerlee was the character who identified the high reeds as equisetacea.

8. **The correct answer is B.** The previous question asked which character was most likely to identify a plant. Lines 17-18 identify Summerlee as the party's botanist and indicate that a botanist is someone who studies plants since Summerlee identifies conifera and cycadaceous plants in these lines. The other answer choices do not support that conclusion.

9. **The correct answer is D.** In this line, the party first sees the dinosaurs, which would be a stunning sight. Choices A and C take the lines too literally. Choice B is unlikely since the party had already seen evidence of dinosaurs.

10. **The correct answer is B.** The author specifies the fact that explorers engaged in "constant activity and travel" instead of hibernating through "the period of darkness" as evidence that the winter at Cape Sheridan was "unique in the experience of Arctic exploration." The other answer choices may seem unique in themselves, but the author does not use them as evidence for the winter's uniqueness.

11. **The correct answer is C.** The author uses *game* to describe something that could provide *fresh meat*, so *wild animals* is the only synonym that makes sense in this context. Choice D can be eliminated since *game* is a noun and *willing* is an adjective.

12. **The correct answer is D.** The narrator makes it clear that the storms at Cape Sheridan disturbed him deeply. Choice A may be true, but there is no specific evidence in the passage that supports it. Choice B is too extreme; the narrator says only that the storms were "frequent." Evidence in the passage contradicts choice C.

13. **The correct answer is B.** These lines state the narrator's feelings about the storm most clearly. The other lines only serve as evidence of *why* he found the storms disturbing.

14. **The correct answer is B.** The other answer choices all describe minor details in the passage, but the question is asking for a shift in the passage's *main* focus.

15. **The correct answer is A.** These are the lines that show where the shift in main purpose takes place. The other lines all take place well after the shift has occurred.

16. **The correct answer is A.** Each answer choice can be used as a synonym of *progress*, but only *journey* makes sense in this particular context. Choice D can be eliminated because *develop* is a verb and *progress* is a noun in this context.

17. **The correct answer is B.** In the passage, the narrator implies that the explorers were stationed in Greenland when he describes the storms he suffered through there. People cannot be "near" the very place they are in, so choice B is a better answer than choice A. According to the map, Cape Morris Jesup is not as close to Ellesmere Island as Greenland is, so choice C is not the best answer. Montreal is not on the map at all, so choice D is incorrect.

18. **The correct answer is D.** The passage specifies that the explorers were stationed in Cape Sheridan, and according to the map, Cape Sheridan is southeast of Cape Columbia. Cape Sheridan is located in Greenland, so choices A and B cannot be correct since they both suggest that the correct answer is at a distance from Cape Sheridan and Greenland. Cape Sheridan is southwest of Cape Morris Jesup, not southeast of it.

19. **The correct answer is A.** The author is mainly interested in proving that there are similarities among the bodies of all animals. Choice B misinterprets the first sentence of the passage. Choice C mistakes an example in the passage for the passage's main purpose. Choice D is an inaccurate exaggeration of the passage's main purpose.

20. **The correct answer is C.** Each answer choice is a synonym of *slight*, but *minor* makes the most sense in this particular context. *Thin* is too suggestive of physical appearance, so it is not as strong a synonym for *slight* in this context as *minor* is.

21. **The correct answer is A.** This statement is intended to show that the idea that all animals share similarities is so obvious that there does not seem to be much sense in discussing it at length. Choice B misinterprets the statement. Choice C is too extreme an interpretation of the statement. Choice D suggests a comparison that is never made in the passage.

22. **The correct answer is A.** The author specifically states that people are considered to be closely related when they share parents. Although the author uses brothers as an example for this, choice B is untrue because those people could be sisters or brothers and sisters. Choice C is simply untrue. Choice D is true in itself, but it is not something that can be determined from the passage.

23. **The correct answer is C.** The author explicitly states that people are considered to be closely related when they share parents. Choice B implies this but is not as explicit as choice C is. Choices A and D do not suggest it at all.

24. **The correct answer is D.** According to the passage, the monkey's arm and the bird's wing have different purposes. Choice A is simply untrue. Choice B is true of a bird's wing, not a monkey's arm. Choice C is true of a monkey's arm, not a bird's wing.

25. **The correct answer is A.** These lines show that a monkey's arm and a bird's wing have different purposes or "duties." Choices B and D show how they are similar.

26. **The correct answer is C.** The passage is mainly about how different animals share similarities, and the final paragraph uses the comparisons of monkey's arms and bird's wings as an example of that idea. The main idea had already been stated clearly, so choice A is not the best answer. Choice B is simply untrue. Choice D is a detail from the paragraph, not its main purpose.

27. **The correct answer is D.** The idea that the earliest birds were related to reptiles can only be learned from the diagram. Choice A cannot be determined from either the passage or the diagram. The information in choices B and C is included in both the diagram and the passage.

28. **The correct answer is B.** This claim from the passage is clearly visible in the diagram. Choices A and C are stated in the passage but are not supported by the diagram. Choice D is visible in the diagram but is not mentioned in the passage.

29. **The correct answer is B.** Each answer choice can be used as a synonym of *challenge*, but *confrontation* makes the most sense in this particular context.

30. **The correct answer is D.** Stevens suggests that the suffrage protests were inherently harmless yet provoked strong reactions eventually. Only the first protest did not surprise the press and the subsequent ones were not soon forgotten, so choice A is not correct. There is no evidence to support choice B. Choice C was a goal of the protests, but Stevens does not indicate whether or not that goal was achieved.

31. **The correct answer is A.** These lines show that the suffrage protests were inherently harmless ("a reasonably mild and gentle thing to have done") yet provoked strong reactions ("caused a profound stir") eventually. Choice B merely describes what happened at the protest. Choice C merely describes the goal of the protest. Choice D only describes the reaction to the first protest.

answers diagnostic test

32. The correct answer is B. Evidence in the passage supports the conclusion that the press believed suffragettes should have given up on their cause. That is the opposite of choice A. Evidence implies that the press thought women should not have fought for any causes, so choice C is not the best answer. There is no evidence to support choice D.

33. The correct answer is B. The press' unsupportive, negative descriptions in these lines ("undesirable" . . ."unwomanly" …"dangerous") imply that it generally thought women should have given up on their fight for suffrage. Choice A says nothing about the press' reaction. Choice C is unclear about whose opinions it reflects. Choice D implies the opinions of Democrats and Republicans but not the press, specifically.

34. The correct answer is A. Each answer choice can be used as a synonym of *ran*, but *streamed* makes the most sense in this particular context.

35. The correct answer is D. This is the most specific definition of how the figurative phrase is used in line 26-27. Choice A is too literal. Choice B does not define the phrase accurately. Choice C is not as specific as choice D is.

36. The correct answer is C. These lines describe the joy the women felt while irritating their opponents and the pleasure they took in knowing that their opponents suffered more than the women did. Choice A is too general; it does not necessarily apply to every situation. Choice B is just a detail in the paragraph. Choice D is not the paragraph's main purpose.

37. The correct answer is C. Throughout the paragraph, Stevens describes examples of how opponents to women's suffrage failed to generate much support. The other answer choices are all details in the paragraph but fail to capture its central claim.

38. The correct answer is B. The anti-suffrage Democrat hoped that the women would grow tired of their fight and withdraw, or stand down. Choice A is incorrect because although this is the most familiar definition of *retire*, the word does not refer to work in this case. Choice C is incorrect because *retire* does not refer to the women's hope, but rather their presence in the movement. Choice D is another common definition of *retire*, but the Congressman was not concerned about the women going to bed.

39. The correct answer is C. Choices A, B, and C can all be used as synonyms for *fixed*, but only *unchanging* makes sense in this particular context. Choice D is an antonym of *fixed*.

40. The correct answer is A. Only choice A suggests that someone who has not studied geology closely may assume that the earth's features have not experienced changes. The other answer choices all suggest an incorrect choice was made when answering the previous question.

41. The correct answer is D. The author suggests that studying both geology and history teaches us about the present. Based on this passage alone, choices A and B apply only to history. Choice C applies only to geology.

42. The correct answer is D. Only choice D states similarities between geology ("the natural world") and history (the "antecedent" "condition of nations"). Choices A and B discuss only geology. Choice C discusses only history.

43. The correct answer is B. Each answer choice can be used as a synonym of *trace*, but *follow* makes the most sense in this particular context. Choice D can be eliminated since *trace* is used as a verb in line 9 and *suggestion* is a noun.

44. The correct answer is A. Both passages explain how geology depends upon changes that occurred in the past. Choices B and D only apply to Passage 1, and these are not the passage's primary purposes in any event. Both passages define *geology*, but they are mostly concerned with other matters, so choice C is not the best answer.

45. The correct answer is C. Even though the author of Passage 1 does not compare geology and history as the author of Passage 2 does, he does explain that geology "deals with the history of the earth." This is sufficient evidence that choice C is a logical conclusion. Choice A is true of geography, not geology. Choice B is true of history, not geology. Choice D is not the best answer because the author of Passage 2 does not discuss geography at all.

46. The correct answer is B. The author of Passage 2 uses a comparison with history to explain geology. He does not mention any other sciences besides geology, so choice A is incorrect. Choices C and D only apply to Passage 1.

47. The correct answer is C. The author of Passage 1 assumes that "a person of ordinary intelligence" might not understand that geology is dependent on past changes. The author of Passage 2 illustrates how geology is dependent on past changes by comparing it to the study of history. Choice B is untrue. Choices A and D do not reach logical conclusions from the information in these passages.

answers diagnostic test

Section 2: Writing and Language Test

1. C	9. D	17. D	24. B	31. C	38. A
2. B	10. B	18. D	25. D	32. C	39. D
3. C	11. D	19. D	26. A	33. B	40. A
4. A	12. B	20. B	27. D	34. C	41. C
5. B	13. B	21. C	28. A	35. B	42. D
6. B	14. D	22. C	29. A	36. D	43. B
7. D	15. A	23. C	30. B	37. B	44. D
8. B	16. B				

1. **The correct answer is C.** Because the sentence starts with "Known as," the verb choice for the underlined text should be different to avoid repetition and awkwardness. Choice B is incorrect because it conveys the opposite of what the writer is trying to say (*Known* and *widely* are the tip-off words that suggest that Johnson is probably not anonymous). Choice D is also incorrect—there is nothing in the passage to suggest that Johnson is disliked for her work at NASA.

2. **The correct answer is B.** As written, the clause "that spanned" is misplaced—is it referring to "contributions" or to "NASA's space program?" Choice B fixes this by changing the order so that "NASA's space program contributions" becomes the noun phrase modified by "which spanned." Choices C and D change the adverb, but the modified phrase isn't clear. Choice D also incorrectly puts a comma before *that*, which is wrong because *that* indicates a restrictive clause and should not be set off with a comma.

3. **The correct answer is C.** The punctuation here is tricky: the underlined text finishes an introductory clause, so that has to be punctuated correctly; and there's also a town and state name, which has its own set of comma rules. The correct answer ends with a comma (which eliminates choice D), but also puts a single comma between the town name and state name (which eliminates choice B).

4. **The correct answer is A.** Of the options, choice A does the best job offering new (but related) details to this paragraph. It confirms that she continued to study math and also mentions her mentor in the subject. Choice B doesn't quite work, because you already know where the school was located, so it's not necessary to repeat where she lived. Choice C should also be eliminated, because the paragraph focuses on her time at school, and the next paragraph does too—it seems too early to start talking about her later job at NASA. Choice D essentially just repeats the information that is stated much more succinctly in "advanced math classes," so it is an unnecessary detail.

5. **The correct answer is B.** This paragraph needs some kind of transition to make the jump in topic from her math studies to her efforts as a civil rights pioneer. Choice D is close, but it creates two abrupt sentences at the beginning of the paragraph when there should be more of a flow. Choice B does this by mentioning her studies but also setting up the next sentence by suggesting there is more to Johnson than her academics. Choice A does the same thing, but "so yeah" does not match the informative tone of this passage and sets up a more conversational tone.

6. **The correct answer is B.** *Although* and *though* are similar: as conjunctions, they both mean "in spite of something." In this sentence, however, we need the adverb version of *though*, which means "however" or "nonetheless." *Still* and *so* (choices C and D) can be used as adverbs, but don't match the context of the sentence.

7. **The correct answer is D.** The sentence should be more specific about which aeronautics laboratory she joined. Choice D is the most specific option here. Choice B is grammatically accurate but lacks the same level of information as choice D. Choice C makes the sentence even more vague.

8. **The correct answer is B.** The word *space* is a common noun and should not be capitalized, which eliminates choices A and C. In this context there is no specific space being referred to, so adding *the* (choice D) is also not correct.

9. **The correct answer is D.** This is the only option that gives specifics about what she worked on during her career at NASA. Choice A just states that she worked for NASA for a long time, which doesn't tell you anything about what she achieved there. Choice B is about her personal life, not her career at NASA. Choice C is about an event in her later life, not her career at NASA at the time.

10. **The correct answer is B.** The strongest detail point at this place in the passage would give a concrete example of the invaluable work Johnson did for NASA's space programs. Choice B gives a specific example that backs up the point made. Choice A is incorrect because although this is an interesting fact, it is not relevant to the information presented in this paragraph, which discusses Johnson's professional accomplishments. Choice C is incorrect because Johnson's honors are discussed in the final paragraph. Choice D is incorrect because it is too vague and is out of place in this paragraph.

11. **The correct answer is D.** Choice A introduces new information rather than relating to the passage as a whole. Choice B would make a good concluding sentence, but it doesn't offer any insight into the passage's main point. Choice C is very vague and, like choice A, adds new information rather than summarizing the passage.

12. **The correct answer is B.** As written, the underlined text is awkward and introduces overlapping information. Choice B simplifies this by starting with the date, quickly identifying Jerry Brown, and summarizing his declaration of the drought. Choice C contains a fragment. Choice D removes necessary details, simplifying the sentence *too* much. Choice B is a better option.

13. **The correct answer is B.** The underlined text is a list of items, but each item needs to be presented equally. Choice B makes each list item an equal noun: *precipitation, soil moisture,* and *groundwater.* Choice C unnecessarily adds *levels* to each item, making the list more confusing. Choice D resolves the issue by leaving out most of the list, which is not helpful for the reader.

answers diagnostic test

14. **The correct answer is D.** Choice A creates an incomplete sentence. Choice B changes the meaning of the sentence by taking the *emergency* detail out of it. Choice C is better than A or B but is a needlessly wordy version of choice D. Choice D is the most effective option.

15. **The correct answer is A.** The underlined text is an effective transition because it tells the reader that the topic is shifting from California specifically to the broader topic of water conservation. Choice B is incorrect because the paragraph is not about California specifically. Choice C is incorrect because there's no information in the passage that tells you that water restrictions are always the best solution. Choice D is incorrect because it sets up the information that follows as a contradiction, when the writer is just expanding the details about how to deal with droughts. It also creates a fragment.

16. **The correct answer is B.** The verb should match the other items in the bulleted list. In this case, that's the present participle (choice B). Choice C is past tense, and choices A and D are the simple present tense.

17. **The correct answer is D.** The bullet point talks about appliances, so you can use the chart to provide examples of household appliances that use water. *Leaks* (choice A) aren't an appliance, so that doesn't fit here. Sprinklers aren't included by name on the chart, so choices B and C are out. Choice D presents a list of items that line up with the info presented in the pie chart.

18. **The correct answer is D.** Based on the chart, the biggest use of fresh water is thermoelectric power (choice B). However, that is not one of the items included on the bulleted list, and the sentence specifically refers only to the bullets listed. Choice C is incorrect because industrial usage is only about 5 percent of fresh water use. Of the possible items left, agricultural irrigation is the biggest user of fresh water and, therefore, has the potential for the most impact.

19. **The correct answer is D.** This choice correctly acknowledges that thermoelectric is the biggest water user, while also making a point about household usage (which ties it to the bulleted list). Choice A may be true but, given that the chart suggests that domestic water use is one of the smallest areas of water usage, it presents an incomplete picture. Choice B is incorrect, based on the info in the graph. Choice C is also incorrect, as you see by the percentages in the chart.

20. **The correct answer is B.** *Largest* (choice A) is a superlative, and the article *a* tells you that you're comparing an indefinite number of items, so *largest* doesn't really work here. *Larger* (choice B) works because it helps the reader compare state water usage to the total number of other types of water usage. *Large* (choice C) isn't specific enough, because it doesn't tell you anything about state water usage vs. total water usage. Choice D is incorrect because when you have the prefix *–er*, you don't need to add *more* (it's redundant).

21. **The correct answer is C.** Use *fewer* when you can assign a specific number to the items, and *less* if it's an undetermined amount. Here, *water* is an indefinite noun, so *less* (choice C) is correct. Choice B is the opposite of what the writer is trying to express in the sentence. Choice D also uses the incorrect adjective *few*.

22. **The correct answer is C.** The overall passage is about drought, not necessarily California, so it makes the most sense to start with the general explanation of drought conditions (Paragraph 2). That eliminates choice D. Paragraph 3 is a natural transition to talking about California, so paragraph 1 would be most logical placed between paragraphs 3 and 4.

23. **The correct answer is C.** As written, the underlined text is far too wordy. It is also redundant, because *digital* and *electronic* are conveying the same idea here. Choice C tones it down by keeping just two *mores* and *digital.* In choice B, the ellipsis doesn't work because it's unclear what the author is taking out—and also because the text is not a direct quote. Choice D's *etc.* is confusing, and the reader doesn't know what *etc.* means in this case.

24. **The correct answer is B.** While the passage is about jobs that require coding, this sentence is a general statement about jobs and is not particularly relevant to how coding fits into future employment. The next paragraph is about coding specifically, so this sentence isn't a good transition (choice C). It also doesn't provide essential information about coding (choice D).

25. **The correct answer is D.** This sentence has a short list of two items (*computer programmers* and *other tech industry professionals*), so there's no comma necessary to separate those. That eliminates choices A and C. In fact, there's no punctuation of any kind necessary to separate them, so choice B is out as well.

26. **The correct answer is A.** The writer is giving a definition of coding, so it is appropriate to set that off with parentheses. She could also have used a pair of em dashes or commas. Choice B removes all punctuation and turns the sentence into a confusing, incomplete fragment. Choices C and D create run-on sentences by unnecessarily adding *or* to the mix.

27. **The correct answer is D.** As written, the underlined text suggests that the computer programmers, not their coding skills, are portable. Choice D rewrites that introductory clause in a way that makes it clear that the writer is talking about the skills. Choice B is incorrect because it unnecessarily repeats "computer programmers" even though the rest of the sentence already indicates that it's talking about computer programmers. Choice C creates a run-on sentence.

28. **The correct answer is A.** The writer is trying to create an image of increased opportunity, so *producing* works well here. Choice B is the opposite of what the rest of the paragraph presents. Choice C, *paraphrasing*, doesn't match the context of the sentence. Choice D is closer, but there's no information in the passage that talks about how people feel about digital media, so choice A is a better option.

29. **The correct answer is A.** This sentence acts as a transition to the list of jobs, so it is relevant. Choice B is too specific and would work better as part of the paragraph about user experience designers. Choice C is an irrelevant detail—the passage is about coding, so it doesn't really make sense to start talking about other kinds of jobs here. For choice D, there isn't enough information given about the jobs to tell whether every one of them requires knowledge of graphic design software.

30. **The correct answer is B.** *And* coordinates the sentence to let the reader know that the writer is listing two equal pieces of information that complement each other. Choice C sets up an unnecessary cause-effect relationship. Choice D is wordier than it needs to be.

31. **The correct answer is C.** The underlined text feels repetitive because of *use* and *users* both appearing in it. The best way to make this a more efficient sentence is to cut it down to just the necessary words. Choice C does this by letting *users* tell the reader that users are, in fact, using the products. It cuts down on unnecessary noise in the sentence.

32. **The correct answer is C.** The pronoun *it* is confusing here—what is it referring to? The writer is talking about making changes to the website or app, so the more specific noun *product* helps make the sentence clearer. Choices B and D are incorrect because they change the meaning of the sentence altogether.

33. **The correct answer is B.** In choice A, Georgia is near the bottom of the list, so it shouldn't be included as a top hotspot. Choice B takes the top two states and uses that to make a conclusion about employment, which works. Choice C is incorrect because the chart just shows the top states—it doesn't necessarily mean that no other states have tech jobs. Choice D attaches the wrong data to New Jersey.

34. **The correct answer is C.** The next part of the sentence tells the reader that Shakespeare wrote many plays. *Prolific* (choice C) means "productive," so that definition fits with the context of the sentence.

35. **The correct answer is B.** The pronoun is confusing and suggests that Shakespeare himself is being handed down from generation to generation. Rather, the writer is trying to say that his work is being handed down, so choice B is the best answer. Choice C has a mismatch between the plural noun *plays* and the single form of the verb *is*. Choice D is incorrect because it's not accurate—it's his plays, not his name, being handed down.

36. **The correct answer is D.** As written, the underlined text is a fragment. Choice B is a possibility: it is grammatically correct, but having *in fact* inserted into the middle of the sentence is awkward. Choice C is awkward as well. Choice D has a clear transition at the beginning (*In fact,*) and keeps the main clause of the sentence clear and intact.

37. **The correct answer is B.** The paragraph is about the questions surrounding Shakespeare's authorship, so it would be relevant to add information about when questions started coming up. The writer's personal preferences don't fit because this is an informational passage, not a persuasive or personal one. The types of plays Shakespeare wrote might be relevant elsewhere in the passage, but this information doesn't really fit with the main topic of the paragraph. The same goes for biographical details about Shakespeare's death and burial.

38. **The correct answer is A.** The paragraph is talking about potential "Shakespeare" writers, and choice A not only stays on that topic, but also offers more information about why these men might be good candidates. Choice B is repetitive (the previous sentence mentions that the other men were playwrights), and focuses on Christopher Marlowe alone. Choice C would be relevant if the paragraph were about England's history during Shakespeare's time, but that's not the case. Choice D talks about a modern project that has nothing to do with the authorship debate.

39. **The correct answer is D.** The verb *to have* should match the subject noun, *accusations*. Because that noun is plural, the verb should be as well. Choices B and C match the number, but they don't agree with the present tense of the sentence (as suggested by *current* earlier in the sentence).

40. **The correct answer is A.** All three of the sentences add information about why there are questions about the authorship of Shakespeare's plays. Sentence 1 introduces the topic; sentence 2 explains why there are questions; and sentence 3 explains why people would doubt the level of Shakespeare's writing ability.

41. **The correct answer is C.** While the sentence is talking *about* questions, it is not actually a question (choice A). An exclamation point (choice B) doesn't really match the tone of the writing, because this is a calm, informational passage. An ellipsis (choice D) should only be used as a pause in a conversation (which this is not) or to show that specific text has been skipped. It should not come at the end of a sentence if it's not part of a quote.

42. **The correct answer is D.** If an adjective clause is describing a person, use *who* (choice D). If it's describing an object or a concept, use *that* (choice A) or *which* (choice B).

43. **The correct answer is B.** The writer is talking about the current status of the debate, so using the past tense (choice A) or the future tense (choices C and D) is incorrect. Choice B is the present tense, so it works with the rest of the sentence.

44. **The correct answer is D.** The sentence is a good closing sentence for the passage: it summarizes both sides of the debate and also restates the idea that there is little evidence either way. Sentence 2 flows most logically after sentence 1, and sentence 3 refers directly to sentence 2. The new sentence would fit best at the end of the paragraph.

Section 3: Math Test—No Calculator

1. A	5. C	9. D	12. C	15. 60
2. A	6. D	10. A	13. D	16. 17
3. B	7. B	11. A	14. 22	17. $\dfrac{7}{2}$
4. A	8. D			

1. **The correct answer is A.** The quartiles are located at the two outer vertical lines forming the box portion of the boxplot (the median is represented by the middle line within the box). From the graph, you can see that the first quartile is 20 and the third quartile is 90. So, their average is $\dfrac{20 + 90}{2} = 55$. Choice B is the interquartile range, choice C is the median, and choice D is the range.

2. **The correct answer is A.** The locust population triples monthly, so the form of the function describing the size of the population in terms of time, where t is measured in months, is $f(t) = A \cdot 3^t$, where A represents the initial population size. If the corn crop is decimated at the same rate, then $\dfrac{1}{3}$ of the crop area is decimated each month and $\dfrac{2}{3}$ of the crop will remain untouched. Since there are initially 580 million square feet of land devoted to corn crops, it follows that the number of square feet that remain untouched by the locusts after t months is $c(t) = 580 \cdot \left(\dfrac{2}{3}\right)^t$. Choice B uses the rate $\dfrac{1}{3}$ instead of the amount remaining; choice C assumes that the crop area grows by a factor of 3 each month; and choice D says that the crop area grows by a factor of $\dfrac{3}{2} = 1.5$ each month.

3. **The correct answer is B.** The slope is $m = \dfrac{6 - 2}{-2 - 6} = \dfrac{4}{-8} = -\dfrac{1}{2}$. Using the point-slope formula with the point $(-2, 6)$ yields the following equation:

$$y - 6 = -\dfrac{1}{2}(x + 2)$$

$$y = -\dfrac{1}{2}x - 1 + 6$$

$$y = -\dfrac{1}{2}x + 5$$

Therefore, the y-intercept is $(0, 5)$. Choice A is the result of using a slope of -2; choice C is the result of using a slope of $\dfrac{1}{2}$, and choice D is the result of using a slope of 2.

4. **The correct answer is A.** First, find the hypotenuse of the right triangle appearing on the right side of the following diagram:

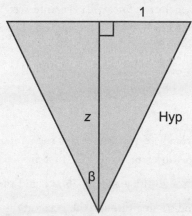

Since the triangle is isosceles, the hypotenuse of the right triangle appearing on the left side of the diagram is also $\sqrt{1+z^2}$. Moreover, the height bisects the base. Thus, the right triangle on the left side of the diagram has dimensions as labeled below:

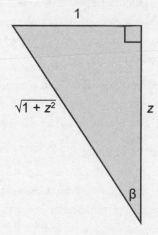

5. **The correct answer is C.** First, "z% of ninety hens produce one egg daily" translates to $\frac{z}{100}\cdot 90$. The phrase, "of these, p% are multicolored" translates to $\frac{p}{100}\cdot\left(\frac{z}{100}\cdot 90\right)$. Finally, if q% will have two yolks, then the phrase "of these, q% are NOT double-yolked" translates to $\left(1-\frac{q}{100}\right)\cdot\left[\frac{p}{100}\cdot\left(\frac{z}{100}\cdot 90\right)\right]$. Now, simplify:

$$\left(1-\frac{q}{100}\right)\left[\frac{p}{100}\cdot\left(\frac{z}{100}\cdot 90\right)\right]=$$

$$\left(\frac{100-q}{100}\right)\left[\frac{90pz}{10000}\right]=\left(\frac{100-q}{100}\right)\left[\frac{9pz}{1000}\right]$$

$$=\frac{9pz(100-q)}{10^5}$$

Choice A is the number of multicolored, double-yolked eggs expected daily. Choice B is the number of double-yolked eggs that are not multicolored. Choice D is the number of eggs that are neither multicolored nor double-yolked.

6. **The correct answer is D.** Let R be the radius of the base (in inches). The diameter is $2R$ inches and the height is $H = 6 + D = 6 + 2R$ inches. The following function gives the surface area of the table:

$$S(R) = 2\pi R^2 + 2\pi RH$$

$$= 2\pi R^2 + 2\pi R(6 + 2R)$$

$$= 2\pi R^2 + 12\pi R + 4\pi R^2$$

$$= 6\pi R^2 + 12\pi R$$

$$= 6\pi R(R + 2)$$

Choice A uses the diameter instead of the radius when expressing the height. Choice B is incorrect because 6 is subtracted instead of added in the height expression. Choice C is the volume.

answers diagnostic test

7. **The correct answer is B.** The percentage increase is computed by subtracting the two quantities, dividing by the quantity *you started with*, and then multiplying by 100:

$$100 \times \frac{60,000 - 42,000}{42,000}\%$$

In choice A, you forgot to multiply by 100. In choices C and D, you divided by the wrong quantity and did not multiply by 100.

8. **The correct answer is D.** The value of x quarters is $0.25x$ dollars. This must be greater than or equal to 75 dollars. This can be written as the inequality $0.25x \geq 75$. The value of y one-dollar bills is y dollars. The sum of the values of x quarters and y one-dollar bills must be strictly less than 350 dollars. This can be written as the inequality $0.25x + y < 350$. So, the system in choice D is correct. Choice A has y instead of xy in the first inequality; choice B uses 25 instead of 0.25; and choice C also uses 25 instead of 0.25 and multiplies this value by y instead of x in the second equation.

9. **The correct answer is D.** Since zero is on one side of the equation, set each factor equal to zero and solve for x:

$$c_1 x = 0 \implies x = 0$$
$$x + c_2 = 0 \implies x = -c_2$$

Since c_2 is assumed to be positive, it follows that $-c_2$ is negative. So, these two solutions are distinct and real. Choices A and C have two complex conjugate solutions, and choice B has one real solution.

10. **The correct answer is A.** The system has no solution when the lines have the same slope, but the y-intercepts are different since then the two lines will never intersect. Write each line in slope-intercept form by solving for y:

$$\begin{cases} y = -\dfrac{k}{2}x + \dfrac{1}{2} \\ y = -\dfrac{k}{3}x + \dfrac{2}{3} \end{cases}$$

From here, you can see that the y-intercepts are different, with the first line passing through the y-axis at $\left(0, \dfrac{1}{2}\right)$ and the second passing through the y-axis at the point $\left(0, \dfrac{2}{3}\right)$. Also, you can see that the slope of the line given by the first equation is $-\dfrac{k}{2}$, and the slope of the line given by the second equation is $-\dfrac{k}{3}$. These slopes are equal only when $k = 0$. When $k = 0$, these will be two parallel horizontal lines. For all other choices, the system has a unique solution because in each case, the slopes of the two lines are different.

11. **The correct answer is A.** Restrict attention to the column for Candidate B; the sample size is 207. Of these, 101 of the votes came from Samoa. So, the probability is $\dfrac{101}{207}$. In choice B, the sample size is not restricted to those who voted for Candidate B. In choice C, the probability is configured to the row for Samoa instead of the column for Candidate B. Choice D is the ratio of votes for Candidate B that came from Samoa township versus the other two townships.

12. **The correct answer is C.** Since there is overlap in the two events "vote is for third-party candidate" and "vote came from McCracken township," use the addition formula. Note that P("vote is for third-party candidate") $= \frac{55}{480}$, P ("vote came from McCracken township") $= \frac{174}{480}$, and P("vote is for third-party candidate" AND "vote came from McCracken township") $= \frac{1}{480}$. So, P ("vote is for third-party candidate" AND "vote came from McCracken township") $= \frac{55}{480} + \frac{174}{480} - \frac{1}{480} = \frac{228}{480} = \frac{19}{40}$.

Choice A is the probability that the vote is for the third-party candidate; choice B is the probability that the vote came from McCracken township; and in choice D, you forgot to subtract $\frac{1}{480}$.

13. **The correct answer is D.** If the temperature is reduced by 50 percent, replace T by $0.5T = \frac{1}{2}T$ in the formula $I = \sigma T^4$. Doing so yields $\overline{I} = \sigma\left(\frac{1}{2}T\right)^4$ $= \sigma\left(\frac{1}{2}\right)^4 T^4 = \frac{1}{16}\sigma T^4 = \frac{1}{16}I$. The other choices are a result of an incorrect application of the exponent rules or a computational error when computing a power.

14. **The correct answer is 22.** Let x be the smallest of three consecutive even integers. Then, the other two integers are $x + 2$ and $x + 4$. Sum the three integers, set the sum equal to 60, and solve for x:

$$x + (x + 2) + (x + 4) = 60$$
$$3x + 6 = 60$$
$$3x = 54$$
$$x = 18$$

So, the integers are 18, 20, and 22. The largest one, therefore, is 22.

15. **The correct answer is 60.** First, determine the equation for the quadratic function. The vertex is $(20, -1,200)$. So, the form of the function is $P(x) = A(x - 20)^2 - 1,600$. The constant A must be positive since the parabola opens upward. Its value is determined by substituting the point $(0, -800)$ into the equation:

$$-1,200 = A(0 - 20)^2 - 1,600$$
$$400 = 400A$$
$$1 = A$$

So, the equation is $P(x) = (x - 20)^2 - 1,600$. Now, to find the break-even point, set this equal to zero and solve for x:

$$(x - 20)^2 - 1,600 = 0$$
$$(x - 20)^2 = 1,600$$
$$x - 20 = \pm\sqrt{1,600} = \pm 40$$
$$x = 20 \pm 40$$
$$x = -20, 60$$

Therefore, the company must sell 60 chairs to break even.

16. **The correct answer is 17%.** Let $3x$ represent the number of hours spent pruning trees, and $7x$ the number of hours spent mowing lawns. Using the given ratio yields the equation $3x + 7x = 60$, which is equivalent to $10x = 60$. So, $x = 6$. As such, last year he spent $3(6) = 18$ hours weekly pruning trees. Approaching this year in the same manner yields the equation $3x + 7x = 70$, so that now $x = 7$. So, this year he expects to spend $3(7) = 21$ hours weekly pruning trees and bushes. The percent increase, therefore, is $\frac{21-18}{18} = \frac{1}{6} = 16\frac{2}{3}\%$, which we round to 17%.

17. **The correct answer is** $\frac{7}{2}$. The vertex of the parabola with this equation is $(-4, -2)$. Since $m(x)$ is a translation of $q(x)$, its graph is also a parabola. The graph of $m(x)$ is obtained from the graph of $q(x)$ by shifting the graph of $q(x)$ to the right a units and down $2a$ units. So, the vertex of $m(x)$ is $(-4 + a, -2 - 2a)$. Thus, the minimum value of $m(x)$ is $-2 - 2a$. Set this equal to -9 and solve for a:

$$-2 - 2a = -9$$
$$-2a = -7$$
$$a = \frac{7}{2}$$

Section 4: Math Test—Calculator

1. A	**8.** A	**14.** C	**20.** C	**26.** A
2. C	**9.** B	**15.** D	**21.** A	**27.** D
3. B	**10.** D	**16.** A	**22.** D	**28.** 2
4. A	**11.** C	**17.** B	**23.** B	**29.** 0.13
5. D	**12.** A	**18.** C	**24.** C	**30.** 720
6. A	**13.** C	**19.** A	**25.** B	**31.** 4
7. B				

1. **The correct answer is A.** Since −2, 0 and 3 are the zeros of a third-degree polynomial with leading coefficient equal to 1, $p(x)$ can be written as $p(x) = x(x + 2)(x − 3)$. Expand this by FOILing the last two expressions and then distributing the x through the resulting trinomial:

$$p(x) = x(x + 2)(x − 3)$$
$$= x(x^2 − x − 6)$$
$$= x^3 − x^2 − 6x$$

Now, set this equal to $p(x) = x^3 + Bx^2 + Cx$ and identify B as −1 and C as −6. Therefore, $\frac{B}{C} = \frac{−1}{−6} = \frac{1}{6}$. Choice B identifies the coefficient of the squared term incorrectly, choice C has the wrong sign, and choice D has the wrong sign and is the reciprocal of the correct answer.

2. **The correct answer is C.** The number of followers gained from each testimonial posted is 4, so she gains $4T$ followers from T posted testimonials. Similarly, the number of followers gained each time someone else shares her business page is 2, so she gains $2S$ followers for S different shares of her business page. The sum of these quantities must be strictly larger than 750. This yields the inequality $4T + 2S > 750$. Choice A interchanges the coefficients of T and S; choice B does this as well, but also uses greater than or equals instead of strictly greater than. Choice D also should have used a strict inequality (but the coefficients used are correct).

3. **The correct answer is B.** The number of hours it takes to produce x standard model tractors is $50x$, and the number of hours it takes to produce y deluxe model tractors is $80y$. So, the total labor needed to manufacture both types of tractors is described by the inequality $50x + 80y \leq 1{,}800$. The storage capacity restriction is given by the inequality $x + y \leq 30$. So, the system describing this scenario is given by choice B. Choices A and D should consist of two inequalities, not equations, and choice C should not have a strict inequality.

4. **The correct answer is A.** The slope of this linear function is $m = \frac{2a − a}{4a − (−2a)} = \frac{a}{6a} = \frac{1}{6}$. Using the point-slope formula with the point $(4a, 2a)$ yields the following equation:

$$y − 2a = \frac{1}{6}(x − 4a)$$
$$y = \frac{1}{6}x − \frac{2}{3}a + 2a$$
$$y = \frac{1}{6}x + \frac{4}{3}a$$

So, the function's equation is $f(x) = \frac{1}{6}x + \frac{4}{3}a$. Choice B is the result of using the wrong sign on the x-coordinate in the point-slope formula. Choice C is the result of not distributing in the point-slope formula. Choice D is the result of using the wrong sign on the x-coordinate and not distributing in the point-slope formula.

5. **The correct answer is D.** The trendline describes the basic pattern evident by the behavior of the clear majority of the points of a scatterplot. Outliers influence the formation of the trendline but not as heavily as does the bulk of the data points. The trendline for this data set is shown below:

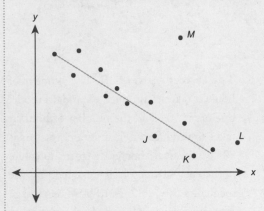

The point that deviates the most from this trendline is point M.

6. **The correct answer is A.** Use the distributive property and combine like terms, as follows:

$$-z + 2\{z - 3(2 - 3z)\} = z - 30$$
$$-z + 2\{z - 6 + 9z\} = z - 30$$
$$-z + 2\{10z - 6\} = z - 30$$
$$-z + 20z - 12 = z - 30$$
$$19z - 12 = z - 30$$
$$18z = -18$$
$$z = -1$$

So, the value of $\left(\frac{z}{1-z}\right)^{-1}$ is $\left(\frac{-1}{1-(-1)}\right)^{-1} = \left(\frac{-1}{2}\right)^{-1} = -2$. In choice B, you did not apply the exponent -1. In choice C, you incorrectly multiplied the base and the exponent. In choice D, you made a sign error when computing the denominator.

7. **The correct answer is B.** The graph of the second equation is the circle shown below:

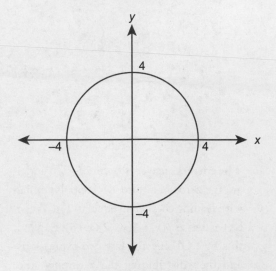

The only way such a system can have a unique solution is if the graph of the linear function is tangent to the circle. If $m = 0$, the line is horizontal. The only two horizontal lines that are tangent to this circle are $y = 4$ and $y = -4$. The line given by choice B is the former of these choices and is therefore the answer. Choices A and D intersect the circle twice, while choice C does not intersect the circle even once.

8. **The correct answer is A.** First, determine the equation of the function $v(t)$. Use the two labeled points $(0, 0.2)$ and $(2.5, 0.6)$ to find the slope: $m = \dfrac{0.6 - 0.2}{2.5 - 0} = \dfrac{0.4}{2.5} = 0.16$. Since the y-intercept is $(0, 0.2)$, the equation of the function in slope-intercept form is $v(t) = 0.16t + 0.2$. Next, set this equal to 3.4 miles and solve for t:

$$0.16t + 0.2 = 3.4$$
$$0.16t = 3.2$$
$$t = \frac{3.2}{0.16} = 20 \text{ hours}$$

So, it took 20 hours for the fog to lift enough so that the visibility was 3.4 miles. Choices B and D are the result of arithmetic mistakes, and choice C is derived by using half hours rather than hours for the time intervals.

9. **The correct answer is B.** You must also take the square root of $\pi\sigma$ in the denominator to get a formula equivalent to $L = 4\pi R^2 \sigma T^4$. The formulas in the other choices are the results of dividing by various terms and using the exponent rules in various ways.

10. **The correct answer is D.** Since the question asks about a randomly selected patient in the study, add the entries in the first column to find the total number of people who had a decline in skin quality and divide by the number of participants, which is 1,000. Doing so yields $\dfrac{85}{1,000} = 0.085$. Choice A focuses only on those who have had severe psoriasis and involves an arithmetic error. In choice B, you mistakenly divided by 500 instead of 1,000. Choice C is a conditional probability.

11. **The correct answer is C.** The system must consist of two equations that are multiples of each other. First, find the equation of the line shown. Using the point $(-6, 9)$ and $(3, 0)$, the slope is $m = \dfrac{9 - 0}{-6 - 3} = -1$. So, using the point-slope formula with the point $(3, 0)$ yields the equation $y - 0 = -(x - 3)$, or equivalently $y = -x + 3$. Note that the equation $-3y = 3x - 9$ is equivalent to this equation (upon division of both sides by -3). Thus, the system in choice C has the solution set shown. Choice A has no solution because the lines are parallel. Choice B has infinitely many solutions, but its solution set consists of a line different from the one shown. Choice D has a unique solution since the slopes of the lines are different.

12. **The correct answer is A.** For a blood pressure reading to be classified as normal according to the chart, the reading on the systolic blood pressure graph must be strictly less than 120 *and* the reading on the diastolic blood pressure graph must be strictly below 80. This occurs at two times: $t = 4$ and $t = 22$. Choice B is the number of times for which the reading on the systolic blood pressure graph equals 120 *and* the reading on the diastolic blood pressure graph equals 80. Choice C is the number of times for which *either* the reading on the systolic blood pressure graph is strictly less than 120 *or* the reading on the diastolic blood pressure graph is strictly below 80. Choice D is the number of points, total, on both graphs at which *either* the reading on the systolic blood pressure graph is strictly less than 120 *or* the reading on the diastolic blood pressure graph is strictly below 80.

answers diagnostic test

13. **The correct answer is C.** There is one point on the systolic graph with a y-coordinate between 140 and 159, and there is one point on the diastolic graph with a y-coordinate between 90 and 99. Since the times at which they occur are different, the proportion of the time that the reading is classified as "High Blood Pressure—STAGE 1" is $\frac{2}{13}$. Choices A and B include the times at which the reading is classified as "High Blood Pressure—STAGE 2," and choice D excludes one of the points.

14. **The correct answer is C.** Factor all expressions and then cancel factors common to the numerator and denominator:

$$\frac{2-x}{x^3-4x} \cdot \frac{x-4}{x^2-16} \cdot x^2$$

$$= \frac{-(x-2)}{x(x-2)(x+2)} \cdot \frac{x-4}{(x-4)(x+4)} \cdot x^2$$

$$= -\frac{x}{(x+2)(x+4)}$$

In choice A, you canceled terms instead of factors in the numerator and denominator. In choice B, you factored incorrectly in the denominator and missed the negative sign. In choice D, you incorrectly factored the denominator of the first rational expression of the product.

15. **The correct answer is D.** Since the cost per *half-mile* is $1.50, the cost per mile is $3. So, the cost for m miles is $3m$ dollars. Adding the flat fee of $25 yields the inequality $25 + 3m \leq 40$ for the various lengths m that your ride can be. The inequality in choice A uses the rate for a half-mile; in choice B the correct quantities are multiplied instead of added, and in choice C the rate per mile is incorrectly computed.

16. **The correct answer is A.** Since 15 percent of the pollutants are removed each minute, 85 percent of the pollutants remain. Thus, the exponential function $P(t) = P_0(0.85)^t$ describes the amount of pollutants remaining after t minutes, where P_0 is the initial amount of pollution present. Since 20 percent of the initial amount is equal to $0.20P_0$, the desired equation is $0.20P_0 = P_0(0.85)^t$. In choice B, you used the percentage of pollution removed. In choice C, you used the wrong base. In choice D, you interchanged 20 percent and 85 percent.

17. **The correct answer is B.** Suppose p is the membership in 2010. Since the membership increases by 75 percent each year, it follows that the membership in 2011 is $1.75p$. Applying the 75 percent increase again to $1.75p$ yields the membership of $(1.75)^2p$ for 2012, and finally $(1.75)^3p$ in 2013. So, $z = (1.75)^3p$. Solving for p shows that the membership in 2010 is $p = (1.75)^{-3}z$. Choice A is the membership in 2011, choice is incorrect because it has 0.75 instead of 1.75 as the base, and choice D has a positive rather than a negative exponent.

18. **The correct answer is C.** Let x be the length of an edge of a cube. A cube has twelve edges, all of which are the same length. Since the sum of all twelve edges is 240 inches, use the equation $12x = 240$ to find the length of one edge. Dividing by twelve shows the length of one edge is 20 inches. The area of a face of a cube is the square of an edge, namely $(20 \text{ inches})^2 = 400$ square inches. Be careful of the units being used. Choice A (20) is the length of an edge in inches, not square inches, and choice D (8,000) is the volume of the cube in cubic inches. Choice B results from computing a power incorrectly by multiplying the base and the exponent.

19. **The correct answer is A.** Isolate the radical term, clear the fractions, square both sides, and solve the resulting quadratic equation, as follows:

$$2 + \sqrt{x-1} = 6 - \frac{1}{10}x$$
$$\sqrt{x-1} = 4 - \frac{1}{10}x$$
$$10\sqrt{x-1} = 40 - x$$
$$\left(10\sqrt{x-1}\right)^2 = (40-x)^2$$
$$100(x-1) = 1,600 - 80x + x^2$$
$$100x - 100 = 1,600 - 80x + x^2$$
$$x^2 - 180x + 1,700 = 0$$
$$(x-10)(x-170) = 0$$
$$x = 10, 170$$

Substituting these values into the original equation reveals that 10 is a solution, but 170 is an extraneous solution. So, the solution set is {10}. Choice B uses the wrong sign. Choice C includes an extraneous solution in the solution set. Choice D uses the wrong signs on both terms and includes an extraneous solution.

20. **The correct answer is C.** Since she can store forty logs, the equation $x + y = 40$ describes the storage capacity. The cost for x maple logs is $20x$ dollars, and the cost of y cherry logs is $35y$ dollars. Since she has 1,500 dollars to spend, the cost equation is $20x + 35y = 1,500$. So, the desired system is

$$\begin{cases} x + y = 40 \\ 20x + 35y = 1,500 \end{cases}$$

Solving the first equation for y and dividing both sides of the second equation by 5 yields the equivalent system in choice C. Choice A is incorrect because you should have subtracted y in the first equation. In choice B, you should not have multiplied the terms on the left side of the second equation. Choice D is incorrect because you should have interchanged the right sides of the two equations.

21. **The correct answer is A.** It is convenient to convert to powers of 10 before converting the units. Note that 6 trillion is equal to 6×10^{12}. Now, convert the units as follows:

$$\left(4.75 \times 10^{19}\right) \cancel{\text{miles}} \times$$

$$\frac{1 \ \cancel{\text{light year}}}{\left(6 \times 10^{12}\right) \cancel{\text{miles}}} \times \frac{1 \text{ parsec}}{3.26 \ \cancel{\text{light years}}}$$

$$\approx 2.43 \times 10^{6} \text{ parsecs}$$

In choice B, the power of 10 is incorrect. In choice C, you used the light year-to-parsec conversion factor incorrectly. In choice D, you incorrectly used 6×10^{14} to represent 6 trillion miles.

answers diagnostic test

22. The correct answer is D. Compute the slope, as follows:

$$m = \frac{-\frac{2}{5}b - \left(-\frac{1}{10}b\right)}{\frac{3}{4}a - \left(-\frac{1}{6}a\right)}$$

$$= \frac{-\frac{3b}{10}}{\frac{11a}{12}} = \left(\frac{-3b}{10}\right)\left(\frac{12}{11a}\right) = -\frac{18b}{55a}$$

Choice A involves an error in fraction division, choice B is the reciprocal of the correct answer without the negative sign, and choice C involves a sign error when subtracting.

23. The correct answer is B. Let x be the measure of one of the angles. Then, the other has measure $3x - 20$. Using the fact that the angles are supplementary yields the following equation:

$$x + (3x - 20) = 180$$
$$4x = 200$$
$$x = 50$$

So, the measures of the two angles are 50° and 130°. The smaller angle, therefore, has a measure of 50°. Choice A used the fact that the angles were complementary, choice C is the larger of the two angles, and choice D would be the larger of the two angles had you mistakenly used $3x + 20$ for the measure of the second angle.

24. The correct answer is C. Use the square root method to solve this equation, as follows:

$$(bx)^2 + b = 0$$
$$(bx)^2 = -b$$
$$bx = \pm\sqrt{-b} = \pm i\sqrt{b}$$
$$x = \frac{\pm i\sqrt{b}}{b}$$

So, the solution set is $\left\{\frac{\pm i\sqrt{b}}{b}\right\}$. Choice A is incorrect because it should be imaginary. Choice B is incorrect because you did not square b when simplifying $(bx)^2$. Choice D is the result of an error in the last step of solving for x.

25. The correct answer is B. The density D of the original object is given by $D = \frac{m}{v}$. If m is halved, then the new mass is $\frac{1}{2}m$. If the volume is doubled, then the new volume is $2v$. The resulting density is $\overline{D} = \frac{\frac{1}{2}m}{2v} = \frac{1}{4}\left(\frac{m}{v}\right) = \frac{1}{4}D$. So, the density is one fourth, or a quarter, of the original density. All other choices are the result of arithmetic errors involving fractions.

26. The correct answer is A. The interquartile range is the difference of the third and first quartiles. For highway driving, this difference is $50 - 35 = 15$, and for city driving this difference is $40 - 30 = 10$. So, the difference in the interquartile ranges is $15 - 10 = 5$. Choice B is the interquartile range for city driving, choice C is the interquartile range for highway driving, and choice D is the sum of the interquartile ranges.

27. **The correct answer is D.** The highway driving boxplot has a range of 55 − 20 = 35, while the range of the city driving boxplot is 45 − 25 = 20; therefore, it is nearly double. Also, the middle 50 percent for the highway boxplot is 50 percent larger than the city boxplot. So, the data are much more spread out for highway driving than city driving. Choice A is wrong because the second vertical lines in each of the boxplots do not occur at the same value. Choice B is incorrect because this value occurred for highway driving. Choice C is incorrect since the range of the highway driving data set is nearly double that of the city driving data set.

28. **The correct answer is 2 liters.** Let x be the number of liters of water that she needs to add to get the desired concentration. Of the original 4 liters, 15 percent is the active ingredient, and so the remainder, 85 percent, is water. So, the amount of water in 4 liters of the original mixture is 0.85(4) liters. Of the x liters of water that she is adding, 100 percent is water. So, this gives x liters of water. The sum of these two quantities must be equal to the amount of water in $(4 + x)$ liters of the new 10 percent mixture; this amount of water is 0.90$(4 + x)$. This yields the equation $4(0.85) + x = 0.90(4 + x)$.

Solve for x, as follows:

$$4(0.85) + x = 0.90(4 + x)$$
$$3.4 + x = 0.9(4 + x)$$
$$340 + 100x = 90(4 + x)$$
$$340 + 100x = 360 + 90x$$
$$10x = 20$$
$$x = 2$$

Therefore, she must add 2 liters of water to reach the desired concentration.

29. **The correct answer is 0.13.** Substitute $D = 5$ and $d = 3$ into the formula and simplify:

$$BHN = \frac{2}{\pi \cdot 5\left(5 - \sqrt{5^2 - 3^2}\right)} =$$

$$\frac{2}{5\pi\left(5 - \sqrt{16}\right)} = \frac{2}{5\pi(5 - 4)} = \frac{2}{5\pi} \approx 0.13$$

30. **The correct answer is 720.** Set up a proportion to determine the number of miles to which the length of each side of the rectangle corresponds.

$$\frac{0.75 \text{ inch}}{12 \text{ miles}} = \frac{1.25 \text{ inches}}{x \text{ miles}}$$
$$0.75x = (1.25)(12)$$
$$x = 20$$
$$\frac{0.75 \text{ inch}}{12 \text{ miles}} = \frac{2.25 \text{ inches}}{y \text{ miles}}$$
$$0.75y = (2.25)(12)$$
$$y = 36$$

Therefore, the area is square miles is 200 × 360 = 720 square miles.

31. **The correct answer is 4 centimeters.** Note that triangle AFQ is similar to triangle ABC because all corresponding angles are the same. As such, corresponding sides of the two triangles are in the same proportion. Specifically, $\frac{AF}{FQ} = \frac{AB}{BC}$. Using this yields the following equation in x:

$$\frac{x}{4} = \frac{x + 2}{x + 6}$$
$$x(x + 6) = 4(x + 2)$$
$$x^2 + 6x = 4x + 8$$
$$x^2 + 2x - 8 = 0$$
$$(x - 2)(x + 4) = 0$$
$$x = \cancel{-4}, 2$$

So, $\overline{AB}$ has length 2 cm + 2 cm = 4 cm.

USING YOUR DIAGNOSTIC TEST RESULTS

Now that you've completed this PSAT/NMSQT® exam diagnostic test, it's time to compute your scores. Simply follow the instructions on the following pages, and use the conversion tables provided to calculate your scores. The formulas provided will give you as close an approximation as possible on how you might score on the actual exam.

To Determine Your Diagnostic Test Score

1. After you go through each of the test sections (**Reading, Writing and Language, Math—No Calculator**, and **Math—Calculator**) and determine which answers you got right, be sure to enter the number of correct answers in the box below the answer key for each of the sections.

2. Your total score on this test is the sum of your Evidence-Based Reading and Writing Section score and your Math Section score. To get your total score for each test section, convert the raw score—the number of questions you got right in a particular section—into the "scaled score" for that section, and then calculate the total score. It may sound a little confusing, but we'll take you through the steps.

To Calculate Your Evidence-Based Reading and Writing Section Score

Your Evidence-Based Reading and Writing Section score is on a scale of 160–760. First determine your Reading Test score, and then determine your score on the Writing and Language Test.

1. Count the number of correct answers you got on the **Reading Test Section.** *Remember that there is no penalty for wrong answers.* **The number of correct answers is your raw score.**

2. Go to **Raw Score Conversion Table 1: Section and Test Scores** on page 107. Look in the "Raw Score" column for your raw score, and match it to the number in the "Reading Test Score" column.

3. Do the same with the **Writing and Language Test Section** to determine that score.

4. Add your **Reading Test score** to your **Writing and Language Test score**.

5. Multiply that number by 10. This is your **Evidence-Based Reading and Writing Section score**.

To Calculate Your Math Section Score

Your Math score is also on a scale of 160–760.

1. Count the number of correct answers you got on the **Math Test—No Calculator Section** and the **Math Test—Calculator Section**. *Again, there is no penalty for wrong answers.* **The number of correct answers is your raw score.**

2. Add the number of correct answers on the **Math Test—No Calculator Section** and the **Math Test—Calculator Section**.

3. Use the **Raw Score Conversion Table 1: Section and Test Scores** on page 107 and convert your raw score into your **Math Section score**.

To Obtain Your Total Score

Add your score on the **Evidence-Based Reading and Writing Section** to the **Math Section** score. This is your **Total Score** on this test, on a scale of 320–1520.

SUBSCORES, TEST SCORES, AND CROSS-TEST SCORES

Test scores, subscores, and cross-test scores offer you greater details about your strengths and weaknesses in certain areas within reading, writing, and math, which can help you evaluate your current skill set and determine which areas you need to focus on most to make improvements. Your scores on the PSAT/NMSQT® exam can also be used to help you predict—and further prepare for—the SAT® exam.

PSAT/NMSQT® Subscores

Subscores on the official PSAT/NMSQT® exam are designed to reflect your performance in a range of key skill areas. You should use your scores to help guide your future study following the exam, and to help guide your preparation for the SAT® exam. Subscores range from 1–15, and include the following areas: Heart of Algebra, Problem Solving and Data Analysis, Passport to Advanced Math, Expression of Ideas, Standard English Conventions, Words in Context, and Command of Evidence.

Computing Your Subscores for the Diagnostic Test

Heart of Algebra

The **Heart of Algebra subscore** is based on questions from the **Math Test** that focus on linear equations and inequalities. Add up your total correct answers from these questions:

- Math Test—No Calculator: Questions 3, 6, 8, 10, 14
- Math Test—Calculator: Questions 2, 3, 6, 8, 11, 15, 18, 20, 21, 23, 29

Your Raw Score = the total number of correct answers from all of these questions.

Use the **Raw Score Conversion Table 2: Subscores** on page 109 to determine your **Heart of Algebra** subscore.

Problem Solving and Data Analysis

The **Problem Solving and Data Analysis subscore** is based on questions from the **Math Test** that focus on quantitative reasoning, the interpretation and synthesis of data, and solving problems in rich and varied contexts. Add up your total correct answers from these questions:

- Math Test—No Calculator: Questions 1, 5, 7, 11, 12, 16
- Math Test—Calculator: Questions 5, 10, 12, 13, 17, 25-28, 30

Your Raw Score = the total number of correct answers from all of these questions

Use the **Raw Score Conversion Table 2: Subscores** on page 109 to determine your **Problem Solving and Data Analysis** subscore.

Passport to Advanced Math

The **Passport to Advanced Math subscore** is based on questions from the **Math Test** that focus on topics central to your ability to progress to more advanced math, such as understanding the structure of expressions, reasoning with more complex equations, and interpreting and building functions. Add up your total correct answers from these questions:

- Math Test—No Calculator: Questions 2, 9, 13, 15, 17
- Math Test—Calculator: Questions 1, 4, 7, 9, 14, 16, 19, 22, 24

Your Raw Score = the total number of correct answers from all of these questions

Use the **Raw Score Conversion Table 2: Subscores** on page 109 to determine your **Passport to Advanced Math** subscore.

Expression of Ideas

The **Expression of Ideas subscore** is based on questions from the **Writing and Language Test** that focus on topic development, organization, and rhetorically effective use of language. Add up your total correct answers from these questions in Section 2: Writing and Language Test:

- Questions 1, 4, 5, 9, 11, 12, 14, 15, 17-19, 22-24, 27-29, 32-34, 37, 38, 40, 44

Your Raw Score = the total number of correct answers from all of these questions

Use the **Raw Score Conversion Table 2: Subscores** on page 109 to determine your **Expression of Ideas** subscore.

Standard English Conventions

The **Standard English Conventions subscore** is based on questions from the **Writing and Language Test** that focus on sentence structure, usage, and punctuation. Add up your total correct answers from these questions in Section 2: Writing and Language Test:

- Questions 2, 3, 6-8, 10, 13, 16, 20, 21, 25, 26, 30, 31, 35, 36, 39, 41-43

Your Raw Score = the total number of correct answers from all of these questions

Use the **Raw Score Conversion Table 2: Subscores** on page 109 to determine your **Standard English Conventions** subscore.

Words in Context

The **Words in Context subscore** is based on questions from the **Reading Test** and the **Writing and Language Test** that address word/phrase meaning in context and rhetorical word choice. Add up your total correct answers from these questions in the following sections:

- Reading Test: Questions 4, 6, 11, 16, 20, 29, 34, 38, 39, 43
- Writing and Language Test: Questions 1, 6, 15, 21, 28, 32, 34, 42

Your Raw Score = the total number of correct answers from all of these questions

Use the **Raw Score Conversion Table 2: Subscores** on page 109 to determine your **Words in Context** subscore.

Command of Evidence

The **Command of Evidence subscore** is based on questions from the **Reading Test** and the **Writing and Language** Test that ask you to interpret and use evidence found in a wide range of passages and informational graphics, such as graphs, tables, and charts. Add up your total correct answers from these questions in Sections 1 and 2:

- Reading Test: Questions 2, 8, 13, 15, 23, 25, 31, 33, 40, 42
- Writing and Language Test: Questions 4, 9, 10, 17-19, 29, 33, 37, 38

Your Raw Score = the total number of correct answers from all of these questions

Use the **Raw Score Conversion Table 2: Subscores** on page 109 to determine your **Command of Evidence** subscore.

PSAT/NMSQT® Test and Cross-Test Scores

When you take the official PSAT/NMSQT® exam, you'll receive three additional test scores (alongside your total score and section scores) on a range of 8–38. These test scores are designed to show how you performed on the content covered in each of the test sections: Reading, Writing and Language, and Math.

You'll also receive two cross-test scores on the official PSAT/NMSQT® exam, which will reflect your performance in the following content domains (which span all test sections): **Analysis in History/ Social Studies**, and **Analysis in Science**. These scores will also be in the range of 8–38, and will help you further analyze your current skill level.

Computing Your Cross-Test Scores for the Diagnostic Test

Use the following to determine your cross-test scores for the diagnostic test:

Analysis in History/Social Studies

Add up your total correct answers from these questions:

- Reading Test: Questions 10-18, 29-38
- Writing and Language Test: Questions 1, 4, 5, 9-11
- Math Test—No Calculator: Questions 5-7, 11, 12, 16
- Math Test—Calculator: Questions 2, 3, 17, 30

Your Raw Score = the total number of correct answers from all of these questions.

Use the **Raw Score Conversion Table 3: Cross-Test Scores** on page 111 to determine your **Analysis in History/Social Studies** cross-test score.

Analysis in Science

Add up your total correct answers from these sections:

- Reading Test: Questions 19-28, 39-47
- Writing and Language Test: Questions 12, 14, 15, 17-19

- • Math Test—No Calculator: Questions 2, 13
- • Math Test—Calculator: Questions 8-10, 12, 13, 16, 21, 28, 29

Your Raw Score = the total number of correct answers from all of these questions

Use the **Raw Score Conversion Table 3: Cross-Test Scores** on page 111 to determine your **Analysis in Science** cross-test score.

Raw Score Conversion Table 1: Section and Test Scores

Raw Score (# of correct answers)	Reading Test Score	Writing and Language Test Score	Math Section Score	Raw Score (# of correct answers)	Reading Test Score	Writing and Language Test Score	Math Section Score
0	8	8	160	25	26	25	560
1	9	9	190	26	26	26	570
2	10	10	210	27	27	27	580
3	11	11	240	28	27	27	580
4	12	12	270	29	28	28	590
5	14	13	290	30	28	28	600
6	15	14	320	31	29	29	610
7	16	14	340	32	29	29	620
8	16	15	360	33	30	30	630
9	17	15	370	34	30	30	640
10	18	16	390	35	31	31	650
11	18	16	400	36	31	32	670
12	19	17	420	37	32	32	680
13	19	18	430	38	32	33	690
14	20	18	440	39	33	34	710
15	20	19	460	40	34	35	720
16	21	20	470	41	34	36	730
17	21	20	480	42	35	37	730
18	22	21	490	43	36	37	740
19	22	21	500	44	37	38	740
20	23	22	510	45	37		750
21	23	23	520	46	38		750
22	24	24	530	47	38		760
23	24	24	540	48			760
24	25	25	550				

Conversion Equation 1: Section and Test Scores

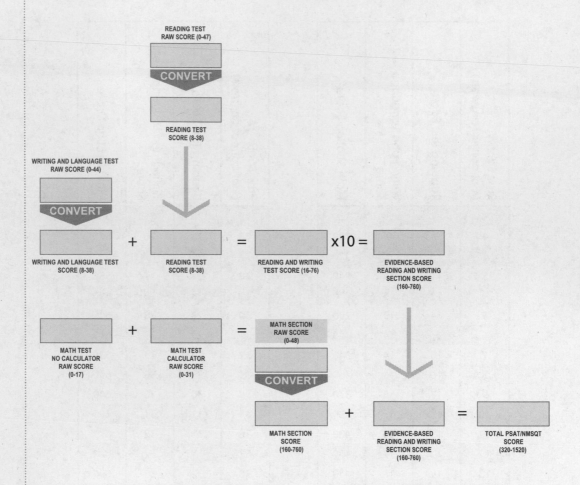

Raw Score Conversion Table 2: Subscores

Raw Score (# of correct answers)	Heart of Algebra	Problem Solving and Data Analysis	Passport to Advanced Math	Expression of Ideas	Standard English Conventions	Words in Context	Command of Evidence
0	1	1	1	1	1	1	1
1	3	3	5	2	2	2	2
2	4	4	7	3	3	3	3
3	5	5	8	4	3	3	4
4	6	6	9	4	4	4	5
5	7	7	10	5	4	5	6
6	8	8	11	6	5	6	7
7	8	8	12	6	6	6	8
8	9	9	13	7	6	7	8
9	10	10	14	7	7	8	9
10	10	11	15	8	7	9	9
11	11	11	15	8	8	10	10
12	12	12	15	9	8	10	11
13	13	13	15	9	9	11	11
14	14	14	15	10	9	12	12
15	15	15		10	10	13	13
16	15	15		11	10	14	14
17				12	11	15	15
18				12	12	15	15
19				13	13		
20				13	15		
21				14			
22				15			
23				15			
24				15			

Conversion Equation: 2 Subscores

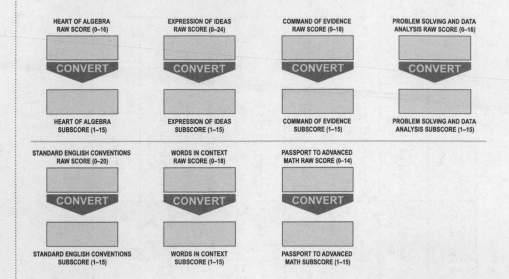

Raw Score Conversion Table 3: Cross-Test Scores

Raw Score (# of correct answers)	Analysis in History/Social Studies Cross-Test Score	Analysis in Science Cross-Test Score
0	8	8
1	9	12
2	11	15
3	12	16
4	14	17
5	15	18
6	16	18
7	17	19
8	18	20
9	19	21
10	20	22
11	21	23
12	22	24
13	23	25
14	24	26
15	25	26
16	26	27
17	26	28
18	27	28
19	28	29
20	29	30
21	30	31
22	30	31
23	31	32
24	32	33
25	32	34
26	33	35
27	34	36
28	35	37
29	36	37
30	37	38
31	37	38
32	38	38

Conversion Equation 3: Cross-Test Scores

TEST	ANALYSIS IN HISTORY/SOCIAL STUDIES		ANALYSIS IN SCIENCE	
	QUESTIONS	RAW SCORE	QUESTIONS	RAW SCORE
Reading Test	10-18; 29-38		19-28; 39-47	
Writing and Language Test	1, 4, 5, 9-11		12, 14, 15, 17-19	
Math Test—No Calculator	5-7; 11, 12, 16		2, 13	
Math Test—Calculator	2, 3, 17, 30		8-10; 12, 13, 16, 21, 28, 29	
TOTAL				

ANALYSIS IN HISTORY/
SOCIAL STUDIES
RAW SCORE (0–32)

ANALYSIS IN SCIENCE
RAW SCORE (0–32)

CONVERT

CONVERT

ANALYSIS IN HISTORY/
SOCIAL STUDIES
CROSS-TEST SCORE (8-38)

ANALYSIS IN SCIENCE
CROSS-TEST SCORE (8-38)

PART III

PSAT/NMSQT® EXAM READING TEST STRATEGIES

Chapter 3   Evidence-Based Reading Strategies

Evidence-Based Reading Strategies

OVERVIEW

- **Words in Context Questions**
- **Analysis in History/Social Studies and Science Questions**
- **Command of Evidence Questions**
- **All About Paired Passages**
- **Four Reading Passage Walkthroughs**
- **Evidence-Based Reading Practice Questions**
- **Answer Key and Explanations**
- **Summing It Up**

You've probably taken some multiple-choice reading tests during your school career. You know—the ones that require you to read a short reading passage and answer multiple-choice questions that test your ability to recall details from the passage, make inferences about it, define vocabulary words in it, and so on. That's basically what you'll have to do on the PSAT/NMSQT® Reading Test, though the passages and questions may be a bit more complex than the ones you've encountered in the past. That's because the intention of the test is to measure how ready you are for the more complex next phase of your schooling career: college. Don't worry, though—this chapter will tell you all you'll need to know to master the passages and questions you'll face on test day.

The Reading Test consists of six passages, two of which are paired, and 47 questions. The passages/passage pairs are roughly 550-750 words long and come in four varieties:

- A **Literature** passage excerpted from a classic or contemporary work of fiction

- A **History** passage excerpted from an important U.S. founding document or speech or one that examines an important historical event

- A **Social Studies** passage about economics (the study of money matters), psychology (the study of the mind), or sociology (the study of human societies and culture)

- Two **Science** passages that may deal with such subtopics as earth science, biology, chemistry, or physics

We'll walk you through these passage types in greater detail a bit later in this chapter so you will have a very clear idea of how they tend to be structured and the kinds of questions that accompany them. Those questions will include:

- **Words in Context** questions, which test your ability to identify the specific ways words and phrases are used in the passages

- **Analysis in History/Social Studies and Science** questions, which are much broader in scope and require you to examine hypotheses, interpret data, and consider implications
- **Command of Evidence** questions, which will require you to locate information in the passages that support your answers to analysis questions

Some questions on the PSAT/NMSQT® Reading Test require you to find information stated directly in the passage. Other questions will require you to interpret ideas that are not stated directly.

Some passages will also include informational graphics such as graphs, tables, charts, diagrams, and maps. You will have to interpret and analyze such materials in the same way you will interpret and analyze the text passages they accompany. Although informational graphics may include numerical information, they won't be used to test your math skills. Remember that this is the Reading Test, and only reading comprehension skills are required.

In this chapter, we'll introduce you to the different kinds of questions that appear on the PSAT/ NMSQT® Reading Test and how those questions are asked. You'll learn a lot about the four passage types as we walk you step-by-step through some sample passages. Along the way, you'll learn some valuable tips on the kinds of information and structures common to these passage types and the best ways to spot the information you'll need to answer the questions that follow. You'll get the chance to put your new skills to the test by answering sample questions at the end of each walkthrough.

Finally, there are twenty more practice questions at the end of the chapter. Answering these will give you a good idea of what you will be required to do on test day.

WORDS IN CONTEXT QUESTIONS

Words are the basic elements of any reading selection. If you don't understand how vocabulary is used within a passage, you're going to have a very hard time understanding its overall meaning. The ability to interpret how a writer uses words within a particular context is one of the most important reading skills to master. The **Words in Context** questions on the PSAT/NMSQT® Reading Test will put those skills to the test.

Words in Context questions can be tricky because many words have more than one meaning. Take a basic word such as *hear*. Its most common definition is "to perceive by listening." However, that is not the only meaning of *hear*. It can also mean:

- *to understand*, as in "Don't worry, I hear what you're saying."
- *to learn*, as in "Did you hear the news about Jenny?"
- *to consider a court case*, as in "The judge will hear the case today."

When a word has multiple meanings, you can identify how it is being used by its context, meaning the way it is used in a particular piece of writing. For example, if *hear* is used in the sentence "The judge will hear the case today," you should conclude that *hear* does not mean "to learn" in this particular context.

You will need to use your ability to identify how words are used in particular contexts on the PSAT/NMSQT® Reading Test. In fact, a minimum of two Words in Context questions will accompany *each* passage or passage pair. They are always phrased the same way:

> *As used in line X, "[vocabulary word]" most nearly means …*

However, these are not the only kinds of Words in Context questions you'll find. Other questions will test your ability to identify the meanings of entire phrases. These phrases will often be figurative, which means they should not be taken literally. If someone were to tell you, "You're getting under my skin," it would be pretty weird to take that phrase literally. Most likely, that person is using the phrase figuratively and intends it to mean "You're bothering me."

Once again, context is the key to identifying the meaning of such figurative phrases. For example, take a look at this sentence group:

> *Can you please stop asking me the same question over and over again? You're starting to get under my skin.*

What's happening here? Someone is asking the same question over and over, which can be really bothersome. You can use that context-based information to interpret "You're starting to get under my skin" as "You're starting to bother me."

Here are a few ways questions that require you to identify how phrases are used in context may be asked on the PSAT/NMSQT® Reading Test:

- *In the passage, when the main character says, "that's a real pickle" (line 10), she most probably means …*

- *Which choice most closely captures the meaning of the figurative "horse of a different color" referred to in line 5?*

Words in Context questions may also require you to understand how writers use words to shape the meaning, style, and tone of a passage. For example, think about how a writer may describe the sky.

> *The sky was full of clouds.*

OK, we know a little about that sky. It has a lot of clouds in it. However, the writer's wording does very little to shape the meaning, style, or tone of that sentence.

How about this?

> *A serene expanse of delicate clouds drifted across the sky.*

Now we have some tone. The writer's use of descriptive words such as *serene*, *delicate*, and *drifted* all work toward shaping a peaceful tone. On the PSAT/NMSQT® Reading Test, you will have to interpret such descriptive words and identify their purpose in shaping meaning, style, or tone. These questions will probably look something like this:

- *The author's use of the word "sunny" (line 12) mainly serves to …*

- *The statement "the hills frowned down upon us" (line 55) mainly serves to …*

At the end of this chapter, you will get some opportunities to answer various Words in Context questions.

TIP

When answering Words in Context questions, try replacing the word you must define in the sentence with each answer choice. Select the answer choice that makes the most sense when used in place of the word you are defining.

TIP

Reading a lot in your spare time is a great way to familiarize yourself with a variety of figurative phrases. Always pay special attention to phrases that do not make literal sense but can be defined by the words and ideas around them.

ANALYSIS IN HISTORY/SOCIAL STUDIES AND SCIENCE QUESTIONS

Five of the six passages you will read on the PSAT/NMSQT® Reading Test fall under the subjects of history, social studies, or science. That means they are particularly important and get a question category all their own: **Analysis in History/Social Studies and Science**.

Analysis in History/Social Studies and Science questions cover a lot of areas, though they all basically require you to examine hypotheses, interpret data, and consider effects of decisions. Yes, those are very general requirements, but the individual questions on the PSAT/NMSQT® exam are pretty specific in their focus. These questions require you to do the following:

1. Identify information and ideas explicitly stated in the passage. Examples of these questions include:

   - *According to the passage, what is the first step of the experiment?*
   - *Based on the passage, what is the main geological feature of the region?*
   - *The author makes which point about psychology?*

2. Draw reasonable inferences and logical conclusions from the passage. Examples of these questions include:

   - *Based on the passage, the author would most likely agree with the idea that …*
   - *The passage characterizes American culture as complex in that …*

3. Identify explicitly stated or implicit relationships (cause-effect, compare-contrast, sequence, etc.) between and among individuals, events, or ideas. Examples of these questions include:

   - *What does the first theory say about the second theory?*
   - *According to the passage, what was the direct result of the study?*
   - *According to the passage, one similarity between the first theory and the second theory is that they both …*

4. Determine the main or most likely purpose of a passage or of a particular part of a passage. Examples of these questions include:

   - *The main purpose of the passage is to …*
   - *The main purpose of the final paragraph of the passage is to …*
   - *In the context of the passage, the main purpose of lines 1–4 ("The theory … conclusion.") is to …*

5. Describe the overall structure of a passage. An example is:

   - *Over the course of the passage, the main focus shifts from …*

You will see a number of these question types among the twenty practice questions you will answer at the end of this chapter.

COMMAND OF EVIDENCE QUESTIONS

You won't be able to get away with just drawing conclusions and making inferences on the PSAT/NMSQT® Reading Test. Often, you will be expected to back up those conclusions and inferences with evidence stated in the passages explicitly. You'll do this by answering **Command of Evidence** questions.

At least two Command of Evidence questions accompany *each* passage or passage pair on the PSAT/NMSQT® Reading Test. These Command of Evidence questions are interesting for two reasons. First of all, they are always phrased the exact same way:

> *Which choice provides the best evidence for the answer to the previous question?*

Just by reading that example question, you may have recognized the other unique thing about these questions—these are the only questions that depend on other questions. They ask you to find the evidence in the passage that supports your answer to the question that preceded it.

The answer choices are pretty uniform, too: they always consist of the line numbers and first and final words of the evidence in the passage. So a complete Command of Evidence question will look something like this:

> Which choice provides the best evidence for the answer to the previous question?
>
> **A.** Lines 1–3 ("Nothing … people.")
>
> **B.** Lines 4–5 ("From the … alone.")
>
> **C.** Lines 6–10 ("Other … West.")
>
> **D.** Lines 11–14 ("And the … existence.")

The good thing about these Command of Evidence questions is that you should already know what evidence you used to answer the preceding Analysis in History/Social Studies and Science question, so answering a Command of Evidence question is more like showing your work than answering a fresh, new question. The bad thing about them is that you may choose the wrong answer if you have answered the preceding question incorrectly. However, while locating the evidence to support your answer to that preceding question, you may realize that you answered it incorrectly and need to select an answer that can actually be supported with evidence in the passage. So that's another way the Command of Evidence question is unique: it is the only question type that can help you correct questions you answered incorrectly!

There are other types of Command of Evidence questions. Some questions may require you to identify claims that *do not* relate to the preceding questions. Others will require you to make connections between passages and informational graphics or two passages in a passage pair. Here are examples of these other Command of Evidence questions you will find on the exam:

1. Questions that require you to cite the evidence that best supports a given claim or point. For example:

   • *Which of the following is cited in the passage as an indicator of the experiment's effectiveness?*

TIP

Underlining important supporting details while reading passages on the PSAT/NMSQT® exam may be really helpful when answering Command of Evidence questions. The details you underline may turn out to be the evidence you will need to identify.

ALERT

Some Command of Evidence answer choices may relate to incorrect answer choices in the previous question. This can be a problem if you selected one of those incorrect answer choices in the previous question.

TIP

Sometimes authors make their claims very clear by announcing them with key phrases such as "I believe" or "My point is …" They might also signal counterclaims with words and phrases such as "but," "however," and "on the other hand."

2. Questions that require you to identify claims and counterclaims explicitly stated in the passage or determine implicit claims and counterclaims from the passage. For example:

   • *The central claim of the first paragraph (lines 1–12) is that …*

3. Questions that require you to assess how an author uses or fails to use evidence to support a claim or counterclaim. For example:

   • *Which choice best supports the claim that the experiment was a success?*

4. Questions that require you to analyze information presented quantitatively in such forms as maps, diagrams, graphs, tables, and charts and/or relate that information to other information presented in text. For example:

   • *What do the results in the graph prove about the passage?*

   • *In what way does the table contradict the passage?*

   • *Which claim from the passage is most directly supported by the map?*

5. Questions that require you to synthesize, or combine, information and ideas you read when faced with a paired set of texts. For example:

   • *The primary purpose of each passage is to …*

   • *Both authors would most likely agree with which statement about the experiment?*

   • *In the passages, a significant difference in how the two authors discuss the experiment is that the author of Passage 1 indicates that*

   • *Assuming that she agrees with the assertions in the final paragraph of Passage 1, the author of Passage 2 would most likely recommend which course of action?*

Now that you have an idea about the kinds of questions that accompany paired passages, it's time to learn more about what you can expect from the passages themselves.

NOTE

Only two passage types are presented in pairs on the PSAT/NMSQT® Reading Test: History and Science.

ALL ABOUT PAIRED PASSAGES

There are six passages on the PSAT/NMSQT® Reading Test, but two of them are paired. There will always be some sort of connection between the passages in a pair. Perhaps they will offer differing opinions about the same topic. Perhaps one passage will develop upon ideas in the other passage. Perhaps they will simply be the same type of passage, such as a pair of presidential addresses. Your job will be recognizing and analyzing the differences, similarities, and other relationships between those two pieces of writing.

The passages in a pair are not as long as the other passages in the exam. They are more like two half-length passages, adding up to a total of 550 to 750 words between them.

TIP

You can anticipate the answers to questions that might accompany paired passages by jotting down their similarities, differences, and other relationships while reading them.

Their questions are paired as well. Some questions will relate only to the first passage, known as Passage 1. Other questions will ask only about the second passage, known as Passage 2. These two question types will look like the majority of Words in Context, Analysis in History/Social Studies and Science, and Command of Evidence questions you'll find on the rest of the exam.

The final types of questions ask about both passages. They will look like the fifth type of questions you read about in the previous section on Command of Evidence questions. You will see more examples of these question types in the sample passage pair we'll walk you through in the next section of this chapter.

FOUR READING PASSAGE WALKTHROUGHS

Now that you have a good idea of the kinds of passages and questions you'll encounter on the PSAT/NMSQT® Reading Test, it's time for a deeper examination. In this section, we'll explore actual PSAT/NMSQT® exam-style passages and questions together. Look for the gray boxes throughout this section. Using the information and expert advice they provide, we will walk you through it all to help you spot what makes each passage type unique and what you should look for when taking notes and preparing to answer questions. You will also read detailed explanations of why each answer choice is right or wrong.

Literature Walkthrough

Questions 1-3 are based on the following passage.

This passage is adapted from *Black Beauty* by Anna Sewell, originally published in 1877.

> Every reading passage on the PSAT/NMSQT® exam begins with a short introduction such as this one. Be sure to read the introduction carefully because questions may refer to the author or title of the passage by name. Also take note of when the passage was published. That information may also be relevant to the questions that follow.

No doubt a horse fair is a very amusing place to those who have nothing to lose; at any rate, there is plenty to see.

> OK, we're only on the first sentence of the passage and the author is already revealing key details. From this opening line, we know the setting of the passage: a horse fair. Chances are, horses are going to be important to the story that follows.

Long strings of young horses out of the country, fresh from the marshes; and droves of
Line shaggy little Welsh ponies, no higher than Merrylegs; and hundreds of cart horses of all sorts,
5   some of them with their long tails braided up and tied with scarlet cord; and a good many
like myself, handsome and high-bred, but fallen into the middle class, through some accident
or blemish, unsoundness of wind, or some other complaint. There were some splendid
animals quite in their prime, and fit for anything; they were throwing out their legs and
showing off their paces in high style, as they were trotted out with a leading rein, the groom
10   running by the side. But round in the background there were a number of poor things, sadly
broken down with hard work, with their knees knuckling over and their hind legs swinging
out at every step, and there were some very dejected-looking old horses, with the under lip
hanging down and the ears lying back heavily, as if there were no more pleasure in life, and
no more hope; there were some so thin you might see all their ribs, and some with old sores
15   on their backs and hips. These were sad sights for a horse to look upon, who knows not but
he may come to the same state.

TIP

Reading actively and reading closely are strong methods for reading passages effectively. To read actively, you read the passage quickly to get a general idea of its information and take simple notes to keep track of key details and ideas. Next you read closely by reading the questions to get an idea of the details and ideas you will really need to know and rereading the passage carefully, watching for anything that will help you to answer those questions.

NOTE

Elements such as characters, dialogue, and setting tend to be unique to Literature passages.

Read carefully, because the narrator is revealing who he is in this paragraph when he says that there were "a good many" horses "like myself." Based on that short phrase, we know that this passage is being narrated from the first-person point of view…or maybe we should say the "first-horse point of view," because by comparing himself to the other horses, we can conclude that our narrator is also a horse. See, we were right—horses are very important to this story!

Another important thing to note when reading any paragraph is its main idea. So what is this paragraph mainly doing? It is describing the horses at the fair and drawing a contrast between the "splendid" horses "quite in their prime" and the "poor" horses "in the background" that are old and run down. The narrator is also giving us a glimpse into his own state of mind when he says that those poor horses "were sad sights for a horse to look upon." Since our narrator is a horse, he is clearly one of those horses who feels sad when he sees the poor ones in the background. In particular, he feels sad because he thinks of how other, currently healthy, horses may one day "come to the same state." Might he be such a horse? That's something to consider.

NOTE

Paragraphs tend to have their own main idea or purpose distinct from the passage as a whole. Some questions may ask you to identify the main idea or purpose of a passage as a whole, while others may ask only for the main idea or purpose of a particular part of a passage.

There was a great deal of bargaining, of running up and beating down; and if a horse may speak his mind so far as he understands, I should say there were more lies told and more trickery at that horse fair than a clever man could give an account of. I was put with two or
20 three other strong, useful-looking horses, and a good many people came to look at us. The gentlemen always turned from me when they saw my broken knees; though the man who had me swore it was only a slip in the stall.

Now the narrator is shifting his attention from his fellow horses to the people who would buy or sell them. The narrator characterizes these people as liars by saying "I should say there were more lies told and more trickery at that horse fair than a clever man could give an account of." That might be an important detail to jot in your notes. We also learn a new detail about the narrator: although he is grouped with the strong horses, he also has broken knees, which may explain why he felt so sad when seeing the broken down horses and why he thinks of how he too "may come to the same state" as he'd said in the previous paragraph.

The first thing was to pull my mouth open, then to look at my eyes, then feel all the way down my legs, and give me a hard feel of the skin and flesh, and then try my paces. It was
25 wonderful what a difference there was in the way these things were done. Some did it in a rough, offhand way, as if one was only a piece of wood; while others would take their hands gently over one's body, with a pat now and then, as much as to say, "By your leave." Of course I judged a good deal of the buyers by their manners to myself.

In this paragraph the narrator is explaining how the various customers at the fair treat him. He has his mouth pulled open, his eyes examined, and his legs grabbed. He explains that different people check him out differently ("It was wonderful what a difference there was in the way these things were done."). Some would be "rough," "offhand," and treat him as if he were "only a piece of wood." Other customers were gentle. The contrast between these treatments may be important in the questions that follow since the narrator spends a good deal of the paragraph describing it. Make a note of it.

30 There was one man, I thought, if he would buy me, I should be happy. He was not a gentleman, nor yet one of the loud, flashy sort that call themselves so. He was rather a small man, but well made, and quick in all his motions. I knew in a moment by the way he handled me, that he was used to horses; he spoke gently, and his gray eye had a kindly, cheery look in it.

In the final paragraph of this excerpt, the narrator focuses on one particular customer. Clearly, this is one of the gentler customers, since the narrator concludes that "if he would buy me, I should be happy." The narrator confirms this by using such key words as "gently," "kindly," and "cheery" to describe the man's behavior and appearance. Take note of these details but also keep in mind that not everything you note will be relevant to the questions that follow. You are just anticipating what the questions *might* ask by noting main ideas and important details.

Now let's look at the type of questions that would accompany this type of passage.

1. What does the narrator's reaction to the horses in the background say about his state of mind?
   A. He is feeling extremely hopeless.
   B. He is concerned about his own future.
   C. He feels nothing but concern for the horses in the background.
   D. He is glad that he is not one of the horses in the background.

You may recall the wording of this question from one of the examples in the section on Analysis in History/Social Studies and Science questions in this chapter. This is a question that tests your ability to recognize and understand relationships. The relationship in this question is the one between the narrator's reactions and feelings. So how does he react when he sees those "poor" horses "in the background"? Remember that we took note of how the narrator thinks they are "sad sights for a horse to look upon." So we can begin by eliminating any answer choices that do not reflect that sadness. Choice D suggests that the narrator feels "glad," so go ahead and eliminate that one. The other choices all suggest sadness, but they cannot all be correct. So what else does the narrator think when he sees those poor horses? As we noted, he thinks about how currently healthy horses may come to the same poor state one day. Also recall that the narrator is worried about his broken knees, which means he isn't completely healthy and really could suffer the same fate as the horses in the background one day. Choice B reflects that concern best. **The correct answer is B.**

TIP

Always take special note of the descriptive words in a passage. The words authors use to describe people, things, and situations in a passage may help you draw conclusions or make inferences about tone, attitude, or a character's mental state.

2. Which choice provides the best evidence for the answer to the previous question?

   A. Lines 7-8 ("There were ... anything;")

   B. Line 10 ("But round ... things,")

   C. Lines 15-16 ("These were ... state.")

   D. Line 17 ("There was ... down;")

So now we need to provide some proof for our conclusion in the previous question. That means this is one of those Command of Evidence questions that will appear twice after every passage you read on the PSAT/NMSQT® Reading Test. The good news is that we've already done the heavy work to answer this question. We concluded that seeing the poor horses in the background made the narrator "concerned about his own future" because he says that those horses "were sad sights for a horse to look upon, who knows not but he may come to the same state." So is that line from the passage one of our answer choices? Yes, indeed it is! **The correct answer is C.** It is much more specific about the narrator's state of mind than choice B, which notes that those background horses were poor but does not say very much about how that makes the narrator feel. Choice A doesn't have anything to do with the poor horses—it describes the healthy ones. Therefore, choice A should be easy to eliminate. Choice D should also be easy to eliminate since it doesn't even appear in the same paragraph as the one that describes the poor background horses. It is on to a new topic altogether: the customers and horse sellers trying to strike bargains.

3. Based on the passage, when the narrator says that he felt like he was being treated "as if one was only a piece of wood" (line 26), he most probably means that he feels like he is being treated

   A. like a useful piece of material.

   B. with great care and tenderness.

   C. the same way the horses are treated.

   D. as if he were a mere object.

Once again we must consider the narrator's feelings, but this is not another Analysis in History/Social Studies and Science or Command of Evidence question. In fact, it is a Words in Context question, and this particular one is testing your ability to define figurative language. The figurative language used in this question is a simile, which is a comparison between two unlike things. The narrator, a horse, is comparing himself to a piece of wood, and I'm sure you'll agree that horses and pieces of wood are very different. So why does he feel like a piece of wood in line 26? Think back to our notes and the contrast the narrator is making in this paragraph. He is contrasting how rough customers treat him with the way gentle customers treat him. The line about how some treat him as if he "was only a piece of wood" is part of the description of how the rough customers treat our narrator. That means it must have negative connotations. So you can eliminate any choice that makes this simile seem positive. Choice A makes it seem as though the simile is used to show that the rough customers make the narrator feel "useful," which is pretty positive. Eliminate choice A. Choice B is even more positive. Eliminate that one too. Choice C is more neutral and the narrator is not comparing the way he is treated to the ways other horses are treated when he says that some customers make him feel like he is "only a piece of wood." Eliminate choice C. That leaves choice D, which does have negative connotations. No living creature wants to feel like "a mere object." **The correct answer is D.**

Social Studies Walkthrough

Questions 4-6 are based on the following passage and supplementary material.

> So now we're on to a totally different subject: social studies. That means we probably won't be dealing with a lot of the literary elements in the previous passage: setting, characters, dialogue, a narrator who turns out to be a horse, etc. In fact, it looks like we might be dealing with something very different. Read that introduction above carefully. Note that it mentions that you will not only be reading a passage, but you will also be reading "supplementary material." On the PSAT/NMSQT® exam, supplementary material means an informational graphic, so expect this passage to include a chart, table, graph, map, or diagram.

This passage is adapted from *Thought Culture or Practical Mental Training* by William Walker Atkinson, originally published in 1909.

What is thought? The answer is not an easy one, although we use the term familiarly almost every hour of our waking existence. The dictionaries define the term *thought* as follows: "The act of thinking; the exercise of the mind in any way except sense and

Line perception; serious consideration; deliberation; reflection; the power or faculty of thinking;

5 the mental faculty of the mind; etc." This drives us back upon the term, "to think," which is defined as follows: "To occupy the mind on some subject; to have ideas; to revolve ideas in the mind; to cogitate; to reason; to exercise the power of thought; to have a succession of ideas or mental states; to perform any mental operation, whether of apprehension, judgment, or illation; to judge; to form a conclusion, to determine; etc."

> As you should remember, each Social Studies passage deals with one of three different subtopics: economics, psychology, or sociology. This passage's subtopic is psychology, which is the study of the mind. We already know that because this opening paragraph is about human thought. It is a very basic introduction to the topic more concerned with defining what "thought" is than anything else. The author defines thought with a pretty long quotation that looks like it was taken from a dictionary. However, we cannot be sure of that because the author does not provide a source for this quotation.

10 Thought is an operation of the intellect. The intellect is: "that faculty of the human soul or mind by which it receives or comprehends the ideas communicated to it by the senses or by perception, or other means, as distinguished from the power to feel and to will; the power or faculty to perceive objects in their relations; the power to judge and comprehend; also the capacity for higher forms of knowledge as distinguished from the power to perceive and

15 imagine."

> Defining a term is also the main purpose of this second paragraph. This time the term is *intellect*. Once again the author uses an extended, uncredited quotation to define the term.

When we say what we "think," we mean that we exercise the faculties whereby we compare and contrast certain things with other things, observing and noting their points of difference and agreement, then classifying them in accordance with these observed agreements and differences. In *thinking* we tend to classify the multitude of impressions
20   received from the outside world, arranging thousands of objects into one general class, and other thousands into other general classes, and then sub-dividing these classes, until finally we have found mental pigeon-holes for every conceivable idea or impression. We then begin to make inferences and deductions regarding these ideas or impressions, working from the known to the unknown, from particulars to generalities, or from generalities to particulars, as
25   the case may be.

> The key term of the third paragraph is *think*, the verb form of the noun *thought* that was the main focus of the first paragraph. The author switches up the format a bit by not using another uncredited quotation to define this paragraph's key term. Yet it is as thorough and detailed a definition as the quotations in the previous two paragraphs. This might be a good time to make a quick note of the term being defined in each of the first three paragraphs, so if you have to answer a question about any of those terms, you can refer back to the relevant paragraph quickly. Once again, those terms are *thought* (paragraph 1), *intellect* (paragraph 2), and *think* (paragraph 3).

It is this faculty or power of thought—this use of the intellect, that has brought man to his present high position in the world of living things. In his early days, man was a much weaker animal than those with whom he was brought into contact. The tigers, lions, bears, mammoths, and other ferocious beasts were much stronger, fiercer, and fleeter than man, and
30   he was placed in a position so lacking of apparent equal chance of survival, that an observer would have unhesitatingly advanced the opinion that this weak, feeble, slow animal must soon surely perish in the struggle for existence, and that the "survival of the fittest" would soon cause him to vanish from the scene of the world's activities. And, so it would have been had he possessed no equipment other than those of the other animals; viz., strength, natural
35   weapons and speed. And yet man not only survived in spite of these disadvantages, but he has actually conquered, mastered and enslaved these other animals which seemed likely to work his destruction. Why? How?

> The author is now done defining and putting those terms he defined into context by explaining how they relate to the development of humans (sorry… the use of *man* to describe both men and women is lazy and not inclusive, but it is something you may see in PSAT/NMSQT® Reading passages as well as a lot of other texts). He draws a contrast between humans and animals, noting how creatures such as "tigers, lions, bears, mammoths, and other ferocious beasts" could rely on their strength and humans had to develop their intellects to compete with animals in the wild.

This feeble animal called *man* had within him the elements of a new power—a power manifested in but a slight degree in the other animals. He possessed an intellect by which he
40   was able to deduce, compare, infer (and) reason…

> In this short paragraph, the author reaches a significant conclusion directly related to the previous paragraph: the triumph of humans over animals is evidence that intellect is more powerful than physical strength.

He sheltered himself, his mate and his young, from the fury of the storm, first by caves and afterwards by rude houses, built in inaccessible places, reached only by means of crude ladders, bridges, or climbing poles. He built doors for his habitations, to protect himself from the attacks of these wild enemies—he heaped stones at the mouth of his caves to keep them
45 out. He placed great boulders on cliffs that he might topple them down on the approaching foe. He learned to hurl rocks with sure aim with his strong arm. He copied the floating log, and built his first rude rafts, and then evolved the hollowed canoe. He used the skins of animals to keep him warm—their tendons for his bowstrings. He learned the advantages of cooperation and combined effort, and thus formed the first rudiments of society and social
50 life. And finally—man's first great discovery—he found the art of fire making.

> The author continues to build on the previous paragraph, giving examples of how humans have used their superior intellect to do things animals cannot do. He describes a number of these achievements, such as the ability to build houses, use basic tools such as ladders and poles, build doors to lock out enemies, use boulders and rocks as weapons of defense, create primitive conveyances such as canoes, make clothing, form societies, and make fire. These are all new details to the passage, so any question that refers to such achievements should send you back to this final paragraph of the passage for a close review.

A Timeline of Human Development	
Development	**Years Ago (approximately)**
Ability to form basic societies	13,000,000
Ability to use primitive tools	2,500,000
Use of fire	1,700,000
Ability to use advanced tools	500,000
Ability to craft art, use language, and think abstractly	200,000

> And here's our informational graphic. It is a timeline in the form of a table. Don't bother studying it too hard until you see the questions that relate to it, but take note of the events it chronicles. Do you remember where events such as these were discussed in the passage? That's right: the final paragraph. So, chances are there will be questions that require you to draw connections between information in the final paragraph of the passage and the table that follows it.

NOTE

Most of the questions that follow passages with supplementary material will not involve the informational graphic. They will be standard passage-related questions.

4. Which of the following is cited in the passage as an indicator of thinking?

   A. The capability of seeing the outside world

   B. The ability to compare and contrast

   C. The faculty of the mind that comprehends

   D. Everything that occupies our waking existence

This question is asking for some support for a general idea in the passage. That general idea is "thinking." Do you remember when we made a note of the paragraph that mainly focuses on that verb form of *thought*? That means we should probably review the third paragraph to find the answer to this question. That paragraph does refer to receiving impressions of "the outside world," but it doesn't exactly use the capability of seeing the outside world as an indicator of thinking. After all, any animal can see the outside world. Choice A probably is not the best answer. However, the author very explicitly uses the human faculty to "compare and contrast certain things with other things" as an indicator of thinking in the paragraph. That means choice B is likely our correct answer. You'd have to go back to the second paragraph to find the words in choice C, which refer to that paragraph's main topic, the intellect, not thinking. Eliminate choice C. The words in choice D appear even earlier in the paragraph—right at the beginning where the author defines "thought." "[E]verything that occupies our waking existence" isn't even part of that term's definition. So eliminate choice D, too. That leaves us with a not-so-great answer (choice A) and pretty great one (choice B). Choose the pretty great answer; **the correct answer is B.**

5. Based on information in the table, approximately when did people first use the ladders, bridges, and poles the author describes in the final paragraph of the passage?

   A. 13,000,000 years ago

   B. 2,500,000 years ago

   C. 1,700,000 years ago

   D. 500,000 years ago

Just as we predicted, a question about the informational graphic requires a review of the final paragraph of the passage. That's where the author discusses "ladders, bridges, and poles." Reviewing the table will give us an approximate idea of when people started using such things. According to it, 13,000,000 years ago is when people developed the ability to form basic societies. Of course, ladders, bridges, and poles are not societies, so choice A can't be correct. Ladders, bridges, and poles can be described as tools, so choice B, which shows the approximate period in which people learned to use primitive tools, could be the correct answer. Choice C is the era in which people learned to use fire, so it is not relevant to this question about tools. However, choice D is relevant. So the big question is: are ladders, bridges, and poles primitive or advanced tools? You may have your own opinion on this topic, but what the author says is more important. So, let's look back at the passage where the author describes these tools as "crude," which is a synonym for *primitive*. **The correct answer is B.**

6. According to the passage and the table, man's first great discovery was made

   A. 3,000,000 years ago.

   B. 2,500,000 years ago.

   C. 17,000,000 years ago.

   D. 200,000 years ago.

The key to answering this question is finding out what the author believes to be "man's first great discovery." Remember that we concluded that final paragraph of the passage is likely to be the most relevant to questions related to the table. If you review that paragraph, you will find the key to answering this question in the very last sentence: "And finally—man's first great discovery—he found the art of fire making." So, according to the author, the ability to make fire is "man's first great discovery." That means choice C is without question the best answer since the table indicates that humans first used fire about 17,000,000 years ago. Even if you had trouble with this question, you should have eliminated choice A easily since there is no indication in the table of what people were up to 3,000,000 years ago!

History Walkthrough

Questions 7-9 are based on the following passage.

This passage is adapted from President Harry S Truman's State of the Union Message to Congress, released on January 21, 1946.

> The history passage we are about to walk through together was written by a U.S. president. Questions that accompany these kinds of passages on the Reading Test are likely to refer to the author by name, so don't be surprised when you are asked what President Truman, not "the author," wrote.
>
> Also take note of the date. Clearly, President Truman is not going to be referring to twenty-first century events. That means he may refer to events with which people in 1946 were very familiar but you may not be. Don't worry though. You will not be expected to know anything that is not stated in the passages very clearly.

During the war, production for civilian use was limited by war needs and available manpower. Economic stabilization required measures to spread limited supplies equitably by rationing, price controls, increased taxes, savings bond campaigns, and credit controls. Now,
Line with the surrender of our enemies, economic stabilization requires that policies be directed
5 toward promoting an increase in supplies at low unit prices.

> So here we are in the deep end! President Truman is talking about a war, but he is not specifying which war he means because everyone in 1946 knew he was talking about World War II. However, even if you don't remember your history lessons well, the particular war he is discussing won't be a factor in the questions that follow this passage. Just know that the president is discussing a war that has depleted the country's resources. This paragraph is mainly about how that situation has affected the country and how it needs to be addressed now that the war is over. The good news is that "our enemies" have surrendered. The United States won the war.

We must encourage the development of resources and enterprises in all parts of the country, particularly in underdeveloped areas. For example, the establishment of new peacetime industries in the Western States and in the South would, in my judgment, add to existing production and markets rather than merely bring about a shifting of production. I

TIP

It is important to always read the introduction to every reading passage carefully. That information may be relevant in the questions that follow the passage.

10 am asking the Secretaries of Agriculture, Commerce, and Labor to explore jointly methods for stimulating new industries, particularly in areas with surplus agricultural labor.

We must also aid small businessmen and particularly veterans who are competent to start their own businesses. The establishment and development of efficient small business ventures, I believe, will not take away from, but rather will add to, the total business of all enterprises.

> In these paragraphs, President Truman starts offering solutions for the resource deficiencies he introduced in the first paragraph. These solutions are the kinds of details that may very well be important for answering the questions. Underline them. Put an asterisk next to them. Do something to make a note that these details could be important.

15 Even with maximum encouragement of production, we cannot hope to remove scarcities within a short time. The most serious deficiencies will persist in the fields of residential housing, building materials, and consumers' durable goods. The critical situation makes continued rent control, price control, and priorities, allocations, and inventory controls absolutely essential. Continued control of consumer credit will help to reduce the pressure on

20 prices of durable goods and will also prolong the period during which the backlog demand will be effective.

> Here comes the bad news. Despite the solutions to the resource deficiency problem he offered in the previous two paragraphs, President Truman is now admitting that the problem won't be solved any time soon ("we cannot hope to remove scarcities within a short time."). This paragraph is mainly about how certain measures—namely the control of rent, prices or price of goods, and consumer credit—must continue as long as the scarcity problem persists. Make a short note identifying that main idea in case there's a question that asks you about the money-saving measures that must continue as long as the scarcity problem persists.

While we are meeting these immediate needs we must look forward to a long-range program of security and increased standard of living.

The best protection of purchasing power is a policy of full production and full

25 employment opportunities. Obviously, an employed worker is a better customer than an unemployed worker. There always will be, however, some frictional unemployment. In the present period of transition we must deal with such temporary unemployment as results from the fact that demobilization will proceed faster than reconversion or industrial expansion. Such temporary unemployment is probably unavoidable in a period of rapid change. The

30 unemployed worker is a victim of conditions beyond his control. He should be enabled to maintain a reasonable standard of living for himself and his family.

In this final paragraph, President Truman has turned his attention to the issue of employment, explaining that some people will unfortunately find themselves unemployed as the country works to get its economy back in shape. There's the main idea.

When reading a passage such as this, you may also want to make note of such factors as the author's tone and style, since they are so important to effective writing. In this case, the president's tone is serious and honest yet hopeful, and his style is formal yet easy to comprehend. He does not use a lot of high-level vocabulary that the average person might not understand.

7. As used in line 11, "stimulating" most nearly means
   A. energizing.
   B. interesting.
   C. refreshing.
   D. relaxing.

As is the case with most Words in Context questions, you cannot answer this question without referring to the passage. That's because almost every answer choice is a synonym of *stimulating*. However, only one is a synonym for *stimulating* as it is used in line 11. The sentence in question is: "I am asking the Secretaries of Agriculture, Commerce, and Labor to explore jointly methods for stimulating new industries, particularly in areas with surplus agricultural labor." First of all, let's just make sure that every answer choice is a synonym for *stimulating*. Choice A: *energizing*? Check. Choice B: *interesting*? Check. Choice C: *refreshing*? Check. Choice D: *relaxing*? Uh oh. *Relaxing* is an antonym of *stimulating*, and that's the opposite of a synonym. Eliminate choice D.

It is also useful to identify the part of speech of *stimulating* in this context. It is being used as a verb in line 11, so any answer choice that is not a verb can be eliminated. Choice B is an adjective, so go ahead and eliminate that one, too.

So that leaves us with choices A and C. They're both synonyms for *stimulating*, and they're both verbs. However, *refreshing* implies something that was vital in the past but needs to be re-energized. After all, the prefix *re-* means "again." However, President Truman is talking about stimulating "new industries" in line 11, and something that is new cannot have been anything in the past because it does not have a past. That leaves *energizing* as the best answer choice. **The correct answer is A.**

8. President Truman makes which point about the lack of resources after the war?
   A. Resources will remain scarce for a long time to come.
   B. Resources can be replenished by increasing production.
   C. Resources will never return to their former abundance again.
   D. The lack of resources makes rent and price control unnecessary.

Sometimes the generalness of a question is what makes it tough. This entire passage is about the lack of resources after the war, so the question does not help you to hone in on one particular part of the passage. So the best you can do is take a deep breath and dive back in. But first, read each

TIP

When reading actively, you may find yourself taking note of details that won't actually be relevant to the questions that follow. That is normal and nothing to worry about unless you find yourself wasting a lot of time with your note taking. Just be sure to take notes efficiently and make sure that the process is not eating into your reading/question-answering time too much.

TIP

There isn't really any way to anticipate which words might be used in Words in Context questions, so don't bother underlining or making note of particular words while reading the passages.

answer choice carefully so you know what you're looking for when you start scanning the passage again. Is there anything in the passage that supports the idea that "resources will remain scarce for a long time to come"? As a matter of fact, there is. It is the first sentence of the fourth paragraph: "Even with maximum encouragement of production, we cannot hope to remove scarcities within a short time." But before settling on Choice A, let's just make sure that the other answer choices are wrong. Well, that statement at the beginning of the fourth paragraph contradicts choice B, so you can eliminate that one. Choice C has a different problem: it is too extreme. President Truman does not suggest that the scarce resources will *never* return to their former abundance again. He just implies that it will take a while. Eliminate choice C. To evaluate the final answer choice, scan the passage for its key words: "rent and price control." You will find these words in the fourth paragraph, which, again, says the opposite of this answer choice: "The critical situation makes continued rent control, price control, and priorities, allocations, and inventory controls absolutely essential." This means rent and price control will be necessary, not unnecessary. Eliminate choice D and select choice A with confidence. **The correct answer is A.**

9. Which choice provides the best evidence for the answer to the previous question?

    A. Lines 6-7 ("We must … areas.")

    B. Lines 7-9 ("the establishment … production.")

    C. Lines 15-16 ("Even with … time.")

    D. Lines 17-19 ("The critical … essential.")

Here's another one of those Command of Evidence questions that requires you to back up your answer to the previous question with a bit of supporting evidence. Once again, you already did the work when you identified choice A as the best answer based on that line about how "resources will remain scarce for a long time to come." Is that line in one of our answer choices? Yes, it's in lines 15-16 in choice C. **The correct answer is C.**

Also, be mindful of answers such as choice D. Imagine you mistakenly selected choice D, "The lack of resources makes rent and price control unnecessary," as the correct answer to Question 8. You might be tempted to select choice D as the correct answer to Question 9 since its lines are the only ones that mention rent and price control. However, by rereading those lines carefully, you should notice that they actually contradict what choice D in Question 8 says about rent and price control. That can actually be helpful, leading you to change a wrong answer to a previous question to a right answer. So always be sure to read very carefully.

Science Paired Passage Walkthrough

Questions 10-12 are based on the following passages.

Passage 1 is adapted from *The Elements of Geology* by William Harmon Norton, originally published in 1905. Passage 2 is adapted from *The Elements of Geology Adapted to Use of Schools and Colleges* by Justin R. Loomis in 1852.

Our final passage is actually two passages, but, as you may notice, their combined length is about the same as the single passages you've read in the previous walkthroughs. If you read the introduction carefully, you will also know that geology is the subtopic of these two particular science passages, which is the first relationship you should take note of. You may also notice that they are both taken from texts with very similar titles, but their different authors and years of publication should tip you off that they are, indeed, different texts.

Passage 1

In our excursion to the valley with sandstone ledges we witnessed a process which is going forward in all lands. Everywhere the rocks are crumbling away; their fragments are creeping down hillsides to the stream ways and are carried by the streams to the sea, where
Line they are rebuilt into rocky layers. When again the rocks are lifted to form land the process
5 will begin anew; again they will crumble and creep down slopes and be washed by streams to the sea. Let us begin our study of this long cycle of change at the point where rocks disintegrate and decay under the action of the weather. In studying now a few outcrops and quarries we shall learn a little of some common rocks and how they weather away.

> The author's use of personal pronouns such as *our* and *us* indicates that this science passage is written from the first-person point of view, but it is not particularly personal. Rather the main idea of the passage is the disintegration process rocks undergo and characteristics of particular rocks, which the author states explicitly in the final two sentences of this opening paragraph. When the author reveals his or her main idea so clearly, you can save note-taking time by simply underlining those sentences and perhaps jotting down "main idea" next to them.

STRATIFICATION AND JOINTING. At the sandstone ledges we saw that the rock
10 was divided into parallel layers. The thicker layers are known as STRATA, and the thin leaves into which each stratum may sometimes be split are termed LAMINAE. To a greater or less degree these layers differ from each other in fineness of grain, showing that the material has been sorted. The planes which divide them are called BEDDING PLANES.

Besides the bedding planes there are other division planes, which cut across the strata
15 from top to bottom. These are found in all rocks and are known as joints. Two sets of joints, running at about right angles to each other, together with the bedding planes, divide the sandstone into quadrangular blocks.

> Now the author is getting more specific, explaining one of the processes he said he would explain throughout the passage. He makes your job easy by announcing the name of that process in capital letters: "STRATIFICATION AND JOINTING." He continues to indicate key words in capital letters. Don't get used to that though. Most authors don't point out their key details in such an obvious way.

SANDSTONE. Examining a piece of sandstone we find it composed of grains quite like those of river sand or of sea beaches. Most of the grains are of a clear glassy mineral called

TIP

Recognizing relationships between the passages in a passage pair is key to answering questions that deal with both passages.

20 quartz. These quartz grains are very hard and will scratch the steel of a knife blade. They are not affected by acid, and their broken surfaces are irregular like those of broken glass.

TIP

As soon as you begin reading the second passage in any passage pair, you should start thinking about how it relates to the first passage.

> In this final paragraph of the short excerpt that is Passage 1, the author takes a break from explaining geological processes to describe a particular kind of rock called sandstone. Remember that the author explained that learning "a little of some common rocks" was part of his main idea at the end of the first paragraph.

Passage 2

The fossiliferous rocks are divided into seven systems, which are readily distinguished by the order of superposition, lithological characters and organic remains. These systems are the Silurian, the Old Red Sandstone, the Carboniferous, the New Red Sandstone, the Oölitic, *Line* the Cretaceous, and the Tertiary systems. There is also an eighth system now in process of 5 formation.

> Now we're on to our second passage, which you already know is another geology passage. This first paragraph shows that rocks are again our main topic, but Passage 2 deals with them in a different way from Passage 1, which was about the processes and characteristics of different rocks. Passage 2 is apparently more concerned with the "seven systems" of rocks. You may also notice a difference in language. Passage 1 was written in simple, more conversational language. Passage 2 is a bit more technical with terms, such as "fossiliferous," "superposition," and "lithological," that may be unfamiliar to you. Remember that you won't be expected to know any technical terms that are not defined within the passages on the PSAT/NMSQT® Reading Test. Also, make a note of this difference in style between Passage 1 and Passage 2. It could be relevant to the questions that follow the passages.

It is the opinion of some geologists that there is another system situated between the metamorphic rocks and the silurian system. It has been called by Dr. Emmons, who has studied it with much care, the "Taconic System," the Taconic Mountains, in the western part of Massachusetts, being composed of these rocks. It is the lower part of what has been called, 10 in England and Wales, the Cambrian system.

> Here's a bit of a twist. While the author began the passage by specifying that there are seven systems of fossiliferous rocks, he is now revealing that there might be an eighth system. Keep in mind that he is not saying he shares this opinion; he is merely saying that "some geologists" believe it. He also identifies one of those scientists as "Dr. Emmons." That's a good use of evidence to support a claim.

The strata of this system have a nearly vertical position, and consist principally of black, greenish and purple slates, of great thickness. Granular quartz rock, however, occurs in considerable quantity, and in this country two thick and important beds of limestone are found. These limestones are occasionally white and crystalline. Generally, however, as a mass,

15 they are a dark, nearly black rock, with a network of lines of a lighter color. All the clouded marbles for architectural and ornamental purposes are from these beds, and our roofing and writing slates are all obtained from the argillaceous portion of this system.

> In this final paragraph of Passage 2, the author uses a couple of the same terms that the author of Passage 1 used: "strata" and "quartz." Always take note of such common elements between the passages in a pair. The author of Passage 2 is also doing something the author of Passage 1 did: he is describing the appearance and qualities of a particular rock. There's another relationship for your notes.

10. As used in line 4, "form" most nearly means

A. develop.

B. shape.

C. type.

D. start.

Here's another Words in Context question that asks you to define how a multiple-meaning word is used in a particular passage. Although the question does not specify that the word is used in Passage 1, referring to the line number in the question stem will make that clear. Another thing to take note of is that each answer choice is a synonym of *form*; there are no antonyms among them as there were among the answer choices of the last Words in Context question (question 7). That makes this question slightly more challenging.

To meet that challenge, try using each answer choice in place of *form* in line 4.

> When again the rocks are lifted to *develop* (choice A) land the process will begin anew …

Does *develop* make sense in this context? It does, since it makes sense that rocks would be the foundation of land development. We should still check out the other answer choices though.

> When again the rocks are lifted to *shape* (choice B) land the process will begin anew …

Shape isn't exactly nonsensical in this context, but it isn't quite perfect either. The rocks in this line are forming new land, yet the word *shape* implies the reconstruction of land that already exists. Choice A is still looking like the best answer.

> When again the rocks are lifted to *type* (choice C) land the process will begin anew …

Type is a synonym of *form*, but only when it is used as a noun. However, *form* is used as a verb in line 4. Eliminate choice C.

> When again the rocks are lifted to *start* (choice D) land the process will begin anew …

Start is a verb, but it is a bit of an odd choice for this particular context. One might start a process, but *form* is not describing a process, it is describing the thing that is created through a process: land. Land is not really something that is "started." **The correct answer is A.**

NOTE

Several of the questions that follow a passage pair will relate only to one of the two passages. Questions that follow a passage pair will always be very clear about whether they relate to Passage 1, Passage 2, or both passages.

TIP

When answering questions that ask for something the two passages in a pair have in common, begin by eliminating any answer choice that includes details from only one of the passages.

11. The primary purpose of each passage is to

    A. show that rocks are divided into systems.

    B. describe specific kinds of rocks.

    C. define the terms "stratification" and "jointing."

    D. explain particular facets of geology.

The key words "each passage" let us know that this is the first question to involve both Passage 1 and Passage 2 in this passage pair. The question is asking you to identify the most basic common relationship between the two passages. First of all, you should try eliminating any answer choice that applies to only one of the passages. Do both passages involve systems of rocks? Nope. Only Passage 2 does, so go ahead and eliminate choice A. Do they both describe specific kinds of rocks? Yes, they do: Passage 1 describes sandstone and Passage 2 describes quartz. So we're going to hold on to choice B for the time being. Do both passages define the terms "stratification" and "jointing?" Only Passage 2 does this, so you can eliminate choice C. Do both passages explain particular facets of geology? They do, so that leaves choices B and D in the running for correct answer.

Of course, the question is not just asking for any old thing that is common to both passages; it is asking for a "primary purpose" that they have in common. So we can narrow down our choices by eliminating that one that does not describe a primary purpose. Is the primary purpose of each passage to describe specific kinds of rocks? Well, as we know from identifying the main idea of Passage 1, this is *one* of the primary purposes of Passage 1, but Passage 2 is mainly about rock systems even though it does include one paragraph that describes a specific kind of rock. That means choice B is not the ideal answer. Choice D is much more general, but that isn't exactly a problem, and both passages do explain particular facets of geology. **The correct answer is D.**

12. Both authors would most likely agree with which statement?

    A. Limestone is an effective roofing material.

    B. Rocks are worthy of close study.

    C. There is an eighth system of fossiliferous rocks.

    D. Rock disintegration is a long process.

We can use the same method to answer this final question that we did when figuring out the best answer to question 11. First we eliminate any choice that applies to only one of the passages in the pair. That nixes choices A, C, and D, leaving just one choice remaining. Before settling on Choice B, let's just make certain that it is valid. Is there reason to believe that both the author of Passage 1 and the author of Passage 2 probably think that rocks are worthy of close study? Well, they both spend a lot of time subjecting rocks to close study in their passages. So let's go with a "yes" and conclude that **the correct answer is B.** Nice work!

EVIDENCE-BASED READING PRACTICE QUESTIONS

Now that we've walked you through some sample PSAT/NMSQT® Reading Test-like passages and questions, it's time for you to go it alone by reading this next series of passages and answering the twenty practice questions that accompany them. Good luck!

Questions 1-5 are based on the following passage.

This passage is adapted from *Patsy Carroll Under Southern Skies* by Josephine Chase, originally published in 1918.

"Oh, dear!" loudly sighed Patsy Carroll.

The regretful exclamation was accompanied by the energetic banging of Patsy's French grammar upon the table.

Line
5
"Stay there, tiresome old thing!" she emphasized. "I've had enough of you for one evening."

"What's the matter, Patsy?"

Beatrice Forbes raised mildly inquiring eyes from the theme she was industriously engaged in writing.

"Lots of things. I hate French verbs. The crazy old irregular ones most of all. They
10 start out one thing and by the time you get to the future tense they're something entirely different."

"Is that all?" smiled Beatrice. "You ought to be used to them by this time."

"That's only one of my troubles," frowned Patsy. "There are others a great deal worse. One of them is this Easter vacation business. I thought we'd surely have three weeks. It's
15 always been so at Yardley until this year. Two weeks is no vacation worth mentioning."

"Well, that's plenty of time to go home in and stay at home and see the folks for a while, isn't it?" asked Beatrice.

"But we didn't intend going *home*," protested Patsy.

"Didn't intend going home?" repeated Beatrice wonderingly. "*What* are you talking about,
20 Patsy Carroll? *I* certainly expect to go home for Easter."

"You only think you do," Patsy assured, her troubled face relaxing into a mischievous grin.

"Maybe you will, though. I don't know. It depends upon what kind of scheme my gigantic brain can think up.

25 "It's like this, Bee," she continued, noting her friend's expression of mystification. "Father and I made a peach of a plan. Excuse my slang, but 'peach of a plan' just expresses it. Well, when I was at home over Christmas, Father promised me that the Wayfarers should join him and Aunt Martha at Palm Beach for the Easter vacation. He bought some land down in Florida last fall. Orange groves and all that, you know. This land isn't so very far from Palm
30 Beach. He was going down there right after Christmas, but a lot of business prevented him from going. He's down there now, though, and——"

"You've been keeping all this a dead secret from your little chums," finished Beatrice with pretended reproach.

"Of course I have," calmly asserted Patsy. "That was to be part of the fun. I meant to
35 spring a fine surprise on you girls. Your mother knows all about it. So does Mrs. Perry. I went around and asked them if you and Mab and Nellie could go while I was at home during the Christmas holidays. Aunt Martha liked my plan, too. Now we'll have to give it up and go

somewhere nearer home. We'd hardly get settled at Palm Beach when we'd have to come right home again. One more week's vacation would make a lot of difference. And we can't
40 have it! It's simply too mean for anything!"

"It would be wonderful to go to Palm Beach," mused Beatrice. "It would be to me, anyway. You know I've never traveled as you have, Patsy. Going to the Adirondacks last summer was my first real trip away from home. Going to Florida would seem like going to fairy land."

45 Readers of "Patsy Carroll at Wilderness Lodge" are already well acquainted, not only with Patsy Carroll and Beatrice Forbes, but also with their chums, Mabel and Eleanor Perry. In this story was narrated the adventures of the four young girls, who, chaperoned by Patsy's stately aunt, Miss Martha Carroll, spent a summer together in the Adirondacks.

Wilderness Lodge, the luxurious "camp" leased by Mr. Carroll for the summer, had
50 formerly belonged to an eccentric old man, Ebeneezer Wellington. Having died intestate the previous spring, his property and money had passed into the hands of Rupert Grandin, his worthless nephew, leaving his foster-daughter, Cecil Vane, penniless.

Hardly were the Wayfarers, as the four girls had named themselves, established at the Lodge when its owner decided, for reasons of his own, to oust them from his property. A
55 chance meeting between Beatrice and Cecil Vane revealed the knowledge that the latter had been defrauded of her rights and was firm in the belief that her late uncle had made a will in her favor, which was tucked away in some corner of the Lodge.

1. As used in line 14, "business" most nearly means
   A. issue.
   B. company.
   C. industry.
   D. commercial.

2. Based on the passage, which character would most likely agree with the idea that home is the best place to spend a holiday?
   A. Patsy
   B. Beatrice
   C. Father
   D. Aunt Martha

3. Which choice provides the best evidence for the answer to the previous question?
   A. Lines 16-17 ("Well… Beatrice.")
   B. Line 18 ("But we… Patsy.")
   C. Line 19 ("Didn't… wonderingly.")
   D. Lines 19-20 (*What*… Easter.")

4. Which choice most closely captures the meaning of the figurative "peach" referred to in line 26?
   A. good
   B. fruit
   C. edible
   D. strange

5. Over the course of the passage, the main focus shifts from a
   A. conversation between two girls about studying to a discussion of French verbs.
   B. description of how two characters are feeling to an explanation of why they feel the way they do.
   C. conversation between two girls to a narrator's description of one of the girls' previous adventures.
   D. description of how two girls spend their time at school to a description of how they spend their vacations.

Questions 6-10 are based on the following passage and supplementary material.

This passage is adapted from *The Chemistry of Food and Nutrition* by A. W. Duncan, originally published in 1905.

Food is never entirely digested. As a reason against confining ourselves solely to vegetable food, it has been stated that such is less perfectly digested than animal food and that it therefore throws more work on the digestive organs. It is also urged that on this
Line account a greater quantity of vegetable food is required. We have shown elsewhere that, on
5 the contrary, vegetarians are satisfied with a smaller amount of food. Man requires a small quantity of woody fiber or cellulose in his food to stimulate intestinal action and prevent constipation.

It is difficult to determine how much of a food is unassimilated in the body. This is for the reason of the intestinal refuse consisting not only of undigested food, but also of residues
10 of the digestive juices, mucus and epithelial debris…

John Goodfellow has shown that of very coarse wholemeal bread quite 14 percent was undigested, whilst bread made from ordinary grade wholemeal showed 12.5 percent. Such a method of analysis was adopted as it was believed would exclude other than the food waste. The experiments were made on a person who was eating nothing but the bread. It seems
15 probable that a smaller proportion would have remained unassimilated had the bread not formed the sole food… Notwithstanding that fine white bread gave only 4.2 percent and a coarse white bread 4.9 percent of waste, a fine wheatmeal bread is more economical as the same quantity of wheat produces a greater weight of flour richer in proteid and mineral matter. From a large number of experiments with man, it has been calculated that of proteids
20 digested when animal food is eaten 98 percent, from cereals (such as rice) and sugars 8 percent, from vegetables and fruits 80 percent. The difference between the proportions digested of the other food constituents was much less. Although there is here a theoretical advantage in favor of animal food, there are other considerations of far more importance than a little undigestible waste. The main question is one of health. In some dietary experiments
25 of a girl aged 7, living upon a fruit diet, of whom we have given some particulars elsewhere, Professor Jaffa gives the following particulars. During the ten days trial the percentages absorbed were proteids 82.5, fat 86.9, nitrogen free extract 96, crude fiber 80, ash 5.7, heat of combustion in calories 86.7. He says, "generally speaking, the food was quite thoroughly assimilated, the coefficients of digestibility being about the same as are found in an ordinary
30 mixed diet. It is interesting to note that 80 percent of the crude fiber appeared to be digested. The results of a number of foreign experiments on the digestibility of crude fiber by man are from 30 to 91.4 percent, the former value being from mixed wheat and rye, and the latter in a diet made of rice, vegetables and meat."

TABLE OF ANALYSIS OF FOOD.

	Pro-teids.	Fat.	Carbo-hydrates.	Ash.	Cellu-lose.	Re-fuse.	Water.	Calo-ries.	N't'nt Ratio
Wholemeal, G.	14.9	1.6	66.2	1.7	1.6	...	14.0	1577	4.68
Fine Flour, G.	9.3	0.8	76.5	0.7	0.7	...	12.0	1629	8·4
Medium Flour, G....	12.1	0.9	72.2	0.9	0.9	...	13.0	1606	6.13
Bread, Wh'lem'l, G.	12.2	1.2	43.5	1.3	1.8	...	40.0	1086	3.8
,, White, G....	7.5	0.8	53.8	0.9	...	...	37.0	1174	7.4
Macaroni, U..........	13.4	0.9	74·1	1.3	...	...	10.3	1665	5.67
Oatmeal, D.	14.8	9.6	63.3	2.2	1.4	...	8.7	1858	5.72
Maize, American, S.	10.0	4.25	71.75	1.5	1.75	...	10.75	1700	8.12
Rice, husked, U. ...	8.0	0.3	79.0	0.4	...	...	12.3	1630	10.0
Rye Flour, U.	6.8	0.9	78.3	0.7	0.4	...	12.9	1620	11.8
Barley, Pearl, C. ...	6.2	1.3	76.0	1.1	0.8	...	14.6	1584	12.7
Buckwheat Flour, U.	6.4	1.2	77.9	0.9	...	...	13.6	1619	12.6
Soy Bean, C.	35.3	18.9	26.0	4.6	4.2	...	11.0	1938	1.93
Pea-nut, C.............	24.5	50.0	11.7	1.8	4.5	...	7.5	2783	5.2
Lentils, U.............	25.7	1.0	59.2	5.7	...	...	8.4	1621	2.4
Peas, dried, U.	24.6	1.0	62.0	2.9	4.5	...	9.5	1655	2.6
Peas, green, E.U....	7.0	0.5	15.2	1.0	1.7	...	74.6	465	2.3
Haricots, C.	23.0	2.3	52.3	2.9	5.5	...	14.0	1463	2.5
Walnuts, fresh k., C.	12.5	31.6	8.9	1.7	0.8	...	44.5	1565	6.33
Walnut kernels	21.4	54.1	15.2	2.9	1.4	...	5.0	2964	6.33
Filberts, fresh ker., C.	8.4	28.5	11.1	1.5	2.5	...	48.0	1506	8.9
Tomatoes, U..........	1.2	0.2	3.5	0.6	0.5	...	94.0	105	3.3
Grapes, U.	1.0	1.2	10.1	0.4	4.3	25	58.0	335	12.8
Apples, E.U.	0.4	0.5	13.0	0.3	1.2	(25)	84.6	290	35.3
Raisins, E.U..........	2.6	3.3	76.1	3.4	...	(10)	14.6	1605	32.0
Dates, E.U.	2.1	2.8	78.4	1.3	...	(10)	15.4	1615	40.0
Banana, C.D..........	1.71	...	20.13	0.71	1.74	...	75.7	406	11.7

* Numbers indicate percentages of nutrients digested

35　Under calories are shown kilo-calories per pound of food. In the analysis marked *U* the crude fiber or cellulose is included with the carbohydrate, the figures being those given in Atwater's table. He has found that from 30 to 91 percent of the crude fiber was digested, according to the kind of food. The term fiber or cellulose in analytical tables is not a very definite one. It depends upon the details of the method of analysis. In the analyses other than *U*, the cellulose is excluded in calculating the calories. Nutrient ratio is the proportion of the sum of 40　the carbohydrate and fat, compared with the proteid as 1. The fat has first been multiplied by 2.225 to bring it to the same nutrient value as the carbohydrate.

6. Which choice best supports the claim that a vegetarian diet is more efficient than a diet that includes meat?

   A. Line 1 ("Food … digested.")

   B. Lines 1-3 ("As a reason … organs.")

   C. Lines 4-5 ("We have … of food.")

   D. Lines 5-7 ("Man … constipation.")

7. According to the passage, what was the direct result of a girl living on a fruit diet?

   A. The girl was on the diet for 10 days.

   B. The girl had trouble digesting the fruit.

   C. The girl decided to switch to a diet of wheat and rye.

   D. The girl digested 80% of the fiber in her food.

8. Which choice provides the best evidence for the answer to the previous question?

   A. Lines 24-26 ("In some … particulars.")

   B. Lines 26-27 ("During … 82.5")

   C. Line 30 ("It is … digested.")

   D. Line 32 ("the former … rye")

9. In which entry in the table is the cellulose not included with the carbohydrate?

   A. rice

   B. lentils

   C. fresh walnuts

   D. dried peas

10. Which claim from the passage is most directly supported by the table?

    A. The body digests 80% of the proteids in vegetables.

    B. The body digests 8% of the proteids in cereals.

    C. The body digests 80% of the proteids in fruits.

    D. The body digests 98% of the proteids in meat.

Questions 11-15 are based on the following passage.

This passage is adapted from *Dreams* by Henri Bergson, originally published in 1913.

The subject which I have to discuss here is so complex, it raises so many questions of all kinds, difficult, obscure, some psychological, others physiological and metaphysical; in order to be treated in a complete manner it requires such a long development—and we have so
Line little space, that I shall ask your permission to dispense with all preamble, to set aside
5 unessentials, and to go at once to the heart of the question.

A dream is this. I perceive objects and there is nothing there. I see men; I seem to speak to them and I hear what they answer; there is no one there and I have not spoken. It is all as if real things and real persons were there, then on waking all has disappeared, both persons and things. How does this happen?

10 But, first, is it true that there is nothing there? I mean, is there not presented a certain sense material to our eyes, to our ears, to our touch, etc., during sleep as well as during waking?

Close the eyes and look attentively at what goes on in the field of our vision. Many persons questioned on this point would say that nothing goes on, that they see nothing. No
15   wonder at this, for a certain amount of practice is necessary to be able to observe oneself satisfactorily. But just give the requisite effort of attention, and you will distinguish, little by little, many things. First, in general, a black background. Upon this black background occasionally brilliant points which come and go, rising and descending, slowly and sedately. More often, spots of many colors, sometimes very dull, sometimes, on the contrary, with
20   certain people, so brilliant that reality cannot compare with it. These spots spread and shrink, changing form and color, constantly displacing one another. Sometimes the change is slow and gradual, sometimes again it is a whirlwind of vertiginous rapidity. Whence comes all this phantasmagoria? The physiologists and the psychologists have studied this play of colors. "Ocular spectra," "colored spots," "phosphenes," such are the names that they have given to
25   the phenomenon. They explain it either by the slight modifications which occur ceaselessly in the retinal circulation, or by the pressure that the closed lid exerts upon the eyeball, causing a mechanical excitation of the optic nerve. But the explanation of the phenomenon and the name that is given to it matters little. It occurs universally and it constitutes—I may say at once—the principal material of which we shape our dreams, "such stuff as dreams are made
30   on."

Thirty or forty years ago, M. Alfred Maury and, about the same time, M. d'Hervey, of St. Denis, had observed that at the moment of falling asleep these colored spots and moving forms consolidate, fix themselves, take on definite outlines, the outlines of the objects and of the persons which people our dreams. But this is an observation to be accepted with
35   caution, since it emanates from psychologists already half asleep. More recently an American psychologist, Professor Ladd, of Yale, has devised a more rigorous method, but of difficult application, because it requires a sort of training. It consists in acquiring the habit on awakening in the morning of keeping the eyes closed and retaining for some minutes the dream that is fading from the field of vision and soon would doubtless have faded from that
40   of memory. Then one sees the figures and objects of the dream melt away little by little into phosphenes, identifying themselves with the colored spots that the eye really perceives when the lids are closed. One reads, for example, a newspaper; that is the dream. One awakens and there remains of the newspaper, whose definite outlines are erased, only a white spot with black marks here and there; that is the reality. Or our dream takes us upon the open sea—
45   round about us the ocean spreads its waves of yellowish gray with here and there a crown of white foam. On awakening, it is all lost in a great spot, half yellow and half gray, sown with brilliant points. The spot was there, the brilliant points were there. There was really presented to our perceptions, in sleep, a visual dust, and it was this dust which served for the fabrication of our dreams.

11. In the context of the passage, "set aside unessentials" (lines 4-5) and "go at once to the heart of the question" (line 5) mainly serve to show the author's desire to

   A. separate fact from fiction.

   B. appeal to the reader's emotions.

   C. answer the reader's questions.

   D. not waste the reader's time.

12. As used in line 11, "sense" most nearly means

   A. intelligence.

   B. meaning.

   C. feel.

   D. perception.

13. In the context of the passage, the main purpose of the fourth paragraph ("Close ... made on.") is to

   A. show that people can see shapes and colors even when their eyes are closed.

   B. suggest that the images people see while dreaming are related to what their eyes see when closed.

   C. define psychological terms such as "ocular spectra," "colored spots," and "phosphenes."

   D. encourage readers to try simple experiments such as the one described in these lines at home.

14. The quotation "such stuff that dreams are made on" (lines 29-30) mainly serves to

   A. make the writing more interesting.

   B. summarize the main idea of the paragraph.

   C. introduce a question for readers to ask themselves.

   D. explain why people dream about the things they dream about.

15. The central claim of the last paragraph (lines 31-49) is that

   A. the observations of M. Alfred Maury and M. d'Hervey cannot be trusted.

   B. a newspaper seen in a dream may look like a white spot with black marks upon awakening.

   C. dreams are fabricated from a certain kind of visual dust.

   D. Professor Ladd believes that images in our dreams can still be detected after waking.

Questions 16-20 are based on the following passages.

Passage 1 is adapted from *America and the World War* by Theodore Roosevelt, originally published in 1915. Passage 2 is adapted from President John F. Kennedy's inaugural address given in 1961.

Passage 1

Peace is worthless unless it serves the cause of righteousness. Peace which consecrates militarism is of small service. Peace obtained by crushing the liberty and life of just and unoffending peoples is as cruel as the most cruel war. It should ever be our honorable effort to
Line serve one of the world's most vital needs by doing all in our power to bring about conditions
5 which will give some effective protection to weak or small nations which themselves keep order and act with justice toward the rest of mankind. There can be no higher international

duty than to safeguard the existence and independence of industrious, orderly states, with a high personal and national standard of conduct, but without the military force of the great powers; states, for instance, such as Belgium, Holland, Switzerland, the Scandinavian

10   countries, Uruguay, and others. A peace which left Belgium's wrongs unredressed and which did not provide against the recurrence of such wrongs as those from which she has suffered would not be a real peace.

As regards the actions of most of the combatants in the hideous world-wide war now raging it is possible sincerely to take and defend either of the opposite views concerning their

15   actions. The causes of any such great and terrible contest almost always lie far back in the past, and the seeming immediate cause is usually itself in major part merely an effect of many preceding causes. The assassination of the heir to the Austro-Hungarian throne was partly or largely due to the existence of political and often murderous secret societies in Servia which the Servian government did not suppress; and it did not suppress them because the "bondage"

20   of the men and women of the Servian race in Bosnia and Herzegovina to Austria was such a source of ever-present irritation to the Servians that their own government was powerless to restrain them. Strong arguments can be advanced on both the Austrian and the Servian sides as regards this initial cause of the present world-wide war.

Passage 2

Finally, to those nations who would make themselves our adversary, we offer not a pledge but a request: that both sides begin anew the quest for peace, before the dark powers of destruction unleashed by science engulf all humanity in planned or accidental

Line   self-destruction.

5   We dare not tempt them with weakness. For only when our arms are sufficient beyond doubt can we be certain beyond doubt that they will never be employed.

But neither can two great and powerful groups of nations take comfort from our present course—both sides overburdened by the cost of modern weapons, both rightly alarmed by the steady spread of the deadly atom, yet both racing to alter that uncertain balance of terror that

10   stays the hand of mankind's final war.

So let us begin anew—remembering on both sides that civility is not a sign of weakness, and sincerity is always subject to proof. Let us never negotiate out of fear. But let us never fear to negotiate.

Let both sides explore what problems unite us instead of belaboring those problems

15   which divide us.

Let both sides, for the first time, formulate serious and precise proposals for the inspection and control of arms—and bring the absolute power to destroy other nations under the absolute control of all nations.

Let both sides seek to invoke the wonders of science instead of its terrors. Together let us

20   explore the stars, conquer the deserts, eradicate disease, tap the ocean depths, and encourage the arts and commerce.

Let both sides unite to heed in all corners of the earth the command of Isaiah—to "undo the heavy burdens...and to let the oppressed go free."

And if a beachhead of cooperation may push back the jungle of suspicion, let both sides join
25 in creating a new endeavor, not a new balance of power, but a new world of law, where the
strong are just and the weak secure and the peace preserved.

16. According to Passage 1, one similarity between Belgium and Uruguay is that they both

   A. achieved peace but were not punished for their wrongdoings.

   B. served the cause of righteousness by achieving peace.

   C. continued to use excessive military force after achieving peace.

   D. used excessive military force to achieve peace.

17. The main purpose of Passage 2 is to

   A. prove that modern weapons are necessary.

   B. suggest that fear should not motivate negotiations.

   C. explain methods for achieving peace.

   D. show how weakness can tempt adversaries.

18. Both authors would most likely agree with which statement about peace?

   A. It should be achieved at any cost.

   B. It should be achieved cautiously.

   C. It should eliminate the need for weapons.

   D. It can be as cruel as the most cruel war.

19. In the passages, a significant difference in how the two authors discuss achieving peace is that Kennedy indicates that

   A. negotiations are important.

   B. industrious nations must be protected.

   C. war weapons are necessary to maintain peace.

   D. science is the solution to mankind's problems.

20. Assuming that he agrees with the assertions in the final paragraph of Passage 2, President Roosevelt would most likely recommend which course of action to President Kennedy?

   A. Eliminating all hostile powers is the best way to achieve law throughout the world.

   B. Do not allow the military to use excessive force to maintain law throughout the world.

   C. Subjecting weapons of war to inspections is a key to maintaining law throughout the world.

   D. Never allow mere suspicions to affect the way you maintain law throughout the world.

ANSWER KEY AND EXPLANATIONS

Evidence-Based Reading

1. A	5. C	9. C	13. B	17. C
2. B	6. C	10. B	14. A	18. B
3. D	7. D	11. D	15. D	19. A
4. A	8. C	12. D	16. D	20. B

1. **The correct answer is A.** Although each answer choice is a synonym of *business, issue* is the only one that makes sense if used in place of *business* in this particular context. *Commercial* (choice D) is a synonym of *business* only if it is used as an adjective, and *business* is used as a noun in line 14.

2. **The correct answer is B.** Beatrice responds to Patsy's announcement that she does not intend to spend Easter vacation at home with surprise. According to Patsy, she, her father, and her Aunt Martha all prefer the idea of spending the holiday away from home in Palm Beach.

3. **The correct answer is D.** Choice D is the line that most clearly shows Beatrice's surprise at Patsy's announcement that she does not plan to spend the Easter holiday at home and Beatrice's own intentions of spending her own holiday at home. Choice A shows that Beatrice assumes Patsy will spend the holiday at home and Choice C gives an indication of Beatrice's surprise that Pasty will not be doing that, but neither choice is as clear a piece of evidence to support the answer to the previous question as choice D is.

4. **The correct answer is A.** Patsy clearly thinks her plan is good, so choice A is the best answer. Choices B and C are too literal. Patsy gives no indication that she thinks her own plan is strange, so choice D is not the best answer.

5. **The correct answer is C.** The dialogue between the two girls suddenly ends when a narrator interjects to describe Patsy's previous adventures that apparently occurred in another story called "Patsy Carroll at Wilderness Lodge." The first half of the passage is not really concerned with description, so choices B and D are incorrect. The discussion of French verbs is part of the conversation about studying, so choice A is incorrect.

6. **The correct answer is C.** These lines state that vegetarians need to eat less food than meat eaters do, which shows that a vegetarian diet is more efficient than one that includes meat. Choice A is incorrect because it does not specify a vegetarian or meat-eating diet. Choice B implies that a meat-eating diet is superior to a vegetarian one. Choice D is incorrect because it merely points out a positive thing about a diet that includes vegetables, not a vegetarian diet, which consists of nothing but vegetables.

7. **The correct answer is D.** According to the passage, the girl was able to digest 80 percent of the fiber in her food because she was on a fruit-only diet. Choice A is true but it is not a direct result of the girl being on the diet; it is only the duration she was on it. Choices B and C are simply untrue.

8. **The correct answer is C.** Choice C shows the evidence supporting the fact that the girl digested 80 percent of the fiber in her food as a result of being on the fruit-only diet. Choice A merely introduces the fact that she was on the diet; it says nothing about the diet's results. Choice B shows the percentage of proteids she digested, not the

percentage of fiber. Choice D has nothing to do with the girl at all.

9. **The correct answer is C.** According to the passage, all entries marked with a *U* indicate a food in which the cellulose is included with the carbohydrate. Of these answer choices, fresh walnuts is the only entry that is not marked with a *U*.

10. **The correct answer is B.** According to the passage, rice is a cereal, and the table shows that the body digests 8 percent of the proteids in rice. The passage also states that the body digests 80 percent of fruits and vegetables, but the numbers on the table do not support this statement, so choices A and C are incorrect. The passage states that the body digests 98 percent of the proteids in meat, but there are no meats represented on the table, so choice D is incorrect.

11. **The correct answer is D.** The literal phrase "set aside unessentials" and the figurative phrase "go at once to the heart of the question" reveal the author's desire to not waste the reader's time and deliver essential information immediately. Although it refers to "the heart," the figurative phrase has nothing to do with emotions, so choice B is incorrect. Choice C applies to the figurative phrase only when it needs to apply to both phrases.

12. **The correct answer is D.** Although each answer choice can be used as a synonym for *sense*, only choice D makes sense in this particular context. *Sense* means the perception of sight, hearing, and touch.

13. **The correct answer is B.** The passage as a whole is about dreams, and these particular lines suggest that the images people see while dreaming are related to what their eyes see when closed. Choice A may be true, but it fails to relate the lines to the passage's main idea: dreams. Choice C is just a detail in the lines. Although the lines describe a simple

experiment, choice D does not explain their main purpose accurately.

14. **The correct answer is A.** This famous quotation from William Shakespeare basically repeats information stated right before it ("the principal material of which we shape our dreams"), so its only purpose is to make the writing a bit more interesting. It does not summarize the main purpose of the paragraph (choice B), it is not a question (choice C), and it does not explain why people dream about the things they dream about (choice D).

15. **The correct answer is D.** Choice D accurately identifies the central claim of the final paragraph as a whole. Choices A and B are just individual details from the paragraph. Choice C takes a figurative use of the term "visual dust" too literally.

16. **The correct answer is D.** President Roosevelt includes Belgium and Uruguay in a list of "great powers" that used excessive military force to achieve peace. He only specifies that Belgium achieved peace but was not punished for their wrongdoings (choice A) and continued to use excessive military force after achieving peace (choice C), but the correct answer needs to apply to Uruguay too. Choice B does not apply to either country.

17. **The correct answer is C.** Choice C best sums up the main purpose of Passage 2. Choices A, B, and D all refer to individual details in the passage and fail to capture its overall purpose.

18. **The correct answer is B.** President Roosevelt believes that achieving peace could end up consecrating militarism and President Kennedy warns against tempting adversaries by disarming, so both would likely agree that peace should be achieved cautiously. That contradicts choices A and C.

Choice D refers only to Passage 1, and the correct answer must refer to both passages.

19. **The correct answer is A.** Only President Kennedy discusses the importance of negotiations. Choice B is an opinion of President Roosevelt, not President Kennedy. Choice C is a likely opinion of both presidents. Choice D misreads the importance of President Kennedy's discussions of science.

20. **The correct answer is B.** In the final paragraph of Passage 2, President Kennedy emphasizes the importance of law throughout the world. President Roosevelt warns against the use of excessive force in Passage 1, so choice B is the most logical answer. Choice A is much too excessive. Choices C and D seem more like advice President Kennedy would give to President Roosevelt.

SUMMING IT UP

- The PSAT/NMSQT® Reading Test is a multiple-choice test consisting of **47 questions.**
  - All of the information you'll need to answer questions on the PSAT/NMSQT® Reading Test is included in the given text or images.

- There are **six passages** on the PSAT/NMSQT® Reading Test, two of which are paired. Each individual passage and passage pair is roughly 550-750 words long.

- There are four types of passages on the PSAT/NMSQT® Reading Test: **Literature, History, Social Studies,** and **Science**.

  1. The **Literature** passage is excerpted from a classic or contemporary work of fiction.

  2. The **History** passage is excerpted from a US founding document or speech or one that examines an important historical event.

  3. The **Social Studies** passage is about economics, psychology, or sociology.

  4. The two **Science** passages may deal with earth science, biology, chemistry, or physics.

- There are three main question types on the PSAT/NMSQT® Reading Test: **Words in Context, Analysis in History/Social Studies and Science,** and **Command of Evidence**.

- **Words in Context questions** test your ability to identify the specific ways words and phrases are used in the passages. You will need to recognize words for their definitions and for the tone they add to the passage.
  - When answering Words in Context questions, replace the word you must define in the sentence with each answer choice to see which makes the most sense.

- **Analysis in History/Social Studies and Science questions** require you to examine hypotheses, interpret data, and consider implications.
  - **Drawing conclusions** is using clues from a passage to determine what will definitely happen.
  - **Making inferences** is using clues to make an assumption about something that might be true.

- **Command of Evidence questions** require you to locate information in the passages that supports your answers to analysis questions. Their correct answers depend on the questions that precede them. This can be helpful if you happened to answer the previous question incorrectly. In researching the answer to the Command of Evidence question, you might find you've made a mistake and can fix it.

- Some questions will require you to analyze **informational graphics** such as charts, tables, graphs, diagrams, and maps. There is a good chance these questions will ask you to look at information from the passage with information from the image to arrive at the right answer.

- **Paired passages** relate to each other in some significant ways and include questions that refer to each individual passage as well as both passages together. They are always History or Science passages.
  - To help you understand how the passages relate to one another, jot down their similarities, differences, and other relationships while reading them.

PART IV
PSAT/NMSQT® EXAM WRITING AND LANGUAGE TEST STRATEGIES

Writing and Language Strategies

OVERVIEW

- **Command of Evidence Questions**
- **Words in Context Questions**
- **Analysis in History/Social Studies and in Science Questions**
- **Expression of Ideas Questions**
- **Writing and Language Practice Questions**
- **Answer Key and Explanations**
- **Summing It Up**

The Writing and Language Test is one-third of your overall PSAT/NMSQT® exam score and half of the Evidence-Based Reading and Writing section. It's multiple-choice, like most of the PSAT/NMSQT® exam. So, despite the name, you won't actually be asked to write anything. Instead, you're the editor, tasked with reading a piece of writing and figuring out what's wrong with the passage—and what's right. These are practical skills you probably already use all the time for school, so it's just a matter of learning the test's ins and outs and putting those skills to use on test day.

The Writing and Language Test is kind of a PSAT/NMSQT® blitz: you have 35 minutes to read four passages and answer 44 questions. That gives you about 48 seconds per question, including passage reading time. Every Writing and Language Test is based on short reading passages that have words, phrases, or sentences underlined and numbered. Your task will be to read the underlined text and, based on the questions, spot mistakes and correct them. Some passages will also be accompanied by graphs or other supplemental information. For those passages, you may be asked to compare, contrast, or find relationships between the passage and the information presented in the graph.

Each passage in Writing and Language is a nonfiction piece, either whole or an excerpt from a larger essay or article on one of these subjects:

- Careers
- History
- Social Studies
- Humanities
- Science

Unlike on the Reading Test, you won't see excerpts from novels or any fictional narratives. These passages are typically informational, like an essay or paper you might see or write in

Chapter 4

TIP

You don't need to learn any special information for the PSAT/NMSQT® Writing and Language Test. Cramming vocabulary definitions or subject knowledge of history or science won't help you here. The test assesses how you can engage with information you haven't seen before and improve the writing.

college. No matter what the subject matter is, you'll be asked to read each passage with a critical eye and make decisions about what would improve it. The questions will point you to specific parts of each passage and either ask you to modify underlined text or make a decision about the paragraph or passage as a whole.

You don't need to bring any specific knowledge of topics in careers, history, social studies, humanities, or science with you on test day. You'll be using the information right in front of you, as well as your knowledge of grammar, usage, and style.

In most of the questions, you'll be presented with the underlined text and expected to choose the best correction out of four options. There's no specific question asked, but from the directions (and your practice!), you know that you need to pick the best version of the underlined text. Typically, one of those options will be "NO CHANGE," which means the text is fine as is.

In other cases, there will be a specific question that asks you something about an entire paragraph or the passage as a whole, so you can clarify the author's tone or message.

Let's look at a short sample test passage and the related questions that would accompany it on the PSAT/NMSQT® exam.

According to a recent study, 3 out of 5 Americans are not getting enough [1] exercise; the American Board of Physicians [2] recommend that people get a minimum of 30–60 minutes of exercise per day to help boost health. [3]

TIP

Don't be afraid to look at text and decide that it's correct as written. Not every question requires an improvement, so don't feel obligated to find mistakes if the word, sentence, etc., looks correct to you. Always check the other answer choices to make sure, but sometimes NO CHANGE is the way to go.

1. **A.** NO CHANGE
   B. exercise, the
   C. exercise. The
   D. exercise the

2. **A.** NO CHANGE
   B. recommends
   C. recommended
   D. recommending

3. The writer wants to add a supporting detail to close out the paragraph. Which of the following would be appropriate?
   A. Doctors recommend daily exercise.
   B. The study also says that 30 minutes of light cardio exercise can help ward off diseases like diabetes.
   C. Certain types of exercise are not as effective.
   D. High-fiber diets contribute to health as well.

As you can see, Writing and Language questions may ask you to identify punctuation or grammatical errors, or you may be asked to make a decision about expression of ideas such as style, detail, or organization. We'll explore all these question types later in this chapter and in Chapter 5.

On the Writing and Language Test, you will see at least one passage that includes a graph or chart. For these questions, you'll need to consider the information in it to answer the question, as well as to understand how the graph relates to the passage as a whole. You may also need to compare or contrast it to the passage.

Let's look at an example of the kind of graph question used in PSAT/NMSQT® Writing and Language Test, using an expanded version of the previous passage and an associated graph.

According to a recent study, 3 out of 5 Americans are not getting enough [1] exercise; the American Board of Physicians [2] recommend that people get a minimum of 30 – 60 minutes of exercise per day to help boost health. [3] Most people get less than that, and so they fall short of exercise guidelines. [4]

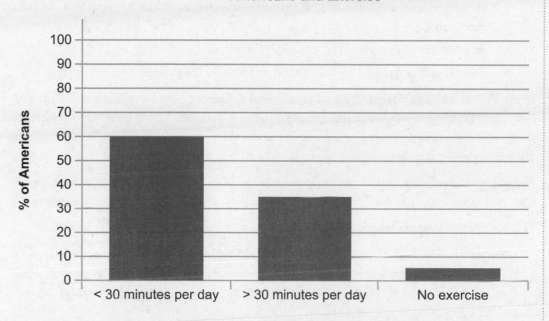

Americans and Exercise

4. According to this passage, which of the following should be indicated in the graph?

   A. Most Americans get more than 30 minutes of exercise per day.

   B. Most Americans get no exercise per day.

   C. Most Americans get less than 30 minutes of exercise per day.

   D. More than half of all Americans get 30 minutes of exercise per day.

This graph is related to the text in the sample passage but might present either a different perspective or information that supports the passage. It's up to you to work out how the information fits in and answer any questions you're asked about this extra info. And don't worry—these charts in the Writing and Language section won't require you to do any math, so no need to fire up your calculator for this section of the test.

COMMAND OF EVIDENCE QUESTIONS

With its focus on reading and writing skills you'll use in college and in everyday life, the PSAT/NMSQT® exam tests your ability to use information given to you and come to your own conclusions about it. For the Writing and Language Test, this means you'll be asked to understand how information is organized or presented in the passage and improve it as necessary. The point is to fix a passage so it presents information in a clear, concise way.

Questions testing these skills are called Command of Evidence questions, which make up about 20 percent of Writing and Language questions. They may ask you to do the following:

- Add a relevant detail or delete an irrelevant one
- Identify how information is used to support (or contrast) the author's argument
- Identify relationships between the passage and any supporting information (graphs, charts, etc.)
- Improve a writer's argument
- Draw conclusions based on information presented in the passage

In the PSAT/NMSQT® Reading Test, Command of Evidence questions typically ask you to find supporting evidence to support themes or narrative elements. In the Writing and Language Test, it's more about improving the way the passage presents and develops information. These are informational articles, so the focus is on presenting information or making an argument effectively.

Rather than just offering you four ways to improve the underlined text, Command of Evidence questions typically ask you to make a specific decision about the underlined text (or the passage in general).

For example, here are the kinds of Command of Evidence questions you might see on test day:

In the past decade, there has been a decline in the health and nutrition of Americans nationwide. It's not only that Americans, as a whole, are not getting enough exercise. [1] <u>Many people are also lacking nutrients in their everyday diet, due in part to the rise in highly processed foods and the easy availability of fast food.</u> [2]

1. Which choice provides information that best supports the claim made by the underlined sentence?

   A. McDonald's had higher profits than ever last year.

   B. Processed foods tend to be higher in sodium and lower in the nutrients found in fruits, vegetables, and whole grains.

   C. People should get about 2,000 calories per day, depending on their size and activity level.

   D. Many people protest the use of GMOs in food.

2. Which choice provides the most logical conclusion to the paragraph?

   A. Doctors recommend eating a serving of fruits and vegetables with every meal to help keep a balanced diet.

   B. Too many kids are overweight these days.

   C. Diet and exercise are the key to health.

   D. Not enough people eat dinner with their families anymore.

Unlike the majority of PSAT/NMSQT® Writing and Language Test questions, in these examples you're not being asked to improve the words on the page. Instead, your task is to find and evaluate information, and make a decision about how that information could be presented most effectively.

Question 1 tells you to support the underlined sentence in the paragraph, so that's your focus. Choice A talks about a specific fast food restaurant, which is unlike the rest of the paragraph. It also talks about revenue, when the sentence in question is talking about nutrition, so this doesn't fit very well with the rest of the sentence. Choice B adds details about processed foods, which does fit with the rest of the sentence. Choice C talks about people's individual nutrition needs, which doesn't quite fit because the sentence is describing how Americans in general eat. Choice D introduces entirely new information on a different topic, which doesn't support the sentence at all. **The correct answer is B.**

To answer question 2, you need to look at the paragraph as a whole and see what the author's argument is. For a question like this, quickly sum up the main idea of the paragraph in your own words. *American diets don't have enough nutritional balance.* Now look at how each answer choice supports that. Choice A is a good option because it talks about how to balance a diet. We have to make sure there aren't any better options, though. On to choice B: this doesn't fit as well, because the paragraph is talking about Americans in general, not adults or kids specifically. Choice C isn't wrong, because it generally fits with the author's point. However, it's vague and doesn't really fit with the argument made in this particular paragraph. Choice D has little to do with any of the information presented in the paragraph, so it would not be a good conclusion. So it's between choice A and choice C, and choice A is a more detailed option that fits well with the whole paragraph. Therefore, **the correct answer is A.**

Command of Evidence questions mean you can't just focus on bits of underlined text—you need to understand what's going on and what the author is trying to say. So how do you give the passage the attention it needs when you have very little time?

The best way to tackle Command of Evidence questions is to read for main points and themes as you go through the passage the first time. When you read the passage before tackling the questions, don't worry about remembering every single detail—that wastes precious time, and you only have seconds to get through your reading before you need to move on to answering questions.

Follow these steps every time you face a new passage:

1. **Read the passage at your normal speed.** You don't want to miss information, but you're also working against the clock. So make sure that you're reading quickly but pretty thoroughly.

2. **Make quick notes as you read.** Underline transition words, key words, and sentences that tell you about the main idea or the author's main argument.

3. **Answer the line- or word-specific questions first**. Then go back to the questions that ask you to identify or add information in the passage.

4. **Use those notes as a guide for any questions that deal with a paragraph or the passage as a whole.** Your breadcrumb trail of underlines and quick notes can help you find the supporting information you need or help you figure out what kind of information fits best with the author's argument.

WORDS IN CONTEXT QUESTIONS

Words in Context questions are some of the most straightforward questions you'll see on the Writing and Language Test. Text is numbered and underlined in the passage, and you'll be given four options to correct the underlined text (or more accurately, three options and a "NO CHANGE"). The answer you choose should be the best possible word that fits in the underlined space.

In these questions, you need to figure out if the underlined word is already correct or if there's an option that fits better with the sentence. To do that, you don't have to know too much about the passage as a whole or the author's overall argument. You want to think smaller: look at the words immediately before and after the underlined word, and figure out what the author is trying to say in this sentence. Once you know that, you can make a judgment about whether the word fits or if it should be changed.

Let's look at a continuation of the passage we started, this time featuring Words in Context questions.

> With this data about Americans' health available to us, it is clear that something needs to be done about this deadly trend, as chronic health issues like diabetes and heart disease [5] <u>choose</u> more lives than ever. For people who want to start down the path to better health, the solution is simple: exercise more and eat healthier. This does not mean everyone should sign up to run a marathon. Rather, many physicians [6] <u>recommend</u> working shorter periods of exercise into the daily routine, whether it's walking or jogging, three to five times per week. Even moderate exercise, 30 minutes a day, can help reduce the risk for diabetes or heart disease. This is a worthwhile investment even for busy people.

5.	A.	NO CHANGE		6.	A.	NO CHANGE
	B.	disrupt			B.	forbid
	C.	claim			C.	perform
	D.	opt			D.	demand

So how would you go about answering these? Let's start with question 5. From the sentence, you know that this word is a verb, an action performed by the nouns *diabetes* and *heart disease*. Because it's a compound noun, the verb should match that as well. All four answer choices meet that criterion. Next look at the words themselves—what do they mean, and would they fit with the sentence? Try plugging each word (or its meaning) into the underlined portion of the sentence.

… diabetes and heart disease _____ more lives than ever.

A. … diabetes and heart disease *choose [pick]* more lives than ever.

B. … diabetes and heart disease *disrupt [disturb]* more lives than ever.

C. … diabetes and heart disease *claim [take]* more lives than ever.

D. … diabetes and heart disease *opt [choose]* more lives than ever.

Choice A is incorrect, because *choosing* lives makes no sense in this context. Choice B is a possibility, because diabetes and heart diseases are illnesses and could disrupt lives. But you need to look at *all* the choices to make sure there's not a better one. Choice C is even better than choice B, because diseases do take lives, and the sentence already used the word *deadly*. Choice D is just a synonym of choice A, so that's out. Once you eliminate choices A and D, you pick the last answer standing that fits the sentence most fully. That's *claim*. **The correct answer is C.**

TIP

Close isn't good enough; you must choose the *best* choice on the PSAT/ NMSQT® exam. One or more answer choices might be a decent answer but definitely not the *best* one.

For question 6, use similar context clues.

> many physicians _____working shorter periods of exercise into the daily routine.

   A.   many physicians *recommend [suggest]* working shorter periods of exercise into the daily routine.

   B.   many physicians *forbid [prohibit]* working shorter periods of exercise into the daily routine.

   C.   many physicians *perform [do]* working shorter periods of exercise into the daily routine.

   D.   many physicians *demand [require]* working shorter periods of exercise into the daily routine.

Choice A is a distinct possibility: doctors prescribe treatment and give advice, so *recommend* (suggest) does work in the sentence. But is it the best option? Choice B seems unlikely, because the sentence and the paragraph are about increasing physical activity, not decreasing it, and forbidding exercise would decrease exercise. Choice C is slightly more realistic, but there's no evidence in the sentence (or the paragraph) that doctors are talking about their own exercise routines. Choice D is a much stronger version of choice A but doesn't quite work here. Doctors can't force anyone to exercise. So **the correct answer is A,** but it was important to rule out all the others before you made that choice.

For Words in Context questions, you have some options if you feel stuck or are faced with words that are totally unfamiliar to you.

   1.   **Sound it out and go by ear.** Try plugging the answer choice words into the sentence. Do any of them sound right? More important, do any of them sound especially wrong, meaning you can eliminate them?

   2.   **Make an educated guess not a random one.** If you're stumped but you can eliminate one or two answer choices, you can then make a more educated guess based on the options left.

The best part about Words in Context questions is that you already have all of the information you need right in front of you, surrounding the underlined word. You don't have to memorize the meaning of every word or know fully what it means—you just need to be able to look at what's around the word to help you arrive at the best answer.

ANALYSIS IN HISTORY/SOCIAL STUDIES AND IN SCIENCE QUESTIONS

The PSAT/NMSQT® Language and Writing Test focuses on your skills in areas that you'll use in school and in regular life. A large part of that is making sure you can 1) engage with writing that talks about history or real-life issues and 2) figure out how that information can be presented most effectively. That's why passages in the Writing and Language Test are about real-life topics instead of literature. The passages you see on test day might be from essays or articles taking a stand on an issue (like the environment) or otherwise presenting factual information, as if you were reading it in a magazine.

Your Analysis in History/Social Studies and in Science subscore shows how well you can read a piece on a real-life issue, analyze what the author is saying, and make it better. These questions aren't

TIP

On the PSAT/NMSQT® exam, there's no penalty for guessing. So if you feel stumped, it's much better to make an educated guess (eliminating as many answer choices as you can) and move on, rather than to leave an item unanswered.

as obvious as, say, the Words in Context questions, because they can ask about a range of different aspects of the passage. These are the questions that ask you to revise the text to be more consistent with the information presented in related graphs, draw conclusions about the information presented, and solve problems that come from real-world history, science and social science issues.

On the Writing and Language Test, you will see at least one passage that includes a graph or chart. For these questions, you'll need to consider the information in the graph to answer the question, as well as understand how the graph relates to the passage as a whole. You may also need to compare or contrast it to the passage to make sure information is presented consistently.

Let's look at a sample Analysis in History/Social Studies and in Science question, using another variation of the passage and chart from earlier in the chapter.

> According to a recent study, 3 out of 5 Americans [7] <u>are getting enough exercise</u>; the American Board of Physicians [8] <u>recommend</u> that people get a minimum of 30–60 minutes of exercise per day to help boost health. [9] [10]

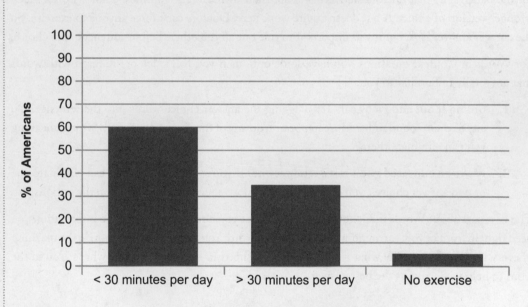

Americans and Exercise

7. Which choice completes the sentence with accurate data based on the graph?

   A. NO CHANGE

   B. are not getting enough exercise

   C. are exercising 30 minutes per day

   D. do not exercise

This question qualifies as an Analysis in History/Social Studies and in Science question because you have to engage with the graph *and* the passage and figure out how to make sure those match up. To answer this question, you need to know what's going on in the graph (60 percent of Americans get fewer than 30 minutes of exercise per day, 35 percent of Americans get more than 30 minutes per day, and 5 percent of Americans get almost no exercise at all). Then you have to make a judgment about what the passage *should* say. In this case, you're asked to make the graph consistent with the passage, so the passage should support the author's argument that most (a majority of 60% + 5%) of Americans get less exercise than doctors recommend. Once you've identified that piece of it, you have your answer: **the correct answer is B.**

Many questions on the Writing and Language Test actually do double duty as Command of Evidence or Expression of Ideas questions, so while it can be difficult to single out the Analysis questions on their own, you can assume that questions that ask you to compare and contrast information will count toward your Analysis in History/Social Studies and in Science subscore.

EXPRESSION OF IDEAS QUESTIONS

Expression of Ideas questions focus on topic development, organization, and effective use of language. These make up more than half of the questions on the Writing and Language Test. These are the opposite of the Words in Context questions because, instead of focusing on one word or phrase at a time, you'll be looking at the bigger picture of either the paragraph or the passage. These questions may ask you to:

- Decide whether a detail is relevant or irrelevant
- Add, delete, or change text
- Identify transitional language that moves effectively from one idea to another
- Combine sentences to make the passage flow better
- Eliminate awkward language and wordiness
- Put sentences in an order that makes more sense
- Make style and tone consistent
- Choose the right words or phrasing to support the author's argument

As the editor/test-taker here, it's your job to make sure that the writer is making his or her points in the best and clearest way possible.

Let's look at a sample passage with Expression of Ideas questions.

(1) While these statistics and trends are alarming, there is hope for the future. (2) [8] A program run by Dr. Marcus Fitch shows how small steps can help reverse a lifetime of bad eating and exercise habits. (3) Dr. Fitch works with senior citizens who are either at risk for cardiovascular disease, or who are already suffering from chronic ailments. (4) In his group of 20 patients, [9] he put all of them on a moderate program of 15-30 minutes per day of light cardio exercise. He also put them on a diet that includes eight daily servings of fruit and vegetables. [10]

8. The writer is considering deleting the underlined sentence. Should the writer do this? Why or why not?

   A. Yes, because it's repetitive, and the next sentence tells you everything you need to know about Dr. Fitch.

   B. No, because it adds detail.

   C. Yes, because the details are unnecessary.

   D. No, because it supports the introductory sentence.

9. Which choice most effectively combines the two underlined sentences?

   A. he put all of them on a moderate program of 15-30 minutes per day of light cardio exercise and a diet

   B. he put all of them on a moderate program of 15-30 minutes per day of light cardio exercise, but also on a diet

   C. he put all of them on a moderate program of 15-30 minutes per day of light cardio exercise, because he also put them on a diet

   D. he put all of them on a moderate program. It was 15-30 minutes per day of light cardio exercise, and a diet

10. The writer wants to add the sentence below? Where should it be located in the paragraph?

Since the creation of the regimen two years ago, nearly three-quarters of the group have seen improvement in their symptoms and overall health.

   A. After sentence 1

   B. After sentence 2

   C. After sentence 3

   D. At the end of the paragraph

These questions aren't just asking you to insert a word or fix grammar. Expression of Ideas questions require you to make a judgment call about how the underlined sentences work as part of the whole paragraph or passage and what you can do to make them work better as puzzle pieces in the passage.

For question 8 (an addition/deletion question), you need to look closely at the answer choices and the paragraph as a whole to figure out whether the sentence fits in the paragraph or whether it should come out. It's important to read all of the answer choices—you want to make sure you're making the right editorial decision. The paragraph is about Dr. Fitch's medical program and what it has done for people's health. Does the underlined text support that? It does; it introduces Dr. Marcus Fitch, backs up the claim that there is hope for the future, and mentions how his program relates to the passage's overall theme of diet and exercise. So if you've decided that it does work well in the passage and should not be deleted, you can eliminate any "yes" choices (A and C). Now you just need to pick the right rationale, and that means you have to consider each answer choice. Choice B is close, but it's vague. Choice D is better because it tells you specifically why the sentence shouldn't be deleted. **The correct answer is D.**

Question 9 is a combining question. These seem tricky, but you shouldn't be too nervous. Most of the time, you can read the sentence in your head and see which option sounds best. If the sentence still sounds choppy or doesn't have enough of a pause, you can eliminate those answers. In this case, choice A pushes the sentences together with the conjunction *and*. Reading it aloud, it seems right—check the other choices, though, before you mark it down. Choice B joins the sentences with the conjunction *but*, which is not correct. The two parts of the thought do not contradict one another. Choice C is out because it makes the two sentences sound like cause and effect (that the doctor put them on a diet *because* of the exercise, which isn't supported by the passage). And choice D makes the sentences even choppier, breaking up the sentence about exercise right in the middle. **The correct answer is A.**

Question 10 is an ordering/reordering question and asks you to decide where this new information should go. The best way to tackle this is to see how it sounds. Try reading the sentence in each of the answer choice spots and see what seems like the most natural fit. In this case, the additional sentence talks about the success of the program, so it makes sense to have it come at the end of the paragraph, after the writer has described the program. **The correct answer is D.**

Expression of Ideas questions may seem like a lot of work, but you should learn to trust your instincts as you prep for the PSAT/NMSQT® exam. If an option feels wrong or just sounds wrong to you, chances are you can eliminate that option and zero in on the better options fairly quickly. These big picture questions may seem more complicated, but the more you practice sifting through passages, the easier it'll come to you on test day.

WRITING AND LANGUAGE PRACTICE QUESTIONS

Now, try some practice questions on your own. Read and carefully analyze the following PSAT/NMSQT® exam-like writing passages. The questions that follow test your evidence-based writing skills.

Directions: Each of the following passages is accompanied by a set of questions. For some questions, you will consider how the passage might be revised to improve the expression of ideas. For other questions, you will consider how the passage might be edited to correct errors in sentence structure, usage, or punctuation. A passage or a question may be accompanied by one or more graphics (such as a table, chart, graph, or photograph) that you will consider as you make revising and editing decisions.

Some questions will direct you to an underlined portion of a passage. Other questions will direct you to a location in a passage or ask you to think about the passage as a whole.

After reading each passage, choose the answer to each question that most effectively improves the quality of writing in the passage or that makes the passage conform to the conventions of standard written English. Many questions include a "NO CHANGE" option. Choose that option if you think the best choice is to leave the relevant portion of the passage as it is.

Questions 1-10 are based on the following passage and supplementary material.

Occupational Therapy

[1] Healthcare careers, especially in the Allied Health fields, are on the rise in [2] <u>general. And occupational</u> therapy is one of the fastest-growing fields in all of healthcare, according to the U.S. Bureau of Labor Statistics. [3]

Healthcare Jobs	+% Change, 2014-2024	Median Annual Wage
Occupational therapy assistants	42.7	$57,870
Physical therapist assistants	40.6	$55,170
Physical therapist aides	39.0	$25,120
Home health aides	38.1	$21,920
Nurse practitioners	35.2	$98,190
Physical therapists	34.0	$84,020
Ambulance drivers	33.0	$23,740
Occupational therapy aides	30.6	$27,800
Physician assistants	30.4	$98,180
Optometrists	27.0	$103,900
Occupational therapists	26.5	$80,150
Diagnostic medical sonographers	26.4	$68,970
Personal care aides	25.9	$20,980
Nurse midwives	24.6	$92,510
Emergency medical technicians/paramedics	24.2	$31,980
Total, all occupations	6.5	$36,200

Source: The U.S. Bureau of Labor Statistics

[4] <u>Occupational therapists, occupational therapy assistants, and occupational therapy aides</u> work with patients who are recovering from illness (such as a stroke), injury, or disability. [5] <u>These Allied Health professionals</u> help patients learn how to manage everyday tasks like moving around, household chores, personal care routines, etc. They create treatment plans to help patients live and work on their own, despite physical challenges. Occupational therapy assistants and aides work with patients to implement these treatment plans and keep track of patient progress. Under the direction of the therapist, assistants and aides help patients do [6] <u>automatic</u> exercises, learn to use devices that can help simplify tasks, and manage patient appointments and records.

(1) To become an occupational therapist, you'll need a master's degree in Occupational Therapy. (2) To become an assistant or an aide, you will need an associate's degree in the field. (3) At

all levels, [7] <u>they</u> also need to be licensed by their states, in addition to these educational requirements. <u>Becoming an occupational therapy professional means committing to a path of education, training, and certification.</u> [8]

For occupational therapists, assistants, and aides, the job outlook is [9] <u>really, really bright!</u> The Bureau of Labor Statistics predicts an average 30% growth in this field over the next ten years, nearly five times the predicted growth of all other occupations. [10]

1. Which of the following would be an effective opening sentence for this passage?

   A. Occupational Therapy is the best career available today—let us tell you why.

   B. There are many careers available in healthcare these days.

   C. If you're looking for a career in healthcare, you might want to consider going into the occupational therapy field.

   D. Let's talk about occupational therapy.

2. A. NO CHANGE

   B. general, and occupational

   C. general. although occupational

   D. general. Occupational

3. Which of the following sentences could best be added here to complete the paragraph with accurate data based on the chart?

   A. Unlike occupational therapists, change in jobs for physical therapists is expected to decline by 34 percent.

   B. Occupational therapists make a median salary of $57,870.

   C. Despite the fact that ambulance driver is the fastest-growing healthcare career, occupational therapy is a popular field, too.

   D. In fact, occupational therapy assistants are the fastest-growing job of all healthcare careers as of 2015.

4. A. NO CHANGE

   B. Occupational therapists, assistants, and aides

   C. Occupational

   D. They

5. A. NO CHANGE

   B. Professionals

   C. Healthcare people

   D. Occupations

6. A. NO CHANGE

   B. unnecessary

   C. therapeutic

   D. difficult

7. A. NO CHANGE

   B. occupational therapy aides

   C. occupational therapy assistants

   D. occupational therapy professionals

8. Where in the paragraph should the underlined sentence be placed?

   A. Before sentence 1

   B. After sentence 1

   C. After sentence 2

   D. After sentence 3

9. A. NO CHANGE
  B. bright.
  C. so, so bright.
  D. the brightest.

10. Which of the following details would be a relevant addition to this passage?
  A. Occupational therapy salaries in comparison to other healthcare career salaries
  B. The benefits of becoming a home health aide
  C. The median annual wage of all Allied Health jobs
  D. What 2024's fastest-growing healthcare career will be

Questions 11-20 are based on the following passage.

Ben Franklin's Turkey

According to a popular American legend, our national bird was very nearly the turkey. When America's founding fathers met to determine the [**11**] fresh United States' symbols [**12**] back then, Benjamin Franklin wanted to propose the turkey to represent the country as the national bird. The turkey ultimately lost out to the symbol we still know today: the majestic bald eagle. Ever since, Americans have enjoyed passing down the [**13**] fact, chuckling about how such a large, clumsy creature was very nearly our national symbol. [**14**]

[**15**] There is only one problem with this legend. The only problem with this legend is the fact that it is not actually true. So how did rumor become accepted as American history? [**16**] And what were Benjamin Franklin's actual feelings about the national bird? What were Benjamin Franklin's actual feelings about the patriotic turkey? Per the story, Franklin felt that the eagle had a "bad character," while the turkey was "respectable…though a little silly, a bird of courage." He even went on to say that the brave turkey would have defended American farms from the British "red coat" soldiers. There are no documented events that show turkeys showing heroism during the Revolutionary War. [**17**]

[**18**] Franklin did write those words to his daughter in a 1784 letter. This letter has been proven to exist. However, what has gotten lost is the context of it: that Franklin was making those comments as a joke after the eagle had already been selected. [**19**] He felt that the new national logo design, featuring the eagle, looked more like a turkey, and made jokes about it. Yet like a game of "Telephone," the story became that Franklin wanted the turkey as the national bird, despite never having seriously or publicly supported that. A private joke to his own daughter became an anecdote that survives to this day.

Although the story continues to be a favorite bit of American lore, the Smithsonian Museum wants to set the record straight, and has devoted museum space to debunking this 200-year-old rumor. As a founding father, Benjamin Franklin was many things to this country [**20**] (founding father, father to a daughter, and more), but unfortunately, turkey-supporter was not one of them.

11. **A.** NO CHANGE

    B. fledgling

    C. united

    D. foraging

12. Which of the following details would fit at this point in the sentence?

    A. after separating from England

    B. under American rule

    C. from all the different kinds of birds

    D. to go with the new flag

13. **A.** NO CHANGE

    B. mystery

    C. tale

    D. book

14. Which of the following would make an effective closing sentence for the first paragraph?

    A. The bald eagle was chosen as the official national bird.

    B. Turkeys were not present at the first Thanksgiving dinner, either.

    C. Ben Franklin was once the Ambassador to France.

    D. It has become a fun bit of trivia to share around the Thanksgiving dinner table.

15. **A.** NO CHANGE

    B. There is only one problem with this legend, the only problem with this legend is the fact that it is not actually true.

    C. There is only one problem with this legend: it is not actually true.

    D. There is only one problem with this legend, and that problem is that it is not actually true.

16. **A.** NO CHANGE

    B. And what were Benjamin Franklin's actual feelings about the national bird and the patriotic turkey?

    C. First, what were Benjamin Franklin's actual feelings about the national bird? Second, what were Benjamin Franklin's actual feelings about the patriotic turkey?

    D. And what were Benjamin Franklin's actual feelings about the national bird … What were Benjamin Franklin's actual feelings about the patriotic turkey?

17. The author wants to delete one of the following sentences from the paragraph. Which is the least relevant to the paragraph as a whole?

    A. The only problem with this legend is the fact that it is not actually true.

    B. So how did rumor become accepted as American history?

    C. Per the story, Franklin felt that the eagle had a "bad character," while the turkey was "respectable … though a little silly, a bird of courage."

    D. There are no documented events that show turkeys showing heroism during the Revolutionary War.

18. Which of the following would make an effective transition for the third paragraph?
   A. In reality,
   B. Also,
   C. Lastly,
   D. So

19. A. NO CHANGE
   B. He felt that the eagle on the new logo looked more like a turkey.
   C. The eagle looked more like a turkey.
   D. The new national logo design featuring the eagle looked more like a turkey, and he made jokes about it.

20. Which choice provides the most relevant set of details?
   A. NO CHANGE
   B. (inventor, advisor, patriot)
   C. (American, letter-writer)
   D. (founding father, writer, inventor)

ANSWER KEY AND EXPLANATIONS

Writing and Language

1. C	5. A	9. B	13. C	17. D
2. B	6. C	10. A	14. D	18. A
3. D	7. D	11. B	15. C	19. B
4. B	8. A	12. A	16. B	20. B

1. **The correct answer is C.** The passage is about healthcare careers, but it also narrows the focus to occupational therapy. This is the only choice that is a complete sentence, and fits with both the tone and the content of the passage.

2. **The correct answer is B.** The two sentences work better when they're joined. The second sentence is related to the first, so, of the given options, choice B does the best job of smoothly joining the sentences and making sure that the relationship is made clear.

3. **The correct answer is D.** This sentence matches the data in the chart: occupational therapy assistants are the fastest-growing career, at 42.7 percent.

4. **The correct answer is B.** It's unnecessary to put *occupational* before each job, given that they're all in the same field. It makes more sense to condense it to one use, and have it describe all three job titles (therapists, assistants, aides). Choice B is the best answer.

5. **The correct answer is A.** This makes it clear who the writer is talking about and also uses a slightly different phrase than "occupational therapists," etc., to break up the repetition of that phrase throughout the passage.

6. **The correct answer is C.** Because these are therapists (and therapy assistants/aides) helping with the exercise, *therapeutic* is the best and most specific word choice here.

7. **The correct answer is D.** *They* is vague, but the start of the sentence tells you that the writer is talking about "all levels" of occupational therapy professionals, so choice D is the most complete choice.

8. **The correct answer is A.** This would be a good introduction/main idea sentence, because the rest of the paragraph is about the steps that someone needs to take to become an occupational therapist, assistant, or aide.

9. **The correct answer is B.** Choice B is the most concise option and is in keeping with the tone of the passage.

10. **The correct answer is A.** Because the passage compares occupational therapy to other healthcare careers (especially in the chart), more details about this topic would fit into the passage.

11. **The correct answer is B.** *Fledgling*, or new, is a better fit in this sentence.

12. **The correct answer is A.** This is the most relevant detail because it lets the reader know *when* this was taking place (after the Revolutionary War, when the United States broke ties with England). It is the best replacement for *back then*.

13. **The correct answer is C.** *Tale*, or story, fits the best with this sentence, and with the passage overall.

14. **The correct answer is D.** Of all the options, choice D is the best because it adds a context detail (it connects turkeys and Thanksgiving) while also supporting the main idea of the passage (that the story, although untrue, has stuck around all this time).

15. **The correct answer is C.** Choice C cuts down on the wordiness of these two sentences, and also joins them correctly with a colon.

16. **The correct answer is B.** These two sentences are repetitive, so you need to condense them into a shorter, more effective sentence.

17. **The correct answer is D.** That detail doesn't really fit with the rest of the paragraph. There is no other information about things that happened during the Revolutionary War, so this information is not relevant to the paragraph (which is about Franklin's comments).

18. **The correct answer is A.** This transition sets up the relationship between what Benjamin Franklin *may* have said and what he actually said.

19. **The correct answer is B.** This sentence is wordy and is redundant because the previous sentence already mentions that Franklin was making a joke.

20. **The correct answer is B.** These details tell the reader more about Benjamin Franklin, while the other options just rehash details the reader already knows from the rest of the passage.

SUMMING IT UP

- The PSAT/NMSQT® Writing and Language Test is a multiple-choice exam that asks you to read a piece of writing and correct errors in grammar, style, and punctuation. You have 35 minutes to read four passages and answer **44 questions**.

- **Writing and Language passages** have words, phrases, or sentences underlined and numbered, which correspond to question numbers. Your task is to select the option that best replaces the numbered and/or underlined part of the passage.

  ○ Some passages will also be accompanied by graphs or other supplemental information. You will be asked questions about how the graph relates to the passage as a whole. You may also need to compare or contrast it to the passage.

  ○ Every Writing and Language passage is nonfiction, covering careers, history, social studies, humanities, or science. You don't need specific knowledge of these topics on test day—all the information will be in the passages themselves.

- **Command of Evidence questions** ask you to fix how information is organized or presented in the passage. Your goal is to edit the passage so it presents information in a clear, concise way that makes the most sense. When faced with Command of Evidence questions, think about how you can improve the way a passage presents information and makes an effective argument. These make up about 20 percent of Writing and Language questions.

  ○ Follow these steps every time you face a new passage to master Command of Evidence questions:

    1. Read the passage at your normal speed.

    2. Make quick notes as you read.

    3. Answer the line- or word-specific questions first.

    4. Use your notes as a guide for any questions that deal with a paragraph or the passage as whole.

- **Words in Context questions** give you options to keep the underlined word or change it to the best possible word for the passage. Look at the words immediately before and after the underlined word, and figure out what the author is trying to say in the sentence.

  ○ Follow these steps to master Words in Context questions:

    1. Plug the answer-choice words into the sentence to see which one sounds right

    2. if you're stuck, try to eliminate one or two answer choices so you can then make a more educated guess.

- **Analysis in History/Social Studies and in Science questions** are often accompanied by a graph—you are being tested on how well you can edit a piece of writing to explain clearly or persuade effectively. Your Analysis in History/Social Studies and in Science subscore is based on how you answer all the questions that accompany the passages.

- **Expression of Ideas questions** test your skills with editing the style and tone of a piece of writing. These make up more than half of the questions on the Writing and Language test. Topics tested include the following:
  - ° Deciding whether a detail is relevant or irrelevant
  - ° Add, delete, or change text
  - ° Identify transitional language that moves effectively from one idea to another
  - ° Combining sentences to make the passage flow better
  - ° Eliminating awkward language and wordiness
  - ° Putting sentences in an order that makes more sense
  - ° Making style and tone consistent
  - ° Choosing the right words or phrasing to support the author's argument

- If an option feels wrong or sounds wrong to you, chances are you can eliminate that option and zero in on a choice that fits better within the style and tone of the passage.

- In most questions, one option will be "NO CHANGE," which means the text is fine as is. Not every question requires an improvement, so don't feel obligated to find mistakes if there are none.

Standard English Conventions

Chapter 5

OVERVIEW

- **Introduction to Standard English Conventions**
- **Conventions of Punctuation Questions**
- **Conventions of Usage Questions**
- **Sentence Structure Questions**
- **Attacking Standard English Conventions Questions**
- **Standard English Conventions Practice Questions**
- **Answer Key and Explanations**
- **Summing It Up**

As we've previously mentioned, the Writing and Language component of the PSAT/NMSQT® exam is designed to gauge your ability to recognize errors in construction, language, style, organization, and grammar and to make corrections as needed, with one key goal: to improve the writing passages provided.

The Writing and Language Test consists of two major components:

- Expression of Ideas
- Standard English Conventions

Keep in mind, Expression of Ideas and Standard English Conventions questions do not appear separately on the exam. They are blended together in the writing passages you'll encounter on test day.

INTRODUCTION TO STANDARD ENGLISH CONVENTIONS

This chapter focuses on **Standard English Conventions** and provides exactly what you need for test success: a comprehensive review of all the topics covered in this skill area and what you can expect to encounter on test day, targeted practice to get you in great test-taking shape, and expert tips, strategies, and advice—to boost your confidence and prepare you for the official PSAT/NMSQT® exam. Remember, being prepared and fully informed *before* test day arrives gives you a real advantage over other test-takers. So let's get started!

What are Standard English Conventions? They are the core rules, standards, and practices that lie at the heart of English writing and language. They are the collectively agreed upon set of guidelines for constructing phrases and sentences, connecting words and thoughts in ways that others can understand, creating written works of every imaginable genre and type, and conveying thoughts that effectively communicate your ideas. It's not difficult to see why this is such an important area—and one worth testing on an exam as important as the PSAT/NMSQT®.

Achieving Test Day Success: Pace Yourself!

The PSAT/NMSQT® Writing and Language Test is a **35-minute exam** that's comprised of **44 multiple-choice questions**. Depending on your test-taking speed, that may not be a great deal of time. Therefore, you'll need to work smart—and at an appropriate pace—in order to achieve success. Use the tools and practice in this book to effectively prepare and develop a pace that works best for you!

Standard English Conventions questions on the PSAT/NMSQT® exam fall into three main categories: conventions of punctuation, conventions of usage, and sentence structure.

Conventions of Punctuation

These questions focus on recognizing and following the rules and standards of appropriate punctuation. On test day, you can expect to encounter a wide array of punctuation issues:

- End-of-sentence punctuation, including periods, exclamation points, and question marks
- Unnecessary and superfluous punctuation
- The correct use and display of parenthetical, tangential, and nonrestrictive items in a sentence
- Series construction, including correctly displaying items in a series, and utilizing commas and semicolons for simple and complex lists
- Within-sentence punctuation, including dashes, colons, and semicolons
- Plural and possessive forms of nouns and pronouns

Conventions of Usage

These questions focus on identifying and adhering to standard writing and language practices. You should be prepared to tackle questions involving these usage issues:

- Recognizing standard conventional English-language expressions and their appropriate use
- Logical comparisons of like vs. unlike terms
- Proper subject-verb agreement
- Possessives and possessive determiners, including contractions and adverbs
- Appropriate pronoun use for clarity
- Correctly identifying and using frequently confused words

Sentence Structure

These questions focus on identifying and fixing issues involving sentence construction:

- Sentence construction and formation
- Parallel structure
- Modifier placement
- Sentence boundaries, including grammatically incomplete and ineffective sentences, inappropriate pronoun shifts, and inappropriate shifts in voice, mood, and verb tense

On test day, you'll encounter issues related to these core topics in a series of carefully constructed passages. Each writing passage will contain a set of targeted multiple-choice questions designed to measure your abilities in these subject areas.

Some questions will refer to underlined portions of text within the passages; others will ask you to consider *adding*, *eliminating*, or *revising* text within the passage to align the writing with the core standards of English writing—always with the goal of improving each passage and making it a more appropriate and effective piece.

We'll now take an in-depth look at the topics that comprise each of the three main categories, along with expert advice and strategies for tackling the types of questions you can expect to encounter on test day. Along the way, you'll also get examples and practice to help you master these concepts and bring your PSAT/NMSQT® score goals within reach.

TIP

The knowledge and skills you've acquired in your English classes will serve you well when tackling Standard English Conventions questions on the PSAT/NMSQT® exam. Use these—and the information in this chapter—to your advantage!

CONVENTIONS OF PUNCTUATION QUESTIONS

At this point in your academic career, you're well aware of the importance of good punctuation. Without it, a piece of writing can devolve into an incoherent and confusing mess.

On the PSAT/NMSQT® exam, Conventions of Punctuation questions will measure your ability to tackle some familiar concepts—including the rules of within-sentence and end-of-sentence punctuation, plural and possessive forms of pronouns and nouns, proper use of nonrestrictive and parenthetical items, and how to assemble items in simple and complex lists. You can expect to encounter a wide array of punctuation issues within the writing passages. It will be your job to identify and fix them appropriately.

Let's take a look at a sample Conventions of Punctuation question that you might encounter on test day:

> Simone was excited about seeing the new exhibit of Egyptian tapestries at the National Art Museum while she was in town for business this week. She arrived on Tuesday and is staying for a week. On Thursday morning, she arrived at the museum and went through the entrance. She was captivated by the museum's massive size. Eager to find her chosen exhibit, she approached the nearest security guard and asked, [1] <u>"Where is the Egyptian tapestry exhibit."</u> The guard directed her to the third floor of the museum.

1. **A.** NO CHANGE
   B. "Where is the Egyptian tapestry exhibit!"
   C. "Where is the Egyptian tapestry exhibit?"
   D. "Where is the Egyptian tapestry exhibit"

This is a common punctuation question involving end-of-sentence punctuation. You'll need to know which punctuation mark is appropriate for a wide variety of sentences on test day. Let's review the underlined quote in the paragraph. If you know what type of punctuation is needed here, that's great—select the answer choice and move on. If you need some more time, let's keep going. The appearance of the word *where* gives us a valuable context clue: it tells us that we're dealing with a question. Now we know that we'll need a question mark to properly punctuate this sentence. Scan the answer choices, and find the correctly punctuated version to make this sentence a proper question. **The correct answer is C.** If you need to make sure, plug it into the sentence and check:

Eager to find her chosen exhibit, she approached the nearest security guard and asked, "Where is the Egyptian tapestry exhibit?"

That's correct, and you can move on with confidence!

End-of-Sentence Punctuation

TIP

Make sure you know the right punctuation for the situation. For example, a question can be asked excitedly, but it still needs to end with a question mark, not an exclamation point.

Like all good things in life, every sentence must eventually come to an end—which means that the one form of punctuation you will *always* see in every complete sentence is end-of-sentence punctuation.

These are probably the very first punctuation marks you learned about:

The period (.): Good for ending most declarative sentences.

1. Example: *Samara returned her physics books to the Northville Regional Library on time.*

The exclamation point (!): Used for ending exclamations, usually to indicate extreme excitement.

2. Example: *I've just been told that I won the grand prize in the annual raffle contest!*

The question mark (?): Absolutely necessary punctuation for ending questions.

3. Example: *Do you know the quickest route to the art museum?*

End-of-sentence punctuation is usually pretty straightforward. You probably already know that you shouldn't end a question with a period or an exclamation with a question mark.

Things get slightly trickier when **quotation marks** are added to the punctuation mix. End-of-sentence punctuation usually belongs *inside* the quotation marks. For example:

Damon asked Shana, "What time is our study group meeting this afternoon?"

Exceptions to the rules do occur, so be careful on test day. For example, when the quotation marks indicate a title, placing end-of-sentence punctuation within the marks might give the impression that the mark is part of the title, as in this example:

Have you seen the movie "The Stranger Returns"?

Commas

Commas are among the most common—and misused—forms of punctuation, so let's take a careful look at them. Some writers overuse **commas**, and using them without rhyme or reason can make your sentences awkward or confusing.

Here's an example of a sentence with way too many commas:

After, Pablo finished dinner with his family, he packed his gym bag, and, drove to football practice.

It's quite a confusing mouthful, and it's a bit difficult to figure out what's happening. Let's take a look at the corrected version:

After Pablo finished dinner with his family, he packed his gym bag and drove to football practice.

This version is much easier to follow, and it only requires one comma!

While there is the odd situation in which the use of a comma is up to the writer, there are almost always very clear rules for comma use. Let's look at some of the most important ones.

Introductory or Transitional Words and Phrases

Commas should be used to offset **introductory words or phrases** from the words that follow, as in the following example:

Unfortunately, Sarah couldn't finish the marathon after she sprained her ankle.

Compound Sentences

Compound sentences consist of two independent clauses, which means that each part of the sentence could be a complete sentence on its own. Each independent clause in a compound sentence with a conjunction needs a comma to separate it.

For example:

Fred is a virtuoso on the clarinet, but Michelle prefers to play the saxophone.

Fred is a virtuoso on the clarinet is the first independent clause. *Michelle prefers to play the saxophone* is the second independent clause. The conjunction is *but* and a comma is used to separate those clauses correctly.

Nonrestrictive Phrases

A **nonrestrictive phrase** is not essential to the meaning of the sentence and should be separated with one comma if it comes at the beginning or end of the sentence and two commas if it is placed in the middle.

Read this sentence:

Dylan's new winter jacket, which has a detachable hood, is perfect for snowboarding.

This sentence would still make sense without the phrase *which has a detachable hood*. It would read *Dylan's new winter jacket is perfect for snowboarding*, which is a perfectly fine sentence. This means

TIP

Commas are *not* needed to separate dependent clauses in complex and compound-complex sentences.

the phrase is nonrestrictive (or nonessential) and should be enclosed in commas. However, if that phrase were restrictive—or essential to the meaning of the sentence—no commas would be needed: *Dylan's new winter jacket with the detachable hood is perfect for snowboarding.*

Series and Lists

Each item in a **simple series or list** should be separated by a comma.

For example:

Tammy bought a new purse, dress, and makeup case at the mall on Tuesday.

In this sentence, a comma also precedes the conjunction *and*, also known as a **serial or Oxford comma**, although this is not a hard and fast rule. Some writers prefer not to use that extra comma. So, the following sentence is also technically correct:

Tammy bought a new purse, dress and makeup case at the mall on Tuesday.

For more complex lists of items, **semicolons** are often used, as in the following example:

I follow the same routine each morning: I get out of bed at 7:00 am; I take a shower; I make breakfast for myself, my cat, and my sister; and I make sure I have my homework, pens, and notebook in my backpack.

When multiple verbs refer to multiple items in a series within a single sentence, you can see how semicolons can come in handy to keep things organized.

Appositives

An **appositive** is a phrase that describes a noun. An appositive contains a noun or pronoun and often one or more modifiers and appears directly before or after the noun it describes. Appositives need to be separated with commas.

For example:

Barry's new puppy Pearl, a silly tan pug, keeps getting into trouble.

In this sentence, the appositive is *a silly tan pug*, and commas are used to separate it correctly.

Quotations

When quoting a complete phrase that someone said, **quotation marks** are needed, and one or more commas is required to separate it from the rest of the sentence. See how the commas are used in these examples:

Cynthia said, "That novel was the worst one I've read this year."

"That novel was the worst one I've read this year," Cynthia said.

"That novel," Cynthia said, "was the worst one I've read this year."

However, if that quotation includes end-of-sentence punctuation, a comma is not needed at the end of it.

TIP

Passages on the PSAT/NMSQT® exam use a comma before a conjunction, but you will not be expected to answer questions about such situations without concrete rules.

For example:

"That novel was the worst one I've read this year!," Cynthia said. **(Incorrect!)**

"That novel was the worst one I've read this year!" Cynthia said. **(Correct!)**

Apostrophes and Possession

Apostrophes are most often used to indicate that a word is a contraction or to show possession in a sentence.

The correct use of apostrophes in **contractions** mostly depends on placing the apostrophe in the right place within a word:

Ca'nt **(Incorrect!)**

Can't **(Correct!)**

You'll also need to recognize when a word that looks like a contraction is not a contraction:

it's (a contraction of *it is*)

its (the possessive form of *it*)

Using apostrophes in possessive words is a little trickier. For the most part, the apostrophe will be placed before the letter *-s*.

For example:

Jonah's guitar

the otter's offspring

However, if the possessive word ends with an *s*, the apostrophe belongs after the *-s*.

For example:

the glasses' lenses

the cactus' spikes

This rule is different when a specifically named person is doing the possessing. For people whose names end in *s*, an apostrophe and an extra *s* are required.

For example:

Lois's car

James's new hoverboard

When more than one noun is doing the possessing, only the last noun in the pair or list needs an apostrophe.

For example:

Myriam and Leslie's sleepover party

The florist and jeweler's shared entrance

Colons

Colons are typically used to introduce a list or series of examples:

> *Miranda brought everything she needed for her upcoming vacation in Paris: her passport, suitcase, and travel guide.*

Colons are also used to offset and emphasize an example:

> *My favorite foreign film ends on a sad note: sometimes love doesn't last forever.*

They can also be placed after a salutation in a letter:

> *To Whom It May Concern:*

And can be used to separate a title from a subtitle in a piece of work like a book or movie:

> *The Mysterious Visitor: Part II*

However, colons should *not* be used to separate objects and verbs or prepositions and objects:

> **Incorrect:** This new TV show is: boring.

> **Correct:** This new TV show is boring.

Semicolons

Don't forget that colons and semicolons are not interchangeable. Each punctuation mark has its own function.

Semicolons can be used in place of conjunctions in compound sentences, joining the independent clauses just as *and, or, but,* or *because* would.

For example:

Archie was nervous about the biology presentation; he had no reason to worry.

As previously mentioned, semicolons are also used in complex lists that contain items with commas, to keep the list from becoming confusing.

For example:

> *This fancy pizza contains only the very best ingredients: olives, which I bought at the outdoor market; basil, which I grew in a pot in my kitchen; and three kinds of cheese, which I got from the best gourmet market in town.*

Dashes

Much like commas, **dashes** tend to get overused and misused. A big problem with dashes is that they're almost never *absolutely necessary* according to the rules of mechanics, so a lot of writers just aren't sure what to do with them. You're about to become one of the lucky few who knows when to use them!

Like the colon, a dash can be used to offset and emphasize a single example:

> *I know whom I would I trust to find me if I were lost in the woods—my dog, Tico.*

Dashes are also useful for indicating a pause or interruption in dialogue, and two dashes can be used to separate an example or examples in the middle of a sentence:

My lunch this afternoon had everything I like—meatballs, melted cheese, and toasted bread—and I couldn't stop eating it!

Parentheses

Sometimes, a few extra details are needed to make a sentence as informative as it can be—but those details aren't always easy to cram into the natural flow of the sentence. In such cases, parentheses are in order. **Parentheses** are often used to enclose additional examples that tend to be a little less relevant to a sentence than the ones you'd place between dashes.

For example:

The Baltimore Orioles (my favorite baseball team) have the best record in the entire league this season.

Unnecessary Punctuation

Altering a piece of writing so it is free from unnecessary or incorrect punctuation is important for making sure it clearly expresses its intended meaning and tone. Just as missing punctuation can lead to awkwardness and confusion, unnecessary punctuation can have the same effect.

Let's look at an example:

Once, the wolf reached the peak of the high, cliff it howled at, the slowly, setting sun.

Don't be concerned if you had trouble reading this sentence. Did the wolf just howl once? What exactly is "the peak of the high"? The meaning and flow of this sentence is clearly being disrupted by its inappropriate punctuation. Its abundance of unnecessary commas makes it confusing and obscures its intended meaning. Commas are among the most overused—and misused—types of internal punctuation, so on test day you should always be on the lookout for unnecessary commas and other forms of punctuation. Let's look at a corrected version of our example:

Once the wolf reached the peak of the high cliff, it howled at the slowly setting sun.

This version is *much* easier to follow and understand.

Make sure you fully understand the Conventions of Punctuation concepts covered here before moving on. Use the examples provided to help ensure that you've mastered these concepts in practice. When you have, use the practice toward the end of the chapter to gauge your skills and guide your preparation moving forward. When you're ready to tackle Conventions of Usage, keep reading!

CONVENTIONS OF USAGE QUESTIONS

Following the rules of sound grammar and usage is essential—in school, in life beyond the classroom, and on the PSAT/NMSQT® exam. Conventions of Usage questions will test your ability to tackle some extremely important writing and language concepts—including the proper use of possessives and determiners, subject-verb agreement, logical comparisons, recognizing conventional English language expressions and their appropriate use, proper pronoun use, and correctly identifying and using frequently confused words.

TIP

Do not skip over portions of passages just because they're not numbered. Sentences that don't correspond to questions directly may contain valuable context clues—and may help you find the correct answers!

TIP

While incorrect punctuation won't necessarily make a sentence sound wrong, poor grammar almost certainly will. Thinking about how sentences sound can help you select the best answers to usage questions.

These questions can appear in a variety of formats on test day; some will be obvious and others will be subtle. This section covers the most essential usage concepts—the ones that you'll need to know and use on test day. Use the practice and review in this chapter to sharpen your skills and get test-ready.

Let's take a look at a sample Conventions of Usage question that you might encounter on test day:

> The school crossing guard waits patiently at the corner for the next group of students who need to cross the street. The students approach and gather at the crosswalk. When the crossing guard gives them the "okay" signal, they begin to move across the street. One of the students [2] race across the street, in front of the others, much to the crossing guard's dismay. That student receives a stern warning about street safety from the crossing guard.

2. **A.** NO CHANGE

   B. races across

   C. racers across

   D. racing across

TIP

Always be on the lookout for answer choices you can quickly eliminate. Even if you're not completely sure of the correct answer, doing so can greatly increase your chances of choosing correctly.

This is a common subject-verb agreement question. Sentences with correct agreement have their subjects and verbs aligned in both form and tense. Let's take a look at the underlined portion of the sentence. A quick scan of the answer choices shows us that a variety of forms of the verb *to race* are on display. This signals us that it's our job to determine the correct verb form needed here in order to correctly answer the question. We first need to determine *who* or *what* is performing the action in order to determine the appropriate verb form for the sentence. Here, *one of the students*, a singular noun, is moving across the street, so the present tense of the singular form of the verb *to race* is needed.

Scan the answer choices and see if you can find the correct singular present verb form for *to race*. In fact, one of the answer choices—choice C—isn't even a verb (*racers*). It's actually a noun, so it can be quickly eliminated.

For this example, **the correct answer is B.** If you need to make sure, plug it into the sentence and check:

> *One of the students races across the street, in front of the others, much to the crossing guard's dismay.*

That's correct, and you can move on with confidence!

Nouns

The subject of any sentence is always a **noun**: the person, place, or thing performing the action that the sentence describes. Some Conventions of Usage questions on the PSAT/NMSQT® exam will likely involve subjects of sentences, often in terms of how they agree with verbs or pronouns.

Before we discuss how nouns interact with other words, let's look at some specific noun forms.

Plural Nouns

The nice thing about nouns is that they really only have two general forms: singular and plural.

- The **singular** form is the most basic: *toad, phone, book, banana,* and *turkey*—these are all nouns in their most basic singular forms.

Making a singular noun **plural** is often as simple as adding the letter *s* to the end (for example: *cup–cups*). Plural nouns get tricky only when they are *irregular*—hard-and-fast rules for creating irregular plural nouns are often tough to apply to a language as complicated as English. We can't simply say that you're *always* safe adding -*es* to the end of all nouns that end in -*o* to make them plural. For example, the plural of *avocado* is *avocados*.

While you're not expected to memorize every single irregular verb for the PSAT/NMSQT® exam, it's a good idea to familiarize yourself with some of the most common, which appear in the following table.

COMMON IRREGULAR PLURAL NOUNS

Noun ends with-	Creating the plural form	Examples
-*f*	change *f* to *v* and add -*es*	**singular**: calf **plural**: calves **singular**: elf **plural**: elves **singular**: half **plural**: halves **singular**: leaf **plural**: leaves **singular**: shelf **plural**: shelves **singular**: thief **plural**: thieves **singular**: wolf **plural**: wolves
-*fe*	change *f* to *v* and add -*s*	**singular**: knife **plural**: knives **singular**: life **plural**: lives **singular**: wife **plural**: wives

Noun ends with-	Creating the plural form	Examples
-is	change to *-es*	**singular:** axis **plural:** axes **singular:** analysis **plural:** analyses **singular:** parenthesis **plural:** parentheses
-o	add *-es*	**singular:** echo **plural:** echoes **singular:** hero **plural:** heroes **singular:** potato **plural:** potatoes **singular:** tomato **plural:** tomatoes
-ous	change to *-ice*	**singular:** louse **plural:** lice **singular:** mouse **plural:** mice
-s	add *-es*	**singular:** class **plural:** classes **singular:** boss **plural:** bosses
-us	change to *-i*	**singular:** alumnus **plural:** alumni **singular:** fungus **plural:** fungi

There are a few other variations of irregular plural nouns that do not involve changing the last letter or two of the singular form. Fortunately, most of these should be very familiar to you.

Nouns that require *-oo-* to be changed to *-ee-* for their plural form:

singular: foot	**plural:** feet
singular: goose	**plural:** geese
singular: tooth	**plural:** teeth

Nouns that require the addition or substitution of *-en* for their plural form:

singular: child	**plural**: children
singular: man	**plural**: men
singular: ox	**plural**: oxen
singular: woman	**plural**: women

Finally, there are the nouns that require no change whatsoever to become plural:

singular: deer	**plural**: deer
singular: fish	**plural**: fish
singular: offspring	**plural**: offspring
singular: series	**plural**: series
singular: sheep	**plural**: sheep
singular: species	**plural**: specics

Collective Nouns

Collective nouns are interesting because they seem like plural nouns since they seem to describe more than one thing.

For example:

- a bunch of sightseers in a *group*
- a group of soldiers in a *squadron*
- several seagulls in a *flock*

However, while the individual nouns in these collections are plural (*sightseers, soldiers, seagulls*), the collections themselves are singular (*group, squadron, flock*). This means that collective nouns must *always* be treated as singular nouns. This will be particularly important when we deal with subject-verb agreement and noun-pronoun agreement in the next section.

Familiarize yourself with some common collective nouns. Remember, all of these nouns are singular, not plural:

army	audience	band	board	class
committee	company	corporation	council	department
faculty	family	firm	flock	group
herd	jury	majority	navy	public
school	senate	society	team	unit

Agreement

When words in a sentence agree, things tend to go smoothly. When they don't, there can be trouble. You can ensure that the elements in sentences don't clash by recognizing when they are—and aren't—in agreement.

Subjects and **verbs** need to agree in terms of number. The same is true of **pronouns** and **antecedents**, which also need to agree in terms of gender.

Subject/Verb Agreement

Every complete sentence has a **subject** and a **verb**. The subject is the noun doing the action. The verb is the action that the subject is doing. Simple, right? Actually, it can be—a sentence with just a subject and a verb can be really simple.

For example:

> *The kangaroo jumps.*

That sentence has only three words, but it's still a complete sentence because it has a subject and a verb. Just as important, the subject and verb agree: the singular subject *kangaroo* agrees with the singular verb *jumps*. (That's right: the verb is singular even though it ends with the letter -*s*.)

Determining whether or not subjects and verbs are in agreement can get a little more complicated in sentences with compound subjects.

For example:

> *The kangaroo and the tarantula jump.*

Neither *kangaroo* nor *tarantula* ends with an-*s*, so they may not look plural, but they work together as a **compound subject** when joined with a conjunction (*and*). This means that they require a plural verb and, as you may have guessed, the plural verb does not end in an extra -*s*.

However, if the conjunction were *or* or *nor*, a singular verb would be required.

For example:

> *Neither the kangaroo nor the tarantula jumps.*

Once again, the compound subject and verb are in agreement.

When dealing with collective nouns, the agreement rule depends on what the collective noun is doing. If every member of the collective noun is doing the exact same thing, it is operating as a single unit and the verb should be singular.

For example:

> *The team meets on Sunday.*

However, if all the members of that team are doing their own things, those members should be specified and a plural verb is required:

> *After a post-meeting dinner, the team return to their homes.*

TIP

Subject-verb agreement can get confusing when there is a word or phrase between the subject and verb. Make sure you have identified the *entire* subject and verb correctly before figuring out whether or not they agree.

TIP

To avoid the debate of using plural or singular verbs with collective nouns, you can force the verb to be plural by adding *members* or *members of* to the sentence: *After a post-meeting dinner, the team members return to their homes.*

Pronoun/Antecedent Agreement

Pronouns and **antecedents** also need to play nice. A pronoun replaces a specific noun. Its antecedent is the noun the pronoun replaces. Since it would sound clumsy to say *Carrie cleans Carrie's apartment*, most writers would replace the second *Carrie* with a pronoun:

> *Carrie cleans her apartment.*

Much better, right? In this sentence, *Carrie* is the antecedent and the pronoun is *her*, a female pronoun. Both are in agreement in this sentence. It is also singular, which is appropriate since Carrie is only one woman.

Now, if the sentence read *Carrie cleans his apartment*, and we know that Carrie is a woman, it would lack pronoun-antecedent agreement in terms of gender (unless, of course, Carrie was cleaning some guy's apartment). If it read *Carrie cleans their apartment*, it would sound as if Carrie were cleaning an apartment owned by two or more people (one of which may or may not be Carrie).

However, *their* would be necessary in a sentence with a **compound antecedent**. For example, maybe Carrie shares her apartment with a friend named Winnie. Then the sentence could read *Carrie and Winnie clean their apartment*. Compound antecedents are a bit more complicated when the conjunction is *or* or *nor* instead of *and*. In such cases, you will select your pronoun based on which antecedent it is nearest.

For example:

> *Neither my friend nor my sons brought **their** coolers to the baseball game.*

> *Neither my sons nor my friend brought **his** cooler to the baseball game.*

Both of these sentences are written correctly. Since the plural antecedent *sons* is closer to the pronoun in the first sentence, the plural pronoun *their* is required. Since the singular antecedent *friend* is closer to the pronoun in the second sentence, the singular pronoun *his* is required.

Now, if your antecedent is a collective noun, selecting the right pronoun depends on what the collective noun is doing and how it is doing it. If every member of the collective noun is doing the exact same thing as a single unit, the singular pronoun is needed.

For example:

> *The research team delivered **its** presentation to the CEO effectively.*

In this example, everyone on the team is working on the same presentation, and the singular pronoun *its* is used correctly. However, if all of the members of that collective noun are doing their own things, a plural pronoun is in order.

For example:

> *The research team delivered **their** individual presentations to the CEO effectively.*

This example describes how the members of the research team handled their individual presentations, and it uses the plural pronoun *their* correctly.

Selecting Pronouns

Selecting appropriate pronouns, given the context of the sentences in which they will appear, is another challenge you should be prepared to face on the PSAT/NMSQT® exam.

Perspective will be a key factor when figuring out the best way to use pronouns on test day. Let's look at a few essential rules:

- A **first person pronoun** (*I, me, we, us*) is necessary when a writer is referring to herself or himself.
- A **second person pronoun** (*you*) is needed when the writer is addressing the reader.
- A **third person pronoun** (*she, he, her, him, they, them*) is needed when the pronoun refers to a person who is neither writing nor reading the passage.

Choosing the right pronoun can be tricky in sentences that pair pronouns with nouns. Which of the following examples is correct?

Rami and I went to buy a new laptop.

Rami and me went to buy a new laptop.

In such cases, try removing the noun and saying the sentence with just the pronoun (*I went to buy a new laptop*; *me went to buy a new laptop*). Chances are, the wrong pronoun will now seem more obvious.

Relative Pronouns

Relative clauses are like adjectives: they exist to describe. **Restrictive relative clauses** cannot stand on their own. You can recognize a relative clause from the presence of a relative pronoun. The **relative pronouns** *who, whom, whose,* and *that* all refer to people; the relative pronouns *that* and *which* refer to things.

The relative clauses in the following sentences are underlined:

Mr. Krendell, <u>who was my science teacher in the eighth grade</u>, is retiring at the end of this year.

The saleswoman <u>with whom you want to meet</u> is not in the office.

London, <u>which is where Sally went on vacation last year</u>, is located in Europe.

Reflexive Pronouns

When a subject needs a pronoun to refer to itself, a reflexive pronoun fits the bill. In fact, *itself* is a **reflexive pronoun**, as is any pronoun that ends with *self* or *selves*.

- There are five **singular reflexive pronouns**: *myself, yourself, himself, herself, itself.*
- There are three **plural reflexive pronouns**: (*ourselves, yourselves, themselves*).

Interrogative Pronouns

To interrogate is to question, and **interrogative pronouns** are used to ask questions. There are five main interrogative pronouns: *whose, who,* and *whom* refer to people exclusively; *what* refers to things exclusively; and *which* can refer to people or things.

A common confusion regarding interrogative pronouns is when to use *who* and when to use *whom*.

- *Who* is used as the **subject** of a question (example: *Who called at 3 a.m. last night?*)
- *Whom* is used as the **object** of a question (example: *To whom am I speaking?*).

The addition of the suffix *-ever* also creates six less common interrogative pronouns: *whatever, whichever, whoever, whomever, whosoever,* and *whomsoever.*

Possessive Pronouns

As mentioned previously, apostrophes are used when indicating that a noun *possesses* something. More often than not, you can just add an apostrophe and an *-s* onto the end of a word to make it possessive.

For example:

That tablet is Renee's.

There is a hockey stick in Sasha's garage.

The extra *-s* is not necessary with a possessive noun that already ends in *-s* but is not someone's name.

For example:

The lions' cubs played in the tall grass.

Those plates' design patterns are quite striking and rare.

Pronouns, however, usually have their very own forms to show possession. Since pronouns such as *his, her, its, their, my, mine, yours, their,* and *theirs* already show possession, they don't need an apostrophe or an extra *-s.*

For example:

*The backpack is **mine**.*

***Their** niece is coming to the library with us.*

***Her** cousin Rhonda is volunteering at the aquarium tomorrow.*

The only pronouns that do need that apostrophe and extra *-s* are *anybody, anyone, everybody, everyone, no one,* and *nobody.*

For example:

***Anybody's** guess is as good as mine.*

***Everybody's** time should be spent helping others.*

Verb Tense

Verbs are words that refer to action, and their **tense** indicates *when* that action happened. Did the action already happen? If so, then the verb is in the **past tense**. Are you still waiting for the action to happen? If so, then the verb is in the **future tense**.

TIP

Remember that **it's** is *not* the possessive form of *it*; it is a contraction of *it is.*

Past, present, and future are the most basic points in time. However, there are quite a few more than three verb tenses. Let's take a quick look at possible verb tenses. You won't have to know these by name on the PSAT/NMSQT® exam, but you should read through and recognize how each sounds.

- **Simple present tense** indicates an action happening now: *I am here.*

- **Present progressive tense** indicates an action happening now that will continue into the future: *I am running*.

- **Present perfect progressive tense** indicates an unfinished action: *I have been studying all day*.

- **Present perfect simple tense** indicates an action that occurred in the past but continues to be relevant: *I have never eaten lasagna.*

- **Past perfect simple tense** indicates an action that occurred in the past but is now complete: *When Vera arrived at the airport, she realized that she had misplaced her wallet.*

- **Past simple tense** indicates an action that happened already: *Last night, I thought about my childhood friends.*

- **Past progressive tense** pairs a past tense verb with a continuous verb ending in -ing: *I was laughing.*

- **Past perfect progressive tense** reflects on an ongoing action from the past: *By the 1990s, hip-hop had been a popular form of music for several years.*

- **Future simple tense** indicates an action that will happen later: *I will be at work by 9:00 a.m.*

- **Future progressive tense** indicates an action that will happen later and continue: *I will be volunteering all day on Sunday.*

- **Future perfect simple tense** indicates the completion of an action that will happen later: *I will have finished vacuuming the bedroom by noon today.*

- **Future perfect progressive tense** indicates an incomplete action that will happen later: *I will have been cleaning for 4 hours by the time my parents arrive.*

Adjectives and Adverbs

As we've already established, the only *completely essential* elements of a sentence are its subject and verb.

For example:

The turtle hides.

Once again, this is a complete sentence. But is it a particularly *interesting* sentence? Writing a sentence with nothing but a subject and a verb is like making soup with nothing but water and tomatoes. Where are the other flavors, the words that give a sentence some unique and memorable character?

In a sentence, **adjectives** (words that describe nouns) and **adverbs** (words that describe verbs, adjectives, and other adverbs) add some extra sentence flavor. Think of them as the spices of a sentence. Let's add some spice to our previous example:

The nervous turtle hides humorously.

Now there's a sentence that paints a more vivid picture! The adjective *nervous* shows that the turtle may be afraid that danger is near. The adverb *humorously* shows us that the turtle must be a funny sight to see. It's certainly a more engaging sentence now.

Let's take a look at the different forms of adjectives and adverbs you should know before taking the PSAT/NMSQT® exam.

Comparative and Superlative Adjectives

Tall! Taller! Tallest! Adjectives and adverbs change form when they are used to make a comparison.

The **comparative** form is used when comparing two things.

comparative adjectives	*This tree is **larger** than the other one.*
	*Pablo feels **more energized** than he did before he rested.*
comparative adverbs	*Today's meeting seemed to go by **more quickly** than last week's meeting did.*
	*Sari is taking her test preparation **more seriously** than she ever has before.*

The **superlative** form is used when comparing three or more things.

superlative adjectives	*Bruce is the **weirdest** pet I own.*
	*Alshad is the **shortest** student in my class.*
superlative adverbs	*Out of everyone in the company, Candice works the **fastest**.*
	*This is the **fastest** I have ever run.*

As you may have noticed, simply adding *-er* to the end of comparative adjectives and *-est* to the end of superlative adjectives is not always enough. Once again, there are a number of exceptions you need to understand to use comparative and superlative adjectives correctly.

Case	Adjective	Comparative	Superlative
One- and two-syllable adjectives ending in *-e* do not need an extra *-e*	*close*	*closer*	*closest*
	large	*larger*	*largest*
	polite	*politer*	*politest*
One-syllable adjectives ending in a consonant need to have that consonant doubled	*big*	*bigger*	*biggest*
	sad	*sadder*	*saddest*
	thin	*thinner*	*thinnest*

Case	Adjective	Comparative	Superlative
One- and two-syllable adjectives ending in –y change that –y to an –i	dry	drier	driest
	heavy	heavier	heaviest
	tiny	tinier	tiniest
Certain adjectives with two or more syllables remain the same but need the addition of *more* for comparatives and *most* for superlatives	beautiful	more beautiful	most beautiful
	complete	more complete	most complete
	important	more important	most important
Irregular adjectives require their own special alterations in the comparative and superlative forms	bad	worse	worst
	far	farther	farthest
	good	better	best
	little	less	least
	many	more	most

For comparative adverbs, adding *more* is usually enough, and superlative adverbs usually only need *most*.

For example:

Lucas giggled **more nervously** than Kim did.

The bicycle rides **most smoothly** on paved roads.

As you may have guessed, there are *exceptions* to this rule, but don't worry—there aren't as many exceptions for adverbs as there are for adjectives. Any adverb that does not end in –*ly* should be treated the same way you would treat it if it were being used to modify a noun instead of a verb.

Adverb	Comparative	Superlative
bad	worse	worst
far	farther	farthest
fast	faster	fastest
good	better	best
hard	harder	hardest
little	less	least
long	longer	longest
loud	louder	loudest
many	more	most
quick	quicker	quickest
soon	sooner	soonest

One thing you need to make sure of on the PSAT/NMSQT® exam is that comparatives and superlatives are actually being used to make a comparison.

You may have seen an advertisement that boasts, *Our product is better*! Well, your product is better than what? Obviously, the implication is that the product is better than other similar products, but the comparison is not correct and complete if that information is not stated directly, as follows:

Our product is better than other similar products!

This may not be the catchiest slogan in the world, but it is a more complete comparison. Remember that incomplete comparisons are incorrect when you're reading Writing and Language passages on the PSAT/NMSQT® exam.

Conventional Expressions

For some students, **conventional expressions** or **idioms** can be confusing because they use words to mean something other than their literal meanings.

For example, if you were to *pull the wool over someone's eyes*, you probably would not *literally* grab a wool scarf and pull it over that person's eyes. However, you may *deceive* them, which is the idiomatic meaning of *pull the wool over someone's eyes*. See what we mean? Idioms can be tricky.

Idiom questions on the PSAT/NMSQT® exam often require you to identify mistakes in their wording. So, even if you don't know what the idiom *bite off more than you can chew* means, you may still have heard it before, and you should be able to recognize that *bite off more than you can see* is not a correctly composed idiom (you may also deduce that biting with your eyes is both difficult and uncomfortable).

Here are some other common idioms that you may encounter:

Idiom	Meaning
Actions speak louder than words.	What one does is more important than what one says.
Back to the drawing board	Time to start all over again!
Barking up the wrong tree	Making the wrong choice
Beat around the bush	Avoid the topic
Bite off more than you can chew	To take on too large a task
Costs an arm and a leg	Very expensive
Cry over spilled milk	Complain about something that cannot be changed
Under the weather	Feel ill
Has a lot on the ball	Is very competent
Hit the sack	Go to bed
Kill two birds with one stone	Accomplish two tasks with a single action

TIP

A good way to become familiar with a wide variety of idioms is to read a lot in your daily life. Writers love to use idioms, and the more you see them, the more comfortable you'll be in facing them on test day.

Idiom	Meaning
Let sleeping dogs lie	Do not provoke a potentially unpleasant situation
Let the cat out of the bag	Reveal a secret
Piece of cake	Easy
Take with a grain of salt	Not take something too seriously
The whole nine yards	Everything

Prepositional Phrases

Prepositions indicate time and direction and are pretty straightforward. **Prepositional phrases**, however, are a bit less straightforward. In fact, they're very similar to idioms in that they cannot be explained with simple rules—you just have to get familiar with them and decide what works best. A prepositional phrase combines a preposition with one or more words. For example, *at home* is a common prepositional phrase. Technically, there is nothing grammatically wrong with saying *in home* (*I didn't go to the park last weekend; I was in home*). However, it simply isn't common to say *I was in home*, and you'll need to be aware of the most commonly used prepositional phrases on test day. Here are a few common prepositions you should remember:

among friends	at work	in the grass	in your mind
at home	at the beach	in the room	on the lawn
at the office	in my heart	in the tree	on the road
at play	in the doorway	in the window	on the roof
at school	in the family	in the yard	on your mind

Frequently Confused Words

The English language contains many **frequently confused words**—words that may look or sound alike but have completely different meanings, so using them interchangeably in your writing can have serious negative consequences. You may encounter these tricky word pairs on the PSAT/NMSQT® exam, and you should be able to identify the correct word required in a sentence given the context.

The following is a list of frequently confused words that you should be aware of—and on the lookout for—on test day.

accept	to receive something
except	the exclusion of something
advice	a recommendation to follow
advise	to recommend something

affect	to influence (*verb*) or an emotional response (*noun*)
effect	a result (*noun*) or to cause (*verb*)
allude	to make an indirect reference to
elude	to successfully avoid
altogether	thoroughly
all together	everyone or everything in a single place
accent	a pronunciation common to a region
ascent	the act of rising or climbing
assent	consent or agreement
brake	a device for stopping a vehicle
break	to destroy into pieces
capital	a major city
capitol	a government building
coarse	feeling rough
course	a path or an academic class series
complement	something that completes another thing
compliment	praise or flattery
conscience	a sense of morality
conscious	awake or aware
dessert	final course in a meal, typically sweet
desert	to abandon
desert	a dry and sandy area
die	to lose life; one of a pair of dice
dye	to change or add color toneflix
hear	to sense sound using an ear
here	in this particular place
hole	an opening
whole	a complete and entire thing
its	the possessive form of *it*
it's	a contraction for *it is*

lead	a type of metal substance
led	past tense of *to lead*
lead	(pronounced *leed*) to guide
loose	not tightly fastened
lose	to misplace
metal	a type of hard substance
medal	an object given in recognition of an accomplishment
mettle	courage or spirit
miner	a worker in a mine
minor	an underage person (*noun*) or less important (*adj.*)
peace	free from war
piece	part of a whole
pedal	a foot-operated lever used for control, as in one found in a vehicle (*noun*) or to move by using the pedals of a vehicle (*verb*)
petal	part of a flower
peddle	to sell
personal	intimate or owned by a person
personnel	employees or staff
plain	simple and unadorned
plane	to shave wood (*verb*) or an aircraft (*noun*)
precede	to come before
proceed	to continue
presence	attendance
presents	gifts
principal	foremost (*adj.*); head figure of a school (*noun*)
principle	a moral conviction or basic truth
reign	to rule
rein	a strap to control an animal (*noun*), or to guide or control (*verb*)
right	correct or direction opposite of left
rite	ritual or ceremony
write	to put words on paper

| road | a path |
| rode | the past tense of *to ride* |

sight	the ability to see or something worth seeing
site	place or location
cite	to document or quote (*verb*)

| stationary | standing still |
| stationery | a type of writing paper |

| than | used in comparison |
| then | at that time or next |

their	possessive form of *they*
there	in a specific place
they're	contraction for *they are*

through	finished or into and out of
threw	past tense of *to throw*
thorough	complete

to	toward
too	also or very (used to show emphasis)
two	number following one

| weak | not strong |
| week | seven consecutive days |

| weather | climate conditions |
| whether | if |

| where | in which place |
| were | past tense of *to be* |

| which | one of a group |
| witch | female sorcerer |

| whose | possessive for *of who* |
| who's | contraction for *who is* |

| your | possessive for *of you* |
| you're | contraction for *you are* |

Logical Comparisons

People make comparisons all the time—both in their daily lives and in writing. The key to making logical comparisons is to make sure that the things being compared are similarly balanced and equivalent. But what happens if we make an **illogical comparison**? Illogical comparisons occur when dissimilar or illogical things are compared, leading to an awkward or confusing result—as in the following example:

Both Saria and Julio have new pet cats. Saria and Julio took their new cats to the veterinarian and had them weighed. According to the vet's scale, Saria's cat is heavier than Julio.

According to the last sentence of this paragraph, *Saria's cat* and *Julio* were weighed on the vet's scale. That certainly doesn't sound right, does it? A review of the earlier portion of the paragraph confirms this—*Saria's cat* and *Julio's cat* were weighed on the vet's scale. We have an illogical comparison to fix. Let's take a look at a corrected version:

Both Saria and Julio have new pet cats. Saria and Julio took their new cats to the veterinarian and had them weighed. According to the vet's scale, Saria's cat is heavier than Julio's cat.

Much better—the problem is solved, the illogical comparison is fixed, and all is well. Be on the lookout for illogical comparisons on the PSAT/NMSQT® exam, and be prepared to fix them.

SENTENCE STRUCTURE QUESTIONS

Sentence structure questions on the PSAT/NMSQT® exam will test your ability to tackle concepts you've covered throughout your life—both in English/language arts classes and in the writing you do in your personal life—including letters, emails, texts, notes, and more. We all know the difference between a well-constructed sentence and one that is rambling and incoherent — and which is more effective.

Let's take a look at a sample Sentence Structure question that you might encounter on test day:

> Ava was nominated to be in charge of Patterson Valley High School's annual fundraiser, which raised funds to help support the school's junior varsity sports teams. Ava was determined to beat this year's fundraising goal and had a lot to do between now and the big event. She still had to create posters to advertise the event, choose an appropriate theme, and [3] <u>decided whether</u> a bake sale or raffle would be more profitable.

3. **A.** NO CHANGE
   B. deciding whether
   C. decides whether
   D. decide whether

This is a common parallel structure question. Sentences with correct parallel structure have all of their parts moving cohesively and in the same tense and direction. You may have noticed something awkward while reading the underlined portion of the sentence. The verb *decided* is written in the *past* tense, while the other action words in the sentence (*create* and *choose*) are in the *present* tense, reflecting the fact that these activities are not yet complete. That's a problem, and on the PSAT/NMSQT® exam it's your job to find and fix such sentence structure issues.

Since the sentence establishes that these events haven't been completed yet (*She still had to...*), we can determine that the present tense is correct for the action that occurs. If you know the present tense of *to decide*, select the answer choice and move on. If you need some more time, scan the answer choices, and plug each into the sentence if needed.

For this example, **the correct answer is D**; *decide whether* is the correct form. If you need to make sure, plug it into the sentence and check:

> *She still had to create posters to advertise the event, choose an appropriate theme, and decide whether a bake sale or raffle would be more profitable.*

That's correct, and you can move on!

Bottom line: Following the rules of good sentence construction and formation helps ensure that your thoughts and ideas are properly communicated to others. The creators of the PSAT/NMSQT® exam recognize how important a skill this is, and the test is designed to make sure your skills in this area are well honed.

Clauses

Just as you can't have a sentence without a subject and verb that express a complete thought, you can't have a sentence without **clauses**.

A subject and verb that express a complete thought is a clause. It's an **independent clause**, because it can stand on its own.

> **Independent clause:** *The puma growls.*

A clause that *can't* stand on its own, even though it has its own subject and verb, is a **dependent** or **subordinate clause**.

> **Subordinate clause:** *when the gazelle leaps over the bushes*

A subordinate clause *needs* to be paired with an independent clause to be part of a complete sentence, like this:

> *The puma growls when the gazelle leaps over the bushes.*

There are four different sentence structures that you'll commonly encounter. Notice that each one *always* includes at least one independent clause.

1. A **simple sentence** has only one independent clause:

    The worm slithers.
    The rhinoceros grunts.

2. A **compound sentence** has two independent clauses that are typically joined in one of two ways:

    With a **conjunction** (for example *if*, *and*, and *but*) to connect the clauses:

    The worm slithers and the rhinoceros grunts.

    With a **semicolon**:

    The worm slithers; the rhinoceros grunts.

TIP

Be on the lookout for comma splices on test day. A semicolon is the only punctuation that can join clauses without a conjunction.

3. A **complex sentence** combines *one* independent clause and at least one subordinate clause:

   When the rain stops, the worm slithers silently in the grass.

4. A **compound-complex sentence** combines at least two independent clauses and one or more subordinate clauses:

   When the rain stops, the worm slithers silently in the grass, but the rhinoceros grunts loudly while it plays in the mud pond.

Conjunctions

You may have noticed the important role that **conjunctions** play in various sentence structures. They are the words that connect clauses and phrases in sentences and help writers clearly and effectively communicate sentences with multiple thoughts and ideas.

When a conjunction joins independent clauses of equal importance, it is known as a **coordinating conjunction**.

For example:

The hamburger was fantastic, but the fries were horrible.

In this compound sentence, *but* is the coordinating conjunction. If you divide the sentence before and after the coordinating conjunction, you will still have two independent clauses of equal importance:

For example:

The hamburger was fantastic.

The fries were horrible.

If a conjunction joins a subordinate clause to an independent clause, it is known as a **subordinating conjunction**.

The vacation that I didn't want to take was actually amazing.

In this sentence, the subordinate clause is *that I didn't want to take*, which is not a complete sentence on its own. The subordinating conjunction is *that*.

Here are some other common coordinating and subordinating conjunctions that you can expect to encounter on the PSAT/NMSQT® exam:

Coordinating Conjunctions	Subordinating Conjunctions
and but, for, nor, or, so, yet	after, although, as, because, before, even though, if, since, that, though, unless, until, when, whenever, whereas, wherever, whether, while, who, why

Fragments and Run-ons

Two of the most common sentence structure errors are **fragments** and **run-ons.** Be on the lookout for these on test day, and make sure you know how to fix them.

A **fragment** is a piece of a sentence and is not complete on its own.

For example:

Walking on the street.

Who was walking on the street? We'll never know until we fix this sentence fragment. This sentence needs a subject, as follows:

The merry mailman is walking on the street.

Mystery solved! The subject-verb pair *mailman is* rescued this sentence from the confusing fragment heap.

Run-on sentences are the opposite of fragments, but they are just as incorrect. They are full of words, but their lack of coherent structure keeps them from expressing ideas clearly.

For example:

The amateur sprinter is jogging on the track, the chilly autumn morning.

This run-on sentence needs a preposition to join its first and second parts (that comma splice does not do the job on its own):

The amateur sprinter is jogging on the track during the chilly autumn morning.

Now it's a clearly expressed thought!

Modifiers

Modifiers, such as adjectives and adverbs, and descriptive phrases and clauses need to be placed correctly in sentences. Otherwise, you can end up with some *very* bewildering thoughts.

Two common modifier issues that you can expect to encounter on the PSAT/NMSQT® exam are misplaced modifiers and dangling modifiers. Let's examine them more closely.

A **misplaced modifier** creates confusion because it's not placed next to the word it's supposed to modify.

For example:

Lawrence walked across the floor because he didn't want to carefully disturb his brother napping in the room below his.

In this sentence, the modifier *carefully* is not where it should be. In fact, its placement makes it seem as though he didn't want to disturb him in a careful way. How do you carefully disturb someone? You have to be conscious and careful about where information is placed in sentences.

The adverb *carefully* would be put to better use modifying *walked*:

Lawrence walked carefully across the floor because he didn't want to disturb his brother napping in the room below his.

Excellent! In this sentence, the modifier *carefully* is no longer misplaced.

Dangling modifiers are often more confusing than misplaced ones. The object they are meant to modify is nowhere in the sentence. Take a look at this sentence:

TIP

Sometimes writers intentionally break the rules and use fragments and run-on sentences creatively to achieve a particular effect, typically referred to as **creative license**. However, as far as the PSAT/NMSQT® Writing and Language Test is concerned, fragments and run-on sentences are *always* wrong and need to be fixed.

Walking along the beach, the ocean waves splashed gently against the pier.

The modifier in this sentence is *Walking along the beach*. But there's a problem: we don't know exactly *who* was walking along the beach. This sentence's lack of a subject leaves the modifier dangling without anything to modify. A subject needs to be added to give the modifier something to do, as follows:

Walking along the beach, Sara listened as the ocean waves splashed gently against the pier.

The addition of the subject *Sara* gives the phrase *Walking along the beach* something to modify.

Parallel Structure

Sentences with correct **parallel structure** have all of their parts moving cohesively and in the same tense and direction. You can't place a word or phrase that's going backward into the past with one that's moving into the future. **Parallel structure** crumbles when groups of words combine different types of phrases, clauses, and parts of speech.

For example:

On Thursday afternoon, I will pay my phone bill, finish my term paper, and went to the post office.

This sentence begins by describing things that are going to happen in the future—*On Thursday afternoon* to be precise. Everything is smooth until that final phrase: *went to the post office*. It's written in the *past tense*, which violates the parallel structure of a sentence that is otherwise written in the *future tense*. Let's take a look at a revised version of the sentence:

On Thursday afternoon, I will pay my phone bill, finish my term paper, and go to the post office.

This version corrects the parallel structure by putting the phrase *went to the post office* into the future tense (*go to the post office*), where it belongs.

Interestingly, a sentence *does not* need to be written entirely in the same tense to be correct. It just needs to be structured correctly.

For example: The sentence *I ate a burrito yesterday, and I am going to eat a sandwich tonight* does *not* violate the rules of good parallel structure.

Correlative Conjunctions

You need to be mindful of parallel structure when dealing with **correlative conjunctions**. These are conjunctions that work in pairs: *either… or*, *neither… nor*, and *not only… but also*. Mixing correlative conjunctions is another violation of parallel structure.

For example:

Neither the pasta or the prime rib could satisfy my dinner cravings.

Neither indicates a negative and *or* indicates a positive. So what does this sentence mean? Do the pasta and prime rib suit the writer's cravings or don't they? We'll only know if the parallel structure is repaired:

Either the pasta or the prime rib could satisfy my dinner cravings.

So now we know this person likes the pasta *and* the prime rib.

ATTACKING STANDARD ENGLISH CONVENTIONS QUESTIONS

Now you should have a better sense of the main topics and types of Standard English Conventions questions that you'll likely encounter on the PSAT/NMSQT® Writing and Language Test. As we've said before, thorough practice and review are your best strategies for achieving your score goals on this important exam.

Let's take the next step on your test-prep journey—with practice questions in the context of a complete passage. We'll also cover proven strategies for effectively attacking questions in the answer explanations that follow.

Read the following passage and answer the questions that follow. Be sure to review the explanations for tackling each question carefully—you'll get valuable tips and strategies for answering Standard English Conventions questions on test day. Good luck!

Edward Gorey: Oddity on Display

You may not immediately recognize the name Edward Gorey, but there's a good chance you'll recognize some of the work he has become famous for. Over the course of Gorey's career as an illustrator and writer, he wrote numerous books and [1] will create countless lasting images of gothic and humorous Victorian characters and scenes, often using his characteristic rough pen and ink drawing style—images that have graced book covers, posters, advertisements and more. Let's take a closer look at the life of this unique twentieth-century American artist.

Edward Gorey was born in 1925 in Chicago and experienced the divorce of his parents as a child—which may have contributed to the plethora of [2] dark eerie and quirky family images that populated his artistic output. It has also been said that [3] Goreys creative side was influenced by his maternal grandmother, who was a greeting card writer and artist. His early years were relatively uneventful and, after studying art for a semester at the School of the Art Institute in Chicago, he eventually left and attended Harvard University; after graduating, he helped found the Poets' Theatre in Cambridge.

Across the span of his career, Gorey created over 100 darkly funny books, complete with his trademark drawing style and such curiously cunning titles as *The Wuggly Ump* and *The Eclectic Abecedarium*. Gorey classified his work as "literary nonsense" and was fond of clever word play and games, which often showed in some of the silly pseudonyms he chose to write under: Ogdred Weary, Raddory Gewe, and Dogear Wryde. Gorey was also responsible for creating a wide array of recognizable book covers and illustrations for such titles as [4] *dracula* and *the war of the worlds*, as well as a host of imaginative children's books. Gorey also had a fondness for theater and created a name for himself in the world of set and costume design—even winning a Tony Award for Best Costume Design for *Dracula*.

Gorey was generally considered a somewhat reclusive figure, spending the majority of [5] their time and life living alone on Cape Cod, Massachusetts. He was a devotee of local theater and created several productions, often featuring puppets of his own design, for nearby playhouses. Upon Gorey's death in 2000, the bulk of his estate assets went to causes to help animals—including cats, dogs, insects, and bats. It would be tough to argue against the claim that, as an artist, Gorey was a unique creative voice who truly marched to the beat of his own drum.

1. **A.** NO CHANGE

   B. will be creating

   C. created

   D. is create

2. **A.** NO CHANGE

   B. dark eerie; and quirky;

   C. dark eerie, and quirky

   D. dark, eerie, and quirky

3. **A.** NO CHANGE

   B. Goreys' creative side

   C. Gorey's creative side

   D. Goreys's creative side

4. **A.** NO CHANGE

   B. Dracula and The War of the Worlds

   C. Dracula and The War of the Worlds

   D. "dracula" and "the war of the worlds"

5. **A.** NO CHANGE

   B. her time

   C. their time

   D. his time

Use What Works Best for YOU!

All of the tips, strategies, and techniques in this book are proven to be effective for tackling the PSAT/NMSQT® exam—but you're a unique individual with a unique test-taking style. What works for someone else might not be the best strategy for you.

On your quest for PSAT/NMSQT® success, your best approach—and one of the best pieces of advice we can offer you—is to test these strategies well in advance of test day to determine if they work well for you.

Bottom line: Use what works for you, and don't spend your time on what doesn't.

Let's carefully break down and analyze the Standard English Conventions questions associated with the passage "Edward Gorey: Oddity on Display." The strategies used to tackle these questions can help you tackle the questions you'll encounter on test day.

1. **A.** NO CHANGE

   B. will be creating

   C. created

   D. is create

Attacking the question: This question is asking you to determine the appropriate verb tense given the context of the sentence. If you're unsure of what type of question you're dealing with, you can often find a clue among the answer choices. In this question, the tense of the verb *to create* is varying, which is your signal regarding what type of question this is.

Now that we know what type of question this is, the next step is to review the sentence in which the underline appears. As written (choice A), the sentence has an issue with parallel structure—the verb *wrote*, referring to Gorey's creative output during his life, is in the past tense while the verb *will create*, referring to the same person, is in the future tense. Now, we need to determine what's the correct tense for this sentence. Since the passage tells us he died in 2000, we know that using the future tense is inappropriate here; the past tense is correct for this sentence and for referring to Gorey's accomplishments while he was alive, so **the correct answer is C**. Choices B and D both contain incorrect verb forms of *to create*.

If you have time, it's always helpful to plug your answer into the sentence to check if it works:

> *Over the course of Gorey's career as an illustrator and writer, he wrote numerous books and created countless lasting images of gothic and humorous Victorian characters and scenes, often using his characteristic rough pen and ink drawing style—images that have graced book covers, posters, advertisements and more.*

Yes, that works, so you can be confident you found the correct answer!

2. **A.** NO CHANGE

   B. dark eerie; and quirky;

   C. dark eerie, and quirky

   D. dark, eerie, and quirky

Attacking the question: This question involves a simple list of items in a sentence. If you quickly recognized the issue while reading the passage and know how to fix it, that's great—quickly answer the question when you encounter it and move on. Remember, the key to developing and maintaining an effective test-taking pace is to save time on the questions that are easier for you so you can have sufficient time to tackle the more challenging questions.

If you need a bit more time to determine the correct answer, let's keep going. Remember, scanning the answer choices can help you to determine what the question is about. We can see that there are variations in comma and semicolon placement throughout the answer choices, so we have a clue that internal punctuation is the theme here.

Remember what we said in this chapter about simple lists of items in sentences—they are separated by commas. As written (choice A), the lack of commas between items creates confusion in the sentence. Choices B and C also fail to correctly separate all of the list items. Let's take a look at choice D. Each of the items in the list of adjectives—*dark, eerie, and quirky*—is correctly separated by a comma. Choice D adds some much needed "comma clarity" to the sentence, and it's the correct answer.

3. **A.** NO CHANGE

   B. Goreys' creative side

   C. Gorey's creative side

   D. Goreys's creative side

Attacking the question: This question involves the correct way to indicate possession in a sentence. In this sentence, the *creative side* that we are referring to belongs to Gorey, so we need to use the correct possessive form of this noun. Remember, apostrophes are used when indicating that a noun *possesses* something. More often than not, you can just add an apostrophe and an *-s* onto the end of the noun to make it possessive.

We can eliminate choice A, as there is no apostrophe. Choice B contains an apostrophe, but it's in the wrong place—this would only be feasible if the name ended in *-s*. Choice D adds the *–'s* to the word, but the person's name is Gorey, not Goreys. Choice C correctly adds the apostrophe to correctly indicate possession—*Gorey's*—and is the correct answer here.

4. **A.** NO CHANGE

    B. *Dracula* and *The War of the Worlds*

    C. *Dracula* and *The War of the Worlds*

    D. *"dracula"* and *"the war of the worlds"*

Attacking the question: This question requires you to recognize the correct way of writing titles of books. In preparation for test day, it's a good idea to be aware of how the titles of creative works—including movies, books, and poems—are commonly handled. Book titles are typically italicized and capitalized. Scan the answer choices and see if you can quickly find the correct answer. Choice B correctly shows how to write the titles of books:

> Gorey was also responsible for creating a wide array of recognizable book covers and illustrations for such titles as *Dracula* and *The War of the Worlds*, as well as a host of imaginative children's books.

5. **A.** NO CHANGE

    B. her time

    C. their time

    D. his time

Attacking the question: Let's place this sentence and the answer choices under our careful analytical lens. The underlined words in the sentence contain a pronoun, and the answer choices have different pronoun forms—so we can quickly determine that we need to put on our "proper pronoun cap" in order to tackle this question.

The first step in determining proper pronoun usage is to figure out the *antecedent*—the noun or nouns that the pronoun is replacing. In this sentence, the underlined pronoun refers to Gorey, who spent time living alone on Cape Cod. Which pronoun among the answer choices should replace Edward Gorey? The singular pronoun *his* should be used to replace the singular masculine noun *Edward Gorey*, so **the correct answer is D**. Let's check the sentence to confirm:

> *Gorey was generally considered a somewhat reclusive figure, spending the majority of his time and life living alone on Cape Cod, Massachusetts.*

This chapter provided you with all the tools you need to achieve success on the PSAT/NMSQT® exam—including a comprehensive review of how Standard English Conventions are tested on the exam, strategies for tackling the types of questions you'll encounter on test day, and targeted practice to build your test-taking skills

Make the most of your time between now and test day to master the concepts covered in this chapter, and you'll set yourself up for success on the PSAT/NMSQT® exam!

STANDARD ENGLISH CONVENTIONS PRACTICE QUESTIONS

Now it's time to put your Standard English Conventions skills to the test! Read and carefully analyze the following full-length writing passage. The questions that follow it are designed to test your ability to recognize and use appropriate English language conventions.

Why Do We Sleep?

Have you ever wondered why you need to [1] sleep. Most individuals end each day with a similar routine—they shut the lights to their bedrooms, climb into bed, and [2] spent the next several hours in a peaceful, unconscious sleep state. However, most of us [3] leads busy lives these days, where each precious waking hour is devoted to some essential task, so it wouldn't be surprising if you've ever wondered why humans spend so much of [4] their time—approximately one-third of our lives on average—asleep and unable to accomplish anything. For those of you who wonder about this, there are good reasons why humans engage in, and need, sleep—and for those of you who think they can short-change themselves by getting by on less sleep, keep reading and consider yourself warned.

Humans spend their entire life either asleep [5] nor awake. The average human adult requires approximately 7 to 8 hours of sleep each night to feel rested and refreshed each [6] day although this number varies based on a wide array of personal factors including age and lifestyle. For most of human history, sleep was a mystery—we knew that it was a facet of life that we all engaged in, but collectively we had little insight as to why it was so essential. This question is particularly curious [7] because: while an organism is asleep it is quite vulnerable to external dangers—from treacherous weather [8] too dangerous predators and more—so the reasons why we need to sleep must be particularly important and compelling to offset this reality. Scientists continue to learn [9] knew things and build our knowledge base on why humans—as well as nearly every other living organism on the planet—requires sleep. Endlessly intrigued about the science behind sleep, citizens will continue to benefit from [10] their ongoing work in this fascinating field. Let's take a closer look.

Learning what happens when a person or animal is deprived of sleep has helped us discover some of sleep's key benefits. Numerous studies have shown that organisms who undergo sleep deprivation, even at modest levels, begin to experience decreased memory and cognitive abilities, and reductions in physical coordination. Serious sleep deprivation has been shown to lead to progressive body failure and even death. Scientists have studied the effects of sleep deprivation on a wide array of common activities—from driving to sports to test-taking and decision-making—and the results indicate the same thing: our brains and bodies simply don't work as well when they are deprived of sleep. In summary, there must be some regenerative quality to sleeping that helps us function at optimal levels while conscious. At times, the urge to sleep can be [11] even strong than the urge to eat.

Recent studies have shown that several essential restorative body functions occur while asleep, [12] including brain plasticity tissue repair muscle growth secretion of important growth hormones, and protein synthesis. Research also suggests that sleep allows humans to conserve precious energy during the nighttime, when resources were typically scarcer during our early history and and when temperatures are colder and more taxing to our bodies. Some scientists contend that sleep also [13] <u>had</u> a protective benefit, keeping humans safer and less vulnerable to injury and physical harm during the night, when our senses are compromised by darkness—anyone who has ever tripped and fallen in a dark room could support this notion.

Despite recent advances in our understanding of sleep and [14] <u>it's</u> benefits, scientists acknowledge that there's still a great deal we don't know about it, and continued research and study will help us further reveal the mysteries that surround this intriguing state of being. Indeed, some of you may be hoping that science advances to the point that we can "conquer" sleep and find a way to be able to devote a full 24 hours of our day to productive and conscious functioning. However, until that day comes, you are well advised to make time in your day to getting enough sleep so that you can function at your absolute [15] <u>weakest</u> each day.

1. **A.** NO CHANGE
   B. sleep
   C. sleep!
   D. sleep?

2. **A.** NO CHANGE
   B. spend
   C. spending
   D. spender

3. **A.** NO CHANGE
   B. lead busy life
   C. lead busy lives
   D. leads busy life

4. **A.** NO CHANGE
   B. his time
   C. her time
   D. your time

5. **A.** NO CHANGE
   B. but awake
   C. or awake
   D. not awake

6. **A.** NO CHANGE
   B. day, although this number varies based on a wide array of personal factors,
   C. day; although this number varies based on a wide array of personal factors;
   D. day. Although this number varies based on a wide array of personal factors.

7. **A.** NO CHANGE
   B. because while
   C. because; while
   D. because, while

8. **A.** NO CHANGE
   B. to
   C. two
   D. through

9. **A.** NO CHANGE
   B. know
   C. now
   D. new

10. A. NO CHANGE
    B. our
    C. scientists'
    D. student's

11. A. NO CHANGE
    B. much strong
    C. less strongest
    D. even stronger

12. A. NO CHANGE
    B. including brain plasticity, tissue repair, muscle growth,
    C. including brain plasticity; tissue repair and muscle growth;
    D. including, brain, plasticity tissue, repair, muscle growth

13. A. NO CHANGE
    B. has
    C. have
    D. having

14. A. NO CHANGE
    B. they're
    C. your
    D. its

15. A. NO CHANGE
    B. nearest
    C. peak
    D. smallest

ANSWER KEY AND EXPLANATIONS

Standard English Conventions

1. D	4. A	7. B	10. C	13. B
2. B	5. C	8. B	11. D	14. D
3. C	6. B	9. D	12. B	15. C

1. **The correct answer is D.** This question is testing your ability to recognize appropriate end-of-sentence punctuation, given the context of the sentence. Let's take a closer look at the sentence under review. It is asking if you've ever wondered why you need to sleep. The fact that you're being asked something should signal you that you are being posed a question—and that means you need a question mark to finish this sentence properly. Choice D correctly includes a question mark at the end of the sentence and is the correct answer. Choice A incorrectly uses a period. Choice B incorrectly leaves off all end punctuation. Choice C incorrectly uses an exclamation point, which should be reserved for exclamations, surprises, and extreme emotional reactions.

2. **The correct answer is B.** This question is testing your ability to recognize and fix issues involving parallel verb structure. Perhaps you noticed that, as written (choice A), the underlined verb *spent* is in the past tense, while the other verbs in the series are in the present tense. Actions in a series should be in the same tense in order to reflect parallel structure. So, we now know that we need to put *spent* into the present tense. *Spend* (choice B) is in the correct present tense and is the correct answer here. Choice C is in the wrong tense and is incorrect. Choice D incorrectly turns the verb into a noun.

3. **The correct answer is C.** This question is measuring your ability to recognize correct subject-verb agreement. In this sentence, the subject *most of us* is in plural form, so

any verb connected to it also needs to be in the plural form. Choices A and D both deploy the singular form of lead (*leads*) and are incorrect. Choices B and C both use the correct plural verb form (*lead*) but use different forms of *life*. Since we're still referring to the plural subject *most of us*, we need to ensure that this word is also in the appropriate plural form. Choice C uses the correct plural form, *lives*, and is the correct answer here. Choice B incorrectly uses the singular form *life*.

4. **The correct answer is A.** In this question, you're being tasked with choosing the correct pronoun form to match the antecedent. In this sentence, the underlined pronoun is meant to take the place of the antecedent humans, a plural noun, so a plural pronoun is needed here. Choice A correctly deploys the plural pronoun *their* and is the correct answer. Choices B, C, and D incorrectly use singular pronoun forms.

5. **The correct answer is C.** This question is designed to test your ability to recognize the appropriate use of correlative conjunctions. As mentioned previously, you need to be mindful of parallel structure when dealing with correlative conjunctions; mixing them violates parallel structure. Most correlative conjunctions are recognizable word pairs: *either… or, neither… nor*, and *not only… but also*. In this example, the author is making the point that humans spend their lives in *either* of two states—asleep or awake. The correct word to accompany *either* and complete the correlative conjunction is *or*,

choice C. Choices A, B, and D all deploy incorrect words to complete the correlative conjunction.

6. **The correct answer is B.** This sentence is tasking you with fixing a run-on sentence (choice A) with appropriate internal punctuation. Run-on sentences can often be addressed and fixed using commas to separate an internal dependent clause, as choice B does. Let's check it to make sure it works correctly:

The average human adult requires approximately 7 to 8 hours of sleep each night to feel rested and refreshed each day, although this number varies based on a wide array of personal factors, including age and lifestyle.

That works, so we can be confident we arrived at the correct answer. Choice C incorrectly uses semicolons, which are typically used for separating complex list items. Choice D incorrectly uses periods to turn the dependent clause into a separate sentence.

7. **The correct answer is B.** This question is designed to test your ability to recognize inappropriate use of internal punctuation within a sentence. As written (choice A), the sentence deploys a colon, which is typically used to set off a list of items. However, we don't have a list of items here, so a colon is inappropriate. A semicolon (choice C) is used to separate complex list items or closely related independent clauses within a sentence, which we don't have here, so this is incorrect as well. Choice D places an unnecessary comma within the sentence and is also incorrect. In fact, no punctuation is needed here at all, and choice B is the correct answer.

8. **The correct answer is B.** Be sure to be on the lookout for commonly confused words on the PSAT/NMSQT®, as we have in this sentence. The underlined portion of the sentence contains the word *too*, which means "also" or "as well." When determining appropriate word choice, make sure you read the entire sentence, so you can make an accurate judgment regarding usage. Does *too* work here? In fact, it does not work here—we're looking at a range of items here, not an additional item, so it is an incorrect word choice given the context. *To* (choice B) is the correct word choice—when given a range of items, it often falls in the "from A to Z" format. The numerical *two* (choice C) and the word *through* (choice D) are also incorrect given the context of the sentence.

9. **The correct answer is D.** We're dealing with another word choice challenge here; in particular, it's a commonly confused words question. As written (choice A), the sentence uses the word *knew*, which is the past tense of "to know." Does that make sense given the context of the sentence? Actually, it doesn't—people don't "learn knew things" in an attempt to build their knowledge base. Is there a word among the answer choices that fits better? Choices B and C also don't fit well within the context of the sentence. *New* (choice D) makes much more sense here—in an effort to build a knowledge base, we learn *new* things.

10. **The correct answer is C.** Here, we have a sentence that at first glance may *seem* structurally correct, but let's delve deeper. When we hit the underlined pronoun in the sentence, are we sure who *their* refers to? Is it the citizen's ongoing work in the field of sleep science and research that we will all benefit from? Choice A certainly doesn't seem correct given what we're told in the rest of the paragraph and passage. Given all we're told in context, it is *scientists'* (choice C) ongoing work that all citizens will continue to benefit from. Choices B and D are incorrect given the context of the sentence and passage.

11. **The correct answer is D.** This question is challenging your knowledge of appropriate comparative adjective usage. This sentence is comparing the strength of two things—the urge to sleep and the urge to eat. Constructing a comparative adjective typically entails adding an -*er* to the end of the adjective (*stronger*), as choice D does correctly. The other answer choices utilize incorrect adjective forms.

12. **The correct answer is B.** This question is testing your ability to correctly separate items in a simple list with the appropriate punctuation within a sentence. The sentence as written (choice A), which fails to separate the list items with any punctuation, is a run-on and is incorrect. Choice B fixes the problem—the items in a simple list within a sentence should be separated by commas. Choice C incorrectly uses semicolons to separate the list items. Choice D incorrectly places commas in the sentence.

13. **The correct answer is B.** In this question, we're trying to determine the appropriate verb given the context of the sentence. As written (choice A), the past tense *had* implies that the protective benefit sleep once had no longer exists, which is incorrect. Since sleep still has the same benefits it always had, the correct verb here is *has* (choice B). Choice C incorrectly uses a plural verb form for the singular *sleep*. Choice D incorrectly uses a future verb tense for a benefit that currently exists.

14. **The correct answer is D.** At first, the sentence as written (choice A) might sound perfectly feasible, but, upon closer inspection, you may notice that the underlined portion contains an incorrect contraction. *It's* is a contraction of *it is* and does not fit in this sentence. A good way to tell if a contraction is being used correctly is to plug the spelled out version into the sentence:

Despite recent advances in our understanding of sleep and *it is* benefits, …

That doesn't make sense, so we know *it's* is wrong. We can now scan the remaining answer choices to see what fits. Choices B and C are both incorrect—they both use incorrect pronouns to replace the antecedent *sleep*. Choice D is the correct answer; *its* fits correctly within the context of this sentence.

15. **The correct answer is C.** In this question, you need to determine which word choice is most appropriate given the context. The information provided throughout the passage is meant to lead us to a clear conclusion—that getting enough sleep helps us to function at our best and most optimal levels. As written (choice A), the word *weakest* conveys the opposite meaning and is incorrect. Choices B and D don't fit in the sentence given the context. *Peak* (choice C) conveys the intended meaning and is the correct answer.

SUMMING IT UP

- The **Writing and Language Test**, one of two tests that comprise the Evidence-Based Reading and Writing section, is a **35-minute test**, and you'll answer **44 questions** that will task you with making qualitative editorial decisions designed to improve the writing passages included in the exam. The two core topic areas on the PSAT/NMSQT® Writing and Language Test are **Expression of Ideas** and **Standard English Conventions**.

- **Standard English Conventions** questions on the PSAT/NMSQT® exam fall into three main categories:

  ○ **Conventions of Punctuation questions** focus on recognizing and adhering to the rules and standards of appropriate punctuation.

  ○ **Conventions of Usage questions** focus on identifying and adhering to standard writing and language practices.

  ○ **Sentence Structure questions** focus on identifying and fixing issues involving sentence construction and sentence formation.

- **End-of-sentence punctuation** includes the period, the exclamation mark, and the question mark. When a sentence ends with quotation marks used to indicate dialogue, the end-of-sentence punctuation is placed within the quotation marks. If the quotation marks indicate a title, and placing end-of-sentence punctuation within the marks might give the impression that the mark is part of the title, the end-of-sentence punctuation is placed after the closing quotation marks.

- **Commas** are used to separate introductory words and phrases, clauses in compound sentences, nonrestrictive phrases, items in a series, appositives, and quotations.

- **Apostrophes** are used to separate letters in contractions and indicate possession. When indicating possession, an apostrophe is usually followed by the letter -*s*. However, no extra -*s* is necessary if the possessing word ends in -*s* and is not someone's name.

- **Colons** are used to introduce a list of items or offset an example.

- **Dashes** are used to offset examples and indicate a pause or interruption in dialogue.

- **Parentheses** often enclose tangential or bonus information that cannot be fit into a sentence naturally.

- Making sure that a piece of writing is free from **unnecessary punctuation** is important for ensuring that it conveys its intended meaning, thoughts, and ideas.

- **Plural nouns** do not always end with -*s*; there are several variations among plural nouns depending on the words' letters. **Collective nouns** are not plural nouns; they are singular.

- **Subjects and verbs** are in agreement when they are in the same form. They both need to be either singular or plural and not a combination of both forms.

- **Pronouns and antecedents**—the words for which the pronouns stand in—need to be in agreement. They need to agree in terms of number, gender, and person.

- **Relative pronouns** signal relative clauses, which are used to describe nouns; **reflexive pronouns** refer back to their subjects; **interrogative pronouns** are used when asking a question; **possessive pronouns** show ownership.

- **Verb tense** indicates when the action the verb describes takes place.

- **Comparative adjectives and adverbs** are used when comparing two things. They usually end in *-er*. **Superlative adjectives and adverbs** are used when comparing three or more things. They usually end in *-est*.

- **Idioms** use words to mean something other than their literal meanings.

- **Prepositional phrases** combine a preposition with other words to indicate direction and time. Their particular word often depends on common usage.

- You may encounter **frequently confused words**—words that may look or sound alike but have completely different meanings—on test day. Be prepared to identify the correct word required in a sentence, given the context.

- **Illogical comparisons** occur when dissimilar or illogical things are compared, leading to an awkward or confusing result.

- **Independent clauses** contain a subject and a verb and make sense on their own. **Subordinate clauses** cannot stand on their own, even though they contain a subject-verb pair. They must be combined with an independent clause.

- **Fragments** are partial sentences that lack either a subject or a verb. They are grammatically incorrect.

- **Run-on sentences** are grammatically incorrect compound or complex sentences that fail to link their parts with the necessary conjunction or punctuation.

- **Modifiers** are words and phrases that describe. **Misplaced modifiers** are not placed next to the words they are supposed to modify. They are grammatically incorrect. **Dangling modifiers** occur when a modifying phrase doesn't have an object to modify in the sentence.

- **Parallel structure** occurs when all groups of words in a sentence are written in the same tense and form. When such words are not in the same tense or form, the sentence is grammatically incorrect. Failing to pair correlative conjunctions correctly also violates parallel structure.

PART V
PSAT/NMSQT® MATH TEST STRATEGIES

Multiple-Choice and Grid-In Math Strategies

Chapter 6

OVERVIEW

- Why Multiple-Choice Math Is Easier
- Why Grid-Ins Are Easier Than You Think
- Multiple-Choice Question Format
- Solving Multiple-Choice Math Questions
- Know When to Use Your Calculator
- Learn The Most Important Multiple-Choice Math Tips

- Grid-In Question Format
- How to Record Your Answers
- Guessing On Grid-Ins Can't Hurt You
- Exercises: Multiple-Choice Math
- Answer Key and Explanations
- Exercises: Grid-Ins
- Answer Key and Explanations
- Summing It Up

WHY MULTIPLE-CHOICE MATH IS EASIER

How can one type of question possibly be easier than another? PSAT/NMSQT® exam multiple-choice math questions are easier than the math tests you take in class because the answers are right there in front of you. As you know from other standardized tests, multiple-choice tests always give you the answer. You just have to figure out which answer is the correct one. So, even if you aren't sure and must guess, you can use the process of elimination to narrow your choices and improve your odds.

The questions in each multiple-choice math section are arranged from easiest to most difficult. The questions don't stick to one content area. They jump around from algebra to geometry to advanced math to data analysis to statistics and back to algebra in no particular pattern and often includes real-world settings.

WHY GRID-INS ARE EASIER THAN YOU THINK

The other type of question that you will see on both the Math Test—No Calculator and Math Test—Calculator sections are grid-ins. These are officially named "student-produced responses," because you have to do the calculations and find the answer on your own; there are no multiple-choice answers from which to choose.

Many students are intimidated by grid-ins. Don't be! Grid-in questions test the exact same mathematical concepts as the multiple-choice questions. The only difference is that there are no answer choices with which to work.

The grid-in questions are in a section of their own and arranged in order of difficulty from easy to hard.

Take a Look at a Grid

The special answer grid has some very different sections. There are blank boxes at the top so you can actually write in your answer. Below the boxes are some ovals that have fraction slashes and decimal points. You fill these in if your answer needs them. The largest section has ovals with numbers in them. You have to fill in the ovals to correspond to the answer you have written in the boxes. Yes, it's a lot to think about, but once you understand how to use them, it's not a big deal.

MULTIPLE-CHOICE QUESTION FORMAT

On the PSAT/NMSQT® Math section, each set of multiple-choice math questions starts with directions and a reference section that look like this:

Directions: For Questions 1–30, solve each problem, select the best answer from the choices provided, and fill in the corresponding oval on your answer sheet. **For Questions 31–38,** solve the problem and enter your answer in the grid on the answer sheet. The directions **before question 31 will** provide information on how to enter your answers in the grid.

ADDITIONAL INFORMATION:

- The use of a calculator is **permitted only in the Math Test—Calculator section**.

- All variables and expressions used represent real numbers unless otherwise indicated.

- Figures provided in this test are drawn to scale unless otherwise indicated.

- All figures lie in a plane unless otherwise indicated.

- Unless otherwise specified, the domain of a given function f is the set of all real numbers x for which is (x) is a real number.

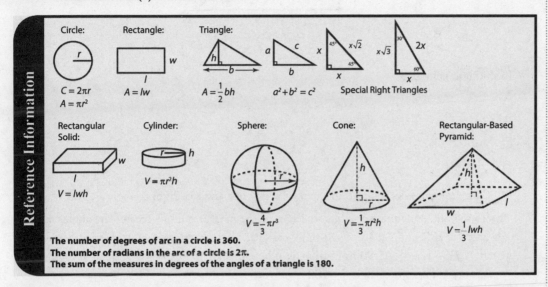

The information in the reference section should all be familiar to you from your school work. Know that it's there in case you need it. But remember: the formulas themselves aren't the answers to any problems. You have to know when to use them and how to apply them.

Some multiple-choice questions ask to solve a given equation or system of equations, while others are presented in the form of word problems. Some include graphs, charts, or tables that you will be asked to interpret. All of the questions have four answer choices. These choices are arranged in numerical order when the answers are numbers, usually from smallest to largest, but occasionally from largest to smallest.

SOLVING MULTIPLE-CHOICE MATH QUESTIONS

These five steps will help you solve multiple-choice math questions:

1. Read the question carefully and determine what's being asked.

2. Decide which math principles apply and use them to solve the problem.

3. Look for your answer among the choices. If it's there, mark it and go on.

4. If the answer you found is not there, recheck the question and your calculations.

5. If you still can't solve the problem, eliminate obviously wrong answers and take your best guess.

Now let's try out these steps on a couple of PSAT/NMSQT® exam-type multiple-choice math questions. We'll start with a geometry problem.

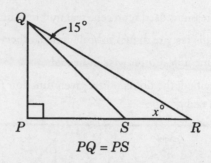

$PQ = PS$

In the figure above, $x =$

A. 15°

B. 30°

C. 60°

D. 75°

1. The problem asks you to find the measure of one angle of right triangle PQR.

2. Two math principles apply: (1) the sum of the measures in degrees of the angles of a triangle is 180, and (2) 45-45-90 right triangles have certain special properties. Since $PQ = PS$, $\triangle PQS$ is a 45-45-90 right triangle. Therefore, angle $PQS = 45°$ and angle $PQR = 45 + 15 = 60°$. Therefore, angle $x = 180 - 90 - 60 = 30°$

3. **The correct answer is B**, 30°.

Let's try the process again with an algebra question.

If x and y are negative numbers, which of the following is negative?

A. xy

B. $(xy)^2$

C. $(x - y)^2$

D. $x + y$

1. The problem asks you to pick an answer choice that is a negative number.

2. The principles that apply are those governing operations with signed numbers. Since x and y are negative, choice A must be positive. As for choices B and C, as long as x and y are not equal to each other, both expressions must be positive. (If they're equal, the expression equals zero, and any number other than zero squared gives a positive result.) Choice D, however, is negative since it represents the sum of two negative numbers.

3. **The correct answer is D.** If you have trouble working with letters, try substituting easy numbers for x and y in each choice.

See, it really doesn't matter what type of math problem it is; stay calm and follow the steps—you will navigate successfully through the Math section!

KNOW WHEN TO USE YOUR CALCULATOR

Calculators are allowed in the PSAT/NMSQT® Math Test—Calculator section, but you won't *need* a calculator to solve any PSAT/NMSQT® math questions. Calculators can be helpful in solving most of the problems, whether you use the calculator for simplifying expressions or graphing equations. But remember that your calculator is not some sort of magic brain. If you don't understand the question in the first place, the calculator won't give you a solution.

Most calculators that you would use in class are allowed. It is best to use whichever calculator you are already comfortable using instead of trying to learn how to use a new one.

The most important thing to remember is to set up your work on paper first, and then plug the information into the calculator. For example, if you have a question that deals with an equation, set up the equation on your scratch paper. Then make your number substitutions on the calculator. This way, you always have something to refer to without having to think, "Oh, no, how did I set that up?" as the seconds tick by.

When you use your calculator, check the display each time you enter numbers to make sure you entered them correctly. Make sure to hit the Clear key after each finished operation, otherwise it could get ugly.

ALERT

Don't automatically reach for your calculator. If it can't help you solve the problem, you'll just waste time fiddling with it. Save the calculator for what it does best, especially simplifying numeric expressions.

LEARN THE MOST IMPORTANT MULTIPLE-CHOICE MATH TIPS

Some of these tips you've heard before; some will be new to you. Whatever the case, read them, learn them, love them. They will help you.

The Question Number Gives A Clue As To How Hard the Question Is

Just as in most of the other PSAT/NMSQT® exam sections, the questions are arranged from easy to hard as you work toward the end. The first third of the questions is easy, the middle third is average but harder, and the final third gets progressively more difficult. Take a look at these three examples. Don't solve them yet (you'll be doing that in a couple of minutes); just get an idea of how the level of difficulty changes from Question 1 to Question 12 to Question 25.

1. If $x - 2 = 5$, then $x =$
   A. -10
   B. $\frac{5}{2}$
   C. 3
   D. 7

12. For how many integers x is $-7 < 2x < -5$?
    A. None
    B. One
    C. Two
    D. Three

25. In a set of five books, no two of which have the same number of pages, the longest book has 150 pages and the shortest book has 130 pages. If x pages is the average (arithmetic mean) of the number of pages in the five-book set, which of the following best indicates all possible values of x?

    A. $130 < x < 150$

    B. $131 < x < 149$

    C. $133 < x < 145$

    D. $135 < x < 145$

TIP

Look for shortcuts. PSAT/NMSQT® exam math problems test your math reasoning, not your ability to make endless calculations. If you find yourself calculating too much, you've probably missed a shortcut that would have made your work easier.

Can you see the difference? You can probably do Question 1 with your eyes closed. For Question 12, you probably have to open your eyes and do some calculations on scratch paper. Question 25 may cause you to wince a little, and then get started on some heavy-duty thinking.

Easy Questions Have Easy Answers—Difficult Questions Don't

The easy questions are straightforward and don't have any hidden tricks. The obvious answer is almost always the correct answer. So, for Question 1, the answer is indeed choice D.

The information for harder questions is not straightforward, and the answers aren't obvious. You can bet that your first-choice, easy answer will be wrong. If you don't believe it, let's take a look at the solution for Question 25.

25. In a set of five books, no two of which have the same number of pages, the longest book has 150 pages and the shortest book has 130 pages. If x pages is the average (arithmetic mean) of the number of pages in the five-book set, which of the following best indicates all possible values of x and only possible values of x?

    A. $130 < x < 150$

    B. $131 < x < 149$

    C. $133 < x < 145$

    D. $135 < x < 145$

Yes, it's difficult mostly because the process you have to use to find the solution is difficult. Let's start by eliminating answer choices. Choice A is designed to fool you. You see the same information that appears in the word problem, so you figure it's got to be right. Wrong. All it does is say that the shortest book is 130 pages, the longest book is 150 pages, and the average is between 130 and 150. Simple and wrong.

Choice B illustrates the reasoning that "no two books have the same number of pages, so the average must be one page more than the shortest book and one page less than the longest." Remember, it's a difficult question, so it's just not that easy an answer.

Let's skip to the correct answer, which is choice D, and find out how we got there. First, you want to find the minimum value for x, so you assume that the other three books contain 131, 132, and 133 pages. So the average would be:

$$\frac{130 + 131 + 132 + 133 + 150}{5} = \frac{676}{5} = 135.2$$

So x must be more than 135. Now assume that the other three books contain 149, 148, and 147 pages. Then the average length of all five books would be:

$$\frac{150 + 149 + 148 + 147 + 130}{5} = \frac{724}{5} = 144.8$$

Then x would be greater than 135 but less than 145.

Be Certain to Answer the Question Being Asked

Suppose that you were asked to solve the following problem:

If $5x + 11 = 31$, what is the value of $x+ 4$?

A. 4

B. 6

C. 8

D. 10

The first step is to solve the equation $5x + 11 = 31$.

$5x + 11 = 31$ Subtract 11 from both sides.

$5x = 20$ Divide both sides by 5.

$x = 4$

Remember that the problem does not ask for the value of x, it asks for the value of $x + 4$, so the answer is actually choice C. Make certain that the answer you select is the answer to the question that is being asked. **The correct answer is C.**

When Guessing at Hard Questions, You Can Toss Out Easy Answers

Now that you know the difficult questions won't have easy or obvious answers, use a guessing strategy. (Use all the help you can get!) When you have less than a clue about a difficult question, scan the answer choices and eliminate the ones that seem easy or obvious, such as any that just restate the information in the question. Then take your best guess.

Questions of Average Difficulty Won't Have Trick Answers

Let's look again at Question 12:

12. For how many integers x is $-7 < 2x < -5$?

A. None

B. One

C. Two

D. Three

This is a bit more difficult than Question 1, but it's still pretty straightforward. There is only one integer between −7 and −5, and that's −6. There's also only one value for integer x so that $2x$ equals

> **ALERT**
>
> Beware of the obvious. Don't be fooled by what look like obvious answers to difficult questions. The answers to difficult questions require some digging. They never jump out at you.

–6, and that is –3. Get it? 2(–3) = –6. So, **the correct answer is B**. Trust your judgment and your reasoning; no tricks here.

It's Smart to Work Backward

Every standard multiple-choice math problem includes four answer choices. One of them has to be correct; the other three are wrong. This means that it's always possible to solve a problem by testing each of the answer choices. Just plug each choice into the problem, and sooner or later you'll find the one that works! Testing answer choices can often be a much easier and surer way of solving a problem than attempting a lengthy calculation.

When Working Backward, Always Start from the Middle

When working on multiple-choice math questions, remember that all of the numeric answer choices are presented in order—either smallest to largest, or vice versa. As a result, it's always best to begin with a middle option, choice B or choice C. This way, if you start with choice C and it's too large, you'll only have to concentrate on the smaller choices. There, you've just knocked off at least two choices in a heartbeat! Now let's give it a test run!

If $\frac{8}{9}y = \frac{9}{4}$, what is the value of y?

A. $\frac{32}{81}$

B. $\frac{1}{2}$

C. 2

D. $\frac{81}{32}$

Start with choice C, because it will be easier to compute with than choice B: $\frac{8}{9}(2) = \frac{16}{9} < \frac{9}{4}$. Since choice C is too small, the only possible answer is choice D.

You can check that $\frac{8}{9}\left(\frac{81}{32}\right) = \frac{9}{4}$

The correct answer is D.

Now, try this testing business with a more difficult question:

In the xy-plane, the line determined by the points $(8, c)$ and $(c, 18)$ passes through the origin. Which of the following could be the value of c?

A. 10

B. 11

C. 12

D. 13

Start with choice C, because it may be easier to compute with than choice B: the line through $(8, 12)$ and $(12, 18)$ is $y = \frac{18-12}{12-8}x + b$. This equation simplifies to $y = \frac{3}{2}x$, which is a line through the origin.

Choice C meets the requirements of the problem. **The correct answer is C.**

It's Easier to Work with Numbers Than with Letters

Because numbers are more meaningful than letters, try plugging them into equations and formulas in place of variables. This technique can make problems much easier to solve. Here are some examples:

If $x - 4$ is 2 greater than y, then $x + 5$ is how much greater than y?

A. 3

B. 7

C. 9

D. 11

Choose any value for x. Let's say you decide to make $x = 4$. All right, $4 - 4 = 0$, and 0 is 2 greater than y. So $y = -2$. If $x = 4$, then $x + 5 = 4 + 5 = 9$, and so $x + 5$ is 11 more than y. **The correct answer is D.**

The cost of renting office space in a building is \$2.50 per square foot per month. Which of the following represents the total cost c, in dollars to rent p square feet of office space each year in the building?

A. $c = 2.50(12p)$

B. $c = 2.50p + 12$

C. $c = \dfrac{2.50h}{12}$

D. $c = \dfrac{12h}{2.50}$

Let $h = 100$, then the rent for one month is \$250, and the rent for one year is \$3,000. The only answer choice that will provide that answer is choice A. **The correct answer is A.**

If a question asks for an odd integer or an even integer, go ahead and pick any odd or even integer you like.

In Problems Involving Variables, Pay Careful Attention to Any Restrictions on the Possible Values of the Variables

Consider the following question:

If $x \geq 2$, which of the following is a solution to the equation $x(x - 3)(x + 4)(x + 2)(3x - 5) = 0$?

A. 2

B. 3

C. 4

D. 5

This equation has five solutions, but the problem is only looking for a solution that is at least 2. Set each of the factors equal to 0 and solve for x. The only answer that is greater than or equal to 2 is 3, choice B. **The correct answer is B.**

Now, consider this slightly different version of the same problem.

If $x < -2$, which of the following is a solution to the equation $x(x - 3)(x + 4)(x + 2)(3x - 5) = 0$?

A. −3

B. −4

C. −5

D. There is more than one solution.

The solutions to the equation can be found by setting each of the factors equal to zero. So $x = 0$, $x - 3 = 0$, $x + 4 = 0$, $x + 2 = 0$, and $3x - 5 = 0$.

These lead to the solutions $x = 0, 3, -4, -2$, and $\frac{5}{3}$ respectively.

Of these five solutions, only −4, choice B, is less than −2. **The correct answer is B.**

Questions in the Three-Statement Format Can Be Solved by the Process of Elimination

You may find a three-statement format in certain questions in the multiple-choice math section. The best way to answer this kind of question is to tackle one statement at a time, marking it as either true or false. Here is an example:

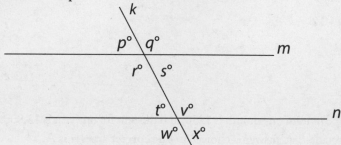

Note: Figure not drawn to scale.

In the figure above, lines k and m intersect at a point, and lines k and n intersect at a different point. If $v + s = p + q$, which of the following statements must be true?

I. $r = w$

II. $t = s$

III. $q = x$

A. I only

B. II only

C. I and II only

D. I, II, and III

Because $v + s = p + q$, we know that $p + q = 180$. Because they both make a straight line, lines m and n must be parallel. Since m and n are parallel, then statements I and II, choice C, must be true. While statement III might be true, it is true only if line k is perpendicular to lines m and n, and that does not have to be true. **The correct answer is C.**

TIP

The test booklet is yours, so feel free to use it for your scratch work. Also, go ahead and mark up any diagrams with length or angle information; it helps. But don't waste time trying to redraw diagrams; it's just not worth it.

When Solving Equations Involving Square Roots or Algebraic Fractions, Make Certain to Check Your Answer

The procedure for solving such equations occasionally results in what are known as *extraneous solutions*. An extraneous solution is a number that is correctly obtained from the equation-solving process, but doesn't actually solve the equation.

Solve for x: $\sqrt{x+4} + 15 = 10$

A. -29

B. -21

C. 21

D. There are no solutions.

Let's solve the equation.

$$\sqrt{x+4} + 15 = 10 \qquad \text{Subtract 15 from both sides}$$
$$\sqrt{x+4} = -5 \qquad \text{Square both sides}$$
$$\left(\sqrt{x+4}\right)^2 = (-5)^2$$
$$x + 4 = 25$$
$$x = 21$$

It appears that the solution is choice C. However, if you check the solution $x = 21$ in the original equation, you will see that it doesn't solve it.

$$\sqrt{x+4} + 15 = 10\,?$$
$$\sqrt{21+4} + 15 = 10\,?$$
$$\sqrt{25} + 15 = 10\,?$$
$$5 + 15 \neq 10.$$

The correct answer is D.

TIP

For multiple-choice math questions, circle what's being asked so that you don't pick a wrong answer by mistake. That way, for example, you won't pick an answer that gives perimeter when the question asks for an area.

Using the Measure of an Angle or a Side of Another Shape Can Help You Find a Measure You Need

In the figure, what is the length of *NP*?

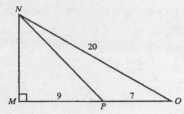

A. 8

B. 9

C. 12

D. 15

This figure is really two right triangles, *NMO* and *NMP*. Since *NM* is a side of both triangles, once you find its length, you can find the length of *NP*. The Pythagorean theorem is what you need:

$$NM^2 + MO^2 = NO^2$$
$$NM^2 + (16)^2 = (20)^2$$

Note that 16 and 20 are multiples of 4 and 5, respectively, so you now know that this is a 3-4-5 right triangle, which means that *NM* = 12.

Since you just found out that triangle *NMP* has sides of 9 and 12, it's also a 3-4-5 right triangle, so *NP* must be 15. **The correct answer is D.**

A Reality Check Can Help You Eliminate Answers That Can't Possibly Be Right

Knowing whether your calculations should produce a number that's larger or smaller than the quantity you started with can point you toward the right answer. It's also an effective way of eliminating wrong answers. Here's an example:

Using his bike, Daryl can complete a paper route in 20 minutes. Francisco, who walks the route, can complete it in 30 minutes. How long will it take the two boys to complete the route if they work together, one starting at each end of the route?

A. 8 minutes

B. 12 minutes

C. 20 minutes

D. 30 minutes

Immediately you can see that choices C and D are impossible because the two boys working together will have to complete the job in less time than either one of them working alone.

TIP

Draw a diagram if none is supplied. Drawing a diagram is a great way to organize information. Mark it up with the information you're given, and you'll have a better idea of what you're looking for.

	Daryl	Francisco
$\dfrac{\text{Actual time spent}}{\text{Time needed to do entire job alone}}$	$\dfrac{x}{20}$	$\dfrac{x}{30}$

$$\frac{x}{20} + \frac{x}{30} = 1$$

Multiply by 60 to clear fractions:

$$3x + 2x = 60$$
$$5x = 60$$
$$x = 12$$

The correct answer is B.

Your Eye Is a Good Estimator

Figures in the standard multiple-choice math section are always drawn to scale unless you see the warning "Note: Figure not drawn to scale." That means you can sometimes solve a problem just by looking at the picture and estimating the answer. Here's how this works:

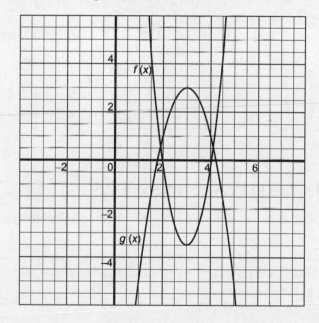

$$f(x) = (x-3)^2 - 3$$
$$g(x) = -2(x-3)^2 + 3$$

Graphs of the functions f and g are shown in the xy-plane above. For which of the following values of x does $f(x) + g(x) = 0$?

A. 1

B. 2

C. 3

D. 4

The sum of the function values is 0 when the function values for *f* and *g* are opposites. That appears to be true at *x* = 3. **The correct answer is C.**

If Some Questions Always Give You Trouble, Save Them for Last

You know which little demons haunt your math skills. If you find questions that you know will give you nightmares, save them for last. They will take up a lot of your time, especially if you're panicking, and you can use that time to do more of the easier questions.

GRID-IN QUESTION FORMAT

Again, here is a sample grid:

HOW TO RECORD YOUR ANSWERS

On the PSAT/NMSQT® exam, each set of grid-in questions starts with directions that look approximately like this:

> **Directions:** For these questions, solve the problem and enter your answer in the grid, as described below, on the answer sheet.

1. Although not required, it is suggested that you write your answer in the boxes at the top of the columns to help you fill in the circles accurately. You will receive credit only if the circles are filled in correctly.

2. Mark no more than one circle in any column.

3. No question has a negative answer.

4. Some problems may have more than one correct answer. In such cases, grid only one answer.

5. **Mixed numbers** such as $3\frac{1}{2}$ must be gridded as 3.5 or $\frac{7}{2}$. If $3\frac{1}{2}$ is entered into the grid as [grid], it will be interpreted as $\frac{31}{2}$, not $3\frac{1}{2}$.

6. **Decimal answers:** If you obtain a decimal answer with more digits than the grid can accommodate, it may be either rounded or truncated, but it must fill the entire grid.

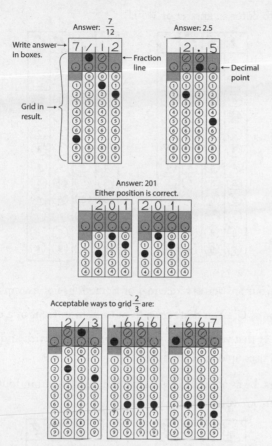

Once you understand the following six rules, you can concentrate just on solving the math problems in this section.

1. Write your answer in the boxes at the top of the grid.

2. Mark the corresponding ovals, one per column.

3. Start in any column.

4. Work with decimals or fractions.

5. Express mixed numbers as decimals or improper fractions.

6. If more than one answer is possible, grid any one.

Now let's look at these rules in more detail:

1. Write your answer in the boxes at the top of the grid. Technically, this isn't required, and it won't affect your PSAT/NMSQT® score. Realistically, it gives you something to follow as you fill in the ovals. Do it—it will help you.

2. Make sure to mark the ovals that correspond to the answer you entered in the boxes, one per column. The machine that scores the test can only read the ovals, so if you don't fill them in, you won't get credit. Just entering your answer in the boxes is not enough!

TIP

Don't use a comma in a number larger than 999. Just fill in the four digits and the corresponding ovals. You only have ovals for numbers, decimal points, and fraction slashes; there aren't any for commas.

3. You can start entering your answer in any column, if space permits. Unused columns should be left blank; don't put in zeroes. Look at this example:

Here are two ways to enter an answer of "150."

4. You can write your answer as a decimal or a fraction. For example, an answer can be expressed as $\frac{3}{4}$ or as .75. You don't have to put a zero in front of a decimal that is less than 1. Just remember that you have only four spaces to work with and that a decimal point or a fraction slash uses up one of the spaces.

For decimal answers, be as accurate as possible but keep it within four spaces. Say you get an answer of .1777; here are your options:

Answers .177 and .178 would both be marked as correct.

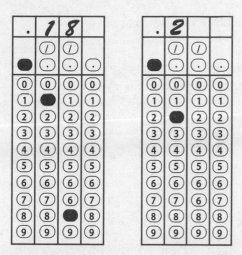

*Answers .18 or .2 would be marked wrong
because they could have been written more accurately in the space provided.*

Fractions do not have to be simplified to simplest form unless they don't fit in the answer grid. For example, you can grid $\frac{4}{10}$, but you can't grid $\frac{12}{16}$ because you'd need five spaces. So, you would simplify it and grid $\frac{3}{4}$.

5. A mixed number has to be expressed as a decimal or as an improper fraction. If you tried to grid $1\frac{3}{4}$, it would be scored as $\frac{13}{4}$, which would give you a wrong answer. Instead, you could grid the answer as 1.75 or as $\frac{7}{4}$.

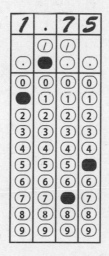  

The above answers are acceptable.   *The above answer is unacceptable.*

6. Sometimes, the problems in this section will have more than one correct answer. Choose one and grid it.

For example, if a question asks for a prime number between 5 and 13, the answer could be 7 or 11. Grid 7 or grid 11, but don't put in both answers.

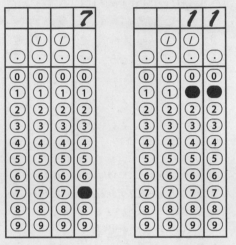

Either answer is acceptable, but not both.

GUESSING ON GRID-INS CAN'T HURT YOU

Unfortunately, you cannot receive partial credit for grid-ins. Your answers are either completely correct or completely incorrect. But no points are deducted for incorrect responses, so guessing is better than leaving a question blank.

EXERCISES: MUTLIPLE-CHOICE MATH

10 Questions • 12 Minutes

For Questions 1–10, solve each problem, choose the best answer from the choices provided, and put a circle around the correct answer. You may use any available space for scratch work.

ADDITIONAL INFORMATION:

- The use of a calculator is permitted.

- All variables and expressions used represent real numbers unless otherwise indicated.

- Figures provided in this test are drawn to scale unless otherwise indicated.

- All figures lie in a plane unless otherwise indicated.

- Unless otherwise specified, the domain of a given function f is the set of all real numbers x for which $f(x)$ is a real number.

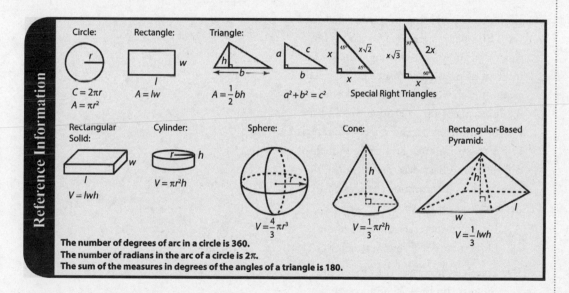

1. In a linear function $f(x)$ with a graph that has a slope of -2.5, if $f(5) = 8$, what is the value of $f(1)$?

    SHOW YOUR WORK HERE

    A. -2

    B. 3

    C. 13

    D. 18

2. If (x, y) is the solution to the system of equations below, what is the value x?

$$\frac{y}{x} = 4$$
$$5(x - 1) = y$$

    A. −20

    B. −5

    C. 5

    D. 20

3. Which of the following is equivalent to the expression $5(3x - 2)(2x + 1)$?

    A. $15x$

    B. $30x^2 - 10$

    C. $30x^2 - 5x - 10$

    D. $25x^2 - 5$

4. Kathleen is preparing to run her first road race. She begins training by doing intervals of running and walking. The longest interval of running increases by a constant amount each week. The first week she runs for intervals of up to 2 minutes at a time. By the ninth week, she runs for intervals of up to 40 minutes at a time. Which of the following best describes how the time Kathleen spends running changes between her first and ninth weeks?

    A. Kathleen increases the time of her longest run by 5 minutes each week.

    B. Kathleen increases the time of her longest run by 4.75 minutes each week.

    C. Kathleen increases the time of her longest run by 4.5 minutes each week.

    D. Kathleen increases the time of her longest run by 4.25 minutes each week.

SHOW YOUR WORK HERE

5. A circle whose center is at the origin passes through the point whose coordinates are (1, 1). What is the area of this circle?

A. π

B. 2π

C. $\sqrt{2\pi}$

D. $2\sqrt{2\pi}$

SHOW YOUR WORK HERE

6. In triangle ABC, $AB = BC$, and $\overline{AC}$ is extended to D. If angle BCD measures 100°, find the number of degrees in angle B.

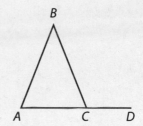

A. 20

B. 40

C. 50

D. 80

7. How many ordered pairs satisfy the system of equations below?

$$x = 3y$$
$$(x-3)^2 + (y-1)^2 = 10$$

A. 0

B. 1

C. 2

D. infinitely many

8. Mario has made 58 successful 3-point shots in basketball this season. The school record is 92 3-point shots. If he makes 3 more 3-point shots each game, which of the following shows how many 3-point shots he will have made after g additional games?

    A. $3 + 58g$

    B. $92 + 3g$

    C. $58 + 3g$

    D. $58 - 3g$

9. A rectangular door measures 5 feet by 6 feet 8 inches. What is the distance from one corner of the door to the diagonally opposite corner?

    A. 8 feet, 2 inches

    B. 8 feet, 4 inches

    C. 8 feet, 8 inches

    D. 9 feet, 6 inches

10. Two ships leave from the same port at 11:30 a.m. If one sails due east at 20 miles per hour and the other due south at 15 miles per hour, how many miles apart are the ships at 2:30 p.m.?

    A. 25

    B. 50

    C. 75

    D. 80

SHOW YOUR WORK HERE

ANSWER KEY AND EXPLANATIONS

Multiple-Choice Math

1. D	3. C	5. B	7. C	9. B
2. C	4. B	6. A	8. C	10. C

1. **The correct answer is D.** If the slope is −2.5 and $f(5) = 8$, then use the slope formula to find $f(1)$.

$$\frac{8 - f(1)}{5 - 1} = -2.5$$
$$\frac{8 - f(1)}{4} = -2.5$$
$$8 - f(1) = -10$$
$$8 + 10 = f(1)$$
$$18 = f(1)$$

2. **The correct answer is C.** If $\frac{y}{x} = 4$ and $5(x - 1) = y$, then $y = 4x$ and $y = 5x - 5$. So, $4x = 5x - 5$ and $x = 5$.

3. **The correct answer is C.** Multiply the expression to find the equivalent one. Use FOIL.

   $5(3x - 2)(2x + 1) = 5(6x^2 + 3x - 4x - 2) =$
   $5(6x^2 - x - 2) = 30x^2 - 5x - 10$

4. **The correct answer is B.** To find the average increase, divide the change in increase by the number of weeks:

$$\frac{40 - 2}{9 - 1} = \frac{38}{8} = 4.75$$

5. **The correct answer is B.**

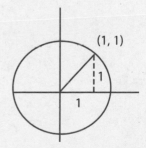

$$1^2 + 1^2 = r^2$$
$$2 = r^2$$
$$Area = \pi r^2 = 2\pi$$

6. **The correct answer is A.** Angle BCA = angle BAC = 80°. There are 20° left for angle B.

7. **The correct answer is C.** Graph the system of equations. Note that the second equation is a circle that is intersected twice by the line.

8. **The correct answer is C.** If Mario already has made 58 shots and will make an additional 3 shots each game, then he will make an additional $3g$ 3-point shots in g games, for a total of $58 + 3g$.

9. **The correct answer is B.**

   5 feet = 60 inches

   6 feet, 8 inches = 80 inches

   This is a 6-8-10 triangle, making the diagonal 100 inches, which is 8 feet 4 inches.

10. **The correct answer is C.** In 3 hours, one ship went 60 miles, the other 45 miles. This is a 3-4-5 triangle as 45 = 3(15), 60 = 4(15). The hypotenuse will be 5(15), or 75.

EXERCISES: GRID-INS

10 Questions • 15 Minutes

Directions: For these questions, solve the problem and enter your answer in the grid following each question, as described below.

1. Although not required, it is suggested that you write your answer in the boxes at the top of the columns to help you fill in the circles accurately. You will receive credit only if the circles are filled in correctly.

2. Mark no more than one circle in any column.

3. No question has a negative answer.

4. Some problems may have more than one correct answer. In such cases, grid only one answer.

5. **Mixed numbers** such as $3\frac{1}{2}$ must be gridded as 3.5 or $\frac{7}{2}$. If $3\frac{1}{2}$ is entered into the grid as [grid image], it will be interpreted as $\frac{31}{2}$, not $3\frac{1}{2}$.

6. **Decimal answers:** If you obtain a decimal answer with more digits than the grid can accommodate, it may be either rounded or truncated, but it must fill the entire grid.

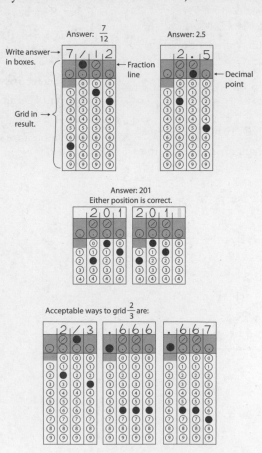

1. Marion is paid $24 for 5 hours of work in the school office. Janet works 3 hours and makes $10.95. How much more per hour does Marion make than Janet? (Ignore the dollar sign in gridding your answer.)

SHOW YOUR WORK HERE

2. If the outer diameter of a cylindrical oil tank is 54.28 inches and the inner diameter is 48.7 inches, what is the thickness of the wall of the tank, in inches?

3. A car has an average mileage of 30 miles per gallon. If one gallon of gasoline costs $3.75, how many miles can the car travel on $20 worth of gasoline?

SHOW YOUR WORK HERE

4. A cube with edges 3 centimeters long is made from solid aluminum. If the density of aluminum is approximately 2.7 grams per cubic centimeter, what is the weight of the cube to the nearest tenth of a gram?

5. $\sqrt{4x + 5} = 6$

If x is a solution of the equation above, what is the value of $4x$?

6. In May, Carter's Appliances sold 40 washing machines. In June, because of a special promotion, the store sold 80 washing machines. What is the percent of increase in the number of washing machines sold?

7. Of the 1,000 students at Jackson High, 53 percent are girls. How many boys are there in the school?

SHOW YOUR WORK HERE

8. The legs of a right triangle measure $\sqrt{2}$ centimeters and $\sqrt{6}$ centimeters. What is the length of the hypotenuse of the right triangle to the nearest tenth of a centimeter?

9. A gallon of water is added to 6 quarts of a solution that is 50% acid. What percent of the new solution is acid?

SHOW YOUR WORK HERE

	①	①	
⊙	⊙	⊙	⊙
⓪	⓪	⓪	⓪
①	①	①	①
②	②	②	②
③	③	③	③
④	④	④	④
⑤	⑤	⑤	⑤
⑥	⑥	⑥	⑥
⑦	⑦	⑦	⑦
⑧	⑧	⑧	⑧
⑨	⑨	⑨	⑨

10. A gasoline tank is $\frac{1}{4}$ full. After adding 10 gallons of gasoline, the gauge indicates that the tank is $\frac{2}{3}$ full. Find the capacity of the tank in gallons.

	①	①	
⊙	⊙	⊙	⊙
⓪	⓪	⓪	⓪
①	①	①	①
②	②	②	②
③	③	③	③
④	④	④	④
⑤	⑤	⑤	⑤
⑥	⑥	⑥	⑥
⑦	⑦	⑦	⑦
⑧	⑧	⑧	⑧
⑨	⑨	⑨	⑨

ANSWER KEY AND EXPLANATIONS

Grid-Ins

1. 1.15	3. 160	5. 31	7. 470	9. 30
2. 2.79	4. 72.9	6. 100	8. 2.8	10. 24

1. **The correct answer is $1.15.** Marion's hourly wage is $\frac{\$24}{5}$, or $4.80. Janet's hourly wage is $\frac{\$10.95}{3}$, or $3.65.

   $4.80 – $3.65 = $1.15

   You would grid 1.15. You do not need to worry about the dollar sign.

2. **The correct answer is 2.79.** The difference of 5.58 must be divided between both sides. The thickness on each side is 2.79 inches. So you would grid in 2.79 as your answer.

3. **The correct answer is 160.**

$$30\left(\frac{20}{3.75}\right) = 160$$

4. **The correct answer is 72.9.**
$$27(2.7) = 72.9$$

5. **The correct answer is 31.**
$$\sqrt{4x+5} = 6$$
$$4x + 5 = 36$$
$$4x = 31$$

6. **The correct answer is 100.** When computing the percent of increase (or decrease), use $\frac{\text{difference}}{\text{original}} \times 100$. In this case, the difference is 80 – 40, which is 40. The original amount sold was 40, so $\frac{40}{40} \times 100 = 100\%$ increase. You would grid 100 as your answer.

7. **The correct answer is 470.** 47 percent of 1,000 are boys. $(0.47)(1,000) = 470$ boys.

8. **The correct answer is 2.8.**
$$\left(\sqrt{2}\right)^2 + \left(\sqrt{6}\right)^2 = \left(\text{hypotenuse}\right)^2$$
$$2 + 6 = \left(\text{hypotenuse}\right)^2$$
$$8 = \left(\text{hypotenuse}\right)^2$$
$$\sqrt{8} = \text{hypotenuse}$$
$$2.8 = \text{hypotenuse}$$

9. **The correct answer is 30.**

	No. of Quarts	% Acid	Amount of Acid
Original	6	0.50	3
Added	4	0	0
New	10		3

$$\frac{3}{10} = 30\%$$

10. **The correct answer is 24.** 10 gallons is $\frac{2}{3} - \frac{1}{4}$ of the tank.

$$\frac{2}{3} - \frac{1}{4} = \frac{8-3}{12} = \frac{5}{12}$$
$$\frac{5}{12}x = 10$$
$$5x = 120$$
$$x = 24$$

SUMMING IT UP

- Follow the five-step plan for answering basic multiple-choice math questions:
  1. Read the question carefully and determine what's being asked.
  2. Decide which math principles apply and use them to solve the problem.
  3. Look for your answer among the choices. If it's there, mark it and go on.
  4. If the answer you found is not there, recheck the question and your calculations.
  5. If you still can't solve the problem, eliminate obviously wrong answers and take your best guess.

- In the Math Test—Calculator section, use a calculator where it can help the most: on basic arithmetic calculations, when calculating square roots and percentages, and comparing and converting fractions.

- Always set up your work on paper, then enter the numbers in your calculator; that way, if your calculation becomes confused, you don't have to try to replicate your setup from memory.

- The question number tells you how hard the question will be, though some questions may be easier for you.

- Work backward from the answer choices. When you do, start with choice B or choice C.

- Try to work with numbers instead of letters. This will help you avoid unnecessary algebraic calculations.

- Figures in the math section are always drawn to scale unless you see a warning. So use your eye as an estimator if you need to.

- When you grid answers to student-produced response questions, follow these six rules:
  1. Write your answer in the boxes at the top of the grid.
  2. Mark the corresponding ovals, one per column.
  3. Start in any column.
  4. Work with decimals or fractions.
  5. Express mixed numbers as decimals or improper fractions.
  6. If more than one answer is possible, grid any one.

- Remember that grid-ins test the same concepts as multiple-choice math.

- The most important advice for grid-ins? Don't be intimidated.

Heart of Algebra and Problem Solving & Data Analysis

Chapter 7

OVERVIEW

- **Heart of Algebra**
- **Arithmetic Essentials**
- **Linear Expressions**
- **Linear Equations and Inequalities in One Variable**
- **Lines and Linear Functions**
- **Systems of Linear Equations**
- **Linear Inequalities in Two Variables**
- **Systems of Linear Inequalities**
- **Problem Solving and Data Analysis**

- **Ratios and Proportions**
- **Density and Rate Problems**
- **Basic Data Analysis**
- **Basic Probability**
- **Heart of Algebra Practice Questions**
- **Problem Solving and Data Analysis Practice Questions**
- **Answer Keys and Explanations**
- **Summing It Up**

This chapter focuses on PSAT/NMSQT® exam math questions that fall into the categories of Heart of Algebra and Problem Solving and Data Analysis. The essence of the questions in these two categories is word problems, word problems, word problems! You will face questions that range from finding the speed of a stream's current, to identifying amounts to invest in two different bank accounts to obtain a desired profit at the end of a year, to determining how long a project will take to complete if two friends work together.

The common link between these two categories of questions is the ability to model a scenario mathematically. You will need to be comfortable with identifying variables and interpreting the information provided to you symbolically so that you can make use of the algebra and geometry rules and methods you have learned in your schoolwork. You will need to set up equations and systems of equations used to solve such problems, interpret parts of equations and inequalities that arise in solving them, and yes, solve some of them algebraically or graphically.

Often, solving such questions will require you to use tools and methods from both categories; for instance, you might need to use algebra to solve a problem involving proportions, percentages, or even geometry. Throughout this chapter, we will review the main tools and techniques needed to tackle questions in both categories, and we will walk you through questions within every tested category so you get a sense of what to expect on test day.

HEART OF ALGEBRA

PSAT/NMSQT® Math Test questions in the **Heart of Algebra** category primarily focus on building, interpreting, and solving linear equations and inequalities and systems thereof. While you need to know how to solve a given equation or system, that ability will get you only part of the way. For instance, you might know how to find the slope-intercept form for the equation of a line, which is a great skill! But on the PSAT/NMSQT® exam, you will need to understand what the slope and y-intercept of a linear equation *tell* you in a real-world scenario. Likewise, you need to be able to build an equation or system of equations that can be used to identify unknowns in a real-world context.

We will review all of this material and share some tips and pitfalls that will be useful to you as you prepare for test day!

ARITHMETIC ESSENTIALS

Questions on simple arithmetic operations are not tested explicitly on the PSAT/NMSQT® exam, but these rules, while simple, are often where students get tripped up—especially when they are being applied in longer, more involved problems. Take some time to carefully review the following rules about integers, so that they're second nature to you on test day.

$-(-a) = a$ for any integer a	$a - (-b) = a + b$ for any integers a, b	Sums of positive integers are positive.
Sums of negative integers are negative.	A product of two negative integers is positive.	A product of one positive and one negative integer is negative.
An integer is *even* if it is a multiple of 2.	An integer is *odd* if it is not a multiple of 2.	

Fraction Basics

A fraction (a.k.a., a **rational number**) is a quotient of two integers, denoted by $\frac{a}{b}$, where $b \neq 0$. A fraction is *simplified* or *in reduced form* if a and b do not share common factors. If $a \neq 0$, the *reciprocal* of $\frac{a}{b}$ can be computed by flipping the fraction over to get $\frac{b}{a}$.

You should be very familiar with the following rules of arithmetic for fractions:

Operation	What to Do (in Words)
Add/Subtract (same denominator)	When fractions have the same denominator, just add/subtract the numerators.
Add/Subtract (different denominators)	When fractions have different denominators, first get a common denominator. Apply it to the fractions and then add/subtract the numerators.
Multiply a Fraction by −1	When multiplying a fraction by −1, you can multiply either the numerator or denominator by −1, but NOT both.
Multiply	When multiplying two fractions, you can simply multiply their numerators and their denominators.
Divide	When dividing two fractions, convert to a multiplication problem.

Beware of These Careless Mistakes!

Here are some common errors students often commit when working with fractions:

- You cannot divide by 0.

- When adding fractions, you do not simply add the numerators and denominators. You must first get a common denominator.

- You cannot pull a fraction apart as a sum of two fractions when the sum occurs in the denominator. For example, $\dfrac{5+8}{3} = \dfrac{5}{3} + \dfrac{8}{3}$, but $\dfrac{3}{5+8} \neq \dfrac{3}{5} + \dfrac{3}{8}$.

- You cannot cancel *terms* in the numerator and denominator. You can only cancel *factors*. For example, $\dfrac{2 \cdot (3+5)}{2} = \dfrac{\cancel{2} \cdot (3+5)}{\cancel{2}}$, but $\dfrac{2+5}{3+2} \neq \dfrac{\cancel{2}+5}{3+\cancel{2}}$.

ALERT

It is common to make these errors when letters replace numbers in an algebraic expression. Remember, these letters represent numbers, so the same rules apply!

Scientific Notation

Large decimals with several digits before and/or after the decimal point are often expressed using so-called **scientific notation**. This notation is a way of expressing the decimal as the product of another decimal with a single digit to the left of the decimal point and an appropriate power of 10. For example:

$$14,201 = 1.4201 \times 10^4 \text{ and } 0.000052 = 5.2 \times 10^{-5}$$

Estimation and Simplification

Estimating quantities is a good skill to have so you can avoid unnecessarily precise calculations when you are simply trying to eliminate choices. The general rule of thumb for rounding is the so-called "rule of 5":

- If the digit to the immediate right of the place to which you wish to round a decimal is 5 or greater, then increase the digit in the place to which you are rounding by 1 and drop all digits to the right. If it is a 9, replace it by 0 and increase the digit to its immediate left by 1. Continue this process until you reach the first digit less than 9. For example, 5.678 rounded to the nearest hundredth is 5.68.

- If the digit to the immediate right of the place to which you wish to round a decimal is less than 5, then simply drop all digits to the right of the place to which you wish to round the decimal. For example, 123.456 rounded to the nearest hundred is 123.

Often, you will need to simplify an arithmetic expression involving different types of numbers (integers, decimals, fractions, etc.) and different arithmetic operations. In order to do so, you must use the following rules that tell us the **order of operations**:

- Step 1: Simplify all expressions contained within parentheses.
- Step 2: Simplify all expressions involving exponents.
- Step 3: Perform all multiplication and division as they arise from left to right.
- Step 4: Perform all addition and subtraction as they arise from left to right.

If there are multiple groupings, apply the same steps *within* each grouping.

LINEAR EXPRESSIONS

A **linear expression** is one involving constants and single variables raised to the first power. Some examples are:

- 6
- $x + 3$
- $2(x - 4)$
- $5x + 2y - 4$
- $6(s - 3(s + 5))$

A typical question on the PSAT/NMSQT® exam involves formulating such an expression as a mathematical representation of a problem in real-world context. For example, here is a scenario in which you would have to design your own expression.

> When installing windows, a local contractor generally charges $350 per window for installation, plus a flat recycling fee of $150 for the project. He decides to give Paul a 5% discount on the whole job. Form a linear expression that represents Paul's total bill, in dollars, for buying w windows.

The standard cost of a job involving w windows is $(350w + 150)$ dollars.

A 5% discount applied to this amount is $0.05(350w + 150)$.

Subtract this discount from the standard cost to obtain
$(350w + 150) - 0.05(350w + 150) = 0.95(350w + 150)$ dollars.
This is Paul's bill for buying w windows.

LINEAR EQUATIONS AND INEQUALITIES IN ONE VARIABLE

It is important to understand the difference between an *expression* and an *equation*. In an **expression**, a desired value is obtained by substituting in different values for the variable(s). An **equation**, on the other hand, equates two expressions. The goal of solving an equation is to identify value(s) of the unknown that make the problem true. The PSAT/NMSQT® exam focuses on **linear equations**, which equate two linear expressions.

Solving Linear Equations and Inequalities

Solving linear equations and inequalities is a skill that you have likely been drilled on extensively! Remember, the general strategy is to first simplify the expressions on both sides of the equal sign or inequality sign using the order of operations, combining like terms along the way. The exception to this rule occurs when an equation or inequality involves fractions. In this case, multiply both sides of the equation or inequality by the least common denominator (LCD) of all fractions appearing on either side to clear the fractions first. This will make the equation or inequality easier to manipulate. Then, move the variable terms to one side and the constant terms to the other and simplify. Finally, divide by the coefficient of the remaining single variable term.

One key difference to keep in mind for inequalities: If you multiply or divide by a negative number, you must reverse the inequality sign.

Consider the following example:

If $\left[\dfrac{1-x}{3}\right] - \dfrac{3}{2}(2x-1) = \dfrac{4}{5}$, what is the value of $35 - 200x$?

First, multiply both sides of the equation by 30 (the LCD of 2, 3, and 5) to clear the fractions. Then, apply the distributive property and solve for x:

$$\left[\frac{1-x}{3}\right] - \frac{3}{2}(2x-1) = \frac{4}{5}$$
$$10(1-x) - 45(2x-1) = 6(4)$$
$$10 - 10x - 90x + 45 = 24$$
$$-100x + 55 = 24$$
$$-100x = -31$$
$$x = \frac{31}{100}$$

Don't stop there! Remember, the question asks for the value of $35 - 200x$:

$$35 - 200x = 35 - 200\left(\frac{31}{100}\right)$$
$$= 35 - 62$$
$$= -27$$

ALERT

Remember to balance the equation or inequality when solving it—whatever is done to one side *must* be done to the other.

NOTE

Any purely mechanical question on the PSAT/NMSQT® exam that involves solving linear equations or inequalities will likely involve some sort of twist, like computing a different quantity using the solution of the equation.

TIP

Always stop to make sure you are answering the exact question asked. Don't do the hard work of calculating the math correctly just to rush and select a choice that does not complete the problem.

Sometimes, a linear equation will involve multiple variables, where you will be asked to solve for one of them in terms of the others. The same procedure applies. For instance, you can solve the equation $y - y_1 = m(x - x_1)$ for x as follows:

$$y - y_1 = m(x - x_1)$$

$$\frac{y - y_1}{m} = x - x_1$$

$$x_1 + \frac{y - y_1}{m} = x$$

Alternatively, you could use the distributive property on the right side first:

$$y - y_1 = m(x - x_1)$$

$$y - y_1 = mx - mx_1$$

$$y - y_1 + mx_1 = mx$$

$$\frac{y - y_1 + mx_1}{m} = x$$

The two solutions *look different* but are actually equivalent. You can see this by simplifying the fraction in the second solution as follows:

$$\frac{y - y_1 + mx_1}{m} = \frac{y - y_1}{m} + \frac{\cancel{m}x_1}{\cancel{m}} = \frac{y - y_1}{m} + x_1 = x_1 + \frac{y - y_1}{m}$$

The ability to manipulate expressions like this will be indispensable on the PSAT/NMSQT® exam!

Linear inequalities come in two varieties. One form is what you get by replacing the equal sign in a linear equation with any one of the four inequality signs. The other is a so-called **double inequality,** which is really *two* linear inequalities in one, such as the following:

$$2x < 3x - 4 \leq 2x + 5$$

$$1 - 4x \geq 3(2 - x) + 5 \geq 2(3 - 2x)$$

Double inequalities are treated a bit differently than single linear inequalities. The goal here is to isolate the variable in the middle and have only constants in both outer parts of the double inequality.

The following is an example of how to solve such an inequality.

Solve for x: $1 - 4x \geq 3(2 - x) + 5 \geq 2(3 - 2x)$.

First, simplify all linear expressions in the double inequality.

$$1 - 4x \geq 3(2 - x) + 5 \geq 2(3 - 2x)$$

$$1 - 4x \geq 11 - 3x \geq 6 - 4x$$

Then, add $4x$ to all three parts of the resulting double inequality to remove the x-terms from the outer expressions.

$$1 \geq 11 + x \geq 6$$

Finally, subtract 11 from all three parts of *that* double inequality to arrive at the solution set:

$$-10 \geq x \geq -5$$

Building Linear Equations in Context

While solving linear equations is an important skill to master, setting them up to solve an applied problem (a word problem) is the next step—and is a skill often tested on the PSAT/NMSQT® exam.

Here is an example of a test-like question.

Suppose you spend $3,000 on a one-time cost for videography equipment for a small business you are starting. For each session, you earn $500, but each session costs $25 in electricity, $40 in materials, and 15% in taxes on the full amount a customer pays. Build an equation that could be used to determine the number of video-shooting sessions you need to conduct to *break even*, meaning that your profit equals your expenses.

Let x represent the number of video-shooting sessions conducted. We need to determine an expression for the cost of conducting x video-shooting sessions and an expression for the profit earned from conducting x video-shooting sessions.

For each video-shooting session, you must pay $65 and 15% of $500, which is $75. So, each video-shooting session costs $140 and, as such, x video-shooting sessions cost $140x$. Your profit from x video-shooting sessions is $500x$.

Finally, for total cost, we must include the initial $3,000 used to purchase equipment. So, the cost is $3,000 + 140x$ dollars. Equating this expression to the profit, $500x$ dollars, gives the equation $3,000 + 140x = 500x$. The solution of this equation would give the break-even point.

The following problem requires you to set up an equation and then solve it to come to the final answer.

Two Internet providers offer different prices for a standard monthly plan. Company A charges $150 for setup and $75 per month for a basic channel lineup. Company B charges $200 for setup and $50 per month for the same lineup. After how many months will the total charges for each company be the same?

Let m be the number of months. Then, the cost for Company A is $150 + 75m$, and the cost for Company B is $200 + 50m$. Setting the two expressions equal to each other yields $150 + 75m = 200 + 50m$.

Subtract 150 from each side and $50m$ from each side to get $25m = 50$. Divide each side by 25 to conclude that $m = 2$. The charges will be the same after 2 months.

Building Linear Inequalities in Context

Setting up a linear inequality to solve an applied problem is comparable to setting up a linear equation; you just need to make sure you are using the correct inequality sign. Consider the following problem.

Richard has $30.50 that he plans to spend on truffles and chocolate-covered strawberries. Each truffle costs $2.75, and each strawberry costs $3.25. If Richard buys 3 truffles and x strawberries,

ALERT

You can be sure the PSAT/NMSQT® exam will give you answer choices that *look* correct but have inequality sign errors!

TIP

In word problems, pay attention to phrases such as "at most," "fewer than," and "at least as many," as they provide clues as to the direction of the inequality sign.

set up an inequality to represent the possible number of strawberries he can buy, assuming there is no tax.

The 3 truffles cost 3($2.75) = $8.25. The total cost of the strawberries is $3.25x$ since each one costs $3.25. Thus, the total cost is $3.25x + 8.25$ dollars. This amount must be less than or equal to $30.50, so the desired inequality is $3.25x + 8.25 \leq 30.50$.

LINES AND LINEAR FUNCTIONS

Let's continue our discussion of linear equations by looking at how they translate to graphs. You will recall from schoolwork in algebra that the equation of a line is often expressed in **slope-intercept form**, which is $y = mx + b$, where m and b are real numbers.

- The parameter b is the **y-intercept** and indicates where the graph of the line crosses the y-axis at the point $(0, b)$.

- The parameter m is the **slope** (which measures steepness of the line, or the change in y-value per unit change in x-value). It is the "rate of change of y with respect to x." The slope of a line is the same no matter what two points on the line you use to compute it. Indeed, if two points (x_1, y_1) and (x_2, y_2) are on the line, then the slope is computed as the "change in y over the change in x," written symbolically as $\dfrac{y_1 - y_2}{x_1 - x_2} = \dfrac{y_2 - y_1}{x_2 - x_1}$.

  ○ If m is positive, then the graph of the line rises from left to right.
  ○ If m is negative, it falls from left to right.
  ○ If $m = 0$, then the equation becomes $y = b$ and the graph is a horizontal line.
  ○ The graph of the equation $x = a$ is a vertical line and is said to have *no slope*.

If (x_1, y_1) is a point on the line and you know its slope m, then the most convenient way to get the equation of the line is to use the **point-slope form**, which is $y - y_1 = m(x - x_1)$.

When graphing a line with equation $y = mx + b$, first plot the y-intercept (the b-value). Next, use the slope to obtain another point on the line. For instance, if $m = \dfrac{2}{3}$, to get a second point on the line starting at y-intercept $(0, b)$, move 2 units up and 3 units right and place a point. You can apply this process again at the new point to get a third point on the line, and so on.

Alternatively, you can think of $\dfrac{2}{3}$ as $\dfrac{-2}{-3}$ and move 2 units down and 3 units left and place a point. Notice that doing so results in a line that slants upward from left to right. If the slope were $-\dfrac{2}{3}$, then you think of the slope as either $\dfrac{-2}{3}$ or $\dfrac{2}{-3}$. So, starting at point $(0, b)$, move 2 units down and 3 units right and place a point, or move 2 units up and 3 units left and place a point. Doing so results in a line that slants downward from left to right.

TIP

You can transform point-slope form into slope-intercept form by distributing the m on the right side using FOIL and moving the y_1 to the right.

Usually, questions on the PSAT/NMSQT® exam involving lines are posed in one of the following ways. Check out the most common calculations you'll be asked on test day, paired with a good method of attack:

Problem Type	Method of Attack
1. You have a point and a slope (either written or by way of a graph) and must find the equation of the line.	Use point-slope formula immediately.*
2. You have two points on a line (either written or by way of a graph) and must determine either the slope or the equation of the line.	First, find the slope of the line using $$m = \frac{y_1 - y_2}{x_1 - x_2} = \frac{y_2 - y_1}{x_2 - x_1}.$$ Then use point-slope formula to find its equation.*
3. You are given a table of points that describe a linear relationship between two variables x and y and must determine the equation of the line.	Use any two of the points to find the slope using $$m = \frac{y_1 - y_2}{x_1 - x_2} = \frac{y_2 - y_1}{x_2 - x_1}.$$ Then, use any of the points from the table with the slope to find the equation of the line using the point-slope formula.

*You might need to transform this into slope-intercept form, depending on the answer choices provided.

The following question tests your understanding of how to find the x-intercept of a line, assuming it is not horizontal.

Assume that k is a nonzero real number. What is the x-intercept of the line whose equation is given by $-\frac{k}{3}x + 2y = 3k$?

To find the x-intercept, let $y = 0$ in the given equation to obtain $-\frac{k}{3}x = 3k$. Solving for x yields $-\frac{k}{3}x = 3k \Rightarrow x = \left(-\frac{3}{k}\right)(3k) = -9$. Note that this is independent of k, so the graph of the line $-\frac{k}{3}x + 2y = 3k$ crosses the x-axis at $(-9, 0)$ for any nonzero value of k.

You might also be asked to interpret the meaning of an x-intercept in an applied context, as in the following example:

A small company earns a profit of y dollars with the sale of x security system packages per the following graph.

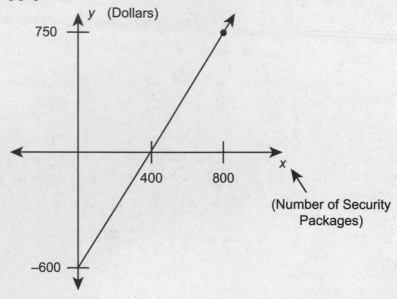

What is the meaning of the x-intercept of this graph in this scenario?

Note that the profit is negative to the left of $x = 400$, zero at $x = 400$, and positive to its immediate right. This suggests that prior to selling 400 security system packages, the company was in debt and that the moment it sold 400, the debt was completely diminished. Hence, $x = 400$ is the break-even point.

Function Notation

Function notation can be used in place of the variable y. A **linear function** has the form $f(x) = mx + b$, where m and b are real numbers. The constants m and b play the same roles as for lines. Everything you know about lines applies here; the only change is the use of function notation. To illustrate this fact, consider the following example:

Suppose $f(x)$ is a linear function. If $f(4) = -1$ and $f(2) = -5$, find the equation for $f(x)$.

First, determine the slope. The x-values in this case are 4 and 2, and the y-values are the solutions, or -1 and -5:

$$\text{slope} = m = \frac{-1 - (-5)}{4 - 2} = \frac{4}{2} = 2$$

The notation $f(4) = -1$ means that the point $(4, -1)$ is on the graph of $y = f(x)$. So, using the point-slope formula, and knowing the slope is 2, the equation of the line passing through these two points is $y - (-1) = 2(x - 4)$. This is equivalent to $y = 2x - 7$. Since $y = f(x)$, the linear function is $f(x) = 2x - 7$.

A linear function can also be described tabularly. In fact, sometimes questions on the PSAT/NMSQT® exam require you to determine if a function is linear based on a table of values or to compute its average rate of change (i.e., its slope) based on such values. Consider the following example.

Consider the following two tables of values (I) and (II). Determine which, if either, *can* describe a linear function. If it *does* describe a linear function, determine the *y*-value when $x = 4$.

(I)			(II)	
x	y		x	y
−1	0		2	2
1	4		5	4
3	8		7	6
7	16		10	8

The way to determine if a function defined tabularly is linear is to see if the slope computed using *any* two points is the same number. Using the first two points in the table for (I) reveals a slope of $\frac{4-0}{1-(-1)} = \frac{4}{2} = 2$. Trying all points in (I), no matter which two points you choose from the table, the slope is 2. So, this can describe a linear function. To determine its *y*-value at $x = 4$, use the slope formula with the point $(4, y)$ and any other point listed in the table. Let's try $(-1, 0)$ for simplicity. This gives the equation $\frac{y-0}{4-(-1)} = 2$, which is equivalent to $\frac{y}{5} = 2$, so $y = 10$ when $x = 4$.

Regarding table (II), using the first two points reveals a slope of $\frac{4-2}{5-2} = \frac{2}{3}$. However, using the second and third points in the table reveals a slope of $\frac{6-4}{7-5} = 1$, which is different! Hence, this cannot describe a linear function.

You can attack applied problems in the same manner.

Michelle goes to an annual fall clearance sale at the local T-shirt emporium. The charge is $8 to enter the sale and then $3.50 per T-shirt purchased. Determine a linear function that describes Michelle's cost $C(t)$, in dollars, for buying t T-shirts and interpret the meaning of the solution of the equation $C(t) = d$, where d is given in dollars.

First, the cost to enter the sale, even if you buy nothing, is $8. Then, the cost for purchasing t T-shirts is $3.50t$ dollars. So, the total cost is the sum of these two, $8 + 3.50t$ dollars. Hence, $C(t) = 8 + 3.50t$. In this context, the solution of the equation $C(t) = d$ is the number of T-shirts one can purchase if he or she were to spend d dollars.

TIP

Often, variables other than x and y will be used in questions on the PSAT/NMSQT® exam. This often throws students! Just remember that the variable that plays the role of what you are used to calling "x" is the input variable, and the one that plays the role of what you typically think of as "y" is the output variable.

SYSTEMS OF LINEAR EQUATIONS

A **system of linear equations** is a pair of linear equations involving two variables, say x and y, that must be satisfied *at the same time*. Solving such a system means finding ordered pairs (x, y) that satisfy *both* equations—not just one or the other! There are three possible outcomes:

Number of Solutions	Interpretation
0	The lines are parallel (their slopes are the same). So, there is no point that is on both lines simultaneously.
1	The lines intersect in a single point. So, the intersection point *is* the solution of the system.
Infinitely many	The graphs of the lines are identical; the equations are constant multiples of each other. So, every point on the line is a solution of the system.

TIP

There are two algebraic methods that you can use to solve a system: the *elimination method* and the *substitution method*. Both are useful in different situations, so make certain to review them from your algebra course.

The following question is as "purely mechanical" as they get on the PSAT/NMSQT® exam.

If (x, y) is a solution of the linear system $\begin{cases} -2y = 1 - x \\ x + 4y = 19 \end{cases}$, what is the value of $\dfrac{4x}{y - x}$?

First, rewrite the system so the variables are lined up, as follows:

$$\begin{cases} x - 2y = 1 \\ x + 4y = 19 \end{cases}$$

Now, multiply the first equation by -1 (to get $-x + 2y = -1$) and then add it to the second equation so that the x-terms cancel. This yields the equation $6y = 18$, so that $y = 3$. Now, plug this value of y into either equation and solve for x to get $x = 7$. So, the solution of the system is $(7, 3)$. But, we are not yet done! (Remember—you must double-check to make sure you are answering the question completely.) Substitute these values into the rational expression $\dfrac{4x}{y - x}$ and simplify:

$$\frac{4x}{y - x} = \frac{4 \cdot 7}{3 - 7} = -\frac{4 \cdot 7}{4} = -7$$

The algebraic questions about linear systems on the PSAT/NMSQT® exam you are more likely to encounter involve identifying the value of some constant that ensures that a system has 0, 1, or infinitely many solutions. For instance, consider the following problem:

Let a be a real number and consider the following system:

$$\begin{cases} 8y - ax = 20 \\ 2y + 3x = 5 \end{cases}$$

For which value of a does the system have more than one solution?

The two equations must be constant multiples of each other in order for the system to have more than one solution. If you multiply both sides of the second equation by 4, you get $8y + 12x = 20$. This means that if you identify a as -12, the equations will be constant multiples of each other, and the system will have more than one solution.

Modeling questions that involve building and solving linear systems are commonplace on the PSAT/ NMSQT® exam. The following is a typical "mixture problem" for which there are numerous variants.

> A groundskeeper needs to make 50 gallons of insect repellant that has a concentration of 6.1% to spray a yard of an estate. Currently, he only has containers of 4.1% and 10.3% concentrations. Formulate a system that can be used to determine the number of gallons of each concentration that he must use.

Let x be the number of gallons of 4.1% insect repellant and y the number of gallons of 10.3% insect repellant. One equation that we need to prescribe should describe the total number of gallons that must be used to get the desired amount. Since he needs 50 gallons of solution and only these two types of solutions are used, that equation is simply $x + y = 50$. The second equation needed is one that describes the concentrations. For this one, observe that $0.041x$ is the amount of active ingredient in x gallons of 4.1% insect repellant, and $0.103y$ is the amount of active ingredient in y gallons of 10.3% insect repellant. The sum of these two quantities must equal the amount of active ingredient in 50 gallons of 6.1% insect repellant, which is $0.061(50) = 3.05$. So, the second equation is $0.041x + 0.103y = 3.05$. So, the system used is given by the following:

$$\begin{cases} x + y = 50 \\ 0.041x + 0.103y = 3.05 \end{cases}$$

Other Applied Linear System Problem Types

Believe it or not, while problems like the following may appear to be quite different, they are really just variations of the previous example.

- *Investment problems:* How much of an original amount p dollars does one invest in account A at interest rate r% and in account B at interest rate s% to get d dollars in interest after one year?

- *"Ticket-type" problems:* If adult tickets each cost a dollars and child tickets each cost b dollars and you need to buy a total of fifty tickets, how many of each type are purchased if d dollars are spent on the entire lot?

LINEAR INEQUALITIES IN TWO VARIABLES

We reviewed linear equations in two variables (for instance, $ax + by = c$) earlier in this chapter. What if now instead of an equal sign, we use an inequality sign? For instance, how do we visualize a linear *inequality* in two variables, such as $5x - 3y < 1$? It turns out that the approach involves only two steps beyond graphing a linear equation.

First, you graph the line $5x - 3y = 1$. If the inequality sign is strict (that is, < or >), then you *dash* the line. If the inequality sign includes equals (that is, ≤ or ≥), then you draw the line normally.

Next, you choose a point not on the line—any point will do. Substitute it into the inequality. If the resulting statement is false (like $4 < 0$), then you shade on the other side of the line. If the resulting statement is true, then you shade on the side of the line containing that point. And, that's it! We say the **solution set** of the inequality is the shaded region *plus* the line itself when the inequality sign is either $\leq$ or $\geq$ (since points *on* the line satisfy the "equals" part of the inequality).

Applied problems involving linear inequalities of two variables do not appear as often as other types of Heart of Algebra problems on the PSAT/NMSQT® exam, but they do arise occasionally.

As part of a dieting plan, Sam eats prefixed meals and engages in prescribed exercise routines. For each prefixed meal Sam eats, he gains 330 calories, and for each prescribed exercise routine he completes, he loses 110 calories. If his total calorie count for the day cannot exceed 1,320 and he must eat at least four meals per day, formulate a linear inequality to describe all combinations of number of prefixed meals to be consumed and number of prescribed exercise routines to be completed, and sketch its solution set.

Let x denote the number of prefixed meals Sam eats and y denote the number of prescribed exercise routines he completes. The calories gained from eating x meals is $330x$, and the number of calories lost by completing y prescribed exercise routines is $110y$. So, his total calorie consumption for the day is $330x - 110y$. This must be no more than 1,320. This leads to the inequality $330x - 110y \leq 1,320$. Dividing both sides by 110 yields the equivalent, yet simpler-to-use, inequality $3x - y \leq 12$.

To graph the solution set, note that x and y are both nonnegative quantities, so we only care about the graph in the first quadrant. Moreover, it is assumed that he must eat at least 4 meals per day. So, x must be no less than 4. Start by graphing the line $y = 3x - 12$. Choose the point $(5, 1)$, for instance. Substitute it into the inequality $3x - y \leq 12$; the result is $3(5) - 1 \leq 12$, which is false. So, shade above the line. Therefore, the solution set is as follows:

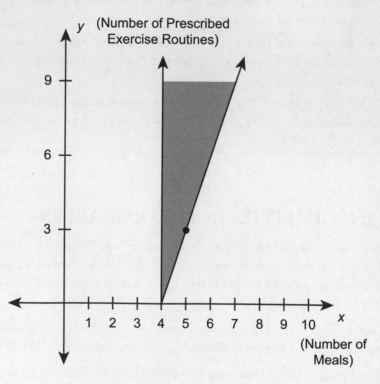

SYSTEMS OF LINEAR INEQUALITIES

Describing some scenarios requires the use of more than one linear inequality in two variables, just as some scenarios must be described by a system of linear equations. The approach used to visualize the solution set, as well as build a system of linear inequalities, is essentially the same as it is for doing so for a single linear inequality in two variables—we just do everything twice and hunt for the intersection.

Let's take a look at this concept in action.

A company specializes in making large metal numbers that can be affixed to house siding to show its address. The company offers two categories of its numbers: standard and "artistically eccentric." Each standard number requires 3 hours of metal work and 4 hours of detail work, while each artistically eccentric number requires 3 hours of metal work and 9 hours of detail work. The company employs 3 metal workers (each who work at most 30 hours per week) and 5 detail workers (each who work at most 25 hours per week). Formulate a system of linear inequalities describing the number of hours spent on metal work and the number of hours spent on detail work for the numbers manufactured in a typical week.

Let x be the number of standard numbers manufactured in one week and y the number of artistically eccentric numbers manufactured in one week. First, note that $x \geq 0$ and $y \geq 0$, since they are count variables. Next, develop an inequality describing the number of hours spent on metal work for a typical week. The number of hours spent on metal work in manufacturing x standard numbers is $3x$ and the number of hours spent on metal work in manufacturing y artistically eccentric numbers is $3y$. The total number of hours, therefore, spent on metal work is $3x + 3y$. Since there are 3 metal workers, each working at most 30 hours per week, at most $3(30) - 90$ hours are spent each week on metal work. This yields the inequality $3x + 3y \leq 90$.

Similarly, develop an inequality describing the number of hours spent on detail work for a typical week. The number of hours spent on detail work in manufacturing x standard numbers is $4x$ and the number of hours spent on detail work in manufacturing y artistically eccentric numbers is $9y$. The total number of hours, therefore, spent on detail work is $4x + 9y$. Since there are 5 detail workers, each working at most 25 hours per week, at most $5(25) = 125$ hours are spent each week on detail work. This yields the inequality $4x + 9y \leq 125$. So, the desired system of linear inequalities is given by

$$\begin{cases} 3x + 3y \leq 90 \\ 4x + 9y \leq 125 \end{cases}$$

PROBLEM SOLVING AND DATA ANALYSIS

Many questions that fall into the **Problem-Solving and Data Analysis** category of the PSAT/NMSQT® exam deal with realistic scenarios and often involve data displayed graphically or tabularly. For instance, you might see questions that deal with science-related topics such as experimental research, sociological and population studies, and organic materials in the environment. Other PSAT/NMSQT® exam questions will ask you to solve problems in the context of history and government—charts of election data, for example. This is no accident, as the creators of the exam have

TIP

Tips for solving PSAT/NMSQT® exam math questions posed in real-world contexts:

- Extract all known information and draw a diagram, if appropriate.
- Translate the question into mathematical language.
- Keep careful track of units.

expended tremendous effort to create a test format that better reflects the math you might need to use in your real life.

RATIOS AND PROPORTIONS

A **ratio** is a comparison of one quantity x to another quantity y. It is interpreted as "for every x of one type, there are y of the second type," and it is often expressed as a fraction $\frac{x}{y}$. The order in which a ratio is expressed is important because, after all, it is a fraction. For example, suppose a fruit vendor sells two apples for every eight bananas she sells. We can say the ratio of apples to bananas is 2:8 and write the fraction $\frac{2}{8}$. This conveys the same information. However, since $\frac{2}{8} \neq \frac{8}{2}$, reversing the order in which the numbers are written, without also bringing along the actual quantity type, does not result in an equivalent ratio.

Ratios can often be simplified just like fractions. For instance, the ratio describing the scenario "there are five dead batteries for every twenty-five working batteries" is $\frac{5}{25}$, which is equivalent to $\frac{1}{5}$. This simplified fraction can be used to express the scenario equivalently as "there is one dead battery for every five working batteries."

A **proportion** is an equation relating two ratios: for example, $\frac{a}{b} = \frac{c}{d}$. Proportions arise when solving many different types of problems, including changing units of measure, geometric questions involving similar triangles, and good-old recipe questions. Proportions are often formulated when one ratio is known and one of the two quantities in an equivalent ratio is unknown.

> A marine biologist wants to estimate the population of gray squirrels in a small, protected, isolated forest. She catches forty gray squirrels, tags them, and returns them to the forest. The next day, she catches sixty gray squirrels and discovers that fifteen of them are tagged. What is the size of the gray squirrel population?

Set up a proportion to find the total number m of gray squirrels in the forest. If the tagged gray squirrels disperse throughout the forest in the same manner as those untagged, it is sensible to set up the proportion, "fifteen tagged gray squirrels is to sixty captured gray squirrels as forty tagged gray squirrels is to the total gray squirrel population m." We express this in fractional form as $\frac{15}{60} = \frac{40}{m}$. To solve for m, we cross-multiply to get $15m = 40(60)$, so that $m = 160$.

Unit Conversions

Keeping careful track of units is crucial when solving real-world ratio-type problems, and doing so can help guide you on the right path to solving some difficult problems. The ability to convert from one unit to another is also a necessity when solving many PSAT/NMSQT® Math Test problems.

Familiarity with basic unit conversions, like hours to seconds, miles to feet, etc., is important, but the PSAT/NMSQT® exam will have you converting units involving rates of change and working with unfamiliar units, which is often confusing because it *looks different*. The secret? The same technique of converting from one type of unit to another applies *no matter what units you have*. You very likely will encounter units that you've never seen before. Don't panic! When new units are involved, you

TIP

Incorrect answer choices will typically include common errors involving the arithmetic of fractions or careless errors one typically makes when solving simple equations.

must be provided a unit conversion factor, and then the problem becomes the same as those involving familiar units.

The following problem is on the difficult side but becomes more manageable if you take it one step at a time.

> A race car can accelerate from 0 miles per hour to 80 miles per hour in 3.1 seconds. What is the approximate acceleration expressed in feet per minute^2?

The first thing to notice is that your end result must be expressed in feet per minutes^2, but we are starting with miles, hours, and seconds. Begin by writing down the conversion factors:

$$1 \text{ mile} = 5{,}280 \text{ feet}$$

$$1 \text{ hour} = 60 \text{ minutes} = 3{,}600 \text{ seconds}$$

$$1 \text{ minute}^2 = (60 \text{ seconds})^2 = 3{,}600 \text{ seconds}^2$$

Now, start the conversion process. Let's first tackle "80 miles per hour" into feet per second:

$$\frac{80 \text{ miles}}{1 \text{ hour}} \times \frac{5{,}280 \text{ feet}}{1 \text{ mile}} \times \frac{1 \text{ hour}}{3{,}600 \text{ seconds}} = \frac{80(5{,}280) \text{ feet}}{3{,}600 \text{ seconds}} \approx 117.3 \text{ }^{\text{feet}}\!/_{\text{sec}}$$

So, the acceleration, in feet per second^2, is:

$$\frac{117.4 \text{ }^{\text{feet}}\!/_{\text{sec}}}{3.1 \text{ sec}} \approx 37.871 \text{ }^{\text{feet}}\!/_{\text{sec}^2}$$

We are nearly done. The problem asks for the acceleration in feet per *minute*^{2}. So, use the fact that

$1 \text{ minute}^2 = 3{,}600 \text{ seconds}^2$ to get $\dfrac{37.871 \text{ feet}}{\text{sec}^2} \times \dfrac{3{,}600 \text{ sec}^2}{1 \text{ min}^2} = 136{,}336 \text{ }^{\text{feet}}\!/_{\text{min}^2}$.

Percentages

The word **percent** literally means "per hundred." Problems involving percentages can be whittled down to three varieties:

Problem Type	Method Used to Solve the Problem
Compute $x\%$ of y.	Convert $x\%$ to a decimal and multiply by y.
What percent of x is y?	Divide y by x, and then convert into a percent.
x is $y\%$ of what number z?	Convert $y\%$ to a decimal, multiply it by z, and set equal to x. Solve for z.

Consider the following applied problems, which test your knowledge of percentages in different contexts.

> A sporting goods store marked down all its skiing equipment by 35%. The following week, the remaining items were marked down again 20% off the sale price. When Cherlyn bought two snow suits and a pair of skis, she presented a coupon that gave her an additional 15% off. What percentage of the original price did Cherlyn save?

Let p be the original price of the items Cherlyn purchased. The exact value of p is not relevant to this problem; what we're looking for is what percentage of it Cherlyn ends up saving. The price during the first week of the sale is $p - 0.35p = 0.65p$. The price of these items the next week, prior to the coupon, is $0.65p - 0.20(0.65p) = 0.65p - 0.13p = 0.52p$. (The important point here is that subsequent discounts are applied to the most recent price each time!) Finally, applying the 15% coupon yields the price $0.52p - 0.15(0.52p) = 0.52p - 0.078p = 0.442p$. Cherlyn paid 44.2% of the original price. Therefore, she saved 55.8% of the original price.

> A study is being conducted to understand the contaminants present in a large lake. Out of a total of s samples, it is found that 95% contain some contaminants, and, of those, 3% contain dangerous contaminants such as lead. Devise an expression that represents the number of all samples that contain dangerous contaminants.

As fractions, the two percentages can be written as $\dfrac{95}{100}$ and $\dfrac{3}{100}$. Since the 3% is of the 95%, multiply them and apply the product to s to find the total number. Thus, the number of all samples with dangerous contaminants is $\left(\dfrac{95}{100}\right)\left(\dfrac{3}{100}\right)s = \dfrac{285s}{10,000} = \dfrac{57s}{2,000}$.

- Chances are, you will see a question about **percent increase** or **percent decrease** on the PSAT/NMSQT® exam.
- If a quantity Q is increased to value P, then the percent increase is defined as $\dfrac{P-Q}{Q} \times 100\%$.
- If a quantity Q is decreased to value P, then the percent decrease is defined as $\dfrac{Q-P}{Q} \times 100\%$.

DENSITY AND RATE PROBLEMS

Students tend to be comfortable with geometric problems involving perimeter, area, and volume, but the concept of **density** often seems like a curveball. The following formula is an intuitive way to think about density:

$$\text{Density} = \frac{\text{Number of "individuals"}}{\text{Total "space"}}$$

Here, "individuals" could be people, fish, amount of chemical, etc., and "space" is typically amount of square footage or volume. The following example is an easy question testing your knowledge of density.

> Ecologists have approximated that there are 25 mountain lions per square mile in a certain national forest. If the entire forest takes up 35 square miles, what is the number of mountain lions in the entire forest?

This problem requires us to solve the formula $\text{Density} = \dfrac{\text{Number of "individuals"}}{\text{Total "space"}}$ for number of "individuals." In this problem, total "space" = 35 square miles and density = 25. Cross-multiply to obtain $(25)(35) = 875$ mountain lions in the entire forest.

The next example is somewhat more complicated, as it involves rates together with the notion of density.

ALERT

The denominator is always the original quantity, not the quantity that results due to an increase or decrease.

NOTE

Density problems involve three unknowns, and you could be asked to identify the value of any of them on the PSAT/NMSQT® exam.

A large mixing tank contains 250 gallons of pure water. A solution of water containing 6 grams of salt per gallon is pumped into this tank at the rate of 2.5 gallons per minute. What is the approximate concentration (in grams per gallon) of salt in the tank after 3 hours?

The number of gallons of liquid entering the tank in 3 hours is 2.5(180) = 450 gallons (since 1 hour = 60 minutes). The number of grams of salt entering the tank in 3 hours, therefore, is 6(450) = 2,700 grams. Now, at the 3-hour mark, the tank contains 250 + 450 = 700 gallons of liquid, and within this liquid, 2,700 grams of salt are dissolved. Therefore, the concentration of salt in the tank after 3 hours is $\frac{2,700}{700}$, or about 3.86 grams per gallon.

Word problems involving rates are also common on the PSAT/NMSQT® exam. The key formula to remember is **distance = rate × time**. The following is a typical word problem involving rates.

Two brothers live 540 miles apart and wish to exchange cars. They follow the same road, traveling toward each other. One brother obeys the speed limit and travels at a speed of 65 miles per hour, while the other is somewhat more impatient and travels at an average speed of 80 miles per hour. Formulate an equation that can be used to determine the amount of time, in hours, it will take the brothers to meet.

The unknown is the time t at which they meet. At this time, one brother travels a distance of $65t$ and one brother travels a distance of $80t$, where we have used distance = speed × t. The sum of these distances must be the initial distance they were apart, which is 540 miles. So, the desired equation is $65t + 80t = 540$.

BASIC DATA ANALYSIS

Problems that involve actual data, whether expressed graphically or tabularly, play a prominent role on the PSAT/NMSQT® exam. You might be asked to make an inference from a graph obtained by "fitting" data to a curve. Or, you might be asked to compute or interpret a numerical measure (like mean, median, or range) of an actual data set in an applied context. Different still, you might be asked to make an inference about the nature of a large population based on data obtained from a sample. Such questions will appear throughout the math exam, so sharpening your data analysis skills will benefit you greatly.

Finding Averages

Questions concerning computing and interpreting numerical measures related to a data set (such as mean, median, and mode) occur on virtually every PSAT/NMSQT® exam.

- To compute the **mean** of a list of numbers, simply add the numbers and divide by how many numbers you added.

- To find the **median**, arrange the numbers in increasing order; if there is an odd number of data values, the value in the middle position is the median, and if there is an even number of data values, the average of the values in the two middle positions is the median.

- The **mode** is the data value that occurs most frequently in a data set. If there are two such values, the data set is called **bimodal**. If there is no such value, we simply say there is *no mode*.

ALERT

If the value "0" is included in a data set, you must include it in the count of the number of data points when computing the mean. For instance, the mean of the list of numbers 0, 2, 5, 5 is $\frac{12}{4}$ = 3, not $\frac{12}{3}$ = 4!

On the exam, data will usually be presented within an applied context. The most common presentation is within a frequency table, as in the following example.

Bowlers in an amateur league play six games during a weekend statewide bowling tournament. The following table displays the number of "turkeys" (three strikes in a row) scored by all players during the games they played that weekend.

Number of Turkeys Bowled	Frequency
0	19
1	15
2	2
3	8
4	9
5	7
6	0
7	6
8	0
9	4
10	0
11	0
12	2

ALERT

You must include the frequency of the data value "0" in the total count when computing the mean.

How many bowlers participated in the tournaments, and what are the mean and median number of turkeys bowled that weekend?

The number of bowlers is the sum of the numbers in the right column, which is 72.

Since there are 72 total scores, the median of this data set is the average of the 36th and 37th outcome, which is $\frac{2+3}{2} = 2.5$.

The mean is computed as a "weighted average," as follows:

$$\frac{19(0) + 15(1) + 2(2) + 8(3) + 9(4) + 7(5) + 0(6) + 6(7) + 0(8) + 4(9) + 0(10) + 0(11) + 2(12)}{72} = \frac{216}{72} = 3$$

The data in the above example could have been displayed using the following graph:

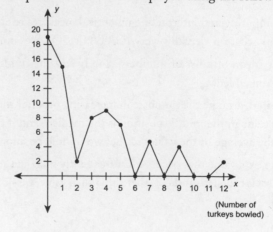

(Number of turkeys bowled)

The answer to the question is the same, but the way you initially extract the information is different. Specifically, the frequency of each "number of turkeys bowled" is the height of the points in the graph. Once you have this information, you can proceed as above.

The following question is more conceptual in nature and requires you to think about how the median is computed independent of an applied context.

> In a data set comprised of at least five values, every data value is 20 except for one value, which equals 1. What can be said about the median of this data set?

If the values are placed in order, the first value will be 1 and the values thereafter will be 20. There would simply need to be three data values in the data set to ensure the median is 20. And so, since there are at least five data values, the middle value must be 20. This is true if the data set has five values or 500 values! So, we conclude that the median of such a data set is 20.

Sometimes, a question straddles the line between data analysis and algebra, as in the following example. Questions like this, which require you to use two different skill sets together, are among the more difficult questions on the exam

> A botanist's lab notebook shows the average percentage levels of carbon dioxide in a closed chamber kept at a constant temperature of 75 degrees Fahrenheit, inside of which tomato plants are being grown using a newly developed nutrient solution. The following table shows the recorded levels.

Day	%-Level of Carbon Dioxide
Monday	6.5%
Tuesday	6.1%
Wednesday	?
Thursday	5.1%
Friday	5.3%
Average for the Week	5.5%

There is a smudge in the lab notebook in the place where the Wednesday reading was recorded. What was this reading?

Let x represent the missing reading. To compute the average of five readings, add them and divide by 5. For the moment, we drop the percent sign, and affix it to the final value of x.

$$\frac{6.5 + 6.1 + x + 5.1 + 5.3}{5} = 5.5$$

$$\frac{23 + x}{5} = 5.5$$

$$23 + x = 27.5$$

$$x = 4.5$$

So, the missing reading is 4.5%.

ALERT

Avoid the temptation to estimate the mean and median from a graph. The close, but wrong, answer obtained by doing so is typically included as a wrong answer choice.

Visual Displays of Data

There are many ways of visualizing data—bar graphs, pie charts, line graphs, scatterplots, and boxplots are just a few. You are likely more familiar with some of these types than others. The two types that are the least familiar are scatterplots and boxplots, so we'll focus our attention on those.

A **scatterplot** is a way of representing a relationship by plotting data points, represented as ordered pairs (x, y), on a coordinate plane. With scatterplots, any evident pattern of data points (or lack of a pattern) is of interest; it tells you something about the relationship between the two variables. When reviewing a scatterplot, you should ask yourself whether the points are close together or far apart and if they are clustering around a certain part of the graph or a line (or if they aren't).

> A study investigates the question, "Is the value of an extended warranty on electronics worth its cost?" One hundred middle-aged men and women were asked how much they spent on extended warranties in the last five years and their satisfaction level (on a scale of 0 to 10, where 0 represents "extremely unsatisfied" and 10 represents "extremely satisfied"). The following scatterplot describes the relationship between amount spent on purchasing extended warranties and satisfaction level. Describe any pattern in the data.

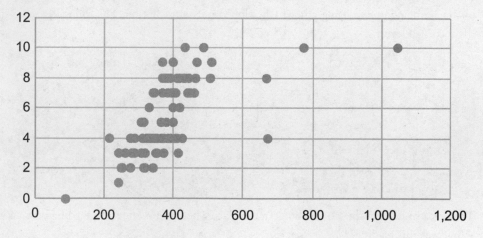

Satisfaction Level versus Amount Spent on Warranties

From this scatterplot, we can infer that generally, the more one spent on extended warranties, the greater their satisfaction, since the points are tightly packed together and rise from left to right as the dollar amount increased from 200 to 400. This trend can be described even more precisely by fitting a "best fit line" (called a regression line) to the scatterplot.

For this scatterplot, the points are in a positive correlation because they are close together and traveling toward the right as the x-values increase. A negatively correlated scatterplot would involve points that fell as the x-value increased. That is, as the x-values increase, so do the corresponding y-values.

Box plots are another useful way to describe a data set; they show the largest and smallest values and the 25%, 50%, and 75% locations (called the quartiles) in the data set. Let's walk through a problem so you can see how to interpret this type of data representation.

Two hundred 65-year-old women who have been diagnosed with shingles at some point in their lives are asked to provide the earliest age at which they received their first diagnosis. Their responses are summarized in the following boxplot:

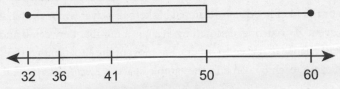

Describe the five-number summary for this data set.

From the given box plot, we know the following:

1. Lowest value in the data set = 32

2. Highest value in the data set = 60

3. **2nd Quartile** (also called the **median**) = 41; this tells you the middle of the data set. So, half of these women received their first shingles diagnosis no later than their very early 40s.

4. **1st Quartile** (also called the **lower quartile**) = 36; 25% of the data is less than this value (the left-most line of the graph). From this, we know that 25% of these women received their first shingles diagnosis between 32 and 36, inclusive, years of age.

5. **3rd Quartile** (also called the **upper quartile**) = 50; 25% of the data is greater than this value (the right-most line of the graph). From this, we know that 25% of these women received their first shingles diagnosis between 50 and 60, inclusive, years of age.

Other useful measures that can be computed using the information provided by a box plot are the range and interquartile range.

- The **range** of a dataset is the difference between the highest and lowest data values.

- The **interquartile range** is the difference between the 3rd and 1st quartiles, so it indicates the size of the spread of the half of the data set.

Finally, the spread of the values in a data set around the mean is called the **standard deviation**. You will not be asked to actually compute a standard deviation on the PSAT/NMSQT® Math Test, but you may be asked how its value changes if the data values are uniformly increased or decreased by the same value. In that case, all of the data values move in the same direction by the same amount, so their spread is unaffected.

BASIC PROBABILITY

Any process that involves uncertainty or chance (e.g., predicting the stock market or weather, guessing what percentage of voters will support a new amendment, or simply rolling a die) falls into the category of probability.

An **outcome** is the result of a single trial of a probability experiment. The collection of all outcomes is the **sample space**. For instance, if you roll a typical six-sided die and record the number of the face that results, the outcomes are the labels on the faces, or $S = \{1, 2, 3, 4, 5, 6\}$. An **event** is a subset of the sample space and is described using one or more conditions. For instance, $E = \{2, 4, 6\}$ represents the event that "the die lands on an even number."

We encounter chance in our everyday lives—for example, the percent chance of your city being hit by a winter storm or the likelihood a professional basketball player will make a half-court shot. The **probability** of an event A occurring, denoted by $P(A)$, is a number between 0 and 1, inclusive, that describes the percent chance that event A occurs. For most of the situations you will encounter on the PSAT/NMSQT® exam, each outcome in the sample space is *equally likely*. So, if the sample space contains N outcomes, then the probability of any *one* of them occurring is $\frac{1}{N}$. More generally, if an event A contains k different outcomes, then $P(A) = \dfrac{\text{Number of outcomes in } A}{\text{Number of possible outcomes}} = \dfrac{k}{N}$.

For instance, when rolling a die, the event "the die lands on an even number" is the subset $E = \{2, 4, 6\}$, and all outcomes are equally likely, $P(E) = \frac{3}{6} = \frac{1}{2}$. So, there is a 50 percent chance of the die landing on an even number.

A **compound probability** is associated with a compound event formed using unions or intersections of two or more simpler events.

- If A and B are two events, then the event "A **and** B" consists of outcomes that belong to *both* A and B.

- If A and B are two events, then the event "A **or** B" consists of outcomes that belong to *either* event A *or* event B, or both.

  ○ If A and B have no outcomes in common, then $P(A \text{ or } B) = P(A) + P(B)$.

  ○ If A and B do have outcomes in common, then we must account for the overlap when computing the probability. Precisely:

  $$P(A \text{ or } B) = P(A) + P(B) - P(A \text{ and } B)$$

- If A and B are two events that are *independent* of each other (meaning the fact that event A has occurred has no effect on the probability of B occurring, AND the fact that event B has occurred has no effect on the probability of A occurring), then the compound probability $P(A \text{ and } B) = P(A) \times P(B)$. (This type of event often arises in the context of some experiment, like selecting a ball or a card at random, done "with replacement.")

Sometimes, data from an experiment (like a survey) is presented in the form of a frequency table. For instance, suppose you ask a question of 180 people, all randomly chosen, with one of four responses possible. A convenient way to record the data is to tabulate the number of responses (the *frequencies*) for each choice and divide that number by 180 (the total number of responses). This **relative frequency** can be used to make an educated guess about how *the entire population* from which the respondents were chosen would answer this question, assuming there is no blatantly obvious bias in how the participants were selected.

Here is how this concept would be tested on the PSAT/NMSQT® exam.

Hospital records indicated that 80 patients being treated for pneumonia stayed in the hospital for the number of days shown in the following distribution.

Number of days stayed	Frequency
1	15
2	32
3	27
4	4
5	2

Based on this sample, compute the probability that a patient being treated for pneumonia will stay in the hospital for at most 2 days.

Use the relative frequency to determine the percentage of people sampled that satisfies the condition. Then, use that percentage to assign the probability to the event for general pneumonia patients. "At most 2 days" translates to "1 day or 2 days." The number that satisfies this is 15 + 32 = 47. So, the relative frequency is $\frac{47}{80} \approx 0.59$. So, the desired probability is approximately 0.59.

Probability problems are often cast in applied settings for which the data is presented in a two-by-two frequency table. These are the number of outcomes that satisfy each event (which corresponds to an "AND" event in each cell of the table.)

The following table summarizes the results of 500 undergraduates who took the MCAT® exam.

	Scored in the 90th percentile on the MCAT®	Did not score in the 90th percentile on the MCAT®
Completed the 10-week online review course	25	120
Did not complete the 10-week online review course	5	350

I. If one of the surveyed undergraduates is chosen at random, what is the probability that he or she did NOT complete the review course?

II. If an undergraduate did NOT complete the review course, how likely is it for him or her to have scored in the 90th percentile?

I. In this problem, an undergraduate is selected at random from the 500 for which there is information provided in the table. The number who did not complete the review course is the sum of the cells in the bottom row, which is 355. So, the probability that an undergraduate did not complete the review course is $\frac{355}{500} = 0.71$.

II. This problem is different from (I) in a notable way. We are given information about the individual being selected; we know that he or she did *not* complete the review course. This means that we can discard the first row of the table completely and take as our new sample space the bottom row. This is called a **conditional probability**. This has the effect of reducing the number of total outcomes that we use when computing the probability of the desired event, which in this case is that the selected individual scored in the 90th percentile on the MCAT® exam. There are only five such individuals, so the probability of this event is $\frac{5}{355} \approx 0.014$. (Note this is different from $\frac{5}{500} = 0.01$, which would incorrectly take the entire population as the sample space.)

HEART OF ALGEBRA PRACTICE QUESTIONS

1. Amanda is paid double-time for each hour she works beyond 30 hours during the weekdays. Last week, she worked h hours overtime and earned \$785 for the week. Which of the following equations can be used to determine her normal hourly rate, r?

    A. $30r + 2hr = 785$

    B. $30hr = 785$

    C. $785r = 30 + h$

    D. $(30 + h)r = 785$

2. A basketball team scores 93 points from making 35 total baskets. Some are two-point shots and some are three-point shots. How many two-point shots did the team make?

    A. 23

    B. 20

    C. 12

    D. 17

SHOW YOUR WORK HERE

3. A team of entomologists stationed in the Amazon rainforests has been collecting data on the average population growth rate of a new species of insect discovered and the rate of deforestation (in square footage per day). Their findings are summarized by the following graph.

SHOW YOUR WORK HERE

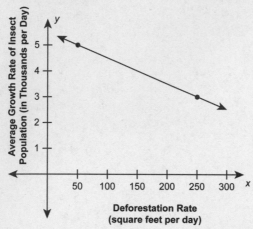

Which of the following best describes the results?

A. For every increase of one square foot of deforestation per day, the rate at which the insect population decreases is 0.01(1,000 per day) = 10 insects per day.

B. As the rate of deforestation increases by 50 square feet per day, the rate at which the insect population grows increases by 1,000 per day.

C. The growth rate of the insect population (in thousands of insects per day) decreases by half for every unit increase in the rate of deforestation (in square footage per day).

D. For every increase of 1,000 thousand insects per day in the growth rate of the insect population, the rate of deforestation increases by 100 square feet per day.

4. You have $600 to spend hosting an anniversary party, where you want to serve baked chicken and sea bass. The baked chicken costs $11.00 per pound, and the sea bass costs $20.50 per pound. A function that relates the pounds of baked chicken and pounds of sea bass you can purchase is $600 = 11.00x + 20.50y$.

What does the x-intercept of this linear function mean in this context?

A. The amount of money you spend on baked chicken

B. The amount of money you spend on sea bass

C. The number of pounds of sea bass you could purchase if you spent the entire $600 on it

D. The number of pounds of baked chicken you could purchase if you spent the entire $600 on it

5. A single-engine, 2-passenger plane flies to an airport 420 miles away. Flying against a head wind, the trip takes 4.2 hours, while the return trip with a tail wind takes 3 hours. What is the wind speed?

A. 140 miles per hour

B. 120 miles per hour

C. 20 miles per hour

D. 10 miles per hour

6. The time U, in minutes, that it takes for a gaming PC to upload files of size x gigabytes to a cloud server is described by the equation $U = 6.1x + 0.9$. What is the minimum number of minutes required to upload a file of size 25,000 megabytes? (Note: 1 gigabyte = 1,024 megabytes). Round your answer to the nearest whole number.

SHOW YOUR WORK HERE

7. Consider the inequality

$$\frac{3}{4}x - \frac{2}{3}\left(\frac{1}{4} - 3x\right) \geq 1 - \frac{1}{2}x.$$ If p is the smallest integer that satisfies this inequality, what is the value of $3 - p^2$?

8. Mick starts walking on a trail at a rate of 4 miles per hour. Ninety minutes later, Rebecca starts jogging on the same trail from where Mick started at 6 miles per hour. How far has Mick walked by the time Rebecca catches up with him?

   A. 4 miles

   B. 6 miles

   C. 12 miles

   D. 16 miles

9. If x is the solution of the equation $2(1-3x) - 4(2x-3) = 1 - 2(1-3x)$, what is the value of x^2?

SHOW YOUR WORK HERE

10. Which of the following regions is the solution set for the following system of inequalities?

$$\begin{cases} 2x - 4y > 8 \\ y \le 2 \end{cases}$$

SHOW YOUR WORK HERE

A.

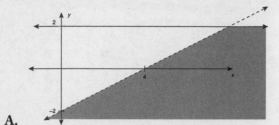

B.

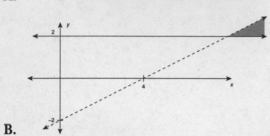

C.

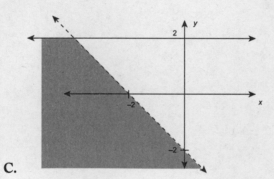

D.

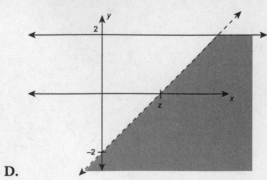

11. To power his leaf blower, Frank needs to make 5 gallons of gasoline-oil fuel mixture with an oil concentration of 15 percent. He has 2 containers of gasoline-oil fuel mixture with oil concentrations of 8.7 percent and 20.5 percent. Which of the following systems can be solved to determine the number of gallons of each type he must use?

SHOW YOUR WORK HERE

A. $\begin{cases} x + y = 5 \\ 29.2(x + y) = 15(5) \end{cases}$

B. $\begin{cases} x + y = 5 \\ 0.087x + 0.205y = 0.75 \end{cases}$

C. $\begin{cases} x + y = 5 \\ 8.7x + 20.5y = 15.0 \end{cases}$

D. $\begin{cases} x + y = 0.75 \\ 0.087x + 0.205y = 5 \end{cases}$

12. What is the smallest value of a for which the solution of the following equation is positive?

$$-2x + 3a = 1 - 2(a - 2x)$$

13. The area A of a trapezoid with base lengths b_1 and b_2 and height h can be computed using the formula $A = \frac{1}{2}h(b_1 + b_2)$. Suppose the area is 522.2 square inches, the height is 11.5 inches, and base b_1 is 5 inches. Which of the following equations shows the length (in inches) of base b_2?

A. $\dfrac{522.2}{11.5} + 5 = b_2$

B. $\dfrac{522.2 - \frac{1}{2}(11.5)}{5} = b_2$

C. $\dfrac{1,044.4}{11.5} - 5 = b_2$

D. $\dfrac{1}{2}(11.5)(522.2 - 5) = b_2$

14. Which of the following is the graph of $4(1 - 2y) = 8x$?

SHOW YOUR WORK HERE

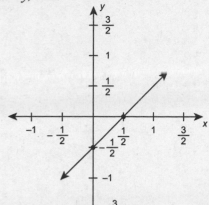

A.

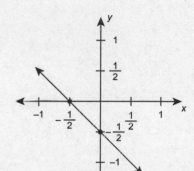

B.

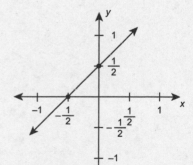

C.

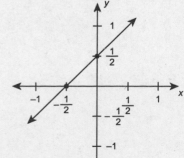

D.

15. The graph of the line $1.4x - 0.7y = 12.25$ passes through the point $(2a, -a)$, where a is a real number. What is the value of a^2?

A. 3.5

B. 12.25

C. 19.14

D. 34.03

SHOW YOUR WORK HERE

16. Let c be a real number. For what value of c does the following system have NO solution?

$$\begin{cases} 2x + cy = -1 \\ -6x - 9y = -1 \end{cases}$$

17. An apple orchard owner pays a local teenager to harvest bushels of apples. He offers her a flat amount of \$50 plus \$15 per bushel harvested. If the teenager's goal is to earn between \$450 and \$600 for this job, which of the following double inequalities describes the range of the number of bushels, b, she needs to harvest to meet her goal?

A. $450 \leq 50 + 15b \leq 600$

B. $450 \leq 15b \leq 600$

C. $450 \leq 15(50 + b) \leq 600$

D. $450 \leq 65 + b \leq 600$

18. The cost to rent rollerblades at a beach boardwalk includes a flat fee of $30 plus a charge of $1.75 for every 15 minutes of use. Which of the following functions describes the total cost, in dollars, for a rental lasting x hours?

   A. $C(x) = 1.75x + 30$

   B. $C(x) = 7x$

   C. $C(x) = 7x + 30$

   D. $C(x) = 3.50x + 30$

19. Two angles are complementary, which means they add up to 90 degrees. The measure of one angle is 5 degrees more than four times the measure of the other angle. What is the measure of the larger of the two angles?

20. Nick starts a lawn mowing business after purchasing equipment for $600. The equation $y + 600 = 75x$ models Nick's net profit, y, after mowing x lawns. What does it mean that $(8, 0)$ is a solution of this equation?

   A. For every eight lawns Nick mows, he earns $75.

   B. Nick's net profit after mowing his first eight lawns is $600.

   C. Nick must mow eight lawns to break even.

   D. Nick starts with $8 before mowing any lawns.

SHOW YOUR WORK HERE

TIP

Question 19 might *seem* like a geometry question, but the skills tested here are purely algebraic!

PROBLEM SOLVING AND DATA ANALYSIS PRACTICE QUESTIONS

1. The following table gives the "honor roll status" classification of freshmen, sophomores, juniors, and seniors at a local high school for the fall semester.

	On Honor Roll	Not on Honor Roll	TOTAL
Freshmen	4	156	160
Sophomore	34	88	122
Junior	69	61	130
Senior	38	50	88
TOTAL	145	355	500

SHOW YOUR WORK HERE

Of the students classified as not being on the honor roll, what proportion are juniors?

A. $\dfrac{61}{500}$

B. $\dfrac{61}{355}$

C. $\dfrac{61}{130}$

D. $\dfrac{294}{355}$

2. A cylindrical-shaped drainage pipe has base diameter $4\frac{1}{2}$ inches and length 10 feet. A contractor needs to create a larger pipe proportional to this one to decrease drainage time. The base of the new pipe must have a diameter of 6 inches. What should be the length the new pipe? Enter your answer **in feet** as a decimal accurate to the tenths place.

3. Every employee of a clothing store receives a $500 holiday bonus in addition to his or her salary. What impact does adding this bonus have on the mean and the range of employee yearly income at this company?

SHOW YOUR WORK HERE

A. The mean increases, but the range remains the same.

B. Both the mean and range increase.

C. The mean remains the same, but the range increases.

D. The mean and range remain the same.

4. Ten teams of oceanographers travel to different parts of the Pacific Ocean in search of a newly identified species of eel. The number of distinct sightings observed during deep-water dives in each team are illustrated below.

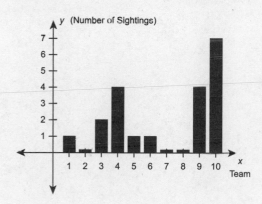

What is the mean number of sightings by these teams?

A. 4

B. 2.9

C. 2

D. 1

5. The speed at which Tanya jogs along a path through the woods during her 90-minute run is graphed below:

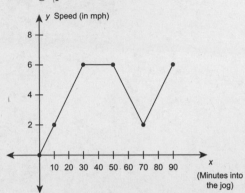

During what time interval is the terrain most likely the most difficult to traverse?

A. Between 0 and 30 minutes

B. Between 30 and 50 minutes

C. Between 50 and 70 minutes

D. Between 70 and 90 minutes

SHOW YOUR WORK HERE

6. Wendell deposits $3,500 in a money market account that earns 2 percent interest at the end of each year. At the end of each year, he reinvests the full amount at the same interest rate. Which of the following tables best describes the approximate amount in Wendell's account for the first four years of investment?

SHOW YOUR WORK HERE

A.

Year	Amount in Savings Bond
1	$4,200
2	$4,900
3	$5,600
4	$6,300

B.

Year	Amount in Savings Bond
1	$3,570
2	$3,710
3	$3,920
4	$4,340

C.

Year	Amount in Savings Bond
1	$3,570
2	$3,640
3	$3,710
4	$3,780

D.

Year	Amount in Savings Bond
1	$3,570
2	$3,641
3	$3,714
4	$3,788

7. Teresa is cleaning out her desk drawer and finds $7.10 in nickels, dimes, and quarters. She has one more than twice as many dimes as nickels, and three times as many quarters as nickels. How many dimes are in the collection?

   A. 7

   B. 15

   C. 21

   D. 43

8. Scott wants to paint his gardening equipment shed. He can apply paint at the rate of 2.5 square feet every 8 seconds. If he must wait 45 minutes after applying one coat of paint before he can begin applying another coat, how long will it take him to apply three coats of paint covering 504 square feet each, rounded to the nearest tenth of an hour?

   A. 1.9 hours

   B. 2.8 hours

   C. 3.8 hours

   D. 4.2 hours

9. During the first year of a two-year internship, a pharmacist-in-training spent 900 hours learning to fill prescriptions and 400 hours studying about dangerous effects of various drugs. Next year, his mentor plans to decrease the intern's time filling prescriptions by 30 percent and increasing the time spent learning about drug effects by 40 percent. By what approximate percentage will the total time spent on these two activities change by making these two adjustments?

   A. 12.5%

   B. 10.0%

   C. 9.2%

   D. 8.5%

SHOW YOUR WORK HERE

10. A state governor proposed an increase in gasoline taxes by 1.3 percent to generate revenue that would be used to repair city infrastructure. Two hundred voters in three different age ranges were asked to provide their opinions. The table below gives the responses.

	Age Range (in Years)			
	21–35	36–55	56–100	TOTAL
Oppose	20	32	40	92
Favor	55	8	10	73
Neutral	5	30	0	35
TOTAL	80	70	50	200

If a voter is chosen at random from those who were not in favor of the issue, what is the probability that the person's age falls in the range 56–100 years?

A. $\frac{1}{5}$

B. $\frac{9}{20}$

C. $\frac{4}{9}$

D. $\frac{11}{20}$

11. An ocean liner is currently traveling at 10 knots but must increase its speed to 13 knots. By approximately how many feet per minute must the ship increase its speed? (Note that 1 knot = 1 nautical mile per hour and 8 nautical miles ≈ 48,609 feet.)

A. 1.69 feet per minute

B. 303.8 feet per minute

C. 911.42 feet per minute

D. 6,076.15 feet per minute

SHOW YOUR WORK HERE

Use the following information to answer questions 12 and 13.

An engineer created the following scatterplot after examining the relationship between the number of watts required to power a lightbulb to gain a desired level of intensity and the life-length of the bulb.

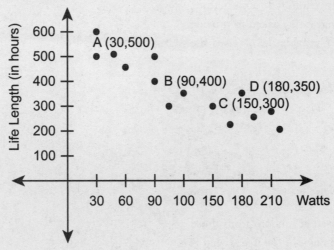

12. What is the life-length of the bulb requiring the most wattage in this sample?

    A. 550 hours

    B. 350 hours

    C. 210 hours

    D. 200 hours

13. What is the median of the ratios of wattage to life-length for the four labeled points?

    A. 2.00

    B. 3.22

    C. 4.44

    D. 6.26

SHOW YOUR WORK HERE

Use the following information to answer questions 14 and 15.

14. A research psychologist conducts a study using medical records of people who were within a certain distance of an explosion and whether they met the criteria for post-traumatic stress disorder (PTSD) within one month of the incident. The data she collected is shown below.

	Met PTSD criteria	Did not meet PTSD criteria	TOTAL
Within 0.1 mile of the explosion	240	80	320
More than 0.1 mile from the explosion	250	630	880
TOTAL	490	710	1,200

If a person known to be within 0.1 mile of the explosion at the time of the incident is chosen randomly, what is the probability that he or she did not meet the criteria for PTSD within one month of the incident?

A. 0.07

B. 0.11

C. 0.25

D. 0.49

SHOW YOUR WORK HERE

15. Given that a person from this sample meets the criteria for PTSD within one month of the incident, how much more likely is it that he or she was within 0.1 mile of the explosion than not at the time of the incident?

A. 1.04 times more likely

B. 2.10 times more likely

C. 4.25 times more likely

D. 10 times more likely

16. A tree-service company wants to get an idea of the extent of tree disease in a rural town. It offers a $25 gift card to 20 neighbors spread randomly throughout the town to select ten trees on their property, at random, and assess whether they are diseased using company-provided criterion. They are to record the percentage of diseased trees and report the information to the company. The company compiled the data they collected as follows:

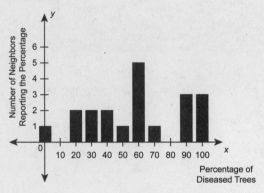

Which of the following is an accurate description of the relationship of mean, to median, to mode?

A. median < mean = mode

B. mean < median = mode

C. mean < median < mode

D. mode < mean < median

SHOW YOUR WORK HERE

17. A social psychologist conducts an experiment to assess the relationship between one's level of social media usage and one's level of self-confidence. She collected her data in the following table:

	High-level of use of social media	Low- to moderate-level of use of social media
Normal to high level of self-confidence	50	88
Below-normal level of self-confidence	61	1

If one of the subjects of this study is selected at random, what is the probability that the person chosen has neither a high-level use of social media nor a below-normal level of self-confidence?

A. 0.25

B. 0.44

C. 0.64

D. 0.98

18. A machine that fills 32-ounce containers of soft soap on a factory assembly line operates for 15 hours per day, 7 days a week. It can fill 980 containers in 25 minutes. How many gallons of soft soap are produced in December, which has 31 days? (Note: 16 cups = 1 gallon and 1 cup = 8 ounces.)

A. 34,997,760

B. 2,187,360

C. 1,093,680

D. 273,420

19. A department store discounts all mattresses by $200 three days before the Christmas holiday to encourage customers to make a purchase. If the store sells seventy-eight mattresses as a result, how does the discount affect the mean and standard deviation of the profit data from the sale mattresses had the discount never been applied to these seventy-eight mattresses?

A. The mean decreases and standard deviation remains the same.

B. The mean will decrease and standard deviation will increase.

C. The mean and standard deviation both remain unchanged.

D. The mean and standard deviation both decrease.

SHOW YOUR WORK HERE

20. Which of the following graphs best shows a strong, negative, nonlinear association between x and y?

SHOW YOUR WORK HERE

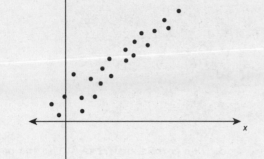

A.

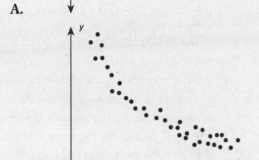

B.

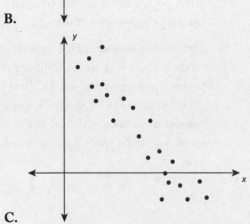

C.

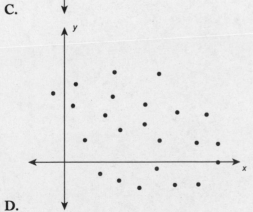

D.

ANSWER KEYS AND EXPLANATIONS

Heart of Algebra

1. A	**6.** 150	**11.** B	**16.** 3
2. C	**7.** 2	**12.** $\frac{1}{5}$	**17.** A
3. A	**8.** C	**13.** C	**18.** C
4. D	**9.** $\frac{9}{16}$	**14.** D	**19.** 73
5. C	**10.** A	**15.** B	**20.** C

1. **The correct answer is A.** The amount she earns for the first 30 hours of work is $30r$. For the h hours she works beyond these initial hours, she earns $h(2r) = 2hr$. The sum of these amounts, $30r + 2hr$, is the amount she earns in the week, $785.

2. **The correct answer is C.** Let x be the number of two-point shots and y the number of three-point shots. The following system of two equations models this scenario:

$$\begin{cases} x + y = 35 \\ 2x + 3y = 93 \end{cases}$$

The first equation is formulated to reflect the fact that 35 total shots were made (some two-point and some three-point). The second equation reflects the number of points of the total 93 attributed to two-point shots and three-point shots.

To solve this system, multiply the first equation by −2 and add to the second to eliminate x:

$$\begin{aligned} -2x - 2y &= -70 \\ \underline{2x + 3y} &= \underline{\ 93} \\ y &= \ 23 \end{aligned}$$

We're not done, since y represents the number of three-point shots, and we are asked to find the number of two-point shots. Substitute y into the first equation to find that $x = 12$.

3. **The correct answer is A.** Use the points $(50, 5)$ and $(150, 4)$ to find that the slope is $-\frac{1}{100} = -0.01$. Since the x-variable is *the rate of deforestation (in square footage per day)* and the y-variable is *rate of insect population growth (in thousands per day)*, and the slope is negative (as the line travels downward from left to right), the interpretation is that for every increase of one square foot of deforestation per day, the growth rate of the insect population decreases by 0.01(1,000 per day) = 10 insects per day.

4. **The correct answer is D.** The x-intercept occurs when $y = 0$, which implies you are buying 0 pounds of sea bass. So, if you solve the equation $600 = 11.00x$ for x, this is the number of pounds of baked chicken you could buy if you spent zero dollars on sea bass.

5. **The correct answer is C.** Set up a system of equations to solve this problem. Let x represent the speed of the plane in still air and y represent the wind speed. Using distance = rate × time, the equation for the "against head wind" trip is $(x - y)(4.2) = 420$, and the equation for the "with tail wind" trip is $(x + y)(3) = 420$. So, we have the following system:

$$\begin{cases} 4.2(x - y) = 420 \\ 3(x + y) = 420 \end{cases}$$

Simplifying by dividing both sides of the first and second equations by 4.2 and 3, respectively, yields the following simpler system with which to work:

$$\begin{cases} x - y = 100 \\ x + y = 140 \end{cases}$$

Adding the two equations enables us to cancel the y-terms, giving us $2x = 240$, so that $x = 120$. Substituting this into the first equation then yields $y = 20$. So, the wind speed is 20 mph.

6. **The correct answer is 150 minutes.** First, convert megabytes to gigabytes:

$$\frac{25,000 \text{ megabytes}}{1} \cdot \frac{1 \text{ gigabyte}}{1,024 \text{ megabytes}}$$

$$\approx 24.41 \text{ gigabytes}$$

Now, substitute $x = 24.41$ into the given equation to determine U:

$U = 6.1(24.41) + 0.9 \approx 149.8$ minutes

Finally, round 149.8 to 150 minutes for your final answer.

7. **The correct answer is 2.** Solve the inequality:

$$\frac{3}{4}x - \frac{2}{3}\left(\frac{1}{4} - 3x\right) \geq 1 - \frac{1}{2}x$$

$$24 \cdot \left[\frac{3}{4}x - \frac{2}{3}\left(\frac{1}{4} - 3x\right)\right] \geq 24 \cdot \left[1 - \frac{1}{2}x\right]$$

$$18x - 16\left(\frac{1}{4} - 3x\right) \geq 24 - 12x$$

$$18x - 4 + 48x \geq 24 - 12x$$

$$66x - 4 \geq 24 - 12x$$

$$78x \geq 28$$

$$x \geq \frac{28}{78}$$

The smallest integer p that satisfies this inequality is $p = 1$. So, $3 - p^2 = 3 - 1 = 2$.

8. **The correct answer is C.** Let x = time Mick walks (in hours). His 90-minute head start equals 1.5 hours. Using distance = rate × time, the distance Mick walks is $4(x + 1.5)$ and the distance Rebecca jogs is $6x$. Equate these expressions and solve for x:

$$4(x + 1.5) = 6x$$

$$4x + 6 = 6x$$

$$2x = 6$$

$$x = 3$$

So, Mick has walked for 3 hours by the time Rebecca catches up with him. Since he walks at 4 miles per hour, he has walked 12 miles.

9. **The correct answer is $\frac{9}{16}$.** Solve for x using the order of operations:

$$2(1 - 3x) - 4(2x - 3) = 1 - 2(1 - 3x)$$

$$2 - 6x - 8x + 12 = 1 - 2 + 6x$$

$$14 - 14x = -1 + 6x$$

$$15 = 20x$$

$$\frac{3}{4} = x$$

So, $x^2 = \left(\frac{3}{4}\right)^2 = \frac{9}{16}$.

10. **The correct answer is A.** The first inequality can be written equivalently as $y < \frac{1}{2}x - 2$; the dashed line in the region corresponds to the line obtained by replacing the < sign by an = sign in this inequality. The graph of the line that forms the boundary for the second inequality is a horizontal line at $y = 2$, and it is solid because the inequality sign includes *equals*. Now, to get the solution set, both inequalities must be satisfied. We want those points that are below both lines, which is precisely what is shown here.

11. **The correct answer is B.** Let x be the number of gallons of 8.7 percent gasoline-oil fuel mixture and y the number of gallons of 20.5 percent gasoline-oil fuel mixture. The first equation describes the total number of gallons of each mixture that must be used to get the desired amount. The second equation describes the concentrations. Observe that $0.087x$ is the amount of oil in x gallons of 8.7 percent gasoline-oil fuel mixture, and $0.205y$ is the amount of oil in y gallons of 20.5 percent gasoline-oil fuel mixture. The sum of these two quantities must equal the amount of oil in 5 gallons of 15 percent gasoline-oil fuel mixture, which is $0.15(5) = 0.75$.

12. **The correct answer is $\frac{1}{5}$.**

$$-2x + 3a = 1 - 2(a - 2x)$$
$$-2x + 3a = 1 - 2a + 4x$$
$$5a - 1 = 6x$$
$$\frac{5a - 1}{6} = x$$

Now, solve the inequality $\frac{5a - 1}{6} > 0$. Cross-multiply by 6 to get $5a - 1 > 0$, which implies $a > \frac{1}{5}$.

13. **The correct answer is C.** First, substitute the given values into the area formula, and then solve for b_2:

$$A = \frac{1}{2}h(b_1 + b_2)$$
$$522.2 = \frac{1}{2}(11.5)(5 + b_2)$$
$$\frac{522.2}{\frac{1}{2}(11.5)} = 5 + b_2$$
$$\frac{522.2}{\frac{1}{2}(11.5)} - 5 = b_2$$
$$\frac{1,044.4}{11.5} - 5 = b_2$$

14. **The correct answer is D.** First, write the given equation in slope-intercept form: $y = -x + \frac{1}{2}$. The y-intercept of this line is $\frac{1}{2}$, and the graph has a negative slope. The graph in choice D is the only one that possesses these characteristics.

15. **The correct answer is B.** Since the point $(2a, -a)$ lies on the given line, it must produce a true statement when it is substituted into its equation. Substitute $2a$ in for x and $-a$ for y, and solve for a:

$$1.4x - 0.7y = 12.25$$
$$1.4(2a) - 0.7(-a) = 12.25$$
$$2.8a + 0.7a = 12.25$$
$$3.5a = 12.25$$
$$a = 3.5$$

So, the value of a^2 is $(3.5)^2 = 12.25$. Choice A is incorrect because it is the value of a, not a^2. Choice C is incorrect because you switched the values and substituted $-a$ for x and $2a$ for y. Choice D is incorrect because you substituted a for y, not $-a$.

16. **The correct answer is 3.** The two lines must have the same slope *and* different y-intercepts for the system to have no solution. Observe that the second equation can be written equivalently as $y = -\frac{2}{3}x + \frac{1}{9}$ and the first one can be written as $y = -\frac{2}{c}x - \frac{1}{c}$. To ensure the lines have the same slope, set the slopes at equal and solve for c: $-\frac{2}{c} = -\frac{2}{3}$ so that $c = 3$. This is the only value of c for which the two lines have the same slope.

    Now, the system will have no solution if the y-intercepts of the two lines *for this value of c* are different. So, check this. The y-intercept of the first equation is $-\frac{1}{c} = -\frac{1}{3}$, which is different from the y-intercept of the second equation, which is $\frac{1}{9}$. So, when $c = 3$, the system has no solution.

17. **The correct answer is A.** The base fee is $50. To that, we add $15b$ dollars, the owner's payment for the teenager harvesting b bushels of apples. So, the total amount earned for b bushels is $50 + 15b$ dollars. This expression should be between 450 and 600, inclusive, to describe teenager's earning goal. This yields the double inequality $450 \leq 50 + 15b < 600$.

18. **The correct answer is C.** Since it costs $1.75 for every 15 minutes of use, it must cost $7.00 per hour to rent the rollerblades. So, the cost for x hours would be $7x$. This, plus the flat fee of $30, yields the total cost of $C(x)$: $C(x) = 7x + 30$ dollars.

19. **The correct answer is 73 degrees.** Let x and y be the measures of the two angles. We know that they must satisfy the following system of equations:

    $$\begin{cases} x + y = 90 \\ y = 4x + 5 \end{cases}$$

    Solve this system using the substitution method. Substitute y from the second equation into the first one and solve for x:

    $$x + (4x + 5) = 90$$
    $$5x + 5 = 90$$
    $$5x = 85$$
    $$x = 17$$

    Substitute this back into the first equation to see that $y = 73$. Thus, the larger of the two angles is 73 degrees.

20. **The correct answer is C.** Let x = eight lawns and y = 0 dollars. If Nick mows eight lawns, his net profit is 0 dollars, meaning that he has covered the expense of equipment he initially purchased to start the business.

Problem Solving and Data Analysis

1. B	6. D	11. B	16. B
2. 13.3	7. B	12. D	17. B
3. A	8. B	13. B	18. D
4. C	9. D	14. C	19. A
5. C	10. C	15. A	20. B

1. **The correct answer is B.** First, you need to fill in the missing information in the table:

	On Honor Roll	Not on Honor Roll	TOTAL
Freshmen	4	156	160
Sophomore	34	88	122
Junior	69	61	130
Senior	38	50	88
TOTAL	145	355	500

We are given that the student is not on the honor roll, so restrict attention to the second column. The sample space is 355, not the entire 500. Of these students, 61 juniors are not on the honor roll. So, the probability is $\frac{61}{355}$.

2. **The correct answer is 13.3 feet.** Let H be the length of the larger cylindrical-shaped pipe. Make certain all units are the same. Change the given length of 10 feet into inches: 10 feet = 120 inches.

Set up this proportion:

$$\frac{4\frac{1}{2} \text{ inches}}{6 \text{ inches}} = \frac{120 \text{ inches}}{H \text{ inches}}$$

Solving for H yields:

$$\left(\frac{9}{2}\right)H = 6(120)$$

$$H = \frac{2}{9}(720) = 160 \text{ inches}$$

Convert to feet:

$$160 \text{ inches} = 13\frac{1}{3} \text{ feet} \approx 13.3 \text{ feet}$$

3. **The correct answer is A.** The mean must increase because all of the data values being added have increased. It will increase by $500. The range remains the same since the bonus is added to every employee's salary. So, if s is the smallest salary and S is the largest salary before the bonus, the range would be $S - s$. After the bonus, $s + 500$ and $S + 500$ are the new smallest and largest salaries, but the difference is $(S + 500) - (s + 500) = S - s$.

4. **The correct answer is C.** Sum the heights of the ten bars and divide by 10.

$$\frac{1 + 0 + 2 + 4 + 1 + 1 + 0 + 0 + 4 + 7}{10} = \frac{20}{10} = 2$$

5. **The correct answer is C.** The speed is decreasing on the interval between 50 and 70 minutes of the jog. So, she is slowing down continuously during this interval of time. Prior to 50 minutes, she was jogging at a constant speed of 6 miles per hour. She then slows down from 50 to 70 minutes and then begins to speed up after 70 minutes. Of all the time periods on the graph, this one is the most likely to indicate a change in terrain that impedes her speed.

6. **The correct answer is D.** Apply 0.02 to $3,500 to get the interest earned in Year 1: (0.02)3,500 = 70. Then, add *that* amount to $3,500 and apply 0.02 to *that* amount to get the interest earned in Year 2: (0.02)3,570 = 71.4. Continue this process to get the amounts for Years 3 and 4.

7. **The correct answer is B.** Let x be the number of nickels in the collection. Then, there are $(2x + 1)$ dimes and $3x$ quarters. Multiplying each number by the value of the respective coin, summing the terms, and equating to $7.10 yields the equation $0.05x + 0.10(2x + 1) + 0.25(3x) = 7.10$.

Solve for x, as follows:

$$0.05x + 0.10(2x + 1) + 0.25(3x) = 7.10$$

$$5x + 10(2x + 1) + 25(3x) = 710$$

$$5x + 20x + 10 + 75x = 710$$

$$100x = 700$$

$$x = 7$$

So, there are $2(7) + 1 = 15$ dimes in the collection.

8. **The correct answer is B.** First, note that since he is applying three coats of paint, the square footage he needs to paint is $3(504) = 1,512$ square feet. Now, determine the number of seconds it takes to apply three coats of paint by solving the proportion:

$$\frac{2.5 \text{ ft.}^2}{8 \text{ sec.}} = \frac{1,512 \text{ ft.}^2}{x \text{ sec.}}$$

Cross-multiplying and dividing by the coefficient of x gives $x = 4,838.4$ seconds. Since there are 60 seconds in 1 minute and 60 minutes in 1 hour, $4,838.4$ seconds $= 80.64$ minutes $= 1.344$ hours.

Now, he must wait 45 minutes $= 0.75$ hour after applying the first coat, and another 0.75 hour after applying the second coat. This adds 1.5 hours to the total time spent on this project. So, it takes him 2.844 hours, which rounds to 2.8 hours, to apply three coats of paint to the shed.

9. **The correct answer is D.** The amount of time the intern will spend filling prescriptions next year is $900 - 900(0.30) = 630$ hours. The amount of time he will spend studying about drug effects next year is $400 + 400(0.40) = 560$ hours. So, the total time he will spend on these two activities next year is 1,190 hours. Since the time spent this year is 1,300 hours, the percent change is

$$\frac{1,300 - 1,190}{1,300} \approx 0.085 = 8.5\%.$$

10. **The correct answer is C.** Since the selection is being made from those sampled who are classified as "not in favor," we must restrict our attention to the first and third columns of the table. This sample space of interest consists of $92 + 35 = 127$ voters, not 200. Of the 127, 40 fall in the age range 56–100 years old. So, the probability is $\frac{40}{90} = \frac{4}{9}$.

11. **The correct answer is B.** Note that 1 nautical mile $= \frac{48,609}{8}$ feet $= 6,076.125$ feet. Convert 10 knots and 13 knots to feet per minute:

10 knots = 10 nautical miles per hour

= 10(6,076.125) feet per hour

= 60,761.25 feet per hour

= 60,761.25 ÷ 60 feet per minute

= 1,012.69 feet per minute

13 knots = 13 nautical miles per hour

= 13(6,076.125) feet per hour

= 78,989.625 feet per hour

= 78,989.625 ÷ 60 feet per minute

= 911.42 feet per minute

Now, subtract these two rates to get 303.8 feet per minute. This is the rate by which the ocean liner must increase its speed.

12. **The correct answer is D.** The point to focus on is the one with the largest x-coordinate. Here, that is when x (the wattage) is 210 watts. The recorded life-length of that bulb is 200 hours at this point.

13. **The correct answer is B.** Compute each ratio, making certain to identify the numerator and denominator as wattage and life-length, respectively:

Point A: $\dfrac{500}{30} \approx 16.67$

Point B: $\dfrac{400}{90} \approx 4.44$

Point C: $\dfrac{300}{150} = 2.00$

Point D: $\dfrac{350}{180} \approx 1.94$

The values are arranged in order, so the median is the average of the second and third ratios: $\dfrac{2.00 + 4.44}{2} = \dfrac{6.44}{2} = 3.22$.

14. **The correct answer is C.** Restrict your attention to the first row of the table since we are given that the person is being selected from the "within 0.1 mile of the explosion" portion of the whole sample. Of these, 80 did not meet the criteria for PTSD within one month of the incident. So, the probability of this event is $\dfrac{80}{320} = 0.25$.

15. **The correct answer is A.** The proportion of the sample consisting of people who met the criteria for PTSD within one month of the incident who were within 0.1 of the mile explosion is $\dfrac{240}{490}$, and the proportion of the sample consisting of people who met the criteria for PTSD within one month of the incident who were more than 0.1 mile from the explosion is $\dfrac{250}{490}$. Let x be how many times more likely it is for a person from this sample to have been within 0.1 mile of the explosion than not. We must solve the linear equation $\left(\dfrac{240}{490}\right)x = \left(\dfrac{250}{490}\right)$. The approximate value of x is 1.04.

16. **The correct answer is B.** The mode is 60—it is the most commonly occurring percentage of diseased trees reported by neighbors in this sample. The median is the average of the 10th and 11th reported percentages (read from smallest to largest), since there were 20 total subjects. The median is therefore 60. And, the mean is given by

$$\frac{0(1) + 10(0) + 20(2) + 30(2) + 40(2) + 50(1) + 60(5) + 70(1) + 80(0) + 90(3) + 100(3)}{20} = \frac{1,170}{20} = 58.5.$$

Thus, mean < median = mode.

17. **The correct answer is B.** Subjects in the upper-right cell of the table satisfy the criteria. Since there are 200 subjects (the sum of all four cells) and 88 of them satisfy the criteria, the probability is $\frac{88}{200} = 0.44$.

18. **The correct answer is D.** First, note that there are 15(31) = 465 hours in December during which the machine operates. Since there are 60 minutes in an hour, this corresponds to 27,900 minutes. Next, let x = number of containers the machine fills during this time. Set up the following proportion:

$$\frac{980 \text{ containers}}{25 \text{ minutes}} = \frac{x \text{ containers}}{27,900 \text{ minutes}}$$

Solving for x yields x = 1,093,680 containers. Since there are 32 ounces in one container, multiplying 1,093,680 by 32 gives 34,997,760 ounces. Finally, to get the number of gallons, divide this by 16(8) = 128 to get 273,420 gallons.

19. **The correct answer is A.** The mean must decrease because all the data values being added have decreased. In fact, each will decrease by $200. The spread (or standard deviation) of the data remains unchanged because the same number is subtracted from all values in the data set.

20. **The correct answer is B.** The relationship is strong because the points are tightly packed together. It is negative because the values fall from left to right. And it is nonlinear because there is a discernible curve to the growth as you move from left to right. In fact, this one resembles exponential decay.

SUMMING IT UP

- The **order of operations** for simplifying algebraic and arithmetic expressions is as follows:

  - **Step 1:** Simplify all expressions contained within parentheses.

  - **Step 2:** Simplify all expressions involving exponents.

  - **Step 3:** Perform all multiplication and division as they arise from left to right.

  - **Step 4:** Perform all addition and subtraction as they arise from left to right.

- If there are multiple groupings, apply the same steps *within* each grouping.

- The general strategy used to solve a linear equation is to first simplify the expressions on both sides of the equal sign or inequality sign using the order of operations, combining like terms along the way. Then, move the variable terms to one side and the constant terms to the other, and simplify. Finally, divide by the coefficient of the single variable term.

- Setting up a linear inequality to solve an applied problem is comparable to setting up a linear equation. Pay attention to phrases such as "at most," "fewer than," and "at least as many," as they provide clues to the direction of the inequality sign.

- The equation of a line is often expressed in **slope-intercept form**, $y = mx + b$, where m and b are real numbers.

- The parameter b is its y-intercept and indicates where the graph of the line crosses the y-axis at the point $(0, b)$.

- The parameter m is the slope (which measures steepness of the line, or the change in y-value per unit change in x-value). It is the "rate of change of y with respect to x."

- A **system of linear equations** is a pair of linear equations involving two variables, say x and y, that must be satisfied *at the same time*. Solving such a system means finding ordered pairs (x, y) that satisfy *both* equations—not just one or the other! There are two algebraic methods that you can use to solve a system: the **elimination method** and the **substitution method**.

- Solving a linear inequality in two variables requires you to draw the line. It is dashed if the inequality is strict ($<$ or $>$) and solid otherwise. To determine the solution set, you select a point off the line and substitute it into the inequality; if the resulting statement is true, shade the region of the xy-plane on the side of the line that contains that point.

- Describing some scenarios requires the use of more than one linear inequality in two variables, just as some scenarios must be described by a system of linear equations. The approach used to visualize the solution set, as well as build a system of linear inequalities, is essentially the same as it is for doing so for a single linear inequality in two variables—we just do everything twice and hunt for the intersection.

- A **ratio** is a comparison of one quantity x to another quantity y. It is interpreted as "for every x of one type, there are y of the second type," and it is expressed as a fraction $\frac{x}{y}$.

- A **proportion** is an equation relating two ratios, say $\frac{a}{b} = \frac{c}{d}$. Proportions arise when solving many different types of problems, including changing units of measure, geometric questions involving similar triangles, and good-old recipe questions!

- Keeping careful track of units is crucial when solving real-world ratio-type problems, and doing so can help guide you on the right path to solving some difficult problems.

- The same technique of converting from one type of unit to another applies *no matter what units you have*! When new units are introduced, you *must* be provided a unit conversion factor, and then the problem becomes the same as those involving familiar units.

- An intuitive way to think about density is the following formula:

$$\text{Density} = \frac{\text{Number of "individuals"}}{\text{Total "space"}}$$

  Here, "individuals" could be people, fish, amount of chemical, etc., and "space" is typically amount of square footage or volume.

- Questions computing measures of center—mean and median—occur on every PSAT/NMSQT® exam.

- To compute the **mean** of a list of numbers, simply add the numbers and divide by how many numbers you added.

- To find the **median**, arrange the numbers in increasing order; if there is an odd number of data values, the value in the middle position is the median, and if there is an even number of data values, the average of the values in the two middle positions is the median.

- Data will be expressed sometimes tabularly and sometimes graphically using bar graphs, line graphs, scatterplots, and boxplots.

- A **scatterplot** is a way of representing a relationship by plotting ordered pairs (x, y) on a coordinate plane. Any discernible pattern, or lack of one, to which the points conform is of interest; it tells you something about the relationship between the two variables.

- **Box plots** are useful for describing a data set in that they show the largest and smallest values and the locations of **quartiles** in the data set.

- The **probability** of an event A occurring, denoted by $P(A)$, is a number between 0 and 1, inclusive, that describes the percent chance that event A occurs. If there are N equally likely outcomes, then the probability of any *one* of them occurring is $\frac{1}{N}$. More generally, if an event A contains k different outcomes, then $P(A) = \dfrac{\text{Number of outcomes in } A}{\text{Number of possible outcomes}} = \dfrac{k}{N}$.

- If A and B are two events, then the event "A **and** B" consists of outcomes that belong to both A and B.

- If A and B are two events, then the event "A **or** B" consists of outcomes that belong to either event A or event B or both.

  ○ If A and B have no outcomes in common, then $P(A \text{ or } B) = P(A) + P(B)$.

  ○ If A and B do have outcomes in common, then we must account for the overlap when computing the probability. Precisely, $P(A \text{ or } B) = P(A) + P(B) - P(A \text{ and } B)$.

Passport to Advanced Math and Additional Topics in Math

OVERVIEW

This chapter focuses on questions that fall into the categories Passport to Advanced Math and Additional Topics in Math. Attention here is placed on more sophisticated types of functions beyond linear ones, like quadratic, polynomial, rational, and exponential functions, as well as elements of geometry and very basic trigonometry. Here, you will find that there are more "purely mathematical" questions, meaning that you will be asked to solve nonlinear equations or dive into the conceptual foundations of functions to analyze situations that are not posed in a real-world context. Of course, given the emphasis of real-world problems on the PSAT/NMSQT® exam, you will certainly also encounter such problems *within* an applied scenario, but less often than you did in the categories discussed in Chapter 7.

While these two categories cover different types of functions and topics than Chapter 7, the way the PSAT/NMSQT® exam tests the math is the same—and your ability to model a scenario mathematically remains very important. You still need to be comfortable identifying variables and interpreting the information provided to you *symbolically* in order to set up equations and functions, as well as systems of nonlinear equations used to solve word problems. Here again, questions on the exam tend to require you to use tools and methods from multiple math categories! For instance, given the relationship between the base radius and height of a cylinder, you may need to determine the height of the cylinder in order to make the volume a certain value. Other possible crossover events will be discussed as you progress through the chapter.

We will review the main tools, techniques, and theorems needed in both the Passport to Advanced Math and Additional Topics in Math categories, and we will discuss a wide range of question types throughout the chapter.

PASSPORT TO ADVANCED MATH

PSAT/NMSQT® exam questions in the Passport to Advanced Math category primarily focus on building functions of various types, interpreting their various parts in applied contexts, and setting up and solving related nonlinear equations and certain systems. As with Heart of Algebra questions, the ability to solve a given equation will get you only part of the way! For instance, you are likely comfortable solving quadratic equations, but can you interpret the meaning of the parameters of a quadratic function used to model a real-world scenario? Likewise, identifying that a graph of a curve is either a polynomial or exponential function is not difficult, but the PSAT/NMSQT® Math Test questions will probe more deeply into your conceptual understanding of these functions.

We will review all of these functions and provide useful tidbits along the way. Let's get started!

INTRODUCTION TO FUNCTIONS

TIP

If you have an actual equation for *f*(*x*), then the way you compute *f*(2) is by substituting 2 in for all *x*'s in the expression.

You likely have encountered equations like $y = 2x^2 - 1$, $y = \dfrac{x}{x+1}$, and $y = e^x$ in your schoolwork. In these, x is the independent variable, and y is the dependent variable. It is often more convenient to replace y to form an equation in **function notation**, where $f(x) = y$—doing so simplifies matters when talking about points on a curve. The sentence, "The graph of the function $f(x)$ contains the point (–2, 7)." can be summed up by simply writing $f(-2) = 7$.

Functions are often described using algebraic expressions, which can then be illustrated by a graph. Two important features of *any* function are its domain and range.

- The **domain** of a function is the set of all values of x that can be substituted into the expression and yield a meaningful output.

- The **range** of a function is the set of all possible y-values attained at some member of the domain.

In the absence of a graph, determining the domain of a function is much easier than specifying its range. The following are methods of finding domains of some common function types that you will encounter on the PSAT/NMSQT® exam:

Function Type	General Form	Domain
Quadratic	$f(x) = ax^2 + bx + c$, where a, b, and c are real numbers	All real numbers
Polynomial	$f(x) = a_n x^n + a_{n-1} x^{n-1} + \ldots a_1 x + a_0$, where $a_0, a_1, \ldots, a_n$ are real numbers	All real numbers
Rational	$f(x) = \dfrac{P(x)}{Q(x)}$, where $P(x)$ and $Q(x)$ are polynomials that do not share any common factors	All real numbers except those values of x in which the denominator $Q(x)$ equals zero
Square Root	$f(x) = \sqrt{ax + b}$, where a and b are real numbers	All real numbers x for which $ax + b \geq 0$
Exponential	$f(x) = A \cdot b^{mx}$, where A, m, and b are real numbers	All real numbers

Do you remember how to add or subtract polynomial expressions like $(2x^3 - x + 5) - (3x - x^3)$? How about multiplying rational expressions like $\dfrac{5x}{2x+1} \cdot \dfrac{4x^2 - 1}{15x^3}$? Regardless of the actual algebraic expression involved, each can be defined as a function. So, knowing how to perform arithmetic operations for general functions and knowing how to determine their domains is important. For the following, let f and g be functions.

- The sum function $(f + g)(x)$ is defined as $f(x) + g(x)$.

- The difference function $(f - g)(x)$ is defined as $f(x) - g(x)$.

- The product function $(f \cdot g)(x)$ is defined as $f(x) \cdot g \cdot (x)$.

- The quotient function $\left(\dfrac{f}{g}\right)(x)$ is defined as $\dfrac{f(x)}{g(x)}$.

The domain of the sum, difference, and product functions is the set of x-values for which **both** $f(x)$ and $g(x)$ are defined; the domain of the quotient function is the set of x-values for which **both** $f(x)$ and $g(x)$ are defined **and** $g(x)$ is not equal to zero.

What is the domain of the function $f(x) = \dfrac{\sqrt{x+1}}{2x-3}$?

The domain of the numerator is the set of x-values for which $x \geq -1$, and the domain of the denominator is the set of all real numbers. But we must discard $x = \dfrac{3}{2}$, since it makes the denominator zero. So, the domain is the set of all real numbers greater than or equal to -1, except $\dfrac{3}{2}$.

Another important combination of functions is the **composition** of f and g, denoted by $(f \circ g)$. This is the function defined by $(f \circ g)(x) = f(g(x))$.

Some PSAT/NMSQT® exam questions will ask you to read functional values from a given graph. Further, you also need to know how to identify x- and y-intercepts, find intervals on which a function is increasing and decreasing by looking at its graphs, determine relative (or absolute) maximum (highest) points and relative (or absolute) minimum (lowest) points, and find the average value of a function on a given interval.

ALERT

In general, $(f \circ g) \neq (f \circ g)$. The order in which you compose two functions matters.

- An **x-intercept of** f is any point of the form $(x, 0)$. You find x-intercept(s) by solving the equation $f(x) = 0$.

- A **y-intercept of** f is the point $(0, f(0))$.

- f is *increasing* on an interval if its graph rises from left to right as you progress through the interval from left to right.

- f is *decreasing* if its graph falls from left to right as you progress through the interval from left to right.

- The **minimum of** f is the y-value of the lowest point on the graph of f.

- The **maximum of** f is the y-value of the highest point on the graph of f.

- The average value of $f(x)$ on an interval from $x = a$ to $x = b$ is defined by $\dfrac{f(b) - f(a)}{b - a}$. This is the slope of the line segment connecting $(a, f(a))$ to $(b, f(b))$.

Let's take a look at the graph of the following polynomial function $p(x)$.

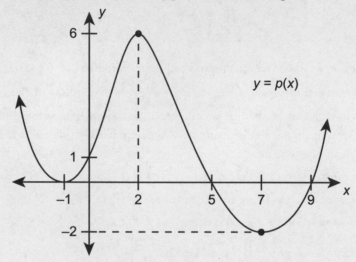

The domain is the set of all real numbers, as indicated by arrowheads affixed to the ends of the graph, suggesting that the upward trend of the graph continues indefinitely to the left and right.

- The range is the set of all real numbers greater than or equal to –2.

- The x-intercepts occur when $x = -1, 5$, and 9; the y-intercept is $(0, 1)$.

- The graph of $p(x)$ is increasing from $x = -1$ to $x = 2$ and to the right of $x = 7$.

- The graph of $p(x)$ is decreasing to the left of $x = -1$ and from $x = 2$ to $x = 7$.

- The minimum of f is –2 (and occurs when $x = 7$); there is no maximum value because the arrowheads affixed to the ends of the curve suggest the graph continues upward indefinitely. (Note that even though the graph levels off at $x = 2$, the y-value there, 6, is not the largest y-value that occurs at any point on the graph.)

The above graph could have easily been incorporated into an applied context. For instance, x could represent the number of units (in thousands) of an item a company manufacturers and $p(x)$ could represent the profit made by manufacturing and selling that number. (Note that in such a case, the graph to the left of the y-axis would be excluded from the problem since you cannot have a negative number of items.) Once the graph is linked to an applied scenario, the intercepts, intervals on which the graph is increasing or decreasing, and the maximum and minimum values all take on specific meaning *in context*. The *x*-intercepts are break-even values, meaning that when a company manufactures and sells that number of units, its profit is zero. The *y*-intercept is the amount of money with which the company starts before production. Intervals on which the graph is increasing indicate that profit is rising, while profit declines on intervals where the graph decreases.

Occasionally, a question concerning the transformation (shifts and reflections) of a function will pop up on the PSAT/NMSQT® exam. The table below summarizes these rules. Assume $c > 0$.

$f(x + c)$	Shifts a graph to the left c units
$f(x - c)$	Shifts a graph to the right c units
$f(x) + c$	Shifts a graph up c units
$f(x) - c$	Shifts a graph down c units
$-f(x)$	Reflects a graph about the x-axis; negate y-values

QUADRATIC EQUATIONS

Quadratic equations, which are of the form $ax^2 + bx + c = 0$, where a, b, and c are real numbers and $a \neq 0$, occur in various forms on every PSAT/NMSQT® Math Test. So, being comfortable with solving them using various methods and understanding the nature of solutions of such equations will improve your overall score.

Several methods can be used to solve quadratic equations: factoring, using the quadratic formula, and completing the square. You must first write the equation in the standard form $ax^2 + bx + c = 0$—which might require moving terms to one side of the equation or using the distributive property—when using any of these techniques.

Solve: $6x^2 - x - 2 = 0$ —Factoring	
Process and Comments	**Illustration of Method**
Whenever possible, factor the quadratic expression into a product of two factors or a single linear factor squared.	$6x^2 - x - 2 = 0$ $(3x - 2)(2x + 1) = 0$ $3x - 2 = 0$ or $2x + 1 = 0$
Once factored, set each factor equal to zero and solve for x.	$x = \dfrac{2}{3}, \ -\dfrac{1}{2}$

Solve: $6x^2 - x - 2 = 0$ —Quadratic Formula	
The solutions of $ax^2 + bx + c = 0$ are given by the formula: $x = \dfrac{-b \pm \sqrt{b^2 - 4ac}}{2a}$	If given $6x^2 - x - 2 = 0$, use $a = 6$, $b = -1$, and $c = -2$ in the formula: $x = \dfrac{-b \pm \sqrt{b^2 - 4ac}}{2a}$ $= \dfrac{-(-1) \pm \sqrt{(-1)^2 - 4(6)(-2)}}{2(6)}$ $= \dfrac{1 \pm \sqrt{49}}{12}$ $= \dfrac{1 \pm 7}{12} = \dfrac{2}{3}, \ -\dfrac{1}{2}$

Solve: $6x^2 - x - 2 = 0$ —Completing the Square

The goal of the method is to rewrite the equation $ax^2 + bx + c = 0$ in the form $a(x - h)^2 + k = 0$. From there, isolate the squared term, take the square root of both sides and solve for x.

The steps of completing the square are:

1. Write the equation in the form $ax^2 + bx + c = 0$.

2. Factor a from the first two terms ONLY to get $a(x^2 + \dfrac{b}{a}x) + c = 0$.

3. To complete the square, add "the square of one-half of the coefficient of x" (that is, $\left(\dfrac{1}{2} \cdot \dfrac{b}{a}\right)^2$) inside the parentheses. Then, on the outside of the parentheses (after the constant term c), subtract $a \cdot \left(\dfrac{1}{2} \cdot \dfrac{b}{a}\right)^2$ to balance it out. Doing so gives the equation

$$a\left(x^2 + \frac{b}{a}x + \left(\frac{1}{2} \cdot \frac{b}{a}\right)^2\right) +$$
$$c - a \cdot \left(\frac{1}{2} \cdot \frac{b}{a}\right)^2 = 0$$

4. Finally, factor the trinomial as a binomial squared:

If $\dfrac{b}{a} < 0$, this factors as

$$a\left(x + \frac{1}{2} \cdot \frac{b}{a}\right)^2 + c - a \cdot \left(\frac{1}{2} \cdot \frac{b}{a}\right)^2 = 0.$$

If $\dfrac{b}{a} > 0$, this factors as

$$a\left(x - \frac{1}{2} \cdot \frac{b}{a}\right)^2 + c - a \cdot \left(\frac{1}{2} \cdot \frac{b}{a}\right)^2 = 0.$$

This method is rarely used to *solve* quadratic equations outright, but the technique is useful when graphing quadratic functions, which we'll cover later in this chapter.

$$6x^2 - x - 2 = 0$$

$$6\left(x^2 - \frac{1}{6}x\right) - 2 = 0$$

$$6\left(x^2 - \frac{1}{6}x + \left(\frac{1}{2} \cdot \left(-\frac{1}{6}\right)\right)^2\right)$$

$$-2 - 6\left(\frac{1}{2} \cdot \left(-\frac{1}{6}\right)\right)^2 = 0$$

$$6\left(x - \frac{1}{12}\right)^2 - \frac{49}{24} = 0$$

$$6\left(x - \frac{1}{12}\right)^2 = \frac{49}{24}$$

$$\left(x - \frac{1}{12}\right)^2 = \frac{49}{144}$$

$$x - \frac{1}{12} = \pm\sqrt{\frac{49}{144}} = \pm\frac{7}{12}$$

$$x = \frac{1}{12} \pm \frac{7}{12} = \frac{2}{3}, \ -\frac{1}{2}$$

If a PSAT/NMSQT® exam question doesn't need an exact solution, but rather asks about the *nature* of the solutions of a quadratic equation—that is, if there are two distinct real solutions, one repeated real solution, or two complex conjugate solutions—you simply need to compute the sign of the radicand $b^2 - 4ac$ (called the **discriminant**) appearing in the quadratic formula.

Sign of Discriminant of $ax^2 + bx + c = 0$	Nature of Solutions
$b^2 - 4ac > 0$	Two distinct real solutions
$b^2 - 4ac = 0$	One repeated real solution
$b^2 - 4ac < 0$	Two complex conjugate solutions

The following examples, which vary in difficulty, are similar to the flavor of the questions on the PSAT/NMSQT® Math Test that examine conceptual understanding of quadratic equations.

Which of the following quadratic equations has a repeated real solution?

A. $8x^2 + 17x = 0$

B. $9x^2 + 6x + 1 = 0$

C. $x^2 + 30x + 2 = 0$

D. $x^2 - 11 = 0$

Compute the discriminant of each equation; the one for which the discriminant = 0 is the equation that has a repeated real solution. **The correct answer is B.** The equation in choice B is the only one with a discriminant of 0:

$$(-6)^2 - 4(9)(1) = 36 - 36 = 0$$

Another way to check: the quadratic equation in choice B, $9x^2 + 6x + 1 = 0$, is equivalent to $(3x + 1)^2 = 0$. The only x-value that satisfies this equation is $x = -\frac{1}{3}$, which is a repeated real solution.

Let's look at another question dealing with quadratic equations.

Given that $x = \frac{1}{2}$ is a solution to the equation $4kx + 1 = 3k^2$ where k is a negative real number, what is the value of k?

Two concepts are being assessed in this problem. First, since $x = \frac{1}{2}$ is a solution to the equation $4kx + 1 = 3k^2$, if you substitute in $x = \frac{1}{2}$, the resulting equation is true. Doing so here yields the following quadratic equation in k: $2k + 1 = 3k^2$, which is equivalent to $3k^2 - 2k - 1 = 0$. Factoring the left side yields $(3k + 1)(k - 1) = 0$. Setting each factor equal to zero and solving for k yields solutions $k = 1$ and $k = -\frac{1}{3}$. Since k is negative, the solution is $k = -\frac{1}{3}$.

QUADRATIC FUNCTIONS

A **quadratic function** has the form $f(x) = ax^2 + bx + c$, where a, b, and c are real numbers and $a \neq 0$. The graph is a U-shaped curve called a **parabola**. The standard form of a quadratic function is $f(x) = a(x - h)^2 + k$, where the vertex is (h, k); any quadratic function can be written in this form using the method of completing the square.

The following are the general characteristics of the graphs of quadratic functions:

- If the coefficient a of x^2 is positive, then the vertex is a minimum point for the graph and the graph looks like a U; if it is negative, then the vertex is a maximum point for the graph and the graph looks like an upside-down U.

TIP

Both accuracy and timeliness are important on the PSAT/NMSQT® exam. If you can factor equations very quickly, feel free to approach this type of problem that way!

TIP

Pay attention to what is ultimately being asked for in a problem. The fact that k is negative is buried slightly in the problem statement. The other solution, $k = 1$, will definitely be listed as a wrong answer choice.

- The x-intercepts (also called **zeros**) are found by solving the equation $ax^2 + bx + c = 0$. There are three possibilities for the type of solutions to this equation:

  1. **Two different real solutions p and q.** The quadratic expression $ax^2 + bx + c$ factors as $(x - p)(x + q)$. In turn, the graph of the parabola has two x-intercepts at $x = p$ and $x = q$. Graphically, this can occur only if the vertex lies above the x-axis and the parabola opens downward, or if the vertex lies below the x-axis and the parabola opens upward.

  2. **One repeated real solution p.** The quadratic expression $ax^2 + bx + c$ factors as $(x - p)^2$. In turn, the graph of the parabola has only one x-intercept at $x = p$. Graphically, this occurs only if the vertex lies *on* the x-axis.

  3. **Two complex conjugate solutions.** The parabola does not cross the x-axis. This can happen one of two ways: either the vertex is above the x-axis and the parabola has a minimum at the vertex, or the vertex lies below the x-axis and the parabola has a maximum at the vertex.

- The graph of a parabola is symmetric about the vertical line passing through its vertex.

TIP

The standard form of a quadratic function is $f(x) = a(x - h)^2 + k$, where the vertex is (h, k).

The following example is typical of a medium-level problem addressing this topic on the PSAT/NMSQT® exam.

The graph of a quadratic function has a vertex of $(-2, 4)$ and passes through the point $(-1, -2)$. What is the equation of this function?

Use the general form of the equation, $f(x) = a(x - h)^2 + k$. Here, $h = -2$ and $k = 4$, so we know that the more specific form of the function is $y = a(x - (-2))^2 + 4 = a(x + 2)^2 + 4$. All that remains is to determine the value of a. To do so, substitute the coordinates of the given point, $x = -1$ and $y = -2$, into the equation:

$$y = a(x + 2)^2 + 4$$

$$-2 = a(-1 + 2)^2 + 4$$

$$-2 = a + 4$$

$$-6 = a$$

NOTE

Typical wrong answer choices include incorrect signs of the vertex in the standard form of the equation. Take extra care when working with multiple negative signs!

So, the equation is $y = -6(x + 2)^2 + 4$.

Sometimes, you will simply be asked to select the correct graph of a given quadratic function, like $f(x) = x^2 + 8x - 9$. For this function, you could eliminate the choice for which the parabola opens downward, because the coefficient of x^2 is positive. To further hone in on the answer, factor the quadratic expression as $(x + 9)(x - 1)$; the graph must cross the x-axis at $x = 1$ and $x = -9$. There will likely be at least one distractor that switches the signs of the zeros or uses different zeros entirely. Finally, if this doesn't do it, put the function into standard form using completing the square—the result of doing so for this function is $f(x) = (x + 4)^2 - 25$—to see that the actual coordinates of the vertex are $(-4, 25)$.

Some problems may appear complicated at first, but a moment's thought and a deep breath can help you see the answer quickly. Such is the case with this example.

If the graph of the function $g(x) = 5(x-3)^2 + k$ never intersects the x-axis, which of the following could be the value of k?

A. -5

B. -4

C. 0

D. 1

The coefficient of x^2, 5, is positive. So, the parabola opens upward. The only way the graph cannot intersect the x-axis is if the y-coordinate of the vertex is positive. (If k were equal to 0, the parabola would be tangent to the x-axis, meaning it has one x-intercept; if it were negative, it would have two distinct x-intercepts.) Hence, from the given choices, $k = 1$ is the only one that works.

Being adept at modeling real-world scenarios involving quadratic functions is important; there are usually one or two such problems testing this skill on the PSAT/NMSQT® exam in one form or another. The following problem requires you to interpret the function in a familiar "ball launch" problem.

The function $h(t) = -4.9t^2 + 19t$ expresses the approximate height h, in meters, of a ball t seconds after it is launched vertically upward from the ground with an initial velocity of 19 meters per second. After approximately how many seconds will the ball hit the ground?

The key here is to know the height of the ball when it hits the ground. At ground level, the height of the ball is 0 meters. So, substitute 0 for $h(t)$ and factor the resulting quadratic expression, as follows:

$$0 = -4.9t^2 + 19t$$

$$0 = -t(4.9t - 19)$$

$$0 = t \text{ and } 0 = 4.9t - 19$$

$$0 = t \text{ and } 4.9t = 19$$

$$0 = t \text{ and } t = \frac{19}{4.9} \approx 3.8$$

Therefore, the ball hits the ground after approximately 3.8 seconds.

The following problem is similar in spirit to the previous example but involves an arithmetic operation on functions.

The following quadratic functions model the heights of two objects launched at the same moment. Assume t represents time and so, $t \geq 0$.

Object 1: $h_1(t) = -16t^2 + 15t + 5$

Object 2: $h_2(t) = -16t^2 + 20t + 1$

Let d be the difference in the height of the second object compared to the first object, assuming that a positive difference indicates that the second object is at a greater height than the first object. What is an expression that describes d in terms of t? Provide an interpretation.

The difference in the height of the second object compared to the first must be $h_2(t) - h_1(t)$, which gives a positive number when the height of Object 2 is greater than the height of Object 1:

$$d = h_2(t) - h_1(t)$$

$$= (-16t^2 + 20t + 1) - (-16t^2 + 15t + 5)$$

$$= -16t^2 + 20t + 1 + 16t^2 - 15t - 5$$

$$= 5t - 4$$

Observe that $h_2(t) - h_1(t) > 0$ when $5t - 4 > 0$, which is equivalent to $t > \dfrac{4}{5}$. In such a case, Object 2 is above Object 1. Similarly, Object 2 is below Object 1 whenever $h_2(t) - h_1(t) < 0$, which occurs for $t < \dfrac{4}{5}$. Finally, Objects 1 and 2 are at the same height when $t = \dfrac{4}{5}$.

POLYNOMIAL EXPRESSIONS

A polynomial expression is a sum or difference of terms consisting of constant multiples of positive integer power, with at least one variable. Some examples are $4x^3 - 2x^2 + 5$, $-x^2y^3 + 5xy^2$, and $5 + xy - 2z^3y$.

A problem or two that asks you to perform an arithmetic operation—addition, subtraction, or multiplication—involving such expressions is typically included on the PSAT/NMSQT® exam. These problems are not difficult, but careless errors involving signs and misusing the distributive property are common pitfalls.

Adding or subtracting polynomial expressions is simply an exercise in combining like terms or terms with the exact same variable parts. Take the following example:

Simplify $2(-x^2y^3 + 5xy^2 - x) - 3(-xy^2 + 3x - 2x^2y)$.

$$2(-x^2y^3 + 5xy^2 - x) - 3(-xy^2 + 3x - 2x^2y)$$

$$= -2x^2y^3 + \underline{10xy^2} - \underline{\underline{2x}} + \underline{3xy^2} - \underline{\underline{9x}} + 6x^2y$$

$$= -2x^2y^3 + 6x^2y + \underline{13xy^2} - \underline{\underline{11x}}$$

Multiplying polynomial expressions involves similar calculations—using the distributive property, followed by combining like terms.

Simplify: $(2x - 3)(x^2 - 2x - 3)$.

$$(2x - 3)(x^2 - 2x - 3) = 2x(x^2 - 2x - 3) - 3(x^2 - 2x - 3)$$

$$= 2x^3 - 4x^2 - 6x - 3x^2 + 6x + 9$$

$$= 2x - 7x^2 + 9$$

The ability to factor polynomials is important, especially when trying to determine values of the variable that make the expression equal to zero (that is, its **zeros**). The following are the common techniques you should review before the exam. Make certain to review your schoolwork notes for practice on these techniques.

Factoring Method	Illustrative Example
GCF (Greatest Common Factor)	$5x^4 + 25x$ factors to $5x(x^3 + 5)$
Difference of Squares	$(a + b)(a - b) = a^2 - b^2$
FOIL (First-Outer-Inner-Last)	$x^4 + 8x^2 - 9$ factors to $(x^2 + 9)(x^2 - 1)$, which further factors as $(x^2 + 9)(x - 1)(x + 1)$

Seldom, if ever, will questions involving factoring be as straightforward as, "Factor this." The need to factor will either be one smaller step of several when solving the problem, or the question will be somewhat more conceptual in nature, like the following example:

> For what real number A can the polynomial $64x^2 + 16Ax + 3A$ be written in the factored form $(mx + n)^2$, where m and n are positive integers?

Start by expanding $(mx + n)^2$ using the FOIL technique:

$$(mx + n)(mx + n)$$

$$m^2x^2 + 2mnx + n^2$$

For $m^2x^2 + 2mnx + n^2 = 64x^2 + 16Ax + 3A$, equate corresponding coefficients, as follows:

$$m^2 = 64$$

$$2mn = 16A$$

$$n^2 = 3A$$

Clearly, $m = 8$ from the first equation. Substituting this into the second equation yields $16n = 16A$. So, $n = A$. Substituting this into the third equation subsequently yields $n^2 = 3n$, so that $n = 0$ or 3. Since n is defined as positive, we conclude that $n = 3$.

POLYNOMIAL FUNCTIONS

A **polynomial function** is a function of the form $f(x) = a_n x^n + a_{n-1} x^{n-1} + \ldots a_1 x + a_0$, where a_0, a_1, $\ldots$, a_n are real numbers and n is a nonnegative integer. We say the polynomial has *degree n*. The three main components of a polynomial $p(x)$ you should be able to define are **x-intercept**, **zero**, and **factor**, defined as follows:

Term	Definition
x-intercept	A point $(a, 0)$ on the graph of $y = p(x)$. $x = a$ is a solution of the equation $p(x) = 0$.
zero	A real number a such that $p(a) = 0$.
factor	An expression of the form $(x - a)$ in which a is a zero of $p(x)$.

The interplay among these three concepts is a topic often assessed on the PSAT/NMSQT® Math Test. Let's walk through a graph together.

The following is the graph of a third-degree polynomial $P(x)$:

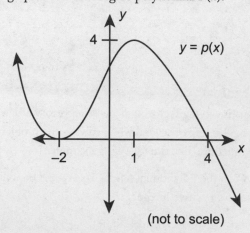

(not to scale)

Determine if each of the following statements is true or false.

I.   The remainder when $P(x)$ is divided by $(x + 2)$ is 0.

II.   The remainder when $P(x)$ is divided by $(x + 2)(x - 4)$ is 0.

III. $P(1)$ is a positive number.

IV. $P(x)$ has three zeros.

I. True. Since the graph of $P(x)$ touches the x-axis at $x = -2$, it follows that -2 is a zero and so, $(x - (-2)) = (x + 2)$ is a factor of $P(x)$.

So, $P(x) = (x + 2) \cdot Q(x)$, where $Q(x)$ is a quadratic expression. Therefore, $\dfrac{P(x)}{x + 2} = \dfrac{(x + 2) \cdot Q(x)}{x + 2} = Q(x)$, with zero remainder.

II. True. Since the graph of $P(x)$ crosses the x-axis at both $x = -2$ and $x = 4$, it follows that both -2 and 4 are zero. So, both $(x + 2)$ and $(x - 4)$ are factors of $P(x)$. So, we can write $P(x)$ as $P(x) = (x + 2)(x - 4)R(x)$, where $R(x)$ is a linear expression:

$$\frac{P(x)}{(x + 2)(x - 4)} = \frac{(x + 2)(x - 4) \cdot R(x)}{(x + 2)(x - 4)} = R(x)$$

III. True. $P(1)$ is the y-coordinate of the point on the graph when $x = 1$. This value is 4, which is positive.

IV. False. A zero of $P(x)$ is an x-intercept. There are only two x-intercepts and so, two zeros.

On the exam, your knowledge of basic graphical properties of polynomials will be assessed algebraically and graphically. Here are a couple of quick facts to know about polynomials:

- The "end behavior" of a polynomial's graph (that is, what it does as the inputs x get very large in either direction) is described exclusively by the term with the highest exponent. So, the graph of $m(x) = x^5 - 3x^3 + 2x - 1$ behaves like $y = x^5$ for very large values of $|x|$.

- If the power of a factor of a polynomial function is even, meaning that the corresponding zero is repeated an even number of times, then the graph of the polynomial is tangent to the x-axis at that zero (and resembles a parabola close by).

The following question assesses your knowledge of zeros of a polynomial given in algebraic form.

Determine which of the following polynomial functions has at its complete set of zeros the set $\{-5, -2, 0, 4\}$. Select all that apply.

I. $p(x) = x(x - 2)(x - 5)(x + 4)$

II. $p(x) = x^2(x + 2)(x + 5)(x - 4)$

III. $p(x) = x(x + 2)(x + 5)(x - 4)$

IV. $p(x) = x(x + 2)^2(x + 5)^3(x - 4)^4$

I. No. The first factor corresponds to the zero 0, but the signs used in the last three binomials are all wrong; the zeros to which they correspond are 2, 5, and −4, respectively.

II. Yes. The values of x that make this polynomial equal to zero are precisely −5, −2, 0, and 4. The fact that one of the factors is squared does not produce another different zero.

III. No. While −2, −5, and 4 are zeros of this polynomial, 0 is not, because $p(0) \neq 0$.

IV. Yes. Just as in the polynomial in II, the values of x that make this polynomial equal to zero are precisely −5, −2, 0, and 4. The fact that the factors are raised to positive integer powers does not produce additional zeros.

RATIONAL EXPRESSIONS AND EQUATIONS

Fractions in which the numerator and denominator are polynomials are called **rational expressions**. Arithmetic with rational expressions is like the arithmetic with numerical fractions—you simply add, subtract, multiply, and divide polynomials, and cancel like factors in the top and bottom as you would when simplifying a fraction involving numbers.

Perform the indicated operations of rational expressions.

I.   Simplify: $\dfrac{10x^2 - 3x - 1}{1 - 2x}$

II. Add and simplify: $\dfrac{12x - 4 - 1}{x^2 - 1} + \dfrac{5 - x}{x^2 - 1}$

III. Subtract and simplify: $\dfrac{x}{a - x} - \dfrac{a}{a + x}$, where a is a nonzero real number

IV. Multiply and simplify: $\dfrac{3x^2 + 3x}{x^2 - 9} \cdot \dfrac{x + 3}{x^2 - 1}$

V.   Simplify this complex fraction: $x - \dfrac{\dfrac{2x + 1}{2}}{x + 1}$

NOTE

A problem similar in spirit to this example could be described graphically instead of algebraically— you could be asked which graph has a prescribed set of zeros.

I. Factor the numerator and cancel any factors appearing in both the top and bottom.

$$\frac{10x^2 - 3x - 1}{1 - 2x} = \frac{(5x+1)(2x-1)}{-(2x-1)} = \frac{(5x+1)\cancel{(2x-1)}}{-\cancel{(2x-1)}} = -(5x+1) = -(5x+1)$$

Notice how we factored a −1 out of the denominator to further simplify. Always look carefully to cancel out all factors you can. Then, when simplifying, keep track of all factors—a common error here would be to drop the −1.

II. Simply add the numerators, keeping the denominator the same, because the two fractions already have the same denominator. Then, simplify the result by canceling any factors appearing in both the top and bottom.

$$\frac{2x - 4}{x^2 - 1} + \frac{5 - x}{x^2 - 1} = \frac{2x - 4 + 5 - x}{x^2 - 1} = \frac{x + 1}{x^2 - 1} = \frac{\cancel{x+1}}{\cancel{(x+1)}(x-1)} = \frac{1}{x - 1}$$

TIP

The commutative property (i.e., the order in which addition and multiplication is performed is irrelevant) is important here because it enabled us to simplify the resulting rational expressions in two instances.

III. First, find a common denominator by simply multiplying the denominators already present: $(a - x)(a + x)$. Express both fractions using this denominator, and then combine and simplify the result by canceling any factors appearing in both the top and bottom:

$$\frac{x}{a - x} - \frac{a}{a + x} = \frac{x(a + x)}{(a - x)(a + x)} - \frac{a(a - x)}{(a - x)(a + x)}$$

$$= \frac{x(a + x) - a(a - x)}{(a - x)(a + x)}$$

$$= \frac{xa + x^2 - a^2 + ax}{(a - x)(a + x)}$$

$$= \frac{x^2 + 2ax - a^2}{(a - x)(a + x)}$$

$$= -\frac{x^2 + 2ax - a^2}{(x - a)(x + a)}$$

The "right" answer can be written in many equivalent forms. For instance:

$$\frac{x^2 + 2ax - a^2}{(a - x)(a + x)} = -\frac{x^2 + 2ax - a^2}{(x - a)(x + a)} = \frac{a^2 - x^2 - 2ax}{(x - a)(x + a)} = \frac{a^2 - 2ax - x^2}{(x - a)(x + a)}.$$

The ability to perform such algebraic manipulations with ease will be very helpful since you do not know in which form answers will be presented on the PSAT/NMSQT® exam.

Sometimes, the rational expressions you will encounter involve arbitrary constants instead of specific numbers. The procedure is exactly the same! Trust your math knowledge.

TIP

Do not multiply the numerators and multiply the denominators *before* factoring. Doing so will create a huge mess that is nearly impossible to simplify.

IV. Factor all expressions and then cancel those common to the top and bottom:

$$\frac{3x^2 + 3x}{x^2 - 9} \cdot \frac{x + 3}{x^2 - 1} = \frac{3x\cancel{(x+1)}}{(x-3)\cancel{(x+3)}} \cdot \frac{\cancel{x+3}}{\cancel{(x+1)}(x-1)} = \frac{3x}{(x-3)(x-1)}$$

Although it might be tempting to do so, do not cancel the 3s in the last fraction. "3" is not a common factor of the numerator and denominator.

V. To simplify a complex fraction, the main goal is to express it in the form of a simple rational expression, meaning no "fractions within fractions." To accomplish that goal here, combine the fractions in the denominator using the LCD of $x + 1$:

$$\frac{2x+1}{x-\dfrac{2}{x+1}} = \frac{2x+1}{\dfrac{x(x+1)}{x+1} - \dfrac{2}{x+1}} = \frac{2x+1}{\dfrac{x(x+1)-2}{x+1}} = \frac{2x+1}{\dfrac{x^2+x-2}{x+1}}$$

Now, multiply the numerator by the reciprocal of the denominator:

$$\frac{2x+1}{\dfrac{x^2+x-2}{x+1}} = (2x+1) \cdot \frac{x+1}{x^2+x-2}$$

Finally, simplify as usual:

$$(2x+1) \cdot \frac{x+1}{x^2+x-2} = \frac{(2x+1)(x+1)}{(x+2)(x-1)}$$

There are no common factors in the top and bottom, so this rational expression is simplified.

Rational expressions can be expressed in different ways, as illustrated in the following example:

Write as a single simplified rational expression: $\dfrac{1}{5x+3} - 3(5x+3)^{-2}$

First, rewrite $3(5x+3)^{-2}$ as $\dfrac{3}{(5x+3)^2}$. Then, using the least common denominator $(5x+3)^2$, subtract the rational expressions and simplify:

$$\frac{1}{5x+3} - \frac{3}{(5x+3)^2} = \frac{5x+3}{(5x+3)^2} - \frac{3}{(5x+3)^2} = \frac{5x+3-3}{(5x+3)^2} = \frac{5x}{(5x+3)^2}$$

As with all the math you'll see on test day, the PSAT/NMSQT® examiners are interested in assessing your ability to model real-world situations. The next example is a typical "upstream-downstream" word problem.

A pontoon boat travels downstream (with the river current) from one dock to another port 45 miles away. The current of the river is 5 miles per hour. The round trip takes 8.4 hours to complete. If the equation describing the situation is $\dfrac{45}{s+5} + \dfrac{45}{s-5} = 8.4$, what does the expression $\dfrac{45}{s-5}$ represent?

Let s be the speed of the pontoon boat in still water. Using the fact that distance = rate × time yields:

	Distance (in Miles)	Rate (in mph)	Time (in Hours)
Downstream	45	$s+5$	$\dfrac{45}{s+5}$
Upstream	45	$s-5$	$\dfrac{45}{s-5}$
Round Trip			8.4

www.petersons.com

ALERT

A common error is writing $3(5x+3)^{-2}$ as $\dfrac{1}{3^2(5x+3)^2}$. The power "–2" applies only to the expression within the parentheses.

TIP

This same type of problem could be posed for airplanes flying with a headwind and tailwind. This is comparable to the pontoon boat traveling in the river against and with the current, respectively.

So, the expression $\frac{45}{s-5}$ represents the number of hours it takes the pontoon boat to complete the upstream portion of the round trip.

The following example is a standard "work" word problem. These come in different varieties, from friends working together to paint a house (or complete some other mundane task) to pumps working together to empty/fill a pool. The trick is to understand the technique used so that you can apply it to *any* setting thrown at you.

> Working together, it takes a laptop computer and a supercomputer 3.5 days to run a numerical analysis program used to model weather patterns. If it takes the supercomputer 6 days to run the program alone, how many days would it take the laptop computer to run the program alone?

Let x equal the number of days it takes the laptop computer to run the program alone. That means that it runs $\frac{1}{x}$ of the program every day. The supercomputer can run the program alone in 6 days, so it completes $\frac{1}{6}$ of the job every day. Working together, the two computers complete the program in 3.5 days, so each day they run $\frac{1}{3.5} = \frac{1}{\frac{7}{2}} = \frac{2}{7}$ of the program. The sum of the individual rates equals the rate working together. So, the following equation can be used to determine the number of days it would take the laptop computer to run the program alone:

$$\frac{1}{x} + \frac{1}{6} = \frac{2}{7}$$

Solving this equation yields the following:

$$\frac{1}{x} + \frac{1}{6} = \frac{2}{7}$$
$$42 + 7x = 12x$$
$$42 = 5x$$
$$x = \frac{42}{5} = 8.4$$

So, it would take the laptop computer 8.4 days to run the program alone.

RADICALS AND RADICAL EQUATIONS

To do well on the PSAT/NMSQT® exam, you should be comfortable working with radicals. Questions that involve radicals are mainly computational in nature—you will need to simplify an expression involving radicals or solve a simple radical equation.

Rule (in Symbols)	Verbal Interpretation
1. $\left(\sqrt{a}\right)^2 = a$	Raising a square root to the 2nd power gives the radicand (the number under the radical symbol).
2. $\sqrt{a^2} = |a|$	Since the square root symbol means the *principal* root, and a could technically be negative, we must take the absolute value of a to get $\sqrt{a^2}$.

Rule (in Symbols)	Verbal Interpretation
3. $\sqrt{a \cdot b} = \sqrt{a} \cdot \sqrt{b}$, whenever $a \geq 0$ and $b \geq 0$.	Square root of a product is the product of the square roots.
4. $\sqrt{\dfrac{a}{b}} = \dfrac{\sqrt{a}}{\sqrt{b}}$, whenever $a \geq 0$ and $b > 0$.	Square root of a quotient is the quotient of the square roots.
5. $\dfrac{1}{\sqrt{a}} = \dfrac{1}{\sqrt{a}} \cdot \dfrac{\sqrt{a}}{\sqrt{a}} = \dfrac{\sqrt{a}}{a}$, whenever $a > 0$.	You can clear a square root from the denominator of a fraction by multiplying top and bottom by it.

Solve for x: $\sqrt{x+10} - 4 = x$.

The strategy is to isolate the radical expression on one side of the equation, so that squaring both sides of the equation eliminates the radical:

$$\sqrt{x+10} = x+4$$
$$\left(\sqrt{x+10}\right)^2 = (x+4)^2$$
$$x+10 = x^2 + 8x + 16$$

Now, solve the resulting quadratic equation. This may or may not factor, so you should know how to use various techniques to solve such equations:

$$x + 10 = x^2 + 8x + 16$$
$$x^2 + 7x + 6 = 0$$
$$(x+6)(x+1) = 0$$
$$x+6 = 0, x+1 = 0$$
$$x = -6, -1$$

Finally, you must check that each of these values satisfies the *original* radical equation, since eliminating the radical as we did could result in **extraneous solutions** (that is, values that satisfy the equation arising from eliminating the radical but do not satisfy the original equation *with* the radical term present):

$$x = -6: \underbrace{\sqrt{-6+10} - 4}_{=\sqrt{4}-4=2-4=-2} \overset{??}{=} -6 \quad \text{NO!}$$

$$x = -1: \underbrace{\sqrt{-1+10} - 4}_{=\sqrt{9}-4=3-4=-1} \overset{??}{=} -1 \quad \text{YES!}$$

So, the only solution is $x = -1$.

EXPONENT RULES AND EXPONENTIAL FUNCTIONS

The exponent rules are a source of common pitfalls! Familiarize yourself with the dos and don'ts of how to deal with exponents; all the main rules are listed in the following table. Assume that the bases a and b are greater than 1 and that the exponents n and m are real numbers.

ALERT

A very common error is to mistakenly say, "The square root of a sum is the sum of the square roots." A quick numerical counter-example shows why this is false:

Correct:
$\sqrt{9+16} = \sqrt{25} = 5$

Incorrect:
$\sqrt{9+16} = \sqrt{9} + \sqrt{16}$
$= 3 + 4$
$= 7$

In particular,
$\sqrt{a^2 + b^2} \neq a + b$.

TIP

Do not forget to check for extraneous solutions when solving radical equations.

Exponent Rule (in Symbols)	Verbal Interpretation
1. $a^0 = 1$	The result of raising any nonzero real number to the zero power is 1.
2. $a^{-n} = \dfrac{1}{a^n}$, $a^n = \dfrac{1}{a^{-n}}$	A term in the numerator that is raised to a negative exponent is equivalent to a term in the denominator with the same base, but positive exponent, and vice versa.
3. $(a \cdot b)^n = a^n \cdot b^n$	When raising a product to a power, apply the power to each term and multiply the results.
4. $\left(\dfrac{a}{b}\right)^n = \dfrac{a^n}{b^n}$	When raising a quotient to a power, apply the power to each term and divide the results.
5. $a^n \cdot a^m = a^{n+m}$	When multiplying terms with the same base raised to powers, add the powers.
6. $\dfrac{a^n}{a^m} = a^{n-m}$	When dividing terms with the same base raised to powers, subtract the powers.
7. $(a^n)^m = a^{n \cdot m}$	When raising a term that is already raised to a power to another power, multiply the powers.
8. If $a = b$, then $a^n = b^n$, for any exponent n.	If two real numbers are equal, then their powers are also equal.

It is common not only to apply the exponent rules incorrectly but also to mistakenly apply rules that do not even exist! The following errors commonly arise when working with exponents.

Statement	Interpretation
$(a + b)^n \neq a^n + b^n$	The power of a sum is not equal to the sum of the powers.
$a^n \cdot b^m \neq (a \cdot b)^{n+m}$	You cannot write the product of terms with different bases raised to different powers as a single product raised to a power.
$-a^2 \neq (-a)^2$	If the negative sign is *outside* the parentheses of a quantity being squared, then the square does not apply to it.

You should be comfortable working with numerical calculations involving exponents, as well as simplifying algebraic expressions involving exponents. Consider the following example.

Write the following expression as a single power of x: $\dfrac{x^{-2} \cdot (x^3)^{-4}}{x^5}$.

Start by simplifying the numerator by applying exponent rule 7 from the table provided, followed by rule 5. Then, apply rule 6:

$$\frac{x^{-2} \cdot (x^3)^{-4}}{x^5} = \frac{x^{-2} \cdot x^{-12}}{x^5} = \frac{x^{-14}}{x^5} = x^{-19}$$

Exponential functions play an important role in modeling real-world scenarios, such as half-life, bacterial and population growth and decay, and financial mathematics (interest-related problems), which frequently appear on the PSAT/NMSQT® exam. Building an exponential function with the form $f(x) = A \cdot b^x$ requires you to identify the two parameters A and b. Here, A is the initial amount present (e.g., an initial population, a principal investment, the amount of a substance, etc.), and $b > 0$ is the growth or decay rate.

If $0 < b < 1$, the function decays toward zero exponentially fast; if b is larger than 1, then the function grows exponentially.

The following examples provide a look at the types of modeling questions you might see on the PSAT/NMSQT® Math Test that involve exponential functions. The first example is a standard "bank account investment" model.

> A meteorologist's salary increases by 3.2% annually. If the starting salary is $65,500, formulate a function that models her salary (in dollars) n years later.

Since the meteorologist's salary increases by 3.2% each year, to get next year's salary, multiply the current year's salary by 1.032. Doing this n times in succession yields the salary for year n. Multiplying the base salary 65,500 by 1.032 n times is equivalent to multiplying 65,500 by $(1.032)^n$. So, the function $f(n) = 65{,}500(1.032)^n$ describes the salary in year n.

The next example is biological in nature and tests your conceptual understanding of exponential functions.

> The formula $P(t) = 30\left(\dfrac{1}{2}\right)^{-t}$, where $t \geq 0$ is measured in minutes, models the number of bacteria observed in a biological experiment. Determine if each of the following statements is true or false.
>
> I.   Every minute, the population increases by 30 bacteria.
>
> II. The maximum number of bacteria is 30.
>
> III. The population doubles every minute.
>
> IV. The population levels off after a half-hour.
>
> V.   The population diminishes by a factor of 2 each minute.

I. False. Thirty bacteria is the initial population only and does not affect the actual growth rate. If the population were to increase by 30 per minute, the function would be linear: $y = 30t$.

II. False. The population size starts at 30 bacteria; it continues to increase with time, so this is not the maximum size. Rather, it is the minimum number of bacteria present.

III. True. Observe that $\left(\dfrac{1}{2}\right)^{-t} = 2^t$, so with every increase in t by 1 minute, the population does indeed double.

IV. False. Using the exponent rules reveals that $P(t) = 30 \cdot 2^t$, which is an increasing function. So, it does not level off as t goes onward.

V. False. Since $\left(\dfrac{1}{2}\right)^{-t} = 2^t$, the population *grows*, rather than diminishes.

Another important skill to master as you prepare for the PSAT/NMSQT® exam is determining the type of function—linear, quadratic, or exponential—you should use to accurately model a scenario.

> Online bidding for an auction of an ultra-rare video game from the '80s started one week ago. Each day, the total number of bids has tripled. If m bids were offered on the first day and this

pattern continues, describe why each of the following functions does or does not accurately describe the total number of bids offered t days after the first day.

A. $f(t) = 3^{mt}$

B. $f(t) = 3m + t$

C. $f(t) = 3mt$

D. $f(t) = m \cdot 3^t$

A. On the upside, this function is exponential, which is on the right track. But you should not include the initial number of bids as part of the actual exponent.

B. This would not represent tripling each day, which is an exponential process. The rate of growth described by this function is one bid per day, and the initial number of bids is $3m$.

C. This function does not show tripling every day. Instead, it shows that the initial amount is a multiple of three times the number of days. This is a *linear* function, while the process described is exponential.

D. This function accurately describes this situation. Since the total triples each day, the number of times you multiply the initial amount, m, by 3 depends on the number of days t. This yields the function $f(t) = m \cdot \underbrace{3 \cdot 3 \cdot \ldots \cdot 3}_{t \text{ times}} = m \cdot 3^t$.

You should also be able to determine if a function described by a small table of values is linear or exponential. The key to making this determination is that the slope between *any* two points of a linear function is the same, while an exponential function grows by the same multiple on intervals of the same length.

LITERAL EQUATIONS

Sometimes, you will be asked to manipulate a formula involving multiple variables. In these cases, the key is to realize that the algebra rules remain unchanged!

The following example deals with a well-known physics formula.

> The formula $F = \dfrac{Gm_1 m_2}{r^2}$ represents the force of gravity, F, between two objects with masses of m_1 and m_2, separated by a distance of r, where G is the gravitational constant. Solve this formula for r.

To solve for r, first isolate the r^2 term on one side of the equation. Then, take the square root of both sides, as follows:

$$F = \frac{Gm_1 m_2}{r^2}$$

$$r^2 = \frac{Gm_1 m_2}{F}$$

$$r = \sqrt{\frac{Gm_1 m_2}{F}}$$

Of course, the formulas can be a bit more complicated and involve different types of functions, as in the following example.

A sample formula describing the total inductance in a parallel circuit in terms of the inductance of its individual parts is given by $\frac{1}{I_T} = \frac{1}{I_1} + \frac{1}{I_2} + \frac{1}{I_3}$. Derive an equivalent formula that is solved for I_2.

There are different ways to go about deriving such a formula. The most expedient is first to isolate the fraction involving I_2:

$$\frac{1}{I_T} - \frac{1}{I_1} - \frac{1}{I_3} = \frac{1}{I_2}$$

Now, express the left side as a single fraction using the least common denominator $I_1 I_3 I_T$:

$$\frac{I_1 I_3 - I_T I_3 - I_1 I_T}{I_T I_1 I_3} = \frac{1}{I_2}$$

Finally, use the property that if $\frac{a}{b} = \frac{c}{d}$, where a, b, c, and $d \neq$ zero, then their reciprocals are equal; that is, $\frac{b}{a} = \frac{d}{c}$. In other words, you can flip the fractions on both sides and the results will still be equal. Doing that here yields the following desired formula:

$$\frac{I_T I_1 I_3}{I_1 I_3 - I_T I_3 - I_1 I_T} = I_2$$

NONLINEAR SYSTEMS

Occasionally, there will be a question on the PSAT/NMSQT® Math Test that asks you to solve a **nonlinear system** of equations. The good thing is that these questions are very predictable—they always involve one linear equation and one quadratic equation, and they rarely, if ever, appear in an applied context. So, you simply need to know the technique used to solve such a system. Take a look at the following example, which has a typical PSAT/NMSQT® exam twist.

Consider the following system:

$$\begin{cases} y = 6x^2 + 15x \\ y - 4x = 10 \end{cases}$$

If (x_1, y_1) and (x_2, y_2) are the two solutions of this system, compute $|x_1 \cdot x_2|$.

To solve this system, first solve both equations for y:

$$\begin{cases} y = 6x^2 + 15x \\ y = 4x + 10 \end{cases}$$

Then, equate the two expressions for y. Doing so will always result in a quadratic equation that you can easily solve for x using the techniques discussed earlier in this chapter:

$$6x^2 + 15x = 4x + 10$$
$$6x^2 + 15x - 4x - 10 = 0$$
$$6x^2 + 11x - 10 = 0$$
$$(2x + 5)(3x - 2) = 0$$
$$x = -\frac{5}{2}, \frac{2}{3}$$

These are the x-coordinates x_1 and x_2, so compute the quantity $|x_1 \cdot x_2|$ as $|x_1 \cdot x_2| = \left| -\frac{5}{2} \cdot \frac{2}{3} \right| = \frac{5}{3}$.

The "twist" referred to above is requiring you to go one step beyond simply solving the system and doing something with the solutions. In this example, this took the form of computing. A different twist on this problem would have been to ask you to compute a quantity involving y_1 and y_2. In such a case, you would need to go one extra step to find the y-values corresponding to the x-values you already found by plugging the x-values back into the original equations.

ADDITIONAL TOPICS IN MATH

Approximately 10 percent of the questions on the PSAT/NMSQT® Math Test will cover skills in the Additional Topics in Math subsection. These questions focus on geometry, basic trigonometry, and complex numbers and occur in both the Calculator and No—Calculator sections. Even though these account for a much smaller percentage of the exam than the other three subsections, the problems tend to be geared toward applied scenarios in which you use familiar geometric formulas (the Pythagorean theorem or the area and volume formulas for simple figures) or involve straight-forward computations using complex numbers or basic trigonometric expressions. That means a careful review of the topics—so you are familiar with what you should do in any given situation—can again lead to quick points on the exam.

SIMILAR AND CONGRUENT TRIANGLES

TIP

Triangles $\triangle ABC$ and $\triangle DEF$ are similar if $\frac{AB}{DE} = \frac{BC}{EF} = \frac{AC}{DF} = k$, where k is a positive number. If this ratio $k = 1$, then the triangles are congruent.

The more complex topics of high school geometry that used to cause students grief on the PSAT/NMSQT® Math Test—such as constructions, sophisticated properties of quadrilaterals, polygons, and circles, proofs—no longer have much of a place on the exam. Deep sigh of relief, right? This leaves only a handful of topics that you are expected to have mastered before you take the test.

Two important rules that all triangles obey are the **Triangle Sum Rule** and **Triangle Inequality**. The Triangle Sum Rule asserts that the sum of the measures of the three angles in any triangle must be 180°, and the Triangle Inequality says that the sum of the lengths of any two sides of a triangle must be strictly larger than the length of the third side. It is impossible to construct a triangle that does not satisfy *both* conditions.

Rest assured, a question that deals with congruent triangles or similar triangles will pop up on the PSAT/NMSQT® Math Test. Two triangles are **congruent** if they have the same three angles *and* the same three sides—such triangles have the same shape *and* size. Relaxing the requirement that they have the same size leads to similarity: two triangles are **similar** if they have the same angles and their corresponding sides have the same ratio.

Try the following example to test your understanding of triangle rules.

In $\triangle ABC$, $\overline{AB} = 11.4$ and $\overline{BC} = 9.6$. Write a compound inequality to represent the possible side lengths of $\overline{AC}$.

Since the sum of any two sides of a triangle must be greater than the third side, $11.4 + 9.6 > \overline{AC}$. So, $\overline{AC} < 21$. But there must be a minimum length that $\overline{AC}$ could be. (For example, if $\overline{AC} = 1$, then $9.6 + 1$ would not be larger than 11.4.) Use the smaller side to create the inequality,

$\overline{AC}$ + 9.6 > 11.4, and solve for $\overline{AC}$ > 1.8. Therefore, $\overline{AC}$ must be greater than 1.8, but less than 21. The inequality solution is: $1.8 < \overline{AC} < 21$.

Modeling problems involving similar triangles often involve the Pythagorean theorem, discussed in the next section.

THE PYTHAGOREAN THEOREM

A **right triangle** has two legs adjacent to the right angle and a **hypotenuse** opposite the right angle. These triangles play an important role in modeling real-world scenarios, as well as in defining the trigonometric functions.

There are two triangles with angle relationships in which we can represent the lengths of all sides using known ratios: 30–60–90 and 45–45–90 triangles.

These are illustrated below:

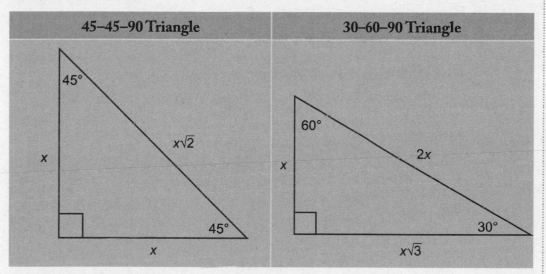

These relationships can be verified using the Pythagorean theorem. The **Pythagorean theorem** expresses the relationship between the sides of a right triangle, stating that $c^2 = a^2 + b^2$, where side c is the hypotenuse and the sides a and b are its legs.

The following is a typical applied problem involving the Pythagorean theorem.

A local state park wants to build a swinging bridge across a small ravine. The ravine measurements and proposed endpoints A and B of the bridge are shown below.

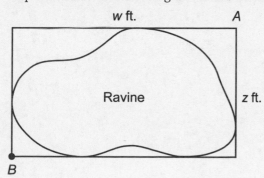

ALERT

The Pythagorean theorem works ONLY for right triangles!

A "simplified" expression need not be the cleanest, simplest-looking choice among the four listed in a multiple-choice problem.

Write a simplified expression that gives the length of the swinging bridge.

Construct a right triangle, as follows:

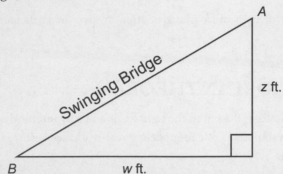

Using the Pythagorean theorem yields the length of AB as $\sqrt{w^2 + z^2}$. This is as simplified as we can get without more information about w and z.

In and of itself, the problem is not difficult. What gets tricky on the PSAT/NMSQT® exam is the presence of distractor choices that throw a wrench in the works. Also, the use of the word "simplified" in the statement of the problem can potentially lure you into certain algebra traps! Here are some common distractors for this problem with an explanation as to why each is wrong.

Incorrect Expression	Why It Is Wrong
$\sqrt{w^2 - z^2}$	You incorrectly identified AB as a leg of the right triangle, rather than as its hypotenuse.
$w - z$	You made the error in the previous row and then incorrectly simplified the radical of a difference.
$w^2 + z^2$	You forgot the square root step from the Pythagorean theorem.
$w + z$	You started with the correct answer $\sqrt{w^2 + z^2}$, but then proceeded to incorrectly simplify the radical of a sum.

PERIMETER OF PLANAR FIGURES

The **perimeter** of a planar region is the sum of the lengths of all portions that make up the outer boundary of the figure. The standard units of measure of length are *inches, feet, yards,* etc.; the metric system is also commonly used (*centimeters, meters,* etc.). In the absence of such specific units, the generic term *units* is affixed to the end of a length measurement.

The following are some standard perimeter formulas.

Figure	Picture	Perimeter Formula
Square		$P = 4s$
Rectangle		$P = 2l + 2w$
Circumference of a circle		Since the diameter d is $2r$, there are two expressions for this formula: $P = 2\pi r = \pi d$.
Length of an arc of a circle		$P = \left(\dfrac{\theta}{180^\circ} \right) \bullet \pi \bullet r$

Among the typical problems that you will encounter on the PSAT/NMSQT® Math Test related to perimeter are those for which you need to compute the perimeter of a composite figure (that is, a figure composed of two or more familiar figures), like the following.

Suppose you start with a circle with diameter d and you create a new circle with triple the radius of the original circle. What is the ratio of the perimeter of the new circle to the original circle?

The perimeter of the original circle is $\pi d = \pi(2r)$. The new circle has radius $3r$, so its perimeter is $\pi(2 \bullet 3r) = 6\pi r$. So, the ratio of the perimeter of the new circle to the original is $6\pi r: 2\pi r$, which is equivalent to 3:1.

NOTE

For any figure, if a new figure is created by increasing or decreasing the lengths of all sides by a factor of k, then the ratio of the perimeter of the new figure to the original is k :1.

AREA OF FAMILIAR FIGURES

The **area** of a planar region is the number of **unit squares** needed to cover it. The standard units of measure of area are *square inches, square feet, square yards,* etc.; the metric system is also commonly used (*square centimeters, square meters,* etc.). In the absence of specific units, the phrase *square units* (or equivalently, *units²*) is affixed to the end of an area measurement.

The following are some standard area formulas.

Region	Picture	Area Formula
Square	*s* ... *s*	$A = s^2$
Rectangle	*l* ... *w*	$A = l \cdot w$
Parallelogram	*h* ... *b*	$A = b \cdot h$ Do not confuse the height (which must be perpendicular to the base) with the measure of the side adjacent to the base.
Triangle	*h* ... *b*	$A = \frac{1}{2} b \cdot h$ The height must be perpendicular to the base.

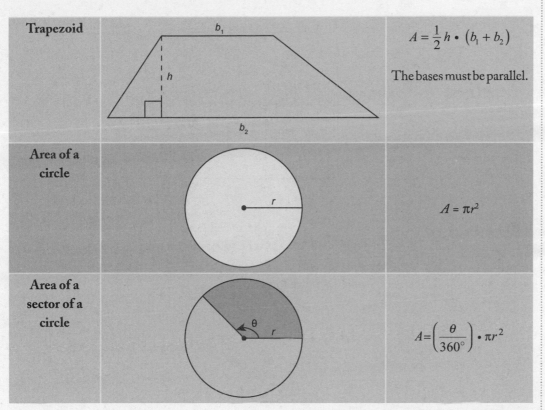

Trapezoid		$A = \frac{1}{2} h \cdot (b_1 + b_2)$ The bases must be parallel.
Area of a circle		$A = \pi r^2$
Area of a sector of a circle		$A = \left(\frac{\theta}{360°} \right) \cdot \pi r^2$

Let's look at how the PSAT/NMSQT® exam will test your knowledge of area. You've read enough by now to know that area questions are sure to contain many layers and steps.

Consider two similar planar figures A and B. If shape A has side lengths that are twice as long as those in shape B, how will the area of shape B differ from the area of shape A?

Intuitively, since area requires you to multiply the length of two dimensions together, if both dimensions are twice as long, then (2 × length) (2 × width) will result in an area that is 4 × (length × width). Hence, the area of shape B will be four times as large as shape A.

Just because a question is geometric in nature, do not think your algebra skills won't enter into the solution! It is likely that you will need to use your algebra-modeling and equation-solving skills when working with perimeter and area questions. Geometry questions on the PSAT/NMSQT® Math Test rarely test just a single concept. Rather, they often require synthesis of algebra and geometry.

Take a look at the following two questions to get a better sense of these concepts.

Square $DEFG$ rests inside square $ABCD$ such that vertex E is on $\overline{AD}$ and vertex G is on $\overline{CD}$. The area of $DEFG$ is 25 and $\overline{AE}$ = x. What is the value of x if the area of $ABCD$ is $x^2 + 64$?

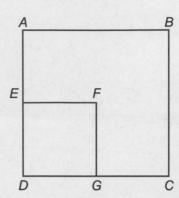

First, since the area of square $DEFG$ is 25 square units, the length of $\overline{ED}$ is 5 units. Since the length of $\overline{AE}$ is x units, it follows that the length of $\overline{AD}$ is $(x + 5)$ units. Since $ABCD$ is a square, all sides have length $(x + 5)$ units. Moreover, the area of $ABCD$, $x^2 + 64$, must be equal to $(x + 5)(x + 5)$. This yields the following equation, which we solve for x:

$$(x + 5)(x + 5) = x^2 + 64$$

$$x^2 + 10x + 25 = x^2 + 64$$

$$10x + 25 = 64$$

$$x = \frac{39}{10} = 3.9$$

Now let's look at another question.

> The length of the radius of circle A is 5 times as long as the radius of circle B. If the radius of circle B is x units, what is the area (in square units) of circle A?

The radius of circle A is $5x$. So, its area is $\pi(5x)^2 = 25\pi x^2$.

SURFACE AREA AND VOLUME OF FAMILIAR SOLIDS

The **volume** of a solid is the number of unit cubes needed to fill it. The standard units of measure of volume are *cubic inches, cubic feet, cubic yards*, etc.; the metric system is also commonly used (*cubic centimeters, cubic meters*, etc.). In the absence of such specific units, we affix the phrase *cubic units* (or equivalently, *units³*) to the end of a volume measurement.

The **surface area** of a solid is the total area all faces of its surface occupy. The standard units of measure are the previously mentioned area measures.

On the exam, you will likely encounter a question involving the volume of standard solids like cones, prisms, pyramids, cylinders, and spheres, as well as composite solids (two or more solids put together). Questions on surface area are somewhat simpler and typically involve rectangular prisms (for which you simply add the area of the six faces to find the surface area). If they involve a different solid, the formula will be provided.

As with questions involving perimeter and area, these problems may or may not be posed in the context of a real-world setting. Or, your algebra skills might be tested under the guise of a volume problem.

If the height of a circular cone equals four times the radius and the surface area is 490π square inches, what is the diameter of the base? (Note: The formula for surface area of a cylinder is $A = 2\pi rh + 2\pi r^2$.)

Let r represent the radius of the base. Then, the height $h = 4r$. Using the surface area formula for a circular cylinder yields the following equation that we must solve for r:

$$490\pi = 2\pi r^2 + 2\pi r(4r)$$
$$490\pi = 2\pi r^2 + 8\pi r^2$$
$$490\pi = 10\pi r^2$$
$$49 = r^2$$
$$7 = r$$

So, the diameter must be 14 inches.

The following two examples are modeling-type problems involving surface area and volume:

Mackenzie wishes to apply three coats of paint to the four walls and ceiling of her exercise room. The ceiling has dimensions 8 feet by 12 feet and the height of the room is 9 feet. If each can of paint can cover 400 square feet of wall, how many cans must she purchase?

First, determine the total surface area to be painted. The exercise room is in the shape of a rectangular prism. Since she will not paint the floor, we modify the typical surface area formula to be the sum of the area of the ceiling and twice the area of two adjacent walls (since opposite walls have the same area). Precisely, the surface area is $\underbrace{(8 \cdot 12)}_{\text{Ceiling}} + \underbrace{2(8 \cdot 9) + 2(12 \cdot 9)}_{\text{Walls}} = 456$ square feet.

She wants to apply three coats of paint, so triple the coverage area to get 1,368 square feet to paint. Since each can covers 400 square feet, she must purchase four cans of paint.

Let's try another one.

Henrique works at an aviary and must purchase a container to store 800 cubic inches of birdseed. The container must fit into a shelf space with height 1.5 feet. To the nearest inch, what is the minimum radius of a cylindrical storage container that can store 800 cubic inches of birdseed?

First, be careful with units! The volume is given in cubic inches while the height is expressed in feet. So, convert 1.5 feet to 18 inches before doing anything else! Now, use the formula for the volume of a cylinder and solve for the radius, as follows.

$$800 = \pi r^2(18)$$
$$r^2 = \frac{800}{18\pi}$$
$$r = \sqrt{\frac{800}{18\pi}} \approx 3.76 \text{ inches}$$

Thus, the radius must be at least 4 inches.

NOTE

When you take the square root, only the positive square root is needed since the radius cannot be negative.

The following problem is of the more conceptual variety.

> A cube has side length s. A new cube is formed with sides half as long as the original cube. Describe the relationship between the volumes of the two cubes.

We need to determine expressions for both cubes and compare them. The volume of the original cube is $V_{original} = s^3$. The length of a side of the new cube is $\frac{1}{2}s$. So, the volume of the new cube is $V_{new} = \left(\frac{1}{2}s\right)^3 = \frac{1}{8}s^3$. Comparing the two formulas, we see that the volume of the new cube is $\frac{1}{8}$ the volume of the original cube.

ANALYTIC GEOMETRY

Drawing geometric figures in the xy-plane is beneficial for various reasons. One, the use of coordinates enables you to compute lengths and slopes of segments more precisely. For example, you can more definitively argue that a quadrilateral is a parallelogram by showing the slopes of opposite sides are equal, which implies the sides are parallel, and you can show the lengths of opposite sides are equal using the distance formula. We review a couple of the most useful concepts from analytic geometry in this section and will walk you through a few sample problems you might encounter.

The **midpoint** of the segment joining two points (x_1, y_1) and (x_2, y_2) in the standard xy-coordinate plane is the point that is equidistant from the two given points. You simply average the x-coordinates and average the y-coordinates to conclude that the midpoint is $\left(\frac{x_1 + x_2}{2}, \frac{y_1 + y_2}{2}\right)$.

The length of the segment joining two points (x_1, y_1) and (x_2, y_2) (a.k.a., the **distance formula**) follows from an application of the Pythagorean theorem. It is given by $\sqrt{(x_2 - x_1)^2 + (y_2 - y_1)^2}$.

You might be asked to simply find the distance between two points, or you may get a more challenging question, such as the following one, which requires you to apply the midpoint and distance formulas together.

A **circle** is the set of points that are a fixed distance r (the radius) from a given point (h, k) (the circle's center). A simple application of the distance formula can be used to conclude the equation of a circle is $(x - h)^2 + (y - k)^2 = r^2$.

The following is a typical analytic geometry question involving circles:

> What is the equation for a circle for which the line segment with endpoints $(-2, -1)$ and $(4, -3)$ is a diameter?

ALERT

Be careful with the signs of the coordinates of a circle's center when writing the equation of a circle in standard form, especially when they are negative!

To write the equation, you must determine the center and radius. First, find the radius by computing the length of this line segment using the distance formula and taking half of it:

$$d = \sqrt{(x_2 - x_1)^2 + (y_2 - y_1)^2} = \sqrt{(-2 - 4)^2 + (-1 - (-3))^2} = \sqrt{36 + 4} = \sqrt{40} = 2\sqrt{10}$$

So, the radius equals $\sqrt{10}$. Next, the center is the midpoint of the given line segment:

$$\left(\frac{(-2) + 4}{2}, \frac{(-1) + (-3)}{2}\right) = (1, -2)$$

Thus, the equation for the circle is $(x - 1)^2 + (y + 2)^2 = 10$.

Remember—the equation for the circle-radius form of a circle with center (h, k) and radius r is the sum of squared differences, not the sum of squared sums:

$$(x - h)^2 + (y - k)^2 = r^2.$$

ELEMENTARY TRIGONOMETRY

The **trigonometric functions** are used to identify the lengths of sides of a right triangle when one side and one angle (instead of two sides) are known. Let θ be an angle and consider the following right triangle.

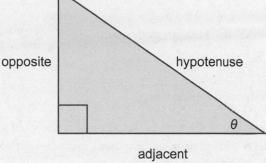

The following three functions play a key role in what is called **right triangle trigonometry**:

Trigonometric Function	Definition
Cosine	$\cos \theta = \dfrac{\text{adjacent}}{\text{hypotenuse}}$
Sine	$\sin \theta = \dfrac{\text{opposite}}{\text{hypotenuse}}$
Tangent	$\tan \theta = \dfrac{\text{opposite}}{\text{adjacent}}$

Questions on the PSAT/NMSQT® Math Test involving trigonometry will be basic and could be simply mechanical or asked within an applied setting. Let's work through an example of each.

If in right triangle ABC, $\sin A = \dfrac{4}{7}$, what is the value of $\cos A$?

First draw a sketch.

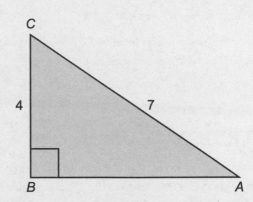

To find the cosine of angle A, you need to determine the length of the adjacent side to angle A, which is segment AB. Using the Pythagorean theorem yields $4^2 + (AB)^2 = 7^2$, so $(AB)^2 = 33$. Thus, $AB = \sqrt{33}$. So, $\cos A = \dfrac{\sqrt{33}}{7}$.

Now we'll look at two real-world applications.

A 70-foot cable is attached to the top of a flagpole and is anchored to the ground. If the cable rises in a straight line at a 55° angle from the ground, formulate a trigonometric expression that represents the height of the flagpole (in feet).

Begin by sketching a diagram:

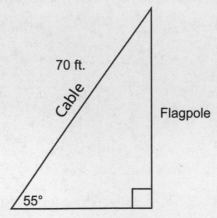

Let x be the height of the flagpole. It is opposite a 55° angle, and the hypotenuse of the triangle is 70 feet. Since sine equals $\dfrac{\text{opposite}}{\text{hypotenuse}}$, we get the formula $\dfrac{x}{70} = \sin 55°$, so that $x = 70\sin 55°$.

The frame of the roof of a church steeple is in the shape of the following right triangle:

Formulate a trigonometric equation that can be used to determine the value of the angle θ.

The lengths of both legs of the triangle are given, but not the hypotenuse. So, the function you want to use is the tangent. Since $\tan \theta = \dfrac{\text{opposite}}{\text{adjacent}}$, we see that $\tan \theta = \dfrac{15}{15}$, or more simply, $\tan \theta = 1$.

COMPLEX NUMBERS

Complex numbers arise when you take the square root of a negative number. The imaginary unit i is defined as $i^2 = -1$. Questions involving complex numbers on the PSAT/NMSQT® exam arise when solving quadratic equations and in the form of basic computational problems involving the following operations:

Definition (in Symbols)	Definition (in Words)
1. Sum $(a + bi) + (c + di) = (a + c) + (b + d)i$	When adding complex numbers, add the real parts and the imaginary parts separately, and form the complex number using those sums.
2. Difference $(a + bi) - (c + di) = (a - c) + (b - d)i$	When subtracting complex numbers, subtract the real parts and the imaginary parts separately, and form the complex number using those sums.
3. Product $(a + bi) \times (c + di) = (ac - bd) + (bc + ad)i$	To multiply two complex numbers, apply the FOIL technique and use the fact that $i^2 = -1$.
4. Complex Conjugate The complex conjugate of $z = a + bi$ is $a - bi$.	To form the complex conjugate of a complex number, change the sign of the imaginary part, but leave the real part the same.
5. Quotient $\dfrac{a + bi}{c + di} = \dfrac{a + bi}{c + di} \cdot \dfrac{c - di}{c - di} = \dfrac{(ac + bd) + (bc - ad)i}{c^2 + d^2}$	To divide two complex numbers, multiply top and bottom by the conjugate of the denominator, and simplify as above.

Perform the following arithmetic operations on complex numbers:

I.   Express the quotient $\dfrac{1 - 3i}{2 + i}$ in the form $a + bi$, where a and b are real numbers.

II. Express the product $(3 + 4i)^2$ in the form $a + bi$, where a and b are real numbers.

III. Express the product $3i(-4 + 3i)(1 - 3i)$ in the form $a + bi$, where a and b are real numbers.

I. To compute this quotient, multiply top and bottom by the conjugate of the denominator, which is $2 - i$. Then, simplify:

$$\frac{1 - 3i}{2 + i} = \frac{1 - 3i}{2 + i} \cdot \frac{2 - i}{2 - i} = \frac{2 - i - 6i + 3i^2}{4 - i^2} = \frac{2 - i - 6i - 3}{4 + 1} = \frac{-1 - 7i}{5} = -\frac{1}{5} - \frac{7}{5}i$$

II. FOIL the product and use the fact that $i^2 = -1$:

$$(3 + 4i)(3 + 4i) = 9 + 12i + 12i + 16i^2 = 9 + 24i - 16 = -7 + 24i$$

ALERT

A typical error when squaring binomials is to forget the middle terms! Remember, $(y + z)^2 \neq y^2 + z^2$.

III. Since multiplication is commutative, you can multiply any two terms first. Let's work from left to right:

$$3i(-4 + 3i)(1 - 3i) = (-12i + 9i^2)(1 - 3i)$$
$$= (-12i - 9)(1 - 3i)$$
$$= -12i + 36i^2 - 9 + 27i$$
$$= 15i - 36 - 9$$
$$= -45 + 15i$$

PASSPORT TO ADVANCED MATH PRACTICE QUESTIONS

1. The formula $r = cs^2(3L - s)$ describes the rebound, r, of a diving board at a position s feet from the fixed end by the ladder. In the formula, L is the length of the diving board, s can range from 0 to L, and c is a positive physical constant. If the board is 8 feet long and the rebound at the very tip of the board is 1.5 feet, what is the value of c? Write your answer as a simplified fraction.

   SHOW YOUR WORK HERE

   A. $\dfrac{3}{2,048}$

   B. $\dfrac{5}{64}$

   C. $\dfrac{1}{16}$

   D. $\dfrac{3}{32}$

2. Assume that $0 < a < b$. Which of the following quadratic equations has two complex conjugate solutions?

   A. $ax^2 + b^2 = 0$

   B. $(ax)^2 - b^2 = 0$

   C. $bax^2 + ax = 0$

   D. $(ax - b)^2 = 0$

3. Suppose $a > 0$. Which of the following quadratic equations has only one real solution?

   A. $x^2 - ax = 0$

   B. $x^2 - 2ax + a^2 = 0$

   C. $x^2 + a = 0$

   D. $x^2 - a = 0$

4. A microbiologist is studying a sample of a particularly virulent form of bacteria. She finds that the function $f(x) = 500 \times 4^x$ represents the number of bacteria cells (in hundred thousands) in a sample after x hours. Which statement correctly describes this situation?

   A. The sample starts with 4 bacteria cells and increases by a factor of 500 every hour.

   B. The sample starts with 500 bacteria cells and quadruples every hour.

   C. The sample starts with 1 bacteria cell and increases by a factor of 500 every hour.

   D. The sample starts with 1,000 bacteria cells and doubles every hour.

5. Which of the following expressions is equivalent to $2(2x - 1) - x(3 - 2x)$?

   A. $2 - x - 2x^2$

   B. $2(x^2 - 2) + 1$

   C. $2x^2 + x - 2$

   D. $3x + 1$

6. Which of the following is equivalent to $\dfrac{3^{-x} \cdot \left(3^{2x}\right)^3}{3^{2+5x}}$?

   A. $\dfrac{1}{3^{10x+2}}$

   B. $3^{8x^3 - 6x - 2}$

   C. $\dfrac{1}{3^{6x^3 + 6x + 2}}$

   D. $\dfrac{1}{9}$

SHOW YOUR WORK HERE

7. The following is the graph of a fourth-degree polynomial $p(x)$.

SHOW YOUR WORK HERE

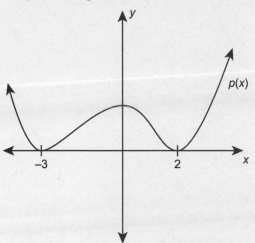

Which of the following is the factored form of this function? Here, a represents a real number.

A. $p(x) = a(x + 3)^2(x - 2)^2$

B. $p(x) = a(x - 3)^2(x + 2)^2$

C. $p(x) = a(x + 3)(x - 2)(x - 1)^2$

D. $p(x) = a(x - 3)(x + 2)(x - 1)^2$

8. Which of the following is equivalent to

$$\frac{5x^2 - 10x}{2(1 - 5x)} \div \frac{10x}{25x^2 - 1}?$$

A. $\dfrac{x(5x + 1)}{2}$

B. $\dfrac{5x^2}{25x^2 - 10x + 1}$

C. $\dfrac{2 + 9x - 5x^2}{4}$

D. $\dfrac{5x^2 - 2 - 9x}{4}$

9. At the beginning of ice hockey practice, Carl had a goal-making percentage of 52.5 percent, having made 165 shots out of 314 attempted so far in the season. He had a great day at practice and made all his goal shots. The number of consecutive goal shots, x, he would need to make at practice to increase his goal shot average to 56 percent can be determined by solving the equation $\frac{165 + x}{314 + x} = 0.56$.

What does the expression $(165 + x)$ represent in this equation?

A. The percentage of goal attempts made.

B. The number of additional goals made to bring the average up to 56 percent.

C. The total number of goals attempted once the average is 56 percent.

D. The total number of goals made to get to an average of 56 percent.

10. What is the solution set for the equation

$2x - 2\sqrt{x} = -1$?

A. Empty set

B. Set of all real numbers

C. $\left\{-\frac{1}{2}, \frac{1}{2}\right\}$

D. $\left\{\frac{1}{2}\right\}$

11. Solve the following equation for x:

$\frac{x + 2}{3(y + 2)} = \frac{x}{2}$

A. $x = \frac{4}{3y + 4}$

B. $x = \frac{3y + 4}{4}$

C. $x = 3y + 1$

D. $x = \frac{1}{3y}$

SHOW YOUR WORK HERE

12. What is the sum of the x-values that are solutions of the equation $-\dfrac{4}{9-x^2} = \dfrac{x}{x+3}$?

SHOW YOUR WORK HERE

13. The value of an LCD television diminishes by 6 percent each year. If the initial cost of the television was $3,750, which of the following expressions represents the amount, in dollars, by which the value of the television decreases between years n and $n + 1$?

    A. $3,750(0.94)^{n+1} - 3,750(0.94)^n$

    B. $3,750[(0.94)^n - (0.94)^{n+1}]$

    C. $3,750(0.94)^{n-(n+1)}$

    D. $3,750(0.94)^{n+1/n}$

14. If $g(x + 3) = x^2 - 3$, for all real numbers x, what is the value of $g(-4)$?

15. Which of the following expressions is equivalent to $(xz^2 - 3x^2z)^2$?

A. $9x^6z^6$

B. $x^2z^4 + 9x^4z^2$

C. $x^2z^4 - 3x^3z^3 + 9x^4z^2$

D. $x^2z^4 - 6x^3z^3 + 9x^4z^2$

SHOW YOUR WORK HERE

16. What is the largest value of x that satisfies the equation $\dfrac{3}{\frac{1}{x} - x} = 2$? Enter your answer as a decimal.

17. The surface area formula for a triangular prism is $S = bh + 2lx + bl$. Which of the following formulas correctly represents l in terms of the other variables?

A. $l = \dfrac{S - h}{2x + 1}$

B. $l = \dfrac{S - bh}{2x + b}$

C. $l = \dfrac{S - 2x - b}{bh}$

D. $l = \dfrac{S - 2x - 1}{h}$

18. Suppose $(3x - 1)(2x + 1)(2x - 1) = 12x^3 + ax^2 - 3x + b$. What is the value of $b - a$?

SHOW YOUR WORK HERE

19. Consider the following system:

$$\begin{cases} y = x^2 - 2x - 15 \\ y - 4x = 1 \end{cases}$$

If (x_1, y_1) and (x_2, y_2) are the two solutions of this system, compute $|y_1 + y_2|$.

20. Suppose the graph of $f(x) = 3x^2 + 6x$ is translated two units to the right and then 4 units up. What is the minimum y-value attained for the translated graph on the interval $(-\infty, \infty)$?

SHOW YOUR WORK HERE

ADDITIONAL TOPICS IN MATH PRACTICE QUESTIONS

1. What is the perimeter of the shaded region below if P is the center of a circle with radius 6 inches and the angle cut out is a right angle?

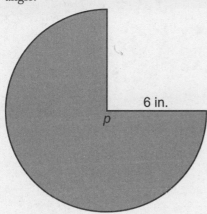

SHOW YOUR WORK HERE

   A. 15 inches

   B. $(12 + 9\pi)$ inches

   C. 9π inches

   D. $(6 + 6\pi)$ inches

2. Consider a circle that has one diameter with endpoints $A\left(2, \frac{1}{2}\right)$ and $B\left(2, -\frac{1}{2}\right)$ and a second diameter with endpoints $C\left(\frac{3}{2}, 0\right)$ and $D\left(\frac{5}{2}, 0\right)$. Which of the following is the equation of this circle?

   A. $x^2 + (y + 2)^2 = \frac{1}{2}$

   B. $x^2 + (y - 2)^2 = \frac{1}{4}$

   C. $(x - 2)^2 + y^2 = \frac{1}{4}$

   D. $(x - 2)^2 + y^2 = \frac{1}{2}$

SHOW YOUR WORK HERE

3. For $i = \sqrt{-1}$, which of the following equals $-8i + (1 - 8i)(1 + 8i)$?

   A. $-63 - 8i$

   B. $1 - 24i$

   C. $65 - 8i$

   D. $57i$

4. For $i = \sqrt{-1}$, which of the following equals $(3 + 4i)^2$?

   A. $-7 + 24i$

   B. $9 + 40i$

   C. $-25 + 24i$

   D. $17i$

5. The circle with equation $(x - 8)^2 + (y + 3)^2 = 49$ lies completely inside a square. What is the least possible length of one of the sides of the square?

6. Which of the following is a simplified formula for the length of the line segment with endpoints $(-a, b)$ and $(-b, -a)$, where a and b represent real numbers?

   A. $\sqrt{2\left(a^2 + b^2\right)}$

   B. $\sqrt{2}\left(a + b\right)$

   C. $\sqrt{2b}$

   D. $2b$

7. The open area in a conservatory is a square lawn bordered by footpaths 150 feet long on each side. The conservatory intends to create a diagonal footpath connecting the northwest corner of the lawn to the southeast corner of the lawn. Approximately how many feet shorter would the new path be than the shortest possible route on the existing footpaths? Round your answer to the nearest foot.

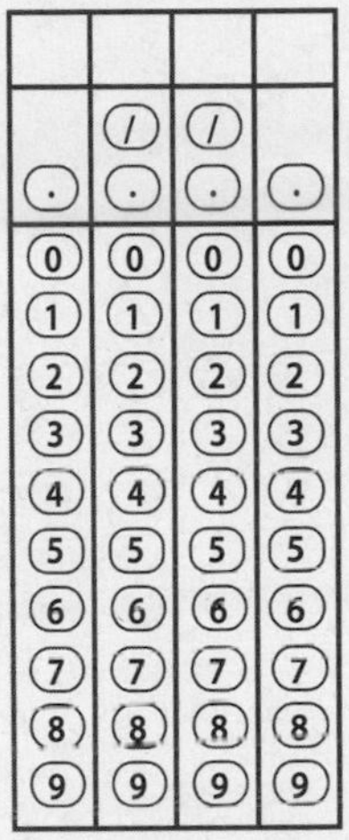

SHOW YOUR WORK HERE

8. The area of a rectangle is $6x^2 + 25x + 25$ square units. If its length is $3x + 5$ units, what is its width, in units?

   A. $2x - 5$

   B. $2x + 5$

   C. $2x + 1$

   D. $\dfrac{6x^2 + 25x + 25}{2}$

9. In $\triangle RST$, if $RS = RT = TS$, then which of the following statements is FALSE?

   A. The sides cannot satisfy the Pythagorean theorem.

   B. All three angles must be acute.

   C. The sum of any two angles in the triangle exceeds 90 degrees.

   D. The triangle can be a right triangle.

10. In the figure below, *ABDF* is a square, and the measurements are as marked. What is the area of the quadrilateral *ACEF*?

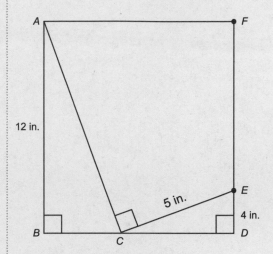

A. 60 square inches

B. 72 square inches

C. 84 square inches

D. 138 square inches

11. What is the area of an equilateral triangle with a perimeter of 30 feet?

A. 75 square feet

B. $100\sqrt{3}$ square feet

C. $25\sqrt{3}$ square feet

D. $50\sqrt{3}$ square feet

12. The length of a narrow rectangular pen is 7 yards more than three times its width. If the area of the pen is 6 square yards, what is the length of the pen, in yards?

A. 9 yards

B. $\frac{2}{3}$ yard

C. 7 yards

D. $\frac{25}{3}$ yards

13. In the figure below, a circle is inscribed within a square. If the perimeter of the square is 80 inches, what is the area of the shaded region, in square inches?

SHOW YOUR WORK HERE

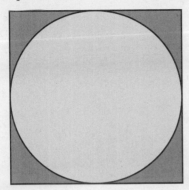

A. $400 + 100\pi$

B. $400 - 100\pi$

C. $80 - 20\pi$

D. $80 + 20\pi$

14. What is the surface area of the following solid?

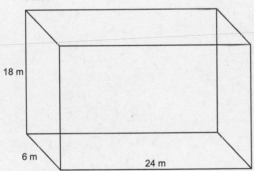

18 m

6 m

24 m

A. 2,052 square meters

B. 1,368 square meters

C. 684 square meters

D. 342 square meters

15. What is the value of x in the following triangle?

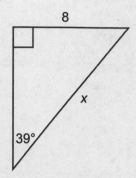

A. $\dfrac{8}{\cos 39°}$

B. $\dfrac{8}{\sin 39°}$

C. $8\sin 39°$

D. $8\cos 39°$

16. The volume of each small conical-shaped traffic cone used in a drivers' education class is 8π cubic inches, and the height is three times the base radius. What is the diameter of the base of each traffic cone? (The formula for volume of a cone is $V = \dfrac{1}{3}\pi r^2 h$.)

17. Consider the shaded region formed between two concentric circles, as shown below.

SHOW YOUR WORK HERE

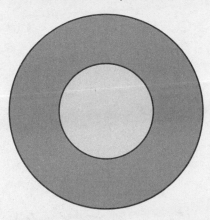

If the radius of the outer circle is 3 times the radius *r* of the inner circle, what is the area of the shaded region in terms of *r*?

A. 5πr square units

B. 2πr² square units

C. 8πr² square units

D. 3πr square units

18. Consider the following triangle.

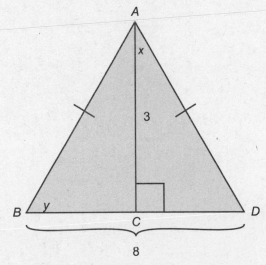

Which of the following is equal to sin(*x*)?

A. tan(*x*)

B. cos(*x*)

C. sin(*y*)

D. cos(*y*)

19. A popular dog chew toy is a hollowed-out sphere into which treats can be inserted. The toy is manufactured by starting with a solid sphere made of rubber with diameter 5 inches and then removing a concentric sphere from the inside of it with diameter 4 inches, thereby leaving a spherical shell with thickness equal to one inch. What is the volume of material comprising this spherical shell? (The formula for volume of a sphere is $V = \frac{4}{3}\pi r^3$.)

A. $\frac{61}{6}\pi$ cubic inches

B. $\frac{32}{3}\pi$ cubic inches

C. $\frac{125}{6}\pi$ cubic inches

D. $\frac{375}{4}\pi$ cubic inches

20. Which of the following can be the lengths of three sides of a right triangle? Assume that a is a positive real number.

A. $a, a, 2a$

B. $5a, 12a, 13a$

C. $4a, 4a, 9a$

D. $a, 2a, 3a$

ANSWER KEYS AND EXPLANATIONS

Passport to Advanced Math

1. A	6. D	11. A	16. 0.5
2. A	7. A	12. 3	17. B
3. B	8. C	13. B	18. 5
4. B	9. D	14. 46	19. 26
5. C	10. A	15. D	20. 1

1. **The correct answer is A.** Substitute $r = 1.5$, $L = 8$, and $s = 8$ (because the rebound is being assessed at the "tip of the board"). This yields the following equation that must be solved for c: $1.5 = c(8)^2(3(8) - 8)$. Solving for c yields the following:

$$c = \frac{1.5}{16 \cdot 64} = \frac{\frac{3}{2}}{16 \cdot 64} = \frac{3}{2,048}$$

2. **The correct answer is A.** Subtract b^2 from both sides, divide by a, and then take the square root. This yields $x = \pm\sqrt{-\frac{b^2}{a}} = \pm i\frac{b}{\sqrt{a}}$, which is a complex conjugate pair of solutions.

3. **The correct answer is B.** Factoring the left side yields $(x - a)^2 = 0$, which has one solution: $x = a$.

4. **The correct answer is B.** The growth factor, 4, is used as the base of a power and is multiplied by the initial value, 500. This means that she started with 500 (hundred thousand) bacteria cells and the number of cells quadruples every hour.

5. **The correct answer is C.** First, use the distributive property to simplify each term in the difference. Then, combine like terms:

$$2(2x - 1) - x(3 - 2x) = 4x - 2 - 3x + 2x^2$$
$$= 2x^2 + x - 2$$

6. **The correct answer is D.** Apply the exponent rules to simplify the expression, as follows:

$$\frac{3^{-x} \cdot \left(3^{2x}\right)^3}{3^{2+5x}} = \frac{3^{-x} \cdot 3^{6x}}{3^{2+5x}}$$
$$= \frac{3^{-x} \cdot 3^{6x}}{3^{5x} \cdot 3^2}$$
$$= \frac{3^{5x}}{3^{5x} \cdot 3^2}$$
$$= \frac{1}{9}$$

7. **The correct answer is A.** The graph has two x-intercepts: -3 and 2. These correspond to the factors $(x - (-3))$ and $(x - 2)$ or equivalently $(x + 3)$ and $(x - 2)$. Since the graph is tangent to the x-axis at both x-values, both factors are squared. Finally, the value of a that would work here is the value that makes $p(0) = 1$.

8. **The correct answer is C.** First, write the division problem as a multiplication problem. Then, factor all parts and cancel like terms:

$$\frac{5x^2 - 10x}{2(1 - 5x)} \div \frac{10x}{25x^2 - 1}$$
$$= \frac{5x^2 - 10x}{2(1 - 5x)} \cdot \frac{25x^2 - 1}{10x}$$
$$= \frac{5x(x - 2)}{-2(5x - 1)} \cdot \frac{(5x - 1)(5x + 1)}{10x_2}$$
$$= \frac{(x - 2)(5x + 1)}{-4}$$
$$= \frac{5x^2 - 9x - 2}{-4}$$
$$= \frac{2 + 9x - 5x^2}{4}$$

9. **The correct answer is D.** The 56 percent is computed by dividing the number of goals made by the number of goals attempted at the end of the practice. So, the numerator represents the total number of goals made to get to an average of 56 percent.

10. **The correct answer is A.** First, isolate the radical term on one side of the equation. Then, square both sides and solve the resulting quadratic equation.

$$2x - 2\sqrt{x} = -1$$
$$2x + 1 = 2\sqrt{x}$$
$$(2x + 1)^2 = \left(2\sqrt{x}\right)^2$$
$$4x^2 + 4x + 1 = 4x$$
$$4x^2 + 1 = 0$$

There are no real values of x that satisfy this equation because the left side is always positive. So, the solution set is an empty set.

11. **The correct answer is A.** Solve for x, as follows:

$$\frac{x + 2}{3(y + 2)} = \frac{x}{2}$$
$$2(x + 2) = x \cdot 3(y + 2)$$
$$2x + 4 = 3xy + 6x$$
$$4 = 3xy + 6x - 2x$$
$$4 = 3xy + 4x$$
$$4 = x(3y + 4)$$
$$x = \frac{4}{3y + 4}$$

12. **The correct answer is 3.** The least common denominator is $(3 - x)(3 + x)$. Multiply both sides of the equation by this expression and solve the resulting equation, as follows:

$$-\frac{4}{9 - x^2} = \frac{x}{x + 3}$$
$$-4 = x(3 - x)$$
$$-4 = 3x - x^2$$
$$x^2 - 3x - 4 = 0$$
$$(x - 4)(x + 1) = 0$$
$$x = -1, \ 4$$

Check each value in the original equation to determine if they work, or if they are extraneous roots:

$x = -1$:

$$-\frac{4}{9 - (-1)^2} \overset{??}{=} \frac{(-1)}{(-1) + 3} \ \Rightarrow \ -\frac{4}{8} \overset{??}{=} \frac{-1}{2}$$

YES!

$x = 4$:

$$-\frac{4}{9 - (4)^2} \overset{??}{=} \frac{(4)}{(4) + 3} \ \Rightarrow \ -\frac{4}{-7} \overset{??}{=} \frac{4}{7}$$

YES!

So, both are solutions of the original equation. The sum of these solutions is $4 + (-1) = 3$.

13. **The correct answer is B.** The value of the television in year n is $3{,}750(0.94)^n$ and its value in year $n + 1$ is $3{,}750(0.94)^{n+1}$. So, the amount by which the value decreases from year n to year $n + 1$ is $3{,}750(0.94)^n - 3{,}750(0.94)^{n+1}$, which is equivalent to $3{,}750\left[(0.94)^n - (0.94)^{n+1}\right]$.

14. **The correct answer is 46.** In order to compute $g(-4)$, we must find the x-value for which $x + 3 = -4$. This value is $x = -7$. So,

$$g(\underbrace{\boxed{-7} + 4}_{=-3}) = (\boxed{-7})^2 - 3 = 49 - 3 = 46$$

15. The correct answer is D. Apply the FOIL method and use the exponent rules wherever needed, as follows:

$$(xz^2 - 3x^2z)^2$$
$$= (xz^2 - 3x^2z)(xz^2 - 3x^2z)$$
$$= (xz^2)^2 - 2(3x^2z)(xz^2) + (3x^2z)^2$$
$$= x^2z^4 - 6x^3z^3 + 9x^4z^2$$

16. The correct answer is 0.5. The first step is to get rid of the complex fraction. Do so by finding a common denominator for the terms in the bottom of the fraction on the left side of the equation. Once that is written as a single fraction, multiply the numerator of the overall fraction on the left side by the reciprocal of the newly created fraction in the denominator. Then, multiply both sides of the equation by the denominator of the resulting fraction and solve the quadratic equation that arises:

$$\frac{3}{\frac{1}{x} - x} = 2$$
$$\frac{3}{\frac{1-x^2}{x}} = 2$$
$$\frac{3x}{1 - x^2} = 2$$
$$3x = 2(1 - x^2)$$
$$3x = 2 - 2x^2$$
$$2x^2 + 3x - 2 = 0$$
$$(2x - 1)(x + 2) = 0$$
$$x = \frac{1}{2}, -2$$

Neither of these values is an extraneous solution because they do not make any denominator throughout equal to zero. So, the larger of the two solutions is $\frac{1}{2}$, which equals 0.5.

17. The correct answer is B. Solve for l, as follows:

$$S = bh + 2lx + bl$$
$$S = bh + l(2x + b)$$
$$S - bh = l(2x + b)$$
$$l = \frac{S - bh}{2x + b}$$

18. The correct answer is 5. Expand the left side and arrange the terms in decreasing order by degree:

$$(3x - 1)(2x + 1)(2x - 1)$$
$$= (6x^2 + x - 1)(2x - 1)$$
$$= 12x^3 + 2x^2 - 2x - 6x^2 - x + 1$$
$$= 12x^3 - 4x^2 - 3x + 1$$

Now, equate corresponding coefficients to the given expression in the question to find that $a = -4$ and $b = 1$. So, $b - a = 1 - (-4) = 5$.

19. The correct answer is 26. To solve this system, solve both equations for y:

$$\begin{cases} y = x^2 - 2x - 15 \\ y = 4x + 1 \end{cases}$$

Use the substitution method to solve this system. Equate the two right sides and solve the resulting quadratic equation for x:

$$x^2 - 2x - 15 = 4x + 1$$
$$x^2 - 6x - 16 = 0$$
$$(x + 2)(x - 8) = 0$$
$$x = -2, 8$$

Substitute each of these into the second equation (for simplicity) to find the corresponding y-coordinates:

$$x_1 = 8 \quad \Rightarrow \quad y_1 = 4 \cdot 8 + 1 = 33$$
$$x_2 = -2 \Rightarrow y_2 = 4 \cdot (-2) + 1 = -7$$

Hence, $|y_1 + y_2| = |33 + (-7)| = |26| = 26$.

20. The correct answer is 1. It is easiest to identify the minimum value of a quadratic function by first putting it into standard form. To do so, complete the square, as follows:

$$f(x) = 3x^2 + 6x$$
$$= 3(x^2 + 2x)$$
$$= 3(x^2 + 2x + 1) - 3$$
$$= 3(x + 1)^2 - 3$$

Looking at this, we can see the graph of $f(x)$ opens upward and has vertex $(-1, -3)$. Its minimum value of the function is the y-coordinate of this point. Translating this graph 2 units right and 4 units up moves the vertex, in particular, to the point $(-1 + 2, -3 + 4) = (1, 1)$. So, the minimum is 1.

Additional Topics in Math

1. B	6. A	11. C	16. 4
2. C	7. 88	12. A	17. C
3. C	8. B	13. B	18. D
4. A	9. D	14. B	19. A
5. 14	10. C	15. B	20. B

1. **The correct answer is B.** The perimeter of this region is the sum of the lengths of the two line segments and the circular arc. Each line segment has length 6 inches since they are both radii of the same circle. So, this contributes 12 inches to the perimeter. Also, using the arc length formula $s = r\theta$ with $r = 6$ inches and $\theta = 270°$ (which we know is the case because the angle between the two radii on the outside of the region is 90 degrees) makes the length of the circular arc $s = \left(\dfrac{270°}{180°}\right)\pi \times 6$ inches $= 9\pi$ inches.

   So, the perimeter of the region is $(12 + 9\pi)$ inches.

2. **The correct answer is C.** Identify the center and radius. The intersection of any two diameters of a circle must be the circle's center. The midpoint of AB and the midpoint of CD are the same point, which is $(2, 0)$. So, this must be the intersection point and the center of the circle. The distance between this center and any of the four endpoints of the line segments AB and CD must be the radius of the circle. This distance is $\dfrac{1}{2}$. So, the equation of the circle is $(x - 2)^2 + y^2 = \left(\dfrac{1}{2}\right)^2$, which is equivalent to $(x - 2)^2 + y^2 = \dfrac{1}{4}$.

3. **The correct answer is C.** Expand the product using FOIL and simplify the resulting expression using the fact that $i^2 = -1$. Then, add like terms:

$$-8i + (1 - 8i)(1 + 8i)$$
$$= -8i + \left(1^2 \cancel{+8i} \cancel{-8i} - (8i)^2\right)$$
$$= -8i + 1 + 64$$
$$= -8i + 65$$
$$= 65 - 8i$$

4. **The correct answer is A.** Expand the product using FOIL and simplify the resulting expression using the fact that $i^2 = -1$:

$$(3 + 4i)(3 + 4i)$$
$$= 9 + 12i + 12i + 16i^2$$
$$= 9 + 24i - 16$$
$$= -7 + 24i$$

5. **The correct answer is 14 units.** For the circle to lie completely inside the square, the side length of the square must be at least as large as the diameter of the circle. The diameter of a circle is twice its radius. The equation of the given circle is in standard form, and so the right side is the square of the radius. Therefore, the radius = 7 units, which means the diameter = 14 units. Thus, the least possible length of a side of such a square is 14 units.

6. **The correct answer is A.** Use the distance formula to find that the length is

$$\sqrt{(-a-(-b))^2 + (b-(-a))^2} = \sqrt{(b-a)^2 + (b+a)^2}$$
$$= \sqrt{b^2 \cancel{-2ab} + a^2 + b^2 \cancel{+2ab} + a^2}$$
$$= \sqrt{2(a^2 + b^2)}$$

This cannot be simplified further.

7. **The correct answer is 88 feet.** The current paths require a trip of 300 feet (150 feet for each of the two sides one must travel along to get from one corner to the other). A diagonal path would form a 45°-45°-90° isosceles right triangle, with the existing paths as its legs. As such, the length of the diagonal path would be $150\sqrt{2}$ feet or approximately 212 feet. The new path would shorten the route by approximately $300 - 212 = 88$ feet.

8. **The correct answer is B.** The area of a rectangle is equal to the product of its length and width. You are given that the area of the rectangle is $6x^2 + 25x + 25$ square units and that its length is $3x + 5$ units. You must determine the other factor that, when multiplied by $(3x + 5)$, yields $6x^2 + 25x + 25$. This factor is $2x + 5$.

9. **The correct answer is D.** The angles opposite equal sides in any triangle have the same measure. Since all three sides are congruent, it follows that all three angles are congruent. Since the sum of the three angles of a triangle must be 180 degrees, the measure of each angle is 60 degrees. Therefore, it is not possible for the triangle to be a right triangle.

10. **The correct answer is C.** The strategy is to find the areas of the two right triangles inside square $ABDF$ and then subtract their sum from the area of the square. To do so, we need to identify the lengths of $\overline{BC}$ and $\overline{CD}$. Using the Pythagorean theorem on triangle CDE shows that $\overline{CD}$ has length 3 units. Since all sides of the square have length 12 inches, $\overline{BC}$ must have length 9 inches. Using the area formula $A = \frac{1}{2}bh$, where b is the base and h is the height of a triangle, we have the following areas:

Area of triangle $ABC =$
$\frac{1}{2}$ (12 in.)(9 in.) = 54 sq. in.

Area of triangle $CDE =$
$\frac{1}{2}$ (4 in.)(3 in.) = 6 sq. in.

The area of the square $ABDF$ is (12 in.) • (12 in.) = 144 sq. in. So, the area of the quadrilateral $ACEF$ is $144 - (54 + 6) = 84$ square inches.

11. **The correct answer is C.** All sides of an equilateral triangle have the same length, so an equilateral triangle with a perimeter of 30 feet must have sides of length 10 feet. This means that the base of the triangle is 10 feet, and the height is the line that divides the equilateral into two 30-60-90 triangles. Since each of these 30-60-90 triangles has a shorter leg of 5 feet (half the base) and a hypotenuse of 10, the longer leg h (the height) must satisfy the Pythagorean theorem: $h^2 + 5^2 = 10^2$, so that $h^2 = 75$ and $h = \sqrt{75} = 5\sqrt{3}$ feet. Substitute these numbers into the area formula:

$\frac{1}{2}bh = \frac{1}{2}(10)(5\sqrt{3}) = 25\sqrt{3}$ square feet

12. **The correct answer is A.** Let w represent the width of the pen. The length is $3w + 7$. The area is given as 6 square yards. Substitute all values into the area formula to solve for w.

$$w(3w + 7) = 6$$
$$3w^2 + 7w - 6 = 0$$
$$(3w - 2)(w + 3) = 0$$
$$w = \frac{2}{3}, \ -3$$

The width of a rectangle cannot be negative, so w must be equal to $\frac{2}{3}$. Thus, the length is $3\left(\frac{2}{3}\right) + 7 = 9$ yards.

13. **The correct answer is B.** The area of the shaded region is the difference between the area of the square and the area of the circle. The perimeter of the square is 80 inches, so the length of each side is 20 inches. The diameter of the circle is also 20 inches since it is tangent to the four sides of the square. The area of this square is $20^2 = 400$ square inches. The area of the circle $\pi(10)^2 = 100\pi$ square inches (since its radius is 10 inches). Therefore, the area of the shaded region is $(400 - 100\pi)$ square inches.

14. **The correct answer is B.** The surface area of a rectangular box is the sum of the areas of the six rectangular faces. The dimensions of the faces are 24 m × 6 m, and 24 m × 18 m, and 6 m × 18 m.

There are two faces with each set of dimensions. So, find the area of each face, multiply it by 2, and add them: $2[24(6) + 24(18) + 6(18)] = 1{,}368$ square meters.

15. **The correct answer is B.** You are given the side length opposite the 39° angle and are trying to find the hypotenuse. Therefore, you must use the sine to relate them: $\sin 39° = \frac{8}{x}$. Solve for x:

$$\sin 39° = \frac{8}{x}$$
$$x \sin 39° = 8$$
$$x = \frac{8}{\sin 39°}$$

16. **The correct answer is 4 inches.** The volume of a right circular cone with height h and radius r is $V = \frac{1}{3}\pi r^2 h$. In this scenario, $V = 8\pi$ and $h = 3r$. Substituting these expressions into the volume formula yields $8\pi = \frac{1}{3}\pi r^2(3r) = \pi r^3$. Solving this equation for r yields $r = 2$ inches. So, the diameter of the base is 4 inches.

17. **The correct answer is C.** The area of the inner circle is πr^2. The radius of the outer circle is 3r, so its area is $\pi(3r)2 = 9\pi r2$. So, the area of the shaded region is $9\pi r^2 - \pi r^2 = 8\pi r^2$ square units.

18. **The correct answer is D.** Since triangle ABD is isosceles, it follows that $\overline{AC}$ is the perpendicular bisector of $\overline{BD}$. Thus, $\overline{BC}$ and $\overline{CD}$ are congruent, so that they each have length 4 units. Observe that $\sin x = \frac{4}{AD}$ and $\cos y = \frac{4}{AB}$. But, since $\overline{AD}$ and $\overline{AB}$ have the same length, we conclude that $\sin(x) - \cos(y)$.

19. **The correct answer is A.** The radius of the large sphere with which the manufacturing process begins is $2.5 = \frac{5}{2}$ inches. The volume of such a sphere is $\frac{4}{3}\pi\left(\frac{5}{2}\right)^3 = \frac{125}{6}\pi$ cubic inches. The sphere to be removed has a radius of 2 inches, so its volume is $\frac{4}{3}\pi(2)^3 = \frac{32}{3}\pi$ cubic inches. So, the volume of the spherical shell is the difference of these two volumes:

$$\frac{125}{6}\pi - \frac{32}{3}\pi = \frac{61}{6}\pi \text{ cubic inches}$$

20. **The correct answer is B.** The two legs and hypotenuse (longest side) of a right triangle must satisfy the Pythagorean theorem. Note that for any positive real number a, $(5a)^2 + (12a)^2 = 169a^2 = (13a)^2$.

SUMMING IT UP

- The **domain** of a function is the set of all values of x that can be substituted into the expression and yield a meaningful output. The **range** of a function is the set of all possible y-values attained at some member of the domain.

- An x-intercept of f is any point of the form $(x, 0)$. You can find all intercepts by solving the equation $f(x) = 0$.

- A y-intercept of f is the point $(0, f(0))$.

- f is *increasing* on an interval if its graph rises from left to right as you progress through the interval from left to right.

- f is *decreasing* if its graph falls from left to right as you progress through the interval from left to right.

- The **minimum** of f is the y-value of the lowest point on the graph of f.

- The **maximum** of f is the y-value of the highest point on the graph of f.

- The average value of $f(x)$ on an interval from $x = a$ to $x = b$ is defined to be $\dfrac{f(b) - f(a)}{b - a}$. This is the slope of the line segment connecting $(a, f(a))$ to $(b, f(b))$.

- The solutions of $ax^2 + bx + c = 0$ are given by the formula $x = \dfrac{-b \pm \sqrt{b^2 - 4ac}}{2a}$.

- A **quadratic function** has the form $f(x) = ax^2 + bx + c$, where a, b, and c are real numbers and $a \neq 0$. The graph is a U-shaped curve called a **parabola**. The standard form of such a function is $f(x) = a(x - h)^2 + k$, where the vertex is (h, k); any quadratic function can be written in this form using the method of completing the square.

- The ability to factor polynomials is important, especially when trying to determine values of the variable that make the expression equal to zero (that is, its **zeros**).

- An x-intercept of a function $p(x)$ is a point $(a, 0)$ on the graph of $y = p(x)$; $x = a$ is a solution of the equation $p(x) = 0$; we call a a zero of $p(x)$, and if $p(x)$ is a polynomial, $(x - a)$ is one of its factors.

- Fractions in which the numerator and denominator are polynomials are called **rational expressions**. The arithmetic of them is like the arithmetic of numerical fractions—you simply add, subtract, multiply, and divide polynomials, and cancel like factors in the top and bottom as you would when simplifying a fraction involving numbers.

- You should be comfortable working with radicals. Specifically, know the following:
  - Raising a square root to the second power gives the radicand.
  - The square root of a product is the product of the square roots.
  - The square root of a quotient is the quotient of the square roots.
  - You can clear a square root from the denominator of a fraction by multiplying top and bottom by it.

- The exponent rules are a source of common pitfalls! Familiarize yourself with the dos and don'ts of how to deal with exponents. Specifically:

  ○ The result of raising any nonzero real number to the zero power is 1.

  ○ A term in the numerator that is raised to a negative exponent is equivalent to a term in the denominator with the same base, but positive exponent, and vice-versa.

  ○ When raising a product to a power, apply the power to each term and multiply the results.

  ○ When raising a quotient to a power, apply the power to each term and divide the results.

  ○ When multiplying terms with the same base raised to powers, add the powers.

  ○ When dividing terms with the same base raised to powers, subtract the powers.

  ○ When raising a term that is already raised to a power to another power, multiply the powers.

  ○ The power of a sum is not equal to the sum of the powers.

- The key to making the determination between a linear and exponential function from a table of points is that the slope between *any* two points of a linear function is the same, while an exponential function grows by the same multiple on intervals of the same length.

- Formulas that involve multiple variables are **literal equations**. The algebra rules remain unchanged when working with them.

- A system consisting of a linear equation and a quadratic equation is solved using the substitution method and can have zero, one, or two solutions.

- The **Triangle Sum Rule** asserts that the sum of the measures of the three angles in any triangle must be 180 degrees, and the **Triangle Inequality** says that the sum of the lengths of any two sides of a triangle must be strictly larger than the length of the third side.

- The **Pythagorean theorem** expresses the relationship between the sides of a right triangle, stating that $c^2 = a^2 + b^2$, where side c is the hypotenuse and the sides a and b are its legs.

- The **perimeter** of a planar region is the sum of the lengths of all portions that comprise the outer boundary of the figure. The **area** of a planar region is the number of unit squares needed to cover it. The **volume** of a solid is the number of unit cubes needed to fill it. The **surface area** of a solid is the total area that its surface occupies in space.

- The midpoint of the segment joining two points (x_1, y_1) and (x_2, y_2) is $\left(\dfrac{x_1 + x_2}{2}, \dfrac{y_1 + y_2}{2} \right)$.

- The length of the segment joining two points (x_1, y_1) and (x_2, y_2) is $\sqrt{(x_2 - x_1)^2 + (y_2 - y_1)^2}$.

- A **circle** is the set of points that are a fixed distance r (called the **radius**) from a given point (h, k) (called the **center**). Its equation is $(x - h)^2 + (y - k)^2 = r^2$.

- The **trigonometric functions** are used to identify the lengths of sides of a right triangle when one side and one angle (instead of two sides) are known.

  ○ $\cos\theta = \dfrac{\text{adjacent}}{\text{hypotenuse}}$

  ○ $\sin\theta = \dfrac{\text{opposite}}{\text{hypotenuse}}$

  ○ $\tan\theta = \dfrac{\text{opposite}}{\text{adjacent}}$

- Complex numbers arise when you take the square root of a negative number. The imaginary unit i is defined as $i^2 = -1$.

  ○ Sum: $(a + bi) + (c + di) = (a + c) + (b + d)i$

  ○ Difference: $(a + bi) - (c + di) = (a - c) + (b - d)i$

  ○ Product: $(a + bi) \times (c + di) = (ac - bd) + (bc + ad)i$

  ○ Quotient: $\dfrac{a + bi}{c + di} = \dfrac{a + bi}{c + di} \cdot \dfrac{c - di}{c - di} = \dfrac{(ac + bd) + (bc - ad)i}{c^2 + d^2}$

PART VI
TWO PRACTICE TESTS FOR THE PSAT/NMSQT® EXAM

Practice Test 1

INTRODUCTION TO THE PRACTICE TEST

On test day, you will see these important reminders on the first page of your exam booklet:

- You must use a No. 2 pencil when taking the test; you may not use a pen or mechanical pencil.
- You may not share any questions with anyone. Doing so could cause your scores to be canceled.
- You are not permitted to take the test booklet out of the testing room.

The general directions for the test will look something like this:

- You may only work on one section at a time.
- If you complete a section before time is called, check your work on that section only. You are not permitted to work on any other section.

The directions for marking your answers will likely include the following recommendations:

- Mark your answer sheet properly—be sure to completely fill in the answer circle.
- Be careful to mark only one answer for each question.
- Don't make any stray marks on the answer sheet.
- If you need to erase your answer, make sure you do so completely.
- Be sure to use the answer spaces that correspond to the question numbers.

You will be able to use your test booklet for scratch work, but you won't get credit for any work done in your test booklet. When time is called at the end of each section, you will not be permitted to transfer answers from your test booklet to your answer sheet.

Scoring on the exam is as follows:

- You will receive one point for each correct answer.
- You will not lose points for wrong answers, so you should attempt to answer every question even if you aren't completely sure of the correct answer.

Your testing supervisor will announce when to open the test booklet, so be sure to wait until you're told to do so. For the purposes of this practice test, be sure you have a timer to set for 60 minutes for the Section 1: Reading Test.

The answer sheets for each test section appear on the next pages.

Following the Answer Key and Explanations section, you will find details on how to score your exam.

Any information, ideas, or opinions presented in any of the passages you will see on the exam that have been taken from other sources or published material do not represent the opinions of the College Board.

PSAT/NMSQT® EXAM ANSWER SHEET

Section 1: Reading Test

1. (A) (B) (C) (D) 11. (A) (B) (C) (D) 21. (A) (B) (C) (D) 30. (A) (B) (C) (D) 39. (A) (B) (C) (D)
2. (A) (B) (C) (D) 12. (A) (B) (C) (D) 22. (A) (B) (C) (D) 31. (A) (B) (C) (D) 40. (A) (B) (C) (D)
3. (A) (B) (C) (D) 13. (A) (B) (C) (D) 23. (A) (B) (C) (D) 32. (A) (B) (C) (D) 41. (A) (B) (C) (D)
4. (A) (B) (C) (D) 14. (A) (B) (C) (D) 24. (A) (B) (C) (D) 33. (A) (B) (C) (D) 42. (A) (B) (C) (D)
5. (A) (B) (C) (D) 15. (A) (B) (C) (D) 25. (A) (B) (C) (D) 34. (A) (B) (C) (D) 43. (A) (B) (C) (D)
6. (A) (B) (C) (D) 16. (A) (B) (C) (D) 26. (A) (B) (C) (D) 35. (A) (B) (C) (D) 44. (A) (B) (C) (D)
7. (A) (B) (C) (D) 17. (A) (B) (C) (D) 27. (A) (B) (C) (D) 36. (A) (B) (C) (D) 45. (A) (B) (C) (D)
8. (A) (B) (C) (D) 18. (A) (B) (C) (D) 28. (A) (B) (C) (D) 37. (A) (B) (C) (D) 46. (A) (B) (C) (D)
9. (A) (B) (C) (D) 19. (A) (B) (C) (D) 29. (A) (B) (C) (D) 38. (A) (B) (C) (D) 47. (A) (B) (C) (D)
10. (A) (B) (C) (D) 20. (A) (B) (C) (D)

Section 2: Writing and Language Test

1. (A) (B) (C) (D) 10. (A) (B) (C) (D) 19. (A) (B) (C) (D) 28. (A) (B) (C) (D) 37. (A) (B) (C) (D)
2. (A) (B) (C) (D) 11. (A) (B) (C) (D) 20. (A) (B) (C) (D) 29. (A) (B) (C) (D) 38. (A) (B) (C) (D)
3. (A) (B) (C) (D) 12. (A) (B) (C) (D) 21. (A) (B) (C) (D) 30. (A) (B) (C) (D) 39. (A) (B) (C) (D)
4. (A) (B) (C) (D) 13. (A) (B) (C) (D) 22. (A) (B) (C) (D) 31. (A) (B) (C) (D) 40. (A) (B) (C) (D)
5. (A) (B) (C) (D) 14. (A) (B) (C) (D) 23. (A) (B) (C) (D) 32. (A) (B) (C) (D) 41. (A) (B) (C) (D)
6. (A) (B) (C) (D) 15. (A) (B) (C) (D) 24. (A) (B) (C) (D) 33. (A) (B) (C) (D) 42. (A) (B) (C) (D)
7. (A) (B) (C) (D) 16. (A) (B) (C) (D) 25. (A) (B) (C) (D) 34. (A) (B) (C) (D) 43. (A) (B) (C) (D)
8. (A) (B) (C) (D) 17. (A) (B) (C) (D) 26. (A) (B) (C) (D) 35. (A) (B) (C) (D) 44. (A) (B) (C) (D)
9. (A) (B) (C) (D) 18. (A) (B) (C) (D) 27. (A) (B) (C) (D) 36. (A) (B) (C) (D)

Section 3: Math Test—No Calculator

1. (A) (B) (C) (D) 4. (A) (B) (C) (D) 7. (A) (B) (C) (D) 10. (A) (B) (C) (D) 12. (A) (B) (C) (D)
2. (A) (B) (C) (D) 5. (A) (B) (C) (D) 8. (A) (B) (C) (D) 11. (A) (B) (C) (D) 13. (A) (B) (C) (D)
3. (A) (B) (C) (D) 6. (A) (B) (C) (D) 9. (A) (B) (C) (D)

Section 3: Math Test—No Calculator

14. 15. 16. 17.

Section 4: Math Test—Calculator

1. Ⓐ Ⓑ Ⓒ Ⓓ   7. Ⓐ Ⓑ Ⓒ Ⓓ   13. Ⓐ Ⓑ Ⓒ Ⓓ   18. Ⓐ Ⓑ Ⓒ Ⓓ   23. Ⓐ Ⓑ Ⓒ Ⓓ

2. Ⓐ Ⓑ Ⓒ Ⓓ   8. Ⓐ Ⓑ Ⓒ Ⓓ   14. Ⓐ Ⓑ Ⓒ Ⓓ   19. Ⓐ Ⓑ Ⓒ Ⓓ   24. Ⓐ Ⓑ Ⓒ Ⓓ

3. Ⓐ Ⓑ Ⓒ Ⓓ   9. Ⓐ Ⓑ Ⓒ Ⓓ   15. Ⓐ Ⓑ Ⓒ Ⓓ   20. Ⓐ Ⓑ Ⓒ Ⓓ   25. Ⓐ Ⓑ Ⓒ Ⓓ

4. Ⓐ Ⓑ Ⓒ Ⓓ   10. Ⓐ Ⓑ Ⓒ Ⓓ   16. Ⓐ Ⓑ Ⓒ Ⓓ   21. Ⓐ Ⓑ Ⓒ Ⓓ   26. Ⓐ Ⓑ Ⓒ Ⓓ

5. Ⓐ Ⓑ Ⓒ Ⓓ   11. Ⓐ Ⓑ Ⓒ Ⓓ   17. Ⓐ Ⓑ Ⓒ Ⓓ   22. Ⓐ Ⓑ Ⓒ Ⓓ   27. Ⓐ Ⓑ Ⓒ Ⓓ

6. Ⓐ Ⓑ Ⓒ Ⓓ   12. Ⓐ Ⓑ Ⓒ Ⓓ

28. 29. 30. 31.

SECTION 1: READING TEST

60 Minutes • 47 Questions

Turn to Section 1 of your answer sheet to answer the questions in this section.

> **Directions:** Each passage or pair of passages below is followed by a number of questions. After reading each passage or pair, choose the best answer to each question based on what is stated or implied in the passage or passages and in any accompanying graphics (such as a table or graph).

Questions 1–9 are based on the following passage.

This passage is adapted from Little Men *by Louisa May Alcott, originally published in 1871.*

"Please, sir, is this Plumfield?" asked a ragged boy of the man who opened the great gate at which the omnibus left him.

"Yes. Who sent you?"

Line   "Mr. Laurence. I have got a letter for the lady."

5   "All right; go up to the house, and give it to her; she'll see to you, little chap."

The man spoke pleasantly, and the boy went on, feeling much cheered by the words. Through the soft spring rain that fell on sprouting grass and budding trees, Nat saw a large square house before him, a hospitable-looking house, with an old-fashioned porch, wide steps, and lights shining in many windows. Neither curtains nor shutters hid the cheerful
10 glimmer; and, pausing a moment before he rang, Nat saw many little shadows dancing on the walls, heard the pleasant hum of young voices, and felt that it was hardly possible that the light and warmth and comfort within could be for a homeless "little chap" like him.

"I hope the lady will see to me," he thought, and gave a timid rap with the great bronze knocker, which was a jovial griffin's head.

15   A rosy-faced servant-maid opened the door, and smiled as she took the letter which he silently offered. She seemed used to receiving strange boys, for she pointed to a seat in the hall, and said, with a nod:

"Sit there and drip on the mat a bit, while I take this in to missis."

Nat found plenty to amuse him while he waited, and stared about him curiously,
20 enjoying the view, yet glad to do so unobserved in the dusky recess by the door.

The house seemed swarming with boys, who were beguiling the rainy twilight with all sorts of amusements. There were boys everywhere, "up-stairs and down-stairs and in the lady's chamber," apparently, for various open doors showed pleasant groups of big boys, little boys, and middle-sized boys in all stages of evening relaxation, not to say effervescence. Two

25 large rooms on the right were evidently schoolrooms, for desks, maps, blackboards, and books were scattered about. An open fire burned on the hearth, and several indolent lads lay on their backs before it, discussing a new cricket-ground, with such animation that their boots waved in the air. A tall youth was practicing on the flute in one corner, quite undisturbed by the racket all about him. Two or three others were jumping over the desks, pausing, now and
30 then, to get their breath and laugh at the droll sketches of a little wag who was caricaturing the whole household on a blackboard.

In the room on the left a long supper-table was seen, set forth with great pitchers of new milk, piles of brown and white bread, and perfect stacks of the shiny gingerbread so dear to boyish souls. A flavor of toast was in the air, also suggestions of baked apples, very tantalizing
35 to one hungry little nose and stomach.

The hall, however, presented the most inviting prospect of all, for a brisk game of tag was going on in the upper entry. One landing was devoted to marbles, the other to checkers, while the stairs were occupied by a boy reading, a girl singing a lullaby to her doll, two puppies, a kitten, and a constant succession of small boys sliding down the banisters, to the
40 great detriment of their clothes and danger to their limbs.

So absorbed did Nat become in this exciting race, that he ventured farther and farther out of his corner; and when one very lively boy came down so swiftly that he could not stop himself, but fell off the banisters, with a crash that would have broken any head but one rendered nearly as hard as a cannon-ball by eleven years of constant bumping, Nat forgot
45 himself, and ran up to the fallen rider, expecting to find him half-dead. The boy, however, only winked rapidly for a second, then lay calmly looking up at the new face with a surprised, "Hullo!"

"Hullo!" returned Nat, not knowing what else to say, and thinking that form of reply both brief and easy.

50 "Are you a new boy?" asked the recumbent youth, without stirring.

"Don't know yet."

"What's your name?"

"Nat Blake."

"Mine's Tommy Bangs. Come up and have a go, will you?" and Tommy got upon his legs
55 like one suddenly remembering the duties of hospitality.

"Guess I won't, till I see whether I'm going to stay or not," returned Nat, feeling the desire to stay increase every moment.

"I say, Demi, here's a new one. Come and see to him;" and the lively Thomas returned to his sport with unabated relish.

1. Based on the passage, when Nat arrives at the house he is

   A. wet from the rain.

   B. suffering from a cold.

   C. in a gloomy mood.

   D. exhausted from his journey.

2. Which choice provides the best evidence for the answer to the previous question?

   A. Line 7 ("Through . . . trees")

   B. Lines 10-12 ("Nat . . . him.")

   C. Lines 15-16 ("A rosy-faced . . . offered.")

   D. Line 18 ("Sit there . . . missis.")

3. Based on the passage, which character would most likely agree with the old proverb that if at first you don't succeed, try, try again?

   A. Nat Blake

   B. Tommy Bangs

   C. Demi

   D. Mr. Laurence

4. Which choice provides the best evidence for the answer to the previous question?

   A. Lines 42-43 ("...one very . . . head...")

   B. Lines 44-45 ("Nat forgot . . . half-dead.")

   C. Line 54 ("Mine's . . . you?")

   D. Lines 58-59 ("...the lively . . . relish.")

5. In the context of the passage, the main purpose of lines 21-22 ("The house . . . amusements.") is to

   A. introduce the story's main characters.

   B. set up the story's main conflict.

   C. establish the setting inside the house.

   D. provide some back story about Nat.

6. As used in line 30, "wag" most nearly means

   A. wiggle.

   B. troublemaker.

   C. sway.

   D. shake.

7. Based on the passage, how did Nat come to the house?

   A. He filled out an application to be accepted there.

   B. The owner of the house sent for him.

   C. Mr. Laurence sent him to the house.

   D. He traveled by carriage.

8. Based on the passage, when Nat says "Don't know yet" (line 51) after Tommy asks Nat if he is the "new boy," Nat most probably means that he is not sure if he

   A. is the newest arrival at the house.

   B. understands Tommy's question.

   C. likes the other boys at the house.

   D. will decide to stay at the house.

9. As used in line 38, "occupied" most nearly means

   A. in use.

   B. engaged.

   C. controlled.

   D. conquered.

practice test 1—Reading

Questions 10–19 are based on the following passage and supplementary material.

This passage is adapted from Democracy and Education *by John Dewey, originally published in 1916.*

Society not only continues to exist by transmission, by communication, but it may fairly be said to exist in transmission, in communication. There is more than a verbal tie between the words common, community, and communication. Men live in a community in virtue
Line of the things which they have in common; and communication is the way in which they
5   come to possess things in common. What they must have in common in order to form a community or society are aims, beliefs, aspirations, knowledge—a common understanding— like-mindedness as the sociologists say. Such things cannot be passed physically from one to another, like bricks; they cannot be shared as persons would share a pie by dividing it into physical pieces. The communication which insures participation in a common understanding
10 is one which secures similar emotional and intellectual dispositions—like ways of responding to expectations and requirements.

Persons do not become a society by living in physical proximity, any more than a man ceases to be socially influenced by being so many feet or miles removed from others. A book or a letter may institute a more intimate association between human beings separated
15 thousands of miles from each other than exists between dwellers under the same roof. Individuals do not even compose a social group because they all work for a common end. The parts of a machine work with a maximum of cooperativeness for a common result, but they do not form a community. If, however, they were all cognizant of the common end and all interested in it so that they regulated their specific activity in view of it, then they would form
20 a community. But this would involve communication. Each would have to know what the other was about and would have to have some way of keeping the other informed as to his own purpose and progress. Consensus demands communication.

We are thus compelled to recognize that within even the most social group there are many relations which are not as yet social. A large number of human relationships in any
25 social group are still upon the machine-like plane. Individuals use one another so as to get desired results, without reference to the emotional and intellectual disposition and consent of those used. Such uses express physical superiority, or superiority of position, skill, technical ability, and command of tools, mechanical or fiscal. So far as the relations of parent and child, teacher and pupil, employer and employee, governor and governed, remain upon this level,
30 they form no true social group, no matter how closely their respective activities touch one another. Giving and taking of orders modifies action and results, but does not of itself effect a sharing of purposes, a communication of interests.

Not only is social life identical with communication, but all communication (and hence all genuine social life) is educative. To be a recipient of a communication is to have an
35 enlarged and changed experience. One shares in what another has thought and felt and in so far, meagerly or amply, has his own attitude modified. Nor is the one who communicates left unaffected. Try the experiment of communicating, with fullness and accuracy, some experience to another, especially if it be somewhat complicated, and you will find your own attitude toward your experience changing; otherwise you resort to expletives and ejaculations.

The following pie chart reflects a 2012 study of how a selection of people spent the majority of their time communicating.

Methods of Communication, 2012

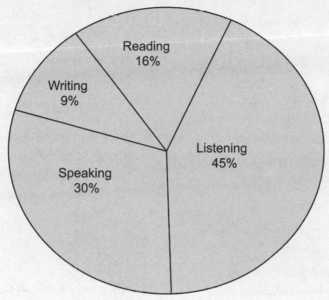

10. The main purpose of the passage is to

   A. argue that communication and common characteristics are the bases of any community.

   B. explain that people don't form societies by living close to each other.

   C. show that information cannot be passed back and forth like bricks.

   D. prove that there is more than a verbal tie between certain words.

11. Which choice provides the best evidence for the answer to the previous question?

   A. Lines 2-3 ("There is . . . communication.")

   B. Lines 3-4 ("Men live . . . in common.")

   C. Lines 7-8 ("Such . . . bricks")

   D. Line 12 ("Persons . . . proximity, . . .")

12. As used in line 13, "removed" most nearly means

   A. indifferent.

   B. impassive.

   C. disinterested.

   D. separated.

13. The passage characterizes relationships that are not social as negative in that they

   A. exist even within the most social groups.

   B. are similar to the ways machines operate.

   C. are common among a large number of humans.

   D. emphasize imbalances of power over mutual care.

14. Which choice provides the best evidence for the answer to the previous question?

    A. Lines 23-24 ("We are . . . social.")

    B. Lines 24-25 ("A large . . . plane.")

    C. Lines 25-28 ("Individuals . . . fiscal.")

    D. Lines 28-31 ("So far . . . another.")

15. Which of the following is cited in the passage as an indicator of how communication changes human experiences?

    A. The exchange of thoughts and feelings that happens during communication.

    B. The idea that social life is identical with communication.

    C. The possibility that other people beside the communicators are affected.

    D. The fact that one can communicate with fullness and accuracy.

16. According to the information in the passage and the pie chart, what percentage of people are most likely to have "enlarged and changed" experiences?

    A. 16 percent

    B. 30 percent

    C. 45 percent

    D. 61 percent

17. According to the passage, what percentage of the people indicated in the pie chart are involved in educative communication?

    A. 39 percent

    B. 45 percent

    C. 61 percent

    D. 100 percent

18. As used in line 25, "plane" most nearly means

    A. flat.

    B. level.

    C. smooth.

    D. airplane.

19. The main purpose of the last paragraph of the passage is to

    A. explain how communication has tightly bonded the world together as methods have advanced.

    B. detail how not only the recipient of information, but also the communicator benefits from sharing knowledge.

    C. explore the anger involved when there are miscommunications.

    D. instruct on how to come up with communication experiments to work on to improve skills.

Questions 20–28 are based on the following passage and supplementary material.

This passage is adapted from The Chemistry, Properties, and Tests of Precious Stones *by John Mastin, originally published in 1911.*

Probably the most important of the many important physical properties possessed by precious stones are those of light and its effects, for to these all known gems owe their beauty, if not actual fascination.

Line
5
When light strikes a cut or polished stone, one or more of the following effects are observed:—it may be transmitted through the stone, diaphaneity, as it is called; it may produce single or double refraction, or polarization; if reflected, it may produce luster or color; or it may produce phosphorescence; so that light may be (1) transmitted; (2) reflected; or produce (3) phosphorescence.

(1) Transmission.—In transmitted light we have, as stated above, single or double
10 refraction, polarization, and diaphaneity.

To the quality of *refraction* is due one of the chief charms of certain precious stones. It is not necessary to explain here what refraction is, for everyone will be familiar with the refractive property of a light-beam when passing through a medium denser than atmospheric air. It will be quite sufficient to say that all the rays are not equal in refractive power in all
15 substances, so that the middle of the spectrum is generally selected as the mean for indexing purposes.

It will be seen that the stones in the 1st, or cubic system, show single refraction, whereas those of all other systems show double refraction; thus, light, in passing through their substance, is deviated, part of it going one way, the other portion going in another direction—
20 that is, at a slightly different angle—so that this property alone will isolate readily all gems belonging to the 1st system.

A well-known simple experiment in physics shows this clearly. A mark on a card or paper is viewed through a piece of double-refracting spar (Iceland spar or clear calcite), when the mark is doubled and two appear. On rotating this rhomb of spar, one of these marks is
25 seen to revolve round the other, which remains stationary, the moving mark passing further from the centre in places. When the spar is cut and used in a certain direction, we see but one mark, and such a position is called its optical axis.

Polarization is when certain crystals possessing double refraction have the power of changing light, giving it the appearance of poles which have different properties, and the
30 polariscope is an instrument in which are placed pieces of double-refracting (Iceland) spar, so that all light passing through will be polarized.

Since only crystals possessing the property of double refraction show polarization, it follows that those of the 1st, or cubic system—in which the diamond stands a prominent example—fail to become polarized, so that when such a stone is placed in the polariscope and
35 rotated, it fails at every point to transmit light, which a double-refracting gem allows to pass except when its optical axis is placed in the axis of the polariscope, but this will be dealt with more fully when the methods of testing the stones come to be considered.

Diaphaneity, or the power of transmitting light:—some rather fine trade distinctions are drawn between the stones in this class, technical distinctions made specially for purposes
40 of classification, thus:—a "non-diaphanous" stone is one which is quite opaque, no light of any kind passing through its substance; a "diaphanous" stone is one which is altogether transparent; "semi-diaphanous" means one not altogether transparent, and sometimes called "sub-transparent." A "translucent" stone is one in which, though light passes through its substance, sight is not possible through it; whilst in a "sub-translucent" stone, light passes
45 through it, but only in a small degree.

Light Rays Hitting a Precious Stone

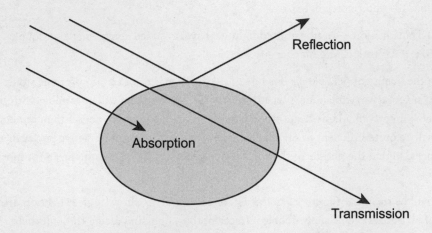

20. According to the passage, those who appreciate precious stones often value the way the stones

   A. polarize light.

   B. leave marks.

   C. are shaped.

   D. refract light.

21. Which choice provides the best evidence for the answer to the previous question?

   A. Lines 9-10 ("Transmission . . . diaphaneity.")

   B. Line 11 ("To the quality . . . stones.")

   C. Lines 12-14 ("It is not . . . air.")

   D. Lines 14-16 ("It will be . . . purposes.")

22. According to the passage, what is the direct result of light passing through certain crystals with double refraction?

   A. polarization

   B. transmission

   C. phosphorescence

   D. production

23. Which choice provides the best evidence for the answer to the previous question?

   A. Lines 28-29 (*"Polarization* . . . light, . . .")

   B. Lines 29-30 ("the polariscope . . . spar, . . .")

   C. Lines 33-34 (". . .those . . . polarized,. . .")

   D. Lines 36-37 (". . .this will . . . considered.")

24. As used in line 19, "substance" most nearly means

A. essence.

B. body.

C. theme.

D. core.

25. The main purpose of the final paragraph of the passage is to

A. introduce and define the term "diaphaneity."

B. define various technical distinctions related to diaphaneity.

C. explain the difference between a translucent and a sub-translucent stone.

D. prove that "diaphaneity" is an extremely complex term.

26. As used in line 39, "class" most nearly means

A. group.

B. lesson.

C. schoolroom.

D. elegance.

27. Based on the passage, which of the following effects is shown on the diagram?

A. phosphorescence

B. double refraction

C. opaque

D. diaphaneity

28. Based on the passage and the graphic, "absorption" might occur in a stone that is

A. non-diaphanous.

B. sub-translucent.

C. diaphanous.

D. translucent.

Questions 29–37 are based on the following passage.

This passage is adapted from "Federalist No. 68. The Mode of Electing the President" by Alexander Hamilton, originally published in 1788.

The mode of appointment of the Chief Magistrate of the United States is almost the only part of the system, of any consequence, which has escaped without severe censure, or which has received the slightest mark of approbation from its opponents. The most plausible
Line of these, who has appeared in print, has even deigned to admit that the election of the
5 President is pretty well guarded. I venture somewhat further, and hesitate not to affirm, that if the manner of it be not perfect, it is at least excellent. It unites in an eminent degree all the advantages, the union of which was to be wished for.

It was desirable that the sense of the people should operate in the choice of the person to whom so important a trust was to be confided. This end will be answered by committing the
10 right of making it, not to any pre-established body, but to men chosen by the people for the special purpose, and at the particular conjuncture.

It was equally desirable, that the immediate election should be made by men most capable of analyzing the qualities adapted to the station, and acting under circumstances favorable to deliberation, and to a judicious combination of all the reasons and inducements
15 which were proper to govern their choice. A small number of persons, selected by their fellow-citizens from the general mass, will be most likely to possess the information and discernment requisite to such complicated investigations.

It was also peculiarly desirable to afford as little opportunity as possible to tumult and disorder. This evil was not least to be dreaded in the election of a magistrate, who was to
20 have so important an agency in the administration of the government as the President of the United States. But the precautions which have been so happily concerted in the system under consideration, promise an effectual security against this mischief. The choice of SEVERAL, to form an intermediate body of electors, will be much less apt to convulse the community with any extraordinary or violent movements, than the choice of ONE who was himself to be
25 the final object of the public wishes. And as the electors, chosen in each State, are to assemble and vote in the State in which they are chosen, this detached and divided situation will expose them much less to heats and ferments, which might be communicated from them to the people, than if they were all to be convened at one time, in one place.

Nothing was more to be desired than that every practicable obstacle should be opposed
30 to cabal, intrigue, and corruption. These most deadly adversaries of republican government might naturally have been expected to make their approaches from more than one quarter, but chiefly from the desire in foreign powers to gain an improper ascendant in our councils. How could they better gratify this, than by raising a creature of their own to the chief magistracy of the Union? But the convention have guarded against all danger of this sort,
35 with the most provident and judicious attention. They have not made the appointment of the President to depend on any preexisting bodies of men, who might be tampered with beforehand to prostitute their votes; but they have referred it in the first instance to an immediate act of the people of America, to be exerted in the choice of persons for the temporary and sole purpose of making the appointment.

29. As used in line 1, "appointment" most nearly means

    A. meeting.

    B. job.

    C. selection.

    D. date.

30. Hamilton makes which point about the American presidential election process?

    A. It is a perfect process.

    B. It is flawed but effective.

    C. Its flaws outweigh its strengths.

    D. It needs to be eliminated completely.

31. Which choice provides the best evidence for the answer to the previous question?

    A. Lines 1-3 ("The mode . . . opponents.")

    B. Lines 3-5 ("The most . . . guarded.")

    C. Lines 5-6 ("I venture . . . excellent.")

    D. Lines 6-7 ("It unites . . . for.")

32. According to Hamilton, electors should

    A. follow the will of the voters completely and uncritically.

    B. outnumber the voters so that the electors' votes constitute a majority.

    C. be uniquely capable of analyzing the effectiveness of potential presidents.

    D. be capable of doing their jobs even if there is tumult and disorder.

33. Which choice provides the best evidence for the answer to the previous question?

    A. Lines 9-11 ("This end . . . conjuncture.")

    B. Lines 12-15 ("It was equally . . . choice.")

    C. Lines 15-17 ("A small . . . investigations.")

    D. Lines 18-19 ("It was also . . . disorder.")

34. The central claim of the fourth paragraph (lines 18-28) is that

    A. having more than one elector prevents the election process from becoming chaotic.

    B. tumult and disorder are evils that the American people should dread.

    C. electors should assemble and vote in the State in which they are chosen.

    D. the American people often try to pressure electors to vote unethically.

35. As used in line 30, "intrigue" most nearly means

    A. fascination.

    B. absorb.

    C. conspiracy.

    D. faithfulness.

36. The main purpose of the final paragraph of the passage is to

    A. prove that all people are capable of falling victim to corruption and special interests.

    B. explain the basic function of the electoral college in the American voting process.

    C. describe the greatest obstacles to a republican form of government.

    D. express the importance of electors who will not be corrupted by special interest groups.

37. The phrase "deadly adversaries" (line 30) mainly serves to show

    A. that corruption can cost people their lives.

    B. that corrupted electors are as bad as murderers.

    C. how corruption does not exist in a democratic government.

    D. how serious a problem corruption is.

Questions 38–47 are based on the following passages.

Passage 1 is adapted from An Elementary Study of Chemistry *by William Edwards Henderson and William McPherson, originally published in 1905. Passage 2 is adapted from* An Introductory Course of Quantitative Chemical Analysis *by Henry Paul Talbot, originally published in 1921.*

Passage 1

    How to distinguish between physical and chemical changes. It is not always easy to tell to which class a given change belongs, and many cases will require careful thought on the part of the student. The test question in all cases is, Has the composition of the substance
Line been changed? Usually this can be answered by a study of the properties of the substance
5 before and after the change, since a change in composition is attended by a change in properties. In some cases, however, only a trained observer can decide the question.

    Changes in physical state. One class of physical changes should be noted with especial care, since it is likely to prove misleading. It is a familiar fact that ice is changed into water, and water into steam, by heating. Here we have three different substances,—the solid ice,
10 the liquid water, and the gaseous steam,—the properties of which differ widely. The chemist can readily show, however, that these three bodies have exactly the same composition, being composed of the same substances in the same proportion. Hence the change from one of these substances into another is a physical change. Many other substances may, under suitable conditions, be changed from solids into liquids, or from liquids into gases, without change in
15 composition. Thus butter and wax will melt when heated; alcohol and gasoline will evaporate when exposed to the air. *The three states—solid, liquid, and gas—are called the three physical states of matter.*

Physical and chemical properties. Many properties of a substance can be noted without causing the substance to undergo chemical change, and are therefore called its *physical properties*. Among these are its physical state, color, odor, taste, size, shape, weight. Other properties are only discovered when the substance undergoes chemical change. These are called its *chemical properties*. Thus we find that coal burns in air, gunpowder explodes when ignited, milk sours when exposed to air.

20

Passage 2

It cannot be too strongly emphasized that for the success of analyses uniformity of practice must prevail throughout all volumetric work with respect to those factors which can influence the accuracy of the measurement of liquids. For example, whatever conditions are imposed during the calibration of a burette, pipette, or flask (notably the time allowed for draining), must also prevail whenever the flask or burette is used.

Line

5

The student should also be constantly watchful to insure parallel conditions during both standardization and analyst with respect to the final volume of liquid in which a titration takes place. The value of a standard solution is only accurate under the conditions which prevailed when it was standardized. It is plain that the standard solutions must be scrupulously protected from concentration or dilution, after their value has been established. Accordingly, great care must be taken to thoroughly rinse out all burettes, flasks, etc., with the solutions which they are to contain, in order to remove all traces of water or other liquid which could act as a diluent. It is best to wash out a burette at least three times with small portions of a solution, allowing each to run out through the tip before assuming that the burette is in a condition to be filled and used. It is, of course, possible to dry measuring instruments in a hot closet, but this is tedious and unnecessary.

10

15

To the same end, all solutions should be kept stoppered and away from direct sunlight or heat. The bottles should be shaken before use to collect any liquid which may have distilled from the solution and condensed on the sides.

The student is again reminded that variations in temperature of volumetric solutions must be carefully noted, and care should always be taken that no source of heat is sufficiently near the solutions to raise the temperature during use.

20

Much time may be saved by estimating the approximate volume of a standard solution which will be required for a titration (if the data are obtainable) before beginning the operation. It is then possible to run in rapidly approximately the required amount, after which it is only necessary to determine the end-point slowly and with accuracy. In such cases, however, the knowledge of the approximate amount to be required should never be allowed to influence the judgment regarding the actual end-point.

25

38. According to Passage 1, one similarity between physical and chemical changes is that they both

    A. affect liquids and solids.

    B. are difficult to detect.

    C. involve a change of odor.

    D. involve a change of composition.

39. Which choice provides the best evidence for the answer to the previous question?

    A. Lines 18-20 ("Many . . . *properties*.")

    B. Line 20 ("Among . . . weight.")

    C. Lines 20-21 ("Other . . . change.")

    D. Lines 22-23 ("Thus . . . air.")

40. As used in line 20, "properties" most nearly means

    A. belongings.

    B. qualities.

    C. homes.

    D. resources.

41. According to Passage 2, every time a particular experiment is performed, it must be

    A. altered to fit changing factors.

    B. done with different pieces of lab equipment.

    C. more accurate than the previous experiment.

    D. performed under the same exact conditions.

42. Which choice provides the best evidence for the answer to the previous question?

    A. Lines 3-5 ("For example . . . is used.")

    B. Lines 9-10 ("It is plain . . . established.")

    C. Lines 11-13 ("Accordingly . . . diluent.")

    D. Lines 13-15 ("It is best . . . and used.")

43. As used in line 17, "solutions" most nearly means

    A. answers.

    B. mixtures.

    C. keys.

    D. explanations.

44. The primary purpose of each passage is to

    A. explain how to perform basic chemistry experiments.

    B. define the term *chemistry* for new science students.

    C. provide basic information about chemistry to students.

    D. describe the differences between physical and chemical properties.

45. Both authors would most likely agree with which statement about scientific work?

    A. Complete consistency is integral to performing scientific work.

    B. Estimations can help to save time while doing scientific work.

    C. Scientific work must always be performed with tremendous care.

    D. Complex scientific work can be performed by any student.

46. A significant difference in how the two authors discuss chemistry is that Passage 2 indicates that it is intended for

    A. professional chemists, while Passage 1 is intended for students.

    B. students who have already read Passage 1.

    C. a more advanced student than Passage 1 is.

    D. students, while Passage 1 is intended for professional chemists.

47. Assuming that he agrees with the assertions in Passage 2, the author of Passage 1 would most likely recommend which course of action to take when evaluating whether or not a substance has undergone a change in chemical composition?

    A. Do not resort to making estimates when making the evaluation.

    B. Be sure to keep the substance away from any heat sources.

    C. Taste the substance to see if it has undergone any changes in flavor.

    D. Make the evaluations more than once using a different burette, pipette, or flask.

STOP! DO NOT GO ON UNTIL TIME IS UP.

practice test 1—Reading

SECTION 2: WRITING AND LANGUAGE TEST

35 Minutes • 44 Questions

Turn to Section 2 of your answer sheet to answer the questions in this section.

Directions: Each passage below is accompanied by a number of multiple-choice questions. For some questions, you will need to consider how the passage might be revised to improve the expression of ideas. Other questions will ask you to consider how the passage might be edited to correct errors in sentence structure, usage, or punctuation. A passage may be accompanied by one or more graphics—such as a chart, table, or graph—that you will need to refer to in order to best answer the question(s).

Some questions will direct you to an underlined portion of a passage—it could be one word, a portion of a sentence, or the full sentence itself. Other questions will direct you to a particular paragraph or to certain sentences within a paragraph, or you'll be asked to think about the passage as a whole. Each question number refers to the corresponding number in the passage.

After reading each passage, select the answer to each question that most effectively improves the quality of writing in the passage or that makes the passage follow the conventions of Standard Written English. Many questions include a "NO CHANGE" option. Select that option if you think the best choice is to leave that specific portion of the passage as it is.

Questions 1–11 are based on the following passage and supplementary material.

When Will We Get to Mars?

In a 1961 speech, President John F. Kennedy outlined his space-related goals to Congress, telling them:

> *"No single space project in this period will be more impressive to mankind, or more important for the long-range exploration of space; and none will be so difficult or expensive to accomplish."*

[1] Eight years later, the U. S. landed a team of two astronauts on the moon. This was a first for humanity. And now, more than fifty years after President Kennedy's historic [2] moon shot speech (as it was later called), there are still impressive and difficult challenges to be had [3] in space namely, sending manned missions to Mars.

[4] There have been a number of Mars exploration programs, which have sent unmanned spacecraft known as "probes" and "rovers" to the planet to research the atmosphere, surface, and chemical composition of Mars. [5] Russia, previously the Soviet Union, China, India, and the United States have all reached Mars's surface, with varying degrees of success. NASA's Viking program, first launched in 1975, was the first to send color panoramic photos of Mars. The programs have grown more complex, over the decades, with the U. S.'s most recent mission—the Mars Science Laboratory's "Curiosity" rover—currently collecting and

sending back data on Mars's climate, geology, and potential for life. **[6]** It is still unclear when any nation's space program will be ready to send a manned mission.

    [7] Here are some reasons the Mars program has been slow to progress. For one, Mars has earned a reputation as a difficult target: more than two-thirds of all Mars-targeted spacecraft have failed without completing their missions. Some of them never even made it to Martian orbit. Most spacecraft that make it to **[8]** Mars's surface either crash, or fall prey to Mars's harsh conditions, like sandstorms, extreme temperature changes, and rough terrain. These missions, successful or not, cost billions of dollars and countless hours spent preparing them.

    With these many risks, it is unsurprising that most countries are hesitant to start planning manned missions. The conditions on the planet are **[9]** unfamiliar for humans, with the lack of oxygen in the atmosphere, the lack of water or food sources, and the potential for dangerous radiation exposure. There are also the logistics of landing; many unmanned missions crash landed due to the thin Martian atmosphere being unable to provide enough friction to slow down the spacecraft enough to land safely. Right now, the risks are too high to attempt that with human passengers rather than technical equipment.

    Still, there is hope. Europe, the U. S., and China are hoping to send human astronauts to Mars within the next 15–20 years, to start **[10]** terraforming the planet for more permanent research facilities or even colonies. Right now, the challenges outweigh the ability of such a program to send human astronauts to Mars, but we're getting there. **[11]**

MISSIONS TO MARS (1971–2016)			
Year	**Mission Name**	**Country**	**Result**
1971	Mariner 8	US	Failure
1971	Kosmos 419	USSR	Failure
1971	Mars 2 Orbiter/Lander	USSR	Failure
1971	Mars 3 Orbiter/Lander	USSR	Success
1971	Mariner 9	US	Success
1973	Mars 4	USSR	Failure
1973	Mars 5	USSR	Success
1973	Mars 6 Orbiter/Lander	USSR	Success/Failure
1973	Mars 7 Lander	USSR	Failure
1975	Viking 1 Orbiter/Lander	US	Success
1975	Viking 2 Orbiter/Lander	US	Success
1988	Phobos 1 Orbiter	USSR	Failure
1988	Phobos 2 Orbiter/Lander	USSR	Failure
1992	Mars Observer	US	Failure

practice test 1— Writing and Language

MISSIONS TO MARS (1971–2016) *continued*			
1996	Mars Global Surveyor	US	Success
1996	Mars 96	Russia	Failure
1996	Mars Pathfinder	US	Success
1998	Nozomi	Japan	Failure
1998	Mars Climate Orbiter	US	Failure
1999	Mars Polar Lander	US	Failure
1999	Deep Space 2 Probes (2)	US	Failure
2001	Mars Odyssey	US	Success
2003	Mars Express Orbiter/Beagle 2 Lander	ESA	Success/Failure
2003	Mars Exploration Rover – Spirit	US	Success
2003	Mars Exploration Rover – Opportunity	US	Success
2005	Mars Reconnaissance Orbiter	US	Success
2007	Phoenix Mars Lander	US	Success
2011	Mars Science Laboratory	US	Success
2011	Phobos-Grunt/Yinghuo–1	Russia/China	Failure
2013	Mars Atmosphere and Volatile Evolution	US	Success
2013	Mars Orbiter Mission (MOM)	India	Success
2016	ExoMars Orbiter/Schiaparelli EDL Demo Lander	ESA/Russia	Success/Failure

[Chart adapted from NASA: http://mars. nasa. gov/programmissions/missions/log/.]

1. **A.** NO CHANGE

   B. Eight years later, the U. S. landed a team of two astronauts on the moon: this was a first for humanity.

   C. Eight years later, the U. S. landed a team of two astronauts on the moon, a first for humanity.

   D. Eight years later, the U. S. landed a team of two astronauts on the moon…this was a first for humanity.

2. **A.** NO CHANGE

   B. "moon shot" speech

   C. "moon shot" Speech

   D. "moon shot speech"

3. A. NO CHANGE
   B. in space. Namely, sending manned missions to Mars.
   C. in space namely, sending manned missions to Mars.
   D. in space—namely, sending manned missions to Mars.

4. Which of the following would be an effective opening sentence for this paragraph?

   A. No country's space program has yet achieved this goal of sending humans to explore Mars.
   B. Mars missions are notoriously difficult.
   C. The U.S. space program has not yet achieved this goal of sending humans to explore Mars.
   D. The movie *The Martian* chronicles the struggles of a U.S. astronaut stranded on Mars.

5. A. NO CHANGE
   B. Russia previously the Soviet Union, China, India, and the United States
   C. Russia; previously the Soviet Union; China, India, and the United States
   D. Russia (previously the Soviet Union), China, India, and the United States

6. Which choice would add a relevant detail from the chart to this sentence?

   A. Because the failure rate has been increasing since 1999,
   B. Although the success rates have been increasing since 1999,
   C. Japan will likely be the first nation to put a manned mission on Mars, but
   D. Given that a joint mission between Russia and China would have the best chance of success,

7. A. NO CHANGE
   B. There are many reasons why the Mars program has been slow to progress.
   C. The Mars program has been slow to progress.
   D. Despite that, there are many reasons why the Mars program has been slow to progress.

8. A. NO CHANGE
   B. Mars'
   C. Mars
   D. Martian's

9. A. NO CHANGE
   B. welcoming
   C. inhospitable
   D. unremarkable

practice test 1— Writing and Language

10. Based on the passage, which of the following is meant by *terraforming*?

   A. Collecting soil from the planet's surface

   B. Making the planet easier for unmanned probes

   C. Making the planet livable for humans

   D. Abandoning

11. The writer wants a concluding sentence that restates the main argument of the passage. Which choice best accomplishes this goal?

   A. NO CHANGE

   B. Various missions to Mars have been unsuccessful, so we might want to consider giving up on this goal.

   C. Although President Kennedy never mentioned Mars in any of his speeches, this would have been his goal as well.

   D. The first person to land on Mars may not even have been born yet.

Questions 12–22 are based on the following passage.

The Freelance Economy

[12] In 2015, the United States Bureau of Labor Statistics estimated that 15. 5 million Americans were self-employed, one million more than in 2014. [13] Someone else also estimated that by 2020, nearly 50% of American employees would be "independent" workers: [14] freelancers, contractors, or temporary employees. What is behind the rise of these independent workers, and what does that mean for people just entering the job market?

(1) One of the main reasons for this rise in freelancing over "traditional" full-time jobs (where someone is an employee of one company at a time, usually with benefits) is economic. (2) [15] Many companies: downsizing and trying to streamline operations to save on costs. (3) This often means eliminating positions, or changing them to a "contract" basis, where employees work on specific projects or for a certain number of hours, without being a full-time employee. [16]

However, much of the growth in this freelancing/contractor movement is due to changing wants and needs of employees themselves. Many people prefer to take jobs that allow them to provide services and build a career while maintaining their independence. [17] Uber are seen as revolutionizing the employment model, with a fleet of independent drivers that are instantly connected with passengers who need rides. This "on demand" approach to freelancing embraces the idea that [18] they should be flexible to meet the demands of their industries.

Freelancing is also an appealing option for people looking to build skills and experience quickly. The traditional job search process has always contained a bit of a [19] continuous, especially at the beginning: companies want to hire people with experience, but how do you gain experience until you're hired? Independent workers take this process into their own hands, building experience and skills on their own terms. [20] According to *Forbes* magazine, the "new economy," a more diverse skill set means more career opportunities.

The growing freelance economy has been helped along by technology as well. Email, devices, and apps [21] allow people to work remotely with others even when they're in different zip codes—or different countries altogether. Arguably the biggest technology piece of this rise in independent workers [22] are the growth of websites and online databases that connect companies which need work done to people who can do it. Rather than going through the traditional hiring process, these sites help freelancers to find and apply for jobs quickly and efficiently.

12. Which of the following would be an effective first sentence of this passage?

    A. NO CHANGE

    B. What is behind the rise of these independent workers, and what does that mean for people just entering the job market?

    C. As the U. S. economy grows and changes, especially with the advent of new technologies, the job market is changing as well.

    D. Let's talk about the new freelance economy.

13. A. NO CHANGE

    B. *Forbes* magazine

    C. Someone Else

    D. The U.S. Bureau of Labor Statistics

14. A. NO CHANGE

    B. freelancers…contractors…or temporary employees

    C. freelancers. Contractors, or temporary employees

    D. freelancers, contractors, or, temporary employees

15. A. NO CHANGE

    B. Many companies are downsizing and trying to streamline operations to save on costs.

    C. Downsizing and trying to streamline operations to save on costs are many companies.

    D. Many companies, downsizing and trying to streamline operations to save on costs.

16. Where in this paragraph should the following sentence be placed?

As a result, some workers are freelancers by economic necessity.

    A. Before sentence 1

    B. After sentence 1

    C. After sentence 2

    D. After sentence 3

17. A. NO CHANGE

    B. Uber people

    C. Companies like Uber

    D. Them at Uber

18. A. NO CHANGE

    B. companies

    C. employees

    D. Uber

19. **A.** NO CHANGE
    B. conundrum
    C. contempt
    D. content

20. **A.** NO CHANGE
    B. According to *Forbes* magazine, in the "new economy;" a more diverse skill set means more career opportunities.
    C. The "new economy" according to *Forbes* magazine, a more diverse skill set means more career opportunities.
    D. According to *Forbes* magazine, a more diverse skill set means more career opportunities in the new economy.

21. **A.** NO CHANGE
    B. allows
    C. allowing
    D. are allowed

22. **A.** NO CHANGE
    B. is
    C. will be
    D. am

practice test 1— Writing and Language

Questions 23–33 are based on the following passage.

The Controversial Electoral College

Although it sounds like a place, the Electoral College is a process. [23] The process by which the United States chooses [24] its next president. [25] In it, voters choose the candidate they want for President, and based on the results of the presidential contest, each state's representatives in the Electoral College cast an official vote for that state's presidential winner. This process is as old as America itself: it gives each state one elector for each Senator and Representative. [26] Yet even though it is enshrined in the Constitution as part of the US's election process, the Electoral College has been controversial almost since day one.

(1) The earliest [27] agreements started over the structure of presidential voting: at the time, the winner of the most votes would become president, and the runner-up would become vice president. (2) Members of the Electoral College would cast two votes: one for the highest vote-getter, and one for the second highest vote-getter. (3) In the election of 1800, this process led to a tie between Thomas Jefferson and Aaron Burr, and then to a long and bitter series of tiebreaker votes in Congress based on political party lines. (4) Outgoing President John Adams was not a factor. (5) Three months and 36 votes later, Jefferson was elected President, and Burr was elected Vice President. (6) However, the damage was done: James Madison and Alexander Hamilton [28] (two of the main architects of the Electoral College) wanted to change the process to prevent it from happening in future elections. [29]

[30] This amendment stated that each member of the Electoral College would cast two separate votes: one for president, and one for vice president. Eventually, the Electoral College would also evolve into a "winner take all" process, where the winner of a state's popular vote would also be the default winner of the state's electoral votes as well.

Still, controversies have happened even after these changes made the process more straightforward. More recently, there have been conflicts when a candidate won the popular vote nationwide (the most votes directly cast by voters), but lost in the [31] electoral college due to the rules, leading to questions about whether the Electoral College should still exist. In the 2000 presidential election, Vice President Al Gore won the national popular vote by a slim margin over Texas governor [32] George W Bush. [33] Still, Florida's 25 electoral votes were hanging in the balance due to a virtual tie and a recount in one of Florida's counties. This battle went to the Supreme Court, which ruled that the recounts would end, and Florida's electoral votes would go to Governor Bush, who had a slight edge in votes before the recount. After the election, many popular vote advocates questioned whether the Electoral College was an outdated system that had no place in modern elections.

23. **A.** NO CHANGE
　　B. The process
　　C. The process, specifically
　　D. Specifically, it is the process

24. **A.** NO CHANGE
　　B. their
　　C. it's
　　D. its'

25. **A.** NO CHANGE
    B. In it, voters choose the candidate they want for President; then, based on the results, each state's representatives in the Electoral College cast an official vote for that state's overall winner.
    C. In it, voters choose the candidate they want for President. Then based on the results of the presidential contest, each state's representatives in the Electoral College cast an official vote for that state's presidential winner. Then that is the winner.
    D. In it, voters choose the candidate they want for President and based on the results of the presidential contest, each state's representatives in the Electoral College cast an official vote for that state's presidential winner.

26. Which of the following details could the writer add here?
    A. That the first president was George Washington
    B. That the Electoral College is detailed in Article II, Section 1, of the U. S. Constitution
    C. The year the Constitution was adopted
    D. The names of people who signed the Constitution

27. **A.** NO CHANGE
    B. communications
    C. contradictions
    D. conflicts

28. **A.** NO CHANGE
    B. two of the main architects of the Electoral College
    C. …two of the main architects of the Electoral College…
    D. (two of the main architects (of the Electoral College))

29. Which of these sentences could be deleted from the paragraph?
    A. Sentence 1
    B. Sentence 2
    C. Sentence 4
    D. Sentence 6

30. Which sentence would be an effective transition sentence for this paragraph?
    A. So yeah, this crisis led to important Constitutional changes.
    B. Soon the Electoral College would be a "winner take all" process.
    C. As a result of this crisis, the 12th Amendment to the Constitution was passed.
    D. This would not be the only controversy related to the Electoral College.

31. **A.** NO CHANGE
    B. electoral College
    C. Electoral college
    D. Electoral College

32. **A.** NO CHANGE
    B. George W. Bush
    C. George w. Bush
    D. George "W" Bush

33. **A.** NO CHANGE
    B. Again,
    C. However,
    D. Similarly,

Questions 34–44 are based on the following passage.

The Poets-in-Chief

When you think of political appointees, poets might not come to mind right away. In the United States, though, the "Poet Laureate" has moved the poetic into the realm of government. [34] By 1986, the United States has had more [35] then 21 people appointed as the national "Poet Laureate," serving as a kind of poet-in-chief, or a national poet-in-residence at the Library of Congress.

[36] The program once existed in a different form. The poets selected to represent the country were known then as "Consultants in Poetry." These included such famous American poets and writers as [37] Robert Frost, the poet who famously read "The Gift Outright" at President John F. Kennedy's inauguration, Elizabeth Bishop, and Gwendolyn Brooks. The Consultants in Poetry were responsible for working with the Library of Congress to promote literacy in general, and awareness of poetry in particular.

In 1985, Senator Spark M. Matsunaga of Hawaii proposed that the title be changed to Poet Laureate Consultant in Poetry (usually shortened to Poet Laureate), with more structure put around their national duties. Each Poet Laureate is nominated by the [38] librarian of Congress. [39] He or she serves a term from October to May. It is a paid position, but is not financed by taxpayer dollars. Rather, a yearly [40] stipend of $35,000 is paid out of an endowment established by businessman and philanthropist Archer M. Huntington.

[41] Anyway, a Poet Laureate has a number of responsibilities: giving an annual lecture and poetry reading of his or her work, [42] hosts events in the Library of Congress's annual poetry series (which is one of the oldest poetry reading traditions in the country), and promoting other poets. These duties are kept to a minimum to give each Poet Laureate time to work on his or her own poetry in the meantime. Together, the U. S. Poets Laureate [43] have brought more than 2,000 poets to read at these events for the Archive of Recorded Poetry and Literature.

Poet Laureates are also welcome to put their own marks on the role and work on their own projects. Joseph Brodsky worked on putting poetry in airports, retail stores, and hotel rooms. Gwendolyn Brooks visited [44] Elementary Schools to encourage young students to read poetry and write their own. In the 1990s, Poet Laureate Rita Dove introduced programs linking poetry and jazz. Each Poet Laureate brings a unique perspective to the role and is encouraged to customize the program during his or her own term.

34. **A.** NO CHANGE
    B. Because of 1986,
    C. Since 1986,
    D. In 1986

35. **A.** NO CHANGE
    B. than
    C. when
    D. of

36. Which of the following would be a strong detail to add to the beginning sentence?

   A. Before the Poet Laureate program was created by an act of Congress in 1986,

   B. The Library of Congress has existed since 1800, and

   C. Poets Laureate have been popular in other countries, so

   D. Throughout different presidents,

37. A. NO CHANGE

   B. Robert Frost the poet who famously read "The Gift Outright" at President John F. Kennedy's inauguration, Elizabeth Bishop, and Gwendolyn Brooks.

   C. Robert Frost—the poet who famously read "The Gift Outright" at President John F. Kennedy's inauguration, Elizabeth Bishop, and Gwendolyn Brooks.

   D. Robert Frost (the poet who famously read "The Gift Outright" at President John F. Kennedy's inauguration), Elizabeth Bishop, and Gwendolyn Brooks.

38. A. NO CHANGE

   B. librarian of congress

   C. Librarian of Congress

   D. Librarian Of Congress

39. A. NO CHANGE

   B. The Librarian of Congress

   C. The President of the United States

   D. The Poet Laureate

40. A. NO CHANGE

   B. fee

   C. bill

   D. charge

41. A. NO CHANGE

   B. Because of this,

   C. As for official duties,

   D. [Delete the text.]

42. A. NO CHANGE

   B. hosted

   C. hosting

   D. host

43. A. NO CHANGE

   B. has

   C. will have

   D. haven't

44. A. NO CHANGE

   B. Elementary schools

   C. elementary Schools

   D. elementary schools

STOP! DO NOT GO ON UNTIL TIME IS UP.

practice test 1—Writing and Language

SECTION 3: MATH TEST—NO CALCULATOR

25 Minutes • 17 Questions

Turn to Section 3 of your answer sheet to answer the questions in this section.

Directions: For **Questions 1–13,** solve each problem, choose the best answer from the choices provided, and fill in the corresponding circle on your answer sheet. For **Questions 14–17,** solve the problem and enter your answer in the grid on the answer sheet. Please refer to the directions before **Question 14** on how to enter your answers in the grid. You may use any available space in your test booklet for scratch work.

NOTES:

1. The use of a calculator is **not permitted.**

2. All variables and expressions used represent real numbers unless otherwise indicated.

3. Figures provided in this test are drawn to scale unless otherwise indicated.

4. All figures lie in a plane unless otherwise indicated.

5. Unless otherwise indicated, the domain of a given function f is the set of all real numbers x for which $f(x)$ is a real number.

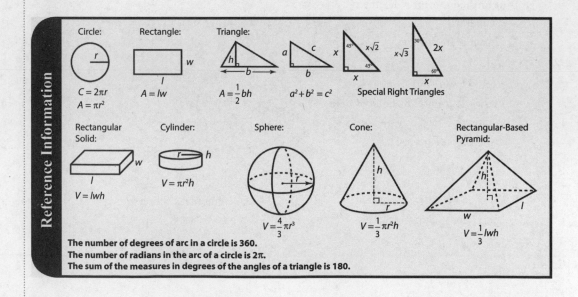

Reference Information

Circle:
$C = 2\pi r$
$A = \pi r^2$

Rectangle:
$A = lw$

Triangle:
$A = \frac{1}{2}bh$

$a^2 + b^2 = c^2$

Special Right Triangles

Rectangular Solid:
$V = lwh$

Cylinder:
$V = \pi r^2 h$

Sphere:
$V = \frac{4}{3}\pi r^3$

Cone:
$V = \frac{1}{3}\pi r^2 h$

Rectangular-Based Pyramid:
$V = \frac{1}{3}lwh$

The number of degrees of arc in a circle is 360.
The number of radians in the arc of a circle is 2π.
The sum of the measures in degrees of the angles of a triangle is 180.

SHOW YOUR WORK HERE

1. Solve for x: $\frac{2}{3}(2 - 3x) = \frac{1}{9}(2x + 1)$

    A. $\frac{11}{20}$

    B. $\frac{13}{20}$

    C. $\frac{11}{5}$

    D. $\frac{13}{5}$

2. O-rings are used to provide a vacuum seal in various mechanical devices. In the following diagram of an O-ring, $\overline{AB}$ and $\overline{CD}$ are outer and inner diameters, respectively.

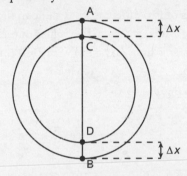

    Suppose $CD = 5$ inches. If the machine used for manufacturing is programmed to produce O-rings for which the length of $\overline{AB}$ is between 5.3 inches and 5.5 inches, inclusive, which inequality can be used to find the range of Δx?

    A. $5.3 \le 5 + \Delta x \le 5.5$

    B. $0.3 \le 5 + 2\Delta x \le 0.5$

    C. $5.3 \le 10 + 2\Delta x \le 5.5$

    D. $5.3 \le 5 + 2\Delta x \le 5.5$

3. Simplify the radical expression: $\sqrt{81x^3} - 5x\sqrt{4x}$.

    A. $\sqrt{61x^3}$

    B. $19x\sqrt{x}$

    C. $-x\sqrt{x}$

    D. $61x\sqrt{x}$

4. A postal supply store wants to determine the dimensions of the base of a rectangular box of height 20 inches to ensure its surface area is as small as possible so it takes up the least amount of space. If the length is 3 inches shorter than twice the width, which of the following functions accurately describes the surface area?

SHOW YOUR WORK HERE

A. $S(x) = 4x^2 + 114x - 120$

B. $S(x) = 40x^2 + 60x$

C. $S(x) = 2x^2 + 57x - 60$

D. $S(x) = 4x^2 + 14x$

Use the following information for Questions 5 and 6.

A stockbroker continually monitors the price of shares of two different stocks, one in the International Markets sector and one in the Emerging Markets sector. The values of each stock during the trading period are shown below. Here, t is time (in hours) with $t = 0$ corresponding to 7 a.m. and $t = 9$ corresponding to 4 p.m.

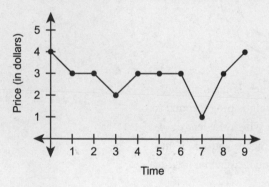

International Market Stock

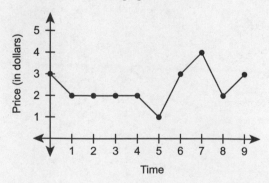

Emerging Market Stock

5. At what hour is the difference in price of the two stocks the greatest?

   A. 10 a.m.

   B. 12 p.m.

   C. 2 p.m.

   D. 4 p.m.

6. If you want to simultaneously sell x shares of the International Market stock and buy x shares of the Emerging Market stock, at which of the following hours would making this trade yield the largest profit?

   A. 10 a.m.

   B. 12 p.m.

   C. 1 p.m.

   D. 2 p.m.

7. If left unchecked, the mosquito population will explode in a tropical environment. Starting with a mosquito population of size 100,000, which of the following functions suggests the most rapid growth of the mosquito population? Assume t is measured in days and the output is measured in tens of thousands.

   A. $f(t) = \dfrac{100}{e^{8t}}$

   B. $g(t) = (50t + 100)^2$

   C. $h(t) = 100e^{5t}$

   D. $j(t) = 50t + 100$

SHOW YOUR WORK HERE

practice test 1— Math— No Calculator

8. Consider the function $y = f(x)$ expressed by the following table of values:

SHOW YOUR WORK HERE

x	-5	1	7	13
y	2	-7	-16	-25

If the function is assumed to be linear, which of these is its equation?

A. $f(x) = \dfrac{2}{3}x + \dfrac{16}{3}$

B. $f(x) = -\dfrac{2}{3}x - \dfrac{4}{3}$

C. $f(x) = \dfrac{3}{2}x + \dfrac{19}{2}$

D. $f(x) = -\dfrac{3}{2}x - \dfrac{11}{2}$

9. There are 127 steps in the tower leading to the roof of Blarney castle, where tourists worldwide gather to kiss the Blarney stone. The steps narrow in width and increase in height as you ascend the staircase. A tourist provides the following approximate count of the various step heights in the staircase:

Step Height (in inches)	Frequency
5	25
6	19
7	18
8	12
9	12
10	12
11	9
12	8
13	5
14	4
15	3

What is the median height of the steps?   **SHOW YOUR WORK HERE**

- **A.** 7 inches
- **B.** 8 inches
- **C.** 9 inches
- **D.** 10 inches

10. Compute $\dfrac{1+2i}{3-2i}$.

- **A.** $\dfrac{1}{13}+\dfrac{2}{13}i$
- **B.** $1+\dfrac{8}{5}i$
- **C.** $\dfrac{1}{3}-i$
- **D.** $-\dfrac{1}{13}+\dfrac{8}{13}i$

11. A botanist needs to plant enough lima bean seeds to ensure that she can yield 400 seedlings after 10 days to use in an experiment. From past records, it is known that $p\%$ of the seedlings will germinate and, of these, $\dfrac{1}{3}$ will die before reaching 10 days. Which equation can be used to determine the number of lima beans, x, the botanist should plant to reach her goal of 400?

- **A.** $px-\dfrac{1}{3}px=400$
- **B.** $x-\dfrac{p}{300}x=400$
- **C.** $\dfrac{p}{100}x-\dfrac{p}{300}x=400$
- **D.** $(0.0p)x-\dfrac{0.0p}{3}x=400$

practice test 1—Math—No Calculator

12. In engineering, the ratio between the critical pressure p_C and initial pressure p_I of a nozzle is described by the formula $\frac{p_C}{p_I} = \left[\frac{2}{k+1} \right]^{\frac{k}{k-1}}$, where k is a physical constant related to expansion and compression. Which of the following expresses p_I in terms of p_C for $k = \frac{5}{4}$?

SHOW YOUR WORK HERE

A. $p_I = \left(\frac{8}{9} \right) \frac{1}{p_C}$

B. $p_I = \left(\frac{9}{8} \right)^5 p_C$

C. $p_I = \left(\frac{9}{8} \right)^{\frac{5}{16}} p_C$

D. $p_I = \left(\frac{9}{2} \right)^5 p_C$

13. Which of the following scatterplots shows a strong negative linear association between variables *x* and *y*?

A.

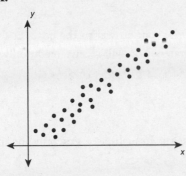

B.

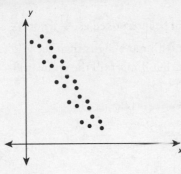

C.

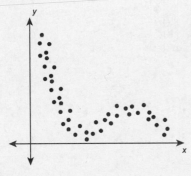

D.

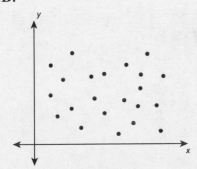

practice test 1 — Math — No Calculator

Directions: For **Questions 14–17,** solve the problem and enter your answer in the grid, as described below, on the answer sheet.

NOTES:

1. Although not required, it is suggested that you write your answer in the boxes at the top of the columns to help you fill in the circles accurately. You will receive credit only if the circles are filled in correctly.

2. Mark no more than one circle in any column.

3. No question has a negative answer.

4. Some problems may have more than one correct answer. In such cases, grid only one answer.

5. **Mixed numbers** such as $3\frac{1}{2}$ must be gridded as 3.5 or $\frac{7}{2}$.

   If $3\frac{1}{2}$ is entered into the grid as 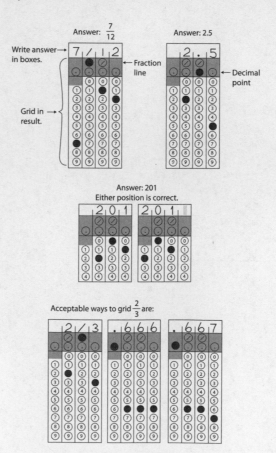 it will be interpreted as $\frac{31}{2}$, not $3\frac{1}{2}$.

6. **Decimal answers:** If you obtain a decimal answer with more digits than the grid can accommodate, it may be either rounded or truncated, but it must fill the entire grid.

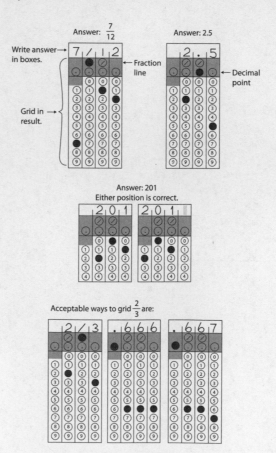

14. A new strain of the influenza virus has begun to emerge this year. Epidemiologists estimate that the median recovery time will increase by 20 percent as compared to last year. The following box plot summarizes the recovery time for a representative sample of people infected with the virus last year.

SHOW YOUR WORK HERE

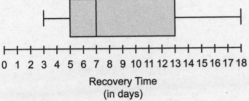

0 1 2 3 4 5 6 7 8 9 10 11 12 13 14 15 16 17 18
Recovery Time
(in days)

What is the expected median recovery time for this year?

15. For what real value of the constant C would the following linear equation have no solution?

$$1 - 3(2x + 3(1 - x)) = Cx$$

16. If x_1 and x_2 are the solutions of the equation $x(x + 2) = 8$, compute $|x_1 \cdot x_2|$.

practice test 1— Math — No Calculator

17. A new version of a canine vaccine is in the last stage of development. Clinical trials are conducted with 200 German shepherd dogs—100 males and 100 females. Data was collected as to whether the dogs exhibited any side effects within 1 day of being administered the vaccine. Here are the results, with some values omitted:

	Exhibited side effects	Did not exhibit side effects
Male Dogs	33	
Female Dogs		42

What is the probability that a dog chosen at random from this sample exhibited side effects? **Round your answer to the nearest hundredth.**

SHOW YOUR WORK HERE

STOP! DO NOT GO ON UNTIL TIME IS UP.

SECTION 4: MATH TEST—CALCULATOR 🖩

45 Minutes • 31 Questions

Turn to Section 4 of your answer sheet to answer the questions in this section.

Directions: For **Questions 1–27,** solve each problem, choose the best answer from the choices provided, and fill in the corresponding circle on your answer sheet. For **Questions 28–31,** solve the problem and enter your answer in the grid on the answer sheet. Please refer to the directions before **Question 28** on how to enter your answers in the grid. You may use any available space in your test booklet for scratch work.

NOTES:

1. The use of a calculator is **permitted.**

2. All variables and expressions used represent real numbers unless otherwise indicated.

3. Figures provided in this test are drawn to scale unless otherwise indicated.

4. All figures lie in a plane unless otherwise indicated.

5. Unless otherwise indicated, the domain of a given function f is the set of all real numbers x for which $f(x)$ is a real number.

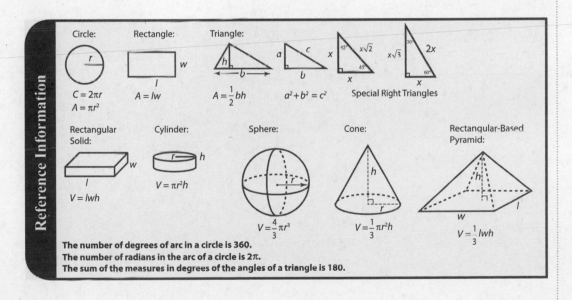

Reference Information

Circle: $C = 2\pi r$, $A = \pi r^2$

Rectangle: $A = lw$

Triangle: $A = \frac{1}{2}bh$

$a^2 + b^2 = c^2$

Special Right Triangles

Rectangular Solid: $V = lwh$

Cylinder: $V = \pi r^2 h$

Sphere: $V = \frac{4}{3}\pi r^3$

Cone: $V = \frac{1}{3}\pi r^2 h$

Rectangular-Based Pyramid: $V = \frac{1}{3}lwh$

The number of degrees of arc in a circle is 360.
The number of radians in the arc of a circle is 2π.
The sum of the measures in degrees of the angles of a triangle is 180.

1. Suppose $a > 1$. Which of the following systems has infinitely many solutions?

SHOW YOUR WORK HERE

A. $\begin{cases} ax + y = 1 \\ x + ay = 1 \end{cases}$

B. $\begin{cases} ay = x + 3 \\ y = 4 + \dfrac{1}{a}x \end{cases}$

C. $\begin{cases} 2y - ax = -1 \\ 3ax = 3 + 6y \end{cases}$

D. $\begin{cases} y + a = 2x \\ y + a = 3x \end{cases}$

2. (x_1, y_1) and (x_2, y_2) are the solutions of the system $\begin{cases} y = f(x) \\ y = 1 - (x - 2)^2 \end{cases}$, and the graph of $f(x)$ is shown below.

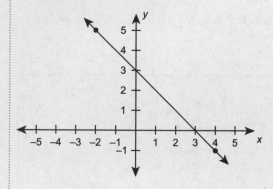

What is the value of $\dfrac{y_1 + y_2}{x_1 + x_2}$?

A. $\dfrac{1}{5}$

B. 1

C. 5

D. 6

Use the following information for Questions 3 and 4:

The following graph describes the relationship between the raccoon and fox populations in a rural portion of Ohio for a typical year:

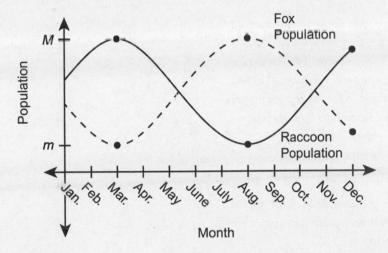

Here, *M* represents the maximum population size over the time period, and *m* is the minimum population size over the time period. The *actual* values of *m* and *M* can differ for the two populations.

3. During which parts of the year is the fox population increasing?

    SHOW YOUR WORK HERE

A. January to March and August to December

B. July to October

C. March to August

D. February to April

practice test 1—Math—Calculator

4. Which of the following is the most plausible explanation for the relationship between the fox and raccoon populations in this area?

SHOW YOUR WORK HERE

A. The populations vary inversely because they compete for the same food source. The fewer raccoons present, the more food will be available for the fox population, which helps it to flourish (and vice-versa).

B. The populations diminish and flourish together.

C. Both populations level off toward a common equilibrium after a few months.

D. There is no discernible relationship between these two populations because both graphs keep going up and down, but during opposite months.

5. Two different missionary teams travel to a village in a third-world country to provide humanitarian assistance after a devastating tsunami. Working alone, Team A can clear debris from one-fourth of the village in 16 days, while it takes Team B 12 days to do the same job alone. How long would it take them to clear the debris from the *entire* village if they work together?

A. $6\frac{6}{7}$ days

B. $24\frac{6}{7}$ days

C. $27\frac{3}{7}$ days

D. $37\frac{5}{7}$ days

6. An artist uses glass-blowing techniques to create beautiful glass vases. Once a vase has been created, its temperature is approximately 1,800°F. To ensure it does not crack, it is placed in a cooling oven so that it cools down slowly at a constant rate, starting at 1,800°F and ending at 60°F. The graph of its temperature over the course of the D days required to reach 60°F is below:

How many days D, to the nearest tenth, does it take the vase to reach 60°F?

A. 7.0

B. 8.9

C. 10.4

D. 12.0

SHOW YOUR WORK HERE

practice test 1— Math — Calculator

SHOW YOUR WORK HERE

7. Zhanna finds a thick rectangular sheet of glass at a scrap shop that she wants to use as a coffee table top. She will affix a wooden border on top of the glass around its perimeter, with the same width all the way around.

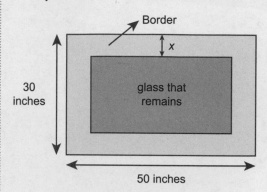

If the area of the entire border needs to be 20 square inches, which equation can be used to determine the width, x, of the border?

A. $1,500 - 160 + 4x^2 = 20$

B. $4x^2 - 160 = 1,500$

C. $20(50 - 2x)(30 - 2x) = 1,500$

D. $160 - 4x^2 = 20$

8. The clock rate of a core processing unit (CPU) describes the frequency at which the chip is running. In 2011, the highest clock rate recorded was 8.805 GHz from an FX-8150 chip, and the close runner-up, the Piledriver chip, had a clock rate of 8.670 GHz. What is the approximate percent increase in clock rate going from the Piledriver chip to the FX-8150 chip?

A. 13.5 percent

B. 1.56 percent

C. 1.53 percent

D. 0.02 percent

9. The perimeter of a small, rectangular apple orchard is 1,500 yards. The length is four yards longer than three times the width. Which system could be used to determine the dimensions of the orchard?

SHOW YOUR WORK HERE

A. $\begin{cases} 2x + 2y = 1,500 \\ x + 4y = 3 \end{cases}$

B. $\begin{cases} 2x + 2y = 1,500 \\ x = 4 + 3y \end{cases}$

C. $\begin{cases} x + y = 1,500 \\ x = 4 + 3y \end{cases}$

D. $\begin{cases} 2x + 2y = 1,500 \\ x = 3 + 4y \end{cases}$

10. What is the solution set for

$$\frac{2x}{x+4} - \frac{2x}{x-4} = 1 ?$$

A. $\left\{ -8 - 4\sqrt{3}, \ -8 + 4\sqrt{3} \right\}$

B. $\{-4, 4\}$

C. $\left\{ -8 - 4\sqrt{5}, \ -8 + 4\sqrt{5} \right\}$

D. $\{0, 16\}$

practice test 1 — Math — Calculator

11. To which system of linear inequalities is this the solution set?

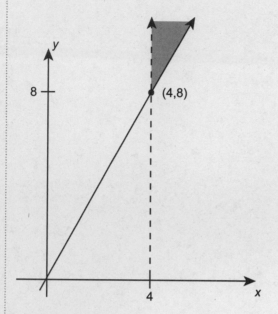

A. $\begin{cases} y \ge \dfrac{1}{2}x \\ x > 4 \end{cases}$

B. $\begin{cases} x > 4 \\ y \ge 2x \end{cases}$

C. $\begin{cases} x < 4 \\ y \le 2x \end{cases}$

D. $\begin{cases} x \ge 4 \\ y > 2x \end{cases}$

12. Solve the inequality:

$1.5 - 2.5(2 - 3x) \ge 1.5x - 2$.

A. $x \ge 0.25$

B. $x \le -0.83$

C. $x \le 4.0$

D. $x \ge -0.45$

13. As part of the sterilization process at a water treatment facility, all water-holding tanks are drained and then cleaned. Once the release valve is opened and after 50 seconds have passed, 900 gallons of water remain in the largest tank. After 2 minutes, 760 gallons remain. Assuming the number of gallons varies linearly with time, how long after the release valve is opened will there be 50 gallons in the tank?

A. 3 minutes, 10 seconds

B. 6 minutes, 15 seconds

C. 7 minutes, 55 seconds

D. 9 minutes, 20 seconds

14. Marty purchases a mattress set at a furniture store during a New Year's Day sale event. He needs it to be delivered to his home. The delivery fee is a flat $55 and the state tax rate is 6 percent. Suppose $f(x)$ is a function that gives the total price of the mattress set x and delivery fee, and that $g(x)$ is a function that gives the price of the mattress set x, after taxes. Both functions are measured in dollars. Which of the following functions gives the total bill if the state taxes are applied before the delivery fee?

A. $(f \circ g)(x)$

B. $(g \circ f)(x)$

C. $f(x) \cdot g(x)$

D. $f(x) + g(x)$

SHOW YOUR WORK HERE

15. Anthropologists conduct a study investigating ethnicity. The study is divided into three meetings scheduled for Monday in three consecutive weeks. The description of these meetings is as follows:

Meeting 1: Initial presentation and open discussion about ethnicity and culture

Meeting 2: Collection of genetic material and completion of questionnaires

Meeting 3: Discussion of results from genetic tests

Originally, z participants attend Meeting 1. Of these, $p\%$ return for Meeting 2, and then $q\%$ of these return for Meeting 3. Which expression represents the number of participants attending Meeting 1 who eventually drop out at some point of the study?

A. $\left(\dfrac{p}{100}\right)\left(\dfrac{q}{100}\right)(z)$

B. $z\left[1-\left(\dfrac{p}{100}\right)\left(\dfrac{q}{100}\right)\right]$

C. $z\left[1-\dfrac{p}{100}-\dfrac{pq}{10,000}\right]$

D. $z-(0.0p)(0.0q)z$

SHOW YOUR WORK HERE

16. The frequency with which crickets chirp depends linearly on the outdoor temperature and is governed by Dolbear's law:

$T = 50 + \left(\dfrac{N - 40}{4} \right)$, where T is the outdoor temperature (in degrees Fahrenheit) and N is the number of chirps per minute. What does the coefficient of N mean in this context?

A. For every increase in N by 4 chirps per minute, the temperature increases by one degree Fahrenheit.

B. The outdoor temperature of 50 degrees Fahrenheit equals $\dfrac{1}{4}$ the number of chirps per minute that occurs when the outdoor temperature is 40 degrees Fahrenheit.

C. For every unit increase in N, the outdoor temperature decreases by $\dfrac{1}{4}$ of a degree Fahrenheit.

D. For every increase in the outdoor temperature by one degree Fahrenheit, the number of chirps per minute increases by $\dfrac{1}{4}$.

17. Which of the following polynomials $p(x)$ satisfies the following criteria?

I. Has two positive zeros and one negative zero.

II. $\dfrac{p(x)}{x - 2}$ is a polynomial.

III. $p(0) = -8$

A. $p(x) = (x + 1)(x + 2)(x - 4)$

B. $p(x) = -2x(x + 1)(x - 1)(x - 2)$

C. $p(x) = \dfrac{1}{2}(x + 8)(x - 1)^2(x - 2)$

D. $p(x) = \dfrac{1}{8}(x - 1)^2(x - 2)(x + 4)$

SHOW YOUR WORK HERE

practice test 1— Math — Calculator

Use the following information for Questions 18 and 19:

The following is an abbreviated, hand-drawn map showing the locations of Benghazi, Libya, and Tripoli, Italy.

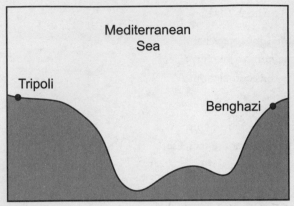

18. The direct, linear distance across the Mediterranean Sea between Tripoli and Benghazi is 404 miles. If the driving distance (obtained by traveling around a highway that conforms to the shape of the shoreline between the two cities) is 53.5% longer, what is the approximate driving distance expressed in kilometers? (Note: 1 kilometer ≈ 0.6214 miles.)

SHOW YOUR WORK HERE

    A. 385.36 kilometers

    B. 620.14 kilometers

    C. 650.14 kilometers

    D. 997.97 kilometers

19. In an enlarged, more detailed version of this map, 1.2 inches represents 75 miles. Approximately how many centimeters would be the linear distance measured from Tripoli directly to Benghazi? (Note: 1 centimeter ≈ 0.3937 inches.)

    A. 0.57 centimeters

    B. 2.54 centimeters

    C. 6.46 centimeters

    D. 16.42 centimeters

SHOW YOUR WORK HERE

20. Consider the function $f(x) = \dfrac{x}{x+3}$. Which of the following functions $g(x)$ is obtained by translating $f(x)$ by one unit to the left and two units down?

   A. $g(x) = -\dfrac{x+5}{x+2}$

   B. $g(x) = \dfrac{3x+9}{x+4}$

   C. $g(x) = \dfrac{3x+3}{x+2}$

   D. $g(x) = -\dfrac{x+7}{x+4}$

21. The fastest recorded speed of an airship (the Zeppelin Luftschifftechnik LZ N07-100) is 112 kilometers per hour, reported in 2004. What is this speed expressed in meters per minute, rounded to the nearest hundredth? (Note: 0.001 kilometer = 1 meter.)

   A. 3.42 meters per minute

   B. 6.72 meters per minute

   C. 186.67 meters per minute

   D. 1,866.67 meters per minute

practice test 1—Math—Calculator

22. A couple is planning to move to a new house. In preparation, they need to purchase several boxes in which to pack their belongings. There are two varieties they need: "Fragile" boxes and "X-Large Bulk" boxes. They need at least thirty Fragile boxes, which cost $8. X-Large Bulk boxes cost $16. They can spend no more than $800 total on boxes. Which graph accurately depicts the various combinations of each type of box they can purchase?

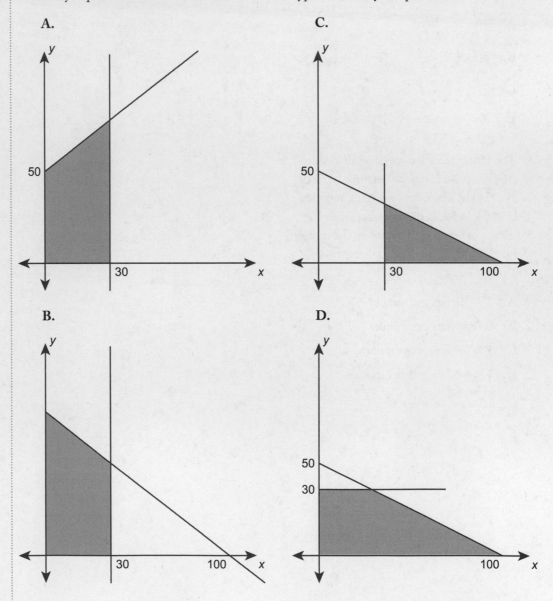

A.

C.

B.

D.

23. Each member of an 11-person committee reviews a job application and provides a rating from 0 to 100. The final score assigned to an applicant is computed by dropping the highest and lowest of the eleven scores and then taking the median of the remaining scores. Which of these following statements is true?

I. The range of the new set of scores must be less than the range of the original set of scores.

II. The medians of the original set of scores and the new set obtained by dropping two scores are the same.

A. I only

B. II only

C. Neither I nor II

D. Both I and II

24. Consider the system

$$\begin{cases} 3x - y = 1 \\ 6x + 2y = -1 \end{cases}$$

Which of the following equations is the result of applying the method of substitution to solve the system?

A. $12x = 1$

B. $4y = -3$

C. $6x + 2(3x - 1) = -1$

D. $9x + y = 0$

SHOW YOUR WORK HERE

practice test 1 — Math — Calculator

25. The following graph shows the number of shots-on-goal that a soccer goalie blocks in each of ten short scrimmage games:

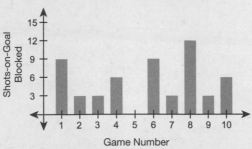

What is the mean number of shots-on-goal blocked?

A. 4.5

B. 5.4

C. 6.1

D. 30.6

26. A salesperson earns a base salary of $42,000 in addition to a 5 percent commission on total sales for the year z. The function $S(z) = 0.05z + 42,000$ describes her earnings. What does $S(75,000) = 45,750$ mean in this context?

A. The amount of commission earned on $75,000 in sales is $45,750.

B. The annual salary earned is $45,750 if the salesperson makes $75,000 in total sales.

C. For every increase of $75,000 in total sales, the annual salary increases by 45,750.

D. The salesperson must make $45,750 in total sales to earn an annual salary of $75,000.

27. Simplify the expression: $-3(2 - x - 2x^2) + 4(x - 2x^2)$.

A. $2x^2 - 7x + 6$

B. $-2x^2 + 7x - 6$

C. $14x^2 - x - 6$

D. $-4x^2 + 3x - 6$

Directions: For **Questions 28–31,** solve the problem and enter your answer in the grid, as described below, on the answer sheet.

NOTES:

1. Although not required, it is suggested that you write your answer in the boxes at the top of the columns to help you fill in the circles accurately. You will receive credit only if the circles are filled in correctly.

2. Mark no more than one circle in any column.

3. No question has a negative answer.

4. Some problems may have more than one correct answer. In such cases, grid only one answer.

5. **Mixed numbers** such as $3\frac{1}{2}$ must be gridded as 3.5 or $\frac{7}{2}$. If $3\frac{1}{2}$ is entered into the grid as [3 1 / 2] it will be interpreted as $\frac{31}{2}$, not $3\frac{1}{2}$.

6. **Decimal answers:** If you obtain a decimal answer with more digits than the grid can accommodate, it may be either rounded or truncated, but it must fill the entire grid.

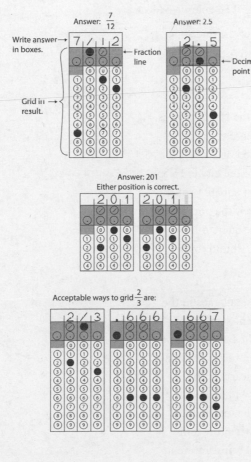

practice test 1— Math — Calculator

28. An E-collar is used to prevent dog patients who have had surgery from licking an incision. The shape of such a collar is as follows:

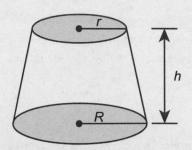

A large puppy is provided an E-collar where the diameter of the larger, circular base is 16 inches, the circumference of the smaller, circular base is 14π inches, and the height between the two bases is 12 inches. What is the volume enclosed by such an E-collar? [Note: The volume of a frustum in the shape of the one above is $V = \dfrac{\pi h}{3}(R^2 + Rr + r^2)$]. **Enter your answer in terms of** π.

29. The City of Manila in the Philippines is recorded as the most densely populated to date, with a population of 1,780,148 people. The total area of the city is 16.55 square miles. How many square yards would each person have if the population were doubled? (Note: 1 square mile = 3,097,600 square yards. Round to the nearest tenth.)

30. Highway bridges have small gaps in the roadway between adjacent sections of the bridge. This gives the bridge room to expand in hotter temperatures. Assume this gap width varies linearly with the temperature. If the gap width measures 2.1 inches when the temperature is 60°F and 1.2 inches when the temperature is 78°F, at what temperature in degrees Fahrenheit would the gap close completely?

SHOW YOUR WORK HERE

31. The budget officer for a dentistry supply company needs to determine the most cost-efficient order to place for parts needed to manufacture dental drills. The following formula is used:

$$Q = \sqrt{\frac{2 \cdot C \cdot p}{s}}$$

In this formula:

- Q is the number of parts ultimately ordered.

- C is the manufacturing cost for making the drill.

- p is the quantity of parts the plant will use in three months' time.

- s is the cost of keeping a completed drill in stock for three months.

Determine the value of s if $Q = 35$, $C = \$4,000$, and $p = 20$. Round your answer to the nearest dollar.

SHOW YOUR WORK HERE

ANSWER KEYS AND EXPLANATIONS

Section 1: Reading Test

1. A	9. A	17. D	25. B	33. B	41. D
2. D	10. A	18. B	26. A	34. A	42. A
3. B	11. B	19. B	27. D	35. C	43. B
4. D	12. D	20. D	28. B	36. D	44. C
5. C	13. D	21. B	29. C	37. D	45. C
6. B	14. C	22. A	30. B	38. A	46. C
7. C	15. A	23. A	31. C	39. D	47. B
8. D	16. D	24. D	32. C	40. B	

READING TEST RAW SCORE

(Number of correct answers)

1. **The correct answer is A.** Information in the passage indicates that Nat was wet from the rain when he arrived at the house. There is no evidence in the passage that supports the conclusions in choices B, C, or D.

2. **The correct answer is D.** This quotation from the servant-maid best shows that Nat was wet from the rain because she points out that he is dripping, and since it is raining outside, it is most likely that he is dripping with rain water. Choice A merely shows that it is raining; it does not show that Nat was in the rain or that he is dripping with it. Choices B and C do not support the idea that he was wet with rain either.

3. **The correct answer is B.** After Tommy falls and hits his head hard while trying to slide down the banister, he gets right back on the banister and tries again. The other characters do not do anything that would support the idea that they'd agree with the proverb.

4. **The correct answer is D.** The lines in choice D show that Tommy returned to sliding down the banister right after falling off of it. Choice A only shows that he fell; it does not show that he plans to try again. Choice B shows only that the boy may have hurt himself. Choice C only reveals who fell off the banister.

5. **The correct answer is C.** Lines 21-22 mainly establish the house's chaotic yet jovial setting. No specific characters are introduced in these lines, so choice A is incorrect. The lines do not set up any conflicts (choice B) or provide a back story (choice D) either.

6. **The correct answer is B.** Each answer choice can be used as a synonym of *wag*, but the word is being used to describe a boy who is drawing droll caricatures in the context of line 30. Only choice B makes sense in that context.

7. **The correct answer is C.** In line 4, Nat explains that Mr. Laurence sent him to the house. There is no evidence to support the other answer choices.

8. **The correct answer is D.** A few lines later, Nat says that he won't know if he is the new boy until he sees "whether I'm going to stay or not," which supports the conclusion in choice D. His immediate fascination with the other boys makes choice C unlikely. There is no evidence to support choices A and B either.

9. **The correct answer is A.** While all of the answer choices are synonyms for *occupied*, only choice A makes sense in the context of line 38: ... *the stairs were* in use *by a boy reading, a girl singing a lullaby to her doll, two puppies* ... . The other synonyms would not make sense if used in place of *occupied* in line 38.

10. **The correct answer is A.** As a whole, the passage makes the case that communication and common characteristics are the bases of any community. The other answer choices are just details in the passage.

11. **The correct answer is B.** Choice B is the topic sentence of the passage, so it is the best evidence to support the answer to the previous question. The other answer choices include details from the incorrect answer choices to the previous question.

12. **The correct answer is D.** In line 13, *removed* is used as a verb, but choices A, B, and C are all adjectives. Choice D is the only verb, and it is the only answer choice that makes sense if used in place of *removed* in line 13.

13. **The correct answer is D.** The author characterizes relationships that are not social in negative terms, expressing the idea that they are based on imbalances of power when they should emphasize mutual care. Choices A, B, and C are all true in themselves, but none really shows how relationships that are not social are negative.

14. **The correct answer is C.** Choice C provides the most complete evidence to support the correct answer to the previous question. Choices A and B include details from the incorrect answer choices to the previous question, failing to indicate the negative aspect of nonsocial relationships. Choice D indicates the negative aspect but does not support the answer to the previous question as specifically as choice C does.

15. **The correct answer is A.** The author cites how "One shares in what another has thought and felt" (line 35) as evidence that communication changes human experiences. The author does not use the other answer choices to indicate how communication changes human experiences.

16. **The correct answer is D.** In lines 34-35, the author writes that "To be a recipient of a communication is to have an enlarged and changed experience." Those who listen and read are the recipients of communication, and 61 percent is the total of the 45 percent of listeners and 16 percent of readers on the chart.

17. **The correct answer is D.** According to lines 33-34 of the passage, "all communication (and hence all genuine social life) is educative." Therefore, the best answer is 100 percent (choice D).

18. **The correct answer is B.** In line 25, *plane* is used as a noun, and the only nouns among the answer choices are *level* (choice B) and *airplane* (choice D). *Airplane* makes no sense in the context of this sentence, so *level* is the best answer.

19. **The correct answer is B.** The final paragraph of the passage discusses how, through communication, both parties gain knowledge of the topic at hand and feel their opinions shift until they crystallize into something more specific and true. Choice A is incorrect because the paragraph does not discuss advancements in communication. Choice C is incorrect because though this paragraph talks about "expletives," its main point is about how communicating is key, and how the absence of it will lead to confusion and unexplored opinions. Choice D is incorrect because the paragraph does not talk about specific experiments one can do to improve how they communicate.

20. **The correct answer is D.** The author only provides evidence that people who appreciate precious stones often value the way the stones refract light. There is no evidence to support the other answer choices.

21. **The correct answer is B.** In these lines, the author calls refraction "one of the chief charms of certain precious stones," which suggests that those who appreciate precious stones might appreciate that particular charm. The other answer choices do not suggest that someone is likely to appreciate the way precious stones refract light.

22. **The correct answer is A.** According to the passage, when light passes through certain crystals with double refraction, the light is polarized.

23. **The correct answer is A.** These lines explicitly explain the direct result of light passing through certain crystals with double refraction. Choices B and C deal with polarization, but they fail to serve as evidence to support the correct answer to the previous question.

24. **The correct answer is D.** In line 18, the author is discussing light passing through the physical substance of stones, so the most sensible answer choice is D, *core*. *Essence* and *theme* do not describe physical objects, so choices A and C are not correct. A body is physical, but one would not really describe a stone as having a body, so choice B is not as strong an answer as choice D is.

25. **The correct answer is B.** The final paragraph is mostly concerned with defining the various technical distinctions related to diaphaneity. By this point in the passage, the term "diaphaneity" has already been introduced, so choice A cannot be correct. Choice C only describes a minor detail in the passage. The author is not trying to prove anything in the passage, so choice D is incorrect.

26. **The correct answer is A.** In line 39, *class* is used to mean a particular group of stones. Choices B, C, and D are all synonyms for *class*, but none makes sense in this particular context.

27. **The correct answer is D.** According to the passage, "diaphaneity" is another term for "transmission," which is shown on the diagram. Choices A and B are not shown on the diagram. Choice C is not an effect.

28. **The correct answer is B.** According to the passage, light only passes through a sub-translucent stone "in a small degree," and the diagram shows that absorption is when light does not pass all the way through a stone. Light does not pass through a non-diaphanous stone at all, so choice A is incorrect. Light passes through diaphanous and translucent stones completely.

29. **The correct answer is C.** This passage is mainly about how the President of the United States is selected, and in this context, *appointment* is a synonym of *selection*. The other choices can be used as synonyms of *appointment* in different contexts but not this particular one.

30. **The correct answer is B.** In the passage, Hamilton points out that there are flaws in the American election process, but it is an effective process overall. The evidence that supports this opinion contradicts the conclusions in choices A, C, and D.

31. **The correct answer is C.** These lines indicate that the American election process is flawed ("it be not perfect") but is very effective overall ("it is at least excellent"). Choices A and B introduce criticisms of the process without indicating that it is very effective overall. Choice D indicates that it is effective without also indicating that it has flaws.

32. **The correct answer is C.** Hamilton provides evidence that he thinks electors should be uniquely capable of analyzing the effectiveness of potential presidents. If choice A were true, there would be no need for electors. Choice B does not make sense. The electors' job is to prevent tumult and disorder from ever occurring, so choice D is not the best answer.

33. **The correct answer is B.** These lines prove that Hamilton believed the electors should be uniquely capable of analyzing the effectiveness of potential presidents ("the immediate election should be made by men most capable of analyzing the qualities adapted to the station"). The other answer choices do not function as evidence that choice C was the correct answer to the previous question.

34. **The correct answer is A.** In the fourth paragraph, Hamilton is mainly saying that having more than one elector is a precaution against the election process becoming chaotic. Choices B and C are minor details in the paragraph.

35. **The correct answer is C.** Only choice C makes sense if used in place of *intrigue* in line 30. Choices A and B are synonyms of *intrigue*, but they are not synonyms of it in this particular context. Choice D is an antonym of *intrigue*, not a synonym of it.

36. **The correct answer is D.** The paragraph is mainly about the importance of electors who will not be corrupted by special interest groups. Hamilton never tries to prove choice A in the passage. Choice B describes the purpose of the passage as a whole, but its final paragraph has a much more specific purpose. Choice C is just one detail in the paragraph.

37. **The correct answer is D.** Hamilton uses the phrase "deadly adversaries" to describe the obstacles of "cabal, intrigue, and corruption." He is using the phrase to say that these obstacles are as serious as death itself. Choices A and B are too literal. Choice C implies a contrast that Hamilton is not actually making in line 30.

answers practice test 1

38. **The correct answer is A.** According to the passage, both liquids (such as water and milk) and solids (such as ice and coal) can undergo physical and chemical changes. Choices B and C make conditions that are sometimes true seem as though they are always true, so they are not the best answer choices. Choice D applies only to chemical changes.

39. **The correct answer is D.** The previous paragraph explicitly states that solids and liquids can undergo physical changes, and this answer choice shows that solids, such as coal, and liquids, such as milk, can as well. Choices A, B, and C do not support the correct answer to the previous question.

40. **The correct answer is B.** Each answer choice can be used as a synonym of *properties*, but only *qualities* makes sense in this particular context. *Belongings* (choice A) and *homes* (choice C) are better suited to human beings than substances. *Resources* (choice D) is not as clear an answer as *qualities* is.

41. **The correct answer is D.** The author emphasizes the importance of always performing particular experiments multiple times under the exact same conditions. Choices A and B contradict that point. Choice C does not make much sense since it is likely the student's goal to perform an experiment accurately every time.

42. **The correct answer is A.** Choices B, C, and D are ways to ensure that the experiment is performed under the same conditions, but they do not state the importance of performing particular experiments under the same conditions every time as clearly as choice A does.

43. **The correct answer is B.** The author states the importance of keeping solutions "away from direct sunlight or heat," which makes sense only if *solutions* refers to something physical. Only *mixtures* refers to a physical substance.

44. **The correct answer is C.** Both of these passages refer to students directly and provide basic information about chemistry: Passage 1 is about the differences between physical and chemical properties, and Passage 2 is about the best way to perform chemistry experiments. Choice A applies only to Passage 2. Choice D applies only to Passage 1. Neither passage defines the term *chemistry*, so choice B cannot be correct.

45. **The correct answer is C.** Passage 1 emphasizes the importance of observing chemical and physical changes carefully, and Passage 2 emphasizes the importance of performing experiments carefully. Choices A and B apply only to Passage 2. Neither passage supports the conclusion in choice D.

46. **The correct answer is C.** Passage 1 is written in more basic language than Passage 2 is and does not get into performing actual experiments as Passage 2 does, so it is logical to conclude that Passage 2 is intended for a more advanced student than Passage 1 is. Both passages are intended for students, not professional chemists, so choices A and D are incorrect. Passage 2 does not build directly on Passage 1, so choice B is incorrect.

47. **The correct answer is B.** The author of Passage 2 states that placing a substance near a heat source could change its temperature and alter findings, so choice B is the best answer. Choice A is incorrect because the author of Passage 2 states that estimations are sometimes appropriate. Only Passage 1 makes any mention of how substances that have undergone changes may taste different, so choice C is incorrect. Choice D contradicts a main point of Passage 2.

Section 2: Writing and Language Test

1. C	9. C	17. C	24. A	31. D	38. C
2. B	10. C	18. C	25. B	32. B	39. D
3. D	11. A	19. B	26. B	33. C	40. A
4. A	12. C	20. D	27. D	34. C	41. C
5. D	13. B	21. A	28. A	35. B	42. C
6. B	14. A	22. B	29. C	36. A	43. A
7. B	15. B	23. D	30. C	37. D	44. D
8. A	16. D				

WRITING AND LANGUAGE TEST RAW SCORE ☐

(Number of correct answers)

1. **The correct answer is C.** This choice connects the two sentences, eliminates wordiness by deleting "This was," and prevents it from becoming a run-on sentence. Choice A is too choppy. Choices B and D use incorrect punctuation to join the sentences.

2. **The correct answer is B.** "As it was later called" tells you that "moon shot speech" is not the official title of this speech, so "speech" should not be capitalized as a proper noun nor included within the quotation marks. That eliminates choices C and D. Choice B is correct because the phrase being quoted is "moon shot."

3. **The correct answer is D.** The em dash sets off the explanatory phrase (*namely, sending manned missions to Mars*). Choice B creates a sentence fragment. Choice C is incorrect because it removes that pause before the phrase, running the sentence together.

4. **The correct answer is A.** The paragraph is about the history of different countries' Mars programs. Choice C is similar but, because the paragraph also talks about European and Asian efforts to reach Mars, it's not the best answer. Choice B is incorrect because it basically repeats the last sentence of the previous paragraph. And choice D doesn't fit at all, because the passage doesn't talk about fictional Mars missions, only real-life ones.

5. **The correct answer is D.** As written, the sentence suggests that *previously the Soviet Union* is a list item like China or the United States, when it's really an adjective phrase describing Russia. Choice D correctly uses parentheses to set this off so that it's separate from the list. Choice B removes any punctuation that would indicate that *previously the Soviet Union* is describing *Russia*. Choice C incorrectly uses semicolons.

6. **The correct answer is B.** If you look at the chart, there have been more successes than failures since 1999. Choice A says the opposite, although there are fewer failures than successes since 1999. Choice C is incorrect because there is no information on the chart to suggest this (and Japan doesn't even appear on the chart after 1998). The chart indicates that the one joint venture between Russia and China since 1999 failed, so there's no information in the chart to support Choice D.

7. **The correct answer is B.** The original phrasing is awkward and doesn't flow well into the paragraph. Choice B does a better job of stating the topic of the paragraph while leading into the main points. It works well with the beginning of the next sentence (*For one,*). Choice C doesn't connect with the rest of the paragraph; it just makes a flat statement. Choice D sets up the paragraph as the opposite of the previous paragraph, which is incorrect.

8. **The correct answer is A.** *Mars* is singular, so the possessive noun should add an apostrophe + *s*. Choice B makes Mars incorrectly plural, while choice C removes the possessive element altogether. Choice D is incorrect because *Martian* is an adjective, not a noun.

9. **The correct answer is C.** Based on the sentence, you know that Mars lacks the elements that humans need (oxygen and water) and also has elements that harm humans (radiation). *Inhospitable* (choice C) is the choice that most closely aligns with that context. *Welcoming* means the opposite, so it is incorrect. And neither *unfamiliar* (choice A) nor *unremarkable* (choice D) really fit in with the rest of the sentence.

10. **The correct answer is C.** The passage is about sending humans to Mars, so it makes the most sense that *terraforming* means getting ready for human visitors. Choice B is incorrect because unmanned probes have been going to Mars without any special changes to the Martian environment. Collecting soil (choice A) might be a step taken in researching what's needed to terraform Mars, but it is not the actual process. Choice D doesn't make sense.

11. **The correct answer is A.** This sentence summarizes the author's main point—that the history of Martian space travel has been difficult, and the logistics of getting there are complicated—while also incorporating the point in the last paragraph that many countries are optimistic about getting there in the next 15–20 years. Choice B doesn't fit with any of the information presented; the author talks about how challenging Mars expeditions have been but does not suggest anywhere that this should not be a goal. Choice C ties back to the first paragraph but has little to do with the rest of the passage. There is not enough information to tell what President Kennedy would have wanted. Choice D is also not a good fit, because the focus of the passage is the missions to Mars, not the people involved in them.

12. **The correct answer is C.** This sentence summarizes the topic of the passage (the economic factors behind the growing number of freelancers) without getting too specific. Choice A is too abrupt to be an introduction. There isn't enough context about what the reader will be learning in the passage. Choice B is fine where it is as the closing sentence of the paragraph, and choice D doesn't fit with the tone of the informative piece.

13. **The correct answer is B.** From the words *someone else*, you can tell that the writer is not talking about the U.S. Bureau of Labor Statistics, so that eliminates choice D. Choice C merely turns the phrase into a proper noun, and it is unlikely that the writer is referring to someone named "Someone Else." That leaves choice B, which is a likely source for the information.

14. **The correct answer is A.** This is a short list of items, and separating them with a comma is correct. The ellipsis in choice B breaks up the sentence incorrectly, and the period in choice C creates a sentence fragment. Choice D adds an unnecessary comma.

15. **The correct answer is B.** The colon in choice A falsely sets up a list and makes the sentence confusing. Choice B turns it into a complete sentence by adding the verb *are* and smoothing out the sentence.

16. **The correct answer is D.** This sentence summarizes the outcome of the details presented in the paragraph, so it makes the most sense as a closing sentence.

17. **The correct answer is C.** To be most clear, you want to specify what Uber is (because the writer hasn't yet mentioned whether it's a person, a company, etc.) Choice C does this most clearly. Choice B doesn't really clarify what the writer is trying to say, and choice D is grammatically incorrect.

18. **The correct answer is C.** From the word *freelancing* in the sentence, you know that the writer is no longer talking about companies (choice B) or Uber (choice D). *Employees* (choice C) makes the sentence clearer.

19. **The correct answer is B.** The context of the sentence suggests that you need a synonym for *problem* or *conflict*, and choice B fits that the best out of the choices.

20. **The correct answer is D.** As written, the sentence is a fragment. Choice D rearranges the sentence to be simpler and clearer, as well as complete. Choice B incorrectly uses a semicolon between clauses. Choice C is also a sentence fragment.

21. **The correct answer is A.** There are three nouns in the subject: *email*, *devices*, and *apps*, so the verb needs to be plural as well. The verb is correct as written. Choice B is a verb for a singular subject. Choice C is a present participle, not a standalone verb. And choice D is not only past tense but also changes the meaning of the sentence.

22. **The correct answer is B.** In this sentence, you have to work a little to figure out the subject: is it the singular *piece* or the plural *independent workers*? In this case it's *piece*, so the verb should be singular (choice B). Choice C is an incorrect plural verb phrase, and choice D is the first-person singular.

23. **The correct answer is D.** The word *specifically* is the transition between the introductory sentence and the details in the paragraph that follow. Choice B removes the transition element, so it is incorrect. Choice C sets up a sentence fragment, so it too is incorrect.

24. **The correct answer is A.** *States* is plural, but *the United States* is one country, so it should be treated as singular here. Also, the singular possessive means there is no apostrophe, so both choices C and D are out. Choice B is a plural possessive, so it is incorrect as well.

25. **The correct answer is B.** The sentence is too wordy and awkward as written, so the writer needs to simplify. Of the options, choice B does this best by inserting a semicolon and breaking it into two main parts. Choice C breaks up the sentence too much, leading to a repetitive set of short sentences. Choice D removes all punctuation, making the sentence even harder to follow.

26. **The correct answer is B.** This sentence is talking about the part of the Constitution that describes the Electoral College, so the location of that specific information would be helpful. The other details may be historically accurate, but they would distract from the writer's point.

27. **The correct answer is D.** From the rest of the passage (including the title), you know that the writer is talking about controversies, or challenges, over the Electoral College. Choice A doesn't fit with that theme. Choice B is too vague and doesn't convey the author's point about the controversy. Choice C doesn't quite work either, because the Electoral College isn't contradicting anything, according to the passage.

28. **The correct answer is A.** This is an explanatory clause, and a single set of parentheses is a great way to set that off. Choice D uses too many parentheses—you don't want to overdo it if you want the sentence to be clear. Choice B removes all pauses and punctuation, turning the sentence into a run-on. Choice C incorrectly uses ellipses to set off the clause.

29. **The correct answer is C.** This paragraph tells the story of the first real challenge to the Electoral College, so any details included should be relevant to that point. The paragraph is about the Jefferson/Burr battle, and the detail about President John Adams has little to do with the rest of the paragraph.

30. **The correct answer is C.** This paragraph is about the changes that would take place after the problems encountered in the election of 1800. *As a result of this crisis…* (choice C) is an effective way to transition from the previous paragraph to the new one. Choice A is similar, but the tone is off from the rest of the passage. Choice B repeats a detail that comes later in the paragraph. Choice D is inappropriate because it doesn't directly relate to the information in this particular paragraph.

31. **The correct answer is D.** From the context of the passage, you notice right away how *Electoral College* has been used throughout. Also, *Electoral College* is a proper noun, so both words should be capitalized.

32. **The correct answer is B.** Middle initials should be followed by a period, not enclosed in quotation marks, so you can eliminate choices A and D. A middle initial is also part of a name and should be capitalized, so choice C is incorrect.

33. **The correct answer is C.** In this sentence, the writer is presenting information that is different from what was presented in the last sentence (that Al Gore was leading overall). The first sentence in the paragraph also used *still*, so it's better to find a different, more specific, transition word for this sentence. *However* (choice C) works because it sets the reader up to know that there is going to be a change. Choice B doesn't work because it suggests that the writer is repeating information, which is not the case. Choice D doesn't work because it makes the reader think that the information presented in each sentence will be the same.

34. **The correct answer is C.** The writer is talking about the entire Poet Laureate program. It may have started in 1986, but *has had* suggests that the writer is including everything that has happened since then, which eliminates choice D. Choice B is incorrect because this is a time relationship, not a cause-and-effect relationship.

35. **The correct answer is B.** *Then* shows time, which is not what the writer is trying to convey; she is trying to make a number comparison, which should be *than*. *When* doesn't work here in this sentence, nor does *of*.

36. **The correct answer is A.** This detail helps to transition from the first paragraph to the second, by offering more information about how the program was created. It builds on the mention of 1986 in the first paragraph. The history of the Library of Congress isn't necessarily relevant here, because the passage focuses specifically on the Poets Laureate. And it focuses on the United States, so a detail about other countries doesn't really fit with this passage's topic.

37. **The correct answer is D.** As written, the sentence looks like *the poet who famously read…* is a poet separate from Robert Frost, Elizabeth Bishop, and Gwendolyn Brooks. It should be set off with appropriate punctuation—in this case, parentheses. Choice B incorrectly pushes together *Robert Frost* and *the poet*. Even though the appositive phrase likely describes Robert Frost, there needs to be a break of some kind. In choice C, there's a mismatch because the writer starts by setting the appositive off with a dash but completes it with a comma.

38. **The correct answer is C.** *Librarian of Congress* is a person's title, so it should be capitalized. However, a preposition in a title (like *of*) should not be capitalized, so choice D may look good at first, but it's incorrect. Choices A and B incorrectly make part of the person's title into common nouns.

39. **The correct answer is D.** The previous sentence ends with *Librarian of Congress*, so it is unclear if the *He or she* refers to the librarian or the poet. The paragraph is about the process for appointing Poets Laureate, so choice D makes the most sense here. There is no other information about presidents or librarians, so these are not likely to be the correct subjects to use here.

40. **The correct answer is A.** The poet is being paid, while most of the options suggest that the poet is paying. *Stipend* is the only choice that clearly states that the Poet Laureate is receiving the money.

41. **The correct answer is C.** The writer needs a transitional phrase, and choice C introduces the new topic: the Poet Laureate's tasks. As written, the choice is too casual for the tone of the passage. Choice B is confusing—the paragraph isn't an effect of the previous topic (what a Poet Laureate's term is). Choice D would leave the paragraph with a too-abrupt start; there needs to be some introduction.

42. **The correct answer is C.** To make sure that you're keeping the list items parallel, make sure the verbs align. *Giving* and *promoting* should tip you off about how the sentence should stay consistent. The past-tense *hosted* (choice B) and the first- or second-person *host* do not match either the tense of the sentence or the third-person subject (*a Poet Laureate*).

43. **The correct answer is A.** The subject is plural (*Poets Laureate*), so the verb phrase should be as well. Choice B is incorrectly matched as a singular helping verb. Choice C suggests that this is happening in the future when there's no indication that the passage is predicting what will happen. Choice D expresses the opposite of what the writer is trying to say.

44. **The correct answer is D.** *Elementary schools* is a common noun (there's no mention of a specific school), so both words should be lowercase.

Section 3: Math Test—No Calculator

1. A	**5.** C	**9.** B	**12.** B	**15.** 3
2. D	**6.** B	**10.** D	**13.** A	**16.** 8
3. C	**7.** C	**11.** C	**14.** 8.4	**17.** 0.46
4. A	**8.** D			

MATH TEST—NO CALCULATOR TEST RAW SCORE ☐

(Number of correct answers)

1. **The correct answer is A.** Start by clearing the fractions by multiplying both sides by 9. Then, apply the distributive property and combine like terms:

$$\frac{2}{3}(2 - 3x) = \frac{1}{9}(2x + 1)$$
$$6(2 - 3x) = 2x + 1$$
$$12 - 18x = 2x + 1$$
$$11 = 20x$$
$$x = \frac{11}{20}$$

Choice B is the result of a minor arithmetic mistake in the last step (adding 1 to both sides instead of subtracting), choice C is the result of not correctly applying the distributive property in the second step, and choice D is the result not applying the distributive property correctly and then making a minor arithmetic mistake.

2. **The correct answer is D.** The length of $\overline{AB}$ is $CD + 2\Delta x$. Using $CD = 5$ with the fact that the bounds AB are 5.3 and 5.5 inches, yields the double inequality $5.3 \leq 5 + 2\Delta x \leq 5.5$. In choice A, Δx should be doubled; in choice B, 5 should be removed from the middle portion of the inequality; and in choice C, you used $2CD$, not CD.

3. **The correct answer is C.** Simplify each radical term and then combine the results:

$$\sqrt{81x^3} = \sqrt{9 \cdot 9 \cdot x^2 \cdot x} = \underline{9x}\sqrt{x}$$
$$5x\sqrt{4x} = 5x\sqrt{2^2 \cdot x} = 5x \cdot \underline{2}\sqrt{x} = 10x\sqrt{x}$$

So,

$$\sqrt{81x^3} - 5x\sqrt{4x} = 9x\sqrt{x} - 10x\sqrt{x} = -x\sqrt{x}$$

Choice A is incorrect because 61 should be outside the radical sign. Choice B is the result of adding the radicals instead of subtracting them, and choice D is the result of an arithmetic error when simplifying square roots of numbers.

4. **The correct answer is A.** Let x be the width of the base (in inches). The length is then $(2x - 3)$ inches. Since the height is 20 inches, the following function gives the surface area:

$$S(x) = 2\left(x(2x - 3) + 20x + 20(2x - 3)\right)$$
$$= 2\left(2x^2 - 3x + 20x + 40x - 60\right)$$
$$= 2\left(2x^2 + 57x - 60\right)$$
$$= 4x^2 + 114x - 120$$

Choice B is the volume, choice C is one-half of the surface area, and choice D is missing the area of two of the six faces of the box.

5. **The correct answer is C.** The difference is $3, and this is larger than the differences at the times provided by the other three choices.

6. **The correct answer is B.** The strategy is to make the trade at a time when the International Market stock is worth the most *and* simultaneously the Emerging Market stock is worth the least. Create the following table to make this determination.

t	Time	International Market Stock Price (in Dollars)	Emerging Market Stock Price (in Dollars)	Profit: International Market – Emerging Market
0	7 a.m.	4	3	1
1	8 a.m.	3	2	1
2	9 a.m.	3	2	1
3	10 a.m.	2	2	0
4	11 a.m.	3	2	1
5	12 p.m.	3	1	2
6	1 p.m.	3	3	0
7	2 p.m.	1	4	–3
8	3 p.m.	3	2	1
9	4 p.m.	4	3	1

From this, we see that the best time to make the trade is 12 p.m.

7. **The correct answer is C.** Exponential functions of the form Ae^{bt}, where A and b are positive constants, grow faster than all the following types of functions:

- other exponential functions for which b is negative
- linear functions
- quadratic functions

The functions in the other three choices all fit into one of these categories. So, the function in choice C exhibits the most rapid growth rate of those listed.

8. **The correct answer is D.** Since it is assumed that the function is linear, the slope can be computed using any two points in the table. Using the first two columns yields the slope $\frac{-7-2}{1-(-5)} = -\frac{3}{2}$. Now, use the point-slope formula for a line with the point $(-5, 2)$ to get the equation $y - 2 = -\frac{3}{2}(x + 5)$. This simplifies to $y = f(x) = -\frac{3}{2}x - \frac{11}{2}$. The slopes of the functions in the other three choices are all incorrect.

9. **The correct answer is B.** The median occurs in the middle position of an ordered data set. Since there are 127 data values here, the one in the 64th position is the median. This value is 8. Choices A and C are off by one in either direction. Choice D is the median of the heights, if you don't consider the frequency (if each occurred once).

10. **The correct answer is D.** Multiply the numerator and denominator by the conjugate of the denominator, which is $3 + 2i$. Then, FOIL the numerator and simplify:

$$\frac{1 + 2i}{3 - 2i} = \frac{1 + 2i}{3 - 2i} \cdot \frac{3 + 2i}{3 + 2i}$$
$$= \frac{3 + 6i + 2i + 4i^2}{9 - 4i^2}$$
$$= \frac{3 + 8i - 4}{9 - 4(-1)}$$
$$= \frac{-1 + 8i}{13}$$
$$= -\frac{1}{13} + \frac{8}{13}i$$

In choice A, you did not multiply the numerator by the conjugate of the denominator. In choice B, you used $i^2 = 1$ instead of -1. Choice C is the result of just dividing the real and the imaginary parts separately.

11. **The correct answer is C.** Let x be the number of lima beans to plant. Note that "$p\%$ of x" equals $\frac{p}{100}x$, and the number of these that die before 10 days is $\frac{1}{3}\left(\frac{p}{100}x\right) = \frac{p}{300}x$. So, the number of plants that make it to 10 days is $\frac{p}{100}x - \frac{p}{300}x$. Setting this expression equal to 400 yields the desired equation. In choice A, you incorrectly used $p\% = p$; in choice B, you did not multiply the first x on the left side by $p\%$; and in choice D, you incorrectly used $p\% = 0.0p$ (for instance, this would mean $100\% = 0.0100$ rather than 1.00).

12. **The correct answer is B.** Substitute $k = \frac{5}{4}$ and simplify:

$$\frac{p_C}{p_I} = \left[\frac{2}{\frac{5}{4} + 1}\right]^{\frac{\frac{5}{4}}{\frac{5}{4} - 1}} = \left[\frac{2}{\frac{5}{1} + \frac{4}{4}}\right]^{\frac{\frac{5}{4}}{\frac{1}{4}}}$$
$$= \left[\frac{2}{\frac{9}{4}}\right]^{\frac{5}{1}} = \left[\frac{8}{9}\right]^5 = \frac{8^5}{9^5}$$

Now, solve for p_I:

$$\frac{p_C}{p_I} = \frac{8^5}{9^5}$$
$$9^5 p_C = 8^5 p_I$$
$$\frac{9^5 p_C}{8^5} = p_I$$
$$\left(\frac{9}{8}\right)^5 p_C = p_I$$

Choice A is the reciprocal of the correct answer, and choices C and D are the results of computing incorrectly with complex fractions.

13. **The correct answer is A.** The association is strong because the points are packed closely together. It is linear because the points conform to a linear-looking pattern. It is negative because the points fall from left to right. Choice B is a strong, positive linear association, choice C is a strong nonlinear association, and choice D is a nonexistent association.

14. **The correct answer is 8.4 days.** The median recovery time from last year is 7 days because in a boxplot, the vertical line contained within the box represents the location of the 50th percentile, which is the median. Twenty percent more than this equals $7(0.2) = 1.4$ days. So, the expected median recovery time for this year is 8.4 days.

15. **The correct answer is 3.** Simplify the left-side of the equation as follows:

$$1 - 3\big(2x + 3(1 - x)\big) = Cx$$
$$1 - 3\big(2x + 3 - 3x\big) = Cx$$
$$1 - 3\big(3 - x\big) = Cx$$
$$1 - 9 + 3x = Cx$$
$$3x - 8 = Cx$$

The only value of C for which this equation has no solution is 3 because in such case, the x-terms cancel, leaving the false statement $-8 = 0$. For all other values of C, subtracting $3x$ from both sides yields the equation $-8 = (C - 3)x$, the solution of which is $x = -\dfrac{8}{C - 3}$.

16. **The correct answer is 8.** First, write the quadratic equation in standard form. (Do *not* set each factor equal to 6!)

$$x(x + 2) = 8$$
$$x^2 + 2x - 8 = 0$$
$$(x + 4)(x - 2) = 0$$
$$x = 4, 2$$

So, $\big|x_1 \cdot x_2\big| = \big|(-4) \cdot 2\big| = 8$.

17. **The correct answer is 0.46.** First, note that the number of female dogs that exhibited side effects is $100 - 42 = 58$ (since 100 female dogs were in the sample and 42 did not exhibit side effects). So, of all dogs in the sample, $33 + 58 = 91$ exhibited side effects. Since the sample consists of 200 dogs, the probability that a dog exhibited side effects is $\dfrac{91}{200} = 0.455$. Rounded to the nearest hundredth, the answer is 0.46.

Section 4: Math Test—Calculator

1. C	**8.** B	**14.** A	**20.** D	**26.** B
2. A	**9.** B	**15.** B	**21.** D	**27.** B
3. C	**10.** C	**16.** A	**22.** C	**28.** 676
4. A	**11.** B	**17.** C	**23.** B	**29.** 14.4
5. C	**12.** A	**18.** D	**24.** C	**30.** 102
6. C	**13.** C	**19.** D	**25.** B	**31.** 131
7. D				

MATH TEST—CALCULATOR TEST RAW SCORE

(Number of correct answers)

1. **The correct answer is C.** First, line up the variables in the equations of the system:

$$\begin{cases} -ax + 2y = -1 \\ 3ax - 6y = 3 \end{cases}$$

   Multiply the first equation by −3. Doing so shows that the two equations are equivalent. So, this system has infinitely many solutions. Choices A and C have one solution, and choice B has no solution.

2. **The correct answer is A.** First, determine the equation for $f(x)$:

   Using the two labeled points, compute the slope as $\frac{5 - (-1)}{-2 - 4} = -1$. Using point-slope formula with the point $(-2, 5)$ yields the equation $y - 5 = -1(x + 2)$, or equivalently $y = -x + 3$. So, $f(x) = -x + 3$. Now, to solve the system

$$\begin{cases} y = -x + 3 \\ y = 1 - (x - 2)^2 \end{cases}$$

   set the expressions equal and solve for x:

$$-x + 3 = 1 - (x^2 - 4x + 4)$$
$$-x + 3 = 1 - x^2 + 4x - 4$$
$$-x + 3 = -x^2 + 4x - 3$$
$$x^2 - 5x + 6 = 0$$
$$(x - 3)(x - 2) = 0$$
$$x = 2, 3$$

   If $x = 2$, then $y = 1$, and if $x = 3$, then $y = 0$. Thus, $x_1 = 2$, $x_2 = 3$, $y_1 = 1$, $y_2 = 0$, so that $\frac{y_1 + y_2}{x_1 + x_2} = \frac{1 + 0}{2 + 3} = \frac{1}{5}$. In choice B, you used the sum of coordinates of the same point in the top and the bottom rather than summing the x-coordinates and y-coordinates; choice C is the reciprocal of the correct answer; and choice D is the product of $(y_1 + y_2)$ and $(x_1 + x_2)$.

3. **The correct answer is C.** The fox population graph rises from left to right during this time period. Choice A is where the fox population is decreasing, and choices B and D represent time periods over which the population increases and decreases.

4. **The correct answer is A.** This is a reasonable, plausible interpretation for this situation when the food supply is finite. Choice B is wrong because the graphs show that when one population rises, the other declines. Choice C is wrong because the graphs are both cyclic and do not level off toward a horizontal line. Choice D is wrong because that observation *is precisely* the relationship being sought!

5. **The correct answer is C.** Organize the given information, as follows:

	Days to complete the job	Portion of job completed per day
Team A	16	$\frac{1}{16}$
Team B	12	$\frac{1}{12}$
Together	t	$\frac{1}{t}$

Add the individual labor (last column, first two rows) and set it equal to the combined label (last column, last row) to get the equation $\frac{1}{16} + \frac{1}{12} = \frac{1}{t}$. Now, solve for t:

$$\frac{1}{16} + \frac{1}{12} = \frac{1}{t}$$
$$3t + 4t = 48$$
$$7t = 48$$
$$t = 6\frac{6}{7} \text{ days}$$

So, the two teams remove one-fourth of the debris in $6\frac{6}{7}$ when they work together. So, it takes $\left(6\frac{6}{7}\right) = 4 \cdot \frac{48}{7} = \frac{192}{7} = 27\frac{3}{7}$ days to remove *all* the debris from the village. Choice A is the time it takes to clear only one-fourth of the debris, and choices B and D involve arithmetic errors with the mixed numbers.

6. **The correct answer is C.** Using the points (0, 1,800) and (1.5, 1,550), find the equation of the line. The slope is

$$m = \frac{1,800 - 1,550}{0 - 1.5} = -\frac{250}{1.5} = \frac{-500}{3}.$$

Since the y-intercept is 1,800, the equation of the line is $y = -\frac{500}{3}x + 1,800$. Now, determine the value of x for which this equals 60:

$$-\frac{500}{3}x + 1,800 = 60$$
$$-\frac{500}{3}x = -1,740$$
$$x = (1,740)\left(\frac{3}{500}\right)$$
$$= \frac{261}{25} = 10.44$$

So, it takes approximately 10.4 days. Choice A is the result of using the point (1, 1,550) instead of (1.5, 1,550), choice B uses 1,550 instead of 1,800 as the y-intercept, and choice D is a significant overestimate.

7. **The correct answer is D.** The area of the glass coffee top without considering the border is (50)(30) = 1,500 square inches. The area of the portion of the coffee top that will appear as glass once the border is affixed to the top is $(50 - 2x)(30 - 2x) = 1,500 - 160x + 4x^2$ square inches.

So, the area of the border itself is the difference of these two expressions:

$$1,500 - (1,500 - 160x + 4x^2) = 160x - 4x^2 \text{ square inches.}$$

Finally, set this expression equal to 20 to get the equation $160x - 4x^2 = 20$. In choice A, you mistakenly set the left side of the equation as the area of the glass remaining after the border is affixed; in choice B, you wrote the area incorrectly on the right side; in choice C, you set an expression on the left side that is not an area.

8. **The correct answer is B.** Observe that $\frac{8.805 - 8.670}{8.670} \approx 0.01557$, or about 1.56 percent. In choice A, you did not divide by the smaller of the two clock rates; in choice C, you did not divide by the correct clock rate; and in choice D, you converted the decimal to a percent incorrectly.

9. **The correct answer is B.** Let x be the length and y be the width. The perimeter of the orchard is described by the equation $2x + 2y = 1,500$, and the given relationship between the length and width is described by the equation $x = 4 + 3y$. This gives the system in choice B. Choice A has a sign error in the second equation, choice C has the perimeter formula wrong, and choice D has the 3 and 4 in the second equation interchanged.

10. **The correct answer is C.** Multiply both sides of the equation by the LCD $(x + 4)(x - 4)$, and then solve the resulting quadratic equation using the quadratic formula:

$$\frac{2x}{x + 4} - \frac{2x}{x - 4} = 1$$

$$(x + 4)(x - 4) \cdot \left(\frac{2x}{x + 4} - \frac{2x}{x - 4} \right) = (x + 4)(x - 4) \cdot 1$$

$$2x(x - 4) - 2x(x + 4) = (x + 4)(x - 4)$$

$$2x^2 - 8x - 2x^2 - 8x = x^2 - 16$$

$$-16x = x^2 - 16$$

$$x^2 - 16x - 16 = 0$$

$$x = \frac{-16 + \sqrt{(-16)^2 - 4(1)(-16)}}{2(1)}$$

$$= \frac{-16 \pm \sqrt{320}}{2} = \frac{-16 \pm 8\sqrt{5}}{2} = -8 \pm 4\sqrt{5}$$

In choice A, you used an incorrect radicand in the quadratic formula. Choice B is the list of restrictions for the equation, and choice D is the result of missing the constant term in the standard form of the quadratic equation.

11. **The correct answer is B.** The equation of the vertical, dashed line is $x = 4$. Since the line is dashed and the region lies to its right, the corresponding inequality is $x > 4$. As for the solid, diagonal line, the y-intercept is 0. Since $(4, 8)$ is on the line, the slope is $\frac{8 - 0}{4 - 0} = 2$. So, its equation is $y = 2x$. Since the line is solid and the region is above it, the corresponding inequality is $y \geq 2x$. Thus, the system to which the region is the solution set is given by choice B. Choice A uses the wrong slope in the first inequality, choice C needs to have both inequality signs reversed, and choice D needs to have the inequality signs in both inequalities interchanged.

12. **The correct answer is A.** First, multiply both sides by 10 to clear the decimals. Then, proceed as you would when solving a linear equation:

$$1.5 - 2.5(2 - 3x) \geq 1.5x - 2$$
$$15 - 25(2 - 3x) \geq 15x - 20$$
$$15 - 50 + 75x \geq 15x - 20$$
$$60x \geq 15$$
$$x \geq \frac{15}{60} = 0.25$$

In choice B, you incorrectly applied the distributive property. Choices C and D are the result of arithmetic or algebraic errors.

13. **The correct answer is C.** You must determine an equation for the function $y = f(t)$ that describes the number of gallons, y, in the tank at time t (in seconds). Since 2 minutes = 120 seconds, we know that the two points (50, 900) and (120, 760) are on its graph. The slope is $\frac{900 - 760}{50 - 120} = \frac{140}{-70} = -2$. Using the point-slope formula with the point (50, 900) yields the equation $y - 900 = -2(t - 50)$, or equivalently $y = -2t + 1,000$. Now, set this equation equal to 50 and solve for t:

$$-2t + 1,000 = 50$$
$$2t = 950$$
$$t = 475 \text{ seconds}$$

Since 1 minutes = 60 seconds, convert 475 seconds to minutes by dividing by 60. Doing so yields 7 minutes, 55 seconds. In choice A, you used the wrong slope. Choices B and D are the result of sign errors.

14. **The correct answer is A.** Note that $f(x) = x + 55$ and $g(x) = 1.06x$. So, $(f \circ g)(x) = f(g(x)) = (1.06x) + 55$. The delivery fee of $55 is not multiplied by 1.06 in this function, so it is added *after* taxes. Choice B is the function if you want to have the delivery fee taxed, choice C does not produce a dollar amount since the result would have units "square dollars," and choice D would mean the tax rate is 106 percent, not 6 percent.

15. **The correct answer is B.** The following are the number of participants who attend each meeting:

Meeting 1: z

Meeting 2: $\left(\dfrac{p}{100}\right)z$

Meeting 3: $\left(\dfrac{q}{100}\right)\left(\dfrac{p}{100}\right)z$

So, the number who drop out of the study *at some point* is the difference:

$$z - \left(\frac{q}{100}\right)\left(\frac{p}{100}\right)z = z\left[1 - \left(\frac{q}{100}\right)\left(\frac{p}{100}\right)\right]$$

Choice A is the number who completed the study, choice C double-counted the participants who dropped out after the first meeting, and choice D does not express percentages correctly as decimals.

16. **The correct answer is A.** Dolbear's law can be written equivalently as $T = \frac{1}{4}N + 40$. This is a linear function, and the coefficient of N, namely $\frac{1}{4}$, is the slope. In this context, this means, "for every *unit* increase in N, the temperature increases by one-fourth of a degree." This is equivalent to saying, "for every increase in N by 4 chirps per minute, the temperature increases by one degree." Choice B is wrong because $N = 40$ for this temperature; choice C is wrong because the temperature is increasing; and choice D involves the wrong increase in chirps per minute.

17. **The correct answer is C.** The zeros of this particular function are $-8, 1$, and 2, obtained by setting each factor equal to zero and solving for x. Substituting 0 in for x shows that $p(0) = -8$. Since $(x - 2)$ is a factor, note that $\frac{p(x)}{x - 2} = \frac{1}{2}(x + 8)(x - 1)^2$, which is a polynomial. So, the polynomial in choice C satisfies all three characteristics. Choice A violates I and II, choices B and D violate III.

18. **The correct answer is D.** Let x be the driving distance. Then, $x = 404 + 0.535(404) = 620.14$ miles. Convert this quantity to kilometers: $(620.14 \text{ miles}) \times \dfrac{1 \text{ kilometer}}{(0.6214 \text{ miles})} \approx 997.97$ kilometers. In choice A, you used the wrong conversion factor. Choice B is the number of miles, and choice C is the linear distance across the Mediterranean Sea converted to kilometers.

19. **The correct answer is D.** Let x be the number of inches representing the direct, linear distance across the Mediterranean Sea from Tripoli to Benghazi. Set up the following proportion:

$$\frac{1.2 \text{ inches}}{75 \text{ miles}} = \frac{x \text{ inches}}{404 \text{ miles}}$$

Solve for x: $(1.2)(404) = 75x$, so that $x = 6.464$ inches. Now, convert to centimeters: $(6.464 \text{ inches}) \times \dfrac{1 \text{ centimeter}}{(0.3937 \text{ inches})} \approx 16.42$ centimeters.

In choice A, you set up the proportion incorrectly. In choice B, you used the wrong conversion factor, and choice C is the number of inches.

20. **The correct answer is D.** The general formula for $g(x)$ is $g(x) = f(x + 1) - 2$. So,

$$g(x) = \frac{x+1}{(x+1)+3} - 2$$
$$= \frac{x+1}{x+4} - 2$$
$$= \frac{x+1-2(x+4)}{x+4}$$
$$= \frac{-x-7}{x+4}$$
$$= -\frac{x+7}{x+4}$$

Choice A is shifted right one unit, not left one unit; choice B is shifted up 2 units, not down 2 units; choice C is shifted right one unit and up two units.

21. **The correct answer is D.** Convert the units as follows:

$$\frac{112 \text{ kilometers}}{1 \text{ hour}} \times \frac{1 \text{ hour}}{60 \text{ minutes}}$$
$$\times \frac{1 \text{ meter}}{0.001 \text{ kilometer}} = \frac{112}{60(0.001)} \text{ meters}\big/\text{minute}$$

Simplify as follows:
$$\frac{112}{60(0.001)} = \frac{112}{60 \cdot \frac{1}{1000}} = \frac{112 \cdot 100}{6}$$
$$\approx 1,866.67 \text{ meters}\big/\text{minute}$$

In choice A, you used the incorrect number of minutes in an hour. In choice B, you applied the conversion factor backwards. In choice C, you used the incorrect number of meters in a kilometer.

22. **The correct answer is C.** Let x be the number of Fragile boxes and y the number of X-Large Bulk boxes. The price inequality is $8x + 16y \le 800$, and the inequality arising from the fact that they need at least thirty Fragile boxes is $x \ge 30$. So, the system of linear inequalities is $\begin{cases} 8x + 16y \le 800 \\ x \ge 30 \end{cases}$,

which is equivalent to $\begin{cases} y \le -\frac{1}{2}x + 50 \\ x \ge 30 \end{cases}$.

To obtain the solution, sketch both lines as solid lines, shade to the right of the vertical line and beneath the diagonal one. This is shown in the region in choice C. In choice A, you graphed the diagonal line incorrectly (it should be decreasing) and shaded to the left of the vertical line. In choice B, you also shaded to the left of the vertical line. In choice D, you graphed $y = 30$ instead of $x = 30$.

23. The correct answer is B. Statement I is false. For example, if the data set were given by 60, 60, 75, 75, 79, 80, 82, 84, 85, 90, 90, the range is 30 before deleting the lowest and highest values (60 and 90), and the range remains the same after the deletion because there were two occurrences of both of those values in the data set. Statement II is true because the median of the original data set of eleven values is the value in the sixth position of the ordered data set. If you remove one value from each end, the low end and high end, the median of the resulting data set of nine values is in the fifth position. This value is the same as the one prior to deletion since one value was removed *from each side* of the median rather from the same side.

24. The correct answer is C. Solve the first equation for y: $y = 3x - 1$. Substitute this expression into the second equation to get the equation $6x + 2(3x - 1) = -1$. In choice A, you used elimination by multiplying the first equation by 2 and adding them. In choice B, you used elimination by multiplying the first equation by -2 and adding them. Choice D is the result of just adding the equations.

25. The correct answer is B. Add the heights of the bars and divide that sum by 10:

$$\frac{9 + 3 + 3 + 6 + 0 + 9 + 3 + 12 + 3 + 6}{10} = 5.4$$

Choice A is the median; choice C is the result of dividing the sum by 9 (likely because you incorrectly discarded 0 as a data value); and choice D is the result of computing a weighted mean.

26. The correct answer is B. Since z represents the yearly sales and $S(z)$ represents the annual salary, $S(75,000) = 45,750$ means that if the salesperson makes \$75,000 in sales, the annual salary will be \$45,750. The other choices misinterpreted the meaning of the input variable in various ways.

27. The correct answer is B. Use the distributive property and then combine like terms, as follows: $-3(2 - x - 2x^2) + 4(x - 2x^2) = -6 + 3x + 6x^2 + 4x - 8x^2 = -2x^2 + 7x - 6$.

Choice A is the negative of the correct answer, choice C is the result of subtracting the expressions instead of adding them, and in choice D, you did not use the distributive property correctly.

28. The correct answer is 676π cubic inches. First, note that $R = 8$ inches, $h = 12$ inches, and $r = 7$ inches. The value of r follows from the circumference formula: $2\pi r = 14\pi$, so that $r = 7$ inches. Use the volume formula $V = \frac{\pi h}{3}(R^2 + Rr + r^2)$ with these values to obtain $V = \frac{\pi(12)}{3}\left(8^2 + 8 \cdot 7 + 7^2\right) = 676\pi$ cubic inches.

29. The correct answer is 14.4 square yards per person. If the population is doubled, there would be 3,560,296 people in the city. The density of square mileage of the city to the number of people equals $D = \dfrac{16.55 \text{ square miles}}{3,560,296 \text{ people}} \approx 0.00000465$ square miles per person. Convert to square yards:

$$\frac{0.00000465 \text{ mile}^2}{1 \text{ person}} \times \frac{3,097,600 \text{ yards}^2}{1 \text{ square mile}}$$

≈ 14.4 square yards per person

30. **The correct answer is 102°F.** First, you must determine the equation. The slope is $\frac{1.2 - 2.1}{78 - 60} = \frac{-0.9}{18} = -\frac{1}{20}$. Using the point-slope formula with the point $(78, 1.2)$ yields the equation $W - 1.2 = -\frac{1}{20}(T - 78)$, or equivalently, $W = -\frac{1}{20}T + 5.1$, where T is the temperature in degrees Fahrenheit and W is the width of the gap (in inches). Now, solve this equation with the width, W, equal to zero:

$$0 = -\frac{1}{20}T + 5.1$$
$$-5.1 = -\frac{1}{20}T$$
$$102 = T$$

31. **The correct answer is 131 dollars.** Substitute the given values into the formula and solve for s:

$$Q = \sqrt{\frac{2 \cdot C \cdot p}{s}}$$
$$35 = \sqrt{\frac{2 \cdot 4,000 \cdot 20}{s}}$$
$$35^2 = \frac{160,000}{s}$$
$$1,225s = 160,000$$
$$s \approx 130.6 \approx 131$$

USING YOUR PRACTICE TEST RESULTS

Now that you've completed the first PSAT/NMSQT® exam practice test, it›s time to compute your scores. Simply follow the instructions on the following pages, and use the conversion tables provided to calculate your scores. The formulas provided will give you as close an approximation as possible on how you might score on the actual exam.

To Determine Your Test Score

1. After you go through each of the test sections (**Reading, Writing and Language, Math—No Calculator**, and **Math—Calculator**) and determine which answers you got right, be sure to enter the number of correct answers in the box below the answer key for each of the sections.

2. Your total score on this test is the sum of your Evidence-Based Reading and Writing Section score and your Math Section score. To get your total score for each test section, convert the raw score—the number of questions you got right in a particular section—into the "scaled score" for that section, and then calculate the total score. It may sound a little confusing, but we'll take you through the steps.

To Calculate Your Evidence-Based Reading and Writing Section Score

Your Evidence-Based Reading and Writing Section score is on a scale of 160–760. First determine your Reading Test score, and then determine your score on the Writing and Language Test.

1. Count the number of correct answers you got on the **Reading Test Section**. *Remember that there is no penalty for wrong answers.* **The number of correct answers is your raw score.**

2. Go to **Raw Score Conversion Table 1: Section and Test Scores** on page 459. Look in the "Raw Score" column for your raw score, and match it to the number in the "Reading Test Score" column.

3. Do the same with the **Writing and Language Test Section** to determine that score.

4. Add your **Reading Test score** to your **Writing and Language Test score**.

5. Multiply that number by 10. This is your **Evidence-Based Reading and Writing Section score.**

To Calculate Your Math Section Score

Your Math score is also on a scale of 160–760.

1. Count the number of correct answers you got on the **Math Test—No Calculator Section** and the **Math Test—Calculator Section**. *Again, there is no penalty for wrong answers.* **The number of correct answers is your raw score.**

2. Add the number of correct answers on the **Math Test—No Calculator Section** and the **Math Test—Calculator Section**.

3. Use the **Raw Score Conversion Table 1: Section and Test Scores** on page 459 and convert your raw score into your **Math Section score.**

To Obtain Your Total Score

Add your score on the **Evidence-Based Reading and Writing Section** to the **Math Section** score. This is your **Total Score** on this test, on a scale of 320–1520.

SUBSCORES, TEST SCORES, AND CROSS-TEST SCORES

Test scores, subscores, and cross-test scores offer you greater details about your strengths and weaknesses in certain areas within reading, writing, and math, which can help you evaluate your current skill set and determine which areas you need to focus on most to make improvements. Your scores on the PSAT/NMSQT® exam can also be used to help you predict—and further prepare for—the SAT® exam.

PSAT/NMSQT® Subscores

Subscores on the official PSAT/NMSQT® exam are designed to reflect your performance in a range of key skill areas. You should use your scores to help guide your future study following the exam, and to help guide your preparation for the SAT® exam. Subscores range from 1–15, and include the following areas: Heart of Algebra, Problem Solving and Data Analysis, Passport to Advanced Math, Expression of Ideas, Standard English Conventions, Words in Context, and Command of Evidence.

Computing Your Test Subscores

Heart of Algebra

The **Heart of Algebra subscore** is based on questions from the **Math Test** that focus on linear equations and inequalities. Add up your total correct answers from these questions:

- o Math Test—No Calculator: Questions 1, 11, 15, 16
- o Math Test—Calculator: Questions 1, 5, 9, 11-13, 15, 16, 18, 22, 24, 26

Your Raw Score = the total number of correct answers from all of these questions.

Use the **Raw Score Conversion Table 2: Subscores** on page 461 to determine your **Heart of Algebra** subscore.

Problem Solving and Data Analysis

The **Problem Solving and Data Analysis subscore** is based on questions from the **Math Test** that focus on quantitative reasoning, the interpretation and synthesis of data, and solving problems in rich and varied contexts. Add up your total correct answers from these questions:

- • Math Test—No Calculator: Questions 5, 6, 9, 12-14, 17
- • Math Test—Calculator: Questions 3, 4, 8, 19, 21, 23, 25, 29, 30

Your Raw Score = the total number of correct answers from all of these questions

Use the **Raw Score Conversion Table 2: Subscores** on page 461 to determine your **Problem Solving and Data Analysis** subscore.

Passport to Advanced Math

The **Passport to Advanced Math subscore** is based on questions from the **Math Test** that focus on topics central to your ability to progress to more advanced math, such as understanding the structure of expressions, reasoning with more complex equations, and interpreting and building functions. Add up your total correct answers from these questions:

- Math Test—No Calculator: Questions 3, 4, 7, 8, 10
- Math Test—Calculator: Questions 2, 6, 7, 10, 14, 17, 20, 27, 31

Your Raw Score = the total number of correct answers from all of these questions

Use the **Raw Score Conversion Table 2: Subscores** on page 461 to determine your **Passport to Advanced Math** subscore.

Expression of Ideas

The **Expression of Ideas subscore** is based on questions from the **Writing and Language Test** that focus on topic development, organization, and rhetorically effective use of language. Add up your total correct answers from these questions in Section 2: Writing and Language Test:

Questions 4, 6, 7, 9-13, 16-19, 23, 26, 27, 29, 30, 33-36, 39-41

Your Raw Score = the total number of correct answers from all of these questions.

Use the **Raw Score Conversion Table 2: Subscores** on page 461 to determine your **Expression of Ideas** subscore.

Standard English Conventions

The **Standard English Conventions subscore** is based on questions from the **Writing and Language Test** that focus on sentence structure, usage, and punctuation. Add up your total correct answers from these questions in Section 2: Writing and Language Test:

- Questions 1-3, 5, 8, 14, 15, 20-22, 24, 25, 28, 31, 32, 37, 38, 42-44

Your Raw Score = the total number of correct answers from all of these questions.

Use the **Raw Score Conversion Table 2: Subscores** on page 461 to determine your **Standard English Conventions** subscore.

Words in Context

The **Words in Context subscore** is based on questions from the **Reading Test** and the **Writing and Language Test** that address word/phrase meaning in context and rhetorical word choice. Add up your total correct answers from these questions in the following sections:

- Reading Test: Questions 6, 9, 12, 18, 24, 26, 29, 35, 40, 43
- Writing and Language Test: Questions 9, 10, 18, 19, 27, 33, 34, 40

Your Raw Score = the total number of correct answers from all of these questions

Use the **Raw Score Conversion Table 2: Subscores** on page 461 to determine your **Words in Context** subscore.

Command of Evidence

The **Command of Evidence subscore** is based on questions from the **Reading Test** and the **Writing and Language** Test that ask you to interpret and use evidence found in a wide range of passages and informational graphics, such as graphs, tables, and charts. Add up your total correct answers from these questions in Sections 1 and 2:

- Reading Test: Questions 2, 4, 11, 14, 21, 23, 31, 33, 39, 42
- Writing and Language Test: Questions: 4, 6, 11, 16, 26, 29, 36, 39

Your Raw Score = the total number of correct answers from all of these questions

Use the **Raw Score Conversion Table 2: Subscores** on page 461 to determine your **Command of Evidence** subscore.

PSAT/NMSQT® Test and Cross-test Scores

When you take the official PSAT/NMSQT® exam, you'll receive three additional test scores (alongside your total score and section scores) on a range of 8–38. These test scores are designed to show how you performed on the content covered in each of the test sections: Reading, Writing and Language, and Math.

You'll also receive two cross-test scores on the official PSAT/NMSQT® test, which will reflect your performance in the following content domains (which span all test sections): **Analysis in History/Social Studies**, and **Analysis in Science**. These scores will also be in the range of 8–38, and will help you further analyze your current skill level.

Computing Your Cross-Test Scores

Use the following to determine your cross-test scores for this test:

Analysis in History/Social Studies

Add up your total correct answers from these questions:

- Reading Test: Questions 10-19, 29-37
- Writing and Language Test: Questions 23, 26, 27, 29, 30, 33
- Math Test—No Calculator: Questions 5, 6
- Math Test—Calculator: Questions 5, 15, 18, 19, 23

Your Raw Score = the total number of correct answers from all of these questions.

Use the **Raw Score Conversion Table 3: Cross-Test Scores** on page 463 to determine your **Analysis in History/Social Studies** cross-test score.

Analysis in Science

Add up your total correct answers from these sections:

- Reading Test: Questions 20-28, 38-47
- Writing and Language Test: Questions 4, 6, 7, 9-11

- • Math Test—No Calculator: Questions 2, 7, 11, 14, 15, 17
- • Math Test—Calculator: Question 8

Your Raw Score = the total number of correct answers from all of these questions

Use the **Raw Score Conversion Table 3: Cross-Test Scores** on page 463 to determine your **Analysis in Science** cross-test score.

Raw Score Conversion Table 1: Section and Test Scores

Raw Score (# of correct answers)	Reading Test Score	Writing and Language Test Score	Math Section Score	Raw Score (# of correct answers)	Reading Test Score	Writing and Language Test Score	Math Section Score
0	8	8	160	25	26	25	560
1	9	9	190	26	26	26	570
2	10	10	210	27	27	27	580
3	11	11	240	28	27	27	580
4	12	12	270	29	28	28	590
5	14	13	290	30	28	28	600
6	15	14	320	31	29	29	610
7	16	14	340	32	29	29	620
8	16	15	360	33	30	30	630
9	17	15	370	34	30	30	640
10	18	16	390	35	31	31	650
11	18	16	400	36	31	32	670
12	19	17	420	37	32	32	680
13	19	18	430	38	32	33	690
14	20	18	440	39	33	34	710
15	20	19	460	40	34	35	720
16	21	20	470	41	34	36	730
17	21	20	480	42	35	37	730
18	22	21	490	43	36	37	740
19	22	21	500	44	37	38	740
20	23	22	510	45	37		750
21	23	23	520	46	38		750
22	24	24	530	47	38		760
23	24	24	540	48			760
24	25	25	550				

Conversion Equation 1: Section and Test Scores

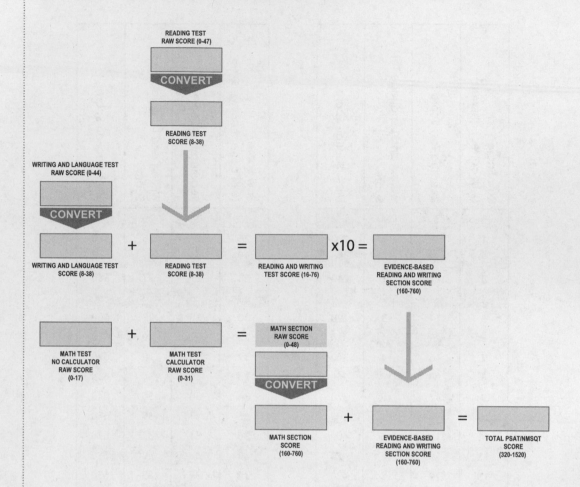

Raw Score Conversion Table 2: Subscores

Raw Score (# of correct answers)	Heart of Algebra	Problem Solving and Data Analysis	Passport to Advanced Math	Expression of Ideas	Standard English Conventions	Words in Context	Command of Evidence
0	1	1	1	1	1	1	1
1	3	3	5	2	2	2	2
2	4	4	7	3	3	3	3
3	5	5	8	4	3	3	4
4	6	6	9	4	4	4	5
5	7	7	10	5	4	5	6
6	8	8	11	6	5	6	7
7	8	8	12	6	6	6	8
8	9	9	13	7	6	7	8
9	10	10	14	7	7	8	9
10	10	11	15	8	7	9	9
11	11	11	15	8	8	10	10
12	12	12	15	9	8	10	11
13	13	13	15	9	9	11	11
14	14	14	15	10	9	12	12
15	15	15		10	10	13	13
16	15	15		11	10	14	14
17				12	11	15	15
18				12	12	15	15
19				13	13		
20				13	15		
21				14			
22				15			
23				15			
24				15			

Conversion Equation 2: Subscores

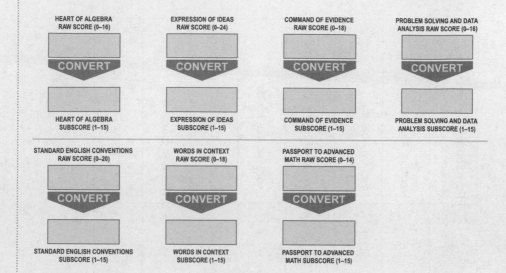

Raw Score Conversion Table 3: Cross-Test Scores

Raw Score (# of correct answers)	Analysis in History/Social Studies Cross-Test Score	Analysis in Science Cross-Test Score
0	8	8
1	9	12
2	11	15
3	12	16
4	14	17
5	15	18
6	16	18
7	17	19
8	18	20
9	19	21
10	20	22
11	21	23
12	22	24
13	23	25
14	24	26
15	25	26
16	26	27

Raw Score (# of correct answers)	Analysis in History/Social Studies Cross-Test Score	Analysis in Science Cross-Test Score
17	26	28
18	27	28
19	28	29
20	29	30
21	30	31
22	30	31
23	31	32
24	32	33
25	32	34
26	33	35
27	34	36
28	35	37
29	36	37
30	37	38
31	37	38
32	38	38

Conversion Equation 3: Cross-Test Scores

	ANALYSIS IN HISTORY/SOCIAL STUDIES		ANALYSIS IN SCIENCE	
TEST	QUESTIONS	RAW SCORE	QUESTIONS	RAW SCORE
Reading Test	10-19; 29-37		20-28; 38-47	
Writing and Language Test	23, 26, 27, 29, 30, 33		4, 6, 7, 9-11	
Math Test—No Calculator	5, 6		2, 7, 11, 14, 15, 17	
Math Test—Calculator	5, 15, 18, 19, 23		8	
TOTAL				

ANALYSIS IN HISTORY/
SOCIAL STUDIES
RAW SCORE (0–32)

CONVERT

ANALYSIS IN HISTORY/
SOCIAL STUDIES
CROSS-TEST SCORE (8-38)

ANALYSIS IN SCIENCE
RAW SCORE (0–32)

CONVERT

ANALYSIS IN SCIENCE
CROSS-TEST SCORE (8-38)

Practice Test 2

INTRODUCTION TO THE PRACTICE TEST

On test day, you will see these important reminders on the first page of your exam booklet:

- You must use a No. 2 pencil when taking the test; you may not use a pen or mechanical pencil.

- You may not share any questions with anyone. Doing so could cause your scores to be canceled.

- You are not permitted to take the test booklet out of the testing room.

The general directions for the test will look something like this:

- You may only work on one section at a time.

- If you complete a section before time is called, check your work on that section only. You are not permitted to work on any other section.

The directions for marking your answers will likely include the following recommendations:

- Mark your answer sheet properly—be sure to completely fill in the answer circle.

- Be careful to mark only one answer for each question.

- Don't make any stray marks on the answer sheet.

- If you need to erase your answer, make sure you do so completely.

- Be sure to use the answer spaces that correspond to the question numbers.

You will be able to use your test booklet for scratch work, but you won't get credit for any work done in your test booklet. When time is called at the end of each section, you will not be permitted to transfer answers from your test booklet to your answer sheet.

Scoring on the exam is as follows:

- You will receive one point for each correct answer.

- You will not lose points for wrong answers, so you should attempt to answer every question even if you aren't completely sure of the correct answer.

Your testing supervisor will announce when to open the test booklet, so be sure to wait until you're told to do so. For the purposes of this practice test, be sure you have a timer to set for 60 minutes for the Section 1: Reading Test.

The answer sheets for each test section appear on the next pages.

Following the Answer Key and Explanations section, you will find details on how to score your exam.

Any information, ideas, or opinions presented in any of the passages you will see on the exam that have been taken from other sources or published material do not represent the opinions of the College Board.

PSAT/NMSQT® EXAM ANSWER SHEET

Section 1: Reading Test

1. Ⓐ Ⓑ Ⓒ Ⓓ   11. Ⓐ Ⓑ Ⓒ Ⓓ   21. Ⓐ Ⓑ Ⓒ Ⓓ   30. Ⓐ Ⓑ Ⓒ Ⓓ   39. Ⓐ Ⓑ Ⓒ Ⓓ
2. Ⓐ Ⓑ Ⓒ Ⓓ   12. Ⓐ Ⓑ Ⓒ Ⓓ   22. Ⓐ Ⓑ Ⓒ Ⓓ   31. Ⓐ Ⓑ Ⓒ Ⓓ   40. Ⓐ Ⓑ Ⓒ Ⓓ
3. Ⓐ Ⓑ Ⓒ Ⓓ   13. Ⓐ Ⓑ Ⓒ Ⓓ   23. Ⓐ Ⓑ Ⓒ Ⓓ   32. Ⓐ Ⓑ Ⓒ Ⓓ   41. Ⓐ Ⓑ Ⓒ Ⓓ
4. Ⓐ Ⓑ Ⓒ Ⓓ   14. Ⓐ Ⓑ Ⓒ Ⓓ   24. Ⓐ Ⓑ Ⓒ Ⓓ   33. Ⓐ Ⓑ Ⓒ Ⓓ   42. Ⓐ Ⓑ Ⓒ Ⓓ
5. Ⓐ Ⓑ Ⓒ Ⓓ   15. Ⓐ Ⓑ Ⓒ Ⓓ   25. Ⓐ Ⓑ Ⓒ Ⓓ   34. Ⓐ Ⓑ Ⓒ Ⓓ   43. Ⓐ Ⓑ Ⓒ Ⓓ
6. Ⓐ Ⓑ Ⓒ Ⓓ   16. Ⓐ Ⓑ Ⓒ Ⓓ   26. Ⓐ Ⓑ Ⓒ Ⓓ   35. Ⓐ Ⓑ Ⓒ Ⓓ   44. Ⓐ Ⓑ Ⓒ Ⓓ
7. Ⓐ Ⓑ Ⓒ Ⓓ   17. Ⓐ Ⓑ Ⓒ Ⓓ   27. Ⓐ Ⓑ Ⓒ Ⓓ   36. Ⓐ Ⓑ Ⓒ Ⓓ   45. Ⓐ Ⓑ Ⓒ Ⓓ
8. Ⓐ Ⓑ Ⓒ Ⓓ   18. Ⓐ Ⓑ Ⓒ Ⓓ   28. Ⓐ Ⓑ Ⓒ Ⓓ   37. Ⓐ Ⓑ Ⓒ Ⓓ   46. Ⓐ Ⓑ Ⓒ Ⓓ
9. Ⓐ Ⓑ Ⓒ Ⓓ   19. Ⓐ Ⓑ Ⓒ Ⓓ   29. Ⓐ Ⓑ Ⓒ Ⓓ   38. Ⓐ Ⓑ Ⓒ Ⓓ   47. Ⓐ Ⓑ Ⓒ Ⓓ
10. Ⓐ Ⓑ Ⓒ Ⓓ   20. Ⓐ Ⓑ Ⓒ Ⓓ

Section 2: Writing and Language Test

1. Ⓐ Ⓑ Ⓒ Ⓓ   10. Ⓐ Ⓑ Ⓒ Ⓓ   19. Ⓐ Ⓑ Ⓒ Ⓓ   28. Ⓐ Ⓑ Ⓒ Ⓓ   37. Ⓐ Ⓑ Ⓒ Ⓓ
2. Ⓐ Ⓑ Ⓒ Ⓓ   11. Ⓐ Ⓑ Ⓒ Ⓓ   20. Ⓐ Ⓑ Ⓒ Ⓓ   29. Ⓐ Ⓑ Ⓒ Ⓓ   38. Ⓐ Ⓑ Ⓒ Ⓓ
3. Ⓐ Ⓑ Ⓒ Ⓓ   12. Ⓐ Ⓑ Ⓒ Ⓓ   21. Ⓐ Ⓑ Ⓒ Ⓓ   30. Ⓐ Ⓑ Ⓒ Ⓓ   39. Ⓐ Ⓑ Ⓒ Ⓓ
4. Ⓐ Ⓑ Ⓒ Ⓓ   13. Ⓐ Ⓑ Ⓒ Ⓓ   22. Ⓐ Ⓑ Ⓒ Ⓓ   31. Ⓐ Ⓑ Ⓒ Ⓓ   40. Ⓐ Ⓑ Ⓒ Ⓓ
5. Ⓐ Ⓑ Ⓒ Ⓓ   14. Ⓐ Ⓑ Ⓒ Ⓓ   23. Ⓐ Ⓑ Ⓒ Ⓓ   32. Ⓐ Ⓑ Ⓒ Ⓓ   41. Ⓐ Ⓑ Ⓒ Ⓓ
6. Ⓐ Ⓑ Ⓒ Ⓓ   15. Ⓐ Ⓑ Ⓒ Ⓓ   24. Ⓐ Ⓑ Ⓒ Ⓓ   33. Ⓐ Ⓑ Ⓒ Ⓓ   42. Ⓐ Ⓑ Ⓒ Ⓓ
7. Ⓐ Ⓑ Ⓒ Ⓓ   16. Ⓐ Ⓑ Ⓒ Ⓓ   25. Ⓐ Ⓑ Ⓒ Ⓓ   34. Ⓐ Ⓑ Ⓒ Ⓓ   43. Ⓐ Ⓑ Ⓒ Ⓓ
8. Ⓐ Ⓑ Ⓒ Ⓓ   17. Ⓐ Ⓑ Ⓒ Ⓓ   26. Ⓐ Ⓑ Ⓒ Ⓓ   35. Ⓐ Ⓑ Ⓒ Ⓓ   44. Ⓐ Ⓑ Ⓒ Ⓓ
9. Ⓐ Ⓑ Ⓒ Ⓓ   18. Ⓐ Ⓑ Ⓒ Ⓓ   27. Ⓐ Ⓑ Ⓒ Ⓓ   36. Ⓐ Ⓑ Ⓒ Ⓓ

Section 3: Math Test—No Calculator

1. Ⓐ Ⓑ Ⓒ Ⓓ   4. Ⓐ Ⓑ Ⓒ Ⓓ   7. Ⓐ Ⓑ Ⓒ Ⓓ   10. Ⓐ Ⓑ Ⓒ Ⓓ   12. Ⓐ Ⓑ Ⓒ Ⓓ
2. Ⓐ Ⓑ Ⓒ Ⓓ   5. Ⓐ Ⓑ Ⓒ Ⓓ   8. Ⓐ Ⓑ Ⓒ Ⓓ   11. Ⓐ Ⓑ Ⓒ Ⓓ   13. Ⓐ Ⓑ Ⓒ Ⓓ
3. Ⓐ Ⓑ Ⓒ Ⓓ   6. Ⓐ Ⓑ Ⓒ Ⓓ   9. Ⓐ Ⓑ Ⓒ Ⓓ

answer sheet

Section 3: Math Test—No Calculator

14.

15.

16.

17.

Section 4: Math Test—Calculator

1. Ⓐ Ⓑ Ⓒ Ⓓ
2. Ⓐ Ⓑ Ⓒ Ⓓ
3. Ⓐ Ⓑ Ⓒ Ⓓ
4. Ⓐ Ⓑ Ⓒ Ⓓ
5. Ⓐ Ⓑ Ⓒ Ⓓ
6. Ⓐ Ⓑ Ⓒ Ⓓ

7. Ⓐ Ⓑ Ⓒ Ⓓ
8. Ⓐ Ⓑ Ⓒ Ⓓ
9. Ⓐ Ⓑ Ⓒ Ⓓ
10. Ⓐ Ⓑ Ⓒ Ⓓ
11. Ⓐ Ⓑ Ⓒ Ⓓ
12. Ⓐ Ⓑ Ⓒ Ⓓ

13. Ⓐ Ⓑ Ⓒ Ⓓ
14. Ⓐ Ⓑ Ⓒ Ⓓ
15. Ⓐ Ⓑ Ⓒ Ⓓ
16. Ⓐ Ⓑ Ⓒ Ⓓ
17. Ⓐ Ⓑ Ⓒ Ⓓ

18. Ⓐ Ⓑ Ⓒ Ⓓ
19. Ⓐ Ⓑ Ⓒ Ⓓ
20. Ⓐ Ⓑ Ⓒ Ⓓ
21. Ⓐ Ⓑ Ⓒ Ⓓ
22. Ⓐ Ⓑ Ⓒ Ⓓ

23. Ⓐ Ⓑ Ⓒ Ⓓ
24. Ⓐ Ⓑ Ⓒ Ⓓ
25. Ⓐ Ⓑ Ⓒ Ⓓ
26. Ⓐ Ⓑ Ⓒ Ⓓ
27. Ⓐ Ⓑ Ⓒ Ⓓ

28.

29.

30.

31.

SECTION 1: READING TEST

60 Minutes • 47 Questions

Turn to Section 1 of your answer sheet to answer the questions in this section.

> **Directions:** Each passage or pair of passages below is followed by a number of questions. After reading each passage or pair, choose the best answer to each question based on what is stated or implied in the passage or passages and in any accompanying graphics (such as a table or graph).

Questions 1–9 are based on the following passage.

This passage is adapted from Flatland *by Edward A. Abbott, originally published in 1884.*

I call our world Flatland, not because we call it so, but to make its nature clearer to you, my happy readers, who are privileged to live in Space.

Imagine a vast sheet of paper on which straight Lines, Triangles, Squares, Pentagons,
Line Hexagons, and other figures, instead of remaining fixed in their places, move freely about, on
5 or in the surface, but without the power of rising above or sinking below it, very much like shadows—only hard with luminous edges—and you will then have a pretty correct notion of my country and countrymen. Alas, a few years ago, I should have said "my universe:" but now my mind has been opened to higher views of things.

In such a country, you will perceive at once that it is impossible that there should be
10 anything of what you call a "solid" kind; but I dare say you will suppose that we could at least distinguish by sight the Triangles, Squares, and other figures, moving about as I have described them. On the contrary, we could see nothing of the kind, not at least so as to distinguish one figure from another. Nothing was visible, nor could be visible, to us, except Straight Lines; and the necessity of this I will speedily demonstrate.

15 Place a penny on the middle of one of your tables in Space; and leaning over it, look down upon it. It will appear a circle.

But now, drawing back to the edge of the table, gradually lower your eye (thus bringing yourself more and more into the condition of the inhabitants of Flatland), and you will find the penny becoming more and more oval to your view, and at last when you have placed your
20 eye exactly on the edge of the table (so that you are, as it were, actually a Flatlander) the penny will then have ceased to appear oval at all, and will have become, so far as you can see, a straight line...

When I was in Spaceland I heard that your sailors have very similar experiences while they traverse your seas and discern some distant island or coast lying on the horizon. The

25 far-off land may have bays, forelands, angles in and out to any number and extent; yet at a
distance you see none of these (unless indeed your sun shines bright upon them revealing the
projections and retirements by means of light and shade), nothing but a grey unbroken line
upon the water.

Well, that is just what we see when one of our triangular or other acquaintances comes
30 towards us in Flatland. As there is neither sun with us, nor any light of such a kind as to
make shadows, we have none of the helps to the sight that you have in Spaceland. If our
friend comes closer to us we see his line becomes larger; if he leaves us it becomes smaller;
but still he looks like a straight line; be he a Triangle, Square, Pentagon, Hexagon, Circle,
what you will—a straight Line he looks and nothing else.

35 You may perhaps ask how under these disadvantageous circumstances we are able to
distinguish our friends from one another: but the answer to this very natural question will
be more fitly and easily given when I come to describe the inhabitants of Flatland. For the
present let me defer this subject, and say a word or two about the climate and houses in our
country.

40 As with you, so also with us, there are four points of the compass North, South, East,
and West.

There being no sun nor other heavenly bodies, it is impossible for us to determine the
North in the usual way; but we have a method of our own. By a Law of Nature with us, there
is a constant attraction to the South; and, although in temperate climates this is very slight—
45 so that even a Woman in reasonable health can journey several furlongs northward without
much difficulty—yet the hampering effort of the southward attraction is quite sufficient
to serve as a compass in most parts of our earth. Moreover, the rain (which falls at stated
intervals) coming always from the North, is an additional assistance; and in the towns we
have the guidance of the houses, which of course have their side-walls running for the most
50 part North and South, so that the roofs may keep off the rain from the North. In the country,
where there are no houses, the trunks of the trees serve as some sort of guide. Altogether, we
have not so much difficulty as might be expected in determining our bearings.

1. What does the narrator suggest about
life in Spaceland as opposed to life in
Flatland?

   A. Life is more complex in Spaceland
than it is in Flatland.

   B. People who live in Spaceland can
move, but shapes in Flatland cannot.

   C. Living in Spaceland is better than
living in Flatland.

   D. People in Spaceland may travel
freely, but the shapes must remain in
Flatland.

2. Which choice provides the best evidence
for the answer to the previous question?

   A. Lines 1-2 ("I call . . . Space.")

   B. Lines 3-4 ("Imagine . . . figures")

   C. Lines 7-8 ("Alas . . . things.")

   D. Lines 9-10 ("In such . . . kind")

3. The passage characterizes the horizon in Spaceland as similar to the inhabitants in Flatland in that they both

    A. look like islands and coastlines.

    B. are only visible while sailing.

    C. are invisible when seen from afar

    D. appear as straight lines in the distance.

4. As used in line 1, "nature" most nearly means

    A. environment.

    B. temperament.

    C. disposition.

    D. type.

5. In the context of the passage, the main purpose of lines 15-22 ("Place . . . line.") is to

    A. give the reader an interesting experiment to perform.

    B. help the reader comprehend the inhabitants of Flatland.

    C. describe the landscape of Flatland to the reader.

    D. show the reader how to detect differences in shapes.

6. Based on the passage, the inhabitants of Flatland have

    A. arms and legs.

    B. dimensions.

    C. identical appearances.

    D. genders.

7. Which choice provides the best evidence for the answer to the previous question?

    A. Lines 42-43 ("There . . . own.")

    B. Lines 43-44 ("By a Law . . . South")

    C. Lines 45-46 ("so that . . . difficulty")

    D. Lines 46-47 ("yet the . . . earth.")

8. Over the course of the passage, the main focus shifts from

    A. the inhabitants of Flatland to compasses in Flatland.

    B. the landscape of Spaceland to the landscape of Flatland.

    C. the inhabitants of Flatland to the climate and houses in Flatland.

    D. the Triangles who live in Flatland to the Squares who live in Flatland.

9. As used in line 52, "bearings" most nearly means

    A. supports.

    B. directions.

    C. manners.

    D. natures.

Questions 10–18 are based on the following passage and supplementary material.

This passage is adapted from Economic Sophisms, *by Frédéric Bastiat, originally published in 1863.*

Which is best for man, and for society, abundance or scarcity? What! you exclaim, can that be a question? Has any one ever asserted, or is it possible to maintain, that scarcity is at the foundation of human well-being?

Line
5 Yes, this has been asserted, and is maintained every day; and I hesitate not to affirm that the *theory of scarcity* is much the most popular. It is the life of conversation, of the journals, of books, and of the tribune; and strange as it may seem, it is certain that Political Economy will have fulfilled its practical mission when it has established beyond question, and widely disseminated, this very simple proposition: "The wealth of men consists in the abundance of commodities."

10 Do we not hear it said every day, "The foreigner is about to inundate us with his products"? Then we fear abundance.

Did not M. Saint-Cricq exclaim, "There is overproduction"? Then he feared abundance.

Do workmen break machines? Then they fear excess of production, or abundance.

Has not M. Bugeaud pronounced these words, "Let bread be dear, and agriculturists will
15 get rich"? Now, bread cannot be dear but because it is scarce. Therefore M. Bugeaud extols scarcity.

Does not M. d'Argout urge as an argument against sugar-growing the very productiveness of that industry? Does he not say, "Beetroot has no future, and its culture cannot be extended, because a few acres devoted to its culture in each department would
20 supply the whole consumption of France"? Then, in his eyes, good lies in sterility, in dearth, and evil in fertility and abundance.

The *Presse*, the *Commerce*, and the greater part of the daily papers, have one or more articles every morning to demonstrate to the Chambers and the Government, that it is sound policy to raise legislatively the price of all things by means of tariffs. And do the
25 Chambers and the Government not obey the injunction? Now tariffs can raise prices only by diminishing the *supply* of commodities in the market! Then the journals, the Chambers, and the Minister, put in practice the theory of scarcity, and I am justified in saying that this theory is by far the most popular.

How does it happen that in the eyes of workmen, of publicists, and statesmen,
30 abundance should appear a thing to be dreaded, and scarcity advantageous? I propose to trace this illusion to its source.

We remark that a man grows richer in proportion to the return yielded by his exertions, that is to say, in proportion as he sells his commodity at a *higher price*. He sells at a higher price in proportion to the rarity, to the scarcity, of the article he produces. We conclude from
35 this, that, as far as he is concerned at least, scarcity enriches him. Applying successively the same reasoning to all other producers, we construct the *theory of scarcity*. We next proceed to apply this theory, and, in order to favor producers generally, we raise prices artificially,

and cause a scarcity of all commodities, by prohibition, by restriction, by the suppression of machinery, and other analogous means.

40 The same thing holds of abundance. We observe that when a product is plentiful, it sells at a lower price, and the producer gains less. If all producers are in the same situation, they are all poor. Therefore it is abundance that ruins society. And as theories are soon reduced to practice, we see the law struggling against the abundance of commodities.

This sophism in its more general form may make little impression, but applied to a
45 particular order of facts, to a certain branch of industry, to a given class, of producers, it is extremely specious; and this is easily explained. It forms a syllogism which is not *false*, but *incomplete*. Now, what is *true* in a syllogism is always and necessarily present to the mind. But *incompleteness* is a negative quality, an absent *datum*, which it is very possible, and indeed very easy, to leave out of account.

50 Man produces in order to consume. He is at once producer and consumer. The reasoning which I have just explained considers him only in the first of these points of view. Had the second been taken into account, it would have led to an opposite conclusion.

Widgets: Supply and Cost

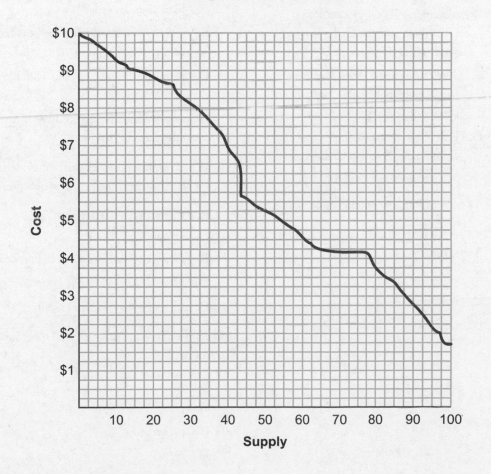

10. Based on the passage, how does the author characterize the idea that abundance is better than scarcity?

    A. An idea with which no one agrees.

    B. A common-sense assumption.

    C. A complete falsehood.

    D. An opinion of the government.

11. Which choice best supports the claim that the daily papers dictate the decisions of the Chambers and the Government?

    A. The daily papers publish articles demonstrating to the Chambers and the Government that it is sound policy to raise prices with tariffs.

    B. After the daily papers argue for placing tariffs on products, the Chambers and the Government place such tariffs on products.

    C. The daily papers, the Chambers, and the Government put in practice the theory of scarcity.

    D. Publicists and statesmen agree that abundance should be dreaded and scarcity is advantageous.

12. As used in line 24, "sound" most nearly means

    A. noise.

    B. sensible.

    C. whole.

    D. unreliable.

13. In the context of the passage, the sentence "Let bread be dear, and agriculturists will get rich"? (lines 14-15) mainly serves to show

    A. support for the value of scarcity over abundance.

    B. how bread can help people to become rich.

    C. why bread was so expensive when this passage was written.

    D. the kind of people who profit from the sales of bread.

14. Based on the passage, the author would most likely agree that

    A. scarcity is better for the economy than abundance is.

    B. scarcity and abundance are of equal value to the economy.

    C. people are wrong to value scarcity over abundance.

    D. scarcity and abundance have little effect on the economy.

15. Which choice provides the best evidence for the answer to the previous question?

    A. Lines 15-18 ("Therefore . . . industry?")

    B. Lines 18-20 ("Does he . . . France?")

    C. Lines 20-28 ("Then . . . popular.")

    D. Lines 29-30 ("How . . . source.")

16. As used in line 50, "consume" most nearly means

    A. eat.

    B. use.

    C. conserve.

    D. spend.

17. Based on the passage, the graph illustrates

    A. the claim that production is excessive.

    B. foreign inundation of products.

    C. the theory of scarcity.

    D. a false syllogism.

18. Based on the passage, the data on the graph best support the opinions of

    A. M. Saint-Cricq.

    B. workmen.

    C. the author.

    D. consumers.

practice test 2—Reading

Questions 19–27 are based on the following passage and supplementary material.

This passage is adapted from Physiology, *by Sir M. Foster, originally published in 1877.*

How is it that we can move about as we do? And first of all let us take one particular movement and see if we can understand that.

For instance, you can bend your arm. You know that when your arm is lying flat on
Line the table, you can, if you like, bend the lower part of your arm (the fore-arm as it is called,
5 reaching from the elbow to the hand) on the upper arm until your fingers touch your shoulder. How do you manage to do that?

Look at the bones of the arm in a skeleton. You will see that in the upper arm there is one rather large bone reaching from the shoulder to the elbow, while in the fore-arm there are two, one being wider and stouter than the other at the elbow, but smaller and more slender at
10 the wrist. The bone in the upper arm is called the **humerus**; the bone in the fore-arm, which is stoutest at the elbow, is called the **ulna**; the one which is stoutest at the wrist is called the **radius**. If you look carefully you will see that the end of the humerus at the elbow is curiously rounded, and the end of the ulna at the elbow curiously scooped out, in such a way that the one fits loosely into the other.

15 If you try to move them about one on the other, you will find that you can easily double the ulna very closely on the humerus without their ends coming apart, and if you notice you will see that as you move the ulna up and down, its end and the end of the humerus slide over each other. But they will only slide one way, what we may call up and down. If you try to slide them from side to side, you will find that they get locked. They have only one movement, like
20 that of a door on its hinge, and that movement is of such a kind as to double the ulna on the humerus.

Moreover, if you look a little more carefully you will find that, though you can easily double the ulna on the front of the humerus, and then pull it back again until the two are in a straight line, you cannot bend the ulna on the back of the humerus. On examining the end
25 of the ulna you will find at the back of it a beak-like projection, which when the bones are straightened out locks into the end of the humerus, and so prevents the ulna being bent any further back. This is the reason why you can only bend your arm one way. As you very well know, you can bend your arm so as to touch the top of your shoulder with your fingers, but you can't bend it the other way so as to touch the back of your shoulder; you can't bring it any
30 further back than the straight line.

Well, then, at the elbow the two bones, the humerus and ulna, are so shaped and so fit into each other that the arm may be straightened or bent. In the skeleton the two bones are quite separate, *i.e.*, they have to be fastened together by something, else they would fall apart. Most probably in the skeleton you have been examining they are fastened together by wires
35 or slips of brass. But they would hold together if you took away the wire or brass slips and bound some tape round the two ends, tight enough to keep them touching each other, but loose enough to allow them to move on each other. You might easily manage it if you took short slips of tape, or, better still, of india-rubber, and placed them all round the elbow, back, front, and sides, fastening one end of each slip to the humerus and the other to the ulna. If

40 you did this you would be imitating very closely the manner in which the bones at the elbow are kept together in your own arm. Only the slips are not made of india-rubber, but are flat bands of that stringy, or as we may now call it fibrous stuff, which in the preceding lessons you learnt to call connective tissue. These flat bands have a special name, and are called **ligaments**.

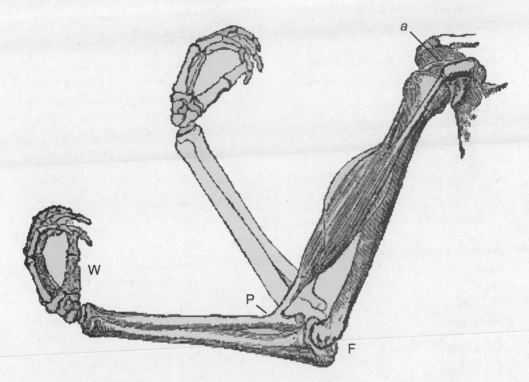

19. The main purpose of the passage is to

   A. explain why humans are able to move in general.

   B. describe each bone in the human arm.

   C. explain how the human arm moves.

   D. define the terms "humerus," "radius," "ulna," and "ligaments."

20. As used in line 12, "curiously" most nearly means

   A. peculiarly.

   B. inquiringly.

   C. inquisitively.

   D. normally.

21. According to the passage, the humerus and ulna are

   A. both bones in the forearm.

   B. not located in the same limb.

   C. not connected rigidly.

   D. both very stout bones.

22. Which choice provides the best evidence for the answer to the previous question?

   A. Line 7 ("Look . . . skeleton.")

   B. Lines 8-10 ("in the fore-arm . . . wrist.")

   C. Lines 10-12 ("The bone . . . radius.")

   D. Lines 12-14 ("If you . . . other.")

23. According to the passage, what is the direct result of moving the ulna?

    A. It slides side to side.

    B. It resembles a hinge.

    C. It slides over the humerus.

    D. It causes the humerus to double.

24. Which choice provides the best evidence for the answer to the previous question?

    A. Lines 15-16 ("If you try . . . apart")

    B. Lines 16-18 ("if you notice . . . other.")

    C. Lines 18-19 ("But they . . . locked.")

    D. Lines 19-21 ("They have . . . humerus.")

25. As used in line 36, "bound" most nearly means

    A. leap.

    B. certain.

    C. compelled.

    D. wrapped.

26. Based on the passage, the lower end of the humerus is marked on the diagram with the letter

    A. a.

    B. F.

    C. P.

    D. W.

27. Which claim from the passage is most directly supported by the diagram?

    A. Line 27 ("This . . . way.")

    B. Lines 17-28 ("as you . . . fingers.")

    C. Line 29 ("you can't . . . shoulder")

    D. Lines 31-32 ("Well . . . bent.")

Questions 28–37 are based on the following passages.

Passage 1 is adapted from President Franklin Delano Roosevelt's first inaugural address, given in 1933. Passage 2 is adapted from President Barack Obama's address before a joint session of the Congress, given in 2009.

Passage 1

Values have shrunken to fantastic levels; taxes have risen; our ability to pay has fallen; government of all kinds is faced by serious curtailment of income; the means of exchange are frozen in the currents of trade; the withered leaves of industrial enterprise lie on every side;
Line farmers find no markets for their produce; the savings of many years in thousands of families
5 are gone.

More important, a host of unemployed citizens face the grim problem of existence, and an equally great number toil with little return. Only a foolish optimist can deny the dark realities of the moment.

Yet our distress comes from no failure of substance. We are stricken by no plague of
10 locusts. Compared with the perils which our forefathers conquered because they believed and were not afraid, we have still much to be thankful for. Nature still offers her bounty and human efforts have multiplied it. Plenty is at our doorstep, but a generous use of it languishes in the very sight of the supply. Primarily this is because rulers of the exchange of mankind's goods have failed through their own stubbornness and their own incompetence, have
15 admitted their failure, and have abdicated. Practices of the unscrupulous money changers stand indicted in the court of public opinion, rejected by the hearts and minds of men.

True they have tried, but their efforts have been cast in the pattern of an outworn tradition. Faced by failure of credit they have proposed only the lending of more money. Stripped of the lure of profit by which to induce our people to follow their false leadership,
20 they have resorted to exhortations, pleading tearfully for restored confidence. They know only the rules of a generation of self-seekers. They have no vision, and when there is no vision the people perish.

The money changers have fled from their high seats in the temple of our civilization. We may now restore that temple to the ancient truths. The measure of the restoration lies in the
25 extent to which we apply social values more noble than mere monetary profit.

Happiness lies not in the mere possession of money; it lies in the joy of achievement, in the thrill of creative effort. The joy and moral stimulation of work no longer must be forgotten in the mad chase of evanescent profits. These dark days will be worth all they cost us if they teach us that our true destiny is not to be ministered unto but to minister to
30 ourselves and to our fellow men.

Passage 2

I know that for many Americans watching right now, the state of our economy is a concern that rises above all others, and rightly so. If you haven't been personally affected by this recession, you probably know someone who has: a friend, a neighbor, a member of your
Line family. You don't need to hear another list of statistics to know that our economy is in crisis,
5 because you live it every day. It's the worry you wake up with and the source of sleepless

nights. It's the job you thought you'd retire from but now have lost, the business you built your dreams upon that's now hanging by a thread, the college acceptance letter your child had to put back in the envelope. The impact of this recession is real, and it is everywhere.

But while our economy may be weakened and our confidence shaken, though we are
10 living through difficult and uncertain times, tonight I want every American to know this: We will rebuild, we will recover, and the United States of America will emerge stronger than before.

The weight of this crisis will not determine the destiny of this Nation. The answers to our problems don't lie beyond our reach. They exist in our laboratories and our universities,
15 in our fields and our factories, in the imaginations of our entrepreneurs and the pride of the hardest working people on Earth. Those qualities that have made America the greatest force of progress and prosperity in human history, we still possess in ample measure. What is required now is for this country to pull together, confront boldly the challenges we face, and take responsibility for our future once more.

20 Now, if we're honest with ourselves, we'll admit that for too long, we have not always met these responsibilities as a Government or as a people. I say this not to lay blame or to look backwards, but because it is only by understanding how we arrived at this moment that we'll be able to lift ourselves out of this predicament.

28. Which choice most closely captures the meaning of the figurative "the withered leaves of industrial enterprise" referred to in line 3?

  A. Industries grow like leaves.

  B. All industries have disappeared.

  C. Industries are plentiful.

  D. Industries are failing.

29. Which choice provides the best evidence for the answer to the previous question?

  A. Line 1 ("Values . . . levels")

  B. Line 2 ("government . . . income")

  C. Lines 2-3 ("the means . . . trade")

  D. Line 4 ("farmers . . . produce")

30. According to Passage 2, the recession has

  A. derailed many people's retirement plans.

  B. affected the neighbors of every American.

  C. stopped colleges from accepting new students.

  D. forced many businesses to declare bankruptcy.

31. Which choice provides the best evidence for the answer to the previous question?

  A. Lines 1-2 ("I know . . . rightly so.")

  B. Lines 2-3 ("If you haven't . . . who has")

  C. Line 6 ("It's the job . . . lost")

  D. Lines 7-8 ("the college . . . envelope.")

32. As used in line 15 of Passage 1, "practices" most nearly means

    A. rehearsals.

    B. applications.

    C. procedures.

    D. customs.

33. As used in line 13 of Passage 2, "weight" most nearly means

    A. mass.

    B. load.

    C. importance.

    D. severity.

34. The primary purpose of each passage is to

    A. condemn the people who caused an economic crisis.

    B. help people through an economic crisis.

    C. ensure people that an economic recession is not permanent.

    D. announce the end of an economic crisis.

35. Both authors would most likely agree with which statement about American citizens?

    A. They need to understand that profit is not the only benefit of working.

    B. They need to be more honest about the economic crises.

    C. They are more powerful than the American government is.

    D. They need to continue to work very hard.

36. A significant difference in how the two presidents discuss the causes of their economic crises indicates that

    A. President Roosevelt is more comfortable placing blame than President Obama is.

    B. President Roosevelt is more encouraging about the end of the economic crisis than President Obama is.

    C. President Obama describes the causes of his economic crisis more specifically than President Roosevelt describes his.

    D. President Obama focuses more on the causes of his economic crisis than President Roosevelt does on his own.

37. Assuming that he agrees with the assertions in the third paragraph of Passage 2, President Roosevelt would most likely recommend which course of action to President Obama?

    A. President Roosevelt would encourage President Obama to publically condemn the people who caused the recession.

    B. President Roosevelt would encourage President Obama to visit laboratories, factories, and universities and emphasize the nonprofit benefits of work.

    C. President Roosevelt would encourage President Obama to not encourage the delusions of foolish optimists.

    D. President Roosevelt would encourage President Obama to work harder to stimulate the farming industry.

practice test 2—Reading

Questions 38–47 are based on the following passage.

This passage is adapted from The New Physics and Its Evolution, *by Lucien Poincaré, originally published in 1907.*

The now numerous public which tries with some success to keep abreast of the movement in science, from seeing its mental habits every day upset, and from occasionally witnessing unexpected discoveries that produce a more lively sensation from their reaction
Line on social life, is led to suppose that we live in a really exceptional epoch, scored by profound
5 crises and illustrated by extraordinary discoveries, whose singularity surpasses everything known in the past. Thus we often hear it said that physics, in particular, has of late years undergone a veritable revolution; that all its principles have been made new, that all the edifices constructed by our fathers have been overthrown, and that on the field thus cleared has sprung up the most abundant harvest that has ever enriched the domain of science.

10 It is in fact true that the crop becomes richer and more fruitful, thanks to the development of our laboratories, and that the quantity of seekers has considerably increased in all countries, while their quality has not diminished. We should be sustaining an absolute paradox, and at the same time committing a crying injustice, were we to contest the high importance of recent progress, and to seek to diminish the glory of contemporary physicists.
15 Yet it may be as well not to give way to exaggerations, however pardonable, and to guard against facile illusions. On closer examination it will be seen that our predecessors might at several periods in history have conceived, as legitimately as ourselves, similar sentiments of scientific pride, and have felt that the world was about to appear to them transformed and under an aspect until then absolutely unknown.

20 Let us take an example which is salient enough; for, however arbitrary the conventional division of time may appear to a physicist's eyes, it is natural, when instituting a comparison between two epochs, to choose those which extend over a space of half a score of years, and are separated from each other by the gap of a century. Let us, then, go back a hundred years and examine what would have been the state of mind of an erudite amateur who had read
25 and understood the chief publications on physical research between 1800 and 1810.

Let us suppose that this intelligent and attentive spectator witnessed in 1800 the discovery of the galvanic battery by Volta. He might from that moment have felt a presentiment that a prodigious transformation was about to occur in our mode of regarding electrical phenomena. Brought up in the ideas of Coulomb and Franklin, he might till
30 then have imagined that electricity had unveiled nearly all its mysteries, when an entirely original apparatus suddenly gave birth to applications of the highest interest, and excited the blossoming of theories of immense philosophical extent.

In the treatises on physics published a little later, we find traces of the astonishment produced by this sudden revelation of a new world. "Electricity," wrote the Abbé Haüy,
35 "enriched by the labour of so many distinguished physicists, seemed to have reached the term when a science has no further important steps before it, and only leaves to those who cultivate it the hope of confirming the discoveries of their predecessors, and of casting a brighter light on the truths revealed. One would have thought that all researches for diversifying the results of experiment were exhausted, and that theory itself could only be augmented by the addition

40 of a greater degree of precision to the applications of principles already known. While
science thus appeared to be making for repose, the phenomena of the convulsive movements
observed by Galvani in the muscles of a frog when connected by metal were brought to the
attention and astonishment of physicists.... Volta, in that Italy which had been the cradle of
the new knowledge, discovered the principle of its true theory in a fact which reduces the

45 explanation of all the phenomena in question to the simple contact of two substances of
different nature. This fact became in his hands the germ of the admirable apparatus to which
its manner of being and its fecundity assign one of the chief places among those with which
the genius of mankind has enriched physics."

Shortly afterwards, our amateur would learn that Carlisle and Nicholson had

50 decomposed water by the aid of a battery; then, that Davy, in 1803, had produced, by the help
of the same battery, a quite unexpected phenomenon, and had succeeded in preparing metals
endowed with marvelous properties, beginning with substances of an earthy appearance
which had been known for a long time, but whose real nature had not been discovered.

38. The central claim of the first paragraph (lines 1-9) is that

A. new scientific research can make people realize that the scientists of their era do not know everything there is to know.

B. new movements in science upset the mental habits of people every day.

C. much of what scientists once believed about physics has been disproved.

D. people generally believe that the scientific findings of their own eras are historically exceptional.

39. As used in line 4, "scored" most nearly means

A. marked.

B. won.

C. gained.

D. slashed.

40. The author makes which point about contemporary scientific research?

A. It has diminished.

B. It has caused a paradox.

C. It is worthy of glory.

D. It is high quality.

41. Which choice provides the best evidence for the answer to the previous question?

A. Lines 10-11 ("It is in . . . laboratorics")

B. Lines 11-12 ("the quantity . . . diminished.")

C. Lines 12-13 ("We should . . . injustice,")

D. Lines 15-16 ("Yet it may . . . illusions.")

42. According to the author, scientific eras should be compared if

    A. one occurs immediately after the other.

    B. they feature very similar discoveries.

    C. they are separated by long periods of time.

    D. one disproves the discoveries of the other.

43. Which choice provides the best evidence for the answer to the previous question?

    A. Line 20 ("Let us take . . . enough")

    B. Lines 21-23 ("it is natural . . . century.")

    C. Lines 23-25 ("go back . . . 1810.")

    D. Lines 26-27 ("suppose . . . Volta.")

44. The statement "casting a brighter light on the truths revealed" (lines 37-38) mainly serves to

    A. illustrate that people assumed science could only clarify existing ideas.

    B. prove that Haüy was ignorant of how science can confound assumptions.

    C. show that people realize that new truths are constantly being learned.

    D. indicate that there are no limits to what science can reveal.

45. Over the course of the passage, the main focus shifts from

    A. the author's own ideas to a long quote from a scientist named Abbé Haüy.

    B. general ideas about science to specific experiments that illustrate those ideas.

    C. descriptions of Galvani and Volta's experiments to Carlisle, Nicholson, and Davy's experiments.

    D. mistakes that scientists often make to the ways those mistakes are corrected.

46. As used in line 46, "germ" most nearly means

    A. virus.

    B. bacteria.

    C. kernel.

    D. origin.

47. According to the passage, one similarity between Galvani and Davy is that they both

    A. made discoveries that forced scientists to rethink what they thought they already knew.

    B. performed work that developed on the experiments of Carlisle and Nicholson.

    C. performed experiments that involved the muscle contractions of frogs.

    D. concluded that all phenomena are caused by the contact of two substances of different natures.

STOP! DO NOT GO ON UNTIL TIME IS UP.

SECTION 2: WRITING AND LANGUAGE TEST

35 Minutes • 44 Questions

Turn to Section 2 of your answer sheet to answer the questions in this section.

Directions: Each passage below is accompanied by a number of multiple-choice questions. For some questions, you will need to consider how the passage might be revised to improve the expression of ideas. Other questions will ask you to consider how the passage might be edited to correct errors in sentence structure, usage, or punctuation. A passage may be accompanied by one or more graphics—such as a chart, table, or graph—that you will need to refer to in order to best answer the question(s).

Some questions will direct you to an underlined portion of a passage—it could be one word, a portion of a sentence, or the full sentence itself. Other questions will direct you to a particular paragraph or to certain sentences within a paragraph, or you'll be asked to think about the passage as a whole. Each question number refers to the corresponding number in the passage.

After reading each passage, select the answer to each question that most effectively improves the quality of writing in the passage or that makes the passage follow the conventions of Standard Written English. Many questions include a "NO CHANGE" option. Select that option if you think the best choice is to leave that specific portion of the passage as it is.

Questions 1–11 are based on the following passage and supplementary material.

A Career in Space

Space may be "the final frontier," but it is also a career path with opportunities for thousands of people who will never wear an astronaut suit. If you've ever been [1] <u>fascinate</u> by space, but are more interested in earth-bound careers [2] <u>(particularly in states like Florida or Texas)</u>, there are jobs in science, engineering, or communications that could be the right path for you.

Engineering

Engineers [3] <u>design: materials</u>, hardware, devices, instruments to collect data, and the spacecraft themselves. By 2024, the United States Bureau of Labor Statistics predicts that there will be more than 171,900 job openings for engineers in the aerospace industry.

Aerospace Engineers. These engineers design, test, and construct aircraft, missiles, and spacecraft. They work with the limitations of an environment to create their designs. For example, [4] <u>for</u> there is no oxygen in space to create thrust, aerospace engineers create rockets that run on liquid oxygen and propellant to artificially create that thrust.

Computer Hardware Engineers. These engineers research, design, develop, and test computer systems and equipment that are used to perform tasks or collect data.

Science

[5] <u>Without a strong understanding of space, what to expect from it, space exploration programs would quite literally never get off the ground.</u> Scientists study all aspects of space, particularly the physics and atmospheric phenomena. The U.S. Bureau of Labor Statistics projects that there will be 8,600 openings in this field by 2024.

Astronomers. Astronomers study objects in the universe, including planets, moons, stars, and entire galaxies. They collect data from equipment here on Earth [6] or equipment in space (like probes and satellites) to further their understanding of how space is laid out.

Atmospheric Scientists. These scientists [7] <u>study weather and climate and include meteorologists.</u> Atmospheric scientists use highly developed instruments and computer programs to do their [8] <u>jobs. Such</u> as using weather balloons, radar systems, and satellites to monitor the weather and collect data.

Communications

[9] Because NASA and other space programs are typically government agencies, it is important to have a link to the rest of the country to let them know about any news and advancements. Media and communications professionals are a growing field in the space industry; the U.S. Bureau of Labor Statistics anticipates that there will be more than 145,000 job openings by 2024, and many of those will be in the aerospace industry.

Technical Writers. Technical writers have the very important role of translating complicated scientific and technological information so that it can be understood by [10] <u>people, including people who are not necessarily experts.</u>

Public Relations Specialists. These media professionals are often the public faces of the space industry. They let the public know what's going on and prepare information for news outlets, blogs, and other public information sources. [11]

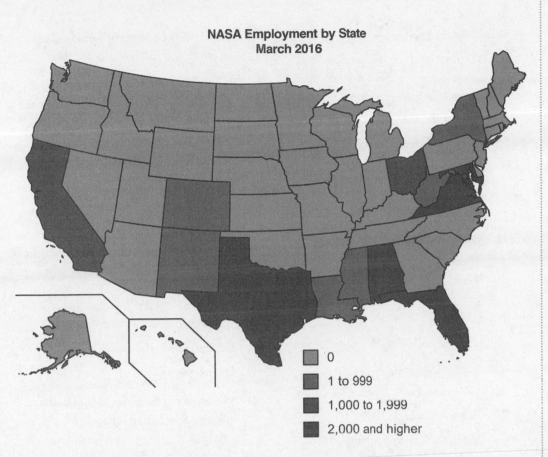

NASA Employment by State
March 2016

- 0
- 1 to 999
- 1,000 to 1,999
- 2,000 and higher

[Source: https://www.bls.gov/careeroutlook/2016/article/careers-in-space.htm]

1. **A.** NO CHANGE
   B. fascinating
   C. fascinated
   D. fascination

2. Which choice completes the sentence with accurate data based on the chart?

   A. NO CHANGE
   B. (particularly in states like Maine or Texas)
   C. (particularly in states like Florida or Nevada)
   D. (particularly in states like California or Michigan)

3. **A.** NO CHANGE
   B. design—materials
   C. design materials
   D. design; materials

4. **A.** NO CHANGE
   B. because
   C. wherein
   D. and

practice test 2— Writing and Language

5. **A.** NO CHANGE

   B. Without a strong understanding of space (what to expect from it), space exploration programs would quite literally never get off the ground.

   C. Without a strong understanding of space and what to expect from it, space exploration programs would quite literally never get off the ground.

   D. Without a strong understanding of space, what to expect from it, and space exploration programs would quite literally never get off the ground.

6. Which of the following details would be effective here?

   A. (like satellites)

   B. (like telescopes)

   C. (like technical equipment)

   D. (as scientists)

7. **A.** NO CHANGE

   B. including meteorologists study weather and climate

   C. study weather, climate, and meteorologists

   D. include meteorologists, who study weather and climate

8. **A.** NO CHANGE

   B. jobs—such

   C. jobs such

   D. jobs? Such

9. Which of the following would make an effective topic sentence for this paragraph?

   A. Science and engineering are not the only paths to a career with NASA.

   B. Science and engineering are essential parts of space exploration.

   C. If you are interested in communications, you should not consider a career with NASA.

   D. Communications is the smallest field within the space industry.

10. **A.** NO CHANGE

   B. people who aren't experts

   C. lay people as well as experts

   D. people

11. Which of the following would make an effective concluding sentence for this passage?

   A. If you want a career in space, you should plan to move to Florida.

   B. Together, all of these professionals form a team that advances our knowledge of space, even if none of them ever leaves Earth.

   C. Aerospace engineers make more money than all other space-related professionals.

   D. In conclusion, space careers are where it's at.

Questions 12–22 are based on the following passage.

The Rise of Techspeak

Technology undoubtedly changes the way we communicate with the world. Once we might have written a letter and waited at least a week while it was delivered. [12] Today, we can write the same information, tap a "send" icon, and have the note read within moments. Yet even as we acknowledge how technology has improved our ability to communicate, it is also important to consider that technology has also [13] effected how and what we communicate.

Technology has created [14] an new vocabulary that has the power to create all-new terms (like "to Google" something) but also to make old ones meaningless. For example, the # key on a phone keypad is rarely called a "pound sign" or a "number sign" anymore, but rather a *hashtag* thanks to social media. In 2016, 500 words and word usages were added to the *Oxford English Dictionary* (*OED*). Of those words, more than fifteen of [15] it were related to technical slang or processes. A few examples of these are *hackability*, *teleconference*, *browsability*, and *YouTuber*. [16]

(1) Also, while you may not find these in the *OED* anytime soon, tech slang has made it more acceptable to abbreviate words in everyday conversation. (2) In an interview with the BBC, University of Bangor honorary linguistics professor David Crystal credits the Internet with normalizing [17] a term like *LOL* (Laugh Out Loud) and *BRB* (Be Right Back), which commonly show up in text messages. (3) Crystal stated that "Language itself changes slowly but the Internet has speeded up the process of those changes so you notice them more quickly." [18]

[19] Oxford University credits social media even more than the Internet at large. Facebook has given extra meanings for terms like *like* (in the context of rating something online), *status*, *profile*, and *friend*, while photo-sharing apps like Instagram have helped [20] prop *selfie* into our collective vocabulary very quickly. No Twitter post is complete without a *hashtag*. And these days, everyone knows that a *troll* [21] is no longer just a fantastical creature who lives under a bridge, but rather an Internet commenter looking for trouble. [22]

12. **A.** NO CHANGE

    B. Today, we can write the same information, tap a "send" icon, and read the note within moments.

    C. Today, we can write the same information…tap a "send" icon…have the note read within moments.

    D. Today, we can write the same information.

13. **A.** NO CHANGE

    B. effaced

    C. affected

    D. affecting

14. **A.** NO CHANGE

    B. a new

    C. the new

    D. as new

15. **A.** NO CHANGE

    B. words

    C. them

    D. it's

16. Which of the following would be an effective sentence to add to this paragraph?

    A. YouTubers are people who post videos on the popular website YouTube.

    B. Therefore, technology has created a new vocabulary that people use every day.

    C. According to Oxford University, only words that meet strict standards of common use are included in the *OED*.

    D. It is unclear whether the rise of techspeak has changed punctuation as well.

17. **A.** NO CHANGE

    B. terms

    C. one term

    D. any terms

18. Where in the paragraph should the following sentence be placed?

    This "techspeak" is not just in our dictionaries now but is also affecting our everyday speech.

    A. Before sentence 1

    B. After sentence 1

    C. After sentence 2

    D. After sentence 3

19. **A.** NO CHANGE

    B. Still, Oxford University credits social media even more than the Internet at large.

    C. More specifically, Oxford University credits social media even more than the Internet at large.

    D. And Oxford University credits social media even more than the Internet at large.

20. **A.** NO CHANGE

    B. propel

    C. propose

    D. repurpose

21. A. NO CHANGE

B. is no longer just a fantastical creature who lives under a bridge, is an Internet commenter looking for trouble.

C. is no longer just a fantastical creature who lives under a bridge. A troll is an Internet commenter looking for trouble.

D. is an Internet commenter looking for trouble, when we used to think a troll was a fantastical creature who lives under a bridge.

22. Which of the following sentences should the writer use as a conclusion for the passage?

A. Selfies are so popular these days that people even buy "selfie sticks" to improve their picture-taking game.

B. The *Oxford English Dictionary* is a living history of our vocabulary trends.

C. Technology undoubtedly changes the way we communicate with the world.

D. As the language evolves with technology, we could soon see the day when a smiley-face emoticon is included forever in the *OED*.

practice test 2—
Writing and Language

Questions 23–33 are based on the following passage.

The National Parks at 100

From "sea to shining sea," the United States is full of [**23**] <u>things</u> that show how diverse and majestic the country's land can be. For over a hundred years, the National Park Service (NPS) has been developing and taking care of these spaces on behalf of all Americans.

[**24**] The National Park Service was created by the National Park Service Organic Act and signed into existence by President Woodrow Wilson. National parks and monuments had previously been managed by the U.S. Department of the Interior, [**25**] <u>but the cause to make them an independent government agency had been taken up by American conservationists Stephen Mather and J. Horace McFarland</u>. This new bureau would be responsible for maintaining all historical parks (like the ones at natural sites like the Grand Canyon) and monuments that were not under state control.

[**26**] The history of parks in the National Park System is as diverse as the country itself. Some of the parks came to be after monuments were created there, but others were acquired under different circumstances. Many of the parks are sprawling pieces of land under federal control. The first national parks actually predated the National Park Service. Yellowstone became a park in 1872, but there was no official state of Wyoming at that point, [**27**] <u>or Alaska either</u>. Similarly, Yosemite Park in California shifted back over to federal government control after [**28**] <u>it</u> was temporarily donated to the state.

National parks are not the only responsibility of the [**29**] <u>National Park Service, however</u>. Manmade monuments fall under the NPS as well. The Lincoln Memorial and the other presidential monuments in Washington, DC, are also managed by the NPS. Historically significant battlefields, like Gettysburg, have also become national parks under the American Battlefield Protection Program (ABPP).

All of these sites [**30**]<u>—geographic parks or historical parks,</u> are staffed by federal park rangers, who are responsible for maintaining the land and educating visitors about the parks' history. These rangers are considered stewards of one of America's best resources.

Together, the NPS manages fifty-nine national parks and 417 total areas [**31**]. Known [**32**] <u>secretly</u> as America's "crown jewels," these park sites are found in all fifty states, plus US territories (District of Columbia, Guam, Puerto Rico, American Samoa, and the Virgin Islands), and they represent the combination of natural beauty and evolving history of the country. [**33**]

23. A. NO CHANGE

    B. natural beauty and unique geographical places

    C. people who come from all walks of life

    D. cultural inspiration taken from backgrounds from all over the world

24. Which choice effectively sets up the information that follows?

    A. Founded as a U.S. government agency in 1916,

    B. In America,

    C. And now getting to the National Park Service,

    D. Because parks have always been a national treasure,

25. A. NO CHANGE

    B. but American conservationists Stephen Mather and J. Horace McFarland sought to make the parks into an independent government agency.

    C. but the cause, taken up by American conservationists Stephen Mather and J. Horace McFarland, to make them an independent government agency.

    D. the cause to make them an independent government agency had been taken up by American conservationists Stephen Mather and J. Horace McFarland.

26. Which of the following sentences should be deleted from the paragraph?

    A. The history of parks in the National Park System is as diverse as the country itself.

    B. Many of the parks are sprawling pieces of land under federal control.

    C. The first national parks actually predated the National Park Service.

    D. Similarly, Yosemite Park in California shifted back over to federal government control after it was temporarily donated to California.

27. Which choice provides information that best supports the claim made by the sentence?

    A. NO CHANGE

    B. although the park was in the Wyoming Territory.

    C. which is why the park is different.

    D. and so the federal government assumed control of the park.

28. A. NO CHANGE

    B. California

    C. the government

    D. the park

29. A. NO CHANGE

    B. National Park Service. However,

    C. National Park Service however.

    D. National Park Service; however.

practice test 2— Writing and Language

30. A. NO CHANGE

B. —geographic parks or historical parks—

C. geographic parks or historical parks

D. , geographic parks, or historical parks,

31. Which of the following adds relevant information to the sentence?

A. occupying more than 84 million acres of land.

B. , which is a lot of parks.

C. , all under the NPS.

D. with more than 4 million visitors per year.

32. A. NO CHANGE

B. only

C. collectively

D. truly

33. In which paragraph would the following sentence be most relevant?

Ranging from the Washington Monument to the Grand Canyon, America's national parks show how the nation enjoys both its history and its natural resources.

A. Paragraph 2

B. Paragraph 3

C. Paragraph 4

D. Paragraph 5

Questions 34–44 are based on the following passage.

Do Multiple Universes Exist?

The idea of multiple universes, existing in [34] parallel with our own, has always been a popular concept in science fiction. The idea that there are worlds similar to our own, or fantastically different [35] (yet still somehow linked, I think?) has great storytelling potential. But is this real? Is it possible that there are other universes out there? [36] Many scientists are intrigued by the possibility. Most believe that our universe exists on its own.

At the most basic level, scientists do not have any concrete evidence that a set of infinite parallel universes [37] (known as the multiverse) exists. Yet they still continue to probe the *idea* of a multiverse, because such a thing could explain some questions about our own universe. For example, it would explain why the basic forces necessary for life, like electromagnetic force between particles, exist at the low end of the range necessary to support life. [38] For example, some physicists also believe that a multiverse would account for physics data oddities that no one has yet been able to resolve.

Some physicists believe that even researching the idea of a multiverse is highly unscientific, not to mention potentially irresponsible. Because this theory cannot be tested and either proven [39] nor disproven, many in the physics world believe that this is not a worthwhile area of study. [40]

From a cultural standpoint, however, the multiverse idea is much more popular. [41] Here, the idea is not so much that physical forces would be different from universe to universe, but rather that anything would be possible. One physicist, Marcelo Gleiser, has suggested on National Public Radio that creatures which do not exist in our world, like fairies, could exist in other universes under different physical conditions, if the multiverse turns out to be real.

[42] Between those who believe that the multiverse theory has potential, there are many dedicated to finding ways to test it. One of the most common lines of research right now is looking at whether there were possibly multiple Big Bang events, in addition to the one believed to have created the universe as we know it. Theoretical physicist Brian Greene has also proposed using the Large Hadron Collider, a particle accelerator that is being used [43] too test other [44] Universe origination theories and the existence of black holes, to see if the multiverse theory has legs.

34. **A.** NO CHANGE
    B. contrast
    C. compliance
    D. peril

35. **A.** NO CHANGE
    B. (yet still somehow linked)
    C. (yet, I think, still somehow linked?)
    D. (yet still somehow linked, I think.)

36. Which choice most effectively combines these sentences?

    A. Many scientists are intrigued by the possibility, most believe that our universe exists on its own.

    B. Intrigued by the possibility, most scientists believe that our universe exists on its own.

    C. Many scientists are intrigued by the possibility—most believe that our universe exists on its own.

    D. Although many scientists are intrigued by the possibility, most believe that our universe exists on its own.

37. **A.** NO CHANGE

    B. known as 'the multiverse'

    C. known as "the multiverse"

    D. "known" as the multiverse

38. **A.** NO CHANGE

    B. Shockingly,

    C. In addition,

    D. In conclusion,

39. **A.** NO CHANGE

    B. or

    C. not

    D. else

40. Which of the following sentences should the writer add here?

    A. Without a broad scientific consensus, few research programs are willing to put academic resources into researching the possibility of the multiverse.

    B. Multiverses will likely be proven real someday.

    C. Others are usually hesitant to talk about the multiverse on the record, because they are scared of the consequences.

    D. Given that there's no universal consensus on the subject, I guess you could call it a multiversal consensus!

41. The writer is considering deleting the underlined sentence. Should the writer do this?

    A. Yes, because it introduces a detail that is not directly related to the topic of the paragraph.

    B. Yes, because it contradicts information in the paragraph.

    C. No, because it explains the main topic of the paragraph.

    D. No, because it is the topic sentence of the whole passage.

42. **A.** NO CHANGE

    B. In

    C. Because

    D. Among

43. **A.** NO CHANGE

    B. two

    C. to

    D. To

44. **A.** NO CHANGE

    B. universe

    C. The Universe

    D. multiverse

STOP! DO NOT GO ON UNTIL TIME IS UP.

practice test 2— Writing and Language

SECTION 3: MATH TEST—NO CALCULATOR

25 Minutes • 17 Questions

Turn to Section 3 of your answer sheet to answer the questions in this section.

> **Directions:** For **Questions 1–13,** solve each problem, choose the best answer from the choices provided, and fill in the corresponding circle on your answer sheet. For **Questions 14–17,** solve the problem and enter your answer in the grid on the answer sheet. Please refer to the directions before **Question 14** on how to enter your answers in the grid. You may use any available space in your test booklet for scratch work.

NOTES:

1. The use of a calculator is **not permitted.**

2. All variables and expressions used represent real numbers unless otherwise indicated.

3. Figures provided in this test are drawn to scale unless otherwise indicated.

4. All figures lie in a plane unless otherwise indicated.

5. Unless otherwise indicated, the domain of a given function f is the set of all real numbers x for which $f(x)$ is a real number.

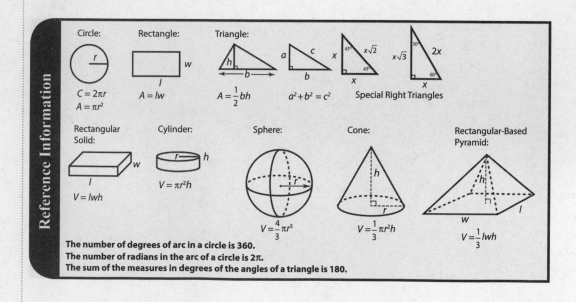

The number of degrees of arc in a circle is 360.
The number of radians in the arc of a circle is 2π.
The sum of the measures in degrees of the angles of a triangle is 180.

1. What is the solution set for the equation $3(x + 2)^2 = 27$?

   SHOW YOUR WORK HERE

   A. $\{7\}$
   B. $\left\{-\dfrac{3}{2}, \dfrac{3}{2}\right\}$
   C. $\{5, 1\}$
   D. $\{-1, 5\}$

2. Pilots flying over Antarctica are concerned that the fuel line will freeze if the temperature gets too low. The freezing point for the fuel mixtures they use lies between −40°F and −58°F. The temperature reading on the plane's panel has an error of ±1.7°F. Which inequality describes the temperatures in degrees Fahrenheit, T, that the gauge can display and the pilot be assured that the fuel line will not freeze?

   A. $T > -41.7$
   B. $T > -38.3$
   C. $-59.7 \leq T \leq -38.3$
   D. $T < -56.3$

3. An international group of educators focused on using virtual reality in the teaching of art history and geography started with 20 founding members. Within one year, membership rose to 950 members worldwide. What is the percent increase in membership for this year?

   A. 465%
   B. 97.9%
   C. 475%
   D. 4,650%

practice test 2— Math — No Calculator

4. If $\left[\dfrac{2-6x}{-4}\right] - \dfrac{2}{3}(3x+1) = \dfrac{1}{6}x$, what is the value of $(4x)^2$?

  A. −7

  B. $\dfrac{25}{256}$

  C. $-\dfrac{7}{4}$

  D. 49

SHOW YOUR WORK HERE

5. By Hooke's law, the amount of work done, W, by a spring on a block, compressing it from an initial position x_1 to a final position x_2, is given by the formula $W = -\left(\dfrac{1}{2}x_2^2 - \dfrac{1}{2}x_1^2\right)$. If $x_1 = 8$ inches, find the position to which the spring compresses the block (as shown in the diagram) if the work done is $\dfrac{39}{2}$ Newtons. (**Note:** A Newton is a unit of force.)

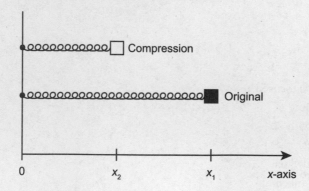

  A. 3 inches

  B. 5 inches

  C. 8 inches

  D. 13 inches

6. Scouts build a teepee by staking the inside pole (*h* feet tall) to four equally spaced points arranged around a circular base, as shown.

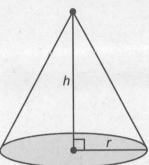

SHOW YOUR WORK HERE

When the center of the base is treated as the origin, the equation of the base is $x^2 + y^2 = 81$. If the scouts have 700 square feet of material to use for the surface and base of the teepee, which of the following expressions represents *h* when all of the material is used?

Note: The surface area of a right circular cone with base radius *r* and height *h* is

$$S = \pi r \left(r + \sqrt{h^2 + r^2} \right).$$

A. $h = \dfrac{700 - 81\pi}{9\pi} - 9$

B. $h = \dfrac{700 - 81\pi}{9\pi}$

C. $h = \sqrt{\left(\dfrac{700 - 81\pi}{9\pi} \right)^2 - 81}$

D. $h = \left(\dfrac{700 - 81\pi}{9\pi} \right)^2 + 81$

7. Let $a > 0$. Consider the following two data sets:

Data Set I: $\{a, 2a, 3a, 4a, 5a\}$
Data Set II: $\{2a, 4a, 6a, 8a, 10a\}$

Which of the following measures, if any, are the same for Data Set I and Data Set II?

A. mean

B. median

C. range

D. none of these

8. The *Michaelis–Menten* formula is a model of enzyme kinetics. It relates the reaction rate v to the concentration, C, of a substance. The formula is $v = \dfrac{V_{max} \cdot C}{K + C}$.

Here, K is the Michaelis constant and V_{max} is the maximum rate achieved by the system. Which of these formulas shows the concentration C in terms of the other variables?

A. $C = \dfrac{v \cdot K}{V_{max} - v}$

B. $C = \dfrac{K}{V_{max} - 1}$

C. $C = \dfrac{v \cdot K}{V_{max} - 1}$

D. $C = \dfrac{v \cdot K}{v - V_{max}}$

SHOW YOUR WORK HERE

Use the following information for Questions 9 and 10.

A survey asked 400 participants to provide their opinions as to how important it is for the new government to address issues arising in the following three areas:

    I.   Equality of international trade agreements

    II. Unemployment rate

    III. International humanitarian efforts

The data collected is summarized in this table; the numerical score and its qualitative meaning are provided in the first column.

	Issue to Address		
	I	II	III
1 *(Very Low Priority)*	80	40	20
2 *(Low Priority)*	90	60	80
3 *(Neutral)*	120	100	90
4 *(Moderate Priority)*	40	10	180
5 *(High Priority)*	70	190	30

9. Compute $|\text{Median}_{\text{I}} - \text{Median}_{\text{II}}|$. Here, Median I is the median response for Issue I and Median II is the median response for Issue II.

   A. 0

   B. 0.5

   C. 0.7875

   D. 1

10. If a participant's rating of Issue III is selected at random, what is the probability that the rate is either a moderate priority or high priority?

    A. 0.175

    B. 0.25

    C. 0.525

    D. 0.75

11. During the airing of a 3-hour telethon devoted to raising money for research on a rare disease, exactly 35 percent of the commercial time (to the minute) was devoted to real-life testimonials. Which of the following could be the total amount of time used for commercials during the telethon?

    A. 75 minutes

    B. 90 minutes

    C. 110 minutes

    D. 120 minutes

12. If $(-2, k)$ and $(4, -1)$ lie on a line, what should be the value of k so the x-intercept of the linc is $(-6, 0)$?

    A. $-\dfrac{17}{2}$

    B. $-\dfrac{2}{5}$

    C. -7

    D. 35

practice test 2— Math — No Calculator

13. Penny travels 800 miles from the university to her home, partly by bus and partly by rental car. The trip takes 9 hours if she travels 240 miles by bus and the rest by rental car. The trip takes 30 minutes longer if she travels 320 miles by bus and the rest by rental car. Which system can be used to find the speeds of the bus, x, and rental car, y, in miles per hour?

SHOW YOUR WORK HERE

A. $\begin{cases} 320x + 480y = 9.5 \\ 240x + 560y = 9 \end{cases}$

B. $\begin{cases} \dfrac{320}{x} + \dfrac{480}{y} = 9.5 \\ \dfrac{560}{x} + \dfrac{240}{y} = 9 \end{cases}$

C. $\begin{cases} \dfrac{x}{360} + \dfrac{y}{480} = 9.5 \\ \dfrac{x}{240} + \dfrac{y}{560} = 9 \end{cases}$

D. $\begin{cases} \dfrac{320}{x} + \dfrac{480}{y} = 9.5 \\ \dfrac{240}{x} + \dfrac{560}{y} = 9 \end{cases}$

Directions: For **Questions 14–17**, solve the problem and enter your answer in the grid, as described below, on the answer sheet.

NOTES:

1. Although not required, it is suggested that you write your answer in the boxes at the top of the columns to help you fill in the circles accurately. You will receive credit only if the circles are filled in correctly.

2. Mark no more than one circle in any column.

3. No question has a negative answer.

4. Some problems may have more than one correct answer. In such cases, grid only one answer.

5. **Mixed numbers** such as $3\frac{1}{2}$ must be gridded as 3.5 or $\frac{7}{2}$. If $3\frac{1}{2}$ is entered into the grid as [grid] it will be interpreted as $\frac{31}{2}$, not $3\frac{1}{2}$.

6. **Decimal answers:** If you obtain a decimal answer with more digits than the grid can accommodate, it may be either rounded or truncated, but it must fill the entire grid.

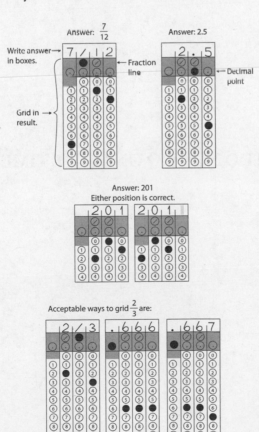

14. A clinical psychology intern spends 56 hours per week in training. The number of hours she spends conducting therapy and the number of hours conducting research are in a 6:2 ratio. How many hours does she spend conducting therapy?

SHOW YOUR WORK HERE

15. If x is the solution of the equation

$$4\sqrt{1-x} - 36 = 0, \text{ what is } |x|?$$

16. A local cafe averages 500 customers per week for years. Then, seemingly overnight, the owner notices that this weekly average begins to decline by 4 percent each week. If the average number of customers x weeks after this change is described by the function $C(x) = A \cdot b^x$, what is the value of b?

17. If (x, y) is a solution of the following system, what is the value of $(2x - 3y)^{-2}$?

$$\begin{cases} 5x + 1 = 2y \\ y - 2 = x \end{cases}$$

STOP! DO NOT GO ON UNTIL TIME IS UP.

SECTION 4: MATH TEST—CALCULATOR 🖩

45 Minutes • 31 Questions

Turn to Section 4 of your answer sheet to answer the questions in this section.

Directions: For **Questions 1–27,** solve each problem, choose the best answer from the choices provided, and fill in the corresponding circle on your answer sheet. For **Questions 28–31,** solve the problem and enter your answer in the grid on the answer sheet. Please refer to the directions before **Question 28** on how to enter your answers in the grid. You may use any available space in your test booklet for scratch work.

NOTES:

1. The use of a calculator is **permitted.**

2. All variables and expressions used represent real numbers unless otherwise indicated.

3. Figures provided in this test are drawn to scale unless otherwise indicated.

4. All figures lie in a plane unless otherwise indicated.

5. Unless otherwise indicated, the domain of a given function f is the set of all real numbers x for which $f(x)$ is a real number.

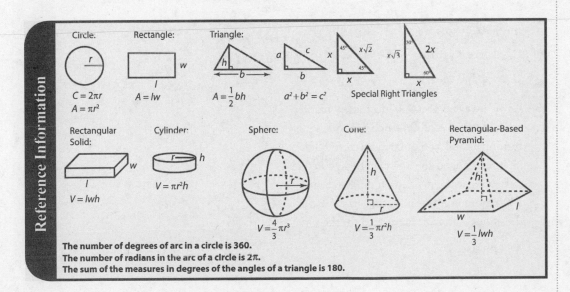

Reference Information

Circle.
$C = 2\pi r$
$A = \pi r^2$

Rectangle:
$A = lw$

Triangle:
$A = \frac{1}{2}bh$

$a^2 + b^2 = c^2$

Special Right Triangles

Rectangular Solid:
$V = lwh$

Cylinder:
$V = \pi r^2 h$

Sphere:
$V = \frac{4}{3}\pi r^3$

Cone:
$V = \frac{1}{3}\pi r^2 h$

Rectangular-Based Pyramid:
$V = \frac{1}{3}lwh$

The number of degrees of arc in a circle is 360.
The number of radians in the arc of a circle is 2π.
The sum of the measures in degrees of the angles of a triangle is 180.

1. A massive network of grooves (or fissures) extends throughout a hillside. Rainwater flows through these grooves, causing erosion. Following a heavy rain, the rate of flow of water through these grooves is 5 grams per each half a second. What is this rate in gallons per minute? (**Note:** 1 gallon of water weighs approximately 3.785 kilograms.)

   A. 3.96×10^{-2} gallons per minute

   B. 3.79×10^{-2} gallons per minute

   C. 1.59×10^{-1} gallons per minute

   D. 7.93×10^{-2} gallons per minute

2. Frank is hiking through Mayan ruins, trying to find an ancient shrine. Suppose his current distance from the shrine is x yards. He walks y feet due east and the GPS indicates that he is now 1,128 yards due north of the shrine. If y is one-fifth of x, approximately how many yards was he originally from the shrine?

   A. 0.1 yards

   B. 230.3 yards

   C. 1,151.3 yards

   D. 1,410.0 yards

3. Lewis invested $30,000 in a money market account and $20,000 in a CD for one year, earning a total of $1,600 in interest. Had he interchanged the amounts he invested in these two accounts, he would have earned $400 more in interest for the year. What is the annual interest rate earned for the CD?

   A. 1.6%

   B. 3.6%

   C. 5.6%

   D. 7.2%

SHOW YOUR WORK HERE

4. Which of the following expressions is equivalent to $(2 - 3x)(3 - 2x)x$?

   SHOW YOUR WORK HERE

   A. $6x + 6x^3$

   B. $6x^2 - 13x + 6$

   C. $-6x^3 - 5x^2 + 6x$

   D. $6x^3 - 13x^2 + 6x$

5. A ball weighing 5 kg is affixed to the end of a string and is rotated about a circle 6 m in diameter. The tension T in the string is given by the formula $T = \dfrac{m \cdot v^2}{r}$, where m is the weight of the ball in kilograms, v is the speed of rotation in meters per second, and r is the radius of its circular path in meters. The maximum possible tension of the string is $30 \; \dfrac{\text{kg} \cdot \text{m}}{\text{sec}^2}$. What is the speed of rotation when the tension of the string is at its maximum?

   A. $3\sqrt{2}$ meters per second

   B. 6 meters per second

   C. 18 meters per second

   D. 36 meters per second

6. The interior angles of a triangle PQR are related as follows: The measure of $\angle P$ is three degrees less than twice the measure of $\angle R$, and the sum of the measures of $\angle P$ and $\angle R$ is 39°. Determine $\mathrm{m}(\angle Q) - \mathrm{m}(\angle P)$, where $\mathrm{m}(\angle P)$ stands for the measure of angle P.

   A. 14°

   B. 25°

   C. 116°

   D. 141°

7. Which of the following expressions is equivalent to the quotient

$$\frac{6x^2 + 5x - 1}{x^2 - 2x} \div \frac{(x+1)\left(36x^2 - 12x + 1\right)}{x - 2}?$$

SHOW YOUR WORK HERE

A. $\dfrac{(6x-1)^3(x+1)^2}{x(x-2)^2}$

B. $\dfrac{6x-1}{x}$

C. $\dfrac{1}{x(6x-1)}$

D. $6x^2 - x$

Use the following information for Questions 8–10.

The following line graphs show the annual export growth and import growth percentages for a large, industrial country for the time period 2006–2016.

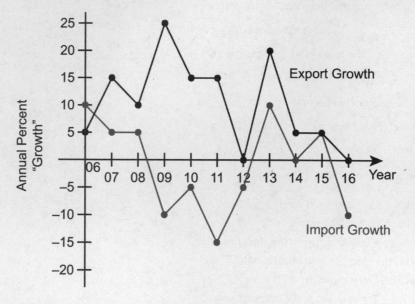

8. During which two consecutive years is the increase in export growth the greatest?

A. 2008 to 2009

B. 2011 to 2012

C. 2013 to 2014

D. 2014 to 2015

9. Three-year averages (that is, averages computed for three consecutive years) are useful predictors of future growth. For how many consecutive-year triples is the three-year import growth average negative? (**Note:** An example of a consecutive-year triple is 2010 – 2011 – 2012.)

   A. 0

   B. 1

   C. 2

   D. 5

SHOW YOUR WORK HERE

10. Which of the following inequalities has a solution set that includes values in the third and fourth quadrants only?

   A. $x > 0$

   B. $y > 0$

   C. $x < 0$

   D. $y < 0$

11. The captain of a private ferry that takes passengers from a tourist town to an island charges a flat fee of $24 per passenger plus $0.40 per minute for the trip. If the ride for a single passenger cost $72, how long was the ride?

   A. 47 minutes, 30 seconds

   B. 1 hour, 20 minutes

   C. 2 hours

   D. 4 hours, 10 minutes

practice test 2— Math — Calculator

12. Part of an urban planning project is to reduce the traffic density on the main road through the city. Currently, there are three cars for every 138 square feet of roadway during rush hour. The addition of two lanes to the existing road will reduce the traffic density during rush hour by 30 percent. What is the approximate density in such case?

SHOW YOUR WORK HERE

A. 1 car for every 35 square feet of roadway

B. 1 car for every 46 square feet of roadway

C. 1 car for every 66 square feet of roadway

D. 1 car for every 92 square feet of roadway

13. Paintballs are formed by inserting paint into a thin plastic spherical shell. The mass m of a spherical shell of outer radius R, density ρ, and thickness of l is given by the formula $m = 4\pi R^2 l\rho$. Which of the following expressions correctly gives the outer diameter of such a spherical shell?

A. $D = \sqrt{m - \pi l\rho}$

B. $D = \sqrt{\dfrac{m}{\pi l\rho}}$

C. $D = \dfrac{1}{2}\sqrt{\dfrac{m}{\pi l\rho}}$

D. $D = 4\sqrt{\dfrac{m}{\pi l\rho}}$

14. Which of the following is the solution set of the inequality $1.6 - 0.8(2 - 5x) < -3.2x$?

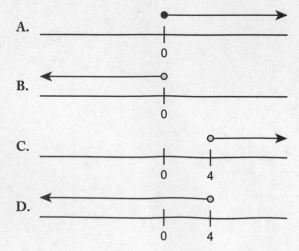

SHOW YOUR WORK HERE

15. A limousine is rented by a portion of a wedding party consisting of p people for $240. The cost is shared equally among all riders. A couple decides to drive their own car, leaving the remainder of the group to pay the same amount. If this results in each person needing to pay $10 more, what is p?

A. 6

B. 8

C. 46

D. 48

16. A solid rocket booster descends to earth upon separation from the space shuttle during its launch. The linear function $y = h(t)$ graphed below describes the relationship between the height of the booster, $h(t)$, above the ocean and the time t of its descent.

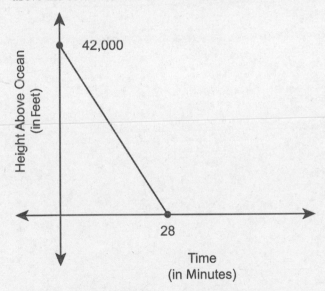

What is the slope of this linear function and what does it mean in this context?

A. 1,500 feet per minute; the booster descends 1,500 feet per minute.

B. −3,000 feet per minute; the booster descends 3,000 feet per minute.

C. −1,500 feet per minute; the height of the booster increases by 1,500 feet per minute

D. −1,500 feet per minute; the booster gets 1,500 feet closer to the ocean per minute.

17. If $f(x) = -5(2x-1)^2 + 1$ and $g(x) = 3 - x$, which of the following equals $(f \circ g)(x)$?

SHOW YOUR WORK HERE

    A. $-(124 + 20x^2)$

    B. $20x^2 - 20x + 7$

    C. $4x^2 - 10x - 124$

    D. $-20x^2 + 100x - 124$

18. Aspiring football quarterbacks practice to master the perfect "spiral" pass. Factors that must be considered are grip, release angle, and rotation speed. An athlete's spiral pass currently has a rotation rate of 0.75 rotations per second. His goal is to achieve a rotation rate of 180 rotations per minute. What would be the percent increase in rotation rate if he were to achieve this goal?

    A. 3%

    B. 75%

    C. 150%

    D. 300%

19. Which of the following is equivalent to $\dfrac{3-2x}{1+2x} - \dfrac{3-x}{x}$?

    A. 0

    B. $-\dfrac{3+2x}{x(1+2x)}$

    C. $\dfrac{-4x^2 + 8x + 3}{2x^2 + x}$

    D. $-\dfrac{x}{1+3x}$

20. Torrential rains pound a southern state for 36 hours. The downpour causes the water level in the river to rise 16 inches. Once the rain stops, it recedes at a constant rate of 1.2 inches every three days. Which equation could be used to determine the number of days, d, it takes for the water level to lower to one-half foot?

    A. $-0.4d + 16 = 6$

    B. $-0.4d + 16 = 0.5$

    C. $-0.25d + 16 = 6$

    D. $-1.2d + 16 = 0.5$

21. What values of a and b make the following equation true for all nonzero values of x and y?

$$\frac{x\left(x^{-3}y^2\right)^2}{y\left(x^2y^4\right)^{-1}} = x^a y^b$$

A. $a = 3, b = 7$

B. $a = -1, b = 0$

C. $a = -3, b = 7$

D. $a = 10, b = -12$

SHOW YOUR WORK HERE

Use the following information for Questions 22 and 23.

The scatterplot below shows the data collected from 10 participants to assess the relationship between the score on a battery of memory tests (scored 0 through 200) and the time necessary for an examinee to subsequently assemble a fifty-piece jigsaw puzzle. The best fit trend line is shown.

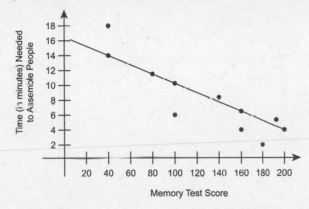

22. How many of the 10 participants have a completion time of the jigsaw puzzle that differs by at least 2 minutes from the time predicted by the trend line for their score on the memory test?

A. 2

B. 4

C. 6

D. 7

23. Based on the trend line, what is the range of predicted times for completing the jigsaw puzzle if the score on the memory test is between 100 and 130, inclusive?

A. Between 8 and 10 minutes

B. Between 7 and 9 minutes

C. Between 9 and 11 minutes

D. Between 10 and 12 minutes

24. Which of the following systems of linear inequalities has an empty solution set?

SHOW YOUR WORK HERE

A. $\begin{cases} x \geq 4 \\ y < 4 \end{cases}$

B. $\begin{cases} y < -3x + 4 \\ y > -3x - 4 \end{cases}$

C. $\begin{cases} y \geq 2x + 3 \\ y < -3 + 2x \end{cases}$

D. $\begin{cases} y \geq 2x \\ y \leq 2x \end{cases}$

25. During a physical fitness test, an examinee endures five 1-minute rounds during which he must complete as many sit-ups as possible. There are three levels of achievement based on the average of these five rounds, as shown in the table below.

SHOW YOUR WORK HERE

Level of Achievement	Average number of sit-ups
Fail	Less than or equal to 50
Satisfactory	Greater than 50, but less than or equal to 80
Superior	Greater than 80

Eric completed 42, 51, 31, and 63 sit-ups during the first four rounds. Which inequality can be used to determine the number of sit-ups he needs during the fifth round to ensure his score, x, lands in the Satisfactory range?

A. $50 \leq \dfrac{42 + 51 + 31 + 63 + x}{5} < 80$

B. $50 < \dfrac{42 + 51 + 31 + 63 + x}{5} \leq 80$

C. $50 \leq \dfrac{42 + 51 + 31 + 63 + x}{5} \leq 80$

D. $50 < 42 + 51 + 31 + 63 + x < 80$

practice test 2— Math — Calculator

26. The following scatterplot shows data relating   **SHOW YOUR WORK HERE**
two variables X and Y:

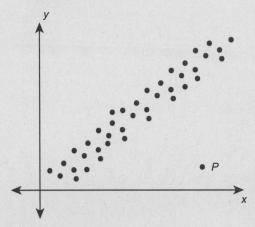

Which of the following is the most accurate
description of the relationship between X and Y?

A. Moderate, positive linear relationship
between X and Y

B. Strong, positive nonlinear relationship
between X and Y

C. Negative linear relationship between X
and Y

D. No discernible relationship between X and
Y because of the presence of the outlier

27. Which of the following is the graph of $-3(2x + y) + 9 = 0$?

A.

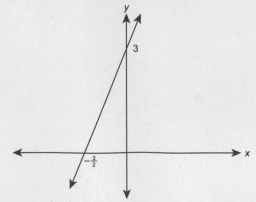

B.

SHOW YOUR WORK HERE

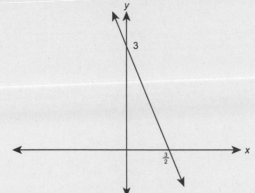

C.

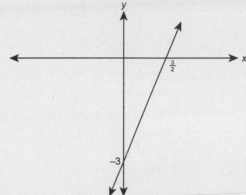

D.

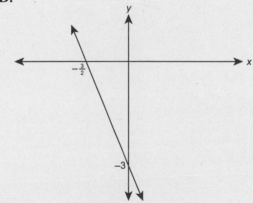

practice test 2— Math — Calculator

Directions: For **Questions 28–31**, solve the problem and enter your answer in the grid, as described below, on the answer sheet.

NOTES:

1. Although not required, it is suggested that you write your answer in the boxes at the top of the columns to help you fill in the circles accurately. You will receive credit only if the circles are filled in correctly.

2. Mark no more than one circle in any column.

3. No question has a negative answer.

4. Some problems may have more than one correct answer. In such cases, grid only one answer.

5. **Mixed numbers** such as $3\frac{1}{2}$ must be gridded as 3.5 or $\frac{7}{2}$. If $3\frac{1}{2}$ is entered into the grid as ![grid showing 3 1 / 2] it will be interpreted as $\frac{31}{2}$, not $3\frac{1}{2}$.

6. **Decimal answers:** If you obtain a decimal answer with more digits than the grid can accommodate, it may be either rounded or truncated, but it must fill the entire grid.

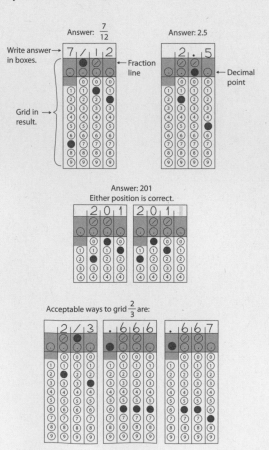

28. A nutritionist wishes to determine if drinking organic chamomile tea versus leading-brand chamomile tea is related to the number of days it takes to recover from a head cold. She conducted an experiment with 200 participants; the results are as follows:

	Takes 4 or fewer days to recover from head cold	Takes more than 4 days to recover from head cold
Drink organic chamomile tea	59	41
Drink leading-brand chamomile tea	38	62

How likely is it to select a participant who drank organic chamomile tea given that it was known that they recovered from the head cold in four or fewer days? Represent your answer as a decimal rounded to the nearest hundredth.

SHOW YOUR WORK HERE

29. A medieval studies enthusiast group is planning to reenact the siege of a certain castle. They have a catapult to launch a boulder over the outer wall and would like it to land 40 yards beyond the frontline of troops. If the wall is 29 yards from the frontline, how far from the frontline should they place the catapult to ensure the boulder reaches peak height directly over the wall?

SHOW YOUR WORK HERE

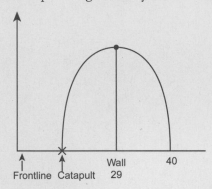

30. Traffic roundabouts are frequently used in lieu of traffic lights in areas prone to hurricanes. An aerial view of a four-prong traffic roundabout, centered at point O, is below:

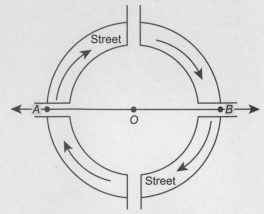

The street is 16 feet wide and the distance across from point A to point B is 76 feet. A paving company needs to know the area of the street used for the roundabout so it can determine the appropriate amount of gravel to use. What is this area? (Enter your answer in terms of π.)

31. For what constant C does the following linear equation have infinitely many solutions?

$$2x - 3[1 - (C + 3x)] = 5 + 11x$$

ANSWER KEYS AND EXPLANATIONS

Section 1: Reading Test

1. C	9. B	17. C	25. D	33. D	41. B
2. A	10. B	18. A	26. B	34. B	42. C
3. D	11. B	19. C	27. D	35. D	43. B
4. A	12. B	20. A	28. D	36. A	44. A
5. B	13. A	21. C	29. D	37. B	45. B
6. D	14. C	22. D	30. A	38. D	46. D
7. C	15. D	23. C	31. C	39. A	47. A
8. C	16. D	24. B	32. C	40. D	

READING TEST RAW SCORE ☐

(Number of correct answers)

1. **The correct answer is C.** The narrator implies that life is better in Spaceland than it is in Flatland. The narrator makes no comparison between the complexity of life in Spaceland and Flatland, so choice A is incorrect. The narrator discusses how the shapes in Flatland move, so choice B is incorrect. The narrator discusses visiting Spaceland, so choice D is incorrect.

2. **The correct answer is A.** By referring to the inhabitants of Spaceland as "privileged" to live in Spaceland, the narrator is implying that it is a better place to live than Flatland is. Choices B, C, and D just describe Flatland without making any direct comparison between life there and life in Spaceland.

3. **The correct answer is D.** The narrator spends the sixth paragraph explaining how the horizon in Spaceland is similar to the inhabitants in Flatland in that they both appear as straight lines in the distance. There is no evidence to support any of the other answer choices.

4. **The correct answer is A.** In line 1, the word *nature* applies to a world, and a world has a particular environment, so choice A is the best answer. Choices B and C would better be applied to a person. Choice D is not as specific as choice A.

5. **The correct answer is B.** The lines are intended to help the reader comprehend how the inhabitants of Flatland look. While the lines are worded like an experiment, choice A does not describe their main purpose accurately. The lines describe the inhabitants of Flatland, not the landscape, so choice C is incorrect. Choice D fails to relate the lines to the passage's specific topic.

6. **The correct answer is D.** Evidence in the passage supports the conclusion that the inhabitants of Flatland have genders. Choice A is never implied in the passage. Choice B is contradicted in the passage. The narrator suggests that the inhabitants of Flatland can tell each other apart, so it is likely that choice C is incorrect.

7. **The correct answer is C.** The narrator's reference to a woman in Flatland indicates that genders exist there. The other answer choices provide no evidence for the conclusion that genders exist in Flatland, which is the correct answer to the previous question.

8. **The correct answer is C.** In the final two paragraphs of the passage, the main focus shifts from the inhabitants of Flatland to the climate and houses in Flatland, and the narrator even announces that this is about to happen at the end of the eighth paragraph. The main topic may shift to compass points in Flatland, but not actual compasses, so choice A is incorrect. Choices B and D do not describe any main focuses in the passage.

9. **The correct answer is B.** As used in this final sentence, the word bearings refers to one's place within a land, and the direction he or she has to go. Choice A is incorrect because bearings are not "supports" within this given context. Choices C and D are incorrect because bearings do not have to do with the subject's manners or nature; they have to do with the narrator's positioning.

10. **The correct answer is B.** In the passage, the author characterizes the idea that abundance is better than scarcity as a common-sense assumption. Choices A and C are both too extreme and contradicted by information in the passage. Choice D is also contradicted by the passage.

11. **The correct answer is B.** It is the only answer choice that actually shows the Chambers and the Government following the dictates of the daily papers. Choice A only shows the papers *trying* to dictate the decisions of the Chambers and the Government. Choices C and D only show that the daily papers, the Chambers, and the Government are in agreement.

12. **The correct answer is B.** Choices A, B, and C are all synonyms of *sound*, but only choice B shows how it is used in this particular context. Choice D is an antonym of *sound*.

13. **The correct answer is A.** The quote is mainly intended to serve as evidence of the support for the value of scarcity over abundance. Choices B, C, and D are too concerned with the specific details of the quote and fail to grasp its overall purpose.

14. **The correct answer is C.** There is evidence in the passage that supports the idea that the author would agree that people are wrong to value scarcity over abundance. That evidence contradicts the conclusions in choices A, B, and D.

15. **The correct answer is D.** In these lines, the author characterizes the belief that scarcity is better than abundance as an "illusion," which suggests that those who share that belief are wrong. Choices A, B, and C merely show that people do share that belief.

16. **The correct answer is D.** Choices A, B, and D are all synonyms of *consume*, but only choice D shows how it is used in this particular context. Choice C is an antonym of *consume*.

17. **The correct answer is C.** According to the passage, the theory of scarcity is the idea that scarcity enriches producers; this graph backs up that theory by showing that the less there is of a product the higher its price.

18. **The correct answer is A.** According to the passage, M. Saint-Cricq feared abundance, and the graph supports the idea that abundance is something to be feared since it shows costs drop as abundance increases. The passage discusses workmen only in terms of how abundance affects their machines, so choice B is not the best answer. The author would likely believe that the information on the graph is incomplete since he says the theory of scarcity is an incomplete syllogism. Consumers are never given a voice in the passage, so choice D cannot be correct.

19. **The correct answer is C.** This passage mainly explains how the human arm moves. Although the author begins the passage by asking "How is it that we can move as we do?" he then focuses on the particular movement of the human arm for the entire passage. So choice A is not the best answer. Choices B and D are only details in the passage.

20. **The correct answer is A.** Only *peculiarly* makes sense if used in place of *curiously* in line 13. Choices B and C would imply that the elbow is capable of thought, so they do not make sense in this context. Choice D is an antonym of *curiously*.

21. **The correct answer is C.** According to the passage, the connection between the humerus and ulna is not rigid. Both bones are not in the forearm, so choice A is incorrect. However, they are both in the arm, so choice B is incorrect, too. There is no mention of whether or not the humerus is stout, so choice D is incorrect.

22. **The correct answer is D.** These lines state that the humerus and ulna fit together loosely, and *loosely* is the opposite of *rigidly*. The other answer choices fail to serve as evidence that choice C was the correct answer to the previous question.

23. **The correct answer is C.** Evidence in the passage supports the fact that the ulna slides over the humerus as the ulna moves. The passage contradicts choice A. The author compares the movement to a hinge, but that is not a direct result of moving the ulna, so choice B is not the best answer. The ulna doubles, not the humerus, so choice D is incorrect.

24. **The correct answer is B.** These are the lines that describe how the ulna slides over the humerus when moved. The lines in the other answer choices do not describe this movement clearly.

25. **The correct answer is D.** Each answer choice can be used as a synonym for *bound*, but only choice D makes sense when describing the attachment of tape around an object.

26. **The correct answer is B.** According to the passage, the elbow is at the end of the humerus, and F marks the elbow on the diagram.

27. **The correct answer is D.** The diagram shows that the arm can be bent at the elbow. Choices A and C describe movements the arm cannot do, and the diagram does not specifically indicate anything the arm cannot do. Choice B describes a movement the arm can do that is not shown on the diagram.

28. **The correct answer is D.** In line 3, President Roosevelt is using the figurative phrase to explain that industries are failing. The word *withering* implies the opposite of choice A. Something that has completely disappeared cannot "lie on every side," as Roosevelt says, so choice B is not the best answer. Choice C fails to interpret the figurative phrase accurately.

29. **The correct answer is D.** These lines are the only ones that show a failing industry: the farming industry. Therefore, they are the only ones that can serve as evidence that choice D was the correct answer to the previous question.

30. **The correct answer is A.** It would not be logical for President Obama to indicate that the recession had resulted in people losing their jobs before they could retire if this were not a common problem, and he does indicate that in his speech. Choices B and C overstate comments in Passage 2. There is no evidence to support choice D.

31. **The correct answer is C.** These are the lines in which President Obama mentions people for whom the recession resulted in losing their jobs before they could retire. The other choices do not support choice A as the correct answer to the previous question.

32. **The correct answer is C.** Each answer choice can be used as a synonym for *practices*, but the only one that makes complete sense in this particular context is *procedures*.

33. **The correct answer is D.** Each answer choice can be used as a synonym for *weight*, but the only one that makes complete sense in this particular context is *severity*.

34. **The correct answer is B.** Passage 1 finds President Roosevelt trying to help Americans though the Great Depression, and Passage 2 finds President Obama trying to help Americans through an economic recession. Choice A is only one purpose of Passage 1. Choice C is only one purpose of Passage 2. Choice D is not a purpose of either passage.

35. **The correct answer is D.** In Passage 1, President Roosevelt emphasizes how profit is not the only benefit of working to encourage Americans to continue to work hard. In Passage 2, President Obama celebrates hard work to encourage Americans to continue working hard to overcome the recession. Choice A only applies to Passage 1. Choices B and C are not really implied in either passage.

36. **The correct answer is A.** President Roosevelt spends much of Passage 1 blaming money changers for the Great Depression, but President Obama emphasizes that he does not wish to "lay blame" in Passage 2. The other answer choices fail to indicate the difference in the ways the two presidents discuss the causes of their problems.

37. **The correct answer is B.** In Passage 1, President Roosevelt speaks out about the importance of working for the pure value of achievement. Therefore, it would make sense that President Roosevelt would encourage President Obama to take similar actions in the workplaces Obama mentions in Passage 2.

38. **The correct answer is D.** The opening paragraph is mainly about how people generally believe that the scientific knowledge of their era will never be expanded in the future. Choice A describes the central claim of the passage as a whole, not the central claim of paragraph 1 alone. Choices B and C are only details in the paragraph.

39. **The correct answer is A.** Each answer choice can be used as a synonym for *scored*, but the only one that makes complete sense in this particular context is *marked*.

40. **The correct answer is D.** Evidence in the passage shows that the author believes that contemporary scientific research is of high quality in general.

41. **The correct answer is B.** These lines state most explicitly the author's point that scientific research is high quality. Choice A can be interpreted this way, but it is not as explicit as choice B. Choices C and D do not support the correct answer to the previous question at all.

42. **The correct answer is C.** The author suggests that scientific eras should be compared only if they are separated by long periods of time. There is no evidence in the passage that supports any of the other answer choices.

43. **The correct answer is B.** These lines show that the author believes scientific eras should be compared if they are separated by long periods of time ("the gap of a century"). Choice A just shows that the author believes this is a salient idea; it does not explain what that idea is. Choices C and D are just examples of that idea.

44. **The correct answer is A.** In this quote, Haüy is using the figurative statement to indicate that people in his time assumed science could only clarify, or "cast a brighter light on," existing ideas.

45. **The correct answer is B.** The first three paragraphs of the passage are about how new scientific discoveries are made in every era despite what people think. The subsequent paragraphs illustrate that idea using specific experiments as evidence. Choices A and C are too specific to describe how the *main* focus of the passage shifts. Choice D fails to describe any part of the passage.

46. **The correct answer is D.** Each answer choice can be used as a synonym for *germ*, but the only one that makes complete sense in this particular context is *origin*.

47. **The correct answer is A.** The passage shows that Galvani's experiments with frogs and Davy's experiments with batteries both resulted in unexpected findings that forced scientists to rethink what they thought they already knew. Choice B applies only to Davy. Choice C applies only to Galvani. Choice D does not apply to either scientist.

answers practice test 2

Section 2: Writing and Language Test

1. C	9. A	17. B	24. A	31. A	38. C
2. A	10. C	18. A	25. B	32. C	39. B
3. C	11. B	19. C	26. B	33. C	40. A
4. B	12. A	20. B	27. D	34. A	41. C
5. C	13. C	21. A	28. D	35. B	42. D
6. B	14. B	22. D	29. A	36. D	43. C
7. D	15. C	23. B	30. B	37. C	44. B
8. B	16. C				

WRITING AND LANGUAGE TEST RAW SCORE ▢

(Number of correct answers)

1. **The correct answer is C.** The sentence is past tense, so the verb should be a past participle. Choice C is the only one of the choices that fits this bill. Choice B is an adjective, not a verb, and choice D is a noun.

2. **The correct answer is A.** According to the map, the darkest states have the most NASA-related jobs. If you look at the options, Maine, Nevada, and Michigan seem to have no NASA jobs, while Florida, Texas, and California have high numbers. The best option (choice A) contains two states that have high numbers of NASA jobs.

3. **The correct answer is C.** There is no need for any punctuation to separate the verb *design* from its direct objects. For a colon (choice A) to be necessary, there would need to be a noun to act as the direct object of the verb ("design the following") so that the list of items explain what "the following" is. Use of an em dash (choice B) adds an unnecessary break in the sentence flow, and inserting a semicolon (choice D) creates a fragment after the word *design*.

4. **The correct answer is B.** You need a subordinating conjunction here to show the relationship between "there is no oxygen in space to create thrust" and "aerospace engineers create rockets that run on...." Choices A and D are coordinating conjunctions, which don't really fit with the writer's intent to create a cause-effect relationship. Choice B is a subordinating conjunction that works here to show cause. Choice C is a synonym for *where*, which can be a subordinating conjunction but doesn't fit with the sentence.

5. **The correct answer is C.** As written, this is a run-on sentence, so you need to coordinate the sentence. Choice C does this by combining the first two clauses with *and*, and pairing them with the independent clause to create a complex sentence. Choice B tries to break up the sentence with a parenthetical clause but is still missing coordination and subordination that make it a complete sentence. Choice D puts the coordinating conjunction *and* in the wrong spot, making the sentence confusing.

6. **The correct answer is B.** It makes the most sense to include a specific example of equipment here. Choice A is incorrect, because satellites are given as an example of equipment in space in the same sentence. Choice C is too vague and redundant because the sentence already mentions *equipment*. Choice D is also redundant because you already know that scientists are the ones gathering the information.

7. **The correct answer is D.** You want to make sure that you understand what the writer is trying to say. In this case, he is trying to give an example of atmospheric scientists (meteorologists) and also trying to say what they study (weather and climate). Choice D does this most clearly. Choice B is confusing because there are no clear clauses. Choice C incorrectly sets up the sentence as a list of three equally weighted things, which isn't the case.

8. **The correct answer is B.** The text as written (choice A) leaves a sentence fragment dangling. Choice B uses an em-dash to join the sentences while creating a strong pause, so it is the best of these options. Choice C creates a run-on sentence, and choice D sets up a question that doesn't work here.

9. **The correct answer is A.** The paragraph is about the growing number of communications jobs in the industry, so choice A offers a transition from talking about science and engineering to communications. Choice B doesn't fit because it suggests that the paragraph will still be about science and engineering, while the topic is shifting away from them. Choices C and D are statements that aren't supported by any information in the paragraph.

10. **The correct answer is C.** As written, the underlined text is clunky and repetitive. Choice C removes the wordiness. Choice B is problematic because the author is trying to show range (people who are experts in space science and those who are not), so this feels incomplete. Choice D takes out *too* much and takes away from what the author is trying to convey.

11. **The correct answer is B.** The concluding sentence should summarize the ideas and points in the passage as much as possible. Choice A is an idea that may be supported by the chart, but it is not discussed at length in the passage. Choice C is not relevant, because salaries aren't discussed in the passage, so it's not appropriate to use that information at the very end. Choice D doesn't fit with the passage's tone. Choice B is the option that best fits the different threads and details in the passage.

12. **The correct answer is A.** The sentence is a complex one, but each clause is coordinated and all elements (tense, number, etc.) match. Choice B is incorrect because it causes confusion—is the same person sending the note *and* reading it? Choice C is incorrect because it sets up three sections of the sentence with ellipses, when no information is being left out. Choice D cuts off too much of the sentence and removes half of the author's meaning.

13. **The correct answer is C.** To *affect* means "to influence," which is the meaning you want, based on the context of the sentence.

answers practice test 2

14. The correct answer is B. *A* and *an* are both indefinite articles that refer to non-specific phrases, like *new vocabulary*, so one of these is the correct answer—but which one? The first word of the phrase is *new*, which starts with a consonant. That means you go with *a* (choice B). *An* (choice A) is only correct if the word after the article starts with a vowel. Choice C is incorrect because while *the* is an article, it refers to specific nouns. Choice D is incorrect because *as* can be a conjunction, adverb, or preposition, but not an article.

15. The correct answer is C. This is an agreement question. The underlined word, a pronoun, should agree with its antecedent: *words*. *Words* is a plural noun, so the pronoun should be plural as well. Choice B is plural, but it just reuses the word over again instead of using a pronoun to make the sentence less awkward. Choice C is a plural pronoun. Choice D is a singular possessive, so it doesn't fit here.

16. The correct answer is C. The topic of the paragraph is new vocabulary words making old ones obsolete and, of the choices, C does the best at supporting that topic by adding a detail about how the *OED* chooses its new words. Choice A talks about YouTube, which has little to do with the topic, and choice D changes the subject entirely to punctuation, so these are not relevant to the paragraph as a whole. Choice B is incorrect because it's basically a restatement of the first sentence in the paragraph, which is unnecessary.

17. The correct answer is B. This is another agreement question, but this time you're asked to make sure that the noun matches the number of examples given. The writer gives two examples (*LOL* and *BRB*), so the noun they modify should be plural. Choice C is just a restatement of choice A, and choice D suggests that there's no specific number of terms, when in reality the author gives two specific examples.

18. The correct answer is A. This sentence would make a good introductory sentence for the paragraph, because it shifts the topics away from the dictionary words and helps the author make her point about how language changes in general.

19. The correct answer is C. This sentence needs a good transition, which the underlined part of the sentence is lacking. Choice B doesn't quite fit because *still* suggests that the writer is about to present conflicting information, but that isn't the case. *And* (choice D) doesn't quite work either, because the writer is introducing a new point, about social media in particular being responsible for language changes.

20. The correct answer is B. *Prop* means "to lean," which doesn't fit with the sentence. *Propose* means "to suggest," and that doesn't quite fit either. *Repurpose* means "to reuse," which doesn't work with the context of the changing definitions of the words. *Propel*, or pushing forward, works best with the overall meaning of the sentence.

21. The correct answer is A. The sentence is correct as written, with a subordinate clause ("but rather…") supporting the main clause ("everyone knows that a troll is no longer just a fantastical creature who lives under a bridge"). Choice B is a run-on sentence. Choice C unnecessarily chops up the sentence. Choice D is too wordy and awkward, making the sentence less clear.

22. **The correct answer is D.** The conclusion should help summarize the piece, without introducing any stray details. Of these options, choice D does that by using the tone of the passage to suggest what might come next, language-wise. It also summarizes the kinds of changes we've already seen in our language. Choice A adds new and unnecessary information about selfies, which weren't a main topic of the passage. Choice B focuses just on the dictionary, when the rest of the passage included other cultural uses of language as well. Choice C just recycles the opening sentence, and the repetition is unnecessary.

23. **The correct answer is B.** The sentence and the rest of the passage go on to talk about how diverse and majestic the physical land of the country is, specifically its parks. Choice B is the only option that specifically mentions geography and nature. Choice A is not the best selection because it is vague and unfocused. Choice C is incorrect because the passage and sentence focus on land, not people. Similarly, choice D is incorrect because the passage and sentence are not about culture; they're about natural beauty and physical features.

24. **The correct answer is A.** This is an informational paragraph about the founding of the National Park Service, so choice A sets up that topic by starting with the date the service began. Choice B does nothing to set up the information in the paragraph, because you already know that the passage is talking about American parks from the first paragraph. Choice C is an awkward transition. Choice D doesn't work because it sets up a cause-and-effect relationship, which the author doesn't support in the paragraph that follows. The option you choose should work well with the information that comes next in the paragraph.

25. **The correct answer is B.** This is a complex sentence that should be made simpler and clearer, and choice B does that by setting up a straightforward subject and predicate combo: *Stephen Mather and J. Horace McFarland sought to make.* Choice C is incredibly confusing to read. Choice D creates a run-on sentence.

26. **The correct answer is B.** The paragraph is talking about the history of the parks, but choice B describes the layout of the parks, so it doesn't quite fit with the others.

27. **The correct answer is D.** This choice adds information to the sentence that tells you more about the history of the park. That Alaska was not a state at the time does not support anything in the paragraph. Saying that the park was different also does nothing to support the sentence's previous claim, and the reader already knows that the park was in Wyoming.

28. **The correct answer is D.** The pronoun *it* is unclear here, so the writer should clarify what it means. California was likely not donated to itself, so choice B doesn't work. Choice C doesn't fit with the rest of the sentence—why would the government control be donated to the state? "The park" clarifies that Yosemite Park was donated to the state before becoming a federal park.

29. **The correct answer is A.** The transitional word *however* comes at the end of the sentence, but don't be fooled—it should still get a comma to set it off. Choice B incorrectly joins the *however* to the next sentence, which confuses what the writer is trying to say. Choice C removes the comma and creates an incomplete sentence. Choice D incorrectly uses a semicolon when there's no list or complex set of clauses.

30. **The correct answer is B.** This is an appositive phrase and should be set off from the sentence consistently without mixing punctuation. Choice B correctly does this by using two em-dashes to set off the clause. Choice C removes all punctuation around it, causing confusion about what is being described. Choice D has too many commas and makes the appositive phrase look like a list of items instead (*these sites, geographic parks, or historical parks*).

31. **The correct answer is A.** The paragraph is about the geography of parks, so the size of the total land is a relevant statistic. Choice D is close, but because none of the rest of the passage talks about visitors to the park, the information isn't especially relevant here. Choice B adds no new information. Choice C repeats information already presented in the sentence.

32. **The correct answer is C.** The paragraph talks about the parks altogether, so *collectively* (as a group) makes the most sense.

33. **The correct answer is C.** The sentence talks about the range of types of national parks, and so does paragraph 4. Paragraph 2 (choice A) is about the NPS's history, so the sentence doesn't fit there. Paragraph 3 talks about the parks' history. Paragraph 5 discusses park rangers, so the sentence doesn't really fit there, either.

34. **The correct answer is A.** The writer is talking about universes that don't intersect with our own, so *parallel* (choice A) is the best choice. *Contrast* (choice B) sets up a different kind of relationship, when the writer isn't trying to compare our universe and others. *Compliance* (choice C) and *peril* (choice D) don't fit with the context of the sentence.

35. **The correct answer is B.** The passage is an informational one, written mostly in the third person. The writer doesn't insert himself anywhere else, so it doesn't fit with the tone and style of the rest of the passage to insert "I think." Also, because it's informative, the information should be presented in a declarative way, instead of asking a question. This isn't a rhetorical question designed to make the reader think (like the two questions that follow this sentence). Instead, choices A and C, though phrased differently, both make the writer seem unsure of the information he's presenting. Choice D presents the information in a declarative way but is also incorrect because it still shifts the voice of the passage from third person to first person.

36. **The correct answer is D.** Choice D subordinates half of the sentence, while leaving the main clause intact. Choice A creates a run-on sentence using a comma. Choice B changes the meaning of the entire sentence. Choice C also creates a run-on sentence, but uses an em-dash instead of a comma.

37. **The correct answer is C.** The writer is trying to show the specific term that people use for the multiple universes, so this phrase should have quotation marks. Choice B uses apostrophes, and choice D puts the quotation marks around the entirely wrong word.

38. **The correct answer is C.** The writer is trying to add information that is separate from the example, but supports it. *In addition* (choice C) is the only choice that shows the writer is trying to build on her example. Choice B doesn't fit because the information in the sentence isn't especially surprising or a contrast to the information that came before it. The sentence also doesn't summarize the paragraph, so using *in conclusion* (choice D) is incorrect as well.

39. **The correct answer is B.** When setting up choices, a positive choice (*either*) is always paired with *or* (choice B). *Nor* (choice A) goes with the negative choice (*neither*). The sentence already gives you *either*, so *or* is the correct choice for the underlined text. *Not* (choice C) and *else* (choice D) don't fit with the word *either*.

40. **The correct answer is A.** This sentence summarizes the general topic of the paragraph, while closing it out before transitioning to the next paragraph. Choice B contradicts the information that the writer presents in the paragraph—that the multiverse can't be proven or disproven. Choice C doesn't work because there's nothing in the passage that suggests physicists are scared, so it doesn't fit with the passage. Choice D is a totally different tone from the rest of the paragraph and the rest of the passage.

41. **The correct answer is C.** This sentence expands the author's point in the paragraph, helping to transition from the introductory sentence to the supporting details about Marcelo Gleiser's perspective on the issue. It is related to the paragraph's topic, so choice A is incorrect. It also does not contradict information in the paragraph (choice B). The sentence also doesn't necessarily describe the passage as a whole (choice D).

42. **The correct answer is D.** *Between* (choice A) and *among* (choice D) show the relationship between a number of items. *Between* lets you know there are two items, while *among* lets you know that there are more than two. In this case, there are an unspecified number of people who believe in the multiverse, but it is likely more than two, so *among* is correct.

43. **The correct answer is C.** Although it is usually used as a preposition, when paired with a verb, the word *to* (choice C) creates the infinitive (or basic) form of the verb. In this sentence, the underlined word is followed by the verb *test*, so it works. *Too* (choice A) means "also," which doesn't fit with the verb. The number *two* (choice B) also doesn't fit with the verb. Choice D is the correct word, but incorrectly capitalized.

44. **The correct answer is B.** The Collider is already testing our own universe, so *multiverse* (choice D) doesn't work with the sentence. The sentence isn't talking about a specifically named universe, just the general one, so the proper nouns (choices A and C) are out. That leaves the regular common noun *universe* (choice B).

Section 3: Math Test—No Calculator

1. C	5. B	9. B	12. B	15. 80
2. B	6. C	10. C	13. D	16. 0.96
3. D	7. D	11. D	14. 42	17. $\frac{1}{49}$
4. D	8. A			

MATH TEST—NO CALCULATOR TEST RAW SCORE ☐

(Number of correct answers)

1. **The correct answer is C.** Use the square-root method to solve the equation, as follows:

$$3(x + 2)^2 = 27$$
$$(x + 2)^2 = 9$$
$$x + 2 = \pm\sqrt{9} = \pm3$$
$$x = -2 \pm 3$$
$$x = -5, 1$$

Choice A is incorrect because you did not take the square root of both sides, choice B involves an error in solving the linear equation in the last step, and choice D has answers for which the signs are both wrong.

2. **The correct answer is B.** If the outside temperature is less than or equal to −40°, then the fuel line will freeze. Accounting for the error to ensure the most conservative estimate yields the inequality $T > -38.3°$F. Choice A is incorrect because the arrow is applied in the wrong direction. Choice C shows an inequality for which the fuel line would freeze for every temperature satisfying it. Choice D includes temperatures in which the fuel line would freeze.

3. **The correct answer is D.** The percent increase is $\frac{950 - 20}{20} = 46.5$, which equals 4,650 percent. Choice A is incorrect because it needs to be multiplied by 100. In choice B, the wrong number of members is divided. In choice C, you forgot to subtract 20 from 950 in the numerator.

4. **The correct answer is D.** First, multiply by 12 to clear the fractions. Then, solve the resulting linear equation.

$$\left[\frac{2 - 6x}{-4}\right] - \frac{2}{3}(3x + 1) = \frac{1}{6}x$$
$$-3(2 - 6x) - 8(3x + 1) = 2x$$
$$-6 + 18x - 24x - 8 = 2x$$
$$-6x - 14 = 2x$$
$$-14 = 8x$$
$$-\frac{7}{4} = x$$

So, $(4x)^2 = \left(4 \cdot \left(-\frac{7}{4}\right)\right)^2 = (-7)2 = 49$.

Choice A is the value of $4x$. In choice B, you did not use the distributive property correctly. Choice C is the value of x, not $4x^2$.

5. **The correct answer is B.** Substitute $x_1 = 8$ and $W = \dfrac{39}{2}$ into the formula $W = -\left(\dfrac{1}{2}x_2^2 - \dfrac{1}{2}x_1^2\right)$ and solve for x_2.

$$\frac{39}{2} = -\frac{1}{2}\left(x_2^2 - 8^2\right)$$
$$-39 = x_2^2 - 64$$
$$x_2^2 = 25$$
$$x_2 = \cancel{-5}, 5$$

So, the location of the block after the compression is 5 inches to the right of the fixed-end of the spring. In choice A, you subtracted 5 from the original position of the spring prior to compression. Choice C involves an arithmetic error, and in choice D, you assumed it stretched the spring to the right rather than compressing it.

6. **The correct answer is C.** From the equation of the circle, it follows that $r = 9$ feet. Substituting this and $S = 700$ into the formula $S = \pi r(r + \sqrt{h^2 + r^2})$ yields the equation $700 = \pi \cdot 9\left(9 + \sqrt{h^2 + 9^2}\right)$.

Solve for r, as follows:

$$700 = \pi \cdot 9\left(9 + \sqrt{h^2 + 81}\right)$$
$$\frac{700}{9\pi} = 9 + \sqrt{h^2 + 81}$$
$$\frac{700}{9\pi} - 9 = \sqrt{h^2 + 81}$$
$$\frac{700 - 81\pi}{9\pi} = \sqrt{h^2 + 81}$$
$$\left(\frac{700 - 81\pi}{9\pi}\right)^2 = h^2 + 81$$
$$\left(\frac{700 - 81\pi}{9\pi}\right)^2 - 81 = h^2$$
$$\sqrt{\left(\frac{700 - 81\pi}{9\pi}\right)^2 - 81} = h$$

Choice A simplifies the square root of a difference incorrectly. In choice B, you forgot to subtract r^2 after squaring both sides of the equation to get rid of the square root. In choice D, you forgot the square root and should have subtracted, not added, 81.

7. **The correct answer is D.** Each of these measures has double the value for Data Set II as compared to their values for Data Set I, so none of them can be equal for Data Sets I and II.

8. **The correct answer is A.** Solve for C, as follows:

$$v = \frac{V_{max} \cdot C}{K + C}$$
$$v(K + C) = V_{max} \cdot C$$
$$vK + vC = V_{max} \cdot C$$
$$vK = V_{max} \cdot C - vC$$
$$vK = (V_{max} - v)C$$
$$C = \frac{vK}{V_{max} - v}$$

In choice B, you incorrectly canceled like *terms* instead of *factors* in the numerator and denominator. In choice C, you did not use the distributive property correctly. Choice D should be multiplied by −1.

9. **The correct answer is B.** The median response for each of the three categories is the average of the 200th and 201st data values for that category's responses. For issue I, the median is 3, while the median for issue II is $\dfrac{3+4}{2} = 3.5$. So, the difference in the medians is 0.5. Choice A is wrong since the medians are not equal; choice C is the difference in the means for issues I and II; and choice D incorrectly computes the median response for issue II.

10. **The correct answer is C.** Restrict attention to row 3 and use the cells corresponding to scores of 4 and 5 to compute the probability: $\dfrac{180 + 30}{400} = \dfrac{210}{400} = 0.525$. Choice A is the probability that the response is below neutral. In choice B, you divided by 1,200. Choice D mistakenly includes neutral.

answers practice test 2

11. **The correct answer is D.** The only choice that, upon multiplying it by 0.35, yields a whole number is 120. Indeed, note that $0.35(120) = 42$.

12. **The correct answer is B.** First, determine the equation of the line. The slope is $m = \dfrac{k-(-1)}{-2-4} = -\dfrac{k+1}{6}$. Using the point-slope formula with the point $(4, -1)$ yields the equation $y + 1 = -\dfrac{k+1}{6}(x - 4)$, or equivalently $y = -\dfrac{k+1}{6}x - 1 + \dfrac{2}{3}(k + 1)$. Now, substitute $x = -6$ and $y = 0$ and solve for k:

$$0 = -\frac{k+1}{6}(-6) - 1 + \frac{2}{3}(k+1)$$

$$0 = k + 1 - 1 + \frac{2}{3}(k+1)$$

$$0 = \frac{5}{3}k + \frac{2}{3}$$

$$0 = 5k + 2$$

$$5k = -2$$

$$k = -\frac{2}{5}$$

In choice A, you used a y-intercept of $(0, -6)$. Choice C involves an error in solving the linear equation. Choice D ensures the slope is -6, not the x-intercept.

13. **The correct answer is D.** Using distance equals rate times time, we derive two equations, as follows:

Trip 1:

Distance by bus = 240 miles

Speed of bus = x Time = $\dfrac{240}{x}$

Distance by car = 560 miles

Speed of car = y Time = $\dfrac{560}{y}$

Total time for trip = 9 hours

So, the equation is: $\dfrac{240}{x} + \dfrac{560}{y} = 9$.

Trip 2:

Distance by bus = 320 miles

Speed of bus = x Time = $\dfrac{320}{x}$

Distance by car = 480 miles

Speed of car = y Time = $\dfrac{480}{y}$

Total time for trip = 9.5 hours

So, the equation is $\dfrac{320}{x} + \dfrac{480}{y} = 9.5$.

So, the system is $\begin{cases} \dfrac{320}{x} + \dfrac{480}{y} = 9.5 \\ \dfrac{240}{x} + \dfrac{560}{y} = 9 \end{cases}$

In choices A and C, you used "distance equals rate times time" incorrectly, and in choice B, the variables in the equations are mismatched.

14. **The correct answer is 42 hours.** Given the ratio of 6:2, let $6x$ represent the number of hours she spends conducting therapy, and let $2x$ represent the number of hours she spends doing research. Since the total number of hours spent is 56, we can write the equation $2x + 6x = 56$, which is equivalent to $8x = 56$. So, $x = 7$. As such, the number of hours spent conducting therapy session is $6x = 6(7) = 42$.

15. **The correct answer is 80.** Isolate the radical term on one side of the equation, then square both sides and solve for x:

$$4\sqrt{1-x} = 36$$
$$\sqrt{1-x} = 9$$
$$1-x = 81$$
$$x = -80$$

So, $|x| = |{-80}| = 80$.

16. **The correct answer is 0.96.** The quantity A is the original number present, which we interpret here as 500 customers. The quantity b is the percentage that is applied to the number of customers in week x to get the number in week $(x + 1)$. This value is $b = 1 - 0.04 = 0.96$.

17. **The correct answer is $\frac{1}{49}$.** The substitution method is the most efficient one to apply. Substitute the expression for x given by the second equation into the first equation, and solve for y:

$$5(y - 2) + 1 = 2y$$
$$5y - 10 + 1 = 2y$$
$$5y - 9 = 2y$$
$$3y = 9$$
$$y = 3$$

Thus, $x = 3 - 2 = 1$. As such, $(2x - 3y) - 2 = (2 - 9) - 2 = (-7) - 2 = \frac{1}{(-7)^2} = \frac{1}{49}$.

answers practice test 2

Section 4: Math Test—Calculator

1. C	**8.** A	**14.** B	**20.** A	**26.** A
2. C	**9.** D	**15.** B	**21.** C	**27.** B
3. C	**10.** D	**16.** D	**22.** B	**28.** 0.61
4. D	**11.** C	**17.** D	**23.** C	**29.** 18
5. A	**12.** C	**18.** D	**24.** C	**30.** 960
6. C	**13.** B	**19.** B	**25.** B	**31.** $\frac{8}{3}$
7. C				

MATH TEST—CALCULATOR TEST RAW SCORE

(Number of correct answers)

1. **The correct answer is C.** Convert the units, as follows:

$$\frac{5\ \cancel{g}}{\frac{1}{2}\ \text{sec.}} \times \frac{0.001\ \cancel{kg}}{1\ \cancel{g}} \times \frac{1\ \text{gal.}}{3.785\ \cancel{kg}} \times \frac{60\ \cancel{sec.}}{1\ \text{min.}} = \frac{2(0.3)}{3.785}\ \text{gal.}\Big/\text{min.}$$

$$\approx 0.15852\ \text{gal.}\Big/\text{min.} = 1.59 \times 10^{-1}\ \text{gal.}\Big/\text{min.}$$

In choice A, you used 2 seconds instead of $\frac{1}{2}$ second, and in choice B, you did not convert to minutes, showing instead the rate in gallons per second. In choice D, you used the information from the problem as though the rate was 5 grams per second instead of per half-second.

2. **The correct answer is C.** First, draw the following diagram:

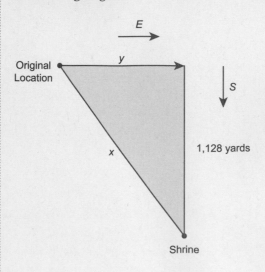

It is given that $y = \frac{1}{5}x$, therefore, by the Pythagorean theorem:

$$\left(\frac{1}{5}x\right)^2 + 1,128^2 = x^2$$

$$\frac{1}{25}x^2 + 1,128^2 = x^2$$

$$1,128^2 = \frac{24}{25}x^2$$

$$\sqrt{\frac{25}{24}(1,128)^2} = x$$

$$x \approx 1,151.3$$

So, Frank was originally about 1,151.3 yards from the shrine. In choice A, you divided y by 5 instead of multiplying it by 5. Choice B is the distance due east that Frank walked. In choice D, you did not square the quantities in the Pythagorean theorem.

3. **The correct answer is C.** Let r_1 be the money market interest rate and r_2 the CD interest rate. Solve the following system:

$$\begin{cases} 30,000\,r_1 + 20,000r_2 = 1,600 \\ 20,000\,r_1 + 30,000r_2 = 2,000 \end{cases}$$

Divide both equations by 100:

$$\begin{cases} 300\,r_1 + 200r_2 = 16 \\ 200\,r_1 + 300r_2 = 20 \end{cases}$$

Multiply the first equation by −2 and the second equation by 3, and then add to get $500r_2 = 28$ so that $r_2 = \dfrac{28}{500} = 0.056$, or 5.6%. Choice A is the money market interest rate, choice B is the result of an arithmetic error, and choice D is the sum of the two interest rates.

4. **The correct answer is D.** FOIL the first two expressions, simplify, and then distribute the x to all terms of the resulting trinomial:

$$(2-3x)(3-2x)x = \left(6 - 9x - 4x + 6x^2\right)x$$
$$= \left(6x^2 - 13x + 6\right)x$$
$$= 6x^3 - 13x^2 + 6x$$

In choice A, you forgot the middle term when FOILing the first two expressions; in choice B, you did not multiply by x; and in choice C, the first two coefficients are wrong.

5. **The correct answer is A.** Suppressing the units momentarily, use the following in the formula: $T = 30$, $m = 5$, and $r = 3$ (half the diameter of 6). Solve the equation for v:

$$30 = \frac{5 \cdot v^2}{3}$$
$$90 = 5 \cdot v^2$$
$$18 = v^2$$
$$v = 3\sqrt{2}$$

In choice B, you used the diameter instead of the radius. In choice C, you forgot to take the square root, and in choice D you used the diameter and forgot to take the square root.

6. **The correct answer is C.** Let $x = \mathrm{m}\,(\angle R)$ and $y = \mathrm{m}\,(\angle P)$. Solve the system:

$$\begin{cases} y = 2x - 3 \\ x + y = 39 \end{cases}$$

Solve using the substitution method. Substitute the expression from the first equation into the second equation and solve for x:

$$x + (2x - 3) = 39$$
$$3x = 42$$
$$x = 14$$

So, $\mathrm{m}\,(\angle R) = 14°$ and $\mathrm{m}\,(\angle P) = 25°$. Since the sum of the angles in a triangle is 180°, we see that $\mathrm{m}\,(\angle Q) = 180° - (14° + 25°) = 141°$. Thus, $\mathrm{m}\,(\angle Q) - \mathrm{m}\,(\angle P) = 116°$. Choice A is the measure of angle R, choice B is the measure of angle P, and choice D is the measure of angle Q.

7. **The correct answer is C.** Factor all expressions and write the division problem as a multiplication problem. Then, cancel like factors in the numerator and denominator:

$$\frac{6x^2 + 5x - 1}{x^2 - 2x} \div \frac{(x+1)\left(36x^2 - 12x + 1\right)}{x - 2}$$
$$= \frac{(6x-1)(x+1)}{x(x-2)} \div \frac{(x+1)(6x-1)(6x-1)}{x-2}$$
$$= \frac{(6x-1)(x+1)}{x(x-2)} \cdot \frac{x-2}{(x+1)(6x-1)(6x-1)}$$
$$= \frac{1}{x(6x-1)}$$

Choice A is the result of multiplying instead of dividing, choice B should have $6x - 1$ in the denominator, and choice D is the reciprocal of the correct answer.

8. **The correct answer is A.** Subtract the y-coordinate of the point of the earlier year from the y-coordinate of the point of the later year for each of the four given choices. The differences for choices A through D are respectively, 15 percent, −15 percent, 5 percent, and 0 percent. So, the largest occurs in choice A.

9. **The correct answer is D.** Work from left to right to determine these. As you do so, you will find the following consecutive-year triples have negative averages: 08–09–10, 09–10–11, 10–11–12, 11–12–13, and 14–15–16.

10. **The correct answer is D.** Check each answer choice to see what part of the xy-coordinate plane is included in the solution set. Choice A includes values in the 1st and 4th quadrants (everything to the right of the y-axis is shaded), choice B includes values in the 1st and 2nd quadrants (everything above the x-axis is shaded), and choice C includes values in the 2nd and 3rd quadrants (everything to the left of the y-axis is shaded). As you can see, only choice D has a solution set that includes the indicated values.

11. **The correct answer is C.** Let x be the number of minutes the ferry ride takes to complete. Since only one passenger went on the ride, the cost of the ferry ride is $(24 + 0.40x)$ dollars. Set this equal to $72 and solve for x:

$$24 + 0.40x = 72$$
$$0.40x = 48$$
$$x = 120 \text{ minutes}$$

Choice A is the result of an error in the final step of solving the linear equation. In choice B, you used the wrong cost per minute. Choice D is the result of adding 24 to both sides of the linear equation instead of subtracting it.

12. **The correct answer is C.** The density of traffic prior to adding the two lanes is given by $D = \dfrac{\text{number of cars}}{\text{square footage}} = \dfrac{3}{138} = \dfrac{1}{46} \dfrac{\text{car}}{\text{sq ft}}$. This means 1 car per 46 square feet of road. A reduction by 30 percent equals

$$\frac{1}{46} - 0.30\left(\frac{1}{46}\right) = \frac{1}{46} - \frac{3}{460} = \frac{7}{460} \frac{\text{cars}}{\text{sq ft}}.$$

To get the density in terms of a single car, divide the numerator and denominator by 7.

$$\frac{7 \div 7}{460 \div 7} \frac{\text{cars}}{\text{sq ft}} \approx \frac{1}{65.7} \frac{\text{car}}{\text{sq ft}}$$

In choice A, you added 30 percent instead of subtracting it. Choice B is the current traffic density. Choice D is a 50 percent reduction.

13. **The correct answer is B.** Substitute $R = \dfrac{D}{2}$ (since the radius is half the diameter) into the formula $m = 4\pi R^2 l \rho$ and solve for D:

$$m = 4\pi\left(\frac{D}{2}\right)^2 l\rho$$
$$m = \pi D^2 l\rho$$
$$\frac{m}{\pi l\rho} = D^2$$
$$D = \sqrt{\frac{m}{\pi l\rho}}$$

In choice A, you subtracted by $\varpi l\rho$ instead of dividing by it. In choice C, you used the radius instead of the diameter, and in choice D, you mistakenly used $R = 2D$ instead of $R = \dfrac{D}{2}$.

14. **The correct answer is B.** Solve for x, as follows:

$$1.6 - 0.8(2 - 5x) < -3.2x$$
$$1.6 - 1.6 + 4x < -3.2x$$
$$7.2x < 0$$
$$x < 0$$

To visualize this on the number line, put an open hole at 0 and draw a ray that extends to the left. This is shown in choice B. Choice A includes 0 (but should not since the inequality is strict) and extends in the wrong direction, choice C is the result of having made sign errors when solving the inequality, and choice D is the result of having made a sign error when solving the inequality and it should not include 4 since it is a strict inequality.

15. **The correct answer is B.** The cost per person for the limousine rental when there are p people splitting the bill is $\dfrac{240}{p}$ dollars, and the cost per person when there are $(p-2)$ people splitting the bill is $\dfrac{240}{p-2}$ dollars. The difference in these costs is 10 dollars. This yields the equation $\dfrac{240}{p-2} - \dfrac{240}{p} = 10$. Solve for p, as follows:

$$\frac{240}{p-2} - \frac{240}{p} = 10$$
$$240p - 240(p-2) = 10p(p-2)$$
$$240p - 240p + 480 = 10p^2 - 20p$$
$$48 = p^2 - 2p$$
$$p^2 - 2p - 48 = 0$$
$$(p-8)(p+6) = 0$$
$$p = \cancel{-6}, 8$$

So, there were originally 8 people sharing the limousine rental. Choice A is the number of people *after* the couple withdraws from the rental, choices C and D are the results of solving a quadratic equation incorrectly; you MUST have zero on one side before solving the equation.

16. **The correct answer is D.** The slope of the linear function is obtained by using the points (0, 42,000) and (28, 0): $m = \dfrac{42,000 - 0}{0 - 28} = -1,500$. The units are feet per minute. This means that the booster's height decreases by 1,500 feet per minute of its descent. Choice A has a positive slope, which would mean the line would rise from left to right; choice B has the wrong slope; and choice C has the booster gaining height instead of falling toward the ocean—a negative slope means the height decreases.

17. **The correct answer is D.** Compute the composition, as follows:

$$(f \circ g)(x) = f(g(x))$$
$$-5[2(3-x)-1]^2 + 1$$
$$-5[5 - 2x]^2 + 1$$
$$-5[25 - 20x + 4x^2] + 1$$
$$-125 + 100x - 20x^2 + 1$$
$$-20x^2 + 100x - 124$$

In choice A, you did not FOIL correctly (the middle terms are missing). Choice B is $(g \circ f)(x)$. In choice C, you did not use the distributive property correctly.

18. **The correct answer is D.** First, convert the quantities to the same units:

$$\frac{180 \text{ rotations}}{1 \text{ minute}} \times \frac{1 \text{ minute}}{60 \text{ seconds}} = \frac{3 \text{ rotations}}{1 \text{ second}}$$

Now, the percent increase is $\dfrac{3 - 0.75}{0.75} = \dfrac{2.25}{0.75} = 3$, or 300 percent. Choice A is not converted to a percent. In choice B, you divided by the wrong rotation rate. Choice C is half the correct rotation rate.

answers practice test 2

19. The correct answer is B. Combine the rational expressions using the least common denominator $x(1 + 2x)$, and then simplify:

$$\frac{3 - 2x}{1 + 2x} - \frac{3 - x}{x}$$
$$= \frac{x(3 - 2x) - (3 - x)(1 + 2x)}{x(1 + 2x)}$$
$$= \frac{3x - 2x^2 - (3 - x + 6x - 2x^2)}{x(1 + 2x)}$$
$$= \frac{3x - 2x^2 - 3 - 5x + 2x^2}{x(1 + 2x)}$$
$$= \frac{-2x - 3}{x(1 + 2x)}$$
$$= -\frac{3 + 2x}{x(1 + 2x)}$$

In choice A, you canceled out common terms, not factors, in the numerator and the denominator; choice C is the result of adding instead of subtracting; and in choice D, you did not use a least common denominator when adding the rational expressions.

20. The correct answer is A. First, determine the equation of the linear function that describes the water level once the rain stops. The y-intercept is 16 inches. The slope is $m = \frac{-1.2 \text{ inches}}{3 \text{ days}} = -0.4$ inch per day. So, the equation of the function is $h(d) = -0.4d + 16$. Since one-half foot is 6 inches, solve the equation $-0.4d + 16 = 6$. In choice B, you did not convert feet to inches; in choice C, you computed the slope incorrectly; and in choice D, you did not convert feet to inches and used the wrong slope.

21. The correct answer is C. Use the exponent rules to write the given expression in the desired form:

$$\frac{x\left(x^{-3}y^2\right)^2}{y\left(x^2y^4\right)^{-1}} = \frac{x^{-5}y^4}{x^{-2}y^{-3}}$$
$$= \frac{x^2y^3y^4}{x^5} = \frac{x^2y^7}{x^5} = x^{-3}y^7$$

So, $a = -3$ and $b = 7$. Choice A has the wrong sign on the a-value. In choice B, you simplified a "power to a power" incorrectly. In choice D, you simplified the quotient of terms with the same base raised to powers incorrectly.

22. The correct answer is B. Measure the vertical distance between the data point and the point on the trend line that lies directly above or below this data point. There are four points (the ones circled below) with the desired distance:

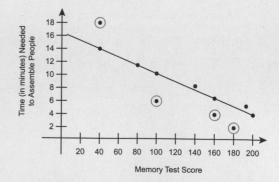

23. The correct answer is C. The range in the input given by $100 \le x \le 130$ corresponds to the output range "9 to 11 minutes, inclusive," using the y-values on the trend line. In choice A, you used the y-coordinates of the data points instead of the trend line, and choices B and D both require different inputs to generate those ranges on the trend line.

24. **The correct answer is C.** The solution set would be the intersection of the region shaded above the line $y = 2x + 3$ and the region below the line $y = -3 + 2x$. But, no point is common to both regions, as seen below:

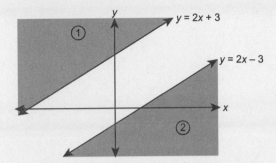

So, the solution set is the empty set for this system. Choice A has a solution—for instance, the point $(5,3)$ satisfies the system; choice B has the entire xy-plane as its solution set, and choice D has the solution set being every point on the line $y = 2x$.

25. **The correct answer is B.** Let x be the number of sit-ups for round five. The average for the five rounds is $\dfrac{42 + 51 + 31 + 63 + x}{5}$. To achieve the "satisfactory" level, one must average more than 50 sit-ups and no more than 80 sit-ups. This is described by the inequality $50 < \dfrac{42 + 51 + 31 + 63 + x}{5} \le 80$. The errors present in the other choices are the correct inclusion or exclusion of one or both endpoints.

26. **The correct answer is A.** The points are packed moderately close together (in that they are not all *on* the same line, but they are not so widely dispersed as to not see the rising pattern that exists among them). The points rise from left to right, so the relationship is positive. And, a trend line reasonably describes this relationship since there is no evident nonlinear curve to which the points conform. Choice B incorrectly describes the relationship as nonlinear, choice C incorrectly says the relationship is

negative, and choice D is wrong because the existence of a single outlier does not inhibit the identification of a relationship.

27. **The correct answer is B.** First, write the given equation in slope-intercept form:

$$-3(2x + y) + 9 = 0$$
$$-3(2x + y) = -9$$
$$2x + y = 3$$
$$y = -2x + 3$$

The y-intercept is 3 and the slope is -2. This is true only of the line in choice B. Choices C and D have the wrong sign on the y-intercept, and choice A has the wrong sign on the x-intercept.

28. **The correct answer is 0.61.** Restrict attention to the first column, which contains 97 outcomes instead of 200. Of these, 59 satisfy the criterion. So, the probability is $\dfrac{59}{97}$. Divide 59 by 97 to get your final answer in decimal form: $59 \div 97 = 0.608$, or 0.61.

29. **The correct answer is 18.** You want the boulder to peak at the wall to give it the best chance of making it over the wall. The maximum value of a parabola that opens downward occurs at its vertex. The vertex occurs exactly halfway between the two x-intercepts. The x-intercept is at $x = 40$ and the vertex is at $x = 29$. So, the other x-intercept occurs 11 yards to the left of 29, namely at 18.

30. **The correct answer is 960π square feet.** The diameter of the outer rim of the traffic roundabout is 76 feet. So, the radius of the larger circle is 38 feet. Since the street is 16 feet wide and occurs on both sides, the diameter of the inner circle is $76 - 32$ feet, or 44 feet. So, its radius is 22 feet. So, the area of the street used for the traffic roundabout is $\pi(38)2 - \pi(22)2 = 960\pi$ square feet.

31. The correct answer is $\frac{8}{3}$. Solve for x, as follows:

$$2x - 3[1 - (C + 3x)] = 5 + 11x$$
$$2x - 3[1 - C - 3x] = 5 + 11x$$
$$2x - 3 + 3C + 9x = 5 + 11x$$
$$11x - 3 + 3C = 11x + 5$$
$$11x + 3C = 11x + 8$$

Since both sides have the same coefficient of x, the only way for the equation to have infinitely many solutions is if the constant terms are equal. So, $3C = 8$. The solution is $C = \frac{8}{3}$.

USING YOUR PRACTICE TEST RESULTS

Now that you've completed the second PSAT/NMSQT® exam, it's time to compute your scores. Simply follow the instructions on the following pages, and use the conversion tables provided to calculate your scores. The formulas provided will give you as close an approximation as possible on how you might score on the actual exam.

To Determine Your Test Score

1. After you go through each of the test sections (**Reading, Writing and Language, Math—No Calculator**, and **Math—Calculator**) and determine which answers you got right, be sure to enter the number of correct answers in the box below the answer key for each of the sections.

2. Your total score on this test is the sum of your Evidence-Based Reading and Writing Section score and your Math Section score. To get your total score for each test section, convert the raw score—the number of questions you got right in a particular section—into the "scaled score" for that section, and then calculate the total score. It may sound a little confusing, but we'll take you through the steps.

To Calculate Your Evidence-Based Reading and Writing Section Score

Your Evidence-Based Reading and Writing Section score is on a scale of 160–760. First determine your Reading Test score, and then determine your score on the Writing and Language Test.

1. Count the number of correct answers you got on the **Reading Test Section**. *Remember that there is no penalty for wrong answers.* **The number of correct answers is your raw score.**

2. Go to **Raw Score Conversion Table 1: Section and Test Scores** on page 550. Look in the "Raw Score" column for your raw score, and match it to the number in the "Reading Test Score" column.

3. Do the same with the **Writing and Language Test Section** to determine that score.

4. Add your **Reading Test score** to your **Writing and Language Test score**.

5. Multiply that number by 10. This is your **Evidence-Based Reading and Writing Section score.**

To Calculate Your Math Section Score

Your Math score is also on a scale of 160–760.

1. 1. Count the number of correct answers you got on the **Math Test—No Calculator Section** and the **Math Test—Calculator Section**. *Again, there is no penalty for wrong answers.* **The number of correct answers is your raw score.**

2. 2. Add the number of correct answers on the **Math Test—No Calculator Section** and the **Math Test—Calculator Section**.

3. 3. Use the **Raw Score Conversion Table 1: Section and Test Scores** on page 550 and convert your raw score into your **Math Section score.**

To Obtain Your Total Score

Add your score on the **Evidence-Based Reading and Writing Section** to the **Math Section** score. This is your **Total Score** on this test, on a scale of 320–1520.

SUBSCORES, TEST SCORES, AND CROSS-TEST SCORES

Test scores, subscores, and cross-test scores offer you greater details about your strengths and weaknesses in certain areas within reading, writing, and math, which can help you evaluate your current skill set and determine which areas you need to focus on most to make improvements. Your scores on the PSAT/NMSQT® exam can also be used to help you predict—and further prepare for—the SAT® exam.

PSAT/NMSQT® Subscores

Subscores on the official PSAT/NMSQT® exam are designed to reflect your performance in a range of key skill areas. You should use your scores to help guide your future study following the exam, and to help guide your preparation for the SAT® exam. Subscores range from 1–15, and include the following areas: Heart of Algebra, Problem Solving and Data Analysis, Passport to Advanced Math, Expression of Ideas, Standard English Conventions, Words in Context, and Command of Evidence.

Computing Your Test Subscores

Heart of Algebra

The **Heart of Algebra subscore** is based on questions from the **Math Test** that focus on linear equations and inequalities. Add up your total correct answers from these questions:

- Math Test—No Calculator: Questions 2, 4, 12, 13
- Math Test—Calculator: Questions 2, 6, 10, 11, 14, 15, 20, 24, 25, 27, 29, 31

Your Raw Score = the total number of correct answers from all of these questions.

Use the **Raw Score Conversion Table 2: Subscores** on page 552 to determine your **Heart of Algebra** subscore.

Problem Solving and Data Analysis

The **Problem Solving and Data Analysis subscore** is based on questions from the **Math Test** that focus on quantitative reasoning, the interpretation and synthesis of data, and solving problems in rich and varied contexts. Add up your total correct answers from these questions:

- Math Test—No Calculator: Questions 3, 7, 9-11, 14
- Math Test—Calculator: Questions 1, 3, 8, 9, 12, 18, 22, 23, 26, 28

Your Raw Score = the total number of correct answers from all of these questions

Use the **Raw Score Conversion Table 2: Subscores** on page 552 to determine your **Problem Solving and Data Analysis** subscore.

Passport to Advanced Math

The **Passport to Advanced Math subscore** is based on questions from the **Math Test** that focus on topics central to your ability to progress to more advanced math, such as understanding the structure of expressions, reasoning with more complex equations, and interpreting and building functions. Add up your total correct answers from these questions:

- Math Test—No Calculator: Questions 1, 5, 8, 15-17
- Math Test—Calculator: Questions 4, 5, 7, 13, 16, 17, 19, 21

Your Raw Score = the total number of correct answers from all of these questions

Use the **Raw Score Conversion Table 2: Subscores** on page 552 to determine your **Passport to Advanced Math** subscore.

Expression of Ideas

The **Expression of Ideas subscore** is based on questions from the **Writing and Language Test** that focus on topic development, organization, and rhetorically effective use of language. Add up your total correct answers from these questions in Section 2: Writing and Language Test:

- Questions 2,4, 6, 9-11, 16, 18, 20, 22-24, 26-28, 31-35, 38, 40, 41, 44

Your Raw Score = the total number of correct answers from all of these questions

Use the **Raw Score Conversion Table 2: Subscores** on page 552 to determine your **Expression of Ideas** subscore.

Standard English Conventions

The **Standard English Conventions subscore** is based on questions from the **Writing and Language Test** that focus on sentence structure, usage, and punctuation. Add up your total correct answers from these questions in Section 2: Writing and Language Test:

- Questions 1, 3, 5, 7, 8, 12-15, 17, 19, 21, 25, 29, 30, 36, 37, 39, 42, 43

Your Raw Score = the total number of correct answers from all of these questions

Use the **Raw Score Conversion Table 2: Subscores** on page 552 to determine your **Standard English Conventions** subscore.

Words in Context

The **Words in Context subscore** is based on questions from the **Reading Test** and the **Writing and Language Test** that address word/phrase meaning in context and rhetorical word choice. Add up your total correct answers from these questions in the following sections:

- Reading Test: Questions 4, 9, 12, 16, 20, 25, 32, 33, 39, 46
- Writing and Language Test: Questions 1, 4, 13, 20, 28, 32, 34, 42

Your Raw Score = the total number of correct answers from all of these questions

Use the **Raw Score Conversion Table 2: Subscores** on page 552 to determine your **Words in Context** subscore.

Command of Evidence

The **Command of Evidence subscore** is based on questions from the **Reading Test** and the **Writing and Language** Test that ask you to interpret and use evidence found in a wide range of passages and informational graphics, such as graphs, tables, and charts. Add up your total correct answers from these questions in Sections 1 and 2:

- Reading Test: Questions 2, 7, 15, 22, 24, 27, 29, 31, 41, 43
- Writing and Language Test: Questions 2, 6, 27, 31, 33, 40, 41

Your Raw Score = the total number of correct answers from all of these questions

Use the **Raw Score Conversion Table 2: Subscores** on page 552 to determine your **Command of Evidence** subscore.

PSAT/NMSQT® Test and Cross-test Scores

When you take the official PSAT/NMSQT® exam, you'll receive three additional test scores (alongside your total score and section scores) on a range of 8–38. These test scores are designed to show how you performed on the content covered in each of the test sections: Reading, Writing and Language, and Math.

You'll also receive two cross-test scores on the official PSAT/NMSQT® exam, which will reflect your performance in the following content domains (which span all test sections): **Analysis in History/ Social Studies**, and **Analysis in Science**. These scores will also be in the range of 8–38, and will help you further analyze your current skill level.

Computing Your Cross-Test Scores

Use the following to determine your cross-test scores:

Analysis in History/Social Studies

Add up your total correct answers from these questions:

- Reading Test: Questions 10-18, 28-37
- Writing and Language Test: Questions 23, 24, 26, 27, 31, 33
- Math Test—No Calculator: Questions 3, 9, 10
- Math Test—Calculator: Questions 3, 8, 9, 12

Your Raw Score = the total number of correct answers from all of these questions.

Use the **Raw Score Conversion Table 3: Cross-Test Scores** on page 554 to determine your **Analysis in History/Social Studies** cross-test score.

Analysis in Science

Add up your total correct answers from these sections:

- Reading Test: Questions 19-27, 38-47
- Writing and Language Test: Questions 34, 35, 38, 40, 41, 44

- Math Test—No Calculator: Questions 2, 5, 8
- Math Test—Calculator: Questions 1, 5, 16, 28

Your Raw Score = the total number of correct answers from all of these questions

Use the **Raw Score Conversion Table 3: Cross-Test Scores** on page 554 to determine your **Analysis in Science** cross-test score.

Raw Score Conversion Table 1: Section and Test Scores

Raw Score (# of correct answers)	Reading Test Score	Writing and Language Test Score	Math Section Score	Raw Score (# of correct answers)	Reading Test Score	Writing and Language Test Score	Math Section Score
0	8	8	160	25	26	25	560
1	9	9	190	26	26	26	570
2	10	10	210	27	27	27	580
3	11	11	240	28	27	27	580
4	12	12	270	29	28	28	590
5	14	13	290	30	28	28	600
6	15	14	320	31	29	29	610
7	16	14	340	32	29	29	620
8	16	15	360	33	30	30	630
9	17	15	370	34	30	30	640
10	18	16	390	35	31	31	650
11	18	16	400	36	31	32	670
12	19	17	420	37	32	32	680
13	19	18	430	38	32	33	690
14	20	18	440	39	33	34	710
15	20	19	460	40	34	35	720
16	21	20	470	41	34	36	730
17	21	20	480	42	35	37	730
18	22	21	490	43	36	37	740
19	22	21	500	44	37	38	740
20	23	22	510	45	37		750
21	23	23	520	46	38		750
22	24	24	530	47	38		760
23	24	24	540	48			760
24	25	25	550				

Conversion Table 1: Section and Test Scores

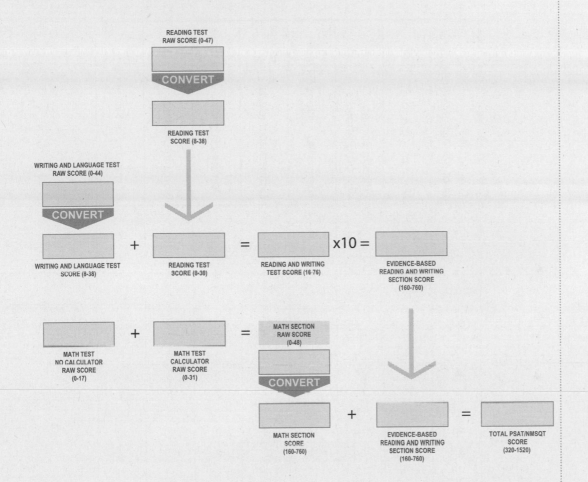

READING TEST
RAW SCORE (0-47)

CONVERT

READING TEST
SCORE (8-38)

WRITING AND LANGUAGE TEST
RAW SCORE (0-44)

CONVERT

WRITING AND LANGUAGE TEST
SCORE (8-38)

+

READING TEST
SCORE (8-38)

=

READING AND WRITING
TEST SCORE (16-76)

x10 =

EVIDENCE-BASED
READING AND WRITING
SECTION SCORE
(160-760)

MATH TEST
NO CALCULATOR
RAW SCORE
(0-17)

+

MATH TEST
CALCULATOR
RAW SCORE
(0-31)

=

MATH SECTION
RAW SCORE
(0-48)

CONVERT

MATH SECTION
SCORE
(160-760)

+

EVIDENCE-BASED
READING AND WRITING
SECTION SCORE
(160-760)

=

TOTAL PSAT/NMSQT
SCORE
(320-1520)

Raw Score Conversion Table 2: Subscores

Raw Score (# of correct answers)	Heart of Algebra	Problem Solving and Data Analysis	Passport to Advanced Math	Expression of Ideas	Standard English Conventions	Words in Context	Command of Evidence
0	1	1	1	1	1	1	1
1	3	3	5	2	2	2	2
2	4	4	7	3	3	3	3
3	5	5	8	4	3	3	4
4	6	6	9	4	4	4	5
5	7	7	10	5	4	5	6
6	8	8	11	6	5	6	7
7	8	8	12	6	6	6	8
8	9	9	13	7	6	7	8
9	10	10	14	7	7	8	9
10	10	11	15	8	7	9	9
11	11	11	15	8	8	10	10
12	12	12	15	9	8	10	11
13	13	13	15	9	9	11	11
14	14	14	15	10	9	12	12
15	15	15		10	10	13	13
16	15	15		11	10	14	14
17				12	11	15	15
18				12	12	15	15
19				13	13		
20				13	15		
21				14			
22				15			
23				15			
24				15			

Conversion Equation 2: Subscores

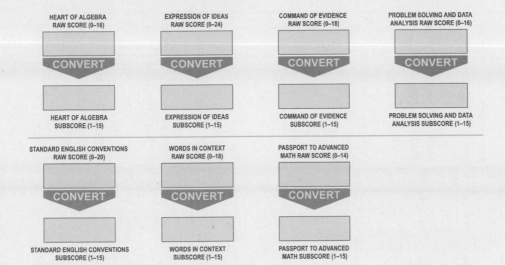

Raw Score Conversion Table 3: Cross-Test Scores

Raw Score (# of correct answers)	Analysis in History/Social Studies Cross-Test Score	Analysis in Science Cross-Test Score
0	8	8
1	9	12
2	11	15
3	12	16
4	14	17
5	15	18
6	16	18
7	17	19
8	18	20
9	19	21
10	20	22
11	21	23
12	22	24
13	23	25
14	24	26
15	25	26
16	26	27

Raw Score (# of correct answers)	Analysis in History/Social Studies Cross-Test Score	Analysis in Science Cross-Test Score
17	26	28
18	27	28
19	28	29
20	29	30
21	30	31
22	30	31
23	31	32
24	32	33
25	32	34
26	33	35
27	34	36
28	35	37
29	36	37
30	37	38
31	37	38
32	38	38

Conversion Equation 3: Cross-Test Scores

TEST	ANALYSIS IN HISTORY/SOCIAL STUDIES		ANALYSIS IN SCIENCE	
	QUESTIONS	RAW SCORE	QUESTIONS	RAW SCORE
Reading Test	10-18; 28-37		19-27; 38-47	
Writing and Language Test	23, 24, 26, 27, 31, 33		34, 35, 38, 40, 41, 44	
Math Test—No Calculator	3, 9, 10		2, 5, 8	
Math Test—Calculator	3, 8, 9, 12		1, 5, 16, 28	
TOTAL				

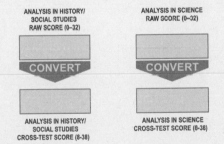

ANALYSIS IN HISTORY/
SOCIAL STUDIES
RAW SCORE (0–32)

CONVERT

ANALYSIS IN HISTORY/
SOCIAL STUDIES
CROSS-TEST SCORE (8-38)

ANALYSIS IN SCIENCE
RAW SCORE (0–32)

CONVERT

ANALYSIS IN SCIENCE
CROSS-TEST SCORE (8-38)

NOTES

NOTES

NOTES